Sustainability & Business Law

Sustainability & Business Law

Edited by

Judd F. Sneirson
SAVANNAH LAW SCHOOL

Nancy E. Shurtz
UNIVERSITY OF OREGON
SCHOOL OF LAW

CAROLINA ACADEMIC PRESS
Durham, North Carolina

Library of Congress Cataloging-in-Publication Data

Names: Shurtz, Nancy E., editor. | Sneirson, Judd F., editor.
Title: Sustainability & business law / Judd F. Sneirson and Nancy E. Shurtz.
Other titles: Sustainability and business law
Description: Durham, North Carolina : Carolina Academic Press, LLC, 2017. | Includes bibliographical references and index.
Identifiers: LCCN 2016052149 | ISBN 9781611639193 (alk. paper)
Subjects: LCSH: Environmental law--Economic aspects--United States. | Sustainable development--Law and legislation--United States. | Social responsibility of business--Law and legislation--United States. | Corporate governance--Law and legislation--United States. | LCGFT: Textbooks.
Classification: LCC KF3775 .S874 2017 | DDC 343.7307--dc23
LC record available at https://lccn.loc.gov/2016052149

e-ISBN 978-1-5310-0680-8

Carolina Academic Press, LLC
700 Kent Street
Durham, North Carolina 27701
Telephone (919) 489-7486
Fax (919) 493-5668
www.cap-press.com

Printed in the United States of America

For Elisa and Mira.
—J.F.S.

For my mother, Pauline Shurtz, who has inspired me to believe that anything is possible.
—N.E.S.

Contents

Preface xi

Chapter 1 Introduction 3

Robert C. Illig, *Al Gore, Oprah, and Silicon Valley: Bringing Main Street and Corporate America into the Environmental Movement* 3

Discussion Questions 7

Chapter 2 · The Fundamentals of Sustainable Business 9

Judd F. Sneirson, *Green Is Good: Sustainability, Profitability, and a New Paradigm for Corporate Governance* 9

Robert W. Kates, Thomas M. Parris, and Anthony A. Leiserowitz, *What Is Sustainable Development? Goals, Indicators, Values, and Practice* 12

Keith H. Hirokawa, *Saving Sustainability* 13

Amory B. Lovins, L. Hunter Lovins, and Paul Hawken, *A Road Map for Natural Capitalism* 16

William McDonough & Michael Braungart, *Cradle to Cradle: Rethinking the Way We Make Things* 28

Discussion Questions 35

Chapter 3 · Sustainability Meets Corporate Governance 37

Thomas Joo, *Global Warming and the Management-Centered Corporation* 37

Judd F. Sneirson, *Doing Well by Doing Good: Leveraging Due Care for Better, More Socially Responsible Corporate Decisionmaking* 41

Kent Greenfield, *Saving the World with Corporate Law* 50

James Gustave Speth, *The Bridge at the End of the World: Capitalism, the Environment, and Crossing from Crisis to Sustainability* 57

Discussion Questions 62

Chapter 4 · Corporate Compliance with Legal Obligations 63

Adam Winkler, *Corporate Law or the Law of Business? Stakeholders and Corporate Governance at the End of History* 63

Cynthia A. Williams, *Corporate Compliance with the Law in the Era of Efficiency* 66

Kent Greenfield, *Ultra Vires Lives! A Stakeholder Analysis of Corporate Illegality* 75

Judd F. Sneirson, *Shareholder Primacy and Corporate Compliance* 84

Discussion Questions 85

Chapter 5 · Entity Choices for Sustainable Businesses 87
Judd F. Sneirson, *Green Is Good: Sustainability, Profitability, and a New Paradigm for Corporate Governance* 87
Dana Brakman Reiser, *Benefit Corporations — A Sustainable Form of Organization?* 90
Antony Page & Robert A. Katz, *Is Social Enterprise the New Corporate Social Responsibility?* 102
Joseph W. Yockey, *Does Social Enterprise Law Matter?* 107
Discussion Questions 126

Chapter 6 · Sustainability and the Securities Laws 129
Thomas Joo, *Global Warming and the Management-Centered Corporation* 129
Cynthia A. Williams, *The Securities and Exchange Commission and Social Corporate Transparency* 132
Starbucks Corporation Fiscal 2014 Global Responsibility Report 152
Dennis D. Hirsch, *Green Business and the Importance of Reflexive Law: What Michael Porter Didn't Say* 154
Discussion Questions 156

Chapter 7 · Sustainable Investing 159
Joakim Sandberg, *Socially Responsible Investment and Fiduciary Duty* 159
Benjamin J. Richardson, *Socially Responsible Investing for Sustainability: Overcoming Its Incomplete and Conflicting Rationales* 170
Susan Gary, *Values and Value: University Endowments, Fiduciary Duties, and ESG Investing* 183
Discussion Questions 190

Chapter 8 · Sustainability and Contract Law 191
Carola Glinski, *Corporate Codes of Conduct: Moral or Legal Obligation?* 191
Michael P. Vandenbergh, *The New Wal-Mart Effect: The Role of Private Contracting in Global Governance* 194
Tory H. Lewis, *Managing Manure: Using Good Neighbor Agreements to Regulate Pollution from Agricultural Production* 207
Discussion Questions 215

Chapter 9 · Sustainability and Taxation 217
Part I: Environmental Taxation 217
Janet E. Milne, *Environmental Taxation: Why Theory Matters* 217
David Malin Roodman, *Environmental Taxes: Adopting a "Polluter Pays" Principle* 226
Janet E. Milne, *Environmental Taxation in the United States: The Long View* 231
Nancy E. Shurtz, *Carbon Pricing Initiatives in Western North America: A Blueprint for Global Climate Change Policy* 237
Discussion Questions for Part I 243

Part II: Tax Subsidies 245
Marilyn A. Brown and Sharon (Jess) Chandler, *Governing Confusion: How Statutes, Fiscal Policy, and Regulation Impede Clean Energy Technologies* 245
Office of Management and Budget, *2015 Budget of the United States Government* 252
Mona Hymel, *Consumerism, Advertising and Tax Policy* 256
Alan S. Lederman, *How Powerful Is the Nuclear Reactor Income Tax Credit?* 261
Viva Hammer, *Alternative Energy Gets a Second Wind* 263
Nancy Shurtz, *Carbon Pricing Initiatives in Western North America: A Blueprint for Global Climate Change Policy* 265
Discussion Questions for Part II 267

Chapter 10 · Sustainability, Torts, and Crimes 269
Carola Glinski, *Corporate Social Responsibility and the Law* 269
Nina A. Mendelson, *A Control-Based Approach to Shareholder Liability for Corporate Torts* 274
Christopher H. Schroeder, *Lost in the Translation: What Environmental Regulation Does That Tort Cannot Duplicate* 281
John P. Manard, Jr., Patrick O'Hara, Kelly R. Blackwood, *Katrina's Tort Litigation: An Imperfect Storm* 292
David M. Uhlmann, *Environmental Crime Comes of Age: The Evolution of Criminal Enforcement in the Environmental Regulatory Scheme* 294
Discussion Questions 306

Chapter 11 · Sustainability and Work Law 307
Brett H. McDonnell, *Strategies for an Employee Role in Corporate Governance* 307
Iris Marion Young, *Responsibility and Global Labor Justice* 315
Jeffrey Pfeffer, *Building Sustainable Organizations: The Human Factor* 321
Discussion Questions 330

Chapter 12 · Sustainability and International Law 331
David Kinley & Junko Tadaki, *From Talk to Walk: The Emergence of Human Rights Responsibilities for Corporations at International Law* 331
Pini Pavel Miretski and Sascha-Dominik Bachmann, *The UN Norms on the Responsibility of Transnational Corporations and Other Business Enterprises with Regard to Human Rights: A Requiem* 348
Paulette L. Stenzel, *Why and How the World Trade Organization Must Promote Environmental Protection* 362
Discussion Questions 374

Chapter 13 · Sustainability, Bankruptcy, and Commercial Law 377
Jared Diamond, *Collapse: How Societies Choose to Fail or Succeed Big Businesses and the Environment: Hardrock Mining Operations* 377
Jackie Gardina, *What if BP Were to File for Bankruptcy?* 383
Heather Hughes, *Enabling Investment in Environmental Sustainability* 393
Discussion Questions 400

Chapter 14 · Sustainability and Intellectual Property Law 401
Michael A. Gollin, *Using Intellectual Property to Improve Environmental Protection* 401
Joshua Sarnoff, *The Patent System and Climate Change* 409
Eric L. Lane, *Consumer Protection in the Eco-Mark Era: A Preliminary Survey and Assessment of Anti-Greenwashing Activity and Eco-Mark Enforcement* 417
Discussion Questions 426

Appendix · Sustainable Business in Practice 427
Matthew Tueth, *Fundamentals of Sustainable Business: A Guide for the Next 100 Years* 427

Notes on the Contributing Authors 443
Table of Cases 447
Index 449

Preface

There is a growing trend in business and business law towards sustainability—doing business with a focus on a firm's environmental and social as well as financial performance. Some business leaders believe that sustainability is a moral imperative while others feel that, moral or not, there is money to be made in "green business." Regardless of motives, businesses wishing to act sustainably will face myriad legal questions at the crossroads of business law and sustainability, such as whether a company may legally devote resources to sustainability at the expense of shareholder profits, whether public companies must disclose facts about their environmental and social performance, and whether the tax system and other areas of business law encourage, discourage, or are indifferent to sustainable business.

This book will explore these questions, studying diverse materials on sustainability as it relates to a wide range of business law topics, including corporate and securities law, contracts, commercial law, taxation, work law, torts, criminal law, international law, and intellectual property. Within each topic, we have endeavored to select readings that present a complete picture of the issues and raise varying viewpoints. We have also included discussion questions at the end of each chapter to invite readers to compare and contrast the readings, raise additional issues within each topic, and provoke thoughtful class discussion. We hope the book not only informs and stimulates debate on the role of law in furthering sustainability, but also, where possible, includes and inspires proposals for change.

Before we begin, a short note on editing. For the sake of brevity and focus, we have cut a great deal of fascinating material as well as most citations from each of the selections we have included. We encourage those readers interested in learning more to seek out the original works in their entirety and consult the sources cited therein. To make that process easier, we have retained the authors' footnote numbering and indicate with ellipses where we have redacted any text. We also took minor liberties with section headings to make our edited excerpts more readable.

This book would not be possible without the help and support of many others. First and foremost, we would like ot thank our contributing authors for graciously permitting us to excerpt and reprint their works here, and to Yuken Teruya for generously contributing his "Green Economy" art for the cover. Thanks also to our secretaries—Jill Elizabeth, Pat Hancock, and Sonya Jackson—for their help with this book over the years, and to our research assistants and the students in our sustainable business law classes for their inspiration, comments, and suggestions on earlier drafts. Thanks as well to the folks at Carolina Academic Press for their editorial work and advice, and, finally, a big thank you to our families for all their support and encouragement.

J.F.S.

N.E.S.

Sustainability & Business Law

Chapter 1

Introduction

Has the time come for sustainable business? The following reading suggests that it has, and points to recent moves on Main Street and on Wall Street as evidence. Do you agree with the author's assessment?

Robert C. Illig, *Al Gore, Oprah, and Silicon Valley: Bringing Main Street and Corporate America into the Environmental Movement*[*]

From an outsider's perspective, something momentous appears to be happening in the United States today with respect to climate change remediation. People seem to be thinking and talking about global warming in a qualitatively different manner. The tone of the debate has shifted. New players have emerged.

The shift started around the time of the Democratic Party's victory in the 2006 midterm elections and culminated in late 2007.... In particular, two events transpired during th[ose] eighteen months that embody the change and may help us to better understand what is at stake. Interestingly enough, they both involved former Vice President Al Gore.

Al Gore

What did Al Gore do in 2007 that was different and unexpected? How did his actions help to change the terms of the climate change debate? The obvious—but incorrect—answer is that he was awarded the Nobel Peace Prize.... Instead, Al Gore did something that is symbolic of a much deeper shift in the conversation. In December of 2006, Al Gore appeared on the Oprah Winfrey Show.

Oprah

Oprah has mass appeal. Hers is one of the highest-rated daytime talk shows in the history of television, drawing an estimated forty-six million viewers each week.... Oprah's appeal is broad. She moves more than just the cognoscenti. She moves middle America. And in December of 2006, Oprah threw her entire support behind Al Gore and "An Inconvenient Truth." Not once, at the end of the show, but almost every time she cut to a commercial or came back from one, she looked straight at the camera—straight at the viewers—and said, DVD in hand, "Every household should own this movie."

* Originally published in 23 Journal of Environmental Law & Litigation 223 (2008). Reprinted with permission.

Many events are contributing to the widening concern regarding climate change among mainstream Americans. Certainly, it matters for public opinion that the Democrats won the 2006 midterm Congressional elections. It matters that the science of climate change continues to become stronger. Hurricane Katrina, though an inconceivable tragedy in itself, moved many people's thinking in a positive direction. Younger Evangelicals are re-thinking their approach to environmental stewardship. In the future, historians may well identify some of these developments as being the causes of America's recent change in attitude toward the environment. However, for a single moment of theater—for an image that captures the meaning and import of what has transpired—it is difficult to trump Oprah's very public embrace of Al Gore.

What Al Gore and Oprah symbolize, then, is that the terms of the debate have begun to change. Just as there was once a moment when it became socially unacceptable to be identified as a racist, it is now becoming socially unacceptable to be anything other than green. And as with racism, we may disagree over what is or is not green, but we all now agree that green is good and normal and just. Though some people may secretly be polluters at heart, they can no longer say so in polite society. Thus, green can no longer be dismissed as the purview of some leftist fringe element that wants to take us back to the Stone Age. Rather, it is now part of the mainstream culture. The vocabulary of the national conversation is changing, and hearts and minds will follow.

Corporate America

... Businesses, of course, are deeply impacted by consumer trends. As a result, businesses listen to Oprah. And, indeed, businesses are hearing in climate change remediation the sound of opportunity. In particular, companies that sell products and services at retail are responding with a plethora of green initiatives. Everyone these days has become "green." General Electric is green. Ford and GM are green. The oil companies are green. Even Wal-Mart is green.

At first blush, this greening of American business feels insincere. It is easy to dismiss the many environmental initiatives one encounters daily in the newspapers and on the television as old economy businesses doing old economy things. One doesn't really believe them in their greenness. One sees only opportunism. One sees businesses trying to re-make the environmental movement into a brand.

The greening of American business is a significant development, however, and it has tangible benefits. First, it impacts the margins. If GM is determined to make a three-ton Cadillac Escalade, then it can't hurt to incorporate some hybrid technology to take the edge off. Meanwhile, Wal-Mart's impact on the behavior of producers is almost beyond calculation. As one of the largest companies in the history of the world, ... everything Wal-Mart does to improve its carbon footprint, no matter how cynical or over-hyped, makes a difference. Certainly, such small, incremental changes are insufficient on their own to turn the tide on a problem as vast and intractable as climate change. However, they do add up and they do help.

Second, it is symbolic of a shift in the thinking of American businesses with regard to climate change. In the past, many businesses denied the underlying science of global warming and sought to defeat legal reforms such as the 1997 Kyoto Protocol that were aimed at remediating climate change. Recently, however, business thinking about the environment has undergone a sea change. Many business leaders now view climate change not as the enemy but as an opportunity. As a result, Corporate America has joined the environmental movement.

We are now living in an America, as embodied by Oprah's embrace of Al Gore, in which mainstream consumers and consumer-oriented businesses are joining forces with environmental activists in response to the dangers posed by climate change....

Silicon Valley

Having appeared on Oprah at the tail end of 2006, Al Gore did something in 2007 that is symbolic of a change that may prove even more significant in the long-run. He joined the firm of Kleiner Perkins Caufield & Byers.

Kleiner Perkins is one of the nation's oldest and most successful venture capital funds. Its managers found Amazon. They found Sun Microsystems and AOL. They found Google and Compaq and Lotus and Netscape. They found Genentech, Intuit, Travelocity, Symantec, and literally hundreds of other hugely successful technology start-ups.... Kleiner Perkins, at a very early stage, recognized the potential of these firms and provided them the funding, connections, and expertise that they needed to become some of the world's largest and most influential companies. And the principals at Kleiner Perkins didn't just talk. They gambled real dollars on the futures of these businesses. Along with other storied venture capital firms like Sequoia and Benchmark Capital, these are the people who fuel innovation.

In dollar terms as well, Kleiner Perkins has real heft. Its website, for example, lists over one hundred portfolio companies that it has taken public. In terms of investable cash, its latest fund raised over $600 million. Moreover, Silicon Valley as a whole is much larger. In 2006, for example, investors added about twenty-five billion dollars of new money into venture capital funds.

What should get the attention of environmentalists, however, is not so much the size and influence of Al Gore's new business partners, but the fact that they've been right so often in the past. So it is that when the best minds in the venture capital industry start talking green—and when they support such talk by paying Al Gore real dollars in exchange for his connections and knowledge of the green marketplace—environmental leaders should take pause.

What Al Gore's new partnership symbolizes, then, is the promise that is inherent in the joining of entrepreneurship and environmentalism. In fact, the entire venture capital industry, Kleiner Perkins and Al Gore included, believe that green technology innovation will transform the world.

... [A]lthough it may sometimes appear that venture capitalists are the equivalent of gamblers in high-priced suits, freely tossing money at every wild, unproven idea, they really cannot afford to take such risks. Certainly, many of the ventures they back fail outright or succeed only modestly. However, unless at least some of them resulted in huge successes, venture capitalists would be out of business. They are, in other words, much more risk-averse than is popularly imagined.

The partners at Kleiner Perkins are very serious people, representing very serious investors. Their goal is neither publicity nor social change; it is profit. As a result, when they start to see their financial future linked to Al Gore, we should recognize that they too have become part of the environmental movement. Moreover, their history of past success should give us real reason for optimism.

Fellow Travelers

The partnership of Al Gore and Kleiner Perkins, not to mention Oprah's public embrace of "An Inconvenient Truth," suggests that American environmentalism is being transformed into a big-tent social movement. No longer will it be comprised only of those on the left. Instead, going forward, it will encompass groups with very different ideas about non-environmental issues and about what it means to be environmental stewards. The traditional American left, in other words, is about to find itself standing shoulder-to-shoulder with middle America and big business.

... Businesses will never seek to protect the environment as an end in itself. Their goal, as their critics contend, will always be to enhance shareholder value. Certainly, we should not overstate this proposition. Corporations are fictional legal entities that lack a physical persona. As such, they are operated by a diverse group of human beings with goals and values that are not limited to the financial well-being of their investors. As with any group of people, some are nice, some are not. Some genuinely care about the environment, some don't.

Nonetheless, business leaders do operate within certain constraints, both legal and normative, and the chief among them is the norm that the goal of business is to make a profit. Thus, while much of the new interest in the green economy may constitute a heartfelt response by concerned business managers, the real issue for most will always be the economic opportunity that the green economy represents.

In this respect, however, the profit-maximization goal of corporate America can be turned on its head and used to the advantage of the environmental movement. Changing attitudes among consumers, for example, can be transformed into both camouflage and impetus. Business leaders who want to become green will now have justification to do so. Meanwhile, those who don't support the environmental agenda may believe they must in order to remain competitive.

... [I]n the next phase of the movement, we must ... support green entrepreneurship and create incentives for change. Businesses will seize upon policies that support alternative and renewable energy sources, tax incentives for green technology innovation, higher fuel standards on cars, and an effective carbon tax. However, they will respond just as aggressively to poor or misaligned incentives. Thus, we need to be ever so careful about how business opportunities are created.

Even as the focus of the environmental movement shifts to include business, the law will continue to play an absolutely crucial role. If we shape the regulatory and policy landscape properly, we can shape the response of business. On the other hand, if we mismanage this opening, conducting politics as usual, we will squander an important opportunity to enlist the incredible power and entrepreneurial spirit of the American economy in the fight to create a more sustainable world.

Discussion Questions

1. Illig's observation that Corporate America has taken notice of green business opportunities suggests that the market is pushing American businesses toward sustainability. Should the government do anything to encourage this shift and, if so, should it act through tax incentives, legislative mandates, or other mechanisms?

2. Are venture capital firms, like Kleiner Perkins, the best avenue for creating sustainable businesses?

3. The market for investment capital and perhaps markets for goods and services both seem to reward green business plans and efforts. Does the market for labor similarly reward sustainable businesses? In other words, do you think a typical college graduate would prefer to work for a "green" company? Do you think she would take such a job over one that pays better? According to one study, workers would be willing to take a 15 percent pay cut in order to work for the more socially responsible firm. *See* Cliff Zukin and Mark Szeltner, *Talent Report: What Workers Want in 2012*, available at http://netimpact.org.

4. Do motivations matter? For example, does it matter whether Wal-Mart or some other business engages in sustainable business practices in order to cut costs and increase profits, and is completely indifferent to the planet, its employees, and its suppliers? In answering these questions consider the impact a business the size of Wal-Mart can make in terms of energy conservation as well as the impact it can have on the market for consumer goods.

5. Not every sustainable business decision or practice turns a profit (although studies show they do on the whole). What can or should be done to encourage businesses to take the steps that the market does not encourage?

6. Do you agree with Illig that environmentalism has become or is becoming a "big-tent social movement"? If he is wrong in his assessment, what does that mean for the future of sustainable business?

7. Illig published this essay in 2008; does it still ring true today? Have we seized or squandered the opportunity he identified? Does that opportunity still present itself?

8. Check the Internet to see what GM, GE, Wal-Mart, or any other company—your favorite brand, your least favorite brand—is currently doing about the environment, social responsibility, and/or sustainability. Do you think its motivation is profit, good corporate citizenship, or some combination of the two?

9. Now pick a business you suspect has little opportunity or inclination to "go green." What does it claim to be doing about the environment, social responsibility, and/or sustainability? Are you surprised about (or skeptical of) its claims?

Chapter 2

The Fundamentals of Sustainable Business

What is sustainability and how does it interact with business law? This chapter's readings focus on this first question. The first excerpt offers a brief overview of sustainability and sets out two ways in which businesses may put sustainability concepts into practice. The second and third readings reflect on the definition of sustainability from an environmentalist's perspective, whereas the fourth and fifth readings approach the topic from business and design perspectives. As you read these materials, consider the authors' various definitions of sustainability and views of sustainable businesses.

Judd F. Sneirson, *Green Is Good: Sustainability, Profitability, and a New Paradigm for Corporate Governance**

Sustainability, according to its first and best-known definition, entails "meeting the needs of the present without compromising the ability of future generations to meet their own needs."[5] The term reflected a concern "that nations [must] find ways to grow their economies without destroying the environment or sacrificing the well-being of future generations."[6] In short, sustainability urges "economic growth, but in a new form."[7] To be sustainable,

> A ... society needs to meet three conditions: its rates of use of renewable resources should not exceed their rates of regeneration; its rates of use of non-renewable resources should not exceed the rate at which sustainable renewable substitutes are developed; and its rates of pollution should not exceed the assimilative capacity of the environment.[8]

---

* Originally published in 94 Iowa Law Review 987 (2008). Reprinted with permission.

5. U.N. World Comm'n on Env't & Dev., Our Common Future 43 (1987) (defining sustainability in the context of sustainable development). This document is commonly known as the "Brundtland Report" after Norwegian Prime Minister Gro Harlem Brundtland, who led the Commission.

6. Andrew W. Savitz with Karl Weber, The Triple Bottom Line: How Today's Best-Run Companies Are Achieving Economic, Social, And Environmental Success—And How You Can Too, at x (2006).

7. John Elkington, Cannibals with Forks: The Triple Bottom Line of 21st Century Business 55 (1998).

8. Id. at 55–56.

concept of sustainability has since expanded beyond economic development into more generally applicable principle that—as governments, businesses, or individuals—our actions must not impinge on future generations' options.

Sustainable businesses aspire to this standard by treading as lightly as possible on the earth and its natural resources and by developing products, services, and technologies that contribute to larger societal efforts to live more sustainably. This sort of business model may include behaviors—such as being more than minimally compliant with environmental regulations, being more than minimally generous towards employees, or paying more for goods and services that are sustainably harvested or humanely produced—that sacrifice profits in the short run. Studies have shown, however, that these practices on the whole pay for themselves and sometimes even enhance profitability. As many firms have shown and seem to believe, it is quite possible, and profitable, to "do well by doing good."

Two complementary ways of operationalizing sustainability in business have emerged in the management literature: one that applies a "triple bottom line" approach to measuring corporate performance and success, and a second method that calls for businesses to "gear up" through increasingly pervasive levels of sustainability.

The Triple Bottom Line

The triple-bottom-line approach to sustainable business views corporate performance and success in three separate dimensions: "economic prosperity, environmental quality, and social justice."[12] That is, in addition to "the traditional bottom line of financial performance (most often expressed in terms of profits, return on investment (ROI), or shareholder value)," sustainable firms must also mind "their impact on the broader economy, the environment, and on the society in which they operate."[13] By using this approach in its accounting, a firm can measure its financial success as well as the extent to which it is "reducing (or increasing) the options available to future generations" during a particular reporting period.[14]

Triple-bottom-line adherents argue that a sustainable mindset not only helps the environment and society, it can also help firms' financial bottom lines. For example, efforts to reduce waste and pollution often result in greater efficiency and the discovery of innovative techniques and materials, all of which in turn can benefit the firm, its workforce, and the environment in both the short and the long runs.[15] Such oppor-

---

12. Elkington, supra note 7, at ix. Because of its tripartite focus, triple-bottom-line sustainability is often described using a three-legged-stool metaphor, where an imbalance among the three legs will cause the stool to topple. The triple bottom line is also often associated with the alliterative tagline "people, planet, profit."

13. Savitz, supra note 6, at xii.

14. Elkington, supra note 7, at 92.

15. Elkington, supra note 7, at 314 (discussing DuPont's successful 99% reduction in toxic emissions at a Texas plant—"achieved through the use of closed-loop recycling, off-site reclamation, selling former wastes as products, and substituting raw materials"—which saved "\$2.5 million of capital and more than \$3 million in annual operating costs"); see also Savitz, supra note 6, passim (containing numerous such anecdotes throughout).

tunities often lurk in the zones where business interests and stakeholder interests overlap, "where the pursuit of profit blends seamlessly with the pursuit of the common good."[16] Thus, an energy company's triple-bottom-line efforts might focus on renewable-energy sources, an automobile company's efforts might focus on fuel efficiency and hybrid and fuel-cell technologies, and a food company's efforts might focus on healthful options and reduced packaging. In each of these examples, a company can better its financial bottom line while also bettering its social and environmental bottom lines.

Gearing Up

A second strategy for incorporating sustainability principles into a business is the "gearing up" framework.[19] Like a manual transmission, the framework is designed to take a company from a level of bare compliance with applicable law to a place where sustainability is a systemic, integrated part of its strategy that transforms its business model and markets. Viewed in this way, sustainability is not just a kinder, gentler way of conducting business; it is a "catalyst for growth and innovation" that can transform an entire industry, with committed, sustainable companies at the leading edge.[21]

The framework's first gear denotes compliance. In this first stage, a firm views the business case for sustainability with skepticism and, aside from generic corporate philanthropy, does little beyond comply with applicable labor and environmental regulations. In second gear, firms voluntarily move beyond mere compliance, view sustainability as legitimate though mostly a public-relations matter, and focus their efforts on "eco-efficiency" and "measuring, managing, and reducing" the direct impact of their operations. Companies that shift into third gear are more proactive in their efforts, often partnering with the government as well as "suppliers, customers, and others in their industry" to innovate sustainable solutions together. By fourth gear, a firm has integrated sustainability principles into its strategy and business processes (starting with product or service development), putting the firm at a competitive advantage in its sector and at the same time creating value for all of its stakeholder groups. In the fifth and highest gear,[26] companies redesign or "reengineer" their business models, financial institutions, and markets to root out underlying causes of non-sustainability at "macro" (planetary ecological limits), "meso" (human-consumption demands), and "micro" (industry and company) levels. To be sure, "for many people, most of the time, four gears is enough, [b]ut there are times when it is necessary to shift into fifth gear, or overdrive."[28]

Nike, the familiar sportswear and equipment company, explicitly follows the gearing-up framework. According to a recent corporate-responsibility report, most

---

16. Savitz, supra note 6, at 22–27.

19. Sustainability Ltd., Gearing Up: From Corporate Responsibility to Good Governance and Scalable Solutions 34–37 (2004).

21. Nike, Inc., Innovate for a Better World: FY05–06 Corporate Responsibility Report 4 (2006).

26. There is also a reverse gear, in which companies simultaneously engage a forward gear and continue unsustainable business practices, either directly or by farming out such activities to others.

28. Sustainability Ltd, supra note 19, at 36.

of its current efforts lie in the fourth, or redesign, gear. The company has deliberately rethought its entire design and production processes to reduce waste; to utilize improved, sustainable, and even reusable materials; and in some cases to eliminate the use of harmful materials altogether. Specifically, the company has, among other efforts, instituted recycling programs that turn used athletic shoes into playing-field surfaces and replaced adhesives with stitching on some of its footwear lines. Nike's efforts at "considered design" present an "enormous opportunity for innovation that can benefit [its] business and society," its supply chain and, one assumes, Nike's entire industry.[33]

Robert W. Kates, Thomas M. Parris, and Anthony A. Leiserowitz, *What Is Sustainable Development? Goals, Indicators, Values, and Practice*[*]

Since the Brundtland Commission first defined sustainable development, dozens, if not hundreds, of scholars and practitioners have articulated and promoted their own alternative definition; yet a clear, fixed, and immutable meaning remains elusive. This has led some observers to call sustainable development an oxymoron: fundamentally contradictory and irreconcilable. Further, if anyone can redefine and reapply the term to fit their purposes, it becomes meaningless in practice, or worse, can be used to disguise or greenwash socially or environmentally destructive activities.

Yet, despite these critiques, each definitional attempt is an important part of an ongoing dialogue. In fact, sustainable development draws much of its resonance, power, and creativity from its very ambiguity. The concrete challenges of sustainable development are at least as heterogeneous and complex as the diversity of human societies and natural ecosystems around the world. As a concept, its malleability allows it to remain an open, dynamic, and evolving idea that can be adapted to fit these very different situations and contexts across space and time. Likewise, its openness to interpretation enables participants at multiple levels, from local to global, within and across activity sectors, and in institutions of governance, business, and civil society to redefine and reinterpret its meaning to fit their own situation. Thus, the concept of sustainability has been adapted to address very different challenges, ranging from the planning of sustainable cities to sustainable livelihoods, sustainable agriculture to sustainable fishing, and the efforts to develop common corporate standards in the U.N. Global Compact and in the World Business Council for Sustainable Development.

Despite this creative ambiguity and openness to interpretation, sustainable development has evolved a core set of guiding principles and values, based on the Brundtland Commission's standard definition to meet the needs, now and in the future, for human, economic, and social development within the restraints of the life support

33. Nike, Inc., supra note 21, at 52.

* Originally published in 47 Environment: Science and Policy for Sustainable Development 8 (2005). Reprinted with permission.

systems of the planet. Further, the connotations of both of the phrase's root words, "sustainable" and "development" are generally quite positive for most people, and their combination imbues this concept with inherent and near-universal agreement that sustainability is a worthwhile value and goal—a powerful feature in diverse and conflicted social contexts.

Importantly, however, these underlying principles are not fixed and immutable but the evolving product of a global dialogue, now several decades old, about what sustainability should mean. The original emphasis on economic development and environmental protection has been broadened and deepened to include alternative notions of development (human and social) and alternative views of nature (anthropocentric versus ecocentric). Thus, the concept maintains a creative tension between a few core principles and an openness to reinterpretation and adaptation to different social and ecological contexts.

Sustainable development thus requires the participation of diverse stakeholders and perspectives, with the ideal of reconciling different and sometimes opposing values and goals toward a new synthesis and subsequent coordination of mutual action to achieve multiple values simultaneously and even synergistically. As real-world experience has shown, however, achieving agreement on sustainability values, goals, and actions is often difficult and painful work, as different stakeholder values are forced to the surface, compared and contrasted, criticized and debated. Sometimes individual stakeholders find the process too difficult or too threatening to their own values and either reject the process entirely to pursue their own narrow goals or critique it ideologically, without engaging in the hard work of negotiation and compromise. Critique is nonetheless a vital part of the conscious evolution of sustainable development—a concept that, in the end, represents diverse local to global efforts to imagine and enact a positive vision of a world in which basic human needs are met without destroying or irrevocably degrading the natural systems on which we all depend.

Keith H. Hirokawa, *Saving Sustainability*[*]

Is sustainability void for vagueness?... Lawrence MacDonnell notes, "The virtue of sustainability as a concept sufficiently broad to embrace contemporary thinking about human objectives becomes the curse of vagueness when the discussion shifts from the general to the specific."[23] This ... mirror[s] [Robin] Craig and [Melinda] Benson's point: if sustainability cannot generate predictability by formulating a certain metric, then it cannot help us generate effective policy prescriptions.[†] Without knowable goals, sustainability fails to provide a basis from which to judge some programs

---

* Originally published in Rethinking Sustainability to Meet the Climate Change Challenge (Jessica Owley & Keith Hirokawa eds., 2015). Reprinted with permission.

23. Lawrence J. MacDonnell, Sustainable Use of Water Resources, 12 Natural Resources & Environment 97 (1997).

† [Robin Kundis Craig & Melinda Harm Benson, Replacing Sustainability, 46 Akron Law Review 841 (2013).]

as "more sustainable" than others. Then it is "greenwashing" all the way down. Once again, this attack on sustainability misconstrues the meaning and value of the term. Sustainability was never intended to facilitate leadership by target; the term was premised on the idea of leadership by process.

The sustainability program was intended to be revolutionary; a shift was needed away from "business as usual" toward a reorganization of values that accounted for a wider audience, a broader definition of "need," and a more inclusive understanding of value in natural resources. Accordingly, sustainability began with the idea that the relevant environmental, economic, and social considerations cannot be accomplished when viewed in isolation. Instead, the decisionmaking process must incorporate a vocabulary that sufficiently accommodates the perspectives from each of the triple-bottom-line elements. This is a pluralistic process.

To say that the concept of sustainability only has meaning in a pluralistic framework is to shoulder the governmental decisionmaking process with the task of being inclusive and pragmatic, where the strategies adopted to resolve current problems illustrate a commitment to long-term human welfare. Far from being impractical, this version of sustainability parallels good governance. For instance, Executive Order No. 13514 requires federal agencies to engage in sustainability planning.

> In order to create a clean energy economy that will increase our Nation's prosperity, promote energy security, protect the interests of taxpayers, and safeguard the health of our environment, the Federal Government must lead by example. It is therefore the policy of the United States that Federal agencies shall increase energy efficiency; measure, report, and reduce their greenhouse gas emissions from direct and indirect activities; conserve and protect water resources through efficiency, reuse, and stormwater management; eliminate waste, recycle, and prevent pollution; leverage agency acquisitions to foster markets for sustainable technologies and environmentally preferable materials, products, and services; design, construct, maintain, and operate high performance sustainable buildings in sustainable locations; strengthen the vitality and livability of the communities in which Federal facilities are located; and inform Federal employees about and involve them in the achievement of these goals.[24]

Notably, the executive order does not envision a static view of the environment, and, in the meantime, does not merely give passing reference to a vague notion of sustainability. Instead, the executive order directs federal agencies to develop and implement programs for the efficient use and assessment of natural resource needs.

Sustainability programs are neither formulaic nor universal. As Andrew Light notes, we are often faced with problems that do not lend themselves to quick and easy solutions. Ongoing inquiry is not synonymous with paralysis, and as Light points out, "inquiry into social problems need not come to an end in order for action to

---

24. Federal Leadership in Environmental, Energy, and Economic Performance, Exec. Order No. 13514 (Oct. 5, 2009).

take place." Hence, "[w]hen we feel the urgency to act, in order to provide aid to nature, we will need temporary stopping places in our ongoing conversation on how to best act for nature and how best to interpret the needs of nature."[26]

Another way of making this point is, as [Paul] Thompson notes, to accept the contingencies of integrity in decisionmaking: "pragmatists do not understand the connection between ethics and policy as one of applying the correct moral theory to a specific situation."[27] Hence, although many claim vague policy statements translate into ineffective regulatory frameworks, vagueness may not be a vice. As [Bryan] Norton observes, "[d]iscussions of social values must inform decisions regarding what to monitor and what models should be constructed; meanwhile, information about natural dynamics and likely impacts on them by human activities must inform and shape our understanding of what we value."[28] Norton's point is that sustainability is pragmatic, contingent, and contextual.

With this understanding, applying sustainability to the challenges of climate change may facilitate an understanding of the character of the climate challenge without subjecting the understanding to the rhetorical commitments of any particular principle; the pragmatic view is that sustainability is contingent in a way that can be open to principled dialogue. Hence, sustainability embraces contingency, but not to the point of skepticism:

> This postmodern conception of objectivity ... admits that the world is contingent, but it nevertheless locates an external check—in the form of community, including people with different perspectives and interests—on our subjective beliefs. This community-based approach to supporting our beliefs relies upon deliberation and disagreement to identify weak links in the web of our common beliefs as its participants seek ways to reach agreement on what to do within a diverse community of inquirers.[29]

Most sustainability advocates are comfortable with the vagueness. As Thompson admits, "We want to pursue sustainability, but we don't really want to be very clear or honest about what that means."[30] Yet, clarity may not be what is required. Thompson identifies pragmatic principles to guide the sustainability program, he notes that, "sustainability indicates a possible state of a airs that we understand as a social goal. We can (and should) ask whether this state of affairs obtains in fact, but by seeing it as a goal, as a morally or politically desirable state of affairs, our interest in sustainability is much more than a matter of scientific curiosity."[31]

---

26. Andrew Light, Compatibilism in Political Ecology, in Environmental Pragmatism 178 (Andrew Light & Eric Katz eds., 1996).

27. Paul B. Thompson, Pragmatism and Policy: The Case of Water, in Environmental Pragmatism 187–88 (Andrew Light & Eric Katz eds., 1996).

28. Bryan G. Norton, Integration or Reduction: Two Approaches to Environmental Values, in Environmental Pragmatism, supra note 27, at 226.

29. Id. at 566.

30. Paul B. Thompson, The Agrarian Vision: Sustainability and Environmental Ethics 235 (2010).

31. Id. at 223.

Amory B. Lovins, L. Hunter Lovins, and Paul Hawken, *A Road Map for Natural Capitalism**

... The earth's ability to sustain life, and therefore economic activity, is threatened by the way we extract, process, transport, and dispose of a vast flow of resources—some 220 billion tons a year, or more than 20 times the average American's body weight every day. With dangerously narrow focus, our industries look only at the exploitable resources of the earth's ecosystems—its oceans, forests, and plains—and not at the larger services that those systems provide for free. Resources and ecosystem services both come from the earth—even from the same biological systems—but they're two different things. Forests, for instance, not only produce the resource of wood fiber but also provide such ecosystem services as water storage, habitat, and regulation of the atmosphere and climate. Yet companies that earn income from harvesting the wood fiber resource often do so in ways that damage the forest's ability to carry out its other vital tasks.

Unfortunately, the cost of destroying ecosystem services becomes apparent only when the services start to break down....

The reason companies (and governments) are so prodigal with ecosystem services is that the value of those services doesn't appear on the business balance sheet. But that's a staggering omission. The economy, after all, is embedded in the environment. Recent calculations published in the journal *Nature* conservatively estimate the value of all the earth's ecosystem services to be at least $33 trillion a year. That's close to the gross world product, and it implies a capitalized book value on the order of half a quadrillion dollars. What's more, for most of these services, there is no known substitute at any price, and we can't live without them.

This article puts forward a new approach not only for protecting the biosphere but also for improving profits and competitiveness. Some very simple changes to the way we run our businesses, built on advanced techniques for making resources more productive, can yield startling benefits both for today's shareholders and for future generations.

This approach is called natural capitalism because it's what capitalism might become if its largest category of capital—the "natural capital" of ecosystem services—were properly valued. The journey to natural capitalism involves four major shifts in business practices, all vitally interlinked:

- Dramatically increase the productivity of natural resources. Reducing the wasteful and destructive flow of resources from depletion to pollution represents a major business opportunity. Through fundamental changes in both production design and technology, farsighted companies are developing ways to make natural resources—energy, minerals, water, forests—stretch 5, 10, even 100 times further than they do today....

* Originally published in 77 Harvard Business Review 145 (1999). Reprinted with permission.

- Shift to biologically inspired production models. Natural capitalism seeks not merely to reduce waste but to eliminate the very concept of waste. In closed-loop production systems, modeled on nature's designs, every output either is returned harmlessly to the ecosystem as a nutrient, like compost, or becomes an input for manufacturing another product. Such systems can often be designed to eliminate the use of toxic materials, which can hamper nature's ability to reprocess materials.
- Move to a solutions-based business model. The business model of traditional manufacturing rests on the sale of goods. In the new model, value is instead delivered as a flow of services—providing illumination, for example, rather than selling lightbulbs. This model entails a new perception of value, a move from the acquisition of goods as a measure of affluence to one where well-being is measured by the continuous satisfaction of changing expectations for quality, utility, and performance. The new relationship aligns the interests of providers and customers in ways that reward them for implementing the first two innovations of natural capitalism—resource productivity and closed-loop manufacturing.
- Reinvest in natural capital. Ultimately, business must restore, sustain, and expand the planet's ecosystems so that they can produce their vital services and biological resources even more abundantly. Pressures to do so are mounting as human needs expand, the costs engendered by deteriorating ecosystems rise, and the environmental awareness of consumers increases. Fortunately, these pressures all create business value.

Natural capitalism is not motivated by a current scarcity of natural resources. Indeed, although many biological resources, like fish, are becoming scarce, most mined resources, such as copper and oil, seem ever more abundant. Indices of average commodity prices are at 28-year lows, thanks partly to powerful extractive technologies, which are often subsidized and whose damage to natural capital remains unaccounted for. Yet even despite these artificially low prices, using resources many-fold more productively can now be so profitable that pioneering companies—large and small—have already embarked on the journey toward natural capitalism.

Still the question arises—if large resource savings are available and profitable, why haven't they all been captured already? The answer is simple: scores of common practices in both the private and public sectors systematically reward companies for wasting natural resources and penalize them for boosting resource productivity. For example, most companies expense their consumption of raw materials through the income statement but pass resource-saving investment through the balance sheet. That distortion makes it more tax efficient to waste fuel than to invest in improving fuel efficiency. In short, even though the road seems clear, the compass that companies use to direct their journey is broken. [L]et's map the route toward natural capitalism.

Dramatically Increase the Productivity of Natural Resources

In the first stage of a company's journey toward natural capitalism, it strives to wring out the waste of energy, water, materials, and other resources throughout its production systems and other operations. There are two main ways companies can do this at a profit. First, they can adopt a fresh approach to design that considers industrial systems as a whole rather than part by part. Second, companies can replace old industrial technologies with new ones, particularly with those based on natural processes and materials.

Implementing Whole-System Design. Inventor Edwin Land once remarked that "people who seem to have had a new idea have often simply stopped having an old idea." This is particularly true when designing for resource savings. The old idea is one of diminishing returns—the greater the resource saving, the higher the cost. But that old idea is giving way to the new idea that bigger savings can cost less—that saving a large fraction of resources can actually cost less than saving a small fraction of resources. This is the concept of expanding returns, and it governs much of the revolutionary thinking behind whole-system design. Lean manufacturing is an example of whole-system thinking that has helped many companies dramatically reduce such forms of waste as lead times, defect rates, and inventory. Applying whole-system thinking to the productivity of natural resources can achieve even more.

[The authors then describe how Interface Corporation, a manufacturer of materials for commercial interiors, redesigned the pipes in its pumping system to be thinner, shorter and straighter, demonstrating "how simple changes in design mentality can yield huge resource savings and returns on investment."]

Whole-system thinking can help managers find small changes that lead to big savings that are cheap, free, or even better than free (because they make the whole system cheaper to build). They can do this because often the right investment in one part of the system can produce multiple benefits throughout the system. For example, companies would gain 18 distinct economic benefits—of which direct energy savings is only one—if they switched from ordinary motors to premium-efficiency motors or from ordinary lighting ballasts (the transformer-like boxes that control fluorescent lamps) to electronic ballasts that automatically dim the lamps to match available daylight. If everyone in America integrated these and other selected technologies into all existing motor and lighting systems in an optimal way, the nation's $220-billion-a-year electric bill would be cut in half. The after-tax return on investing in these changes would in most cases exceed 100% per year.

The profits from saving electricity could be increased even further if companies also incorporated the best off-the-shelf improvements into their building structure and their office, heating, cooling, and other equipment. Overall, such changes could cut national electricity consumption by at least 75% and produce returns of around 100% a year on the investments made. More important, because workers would be more comfortable, better able to see, and less fatigued by noise, their productivity and the quality of their output would rise. Eight recent case studies of people working in well-designed, energy-efficient buildings measured labor productivity gains of 6% to 16%. Since a typical office pays about 100 times as much for people as it does for energy, this increased productivity in people is worth about 6 to 16 times as much as eliminating the entire energy bill.

Energy-saving, productivity-enhancing improvements can often be achieved at even lower cost by piggybacking them onto the periodic renovations that all buildings and factories need. A recent proposal for reallocating the normal 20-year renovation budget for a standard 200,000-square-foot glass-clad office tower near Chicago, Illinois, shows the potential of whole-system design. The proposal suggested replacing the aging glazing system with a new kind of window that lets in nearly six times more daylight than the old sun-blocking glass units. The new windows would reduce the flow of heat and noise four times better than traditional windows do. So even though the glass costs slightly more, the overall cost of the renovation would be reduced because the windows would let in cool, glare-free daylight that, when combined with more efficient lighting and office equipment, would reduce the need for air-conditioning by 75%. Installing a fourfold more efficient, but fourfold smaller, air-conditioning system would cost $200,000 less than giving the old system its normal 20-year renovation. The $200,000 saved would, in turn, pay for the extra cost of the new windows and other improvements. This whole-system approach to renovation would not only save 75% of the building's total energy use, it would also greatly improve the building's comfort and marketability. Yet it would cost essentially the same as the normal renovation. There are about 100,000 twenty-year-old glass office towers in the United States that are ripe for such improvement.

Major gains in resource productivity require that the right steps be taken in the right order. Small changes made at the downstream end of a process often create far larger savings further upstream. In almost any industry that uses a pumping system, for example, saving one unit of liquid flow or friction in an exit pipe saves about ten units of fuel, cost, and pollution at the power station.

Of course, the original reduction in flow itself can bring direct benefits, which are often the reason changes are made in the first place. In the 1980s, while California's industry grew 30%, for example, its water use was cut by 30%, largely to avoid increased wastewater fees. But the resulting reduction in pumping energy (and the roughly tenfold larger saving in power-plant fuel and pollution) delivered bonus savings that were at the time largely unanticipated.

To see how downstream cuts in resource consumption can create huge savings upstream, consider how reducing the use of wood fiber disproportionately reduces the pressure to cut down forests. In round numbers, half of all harvested wood fiber is used for such structural products as lumber; the other half is used for paper and cardboard. In both cases, the biggest leverage comes from reducing the amount of the retail product used. If it takes, for example, three pounds of harvested trees to produce one pound of product, then saving one pound of product will save three pounds of trees—plus all the environmental damage avoided by not having to cut them down in the first place.

The easiest savings come from not using paper that's unwanted or unneeded. In an experiment at its Swiss headquarters, for example, Dow Europe cut office paper flow by about 30% in six weeks simply by discouraging unneeded information. For instance, mailing lists were eliminated and senders of memos got back receipts indicating whether each recipient had wanted the information. Taking those and other small steps, Dow was also able to increase labor productivity by a similar proportion because people could focus on what they really needed to read. Similarly, Danish hearing-aid maker Oticon saved upwards of 30% of its paper as a by-product of redesigning its business processes to produce better decisions faster. Setting the default on office printers and copiers to double-sided mode reduced AT&T's paper costs by about 15%. Recently developed copiers and printers can even strip off old toner and printer ink, permitting each sheet to be reused about ten times.

Further savings can come from using thinner but stronger and more opaque paper, and from designing packaging more thoughtfully. In a 30-month effort at reducing such waste, Johnson & Johnson saved 2,750 tons of packaging, 1,600 tons of paper, $2.8 million, and at least 330 acres of forest annually. The downstream savings in paper use are multiplied by the savings further upstream, as less need for paper products (or less need for fiber to make each product) translates into less raw paper, less raw paper means less pulp, and less pulp requires fewer trees to be harvested from the forest. Recycling paper and substituting alternative fibers such as wheat straw will save even more.

Comparable savings can be achieved for the wood fiber used in structural products. Pacific Gas and Electric, for example, sponsored an innovative design developed by Davis Energy Group that used engineered wood products to reduce the amount of wood needed in a stud wall for a typical tract house by more than 70%. These walls were stronger, cheaper, more stable, and insulated twice as well. Using them enabled the designers to eliminate heating and cooling equipment in a climate where temperatures range from freezing to 113°F. Eliminating the equipment made the whole house much less expensive both to build and to run while still maintaining high levels of comfort. Taken together, these and many other savings in the paper and construction industries could make our use of wood fiber so much more productive that, in principle, the entire world's present wood fiber needs could probably be met by an intensive tree farm about the size of Iowa.

Adopting Innovative Technologies. Implementing whole-system design goes hand in hand with introducing alternative, environmentally friendly technologies. Many of these are already available and profitable but not widely known. Some, like the "designer catalysts" that are transforming the chemical industry, are already runaway successes. Others are still making their way to market, delayed by cultural rather than by economic or technical barriers.

The automobile industry is particularly ripe for technological change. After a century of development, motorcar technology is showing signs of age. Only 1% of the energy consumed by today's cars is actually used to move the driver: only 15% to 20% of the power generated by burning gasoline reaches the wheels (the rest is lost in the engine and drive-train) and 95% of the resulting propulsion moves the car, not the driver. The industry's infrastructure is hugely expensive and inefficient. Its convergent products compete for narrow niches in saturated core markets at commoditylike prices. Auto making is capital intensive, and product cycles are long. It is profitable in good years but subject to large losses in bad years. Like the typewriter industry just before the advent of personal computers, it is vulnerable to displacement by something completely different.

Enter the Hypercar. Since 1993, when Rocky Mountain Institute placed this automotive concept in the public domain, several dozen current and potential auto manufacturers have committed billions of dollars to its development and commercialization. The Hypercar integrates the best existing technologies to reduce the consumption of fuel as much as 85% and the amount of materials used up to 90% by introducing four main innovations.

First, making the vehicle out of advanced polymer composites, chiefly carbon fiber, reduces its weight by two-thirds while maintaining crashworthiness. Second, aerodynamic design and better tires reduce air resistance by as much as 70% and rolling resistance by up to 80%. Together, these innovations save about two-thirds of the fuel. Third, 30% to 50% of the remaining fuel is saved by using a "hybrid-electric" drive. In such a system, the wheels are turned by electric motors whose power is made onboard by a small engine or turbine, or even more efficiently by a fuel cell. The fuel cell generates electricity directly by chemically combining stored hydrogen with oxygen, producing pure hot water as its only by-product. Interactions between the small, clean, efficient power source and the ultralight, low-drag auto body then further reduce the weight, cost, and complexity of both. Fourth, much of the traditional hardware—from transmissions and differentials to gauges and certain parts of the suspension—can be replaced by electronics controlled with highly integrated, customizable, and upgradable software.

These technologies make it feasible to manufacture pollution-free, high-performance cars, sport utilities, pickup trucks, and vans that get 80 to 200 miles per gallon (or its energy equivalent in other fuels). These improvements will not require any compromise in quality or utility. Fuel savings will not come from making the vehicles small, sluggish, unsafe, or unaffordable, nor will they depend on government fuel taxes, mandates, or subsidies. Rather, Hypercars will succeed for the same reason that people buy compact discs instead of phonograph records: the CD is a superior product that redefines market expectations. From the manufacturers' perspective, Hypercars will cut cycle times, capital needs, body part counts, and assembly effort and space by as much as tenfold. Early adopters will have a huge competitive advantage—which is why dozens of corporations, including most automakers, are now racing to bring Hypercar-like products to market.*

In the long term, the Hypercar will transform industries other than automobiles. It will displace about an eighth of the steel market directly and most of the rest even-

* [The commercialization of the Hypercar began in 2014 with the production of the electric BMW i3 and the Volkswagen XL1.—Eds.]

tually, as carbon fiber becomes far cheaper. Hypercars and their cousins could ultimately save as much oil as OPEC now sells. Indeed, oil may well become uncompetitive as a fuel long before it becomes scarce and costly. Similar challenges face the coal and electricity industries because the development of the Hypercar is likely to accelerate greatly the commercialization of inexpensive hydrogen fuel cells. These fuel cells will help shift power production from centralized coal-fired and nuclear power stations to networks of decentralized, small-scale generators. In fact, fuelcell-powered Hypercars could themselves be part of these networks. They'd be, in effect, 20-kilowatt power plants on wheels. Given that cars are left parked—that is, unused-more than 95% of the time, these Hypercars could be plugged into a grid and could then sell back enough electricity to repay as much as half the predicted cost of leasing them. A national Hypercar fleet could ultimately have five to ten times the generating capacity of the national electric grid.

As radical as it sounds, the Hypercar is not an isolated case. Similar ideas are emerging in such industries as chemicals, semiconductors, general manufacturing, transportation, water and waste-water treatment, agriculture, forestry, energy, real estate, and urban design. For example, the amount of carbon dioxide released for each microchip manufactured can be reduced almost 100-fold through improvements that are now profitable or soon will be.

Some of the most striking developments come from emulating nature's techniques. In her book, *Biomimicry*, Janine Benyus points out that spiders convert digested crickets and flies into silk that's as strong as Kevlar without the need for boiling sulfuric acid and high-temperature extruders. Using no furnaces, abalone can convert seawater into an inner shell twice as tough as our best ceramics. Trees turn sunlight, water, soil, and air into cellulose, a sugar stronger than nylon but one-fourth as dense. They then bind it into wood, a natural composite with a higher bending strength than concrete, aluminum alloy, or steel. We may never become as skillful as spiders, abalone, or trees, but smart designers are already realizing that nature's environmentally benign chemistry offers attractive alternatives to industrial brute force.

Whether through better design or through new technologies, reducing waste represents a vast business opportunity. The U.S. economy is not even 10% as energy efficient as the laws of physics allow. Just the energy thrown off as waste heat by U.S. power stations equals the total energy use of Japan. Materials efficiency is even worse: only about 1% of all the materials mobilized to serve America is actually made into products and still in use six months after sale. In every sector, there are opportunities for reducing the amount of resources that go into a production process, the steps required to run that process, and the amount of pollution generated and by-products discarded at the end. These all represent avoidable costs and hence profits to be won.

Redesign Production According to Biological Models

In the second stage on the journey to natural capitalism, companies use closed-loop manufacturing to create new products and processes that can totally prevent waste. This plus more efficient production processes could cut companies' long-term materials requirements by more than 90% in most sectors.

The central principle of closed-loop manufacturing, as architect Paul Bierman-Lytle of the engineering firm CH2M Hill puts it, is "waste equals food." Every output of manufacturing should be either composted into natural nutrients or remanufactured into technical nutrients—that is, it should be returned to the ecosystem or recycled for further production. Closed-loop production systems are designed to eliminate any materials that incur disposal costs, especially toxic ones, because the alternative—isolating them to prevent harm to natural systems—tends to be costly and risky. Indeed, meeting EPA and OSHA standards by eliminating harmful materials often makes a manufacturing process cost less than the hazardous process it replaced. Motorola, for example, formerly used chlorofluorocarbons for cleaning printed circuit boards after soldering. When CFCs were outlawed because they destroy stratospheric ozone, Motorola at first explored such alternatives as orange-peel terpenes. But it turned out to be even cheaper—and produce a better product—to redesign the whole soldering process so that it needed no cleaning operations or cleaning materials at all.

Closed-loop manufacturing is more than just a theory. The U.S. remanufacturing industry in 1996 reported revenues of $53 billion—more than consumer-durables manufacturing (appliances; furniture; audio, video, farm, and garden equipment). Xerox, whose bottom line has swelled by $700 million from remanufacturing, expects to save another $1 billion just by remanufacturing its new, entirely reusable or recyclable line of "green" photocopiers. What's more, policy makers in some countries are already taking steps to encourage industry to think along these lines. German law, for example, makes many manufacturers responsible for their products forever, and Japan is following suit.

Combining closed-loop manufacturing with resource efficiency is especially powerful. DuPont, for example, gets much of its polyester industrial film back from customers after they use it and recycles it into new film. DuPont also makes its polyester film ever stronger and thinner so it uses less material and costs less to make. Yet because the film performs better, customers are willing to pay more for it. As DuPont chairman Jack Krol noted in 1997, "Our ability to continually improve the inherent properties [of our films] enables this process [of developing more productive materials, at lower cost, and higher profits] to go on indefinitely."

[The authors again use Interface Corporation as an example of a leader in "industrial ecology" with its Solenium floor-covering material.] Solenium lasts four times longer and uses 40% less material than ordinary carpets—an 86% reduction in materials intensity. What's more, Solenium is free of chlorine and other toxic materials, is virtually stainproof, doesn't grow mildew, can easily be cleaned with water, and offers aesthetic advantages over traditional carpets … Solenium is only one part of Interface's drive to eliminate every form of waste.

Change the Business Model

In addition to its drive to eliminate waste, Interface has made a fundamental shift in its business model—the third stage on the journey toward natural capitalism. The company has realized that clients want to walk on and look at carpets—but not necessarily to own them. Traditionally, broadloom carpets in office buildings are replaced every decade because some portions look worn out. When that happens, companies suffer the disruption of shutting down their offices and removing their furniture. Billions of pounds of carpets are removed each year and sent to landfills, where they will last up to 20,000 years. To escape this unproductive and wasteful cycle, Interface is transforming itself from a company that sells and fits carpets into one that provides floorcovering services.

Under its Evergreen Lease, Interface no longer sells carpets but rather leases a floor-covering service for a monthly fee, accepting responsibility for keeping the carpet fresh and clean. Monthly inspections detect and replace worn carpet tiles. Since at most 20% of an area typically shows at least 80% of the wear, replacing only the worn parts reduces the consumption of carpeting material by about 80%. It also minimizes the disruption that customers experience—worn tiles are seldom found under furniture. Finally, for the customer, leasing carpets can provide a tax advantage by turning a capital expenditure into a tax-deductible expense. The result: the customer gets cheaper and better services that cost the supplier far less to produce. Indeed, the energy saved from not producing a whole new carpet is in itself enough to produce all the carpeting that the new business model requires. Taken together, the 5-fold savings in carpeting material that Interface achieves through the Evergreen Lease and the 7-fold materials savings achieved through the use of Solenium deliver a stunning 35-fold reduction in the flow of materials needed to sustain a superior floor-covering service. Remanufacturing, and even making carpet initially from renewable materials, can then reduce the extraction of virgin resources essentially to the company's goal of zero.

Interface's shift to a service-leasing business reflects a fundamental change from the basic model of most manufacturing companies, which still look on their businesses as machines for producing and selling products. The more products sold, the better—at least for the company, if not always for the customer or the earth. But any model that wastes natural resources also wastes money. Ultimately, that model will be unable to compete with a service model that emphasizes solving problems and building long-term relationships with customers rather than making and selling products. The shift to what James Womack of the Lean Enterprise Institute calls a "solutions economy" will almost always improve customer value and providers' bottom lines because it aligns both parties' interests, offering rewards for doing more and better with less.

Interface is not alone. Elevator giant Schindler, for example, prefers leasing vertical transportation services to selling elevators because leasing lets it capture the savings from its elevators' lower energy and maintenance costs. Dow Chemical and SafetyKleen prefer leasing dissolving services to selling solvents because they can reuse the same solvent scores of times, reducing costs. United Technologies' Carrier division, the world's largest manufacturer of air conditioners, is shifting its mission from selling air conditioners to leasing comfort. Making its air conditioners more durable and efficient may compromise future equipment sales, but it provides what customers want and will pay for—better comfort at lower cost. But Carrier is going even further. It's starting to team up with other companies to make buildings more efficient so that they need less air-conditioning, or even none at all, to yield the same level of comfort. Carrier will get paid to provide the agreed-upon level of comfort, however that's delivered. Higher profits will come from providing better solutions rather than from selling more equipment. Since comfort with little or no air-conditioning (via better building design) works better and costs less than comfort with copious air-conditioning, Carrier is smart to capture this opportunity itself before its competitors do. As they say at 3M: "We'd rather eat our own lunch, thank you."

The shift to a service business model promises benefits not just to participating businesses but to the entire economy as well. Womack points out that by helping customers reduce their need for capital goods such as carpets or elevators, and by rewarding suppliers for extending and maximizing asset values rather than for churning them, adoption of the service model will reduce the volatility in the turnover of capital goods that lies at the heart of the business cycle. That would significantly reduce the overall volatility of the world's economy. At present, the producers of capital goods face feast or famine because the buying decisions of households and corporations are extremely sensitive to fluctuating income. But in a continuous-flow-of-services economy, those swings would be greatly reduced, bringing a welcome stability to businesses. Excess capacity—another form of waste and source of risk—need no longer be retained for meeting peak demand. The result of adopting the new model would be an economy in which we grow and get richer by using less and become stronger by being leaner and more stable.

Reinvest in Natural Capital

The foundation of textbook capitalism is the prudent reinvestment of earnings in productive capital. Natural capitalists who have dramatically raised their resource productivity, closed their loops, and shifted to a solutions-based business model have one key task remaining. They must reinvest in restoring, sustaining, and expanding the most important form of capital—their own natural habitat and biological resource base.

This was not always so important. Until recently, business could ignore damage to the ecosystem because it didn't affect production and didn't increase costs. But that situation is changing. In 1998 alone, violent weather displaced 300 million people and caused upwards of $90 billion worth of damage, representing more weather-related destruction than was reported through the entire decade of the 1980s. The increase in damage is strongly linked to deforestation and climate change, factors that accelerate the frequency and severity of natural disasters and are the consequences of inefficient industrialization. If the flow of services from industrial systems is to be sustained or increased in the future for a growing population, the vital flow of services from living systems will have to be maintained or increased as well. Without reinvestment in natural capital, shortages of ecosystem services are likely to become the limiting factor to prosperity in the next century. When a manufacturer realizes that a supplier of key components is overextended and running behind on deliveries, it takes immediate action lest its own production lines come to a halt. The ecosystem is a supplier of key components for the life of the planet, and it is now falling behind on its orders.

Failure to protect and reinvest in natural capital can also hit a company's revenues indirectly. Many companies are discovering that public perceptions of environmental responsibility, or its lack thereof, affect sales. MacMillan Bloedel, targeted by environmental activists as an emblematic clear-cutter and chlorine user, lost 5% of its sales almost overnight when dropped as a U.K. supplier by Scott Paper and Kimberly-Clark. Numerous case studies show that companies leading the way in implementing changes that help protect the environment tend to gain disproportionate advantage, while companies perceived as irresponsible lose their franchise, their legitimacy, and their shirts. Even businesses that claim to be committed to the concept of sustainable development but whose strategy is seen as mistaken, like Monsanto, are encountering stiffening public resistance to their products. Not surprisingly, University of Oregon business professor Michael Russo, along with many other analysts, has found that a strong environmental rating is "a consistent predictor of profitability."

The pioneering corporations that have made reinvestments in natural capital are starting to see some interesting paybacks. The independent power producer AES, for example, has long pursued a policy of planting trees to offset the carbon emissions of its power plants. That ethical stance, once thought quixotic, now looks like a smart investment because a dozen brokers are now starting to create markets in carbon reduction. Similarly, certification by the Forest Stewardship Council of certain sustainably grown and harvested products has given Collins Pine the extra profit margins that enabled its U.S. manufacturing operations to survive brutal competition. Taking an even longer view, Swiss Re and other European reinsurers are seeking to cut their storm-damage losses by pressing for international public policy to protect the climate and by investing in climate-safe technologies that also promise good profits. Yet most companies still do not realize that a vibrant ecological web underpins their survival and their business success. Enriching natural capital is not just a public good—it is vital to every company's longevity.

It turns out that changing industrial processes so that they actually replenish and magnify the stock of natural capital can prove especially profitable because nature does the production; people need just step back and let life flourish. Industries that directly harvest living resources, such as forestry, farming, and fishing, offer the most suggestive examples. Here are three:

- Allan Savory of the Center for Holistic Management in Albuquerque, New Mexico, has redesigned cattle ranching to raise the carrying capacity of rangelands, which have often been degraded not by overgrazing but by undergrazing and grazing the wrong way. Savory's solution is to keep the cattle moving from place to place, grazing intensively but briefly at each site, so that they mimic the dense but constantly moving herds of native grazing animals that co-evolved with grasslands. Thousands of ranchers are estimated to be applying this approach, improving both their range and their profits. This "management-intensive rotational grazing" method, long standard in New Zealand, yields such clearly superior returns that over 15% of Wisconsin's dairy farms have adopted it in the past few years.

- The California Rice Industry Association has discovered that letting nature's diversity flourish can be more profitable than forcing it to produce a single product. By flooding 150,000 to 200,000 acres of Sacramento valley rice fields—about 30% of California's rice-growing area—after harvest, farmers are able to create seasonal wetlands that support millions of wildfowl, replenish groundwater, improve fertility, and yield other valuable benefits. In addition, the farmers bale and sell the rice straw, whose high silica content—formerly an air-pollution hazard when the straw was burned—adds insect resistance and hence value as a construction material when it's resold instead.
- John Todd of Living Technologies in Burlington, Vermont, has used biological Living Machines—linked tanks of bacteria, algae, plants, and other organisms—to turn sewage into clean water. That not only yields cleaner water at a reduced cost, with no toxicity or odor, but it also produces commercially valuable flowers and makes the plant compatible with its residential neighborhood. A similar plant at the Ethel M Chocolates factory in Las Vegas, Nevada, not only handles difficult industrial wastes effectively but is showcased in its public tours.

Although such practices are still evolving, the broad lessons they teach are clear. In almost all climates, soils, and societies, working with nature is more productive than working against it. Reinvesting in nature allows farmers, fishermen, and forest managers to match or exceed the high yields and profits sustained by traditional input-intensive, chemically driven practices. Although much of mainstream business is still headed the other way, the profitability of sustainable, nature-emulating practices is already being proven. In the future, many industries that don't now consider themselves dependent on a biological resource base will become more so as they shift their raw materials and production processes more to biological ones. There is evidence that many business leaders are starting to think this way. The consulting firm Arthur D. Little surveyed a group of North American and European business leaders and found that 83% of them already believe that they can derive "real business value [from implementing a] sustainable-development approach to strategy and operations."

... Natural capitalism ... reintegrat[es] ecological with economic goals. Because it is both necessary and profitable, it will subsume traditional industrialism within a new economy and a new paradigm of production, just as industrialism previously rarianism. The companies that first make the changes we have described ompetitive edge. Those that don't make that effort won't be a problem nately they won't be around. In making that choice, as Henry Ford said, ou believe you can, or whether you believe you can't, you're absolutely

William McDonough & Michael Braungart, *Cradle to Cradle: Rethinking the Way We Make Things**

Waste Equals Food

Nature operates according to a system of nutrients and metabolisms in which there is no such thing as waste. A cherry tree makes many blossoms and fruit to (perhaps) germinate and grow. That is why the tree blooms. But the extra blossoms are far from useless. They fall to the ground, decompose, feed various organisms and microorganisms, and enrich the soil. Around the world, animals and humans exhale carbon dioxide, which plants take in and use for their own growth. Nitrogen from wastes is transformed into protein by microorganisms, animals, and plants. Horses eat grass and produce dung, which provides both nest and nourishment for the larvae of flies. The Earth's major nutrients—carbon, hydrogen, oxygen, nitrogen—are cycled and recycled. Waste equals food.

This cyclical, cradle-to-cradle biological system has nourished a planet of thriving, diverse abundance for millions of years.... If humans are truly going to prosper, we will have to learn to imitate nature's highly effective cradle-to-cradle system of nutrient flow and metabolism, in which the very concept of waste does not exist. *To eliminate the concept of waste means to design things—products, packaging, and systems—from the very beginning on the understanding that waste does not exist.* It means that the valuable nutrients contained in the materials shape and determine the design: form follows evolution, not just function. We think this is a more robust prospect than the current way of making things.... With the right design, all of the products and materials manufactured by industry will safely feed [biological and technical] metabolisms, providing nourishment for something new....

The Biological Metabolism

A *biological nutrient* is a material or product that is designed to return to the biological cycle—it is literally consumed by microorganisms in the soil and by other animals. Most packaging (which makes up about 50 percent of the volume of the municipal solid waste stream) can be designed as biological nutrients, what we call *products of consumption.* The idea is to compose these products of materials that can be tossed on the ground or compost heap to safely biodegrade after use—literally to be consumed. There is no need for shampoo bottles, toothpaste tubes, yogurt and

*

ice-cream cartons, juice containers, and other packaging to last decades (or even centuries) longer than what came inside them. Why should individuals and communities be burdened with downcycling or landfilling such material? Worry-free packaging could safely decompose, or be gathered and used as fertilizer, bringing nutrients back to the soil. Shoe soles could degrade to enrich the environment. Soaps and other liquid cleaning products could be designed as biological nutrients as well; that way, when they wash down the drain, pass through a wetland, and end up in a lake or river, they support the balance of the ecosystem.

In the early 1990s the two of us were asked by DesignTex, a division of Steelcase, to conceive and create a compostable upholstery fabric, working with the Swiss textile mill Röhner. We were asked to focus on creating an aesthetically unique fabric that was also environmentally intelligent. DesignTex first proposed that we consider cotton combined with PET (polyethylene terephthalate) fibers from recycled soda bottles. What could be better for the environment, they thought, than a product that combined a "natural" material with a "recycled" one? Such hybrid material had the additional apparent advantages of being readily available, market-tested, durable, and cheap.

But when we looked carefully at the potential long-term design legacy, we discovered some disturbing facts. First, as we have mentioned, upholstery abrades during normal use, and so our design had to allow for the possibility that particles might be inhaled or swallowed. PET is covered with synthetic dyes and chemicals and contains other questionable substances—not exactly what you want to breathe or eat. Furthermore, the fabric would not be able to continue after its useful life as either a technical or a biological nutrient. The PET (from the plastic bottles) would not go back to the soil safely, and the cotton could not be circulated in industrial cycles. The combination would be yet another monstrous hybrid, adding junk to a landfill, and it might also be dangerous. This was not a product worth making.

We made clear to our client our intention to create a product that would enter either the biological or the technical metabolism, and the challenge crystallized for both of us. The team decided to design a fabric that would be safe enough to eat: it would not harm people who breathed it in, and it would not harm natural systems after its disposal. In fact, as a biological nutrient, it would nourish nature.

The textile mill that was chosen to produce the fabric was quite clean by accepted environmental standards, one of the best in Europe, yet it had an interesting dilemma. Although the mill's director, Albin Kaelin, had been diligent about reducing levels of dangerous emissions, government regulators had recently defined the mill's fabric trimmings as hazardous waste. The director had been told that he could no longer bury or burn these trimmings in hazardous-waste incinerators in Switzerland but had to export them to Spain for disposal. (Note the paradoxes here: the trimmings of a fabric are not to be buried or disposed of without expensive precaution, or must be exported "safely" to another location, but the material itself can still be sold as safe for installation in an office or home.) We hoped for a different fate for our trimmings: to provide mulch for the local garden club, with the help of sun, water, and hungry microorganisms.

The mill interviewed people living in wheelchairs and discovered that their most important needs in seating fabric were that it be strong and that it "breathe." The team decided on a mixture of safe, pesticide-free plant and animal fibers for the fabric: wool, which provides insulation in winter and summer, and ramie, which wicks moisture away. Together these fibers would make for a strong and comfortable fabric. Then we began working on the most difficult aspect of the design: the finishes, dyes, and other process chemicals. Instead of filtering out mutagens, carcinogens, endocrine disrupters, persistent toxins, and bioaccumulative substances at the end of the process, we would filter them out at the beginning. In fact, we would go beyond designing a fabric that would do no harm; we would design one that was nutritious.

Sixty chemical companies declined the invitation to join the project, uncomfortable at the idea of exposing their chemistry to the kind of scrutiny it would require. Finally one European company agreed to join. With its help, we eliminated from consideration almost eight thousand chemicals that are commonly used in the textile industry; we also thereby eliminated the need for additives and corrective processes. Not using a given dye, for example, removed the need for additional toxic chemicals and processes to ensure ultraviolet-light stabilization (that is, colorfastness). Then we looked for ingredients that had *positive* qualities. We ended up selecting only thirty-eight of them from which we created the entire fabric line. What might seem like an expensive and laborious research process turned out to solve multiple problems and to contribute to a higher-quality product that was ultimately more economical.

The fabric went into production. The factory director later told us that when regulators came on their rounds and tested the effluent (the water coming out of the factory), they thought their instruments were broken. They could not identify any pollutants, not even elements they knew were in the water when it came into the factory. To confirm that their testing equipment was actually in working order, they checked the influent from the town's water mains. The equipment was fine; it was simply that by most parameters the water coming out of the factory was as clean as—or even cleaner than—the water going in. When a factory's effluent is cleaner than its influent, it might well prefer to use its effluent as influent. Being designed into the manufacturing process, this dividend is free and requires no enforcement to continue or to exploit. Not only did our new design process bypass the traditional responses to environmental problems (reduce, reuse, recycle), it also eliminated the need for regulation, something that any businessperson will appreciate as extremely valuable.

The process had additional positive side effects. Employees began to use, for recreation and additional work space, rooms that were previously reserved for hazardous-chemical storage. Regulatory paperwork was eliminated. Workers stopped wearing the gloves and masks that had given them a thin veil of protection against workplace toxins. The mill's products became so successful that it faced a new problem: financial success, just the kind of problem businesses want to have.

As a biological nutrient, the fabric embodied the kind of fecundity we find in nature's work. After customers finished using it, they could simply tear the fabric off the chair frame and throw it onto the soil or compost heap without feeling bad—even, perhaps, with a kind of relish. Throwing something away can be fun, let's admit it; and giving a guilt-free gift to the natural world is an incomparable pleasure.

The Technical Metabolism

A *technical nutrient* is a material or product that is designed to go back into the technical cycle, into the industrial metabolism from which it came. The average television we analyzed, for example, was made of 4,360 chemicals. Some of them are toxic, but others are valuable nutrients for industry that are wasted when the television ends up in a landfill. Isolating them from biological nutrients allows them to be *upcycled* rather than recycled—to retain their high quality in a closed-loop industrial cycle. Thus a sturdy plastic computer case, for example, will continually circulate as a sturdy plastic computer case—or as some other high-quality product, like a car part or a medical device—instead of being downcycled into soundproof barriers and flowerpots.

Henry Ford practiced an early form of upcycling when he had Model A trucks shipped in crates that became the vehicle's floorboards when it reached its destination. We are initiating a similar practice that is a modest beginning: Korean rice husks used as packing for stereo components and electronics sent to Europe, then reused there as a material for making bricks. (Rice husks contain a high percentage of silica.) The packing material is nontoxic (rice husks are safer than recycled newspapers, which contain toxic inks and particles that contaminate indoor air); its shipping is inclusive in the freight costs the electronic goods would incur anyway; and the concept of waste is eliminated.

Industrial mass can be specifically designed to retain its high quality for multiple uses. Currently, when an automobile is discarded, its component steel is recycled as an amalgam of all its steel parts, along with the various steel alloys of other products. The car is crushed, pressed, and processed so that high-ductile steel from the body and stainless steels are smelted together with various other scrap steels and materials, compromising their high quality and drastically restricting their further use. (It can't, for example, be used to make car bodies again.) The copper in its cables is melded into a general compound and lost to specific technical purposes—it can no longer be used as a copper cable. A more prosperous design would allow the car to be used the way Native Americans used a buffalo carcass, optimizing every element, from tongue to tail. Metals would be smelted only with like metals, to retain their high quality; likewise for plastics.

In order for such a scenario to be practical, however, we have to introduce a concept that goes hand in hand with the notion of a technical nutrient: the concept of a *product of service*. Instead of assuming that all products are to be brought, owned, and disposed of by "consumers," products containing valuable technical nutrients—cars, televisions, carpeting, computers, and refrigerators, for example—would be reconceived as *services* people want to enjoy. In this scenario, customers (a more apt term for the users of these products) would effectively purchase the service of such a product for a *defined user period*—say, ten thousand hours of television viewing, rather than the television itself. They would not be paying for complex materials that they won't be able to use after a product's current life. When they finish with the product, or are simply ready to upgrade to a newer version, the manufacturer replaces it, taking the old model back, breaking it down, and using its complex materials as food for new products. The customers would receive the services they need for as long as they need them and could upgrade as often as desire; manufactures would continue to grow and develop while retaining ownership of their materials.

A number of years ago we worked on a "rent-a-solvent" concept for a chemical company. A solvent is a chemical that is used to remove grease, for example, from machine parts. Companies ordinarily buy the cheapest degreasing solvent available, even if it comes from halfway around the globe. After its use, the waste solvent is either evaporated or entered into a waste treatment flow, to be handled by a sewage treatment plant. The idea behind rent-a-solvent was to provide a degreasing service using high-quality solvents available to customers without selling the solvent itself; the provider would recapture the emissions and separate the solvent from the grease so that it would be available for continuous reuse. Under these circumstances, the company had incentive to use high-quality solvents (how else to retain customers?) and to reuse it, with the important side effect of keeping toxic materials out of waste flows. Dow Chemical has experimented with this concept in Europe, and DuPont is taking up this idea vigorously.

This scenario has tremendous implications for industry's material wealth. When customers finish with a traditional carpet, for example, they must pay to have it removed. At that point its materials are a liability, not an asset—they are a heap of petrochemicals and other potentially toxic substances that must be toted to a landfill. This linear, cradle-to-grave life cycle has several negative consequences for both people and industry. The energy, effort, and materials that were put into manufacturing the carpet are lost to the manufacturer once the customer purchases it. Millions of pounds of potential nutrients for the carpet industry alone are wasted each year, and new raw materials must continually be extracted. Customers who decide they want or need new carpeting are inconvenienced, financially burdened with a new purchase (the cost of the unrecoverable materials must be built into the price), and, if they are environmentally concerned, taxed with guilt as well about disposing of the old and purchasing the new.

Carpet companies have been among the first industries to adopt our product-of-service or "eco-leasing" concepts, but so far they have applied them to conventionally designed products. An average commercial carpet consists of nylon fibers backed with fiberglass and PVC. After the product's useful life, a manufacturer typically downcycles it—shaves off some of the nylon material for further use and discards the leftover material "soup." Alternately, the manufacturer may chop up the whole thing, remelt it, and use it to make more carpet backing. Such a carpet was not originally designed to be recycled and is being forced into another cycle for which it is not ideally suited. But carpeting designed as a true technical nutrient would be made of safe materials designed to be truly recycled as raw material for fresh carpeting, and the delivery system for its service would cost the same as or less than buying it. One of our ideas for a new design would combine a durable bottom layer with a detachable top. When a customer wants to replace the carpeting, the manufacturer simply removes the top, snaps down a fresh one in the desired color, and takes the old one back as food for further carpeting.

Under this scenario, people could indulge their hunger for new products as often as they wish, without guilt, and industry could encourage them to do so with impunity, knowing that both sides are supporting the technical metabolism in the process. Automobile manufactures would *want* people to turn in their old cars in order to regain valuable industrial nutrients. Instead of waving industrial resources good-bye as the customer drives off in a new car, never to enter the dealership again, automobile companies could develop lasting and valuable relationships that enhance customers' quality of life for many decades and that continually enrich the industry itself with industrial "food."

Designing products as products of service means designing them to be disassembled. Industry need not design what it makes to be durable beyond a certain amount of time, any more than nature does. The durability of many current products could even be seen as a kind of intergenerational tyranny. Maybe we want our things to live forever, but what do future generations want? What about their right to the pursuit of life, liberty, and happiness, to a celebration of their own abundance of nutrients, of materials, of delight? Manufacturers would, however, have permanent responsibility for storing and, if it is possible to do so safely, reusing whatever potentially hazardous materials their products contain. What better incentive to evolve a design that does without the hazardous materials entirely?

The advantages of this system, when fully implemented, would be threefold: it would produce no useless and potentially dangerous waste; it would save manufacturers billions of dollars in valuable materials over time; and because nutrients for new products are constantly circulated, it would diminish the extraction of raw materials (such as petrochemicals) and the manufacture of potentially disruptive materials, such as PVC, and eventually phase them out, resulting in more savings to the manufacturer and enormous benefit to the environment.

A number of products are already being designed as biological and technical nutrients. But for the foreseeable future, many products will still not fit either category, a potentially dangerous situation. In addition, certain products cannot be confined to one metabolism exclusively because of the way they are used in the world. These products demand special attention.

When Worlds Collide

If a product must, for the time being, remain a "monstrous hybrid" [that is, "a mixture of materials both technical and biological, neither of which can be salvaged after their current lives"], it may take extra ingenuity to design and market it to have positive consequences for both the biological and technical metabolisms. Consider the unintended design legacy of the average pair of running shoes, something many of us own. While you are going for your walk or run, an activity that supposedly contributes to your health and well-being, each pounding of your shoes releases into the environment tiny particles containing chemicals that may be teratogens, carcinogens, or other substances that can reduce fertility and inhibit the oxidizing properties of cells. The next rain will wash these particles into the plants and soil around the road. (If the soles of your athletic shoes contain a special bubble filled with gases for cushioning—some of which were recently discovered factors in global warming—you may also be contributing to climate change.) Running shoes can be redesigned so that their soles are biological nutrients. Then when they break down under pounding feet, they will nourish the organic metabolism instead of poisoning it. As long as the uppers remain technical nutrients, however, the shoes would be designed for easy disassembly in order to be safely recirculated in both cycles (with the technical materials to be retrieved by the manufacturer). Retrieving technical nutrients from the shoes of famous athletes—and advertising the fact—could give an athletic-gear company a competitive edge.

Some materials do not fit into either the organic or technical metabolism because they contain materials that are hazardous. We call them *unmarketables,* and until technological ways of detoxifying them—or doing without them—have been developed, they also require creative measures. They can be stored in "parking lots"—safe repositories that the producer of the material either maintains or pays a storage fee to use. Current unmarketables can be recalled for safe storage, until they can be detoxified and returned as valuable molecules to a safe human use. Nuclear waste is clearly an unmarketable; in a pure sense, the definition should also include materials known to have hazardous components. PVC is one such example: instead of being incinerated or landfilled, it might instead be safely "parked" until cost-effective detoxification technologies have evolved. As currently made, PET, with its antimony content, is another unmarketable: with some technological ingenuity, items that contain PET, such as soda bottles, might even be upcycled to remove the antimony residues and to create a clean polymer ready for continuous, safe reuse.

Companies might undertake a *waste phaseout,* in which unmarketables—problematic wastes and nutrients—are removed from the current waste stream. Certain polyesters now on the market could be gathered and their problematic antimony removed. This would be preferable to leaving them in textiles, where they will eventually be disposed of or incinerated, perhaps therefore to enter natural systems and nutrient flows. The materials in certain monstrous hybrids could be similarly gathered and separated. Cotton could be composted out of polyester-cotton textile blends, and the polyester then returned to technical cycles. Shoe companies might recover chromium from shoes. Other industries might retrieve parts of television sets and other service products from landfills. Making a successful transition requires leadership in these areas as well as creative owning up.

Should manufacturers of existing products feel guilty about their complicity in this heretofore destructive agenda? Yes. No. It doesn't matter. Insanity has been defined as doing the same thing over and over and expecting a different outcome. Negligence is described as doing the same thing over and over even though you know it is dangerous, stupid, or wrong. Now that we know, it's time for a change. Negligence starts tomorrow.

Discussion Questions

1. According to the John Elkington quote in the first reading, a sustainable society must meet three conditions: "its rates of use of renewable resources should not exceed their rates of regeneration; its rates of use of non-renewable resources should not exceed the rate at which sustainable renewable substitutes are developed; and its rates of pollution should not exceed the assimilative capacity of the environment." Which of these do you think is the most challenging and why?

2. The "triple bottom line" includes financial, social, and environmental components. One commentator describes the concept somewhat differently, writing that sustainable businesses should create "financial benefits for the company, natural world benefits, and social benefits for employees and members of the local community." Matthew Tueth, *Fundamentals of Sustainable Business* 46 (2010) (preferring the term "the triple top line"). Under either formulation, which of the three components do you think is most likely to be ignored or discounted?

3. Sneirson uses an energy company, an automobile company, and a food company to offer examples of sustainable practices. Can you think of other examples, including some general practices that would apply across all industry lines?

4. What are the pros and cons of the two ways Sneirson gives for operationalizing sustainability—the triple bottom line and gearing up? What are their differences and which one is more easily determined?

5. Can you give examples of companies that you believe have not even reached "first gear"? Should these firms be forced to reach at least first gear? If so, how? Can you give examples of companies that you believe have shifted into "overdrive"?

6. Do you prefer the triple-bottom-line approach to the gearing-up approach to sustainable business? Which approach would you choose if you were the CEO of a company? What sorts of barriers would you expect to encounter?

7. Do you agree with Kates et al. and Hirokawa that it is good that sustainability as a concept is vague and malleable? Does it invite "greenwashing" by firms portraying themselves as sustainable when they are in fact not? What are the alternatives?

8. One area in which different stakeholders can come into conflict is in the area of green building. How could the interests of builders and purchasers, landlords and tenants, companies and society conflict? How should such conflicts be resolved? Through bargaining? Local regulation?

9. Western environmentalists have adopted the notion, based on Judeo-Christian ethics, that man is the steward over the natural world and must engage in "enlightened management" of that world. Do you think this anthropocentric idea is superior

to one of "a kinship relationship" that asserts the basic equality of all plants and animals?

10. The "natural capitalism" article describes four major shifts in business practice. What legal or tax changes must be made to ensure that businesses follow this approach?

11. What are some examples of how our current system rewards companies for wasting natural resources? Or penalizes them for boosting resource productivity?

12. One of the intriguing business models mentioned in this chapter is leasing. This can convert a capital expenditure (like the purchase of carpet) into an ordinary operating, currently deductible expense. What other benefits does the leasing model offer?

13. Why would a company consider restoring, sustaining, and expanding their biological resource base? Can you think of any examples of companies that have benefited from this sort of activity?

14. Research a favorite product's lifecycle and determine the origins, distances, and disposability of the product's component parts. Are you surprised? Does your research change the way you view or value the product? Can you think of ways to improve the product through "cradle to cradle" design? For a video of Apple's recycling process, and its disassembling robot "Liam," visit http://apple.co/1SdvFbJ.

15. Do you agree with McDonough and Braungart's contention that "unmarketables" should be stored in "parking lots" until they can be detoxified and returned to safe productive use? Why or why not? If so, who should bear the costs of these parking lots?

16. In her book *Living Downstream,* Sandra Steingraber describes the human and financial costs of the use of industrial toxins. Why do you think many companies do not take human costs into account in their production and operation systems?

17. Are the readings in this chapter too optimistic, suggesting that minor changes in the way firms design things and do business can create win-win situations and solve all of our problems? Can we solve our environmental and social problems without dramatically altering our lifestyles and making sacrifices?

Chapter 3

Sustainability Meets Corporate Governance

With this chapter we begin our survey of different fields of business law and examine how sustainability and sustainable business practices interact with those laws. The first reading offers an overview of the corporate law issues involving sustainability and corporate social responsibility and previews a securities-law issue to be addressed in Chapter 6.* The remaining readings engage the question of whether corporate law permits firms to engage in sustainable business practices at all or whether firms must eschew such considerations in favor of maximizing profits for the company's shareholders. The last excerpt is written by an expert in environmental as opposed to corporate law and advances more sweeping changes. As you read these authors' recommendations, consider whether they would have any meaningful impact, whether they are likely to be adopted, and whether those two considerations might be mutually exclusive.

Thomas Joo, *Global Warming and the Management-Centered Corporation*†

... Some commentators argue that shareholders' governance power has the potential to make corporations serve social interests. I think this view, which I have elsewhere labeled "democratic aspirationalism," is excessively optimistic. There are two reasons for this. First, shareholders' actual governance power is too limited to change corporate policy directly. Second, if shareholder power were increased beyond its current limits, it is far from clear that shareholders would use that power in any significant way to curtail carbon emissions or for any other socially beneficial purpose.

The reality is that corporate-governance power is heavily concentrated in upper management. Thus, ... improving corporate social responsibility through corporate-governance mechanisms should incorporate the perspective of what I have called "hi-

* The terms "sustainable business" and "corporate social responsibility" are often used interchangeably, and corporate law treats both kinds of efforts the same. Because sustainability only recently appeared in the business law literature, some of the excerpted materials speak in terms of a business's social responsibility. That said, sustainability is generally considered to be broader than corporate social responsibility: whereas corporate social responsibility focuses more on a business's responsibility to act ethically and consider its environmental and other impacts, sustainability aims to preserve financial, environmental, and human resources well into the future.

† Originally published in 44 Wake Forest Law Review 671 (2009). Reprinted with permission.

ıcal realism"—that is, acknowledging and taking advantage of the fact that ˌorations are run not by shareholders, but by a small core of top executives, under ıe supervision of a board of directors. [I] will discuss this hierarchical structure and its implications for climate change reform [and] focus on three aspects of corporate governance that seem to have captured the imagination of social-responsibility activists: "corporate democracy," management's fiduciary duty to shareholders, and management's duty to disclose material information....

"Corporate Democracy"

Shareholders participate in and vote on corporate affairs in two primary ways: first, by making and voting on policy proposals, and second, by electing directors. These ostensible powers, however, are largely formalistic and have little direct impact on corporate policymaking.

First of all, shareholder resolutions are typically non-binding; even if a majority of shareholders were to approve a resolution, a corporation could choose to ignore it. Second, the securities laws give management a number of grounds to exclude proposals from the proxy based on their content. When management receives a proposal and wishes to exclude it, it must submit its reasons to the Securities and Exchange Commission ("SEC"). At the same time, management typically requests a "no-action letter" from the Division of Enforcement—that is, an informal assurance that the Division will not advise the SEC to take action against the corporation for the exclusion.

If a proposal were to ask management to take some action with respect to global warming, the most relevant ground for excluding the proposal would probably be that it "deals with a matter relating to the company's ordinary business operations."[11] The SEC has vacillated in its interpretation of this rule. In 1976, the SEC announced that the "ordinary business" rule did not allow exclusion of proposals regarding "matters which have significant policy, economic or other implications inherent in them."[12] In 1992, the SEC repudiated that interpretation on the ground that it was too difficult to apply, and stated that all proposals relating to ordinary business would be excludible.[13] In 1998, however, the SEC reversed itself yet again and returned to the 1976 interpretation: "[F]rom time to time, in light of experience ... and reflecting changing societal views, the Division [of Enforcement] adjusts its view with respect to 'social policy' proposals involving ordinary business."[14]

Whether a global-warming-related proposal raises "significant policy, economic or other implications" remains unclear, however. In 2004, the Nathan Cummings Foundation, a shareholder of The Ryland Group, Inc., one of the nation's largest homebuilders, submitted a proposal requesting that Ryland's board appoint a com-

---

11. See 17 C.F.R. §240.14-8(i)(7)....

12. See N.Y. City Employees' Ret. Sys. v. SEC, 45 F.3d 7, 10 (2d Cir. 1995)....

13. Cracker Barrel Old Country Store, Inc., SEC No-Action Letter, 1992 WL 289095, at *1 (Oct. 13, 1992).

14. Amendments to Rules of Shareholder Proposals, Exchange Act Release No. 40,018, Investment Company Act Release No. 23,200, 63 Fed. Reg. 29,106, 29,108 (May 28, 1998).

mittee to "assess how the company is responding to rising regulatory, competitive, and public pressure to increase energy efficiency and reduce greenhouse-gas emissions and report to shareholders." Ryland sought to exclude the proposal on "ordinary business" grounds. In February 2005, the SEC refused to issue a no-action letter to Ryland. Only four days earlier, however, it had granted Wachovia Bank a no-action letter with respect to its planned exclusion of a similar shareholder proposal by the Service Employees International Union ("SEIU") Master Trust, also on "ordinary business" grounds. Because neither response included a statement of reasons, there is no way to know whether the differing results were simply inconsistent or grounded in differences between the companies' "ordinary business." ... The uncertainty about the viability of proposals may discourage shareholders from incurring the expenses related to developing and submitting proposals....

Even when socially-oriented shareholder proposals are included on the corporate proxy, they tend to fail by significant margins. Indeed, for such proposals, support of ten, sixteen, and twenty-seven percent is considered "impressive." Less than eight percent of the shares voted were cast in favor of the 2005 Ryland proposal. It has been argued that shareholder proposals, even if they fail, shape public opinion by calling attention to social issues. Thus, it might be argued, even if the proposal process cannot directly change corporate behavior, it might help educate the public about global warming, thereby influencing voting and consumer behavior for the better. But it is just as likely, if not more so, that proposals, and shareholders' votes on them, *reflect* rather than cause changes in social norms. The SEC espouses this view....

In 2008, the Nathan Cummings Foundation submitted yet another proposal to Ryland. This proposal was more aggressively worded (and thus more likely to qualify for exclusion). Nonetheless, Ryland apparently did not seek to exclude this proposal. It did, however, file a statement in opposition (routine practice when a shareholder proposal is included in the corporate proxy) claiming the proposal was unnecessary because Ryland was already doing its best to reduce energy consumption. The 2008 proposal also failed. It did, however, fare better than the 2005 proposal, receiving 25.4% of the shares voting.

Does the increase in shareholder support illustrate the importance of shareholder proposals as a tool for education? It seems unlikely. The corporate proxy is a poor forum for education on new topics. Proxy rules limit a proposal's supporting statement to 500 words and allow the corporation to print a rebuttal. Moreover, despite the copious ink spilled on the topic by academics (myself included), shareholder proposals are an obscure and esoteric forum compared to television, newspapers, and the Internet. Even among shareholders, shareholder proposals are unlikely to rank highly as a source of information and opinion shaping....

The public is unlikely to be aware of the results of votes on proposals. They are not widely reported unless they are dramatic. After a shareholder vote takes place, the company is required to report the results on a Form 10-Q. An interested party would have to know that the vote had taken place, that the results are reported on the 10-Q, and that 10-Q filings are available on the SEC website. The report would not be filed until the end of the quarter and would not be available for some time after filing....

State Law Fiduciary Duty Litigation

State corporate governance law is routinely criticized for supposedly centering on management's duty to enrich shareholders. Advocates for socially responsible corporate behavior have periodically tried to leverage that supposed duty by arguing that socially responsible reforms would improve the corporate bottom line.[48] But even assuming that an environmental reform, such as producing products with smaller carbon footprints, could increase profitability, that fact would do no more than provide a bit of amateur business advice to management. It would not implicate any legally actionable duty. Although there are some references to management's supposed "duty" to enrich shareholders in corporate case law, it is not a legal duty in any proper sense, because shareholders have no cause of action against management for failure to maximize corporate profits or shareholder wealth.

The central tenet of state corporation law is the "business judgment rule." More of a general orientation than a doctrinal rule, it means that courts are highly deferential to the business decisions of corporate directors and officers. This concept has deep ideological roots in the libertarian aversion to government interference in business. Courts will not review the substantive merits of a business judgment, and thus shareholders have no cause of action against management for an incorrect or unwise business decision. Furthermore, the decisions of managers are presumptively informed, good-faith exercises of business judgment; shareholders must upset this firm presumption (typically by alleging self-serving or otherwise disloyal acts by management) to sustain a cause of action.

Thus, while much is made lately of the supposed profit potential in "going green," no corporation has a legal obligation to pursue such opportunities. As long as they remain legal, "dirty" products and services will remain in great demand. Regardless of whether it would be a poor business judgment to forego the "green" market, it would nonetheless be a business judgment and as such it would not be actionable by shareholders under state corporation law.

If greenhouse-gas regulation were to pass, shareholders might conceivably assert fiduciary duty claims against management for failure to anticipate and prepare for regulation. But given the business judgment rule and the permissiveness of the duty of care, such an argument would have to assert not just an error or even poor judgment, but an abject failure, even a refusal, to become informed.... And after establishing that management failed to prepare for regulation, shareholders would have to assert that management failed to act after the shape of impending regulation became reasonably clear. Such clarity is likely to remain elusive until the eleventh hour, however....

---

48. Robert Clark terms this equation of profit and social responsibility "monism." Robert C. Clark, Corporate Law 681 (1986)....

Even *after* the shape of regulation was to become clear, indeed even after it was implemented, shareholders would still have difficulty asserting a cause of action against management for failing to reduce emissions. For example, under a cap-and-trade scheme, by its very nature, any given corporation could choose to emit and buy credits rather than reduce its emissions. That choice would implicate precisely the kind of business decision typically protected under the business judgment rule (regardless of whether management actually engaged in a sophisticated cost-benefit analysis). Thus, shareholders would almost certainly be unable to challenge such a decision as a corporate-governance matter.

Nor would hard emissions caps (whether independent of, or as an adjunct to, cap-and-trade) necessarily empower shareholders to sue management for failing to reduce emissions. Even when a corporation's actions violate the law, it is extremely difficult for shareholders to hold management liable for failing to prevent the violation. Delaware case law nominally imposes upon directors a duty to monitor the corporation's compliance with its legal and regulatory obligations and its directors' and officers' fiduciary obligations. But this nominal duty in fact adds little or nothing beyond the duty of loyalty and the lenient duty of care.... Moreover, the cases emphasize that the standard is a very lenient one with respect to corporate management.

[The third aspect of corporate governance discussed next is "management's duty to disclose material information." This topic involves securities law more than corporate governance and is discussed in Chapter 6.]

Judd F. Sneirson, *Doing Well by Doing Good: Leveraging Due Care for Better, More Socially Responsible Corporate Decisionmaking**

One of the long-running debates in modern corporate law concerns the proper purpose of the corporation. Must a corporation serve the interests of its shareholders to the exclusion of all other considerations, typically by aiming to maximize shareholder wealth? Or may—or should or must—a corporation also serve other constituencies, such as its creditors, customers, suppliers, employees, and the communities in which it operates insofar as these broader stakeholders' interests better represent the best interests of the corporate enterprise?

Current thinking suggests that, both as a matter of state statutory law and as a consequence of the business judgment rule, corporations may—but need not—consider non-shareholder interests in making business decisions. Indeed, a great many corporations deliberately strive to serve interests beyond just their shareholders, and turn a nice profit in the process. This Article challenges the current thinking to conclude that corporate boards and managers, as a matter of their fiduciary obligation to exercise due care, *must* at least assess and consider the interests of non-shareholder constituencies in reaching all their decisions.

---

* Originally published in 3 Corporate Governance Law Review 438 (2007). Reprinted with permission.

Based as it is on the modern fiduciary duty of due care, this poses only a procedural requirement on corporate decisionmaking. That is, in the end, it does not force managers to yield to non-shareholder interests at all or ever. Yet, by requiring corporate decisionmakers to assess and consider the impact on non-shareholder stakeholders before acting, substantively better decisions, that better take into account all of the corporation's best interests, will likely result....

Corporate Social Responsibility

The corporate social responsibility debate involves two interconnected issues. The first and more obvious one concerns the role of corporations in society. Sometimes this issue appears in other forms—to whom do corporate fiduciaries owe their duties, or what if any role do non-shareholder constituencies like labor, customers, and the public play in modern corporate governance. At bottom, however, these queries are merely different ways to articulate the same concept. No matter how one poses the question, proponents of corporate social responsibility seek through corporate and securities law to encourage—and in some cases to require—a broader, more communitarian role for corporations and thus responsibility to more than just the company's shareholders. Corporate social responsibility critics, for their part, generally prefer corporations to focus exclusively on shareholders and maximizing the return on their investments in the company.

The second aspect of the stakeholder debate concerns monitoring and motivating corporate managers. Corporate social responsibility proposals typically press for managers to have the discretion to make company decisions in the best interests of all of the company's constituencies. Some proposals take this a step further and call for managers to assume affirmative fiduciary obligations to employees, the environment, and other stakeholders as well as to the company's shareholders. Either way, critics charge, such significant discretion makes managers more difficult to monitor, measure in terms of their performance, and otherwise keep in check and on task. Moreover, management theorists add, presenting managers with so many competing constituencies and objectives is likely to obscure overriding corporate goals, such as maximization of the long-term value of the enterprise, rendering the company at a competitive disadvantage.

... Is [corporate social responsibility] good for business?... Proponents of corporate social responsibility in the management literature, like their legal counterparts, argue that managers should make decisions that take into account all of the stakeholders in a firm.[53] One early advocate of stakeholder theory offered seven "principles of stakeholder management," including the following:

---

53. See, e.g., Max B.E. Clarkson, Principles of Stakeholder Management, in Principles of Stakeholder Management 1–2 (1999), available online at http://www.rotman.utoronto.ca/ccbe/; R. Edward Freeman, Strategic Management: A Stakeholder Approach 52 (1984) ("[I]f business organizations are to be successful in the current and future environment then executives must take multiple stakeholder groups into account.").

- Managers should acknowledge and actively monitor the concerns of all legitimate stakeholders, and should take their interests appropriately into account in decisionmaking and operations.... [and]
- Managers should recognize the interdependence of efforts and rewards among stakeholders and should attempt to achieve a fair distribution of the benefits and burdens of corporate activity among them....[54]

Moreover, proponents of stakeholder theory believe that it "contribute[s] to the long-term survival and success of the firm."[55] They posit that stakeholder theory will foster mutually supportive relationships among stakeholders and replace destructive conflicts with "relational wealth."[56] Further, they contend, "socially and ethically responsible practices" often offer a competitive edge with consumers and, according to some studies, positively correlate with financial indicators of corporate performance.[57]

Others agree "that purely financial measures of performance are not sufficient to yield effective management decisions."[58] In a series of *Harvard Business Review* articles, Robert Kaplan and David Norton advanced a variant on stakeholder theory whereby managers balance financial considerations with other measures of future company performance.[59] The result is what they call a

> Balanced Scorecard [of considerations] organized around four perspectives—financial, customer, internal, and innovation and learning. The name reflect[s] the balance ... between short- and long-term objectives, between financial and nonfinancial measures, between lagging and leading indicators, and between external and internal performance perspectives.[60]

Kaplan and Norton have encouraged the scorecard's use both to measure business performance and to manage enterprises so as to optimize future performance. Their idea quickly became popular with many executives and with the public as an attractive way in which to manage a business.

This popularity notwithstanding, some have criticized stakeholder theory and the balanced scorecard model in two major respects. First, critics argue, by making managers accountable to all stakeholder groups, stakeholder theory makes managers accountable to no one and free to pursue their own ends. "To paraphrase the old

54. See Clarkson, supra note 53, at 4.

55. See id. at 2.

56. See id.

57. See id....

58. See Michael C. Jensen, Value Maximization, Stakeholder Theory, and the Corporate Objective Function, 14 Journal of Applied Corporate Finance 8, 17–18 (2001) (paraphrasing Robert S. Kaplan & David P. Norton, The Balanced Scorecard (1996), and agreeing with their premise).

59. See, e.g., Robert S. Kaplan & David P. Norton, The Balanced Scorecard: Measures that Drive Performance, Harvard Business Review 71–79 (Jan.–Feb. 1992); Robert S. Kaplan & David P. Norton, Using the Balanced Scorecard as a Strategic Management System, Harvard Business Review 51 (Jan.–Feb. 1996).

60. See Robert S. Kaplan & David P. Norton, The Balanced Scorecard viii–ix (1996).

adage, when where are many masters, all end up being shortchanged."[63] Second, critics contend that stakeholder theory and the balanced scorecard offer so many objectives that managers are left with no clear objective or direction. Critics predict that the resulting "confusion and lack of purpose ... will handicap the firm in its competition for survival."[65] The firm would be much better off, critics argue, if managers manage the company with a single objective in mind—namely, maximizing long-term shareholder value.

A third approach to the stakeholder debate comes from influential financial economist Michael Jensen.... In what he terms "enlightened stakeholder theory," Jensen posits that the best way to maximize the long-term value of a corporation is not to strive to serve all of the firm's different constituencies, nor is it to focus exclusively on shareholder profits and completely ignore the firm's other stakeholders.[68] Rather, to maximize the long-term value of the firm, corporate managers must gauge and on some level tend to all of the firm's constituencies.[69] He writes,

> [W]e cannot maximize the long-term market value of an organization if we ignore or mistreat any important constituency. We cannot create value without good relations with customers, employees, financial backers, suppliers, regulators, and communities.[70]

Sometimes satisfying these other stakeholders—even at the expense of short-term profits—will increase the long-term value of the firm. Other times, satisfying other stakeholders will not so increase firm value. According to Jensen's enlightened stakeholder theory, to achieve the goal of long-term value maximization, corporate decisionmakers should first assess and consider any effects on all of the firm's various constituencies, and then proceed according to the best interests of the entire enterprise.

The Modern Duty of Due Care

... [T]he fiduciary duty of due care requires that corporate managers exercise that degree of skill, diligence, and care that a reasonably prudent person would exercise in similar circumstances. Corporate directors must thus keep familiar with the business, stay informed about the firm's activities, engage in a general monitoring of the firm's affairs, attend meetings, review financial statements, and make inquiries into dubious matters, raising objections where appropriate and resigning if corrections

63. See Jensen, supra note 58, at 14.

65. See id. at 11.

68. "Value" here means "the sum of the values of all financial claims on the firm—debt, warrants, and preferred stock, as well as equity," not stock value, accounting profits, or earnings per share. See id. at 8, 16–17.

69. See id. at 9. This view is not so far from the team-production model of corporate governance Margaret Blair and Lynn Stout describe in Margaret M. Blair & Lynn A. Stout, A Team Production Theory of Corporate Law, 85 Virginia Law Review 247 (1999) (calling for boards of directors to act as "mediating hierarchs" charged with determining the best use of corporate assets and resolving disputes that arise between shareholders, managers, and other corporate constituencies).

70. See Jensen, supra note 58, at 16....

are not made. Corporate officers must adhere to a similar standard of conduct in their actions and in making their decisions.

While Delaware* corporate law traditionally measured due care according to a substantive standard, it has largely shifted over time to a strictly procedural standard of review. Courts applying modern corporate law thus do not judge business decisions on their merits with the benefit—and potential bias—of hindsight; rather, courts test the process by which managers reach their decisions, ensuring that there is no conflict of interest present and that business decisions are made conscientiously, in good faith, and on reasonably full information. So long as these due-care procedures are followed, courts in effect abstain from further review of the business decision, invoking the business judgment rule.

Consequently, corporate managers enjoy considerable discretion in the decisions they make. Simply put, if managers follow the required duty of care procedures, their decisions will be largely immune to legal challenges. What is more, Delaware law further widens this discretion in two respects. First, courts measure a director's adherence or departure from the duty of due care requirements according to a permissive gross negligence standard of review, more akin to recklessness than simple negligence. Second, Delaware, and most other states, permit firms to immunize directors—but not officers—from suits seeking damages for due-care breaches. Most corporations take advantage of this opportunity such that even a complete failure to follow the required due-care procedures often will not result in director liability. This effectively leaves injunctive relief as the only remedy that may be obtained for a board's breach of the duty of due care. For example, faced with a board decision reached on less than full information, a court may, at its discretion, enjoin and/or invalidate the decision so that a board may reconsider it in light of the additional, no-longer-missing information.

What this means in terms of the stakeholder debate is that corporate managers may safely take into account non-shareholder constituencies when making their decisions and not fear allegations that they did not sufficiently focus on shareholders and maximizing shareholder wealth. This will certainly be true where managers can articulate some long-term profit-maximizing rationale for their decision, as will usually be the case, but it is equally true in those rare situations where a decision is motivated solely to benefit non-shareholder constituencies and no argument can be made that shareholder profits will eventually and however indirectly accrue.[89]

The constituency statutes many states enacted in the 1980s in response to that decade's surge of corporate takeover activity reaffirm this level of discretion under the duty of due care. That is, most constituency statutes simply make explicit the generally accepted principle, set forth above, that corporate decisionmakers may, but

* [Delaware is the dominant American jurisdiction on corporate law matters.—Eds.]

89. These situations would be exceedingly rare. That said, if there were truly "no rationally related benefits accruing to the stockholders," it might prove problematic under...some Delaware precedents.

do not have to, consider non-shareholder constituencies when making their business decisions.[90] And so, according to both their common law fiduciary duties and according to the constituency statutes, corporate managers enjoy considerable discretion in making their decisions to take into account the interests of the corporation's non-shareholder constituencies.

This is considerable discretion to afford corporate managers, to be sure. However, strong reasons support granting corporate decisionmakers this degree of latitude. First and foremost, such discretion may be necessary for modern corporations to work effectively. That is, because corporate shareholders lack the information, incentives, and coordination to make sound decisions on the firm's behalf, shareholders will prefer to vest true decisionmaking authority in a small, centralized group of managers. For this delegation of authority to be meaningful, managers must be able to exercise this authority fully, freely, and in most instances without constant shareholder interference. In other words, granting managers true authority comes at the expense of accountability.

The traditional rationales behind the business judgment rule likewise support this wide managerial discretion. The most compelling of these is discouraging overly conservative decisionmaking. If managers were too easily held accountable for their bad business decisions, managers might avoid many worthy but risky opportunities and thus forego many potential sources of value. Relatedly, some posit that shareholders—who, after all, have a range of available investment options and may easily and cheaply diversify their stock portfolios—are in a better position than corporate managers to absorb the risk of poor business decisions. Viewed in this way, shareholders can also be said to have assumed the risk of a certain amount of honest and loyal, but in the end bad, business judgments. The business judgment rule also mitigates concerns that courts, with the benefit and bias of hindsight, will more likely than is appropriate fault corporate decisionmakers for their well-intentioned but, it turns out, poor decisions.

In sum, modern corporate law affords managers considerable discretion to manage the firm as best they see fit. So long as there are no conflicts of interest, and managers reach their decisions conscientiously, in good faith, and after considering reasonably full information, their decisions will be not be second-guessed in the courts. Accordingly, corporate law allows—but is not generally understood to require—corporate managers to consider non-shareholder constituencies in making the company's decisions.... [H]ow much information is "reasonably full"? The Delaware precedents require corporate fiduciaries to make their decisions only after obtaining and considering "all material information" that is reasonably available given the circumstances.[98]

90. See, e.g., Ind. Code Ann. §23-1-35-1(d), (f) ("A director may, in considering the best interests of a corporation, consider the effects of any action on shareholders, employees, suppliers, and customers of the corporation, and communities in which offices or other facilities are located, and any other factors the director considers pertinent.")... [T]hese statutes are simply codifications, and not extensions, of existing corporate law rules.

98. See Smith v. Van Gorkom, 488 A.2d 858 (Del. 1985) (quoting Aronson, 473 A.2d at 812, for the requirement that directors avail themselves of "all material information reasonably available to them"); Brehm v. Eisner, 746 A.2d 244, 259 (Del. 2000) ("[I]n making business decisions, directors

And in this context, "material" means "relevant and of a magnitude to be important in carrying out the[ ] fiduciary duty of care in decisionmaking."[99]

Leveraging Due Care

... As the above due-care discussion shows, corporate fiduciaries must, as a matter of their obligation to exercise due care, obtain and consider all reasonably available material information before making company decisions. If they fail to do so, corporate law may protect them from personal liability, but it will not similarly protect their decisions. Rather, decisions reached on less than full information are subject to invalidation in the courts so that managers may reconsider them in light of any additional, no-longer-missing, material information.

How should corporate fiduciaries fulfill this obligation to obtain and consider all reasonably available material information impacting their decisions? Because such information may derive from any of the firm's constituencies, decisionmakers should gauge each of them to determine whether the corporate decision to be made or action to be taken will likely affect them and thus the company. To the extent these effects seem so likely and pronounced that they might constitute the sort of information a reasonable person would want to take into account in making a decision, corporate fiduciaries must further consider these stakeholders' impacts, in good faith, along with any other material information, in reaching their decision of whether and how to take corporate action.

That said, whatever decision corporate fiduciaries ultimately make after giving good-faith consideration to all requisite information will be accorded deference as a properly reached business judgment. This marks a departure both from the conventional view that corporate fiduciaries may—but need not—consider stakeholder interests in making their decisions, and from many progressive proposals that would require corporate boards to cater to certain corporate constituencies in every business decision. Under the view expressed here, as a matter of their fiduciary duty of due care, corporate decisionmakers must in good faith consider the potential impact on each of the firm's stakeholders before making company decisions but in the end can reach whatever decision they feel is in the best interests of the enterprise.

This view of fiduciaries' due-care obligations comports with the progressive corporate law theory, ... [and] with the suggestion in the management literature that, when firms consider all available information in their decisionmaking process, firms reach better and oftentimes more socially responsible decisions. How exactly should corporate actors fulfill this fiduciary obligation to obtain and consider all reasonably available information that is material to their decisions?...

---

must consider all material information reasonably available, and ... the directors' process is only actionable if [it is] grossly negligent.").

99. See Brehm, 746 A.2d at 260 n.49 (applying the materiality standard from TSC Indus., Inc. v. Northway, Inc., 426 U.S. 438, 449 (1976), namely, sufficiently likely and significant such that a reasonable person would consider it to be important)....

A tested model for assessing the materiality of impacts already exists in the National Environmental Policy Act ("NEPA").[117] NEPA is a process-oriented statute that forces federal agencies to assess the environmental consequences of their actions and thereby consider environmental values in their decisionmaking. If NEPA applies to an agency action, the agency must first determine whether a proposal will have "significant environmental impact."[120] If it will have such an effect, the agency must, before taking further action, prepare a formal environmental impact statement that details the specific environmental effects of a proposal and sets forth and analyzes alternatives, including the alternative of taking no action at all. After creating and disclosing the environmental impact statement, allowing an opportunity for public comments, and giving full, good-faith consideration to both, whatever decision the agency reaches will be accorded deference. As in corporate law, so long as the required procedures are followed, courts will respect the results.

If it is unclear whether an action will have significant environmental impact, an agency can conduct a less formal study to gauge whether significant environmental impacts would result and thus whether a full-blown impact statement must be completed. These environmental assessments should

> contain brief discussions of the need for the proposed action, alternatives to the proposed action, the environmental impacts of the proposed action and any alternatives, and a list of agencies and persons consulted during the assessment process.[125]

If in the assessment the agency concludes that an action is not likely to have significant environmental impact, no further action need be taken. If, however, the environmental assessment suggests that an action will have significant environmental impact, then the agency must fulfill the environmental impact statement requirement.

While NEPA has been criticized on various grounds and from various corners, it has been largely successful at injecting underrepresented considerations into decisionmaking processes that tended to unduly stress other values. What is more, NEPA

---

117. See National Environmental Policy Act of 1969, 42 U.S.C. §§ 4321 et seq.

120. See NEPA § 102(2)(C), 42 U.S.C. § 4332(2)(C) (requiring an environmental impact statement for federal actions "significantly affecting the quality of the human environment").

125. See Robert L. Glicksman et al., Environmental Protection: Law and Policy 162 (4th ed. 2003). The Council on Environmental Quality, the body charged with overseeing and implementing NEPA, describes an environmental assessment this way:

> Since an EA is a concise document, it should not contain long descriptions or detailed data which the agency may have gathered. Rather, it should contain a brief discussion of the need for the proposal, alternatives to the proposal, the environmental impacts of the proposed action and alternatives, and a list of agencies and persons consulted.... [T]he Council has generally advised agencies to keep the length of EAs to not more than approximately 10–15 pages.

Forty Most Asked Questions Concerning CEQ's National Environmental Policy Act Regulations, 46 Fed. Reg. 18026 (Mar. 17, 1981); see also Cronin v. U.S. Dep't of Agriculture, 919 F.2d 439, 443 (7th Cir. 1990) ("An environmental assessment is a rough-cut, low-budget environmental impact statement designed to show whether a full-fledged environmental impact statement ... is necessary.").

is widely viewed as having made a positive difference in terms of the substance of agency decisions. Though NEPA's success can be hard to measure, many proposals have been rethought and improved or abandoned as a result of the environmental impact statement scheme and related public disclosures. In fact, according to one study, NEPA has not only improved and protected the environment, it has also improved agency decisionmaking in other ways, including on average saving agencies money. In short, NEPA teaches that more and better information tends to improve end results.

Given the many similarities in procedures and objectives, the corporate fiduciary obligation to exercise due care and act on full information could profit from incorporating certain elements of the NEPA model. It would be impractical, to say the least, for corporations to stop and conduct a formal and detailed analysis akin to an environmental impact statement every time a prospective decision will affect the company's non-shareholder constituencies. Likewise, NEPA's public comment feature has no counterpart in corporate law decisionmaking and therefore seems inapt. Something along the lines of NEPA's environmental assessment, however, would only amount to a minor imposition on corporate decisionmaking yet it would offer a helpful, systematic way for fiduciaries to make the initial assessment of whether the effects of a decision on corporate constituencies would be so material that they must be further considered in the final decisionmaking analysis.

To conduct such a "stakeholder assessment," corporate fiduciaries should articulate the reasons for taking corporate action and develop and consider any alternatives to accomplish the same goal as well as the alternative of taking no action.[133] Decisionmakers should then systematically gauge the likelihood and extent of the effects the decision and its alternatives would have on the company and on each of the company's effected constituencies. These include the corporation's shareholders as well as its employees, creditors, suppliers, customers, the communities in which the firm does business, and the general public. If any of these impacts appear to be material, fiduciaries must then, as a matter of their fiduciary duties, give good-faith consideration to those effects, as well as any other relevant, material information, in making the final decision on how or whether the company should proceed.

The extra effort that a stakeholder assessment would entail is not asking too much. For one thing, it is not asking very much. Corporate law already requires corporate decisions to be made on the basis of all reasonably available material information; a stakeholder assessment merely provides a helpful framework for fulfilling this obligation, albeit in a more holistic, broader-minded way. In addition, once the stakeholder assessment is made, and any obtained material information duly considered, corporate fiduciaries remain free to decide corporate matters according to their good-faith business judgment. That is, a stakeholder procedure would not in any way

---

133. Depending on the level at which the corporate decision is made, the stakeholder assessment could be conducted by a committee of the board of directors, a corporate officer, or a compliance group within the firm.

disrupt the delicate balance of authority and accountability embodied in corporate law's process-oriented duty of due care and concomitant business judgment rule. Most importantly, the stakeholder assessment in large part mirrors what according to the cases and management literature represent best corporate practices. So while stakeholder assessments will require some amount of time and effort, better informed decisions will result, and those decisions have the potential to be both more socially responsible *and* more likely to maximize the long-term value of the firm.

Would stakeholder assessments make any difference either in terms of the quality or cost of corporate decisions or in terms of corporate social responsibility? The question is a good one, particularly given the considerable deference corporate law affords directors and, to a lesser extent, officers in their decisionmaking. To be sure, some corporate decisionmakers might be tempted to simply go through motions of performing a stakeholder assessment, thereby satisfy their fiduciary duty of due care, and then take whatever corporate action they would have taken in the first place. But in the process of conducting and considering a shareholder assessment, even these decisionmakers might uncover better alternatives to the original proposed course of action. Alternatively, those conducting the company's stakeholder assessment might be receptive to stakeholder interests and motivated to take the process seriously. In all events, forcing reluctant fiduciaries to confront the stakeholder effects of their decisions may just broaden their conceptions of the best interests of the corporation to more often include the firm's non-shareholder stakeholders that likewise impact the firm and its value.

Stakeholder assessments would have an even greater impact on those firms that, for whatever reason, do not currently explore alternative courses of action and consider the effects of corporate decisions on non-shareholder constituencies before acting. As the previous materials set forth, these firms stand to gain from such a procedure on at least three levels. Stakeholder assessments would assist these firms' decisionmakers in meeting best information-gathering practices, thereby blunting most shareholder derivative suits for breaching the duty of due care. Stakeholder assessments would also help managers identify less obvious "drivers of value in their business" and thereby enable the company's managers to make decisions most likely to maximize the long-term value of the firm. And, as a result, stakeholder assessments would result in decisions more attuned to corporate social responsibility and the best interests of the entire corporate enterprise.

Kent Greenfield,
*Saving the World with Corporate Law**

... The corporation is immensely successful at creating wealth. But because of the narrow fixation on shareholder benefit imbedded in the market, social norms, and corporate law, non-equity investors (employees, communities, etc.) are often shortchanged in the distribution of the wealth they help create. Even though the corporation

* Originally published in 57 Emory Law Journal 948 (2008). Reprinted with permission.

is a collective enterprise when it comes to inputs, the distribution of the outputs is determined by a body—the board—that is dominated by representatives of only two stakeholders: the shareholders and the senior management. Changing this arrangement has the potential not only to improve the corporation's ability to create wealth but also to address serious and enduring social and economic ills. Almost certainly, if senior managers and the board were required to consider the interests of the firm more broadly—to include the well-being of all investors, equity or non-equity—in their decisionmaking calculus, the firm would be more successful in satisfying the social goal of creating wealth, broadly defined.

I should hasten to make clear that I am not proposing a wholesale revamping of the corporate structure. As discussed [in an omitted section], the structure of hierarchy topped by a board is, by many accounts, a fundamental source of corporations' success. Accordingly, I propose (1) taking advantage of the existing structure's ability to satisfy the objective of creating wealth, but changing the definition of wealth within corporate law to mean the wealth of all the stakeholders rather than just the shareholders; and (2) improving the corporation's structure by diversifying the board to include representatives of stakeholders other than shareholders. I will look at these proposals in turn.

Changing the Corporate Objectives to Include the Well-Being of Non-Equity Investors

... [T]he corporation is a collective enterprise, calling on the resources of a number of contributors to create goods or services for profitable sale.... [T]he reason that society cedes power to corporations is to create wealth, broadly defined. The argument here is that if the managers of the firm were required to consider the interests of the firm more broadly—to include the well-being of all investors, equity or non-equity—in their decisionmaking calculus, the firm would be more successful in satisfying the goal of creating social wealth. More precisely, directors should be held to a fiduciary obligation to all of the firm's stakeholders that varies according to the nature of the stakeholders' contributions to the success of the firm.

Even though this might strike some as being a major change, as it does me, it could be achieved by way of a remarkably simple doctrinal adjustment. Courts could simply hold directors and management to a duty to the firm as a whole, defined as the collection of interests imbedded in the firm, rather than a specific subset of it (the shareholders). This is such a simple shift that some corporate law scholars—most prominently Margaret Blair and Lynn Stout[98]—believe that this is even the best description of *current* corporate law. Indeed, some cases can be read to presume such a broad reading of fiduciary obligations.[99] In any event, such a change in doctrine would not represent a huge transformation.

98. Margaret M. Blair & Lynn A. Stout, A Team Production Theory of Corporate Law, 85 Virginia Law Review 247, 305 (1999).

99. See, e.g., Paramount Comm'ns v. Time, Inc., 571 A.2d 1140, 1148 (Del. 1989); Cheff v. Mathes, 199 A.2d 548 (Del. 1964)....

I believe that the benefits of this change would be significant. First, it would be better for firms themselves over time. One reason for this is that it would encourage stakeholders to make firm-specific investments. Firm-specific investments are great assets for the firm because it can then take advantage of and build on the knowledge and expertise of its investors, suppliers, communities and employees over time. The problem that has bedeviled corporate economists, however, is that the more that a particular stakeholder makes investments that are firm-specific, the greater the risk the stakeholder takes that the firm will collapse, violate some implicit or explicit contract with the stakeholder, or extort concessions from the stakeholder. As the stakeholder becomes more valuable to the company, she also becomes more vulnerable.

Because corporations are a collective effort, the key to sustainability is for those who contribute to the firm to believe that the firm can be trusted. Broad fiduciary obligations would help build this trust, ensuring that *all* stakeholders would be willing to make firm-specific investments. This would help ensure that the firm survives over time.

There is an additional reason why fair allocation of the corporate surplus would inure to the benefit of the firm over time. Numerous studies have shown the truth of what we intuit from our everyday interactions, namely that human beings are "reciprocators."[103] Human beings tend to treat others the way that others treat them. Road rage is the negative example; the norm of giving gifts during the holidays is a positive example. In the working world, people are reciprocators as well. For example, workers who believe that they are treated fairly tend to work harder, be more productive, obey firm rules more often, and be more loyal to their employers. This, in turn, likely makes those firms more profitable than they would have been absent such fair treatment.

Even if one is not convinced that more parity among stakeholders is better for firms themselves, there is an additional reason to push for broader fiduciary duties. When we take society's interest as our ultimate guidepost, society is not concerned exclusively with the maximization of aggregate wealth. Rather, the fairness of the allocation of society's wealth is an important principle in the United States, as well as other democracies. As a society, we look not only at the total social wealth but also at the equality of its distribution. This concern is particularly acute now, as income and wealth inequality in the United States is worsening and compares unfavorably to every other industrialized nation.

Presently, economic fairness is ignored in mainstream corporate law. In fact, a theory of corporate law that is based on the unconstrained ability to contract—the mainstream view—virtually ensures that inequality will be worsened. When people use bargained-for exchange to distribute goods, the weaker bargainer will be less able

103. See, e.g., Robyn M. Dawes & Richard H. Thaler, Cooperation, in The Winner's Curse: Paradoxes and Anomalies of Economic Life 9–11 (Richard H. Thaler ed., 1992) (noting that people tend to reciprocate—"kindness with kindness, cooperation with cooperation, hostility with hostility, and defection with defection"); David Dickinson, Ultimatum Decision-Making: A Test of Reciprocal Kindness, 48 Theory & Decision 151, 153 (2000) (describing a study showing that "individuals will be fair and kind to those that show them kindness, and unkind to those that show them malice")....

to extract concessions from the other. So, unless there is some constraint on the ability of corporations to pass along the lion's share of profit to shareholders, the nation's inequality will worsen over time. A concern for economic fairness is a component of society's interests, and public policy needs to (and does, in a variety of ways) take that value into account.

The question, then, is why *corporate* law should be used to further the interest of fairness, rather than other areas of regulation. The answer to that query harkens back to the previous sections. As noted above, it may simply be more efficient, as a matter of regulatory policy, to use corporate law to redistribute wealth and income than to use other mechanisms. Public policy tools that redistribute wealth and income tend to either work after the initial distribution of financial wealth (e.g., taxes, welfare policy) or to benefit only those at the lowest rung of the economic ladder (e.g., the minimum wage). A stakeholder-oriented corporate law would work at the initial distribution of the corporate surplus and would benefit stakeholders up and down the economic hierarchy. Certainly, if we take economic fairness seriously as a value, we should not blindly accept a corporate law framework that makes fairness less, rather than more, likely.

Changing the Composition of the Board

The best way to realize the potential of the corporation as a progressive force is to adjust the composition of the board so that it contains directors who represent those who invest in the firm in addition to shareholders. At present, shareholders occupy not only a supreme position within the legal framework, being the only beneficiary of management's fiduciary duties, but also within the board itself. Only shareholders vote in elections for corporate directors, and votes are weighed according to the number of shares they own. Once we recognize, however, that corporations are to serve *all* their stakeholders, it becomes clear that the dominance of shareholders within corporate management is a mistake.

Why would a stakeholder board be beneficial? The answer is twofold. First, such a change will inevitably mean that the corporate surplus will be more equitably and efficiently shared, which will help ensure the sustainability (and profitability) of the enterprise over time. Second, a more pluralistic board will improve corporate decisionmaking, which will also help ensure the sustainability (and profitability) of the enterprise over time.

Benefit #1: More Fairness

The first benefit is straightforward. When the board decides how to allocate the corporate surplus, a stakeholder board will behave differently than a shareholder board. The market will be a constraint, to be sure, but the goal of the board will be to allocate the surplus so as to maintain the firm as a going concern. Shareholders will get their proportion, but so will others. In a sense, this conception would use the corporation not only as the mechanism for creation of wealth but its distribution as well.

This is not as jarring as it might seem at first. In the United States, and indeed in most industrialized countries, one of the most important tasks of the state is to redistribute wealth. Mechanisms include the tax and welfare system, minimum wage, and the Social Security program. At base, my proposal is simply to adjust the structure of corporate law so that it can better serve this purpose as well....

The stakeholder board, in an ironic sense, is a genuine realization of the "nexus of contracts" view of the firm. If the firm is best seen as a microcosm of the market, then let us be honest about recognizing all contracts by putting the most important market participants in a position where they can be heard at the decisionmaking level of the firm. The specifics will be difficult, but not impossible: employees could elect a proportion of the board; communities in which the company employs a significant percentage of the workforce could be asked to propose a representative for the board; long-term business partners and creditors could be represented as well.[113]

The specifics do not matter as much as the notion that the board itself should be a place where more than just a shareholder perspective will be heard. As they participate on the board, each stakeholder representative will have the incentive to build and maintain profitability in order to sustain the company over time. Moreover, the board will be the locus of the real negotiations among the various stakeholders about the allocation of the corporate surplus. Even though board members might be selected for their positions in different ways and from different constituencies, each would be held to fiduciary duties to the firm as a whole. Decisions that affect major stakeholders would no longer be made cavalierly without someone on the board being able to anticipate and articulate the likely impact that such a decision would have on the workers, creditors, and other interested stakeholders.

Benefit #2: Better Decisions

This proposal for board pluralism will strike most readers, at least in the United States, as outlandish. But codetermination is common in many countries in Europe and is used to good effect. Perhaps the reason for its success is that, overall, board pluralism makes for better decisions.

[T]he success of corporations [is] based in part on their dependence on a group decisionmaker at the top of the hierarchy. But the benefits of group decisionmaking are drastically mitigated, and sometimes undermined completely, when the group is too homogeneous. In fact, more and more studies show that good decisionmaking requires diversity of viewpoints. As Cass Sunstein has detailed..., conformity among people in a decisionmaking group inevitably breeds error.[116] Dissent is essential, and sometimes "social bonds and affection" can suppress dissent.[117] Sunstein notes, "[I]f strong bonds make even a single dissent less likely, the performance of groups and

113. This form of stakeholder representation could be brought about in any number of ways, but could be achieved merely by defining different classes of stock allocated to different stakeholders, all with their requisite board representatives.

116. See generally [Cass R. Sunstein, Why Societies Need Dissent (2003)].

117. See id. at 27.

institutions will be impaired."[118] He extends the points to corporate boards: "The highest performing companies tend to have extremely contentious boards that regard dissent as a duty and that 'have a good fight now and then.'"[119]

If homogeneity is a flaw, then corporate boards are blemished indeed. At present, corporate boards are among the least diverse institutions in America. A 2002 survey found that 82% of the director positions on Fortune 1000 companies were held by white men, while only 11% were held by white women, 3% by African Americans, 2% by Asian-Americans, and 2% by Hispanics.[120] Adding perspectives other than those of rich, white men will almost certainly improve the quality of business decisions made by the board.

This idea is hardly as radical as it might seem at first. Even mainstream scholars are sometimes found to recognize the benefits of board pluralism. For example, Stephen Bainbridge has said, in the context of suggesting that larger boards are better than smaller boards, that "[m]ore directors will usually translate into more interlocking relationships with other organizations that may be useful in providing resources such as customers, clients, credit, and supplies."[121] Note that Bainbridge sees the benefits of including persons on the board who can speak for and offer insight from various non-equity investors, even though he notably does not include workers in his list. He describes the benefits of this kind of board pluralism as including the ability to address information asymmetries and thus aiding in the creation of strategic alliances. That insight, which seems right, would be true not only for business partners but also for all non-equity investors, including workers. Workers are also, in effect, entering into a strategic alliance with a firm when they invest their time, energy, and futures with the company. Thus, they too "need access to credible information about the competencies and reliability of prospective partners," just as the firm needs credible information about their "competencies and reliability."[124]

---

118. See id.

119. See id. at 28.

120. See Gary Strauss, Good Old Boys' Network Still Rules Corporate Boards, USA Today, Nov. 1, 2002, at 1B.

121. [Stephen M. Bainbridge, Why A Board? Group Decisionmaking in Corporate Governance, 55 Vanderbilt Law Review 1, 43 (2002).]

124. Id. Bainbridge also suggests that boards perform better when a larger board includes a greater number of "specialists" who would aid in both the board's monitoring and service functions. As he says, "complex business decisions require knowledge in such areas as accounting, finance, management, and law. Providing access to such knowledge can be seen as a part of the board's resource gathering function." Boards cannot expect to be, and probably should not be particularly specialized, but they benefit from having specialists among them. While Bainbridge's examples are of investment bankers and attorneys, his reasoning would extend to those having specialized insight about other non-equity investors. As Bainbridge argues, "[L]arger, *more diverse* boards likely contain more specialists, and therefore should get the benefit of specialization." (emphasis added). Bainbridge's focus is more the *size* of boards, but he—perhaps inadvertently—makes my point about the *diversity* of boards, as well.

The worries often expressed about codetermination are overblown. No constituency would have an incentive to hurt the company in order to gain a larger piece of the pie. Even if they did, they would be violating their fiduciary duties to the firm as a whole and could be held to account for their behavior. Second, the possibility of strategic, "rent-seeking" behavior *already* exists in the firm. Directors are currently elected by shareholders only, and shareholders already have incentives in certain circumstances to put their interests ahead of the interests of the firm as a whole. A pluralistic board could actually retard those selfish impulses, because any behavior that benefits one stakeholder at the expense of the firm must be done in full view of the others.

To be sure, making the board less homogeneous will make decisions less tidy, since more views will have to be taken into account and the board will be forced to compromise so that decisions are acceptable to a majority or plurality of stakeholders. But the fact that decisions will be more difficult is not in itself a reason to refuse to improve boards by having them listen to a range of views and perspectives. The real question is whether additional diversity results in decisions that are worth the extra effort. A greater diversity in perspectives and backgrounds within the boardroom will create material benefits to the firm by lessening the risk over time that the board will engage in the defects and systematic mistakes of "groupthink."[125]

On this point, we can gather insight from our experiences outside of business. The notion that decisions produced by a finely wrought process of dialogue and compromise are better than decisions made unilaterally by a uniform group of individuals is widely accepted by institutions other than corporate boards. We recognize in legislative bodies, administrative agencies, school faculties, and non-profit boards that diversity of viewpoints and people increases the likelihood that dissent will be welcomed, important perspectives will be heard, and decisions will be more fully vetted. As Madison argued in the *Federalist Papers*, a pluralistic federal government where power is balanced among many different groups actually *weakens* factions.[126] To make important decisions, one must build coalitions; individual factions cannot act on their own. The same is likely true in corporate governance.

... These principles of good decisionmaking are not new or earth-shaking. They are just systematically ignored in corporate governance. If we imported these insights into corporate law, the strengths of the corporate form could be maintained and then harnessed for a purpose higher than the aggregation of shareholder profit. *Social* wealth could be built; social interests could be internalized into firm decisionmaking; wealth could be more fairly distributed. Perhaps the world will not be saved. But it would be better.

---

125. See, e.g., Sunstein, supra note [116], at 143 (arguing that "defective decisionmaking" is "strongly correlated with structural flaws," such as "insulation and homogeneity"); Bainbridge, supra note [121], at 32 (discussing groupthink).

126. The Federalist No. 10 (James Madison).

James Gustave Speth, *The Bridge at the End of the World: Capitalism, the Environment, and Crossing from Crisis to Sustainability**

... [T]he corporation must be the main object of transformative change: "At the dawn of the twenty-first century, the global corporation stands as the dominant institutional force at the center of human activity and the planet itself.... We must dramatically change the publicly traded, limited liability global corporation, just as previous generations set out to eliminate or control the monarchy."[17]

... What, then should be done to tame the corporation—to make it an instrument of environmental protection rather than a force for environmental destruction? And what are the prospects for such measures, given the power relationships just reviewed?

Action can be envisioned at three levels—three arenas of change, each more far-reaching than the former. First, steps can be taken to encourage voluntary corporate initiatives. Second, corporate accountability can be promoted through regulation and other governmental controls at both national and international levels. And, third, the nature of the corporation itself can be changed.

On the first, voluntary initiatives front, corporations are clearly taking steps to green their operations and products in ways not required by government. Some would say the level of activity is unprecedented, and environmental groups deserve much credit for moving these changes forward. The business press today is crammed with stories:

Business Week, "Green is Good for Business" (May 8, 2006)

Financial Times, "Companies See the Gains of Going Green" (Oct. 2, 2006)

New York Times, "Now Looking Green Is Looking Good" (Dec. 28, 2006)

The green trend is driven by many factors, but prominent among them is a clear-eyed focus on the bottom line. There are more green consumers today, and green is good for corporate image and brand-name products. The *Financial Times* reports, "A string of household names—including General Electric, Wal-Mart, and Unilever—have been lining up to show off their green credentials in an effort to woo customers, at least at the high end of the market.... The UK's Institute of Grocery Distribution reports that sales of 'ethical' products are increasing by 7.5 percent a year, compared with 4.2 percent for conventional products."[19] *Business Week* in 2007 carried a major story on companies that are "doing well by doing good."[20]

---

* Excerpted from James Gustave Speth, *The Bridge at the End of the World: Capitalism, the Environment, and Crossing from Crisis to Sustainability* (Yale University Press 2008), copyright © 2008 James Gustave Speth.

17. John Cavanaugh et al., Alternatives to Economic Globalization: A Better World is Possible 122–24 (2002).

19. Fiona Harvey & Jenny Wiggins, Companies Cash in on Environmental Awareness, Financial Times, Sept. 14, 2006, at 4.

20. Pete Engardio, Beyond the Green Corporation, Business Week, Jan. 29, 2007, at 50, 53.

Demand is also growing for new, solution-oriented technologies and products. GE's wind machine business is booming, as is its overall "Ecomagination" line. Daniel Esty and Andrew Winston's 2007 book *Green to Gold* analyzes these developments in detail. They report, "In a world of constrained natural resources and pollution pressures, the business care for environmental stewardship grows stronger every day. Pressures on companies now come not only from screaming ecoradicals, but also from traditional 'white-shoe' bankers and other asking tough-minded questions about environmental risk and liability. Those who offer solutions to society's environmental problems both mute their potential critics and find expanding markets."[22] Companies that successfully anticipate emerging new directions in public policy and regulatory risk will be ahead of the competition, securing early market share for new products and services and building the institutional know-how required in a changed setting.

As Esty and Winston indicate, keeping critics and government regulators at bay is a factor, too. Corporate worry here is not misplaced. A recent survey of public attitudes in twenty countries found that huge majorities in every country, including the United States, favored tougher regulation to protect the environment. The average level of support for more regulation in the twenty countries was 75 percent. Two-thirds of Americans report that they would like to see major corporations have less influence in the nation, and the number of Americans who see big business as the "biggest threat to the future of this country" has reached the highest point (38 percent) in forty-eight years of polling, although even more Americans fear big government.

Another factor driving change is the emergence of what has been called the "new capitalists." In 1970, a relatively modest number of wealthy individuals controlled corporations. Today, a variety of funds—pension funds, mutual funds, and so on—own more than half of all U.S. stock, up from 19 percent in 1970. These institutional investors seek top returns to be sure, but they have also been increasingly assertive on responsible management and sustainability issues.

Reflecting the trend in business toward embracing the "sustainable enterprise" concept, with its triple bottom line of economy, environment, and society, "corporate social responsibility" has become a catchphrase and CSR an established acronym. CSR can refer to both not-for-profit and for-profit corporate initiatives, provided the for-profit initiatives seem to have a strong social or environmental component. Counted here are the rapidly mounting number of voluntary codes of conduct and product certification schemes operating at both the national and international levels: the Global Reporting Initiative's guidelines for corporate reporting on sustainability; the LEED certification of new green buildings; the Forest Stewardship Council and the Marine Stewardship Council programs for certifying and ecolabeling forest and fish products; the environmental performance principles adopted by major banks; the U.N. Global Compact aimed at promoting good corporate behavior on labor,

22. Daniel C. Esty & Andrew S. Winston, Green to Gold: How Smart Companies Use Environmental Strategy to Innovate, Create Value, and Build Competitive Advantage 304 (2006).

environmental, and human rights issues; the ISO 14000 program; and numerous others. Environmental groups, other nongovernmental organizations and engaged academics have all pressed these issues vigorously.

Reliably Green

... A reliably green company is one that is required to be green by law. Even the best-intentioned manager will avoid actions that are desirable but costly when faced by a competitor lacking a conscience. These environmental regulations and other controls must be promoted at the international level as well as at the national and state levels. My earlier book *Red Sky at Morning* contains a set of prescriptions on what the international community needs to do to make the world of environmental treaties and protocols succeed....

The arena of needed government action also includes an array of worthwhile measures that are not strictly environmental:

1. *Revoke corporate charters.* Most corporate law statues contain provisions allowing government to revoke charters if the corporation has grossly violated the public interest. Making this threat alive and real could have very salutary effects. One way to do this would be to require periodic public reviews and rechartering.

2. *Exclude or expel unwanted corporations.* This tactic has been used extensively in India, for example, by the farmers and consumers who organized the "Monsanto: Quit India" campaign. In the United States there have been campaigns to block Wal-Mart and other giant retailers from various sites.

3. *Roll back limited liability.* Corporate directors and top managers should be personally liable for gross negligence and other major failings. Eventually, personal liability should extend to shareholders in certain cases. That would make buying a company's stock a rather more serious affair and would make management far more circumspect on environmental, labor, and human rights issues.

4. *Eliminate corporate personhood.* There is a nascent movement in the United States to do just that. Spurred by local corporate abuses and corporate claims of due process and First Amendment rights, Porter Township, Pennsylvania, and Arcata, California, both passed (largely symbolic) measures aimed at stripping corporations of the legal fiction of personhood and thus their ability to claim constitutional rights intended for people. Short of outright reversal of a long string of Supreme Court decisions, modification of Supreme Court rulings protecting corporate speech and advertising are overdue.

5. *Get corporations out of politics.* This can best be done by moving to publicly financed elections. The "clean elections" cause is gathering some support. A further step would be to impose tighter restrictions on conflicts of interests by limiting the revolving door between government and corporations and by attending with great care to the process of confirming proposed political appointees.

> 6. *Reform corporate lobbying.* Environmental economist Robert Repetto has urged some important initial steps in this direction. "Should corporate management lobby on public policy issues with broad societal implications, using shareholders' money, with no oversight by shareholders' representatives on the board of directors?" Repetto asks rhetorically in his paper. Repetto notes, "If lobbying on public policy issues is an intrinsic and important aspect of a company's business, then boards of directors, as part of their fiduciary 'duty of care,' have a responsibility to be informed about the company's lobbying activities and positions and to oversee them." He argues in favor of oversight of corporate policy positions and lobbying expenditures by a committee of the corporate board of directors, the majority of whom would be "outside directors with a broad view of the economy and political horizon."[32]

Such ideas are beginning to catch on. In 2006, thirty shareholder resolutions on corporate lobbying were offered; they received average support of 21 percent at annual meetings, double the previous year's support. Further issues that need addressing are corporations that say one thing and lobby for another, sometimes letting trade associations do the dirty work.

The Corporation of the Future

These six points comprise a far-reaching agenda. Others could be added, such as mandating the Securities and Exchange Commission to require a truly sophisticated array of financial and environmental disclosures. Some of the initiatives, like imposing personal liability in certain cases and abolishing corporate personhood, are sufficiently transformative that they could be considered in the third and final category of actions—those that seek to change the nature of the corporation itself. But the major change in the nature of the corporation that is needed now, and that will be essential in the future, is to change the legal mandate that requires the corporation strictly to pursue its own self-interest and to give primacy to maximizing shareholder wealth. The corporation must be, in [Joel] Bakan's words, "reconstituted to serve, promote, and be accountable to broader domains of society than just themselves and their shareholders."[34]

Allen White of the Tellus Institute believes, correctly I think, that "shareholder primacy is the single greatest obstacle to corporate evolution toward a more equitable, humane and socially beneficial institution." He argues for "fundamental changes to the current privilege accorded capital providers and to the legal, regulatory, and financial market structures that enable such privilege to persist. The 'gladiatorial culture' that deifies competitive advantage, efficiency and, above all, shareholder returns is not a corporate culture that comports with [a sustainable economy and a humane society]. The behavior it induces and societal consequences it engenders lay at the

32. Robert Repetto, Best Practice in Internal Oversight of Lobbying Practice (2006).
34. [Joel Bakan, The Corporation: The Pathological Pursuit of Profit and Power 160 (2005)].

heart of the low esteem and high distrust in which the public holds the business community."[35]

The corporation of the future, as envisioned by White and others, must be built around the idea that the wealth produced by the corporation is the joint product of all resource providers—shareholders, employees, unions, future generations, government, customers, communities, and suppliers. Each provides resources for wealth creation over time, and each has a right to expect returns for its contribution: "Framing the corporation as the beneficiary of multiple resource providers opens up horizons for transformation that shareholder primacy stifles. In this [new] framework, the diverse parties that contribute their resources to create goods and services are not simply secondary and dispensable contributors to the production process. Instead, they hold rightful claims to both the surplus generated by the firm as well as to accountability from its board and management. They are, in short, equals, not subordinates to capital providers. This reinterpretation of the nature of the corporation has profound implications for governance, charters and securities laws, as well as the means of corporate wealth distribution.

"Whereas scale, growth and profit-maximization were previously viewed as intrinsic goods and core goals of the corporation, the new corporation marches to a whole different set of principles; namely, those serving the public interest, sustainability, equity, participation and respect for the rights of human beings. Corporate forms [should include] a rich pluralism conforming to global norms that [would] govern business conduct regardless of place, sector or scale." White envisions "a multi-tiered structure in the form of global, regional and local agents, norms, and powers that enables the exercise of citizen rights and democratic control over the corporation. The public purpose of the corporation [should ascend] to preeminence, supported by policies, procedures and instruments that bring democratic process to the forefront of corporate governance."[36]

Is such a future realistic? Certainly, right now, the changes White and others envision are mostly beyond the reach of U.S. politics. But in the future, dissatisfaction with corporations and globalization, already high, is likely to grow. That dissatisfaction could even extend to an increasing number of corporate leaders who feel as trapped and frustrated and worried about the future as many of the rest of us.

It is sometimes said that there are no good answers to today's challenges. The rich array of options for transformative change presented here ... indicates otherwise. With the distrust of corporations and the stirrings already visible, motivation for change is building. What we need are opportunities for transformative change. It seems highly likely that such opportunities will come along, given our crisis-prone world and the dynamics that now govern corporate behavior. And of course, that day can be hastened by citizen demand.

---

35. Allen L. White, Transforming the Corporation 7–8 (2006), available online at Great Transition Initiative, Tellus Institute, www.gtinitiative.org.

36. Id. at 12–17.

Discussion Questions

1. Why should corporate law be at all concerned with fairness, the environment, and the social good? Corporations are designed to make money; why should they not stick to this simple, singular, measurable goal?

2. Joo is very pessimistic about shareholder-led corporate reform. If he is right on the law, are social and environmental activists better off pursuing their agendas in the legislative arena?

3. Institutional shareholders, such as large pension funds, wield significant power. How likely are they to bring social change to corporations and their practices?

4. Sneirson argues that corporate managers need not and should not focus on shareholder profits and yet most mainstream American businesses conduct themselves according to this norm. Do you think that requiring stakeholder assessments would alter this practice and create meaningful change? Do you think this requirement would be too expensive?

5. Greenfield makes two recommendations: broadening corporate objectives to include all stakeholders' wealth, and improving board diversity. Which of these recommendations do you think is more important? Which one is more likely to happen?

6. Do you agree with Greenfield's conclusion that a "fair allocation of the corporate surplus would inure to the benefit of the firm over time"? Why or why not?

7. Speth advocates more radical corporate law reform. Can you think of any other suggestions, radical or not, that might significantly change corporate behavior?

8. Which of Speth's proposals do you think are most important and why? How realistic are his proposals? In thinking about this question, consider this additional fact: corporate law is a matter of state, as opposed to federal, law and so to be effective, Delaware and other business-friendly jurisdictions would have to take part in such reform.

9. Speth's recommendations (including his recommendation to "get corporations out of politics") predate the United States Supreme Court decision in *Citizens United v. Federal Election Commission*, 558 U.S. 310 (2010), which lifted certain restrictions on corporate campaign spending. Does the decision, and the backlash it has caused, improve the chances of meaningful corporate reform?

10. How do you envision the corporation of the future? Are you optimistic or pessimistic?

Chapter 4

Corporate Compliance wit Legal Obligations

The drive to maximize shareholder profits discussed in the previous chapter colors corporate executives' views of their firms' legal obligations. If the profit to be made by breaking a law outweighs the associated penalty—discounted by the likelihood the firm will be caught and made to pay the penalty at whatever point in the future—should the firm break the law in pursuit of corporate profits? This chapter takes up this issue. The first reading notes that most of the recent law reforms affecting sustainability came in the form of environmental, consumer, or employment laws and regulations. Must they be followed? The remaining readings discuss whether corporations must or should comply with such legal obligations or may ignore them in the pursuit of profit.

Adam Winkler, *Corporate Law or the Law of Business? Stakeholders and Corporate Governance at the End of History**

... In the 1960s and 1970s, progressives sought to reform the behavior of corporations by creating new legal regimes outside of corporate law. This era saw an unprecedented wave of what might be termed social welfare laws that were designed in part to benefit corporate stakeholders. Unlike corporate law reforms, however, social welfare legislation of this period sought to cabin managerial discretion over important aspects of hiring, operations, and production. Although this vast array of social welfare legislation is not corporate law per se, it remains a vibrant constraint on managerial decisionmaking, adopted in the name of non-shareholder constituencies of corporations. While corporate lawyers tend to avoid discussing this broader law of business, any attempt to understand how the law shapes and controls corporate decisionmaking will be incomplete without addressing social welfare legislation of this period.

By the mid-1960s, critics of corporate social responsibility were vocal in condemning corporate law reforms allowing corporate charity and the larger pattern those reforms represented: the promotion of non-shareholder interests. No critic was more vocal than University of Chicago economist Milton Friedman. In *Capitalism and Freedom*, Friedman argued that claims that corporations should go "beyond serving the interest

* Originally published in 67 Law and Contemporary Problems 109 (2004). Reprinted with permission.

eir stockholders"[65] were misguided. He continued by stating, "there is one and ly one social responsibility of business—to use its resources and engage in activities designed to increase its profits."[66] To Friedman ... nothing less than the survival of democracy was at stake: "Few trends could so thoroughly undermine the very foundations of our free society as the acceptance by corporate officials of a social responsibility other than to make as much money for their stockholders as possible."[68] But there was also a practical problem: profit maximization gave executives a clear direction in running their businesses, but how were they to define social responsibility?

... Because of its broad social impact, only a distorted view of the firm would see shareholders as the sole constituency group. "A more spacious conception of 'membership,' and one closer to the facts of corporate life, would include all those having a relation of sufficient intimacy with the corporation or subject to its power in a sufficiently specialized way."[71] Some progressive corporate lawyers and activists sought to reward these constituencies—employees, consumers, or the larger public—by reforming the internal mechanisms of corporate governance through codetermination, or exerting their voice through politically motivated proxy fights in corporate elections.

Despite these efforts, corporate governance mechanisms remained relatively immune to non-shareholder constituencies. But progressives recognized another way to empower employees, consumers, and the larger public: legislation outside of corporate law....

Following this model, the late 1960s saw "an unprecedented wave of policy innovation"[76] in the form of social welfare—or quality of life—legislation, as Congress and state legislatures granted broad new protections to workers, consumers, and communities harmed by big business. According to Scott Bowman, "The apparent intransigence and arrogance of certain corporations in refusing to acknowledge or remedy numerous problems associated with public health and safety had nurtured a growing public suspicion that corporations were not socially responsible."[77] Curtailing corporate executives' discretion on whom to hire and promote, how to operate their machinery and equipment, and what products were safe to sell, the laws of this era amounted to "extensive restrictions on business freedom."[78] These laws were not part of corporate law, but they profoundly influenced corporate behavior nonetheless—and did so in the name of non-shareholder constituencies.

---

65. Milton Friedman, Capitalism and Freedom 133 (1962); see also Milton Friedman, A Friedman Doctrine—The Social Responsibility of Business is to Increase Its Profits, N.Y. Times, Sept. 13, 1970 (Magazine) at 33.

66. Id.

68. Id.

71. Abram Chayes, The Modern Corporation and the Rule of Law, in The Corporation in Modern Society 25, 41 (Edward S. Mason ed., 1959).

76. James Q. Wilson, American Politics, Then and Now, Commentary, Feb. 1979, at 40.

77. Scott R. Bowman, The Modern Corporation and American Political Thought: Law, Power, and Ideology 143 (1996).

78. Deborah A. Ballam, The Evolution of the Government-Business Relationship in the United States: Colonial Times to Present, 31 American Business Law Journal 553, 635 (1994).

Consumers were one stakeholder group increasingly in need of new legal protections from corporate managers. Consumers, according to progressive Ralph Nader, were among those harmed directly by corporate irresponsibility. Nader's *Unsafe At Any Speed*—an exposé of built-in safety problems in cars—showed that consumers were vulnerable to cold calculations by automobile executives willing to sacrifice lives in the pursuit of profit.[79] The ensuing harassment of Nader by General Motors caused a scandal, launched Nader's career, resulted in congressional hearings, and eventually proved to be the opening of the era's floodgate of regulation against corporate excesses. Between 1966 and 1972, federal laws were enacted that expanded consumers' rights and limited companies' ability to introduce into the market harmful products: the National Traffic and Motor Vehicle Act, the Consumer Product Safety Act, the Poison Prevention in Packaging Act, the Fair Packaging and Labeling Act, the Federal Meat Inspection Act, the Child Protection Act, and the Flammable Fabrics Act, to list the most important. These laws did not purport to change fiduciary duties. They protected consumers by taking off the table a whole range of options that corporate management had traditionally been within its lawful discretion to choose.

Workers, too, gained expansive new protections from the potentially damaging effects of corporate management's exercise of business judgment. Reflecting concerns about the hazardous conditions of the workplace, Congress passed the Occupational Safety and Health Act (OHSA) in 1970. OSHA aimed to lessen the "mounting toll of industrial injuries" attributable to companies that, in the pursuit of profits for shareholders, sacrificed the health and lives of employees. Also during this period, corporate business confronted new limitations on their hiring and promotion practices in the form of antidiscrimination laws barring companies from discriminating on the basis of race, sex, and religion.

This pattern of restricting corporate management through reforms enacted outside of corporate law also resulted in new protections for communities affected by corporate behavior. The way to protect such communities was not through corporate law reforms, but through the implementation of, for example, environmental laws. As the public awareness of the dangers associated with pollution grew, the blame was placed squarely on big business—the power, petroleum, chemical, and steel industries. By 1972, environmentalism had become a "national obsession" and Congress had passed the Water Pollution Control Act, the Federal Environmental Pesticide Control Act, the Clean Air Act Amendments of 1970, and the Environmental Protection Act. This last law, enacted by unanimous vote, also created a strong, large federal regulatory agency charged with protecting the public health and authorized with "broad powers over a wide range of business decisions."[86]

The public, it seems, was not as troubled as Friedman about identifying the social responsibility of business. By the early 1970s, more than eighty percent of Americans

79. Ralph Nader, Unsafe at Any Speed: The Designed-in Dangers of the American Automobile (1965).

86. David Vogel, Fluctuating Fortunes: The Political Power of Business in America 59, 67–69 (1989).

polled believed that business should provide special leadership in rebuilding inner cities, eliminating racial discrimination, and wiping out poverty.[87] The way to insure that corporations provided such leadership had become clear: reform labor law, consumer protection law, and environmental law, regardless of corporate law's fiduciary duties. Granted, reforms arising in these other areas of law—the broader law of business—did not change corporate law, and applied to all business forms, not merely corporations. Nevertheless, they did amount to legal reforms that fundamentally shaped corporate behavior. To understand the significance—or lack thereof—of the claim that corporate law is witnessing the "end of history" and of the ultimate adoption of shareholder primacy, one must at least recognize that other stakeholders have found protection from corporate management through other areas of law....

Once one looks beyond the corporate law codes and the corporations casebooks, one finds that businesses already face numerous legal requirements to protect non-shareholder constituencies. In the 1920s and 1930s, securities laws and collective bargaining laws were adopted to protect the American economy and its workers from the corruption of Wall Street. In the 1960s, a great blossoming of legislative reform was enacted to restrain corporate management and serve the interests of stakeholders: consumer protection laws, environmental laws, antidiscrimination laws, and occupational safety laws. These areas of law continue to thrive—despite their details varying with shifts in the prevailing political winds—and remain non-trivial constraints on corporate management.

Stakeholder protection and corporate social responsibility are alive and well in the United States. But to see the full extent of these progressive ideals, one has to look outside of corporate law as it is traditionally defined, and look to the broader law of business. It is only by ignoring the success of progressives that one could conclude that corporate law's history is at an end, and perhaps the only meaningful lesson of such claims is that they rest on an artificially narrow understanding of corporate governance. Surely, corporate managers themselves, who must operate within the broader law of business, are aware of the legally imposed duties to protect workers, consumers, and larger communities. Perhaps it is time corporate lawyers—conservative and progressive alike—caught up to this reality.

Cynthia A. Williams, *Corporate Compliance with the Law in the Era of Efficiency*[*]

... Professor (now Judge) Frank Easterbrook and Professor Daniel Fischel set out the following proposition about corporate law compliance: "Managers have no general obligation to avoid violating regulatory laws, when violations are profitable to the firm.... We put to one side laws concerning violence or other acts thought to be *malum in se*."[1]

87. Id. at 42.

* Originally published in 76 North Carolina Law Review 1265 (1998). Reprinted with permission.

1. Frank H. Easterbrook & Daniel R. Fischel, Antitrust Suits by Targets of Tender Offers, 80 Michigan Law Review 1155, 1168 n.36 (1982).

That statement, asserted in a footnote, was elaborated upon only briefly, again in a footnote:

> [M]anagers do not have an ethical duty to obey economic regulatory laws just because the laws exist. They must determine the importance of these laws. The penalties Congress names for disobedience are a measure of how much it wants firms to sacrifice in order to adhere to the rules; the idea of optimal sanctions is based on the supposition that managers not only may but also should violate the rules when it is profitable to do so.[2]

Easterbrook and Fischel's view of corporate compliance with the law ... has obvious intellectual connections to some aspects of law and economics and to the theory of efficient breach of contract, expanded to include efficient breach of public law. While many people might view Easterbrook and Fischel's theory of "efficient breach of public law" as lacking a sound legal and political foundation, a more plausible view (but one that is also flawed) is that of "efficient investment in compliance." That view suggests the maximum amount of money a firm should invest in order to comply with the law is determined by the maximum penalty for violations of a particular law, since it would be economically inefficient to invest more in compliance than one risks in fines.

[T]he conception of law underlying "efficient breach" is similar to the conception underlying "efficient compliance," [in] that both understate the significance of law in a similar way, treating vast realms of law as simply a pricing scheme or set of tariffs on behavior....

Easterbrook and Fischel recognize a narrow subset of laws that truly prohibit certain actions, a subset they would confine to violence and actions that are *mala in se*;[68] beyond that, their concept of the law is as a pricing mechanism, or tax upon various activities.... Thus, "[t]he law establishes a price for the violation, and people then must decide how to respond to the schedule of penalties."[70]

... One central tenet of Easterbrook and Fischel's view is that of rational-choice theory, which is also a central tenet of law and economics. Rational-choice theory is a general theory of decision-making. It posits that people are rational, self-interested, utility maximizers using cost/benefit analysis to make decisions; it has been applied to numerous types of decisions, including decisions about obeying the law. Further, rational-choice theory, as applied to law compliance, asserts that the costs of legal sanctions can be treated like prices in a theory of supply and demand affecting law compliance. The law-as-price view of law is, in essence, rational choice theory interpreted not simply as a descriptive claim about how people respond to legal sanctions, but as two, distinct normative claims.

The first normative claim is the one [Professor Robert] Cooter identified: that the sanctions for violating the law can be treated as the price to be paid for the "right"

2. Id. at 1177 n.57.
68. Id. at 1168 n.36.
70. Id. at 1157.

to violate the law.[77] Inherent in this view of law is the legal voluntarism claim: that particularly with respect to regulatory law, a person can either conform to the law or violate it while accepting the known consequences, and that either choice is an acceptable means for an individual or corporation to fulfill its obligations as a citizen. The second normative claim is that since people and corporations will, and possibly should, make decisions about compliance with law based on a "rational actor's" calculations of costs and benefits, their expectations about the likely outcome of violating the law or investing a certain amount in compliance ought to be recognized as settled expectations upon which they may legitimately rely.

... Another aspect of the law-as-price view of law that is directly derived from rational-choice theory is the tendency to determine whether to obey the law by reference to the likelihood of actually having to pay a penalty for noncompliance, and so discounting penalties by the likelihood of detection and successful enforcement of violations. One articulation of this idea is found in David Engel's article *An Approach to Corporate Social Responsibility.*[89] In that article, Engel defines "corporate voluntarism" or "corporate altruism" (and with it "corporate social responsibility") as instances when corporations "pursue social ends where this pursuit conflicts with the presumptive shareholder desire to maximize profit."[90]

... Among the social goals that Engel considers for which corporations might forego profit-making is "altruistic" corporate obedience to the law, or complying with the substantive standards of the law even when the corporation can escape a liability rule because of non-detection or non-prosecution.[93] The way Engel poses the question is to ask whether a corporation, having determined that it is profitable to violate a given law (given the potential penalty, as discounted by the risks of detection and successful prosecution), should nonetheless act to forbear violating that law based on a cost/benefit calculation using the non-discounted penalty, which Engel assumes equals the full social costs that the corporation's behavior would impose.[94] Note, however, the narrowness of Engel's position: What is defined as altruism is not even "voluntary" obedience to the substantive standards of the law, but rather the corporation's use of a non-discounted penalty in its cost/benefit analysis....

Engel's article also sets out the argument for the "efficient investment in compliance" paradigm. Looking at the particular context of crime, Engel first argues that it is not true that "we criminalize only those acts that we do not want performed in the society at all—regardless of cost."[98] ... [I]nstead of enumerating all of the justifiable "violations," the legislature allows discretion with respect to the penalty; the penalty indicates how much society cares about certain categories of violations.[100] Engel then

77. [Robert Cooter, Prices and Sanctions, 84 Columbia Law Review 1523, 1524–25 (1984).]
89. [David Engel, An Approach to Corporate Social Responsibility, 32 Stanford Law Review 1 (1979).]
90. Id. at 3.
93. Id. at 55....
94. Id. at 38.
98. Id. at 44.
100. Id. at 45.

applies this principle to the corporate context and asserts that "the argument that the socially optimal level of crime is zero seems particularly infirm in the corporate context."[101] This is because reducing corporate crime involves the special costs of corporate law-compliance expenditures, except in the rare instances in which the board actively conducts or condones a pattern of criminal activity. And, with respect to law-compliance expenditures,

> [I]t is not plausible to argue that *every* substantive crime represents a legislative judgment that every corporation should spend an *infinite* amount on an internal auditing system to ensure that *none* of its employees engages in the prohibited conduct. And yet as soon as the argument is diluted at all from this proposition, a moralistic approach to the meaning of substantive criminal law gives no guidance as to *how much* a corporation should spend to reduce lower-echelon crime.[103]

The additional guidance on how much a corporation should spend on law compliance, according to Engel, is found in the penalty levels:

> This is not in itself to suggest ... that it is necessarily appropriate or desirable for corporate management to shape its conduct entirely with a calculated view to legislative penalty levels.... But it is meant to say that not all violations are socially undesirable....[104]

... The [American Law Institute's] law-as-limit position [requiring corporate compliance with laws] and the Easterbrook/Fischel law-as-price position define the ends of a spectrum of views about the meaning of penalties attached to violations of statutes and administrative regulations, and ultimately about the meaning of law. Between those two extremes is an important intermediate position. The major premise of the intermediate position, and the characteristic I take to be definitive of it, is the view that, as a descriptive matter, some law prices behavior and some law limits it, and that most regulatory law, and laws penalizing behaviors that are "merely" malum prohibitum, prices, rather than limits, behavior. For these latter laws, compliance is voluntary for corporations (and individuals) willing to risk paying the price.

[Professor Stephen] Pepper's article in the *Yale Law Journal* ... provides a cogent illustration of the intermediate approach.[106] The issue he addresses is when a lawyer ought to give information to clients on the likely consequences of violating a law or administrative rule and when a lawyer should not provide such information, given the recognition that this information may lead some clients to conclude that it is worthwhile to violate the law and given the recognition that some law violations may cause serious harm to other people. Pepper ... recognizes that advice about enforcement patterns in conjunction with the "modern lawyer's legal realist (and law-and-

101. Id.

103. Id.

104. Id. at 47 n.155.

106. [Stephen L. Pepper, Counseling at the Limits of the Law: An Exercise in the Jurisprudence and Ethics of Lawyering, 104 Yale Law Journal 1545 (1995).]

economics) view of the law may lead the client to respect the law less; to choose to violate the law and chance the consequences."[110]

In addressing this moral and legal dilemma, Pepper explores seven different distinctions in determining when lawyers ought to provide clients with information about enforcement-related aspects of law, including the potential consequences of violating the law. The distinctions he examines are (1) criminal violations ("law as prohibition") versus civil violations ("law as cost"); (2) conduct *malum in se* versus conduct that is *malum prohibitum*; (3) enforced law versus rarely enforced law versus unenforced law; (4) information on enforcement of law versus procedural law versus substantive legal rules; (5) private information versus public information; (6) lawyer-initiated discussions versus client-initiated discussions; and (7) whether it is likely or unlikely that the information will be used to assist unlawful conduct.[112] His discussion of these distinctions says much about the current, academic concept of law and the intermediate law-as-price view.

Thus, Pepper discusses the distinction between giving advice concerning violations of criminal law and violations of civil law, which he suggests is a distinction between conduct that is traditionally understood as truly prohibited (criminal law) versus conduct "to which the law only attaches a cost or penalty" (civil law).[113] So, using this distinction, a lawyer would not give information to the client when it would facilitate a criminal violation, but would be free to give advice about a civil violation. But this distinction does not ultimately prove satisfying to Pepper because it is both over-inclusive and under-inclusive. It is over-inclusive because the reach of the criminal sanction, "which is supposed to mean that conduct is truly prohibited," has been expanded dramatically, extending to violations of major areas of regulatory law that Pepper believes cannot be worthy of true prohibition.[115] It is under-inclusive because some violations of civil tort law, otherwise an area Pepper regards as law as cost, can cause serious injury to other people. A much more important distinction, in Pepper's view, is the *malum in se/malum prohibitum* distinction.

In discussing that distinction, Pepper uses the example of communicating information from a police bulletin board about the frequency of police patrols in given neighborhoods (information that could be quite useful to someone planning a burglary) versus communicating information on the EPA's frequency of testing rural water effluent for compliance with standards for discharging ammonia into the water (information that could be quite useful to a company seeking to discharge ammonia at levels higher than those permitted in the regulations). Using that example, he suggests that "our intuition" that it is wrong to communicate the former to a client but not the latter is based on the *malum in se/malum prohibitum* distinction:

110. Id. at 1554.
112. See id.
113. Id. at 1559.
115. Id. at 1561.

> The discharge may be a technical legal violation, but it may not be wrongful in any other significant sense.... The difference between burglary and this instance of regulatory violation seems to be that the former is clearly wrong in its very nature in addition to being unlawful, and the latter is unlawful, but may or may not be otherwise wrongful.
>
> That difference corresponds to the old distinction between crimes *mala in se*, wrong in their very nature, and crimes *mala prohibita*, crimes wrong only because prohibited by positive law. This distinction also helps in understanding our intuitions concerning the criminal/civil dichotomy.... A prohibition on giving the client legal information that might assist in the commission of a crime rings the right chord when the conduct is something we perceive as "really criminal," but strikes quite another note with vast areas of regulatory law. The *malum in se/malum prohibitum* distinction appears, in older garb, to formulate the difference between law as true prohibition (that is, the identification of conduct not to be tolerated) and law as cost (that is, the identification of conduct to be penalized in some legal fashion, but which *the citizen is still free to choose to do)*.[119]

Based, then, on the concept of law as distinguishing between law-as-limit and law-as-price (which for Pepper essentially tracks the malum in se/malum prohibitum distinction), Pepper proposes the following general standard for guiding lawyers' conduct:

> [W]hen it appears more probable than not that the client will use legal information or advice to facilitate conduct that (1) is clearly prohibited by law *and* (2) involves what is by clear societal consensus a serious and substantial moral wrong, the lawyer shall not provide the client with the legal advice or information.[120]

In counseling clients using the above standard, the lawyer would be guided by the distinctions Pepper discussed:

> Is the legal provision really "law," or has it been eroded by desuetude or enforcement policy into something society appears not to be very concerned about? Is the conduct really prohibited, or *just freighted with a legal cost or penalty?* Is the conduct really wrongful, or just legally prohibited?[121]

In other words, that a particular behavior (such as dumping ammonia in the water at levels beyond that set by the Environmental Protection Agency) is legally prohibited is relevant in determining how a client should be advised, but not determinative. What is determinative is the lawyer's individual assessment of whether the underlying behavior "is really wrongful," that is, whether it "involves what is by clear societal consensus a serious and substantial moral wrong."[124] Only when a violation involves

119. Id. at 1576–77 (emphasis added).
120. Id. at 1578.
121. Id. at 1581 (emphasis added).
124. Id. at 1578.

what is by clear societal consensus a serious and substantial *moral* wrong should the client be denied the information necessary to assess accurately the risks associated with violating the law, even when the lawyer is the one who initiates the discussion about possibly violating the law.

Efficient Breach in the Law

It is an important conceptual development that writers and corporate law thinkers have begun to adopt a view of law that suggests that intentional violations of some categories of law, particularly civil, regulatory law, are relatively unimportant—in fact, so unimportant that they may be characterized as non-culpable—and that some types of penalties for violating the law can be treated as prices or as an alternative system of taxation. Yet, it is far more important that these and related ideas have begun to have an effect on decided cases, suggesting either a right to break the law so long as one is willing to risk the penalties ("efficient breach") or that the amount of money a corporation should invest in compliance with a particular law is a function of the penalty, which also determines the importance of the law and whether the corporation should take it seriously ("efficient compliance")....

Recall Pepper's conclusion that facts concerning the enforcement of law should be communicated to clients, even when those facts may help the client violate the law, except when a potential legal violation also constitutes a serious, morally reprehensible action. Recall also Easterbrook and Fischel's view that managers should violate the law when it is profitable, except if the law concerns violence or other acts that are mala in se. Judge [Douglas] Ginsburg recognized a similar line of demarcation [in *Smith v. National Transportation Safety Board*], suggesting that the obligations of law are equally met by either conformance with the law or violating it and accepting the known consequences, except when a moral or criminal norm is concerned.[229]

These statements reveal a fundamental irony in the law-as-price position. According to these views, there is a narrow realm of positive law that truly commands obedience: law that prohibits *mala in se* actions, such as those constituting violence (Easterbrook and Fischel); actions that are deemed morally reprehensible by a clear social consensus (Pepper); and actions that involve criminal or moral norms (Ginsburg). Often these will be the same thing. All other law, and in particular most regulatory law, is law as cost: "[C]onduct to be penalized in some legal fashion, but which the citizen is still free to choose to do."[230]

In other words, the only law that is binding operates when law is not actually necessary to set the necessary standards of behavior. If the behaviors that are prohibited are wrongful in their very nature, then we do not need law to establish the standards of behavior. We do not need laws against murder to tell us that murder is wrong, nor, in general, do we need laws against rape or kidnapping or child abuse or arson or burglary to communicate the necessary standards of behavior. These things are obviously wrong whether we have laws to define them as wrong or not because these

229. Smith v. Nat'l Transp. Safety Bd., 981 F.2d 1326, 1328 (D.C. Cir. 1993).

230. Pepper, supra note [106], at 1577.

are actions in which there *is* a "clear societal consensus" that they involve "a serious and substantial moral wrong."

Where we need law most, though, given the highly complex, sophisticated, and technological post-industrial nature of society today, is where the law-as-price view of the law would make law impossible: precisely within the broad ambit of regulatory law. There, we definitely need binding law to structure interactions so that there is a level playing field among competitive economic enterprises, so that persons are treated fairly and with respect, and so that industrial practices include considerations of human and environmental health and safety. It is precisely because the issues addressed by regulatory law are so technically complex—composed of interrelated webs of harm, causation, and subtle externalities—and not amenable to determination by reference to obvious moral precepts, that regulatory law is critical. Should airlines maintain their aircraft by a thorough operational review every twenty flights or every one hundred flights? Who knows, but in our society we have empowered a technically expert administrative agency, the FAA, with at least a partial mandate to protect passenger safety, to make that decision and to impose its decision on every industry participant. Should industrial plants discharge ammonia at a level of .050 grams per liter of effluent or at a level of .060 grams per liter? Who knows, but we have empowered the EPA to study the issue, to consider the economic and health effects of permitting discharges of various levels of ammonia, and to make a binding decision. It is precisely because "most of us would not have an immediate answer" about "whether or not it is wrong to discharge .060 grams of ammonia per liter of water effluent" that we need a rule developed by experts who are not self-interested, and we need that rule to be recognized as binding by all industry participants. Therefore, by denying the mandatory nature of regulatory law, the law-as-price view denies us law precisely where we need it most: in the regulatory arena, where there is not a social consensus, where there is not an obvious moral component to the standards the law sets, and where humanistic concerns and economic self-interest collide most acutely.

... In addition to that fundamental irony at the core of the law-as-price theory, there is another serious problem with the theory: the implicit (and in some cases explicit) premise that society is indifferent concerning whether firms choose compliance with the law rather than risking paying the penalty, or even that society is benefited by this approach to law, is demonstrably false.

The efficient breach concept of statutory and regulatory law, which is based on an understanding of law as a series of prices established for the "right" to violate the law, has evolved as a direct extension of the efficient breach of contract theory.... Yet [this] argument fails to acknowledge the significant differences between breach of contract and breach of public law. While ... "few would contest the notion of a 'right' to breach a contract," this insight about private law ... says nothing about whether one also has a "right" to breach public, statutory law.... Admittedly, there is a surface plausibility to the analogy, ... [y]et the analogy ultimately underestimates the differences between breach of contract and breach of statutory law; it also underestimates the extent to which performance of statutory obligations is far superior, from a social viewpoint, to risking paying penalties.

[C]ontract law is a species of private, voluntary law; absent duress, no one is required to enter into most contracts. These are voluntarily undertaken obligations and usually confined to mechanisms of economic exchange.... Public law, on the contrary, is not voluntary in this same sense: one takes on the obligations of citizenship (which include following the law) simply by virtue of enjoying the benefits of society; it is impossible to live in a society without enjoying those benefits, and thereby being required to fulfill the correlative obligations. Indeed, following the law has traditionally been thought of as the absolute *minimum* component of a citizen's duty to her society.[247]

Related to this point is one based on the underlying norms or values of contract law, as opposed to public, statutory law. These norms point in different directions and are effectuated by a different relationship between the individual and her society. Thus, the underlying norms of contract law are autonomy and individualism: "[T]he contract paradigm expresses the basic norm that individuals should be able to agree between and among themselves how to allocate resources."[249] Absent unusual circumstances, society, through the auspices of the courts, will not even enter into the relationship, at least not so far as judging the fairness of the terms of the contract or whether parties should or should not engage in the underlying terms of exchange. In contrast, the underlying norm of regulation is that of social obligation and responsibility, and the process is one of society, through the legislature and administrative agencies, setting out what constitutes minimally acceptable behavior....

Yet another distinction is that parties to a contract can be presumed to know their rights, to know when the contract has been breached (or when at least one party thinks it has been breached), and to be able to insist on compensation as defined in the contract. Even the most ardent advocates of the theory of efficient breach of contract recognize that actual compensation is required, or the goal of the theory (efficiency) will not be well-served.... The same cannot be said about breach of public law: Affected individuals may not know of their rights or that their rights have been infringed upon; or there may be strong disincentives to insisting on one's rights based on the nature of the relationship (for example, employer/employee or landlord/tenant); or public enforcement agencies may not know of law violations, since violators will have every incentive to hide their conduct; or compensation (paying the penalties) may not occur for many reasons unrelated to the underlying conduct, such as the difficulty and expense of enforcing one's rights in court, relative to the amount of money at issue....

But, given the significant differences between "efficient breach of contract" and "efficient breach of public law," society is still the net loser under the Easterbrook/Fischel view of the law even if there is compensation, given the nature of many of

247. [See Lon L. Fuller, The Morality of Law 5 (2d ed. 1969); John Rawls, A Theory of Justice 210 (1971); Christopher D. Stone, Corporate Social Responsibility: What It Might Mean, If It Were Really to Matter, 71 Iowa Law Review 557, 559 (1986).]

249. William Powers, Jr., Border Wars, 72 Texas Law Review 1209, 1211 (1994).

the types of harm caused by failing to comply with one's statutory and regulatory obligations. Since the harm caused by breach of contract is primarily economic, it can often be fully compensated by monetary damages. Significantly, when money damages will not equally compensate a promisee, the courts demand specific performance. [Likewise, i]n the realm of public law, specific performance of statutory obligations is always far superior to having putative defendants paying penalties when the harm to be avoided is not primarily economic. Even in those instances in which the harm to be avoided by a particular statute is purely economic, statutory compliance will usually be preferable....

Kent Greenfield, *Ultra Vires Lives! A Stakeholder Analysis of Corporate Illegality**

Among the fundamental principles of corporate law, as taught in the United States in the early twenty-first century, are these: First, corporations are creatures of unenumerated powers—that is, the doctrine of "ultra vires," which limited corporations to certain purposes and powers, is dead or at least deathly ill; second, the primary obligation of the corporation's managers is to maximize profit; and third, because corporate law is primarily state law and "enabling" in character, it has little to say about matters that go beyond the internal governance of the firm. This [excerpt] questions each of these principles by focusing on the first.

This [excerpt] will argue that, rather than being dead, the ultra vires doctrine remains vibrant in one important way. Although corporations need not enumerate a single purpose for their existence and are not constrained to exercise only specifically identified powers, modern state statutes and articles of incorporation nevertheless charter corporations only for "lawful" purposes. This limitation, though largely overlooked by commentators, is real. It means that corporations are not authorized under their charters to commit crimes or otherwise act unlawfully.... Most importantly, corporate law would provide shareholders [and attorneys general] the right to sue to enjoin corporations' continuing unlawful activities....

The notion that the ultra vires doctrine is still alive is itself worthy of attention.... [I]ts continuing life has implications for what some see as the unyielding duty of corporations and their managers to maximize profits. Indeed, if corporations must obey the law, then they must do so even at times when such obedience is not profitable. The duty to maximize value for the shareholders will be limited by the duty to obey the law. This notion contradicts the views of some of the most prominent scholars in corporate law, who have written that corporations should, with only some small exceptions, seek to maximize profits even when they must break the law in order to do so....

Finally, the notion that the obligation to obey the law is at the heart of the corporate contract means that corporate law cannot be thought of as concerned only with the internal governance of the firm. Rather, because the remaining vestige of the ultra

* Originally published in 87 Virginia Law Review 1279 (2001). Reprinted with permission.

vires doctrine imports into corporate law a concern about general law compliance, corporate law—and corporate law professors and corporate law attorneys—will need to pay attention to a wider range of issues and situations....

The Conflict over the Duty of the Firm to Obey the Law

... By some accounts, corporate crime is growing, and examples of corporations and their responsible managers behaving in unlawful (but non-criminal) ways are numerous as well. Examples of the unlawful activity of U.S. corporations range from routine "union busting," violations of environmental regulations, and price-fixing, to illegal foreign payments, smuggling, and fraud of various kinds. The seriousness of the illegalities range from double-parking to those resulting in deaths. It is widely believed that corporate illegality and crime are "imperfectly regulated by social controls" because corporations cannot be incarcerated, have no conscience, are typically very complex institutions, and are not subject to the same social controls and reputational constraints as individuals.* To be sure, the public policy problem of corporate crime has been the subject of much attention and has been analyzed from a number of different perspectives, including the difficulties of determining the "correct" amount of deterrence and applying the criminal law to large institutions. Most of these efforts to analyze corporate illegality have come from outside of corporate law and from commentators other than corporate law scholars. Perhaps as a result of this inattention, there is no consensus on the question of whether there is an obligation, enforceable within corporate law, on the part of a firm and its managers to obey the law....

The dominant perspective on corporate law ... offers an answer to the question of corporate illegality that strikes many as awkward and untenable. The preeminent [corporate law-and-economics scholars] have suggested that the duty to obey the law is simply a constituent part of the duty to maximize the firm's value. If illegality will profit the company more than it will cost the company, the corporation should break the law. Frank Easterbrook and Daniel Fischel have written that "[m]anagers have no general obligation to avoid violating regulatory laws, when violations are profitable to the firm."[34] Importantly, when a corporation determines whether illegality is likely to be profitable, the "cost" that should be considered is not the penalty or fine; rather, it is the expected penalty, fine, or other costs. That is, a corporation should consider the cost of illegality to be the penalty, fine, or other costs discounted by the chance that the corporation will not be caught in its illegality.

The Rise and Fall of Ultra Vires

... Traditionally, the corporation's powers were limited to the explicit objects of the corporation as defined in the corporate charter. In the words of the Supreme

* [See also the quote attributed to Edward, the First Baron of Thurlow: corporations have "no soul to be damned, no body to be kicked."—Eds.]

34. [Frank H. Easterbrook & Daniel R. Fischel, Antitrust Suits by Targets of Tender Offers, 80 Michigan Law Review 1155, 1168 n.36 (1982).]

Court, "[t]he exercise of the corporate franchise, being restrictive of individual rights, cannot be extended beyond the letter and spirit of the act of incorporation."[68] Through the nineteenth and early twentieth centuries, the ultra vires doctrine was central to corporate law. Limiting the corporation's legal authority to certain powers enumerated in the corporate charter, the doctrine was considered an important tool to protect the state's interest in restricting the power and size of corporations and to protect the shareholders from managerial overreaching....

[Greenfield then detailed the gradual deterioration of the ultra vires doctrine over the years and the reasoning behind it.]

[A]s Justice Brandeis explained in *Liggett* [*Co. v. Lee*], states realized that it was costly for any individual state to attempt to retain a strong policy of limited capacity for corporations.[98] States began to compete for corporate charters by offering statutes that, first, allowed corporations to list any number of authorized activities and powers, and, later, that required no listing of specific powers at all. The story of this state competition for corporate charters is oft-told. Whether a "race to the bottom" or a "race to the top" from the standpoint of shareholder interests, the end result with regard to corporate power was certainly to move away from limiting corporate power and toward broadening corporations' powers to engage in any lawful activity....

The Surviving Vestige of Ultra Vires Doctrine: Illegal Acts

Notwithstanding the many strong reasons for the downfall of the ultra vires doctrine, it did not erode to nothingness. Rather, an important part of the doctrine was retained and survives today. This vestige of the doctrine sets off illegal activities as ultra vires for corporations....

As state statutes did away with the requirement of listing specific corporate purposes and powers, they did not remove the requirement that the corporation's purposes and activities be "lawful" or "legal." The Model Business Corporation Act, for example, states that the articles of incorporation shall set forth "[t]he purpose or purposes for which the corporation is organized which may be stated to be, or to include, the transaction of any or all *lawful* business for which corporations may be incorporated under this Act."[117] The Revised Model Business Corporation Act establishes that "[e]very corporation incorporated under this Act has the purpose of engaging in any *lawful* business."[118] The Delaware statute, in its first section, establishes that "[a] corporation may be incorporated or organized under this chapter to conduct or promote any *lawful* business or purposes."[119] The New York incorporation statute allows that

68. Beaty v. Lessee of Knowler, 29 U.S. (4 Pet.) 152, 167 (1830)....

98. 288 U.S. 517, 554–55 (Brandeis, J., dissenting).

117. Model Business Corporation Act § 54(c) (1979) (emphasis added).

118. Revised Model Business Corporation Act § 3.01(a) (1999) (emphasis added).

119. Del. Code Ann. tit. 8, § 101(b) (emphasis added).

"[a] corporation may be formed under this chapter for any *lawful* business purpose."[120] That states do not limit the lawful activities of corporations obviously does not mean that those states have also chosen not to limit the unlawful activities of corporations.

Articles of incorporation of specific companies tend to track the language of the applicable statutes and thus bolster the notion that the corporations themselves consider their authority as being limited to lawful purposes and activities, as that would be the only power granted by the state. Consider, for example, Unocal's articles of incorporation, which state that the "purpose of the corporation is to engage in any lawful act or activity for which a corporation may be organized" under California law. Nike, Inc. states in its charter that its purpose is "to engage in any lawful activity for which corporations may be organized" under Oregon law....

Another piece of evidence demonstrating that some vestige of the ultra vires doctrine survives is that forty-nine states still have a provision in their state incorporation statutes that allows the state to dissolve a corporation or enjoin it from engaging in ultra vires activities.[127] These provisions are premised, according to one critic of them, "on the notion that the state had an interest in deterring [ultra vires] activity by virtue of its responsibility to protect the public welfare."[128] One critic has called these provisions statutory "dead wood,"[129] and, indeed, if corporations could genuinely be chartered for any purpose whatsoever these provisions would be meaningless. On the other hand, if a limitation on illegal acts is considered a real constraint, then these provisions are anything but refuse. They recognize that the state continues to have a real interest in ensuring that corporations stay within their stated power and authority, that is, conducting their business lawfully.

... [E]ach of the firm's major stakeholders, in whose interest the doctrine was created and in whose interest the doctrine was largely set aside, would still likely prefer that the corporation not engage in unlawful activities. In this section, I argue that it would be unreasonable for the various stakeholders in the firm to agree to the formation of an entity authorized to break the law....

The State.... Would a state want to limit the authority of the firm so that it could further its financial goals through only legal means, or would a state want the firm and its management to have authority under the corporate charter to maximize the value of the firm through unlawful means as well? To ask the question is to answer it. Notwithstanding the competition among states for corporate charters, it is difficult to imagine a state wanting to compete on the basis of its acquiescence to profit making through illegality.

---

120. N.Y. Bus. Corp. Law § (201) (emphasis added).

127. [North Dakota is the one state that lacks such a provision.]

128. [Micahel A. Schaeftler, Ultra Vires—Ultra Useless: The Myth of State Interest in Ultra Vires Acts of Business Corporations, 9 Journal of Corporation Law 81, 85 (1983).]

129. Id. at 93.

The basic reason a state would have no interest in chartering a corporation able to engage in unlawful activities is that, by making something unlawful, the state has already made a judgment that the behavior should be penalized or punished. That is, the state has already determined that the costs of certain acts—whether speeding or fraud or murder—outweigh the benefits of such acts from society's perspective. The state has further determined that such acts need to be punished or penalized in order to bring the behavior of individual or corporate actors into line with society's cost/benefit analysis. It would be logically and politically inconsistent for the state, on the one hand, to establish penalties for certain behavior and then, on the other hand, to agree to authorize the creation of business firms engaged in that very behavior.

... A remaining puzzle is why a particular state would care if corporations chartered under its state law committed unlawful activities in another jurisdiction.... One answer is that the state would suffer large reputational harms if it used corporate law to reinforce only its own laws ... such a state would likely be considered somewhat of a rogue. Corporations chartered in that state might, if nothing else, find it difficult to gain the right to do business in other states. Concerns about reciprocity would also be important. That is, a state would want to protect the laws of other states so that other states would return the favor....

Shareholders. The conventional wisdom within corporate law is that shareholders do not care whether the corporation or its managers are breaking the law, as long as the corporation is maximizing profit and the shareholders' interests are foremost. Indeed, within the dominant ... view of corporate law, ... the only duty of corporate managers is to maximize the long-term value of the firm, and thus long-term profits to shareholders. Even within this paradigm, it will be generally consistent with the profit motive for managers to obey the law because (it is assumed) governments will correctly set the penalties at such a level so as to make it worthwhile to comply with legal strictures and to establish monitoring systems that will steer the corporation clear of illegality. Occasionally, however, breaking the law is profit maximizing....

There is good reason to believe that, ex ante, shareholders would be especially reluctant to agree to a rule that authorized managers to commit unlawful acts on behalf of the corporation. There are several bases for such reluctance....

[One compelling] reason why shareholders would fear a rule giving managers corporate authority to break the law is the reasonable concern that the kinds of illegal acts that corporate executives might commit or have the corporation commit will often hurt shareholders, directly or indirectly. Reports of managers attempting to cheat shareholders through fraud or self-dealing fill business pages and corporate law casebooks. Indeed, a recent study of corporations convicted of federal crimes shows that convictions for fraud constituted twenty-seven percent of all such corporate convictions during the years 1988–96. Fraud was thus the number one crime for corporations during this time frame. Though the statistics do not reveal which "stakeholders" were the victims of such fraud, it does not require a stretch of the imagination to believe that shareholders were among the victims. Thus, shareholders would reasonably fear that allowing managers to commit crimes would result in direct harm to shareholders, and because fiduciary duty suits underdeter such conduct, shareholders will reasonably believe they need another remedy within corporate law.

Shareholders would also fear indirect harm from illegal acts on the basis of a reasonable belief that, over the class of cases, illegal acts will tend to harm the long-term interests of the firm. The costs of unlawful activity, even when managers intend such illegality to benefit the firm, can be high. Unlawful acts can cause harm to the corporation by way of major criminal and civil penalties or other less tangible (though very real) damages such as reputational injuries. Even absent large criminal penalties, the long-term effect of criminal liability on the corporation can often be negative because of adverse reputational effects among customers, employees, governmental actors, and others. As recent research shows, the initial publicity of corporate crime results in a statistically significant loss in the firm's market value. Reputational harm thus hurts shareholders in that the resale value of their shares will tend to be less if the corporation is engaged in illegal activities than if it is not.

Nevertheless, why would shareholders distrust managers' ability to judge the profitability of illegal acts in individual cases? One answer is the moral hazard problem when managers can hide behind the corporate form to avoid individual accountability for the illegal acts of the corporation. Managers can, in part, externalize the risks of the illegality onto the corporation (and its shareholders). This externalization of costs would mean that the decisionmakers would not face the same cost/benefit tradeoff as the corporation as a whole. Thus, shareholders would reasonably fear that allowing illegal acts would result in managers acting illegally more often than the shareholders would prefer.

Also, when managers have a shorter time horizon than shareholders, the managers will likely cause the corporation to break the law more often than the shareholders would prefer. This is particularly true when "the harms caused by corporate conduct may have long latency periods," as is the case with environmental law violations or tortious product defects. As John Coffee noted over twenty years ago, management may be significantly less risk-averse or more interested in short-term profit maximization (at the expense of long-term growth) than the majority of shareholders.[174] If that is true, managers might be more willing to engage in illegalities in order to maximize short-term profits at the expense of the corporation's long-term well-being and reputational interests. Managers might be concerned particularly about the short term because the markets are evaluating the company, and therefore their personal performance, from quarter to quarter. Managers' compensation may be linked to their short-term performance, while investors are typically, according to Coffee, more interested in long-term capital appreciation....

174. John C. Coffee Jr., Beyond the Shut-Eyed Sentry: Toward a Theoretical View of Corporate Misconduct and an Effective Legal Response, 63 Virginia Law Review 1099, 1105–06 & n.13 (1977).

Shareholders have reason to believe that managers' decisionmaking with regard to illegality should not be trusted. Managers might tend to underestimate the chances of getting caught in an illegal act, overestimate the potential benefits of breaking the law, or underestimate the potential penalties.[177] Shareholders could reasonably fear that managers would get caught up in the moment and fail to take proper account of all the various costs that might flow from illegality. A corporate executive "may simply enjoy taking risks, and also find it a means of advancing his career within the corporation (at the possible expense of the corporation)."[178] Moreover, "in computing [a corporation's] own costs and benefits, the corporate manager faces serious miscalculation risks."[179] "Valuation problems are notoriously difficult"[180] in the best of cases, but when the cost/benefit calculation depends on predictions about the actions of any number of government actors, competitors, employees, shareholders, and others, "it is entirely possible that the corporate manager's calculation will overstate the possible returns available from undertaking the deviant course of conduct."[181]

... This argument, it is important to note, is substantiated by recent research that shows that corporate "crime occurs less frequently among firms in which management has a larger ownership stake."[186] This is because, according to the authors, "corporate crime tends not to benefit shareholders" ... "[w]hile past penalties have not been high enough to eliminate corporate crime altogether, they appear to have been high enough to prevent crime from being a good investment for shareholders, ex ante."[189]

... [Another reason shareholders would prefer an ultra-vires limitation is that] shareholders value things other than profit; they are not as strictly self-interested as the above discussion assumes. An individual's decision to invest in a firm does not cause that person to set aside all objectives and values other than making money. Individuals reveal "other regarding preferences" in a range of situations, and studies are beginning to test the robustness of these preferences in the corporate setting. The point is that shareholders need not be saints to respect the interests of other stakeholders in the firm (at least at the margin) or to care about the importance of obeying the law....

Creditors.... [One] reason creditors would not want managers to be empowered to conduct illegal activities is because the creditors might reasonably expect to be

177. The evaluation of risk is notoriously faulty. For example, it has been shown that individuals systematically underestimate the probability of low-risk events....

178. Coffee, supra note [174], at 1105–06 & n.13.

179. [Patrick J. Ryan, Strange Bedfellows: Corporate Fiduciaries and the General Law Compliance Obligation in Section 2.01(a) of the American Law Institute's Principles of Corporate Governance, 66 Washington Law Review 413, 491 (1991).]

180. Id.

181. Id.

186. [Cindy R. Alexander & Marc A. Cohen, Why Do Corporations Become Criminals? Ownership, Hidden Actions, and Crime as an Agency Cost, 5 Journal of Corporate Finance 1 (1999).]

189. [Id. at 22, 32.]

direct victims of illegal activities. If managers were allowed to engage in unlawful acts in order to maximize profit, they would be tempted to transfer economic surplus from creditors to shareholders through fraud or other illegal activities. Creditors would of course have a direct cause of action in such circumstances, but they certainly would not easily approve of a corporate contract that created incentives for managers to engage in such conduct. An ultra vires term would, in effect, give creditors additional insurance that the firm was not defrauding them or otherwise hurting them through illegal acts....

[C]reditors would [also] have reputational reasons to care whether the firm engaged in unlawful acts. Creditors frequently become identified with the firms with whom they deal. When a particular firm is caught in some illegality, the reputational harm can overflow and damage the reputation of that firm's business partners, including creditors and suppliers. Consider, for example, the problem of Nike's contractors in Southeast Asia. These contractors are typically not owned by Nike, yet the accusations of unlawful and irresponsible acts in connection with their treatment of workers have certainly damaged Nike's reputation.... Creditors and suppliers cannot simply assume that the illegal acts of their business partners, if brought to light, would not harm their reputation as well, especially if the relationship is a close one....

Managers and Employees. Managers and employees ... would also prefer that unlawful acts be considered ultra vires for the firm. The reason non-managerial employees would not want corporations to be empowered to commit unlawful acts is fairly straightforward. Like creditors and shareholders, employees have reason to worry that they would be the victim of illegality rather than its beneficiary.... Indeed, when one thinks about profitable illegality, many of the examples that spring to mind—the use of slave labor to build pipelines, the manufacture of clothing in sweatshops, union busting—have to do with the violation of workers' rights.

Moreover, employees would be reluctant to join a corporation that allowed illegality because they would worry that they would be required to participate in such illegality as a condition of employment. Employees would thus be concerned that they would then risk personal liability or prosecution because of their acts on behalf of the corporation. Because non-managerial employees have relatively fixed wages, they would [also] not be in a position to reap many of the benefits of even the profitable illegality of the firm....

Managers (including senior management and the board of directors) would also want a provision setting unlawful acts outside the authority of the firm. The reasons for their preferences in this regard are less obvious than the reasons for the non-managerial employees' preferences. Indeed, one could ask why managers would not want more rather than less authority in the corporate charter, including the authority to have the corporation break the law if profitable to do so. Managers, whose reputation and financial health are much more aligned with the firm's than those of the non-managerial employees, could be said to have the correct incentives to break the law when profitable and to remain lawful when profitable.

Managers, however, would not likely want ... authority for them or the corporation to break the law. Even more than non-managerial employees, managers would worry that their participation in corporate illegality would result in personal liability. Because of their more senior status, managers tend to have more responsibility and the impact of their decisions will be felt more broadly. The risks of personal liability would thus be much greater. Fines would tend to be higher and terms of imprisonment longer....

Implications for Corporate Practice

... [T]he doctrine of ultra vires for unlawful acts is a part of existing corporate law, as a positive matter. The fact that it has been ignored does not mean that it has ceased to exist. Rather, it simply needs to be noticed to be put into action. Shareholder plaintiffs, for example, could bring suits on the basis of these arguments immediately.

... The key implication for corporate practice of an ultra vires doctrine for unlawful acts is that injunctive relief would be available. As when the ultra vires doctrine was more vibrant, individual shareholders could sue to enjoin the corporation from engaging in ultra vires acts, even if such acts were expected to be profitable. Such a right would belong, as it did previously, to each shareholder individually and could be exercised even though every other shareholder was opposed. As the Supreme Court said, "beyond the limits of the act of incorporation, the will of the majority cannot make an act valid; and the powers of a court of equity may be put in motion at the instance of a single shareholder."[214]

Thus, if a shareholder became aware that the corporation was committing a crime or otherwise acting unlawfully, she could sue in the state of incorporation for an injunction against such activity. Importantly, such an injunctive action would not require a showing of damages. [A] shareholder would have an injunctive remedy even if the ultra vires act (under the "modern" doctrine, an unlawful act) were expected or even proven to be profitable.

Of course, the nature of injunctive actions means that this remedy will be available only if shareholders discover that a course of illegality or unlawful behavior is ongoing or that an unlawful act is planned for the future. Though limited, this remedy is nevertheless very powerful. Shareholders may indeed come to learn that their corporation is engaging in unlawful activity and that the governmental entity charged with enforcing the law has declined to do so or that the possible penalties that the government could impose are slight. Another possibility is that shareholders might learn that the corporation is engaging in a series of torts and that the victims of such torts are unlikely to bring actions against the corporation (because, perhaps, as in the case of many environmental torts the injuries will become obvious only years later). In these situations and others like them, shareholders would be able to bring an ultra vires

214. Dodge v. Woolsey, 59 U.S. (18 How.) 331, 343 (1855).

suit against the corporation, asking that the corporation be enjoined from its unlawful activity....

Another way that the ultra vires rule could be enforced is through actions by the corporation itself, either directly or derivatively [by its shareholders], against the corporate manager or director who caused the corporation to act beyond its powers.... [Thus] not only can a shareholder bring an injunctive action to stop a corporation from acting unlawfully, she can sue the responsible corporate officials in a derivative action to recover any losses to the corporation....

... A damages remedy ... would help deter corporations from breaking the law when some penalty or fine or judgment is likely to be imposed on the corporation, since such cost could be recovered from the individuals responsible for causing the corporation to act beyond its authority. This remedy would not, however, deter unlawful behavior if the expected amount of the penalties or fines or judgments were small.

... [T]he ultra vires doctrine [also] provide[s] the incorporating state, through its attorney general, some powerful remedies.... Forty-nine states still retain a provision in their state incorporation statutes that allows the state to dissolve a corporation or enjoin it from engaging in ultra vires activities....

Once an obligation of lawfulness is recognized as being the sine qua non of the modern ultra vires doctrine, the importance of such an obligation becomes clear. It is so important that shareholders have a powerful method to enforce it.... [G]iving shareholders the power to enjoin the corporation's continuing unlawful acts ... will likely be an important part of any effort to keep corporations within the law, whether they be operating in the United States or elsewhere.

Judd F. Sneirson, *Shareholder Primacy and Corporate Compliance*[*]

Corporate law requires fiduciaries to take reasonable steps to ensure that the firm complies with applicable laws, and put into place an information-and-control structure to aid in this effort. In addition to this monitoring obligation, corporate fiduciaries must themselves manage the firm in accordance with applicable laws. A failure to do so—for example, knowing that the firm is out of compliance and failing to act to rectify the situation, or affirmatively causing the firm to break the law—would not only amount to a breach of fiduciary duty, it would also fall outside the scope of the business judgment rule and any director-exculpation charter provisions.

Importantly, this rule holds even where non-compliance, after the payment of any fines, would prove the more profitable course: "Under Delaware law, a fiduciary may not choose to manage an entity in an illegal fashion, even if the fiduciary believes that

* Originally published in 26 Fordham Environmental Law Review 450 (2015). Reprinted with permission.

the illegal activity will result in profits for the entity."[8] Likewise under New York law, directors are liable for illegal acts "even though committed to benefit the corporation."[9]

This raises the question: which laws demand compliance and implicate these corporate fiduciary duties? Should the corporate-law rule apply to all laws and regulations, just laws, just criminal laws, just criminal laws prohibiting *mala in se*, or what? Corporate-law scholarship, primarily from the law-and-economics school of thought, has variously answered this question, with most commentators drawing this line somewhere between laws concerning *mala in se* and those concerning *mala prohibita*. Corporate-law cases are less clear on this point but certainly take a tougher stance than the scholarship recommends: the violation in the principal casebook case involves illegal corporate campaign-finance contributions,[13] and other cases involve a wide range of criminal and civil violations, from the mundane to the serious.[14] The scholarship, in other words, does not accurately describe the corporate law duty to comply with applicable laws....

Discussion Questions

1. Winkler suggests that corporate obligations to the public derive from environmental, consumer, and employment law. Is this desirable or should corporate law also address the needs of stakeholder groups? Do you think sustainability concepts could or should take hold in other areas of the law? If so, which areas?

2. Do you agree with cited authors that some laws ought to be treated as prices? Where would you draw the line between law-as-sanction and law-as-price? Is it ever optimal to disregard laws legislating corporate social responsibility?

---

8. See Metro Comm'n [Corp. BVI v. Advanced Mobilcomm. Techs., 854 A.2d 121, 131 (Del. Ch. 2004)]; see also Desimone [v. Barrows, 924 A.2d 908, 934–35 (Del. Ch. 2007)] ("The knowing use of illegal means to pursue profit for the corporation is director misconduct."); In re Massey, 2011 WL 2176479 at *20 (Del. Ch. May 31, 2011) ("Delaware law allows corporations to pursue diverse means to make a profit, subject to a critical statutory floor, which is the requirement that Delaware corporations only pursue 'lawful business' by 'lawful acts.'"); see also American Law Institute, Principles of Corporate Governance § 4.01 cmt. d ("The concept of profit enhancement is also qualified by the provision in § 2.01(b)(1) that obliges the corporation 'to the same extent as a natural person, to act within the boundaries set by law.'").

9. Miller v. American Telephone & Telegraph Co., 507 F.2d 759, 762 (3d Cir. 1974) (applying New York law).

13. See Miller, 507 F.2d at 761.

14. See, e.g., Scrushy v. Tucker, 70 So. 3d 289, 312–13 (Ala. 2011) (criminal fraud) (applying Delaware law); Louisiana Mun. Police Employees' Ret. Sys. v. Pyott, 46 A.3d 313, 317–18 (Del. Ch. 2012) (marketing Botox for off-label uses in violation of FDA regulations); In re Massey, 2011 WL 2176479 at *5–*10 (Mine Safety and Health Administration violations); Desimone, 924 A.2d at 934–35 (alleged violation SEC and IRS disclosure obligations); Davis v. Dyson, 900 N.E.2d 698, 712–16 (Ill. 2008) (violation of Illinois Condo Act's insurance requirements); Roth v. Robertson, 118 N.Y.S. 351, 353 (Sup. Ct. 1909) (violation of Sunday Blue Laws requiring business closures); see also American Law Institute, Principles of Corporate Governance § 2.01 cmt. g (using a speed-limit example to demonstrate the corporate law obligation to obey the law).

3. According to Tom R. Tyler, *Why People Obey the Law* (2006), people obey the law if they believe it is legitimate and worthy of respect, not because they fear punishment. What does Tyler's hypothesis mean for corporate compliance? Does it comport with the law-as-price view described in this chapter? How can authorities use Tyler's research to improve compliance?

4. The famous Milton Friedman quote about corporate social responsibility reads in full: "[T]here is one and only one social responsibility of business—to use its resources and engage in activities designed to increase its profits *so long as it stays within the rules of the game*." (emphasis added) Would Friedman thus reject the law-as-price view of later law-and-economics scholars?

5. Are you persuaded by Williams's argument that regulatory law is so complex that it is difficult to gauge morally and therefore should be complied with, period?

6. Greenfield suggests that part of the problem is that law and regulation enforcement is less than perfect, such that the prices associated with legal non-compliance are unduly discounted. Does this suggest we need better law enforcement? Stronger penalties? Different penalties? Criminal penalties?

7. Criminal penalties for corporate decisionmakers are rare, but offer a tempting tool to obtain compliance with corporations' legal obligations. Do you think they should be used? For what sorts of violations? We will take a closer look at criminal sanctions in Chapter 10.

8. In light of recent corporate and financial scandals in the headlines, do you believe that society is more or less indifferent to corporate crime? If so, what steps can be taken to increase public scrutiny on firms that break the law?

9. Greenfield's ultra vires theory would leave enforcement to the corporation's shareholders. Is this realistic? Do you agree with Greenfield that shareholders "value things other than profit"?

10. The Environmental Protection Agency maintains a searchable database of environmental violations called the Toxics Release Inventory. See http://www2.epa.gov/toxics-release-inventory-tri-program. What are the compliance track records of the businesses near you?

11. Do you think that "shaming" companies that flout their legal obligations—or requiring companies to disclose their compliance track records—would be effective in changing their behavior?

Chapter 5

Entity Choices for Sustainable Businesses

Earlier chapters suggest that corporations wishing to engage in sustainable business practices may freely do so, and courts will respect such decisions under the business judgment rule. Would other forms of business organizations better suit sustainable businesses, or at least better signal to consumers and investors that the firm is to be managed in this way? This chapter looks at alternatives to the traditional corporation. The first excerpt describes several twists on the corporate form, including a corporation that obtains "B Corporation" status—a sort of "Good Housekeeping" seal of approval from a private certifying organization. The second and third excerpts discuss statutory alternatives, including a low-profit limited liability company or "L3C," benefit corporations, English community interest corporations, and flexible purpose corporations. The final excerpt asks whether this proliferation of new forms of business organization advances or hinders sustainability and situates the benefit corporation trend in larger corporate governance debates.

Judd F. Sneirson, *Green Is Good: Sustainability, Profitability, and a New Paradigm for Corporate Governance**

The shareholder-wealth-maximization principle ... should not discourage corporations from undertaking sustainability efforts, even when those efforts appear to detract in the short term from what would otherwise become shareholder profits. A number of businesses have elected to take this permission to the next level by incorporating an affirmative commitment to sustainable business practices into their corporate identities. In the process, these firms have forged a new paradigm for sustainability and corporate governance: a corporation that is green to its very core.

These efforts follow a common pattern. In their corporate charters, these firms include a statement to the effect that the business will be managed in a sustainable and socially responsible manner.... [S]uch a charter provision becomes the firm's "internal law" ... and binds it, unless and until it is amended. And ... shareholders investing in the firm do so on this basis and thereby accede to this explicit commitment as part of their hypothetical bargain [with management]. The following [paragraphs] discuss three variations of this theme.

* Originally published in 94 Iowa Law Review 987 (2008). Reprinted with permission.

... A B Corporation is a private certification and associated mark signifying that a business meets certain high standards of social and environmental performance.[159] To become a B Corporation and use its mark, a firm must first score high enough on a survey meant to distinguish sincere social and environmental commitments from mere window dressing. Second, an applicant must include in its articles of incorporation the following provision respecting the interests of employees, the community, and the environment:

> In discharging his or her duties, and in determining what is in the best interests of the Company and its shareholders, a Director shall consider such factors as the Director deems relevant, including but not limited to, the long-term prospects and interests of the Company and its shareholders, and the social, economic, legal, or other effects of any action on the current and retired employees, the suppliers and customers of the Company or its subsidiaries, and the communities in which the Company or its subsidiaries operate..., together with the short-term, as well as long-term, interests of its shareholders and the effect of the Company's operations (and its subsidiaries' operations) on the economy of the state, the region and the nation.
>
> Nothing in this Article, express or implied, is intended to create or shall create or grant any right in or for any person or any cause of action by or for any person.

The provision is meant to offer additional protection to corporate fiduciaries who consider the interests of groups other than shareholders in making company decisions and to empower shareholders (but not other groups) to hold fiduciaries accountable for not doing so. By enshrining these values in the firm's charter, they are "more likely ... [to] survive new investors, new management, and even, someday, new owners."[163]

The Oregon legislature amended its corporations code in 2007 to effect a similar option.[164] Oregon law now expressly permits its corporations to include in their articles of incorporation "[a] provision authorizing or directing the corporation to conduct the business of the corporation in a manner that is environmentally and socially responsible."[165] Thus, firms may either "authorize" their decisionmakers to act in an environmentally and socially responsible manner, "direct" them to do so, or remain silent on the issue.

---

159. See Certified B Corp., About B Corp., http://www.bcorporation.net/about (explaining what B corporations are). Other examples of private certification arrangements are the Orthodox Union certification for kosher products, the Leadership in Energy and Environmental Design ("LEED") system for certifying "green" buildings, and the Quality Assurance International organic food certification....

163. See Certified B Corp., About B Corp., http://www.bcorporation.net/about ....

164. See H.B. 2826, 74th Leg. Assem., Reg. Sess. (Or. 2007) (codified at Or. Rev. Stat. §60.047(2)(e) (Supp. 2008)). The bill went into effect on January 1, 2008.

165. Or. Rev. Stat. §60.047(2)(e). The statute's reference to environmental and social responsibility deliberately reflects the triple-bottom-line conception of sustainability....

Even though the "authorizing" version effectively reaffirms the business-judgment rule, the provision's proponents consider such charter language useful.... [T]he provision helps dispel the common misconception that corporate boards have a legal obligation to maximize shareholder profits and may not take into account, and sacrifice profits to benefit, other stakeholder groups.... [The] law will hopefully enlighten corporate decisionmakers (and their attorneys) on this point and embolden them to take a broader view of their roles.

The "directing" language literally mandates that the firm be run in an environmentally and socially responsible manner, like the B Corporation form charter provision quoted above. Also like the B Corporation provision, the optional Oregon provision is not meant to confer any legal rights or standing on nonshareholder groups, and it leaves any enforcement primarily to the company's shareholders—just as it stands under current corporate law.

A third variation on this theme is a voluntary charter provision along the lines described above but without the attendant marketing or statutory endorsement. Jurisdictions permit such provisions, and indeed companies have long included them. To take one prominent example, The Washington Post Company's certificate of incorporation states that its corporate purpose is "to publish ... an independent newspaper dedicated to the welfare of the community and the nation, in keeping with the principles of a free press."[174] In its 1971 offering prospectus, The Post noted: "Publishing The Post in keeping with those principles has involved and will continue to involve substantial expenses (not necessarily compensated for by increased revenues) incurred in endeavoring to achieve and to maintain editorial excellence and independence as well as to provide outstanding news collection and reporting."[175] Similarly, a Portland, Oregon sportswear company included a sustainability pledge in its charter, stating that the duty of directors shall be to make money for shareholders but not at the expense of the environment, human rights, public health and safety, dignity of employees, and the welfare of the community in which the company operates.[176] This mandate can be amended, to be sure, but only by a supermajority shareholder vote [per that company's charter].

These variations raise interesting corporate-governance questions, including who is to prosecute when fiduciaries fail to live up to these internal obligations and how are such prosecutions to be decided. The B Corporation language and the Oregon law's legislative history both indicate that only shareholders can bring derivative actions to enforce these provisions, and both purport not to confer standing and additional rights on nonshareholder constituencies. As for the second question, ... a charter mandate to act sustainably [sh]ould be governed by the business-judgment rule. That is, disinterested, informed, good-faith decisions—about how sustainable

174. Washington Post Co., Certificate of Incorporation, art. 3. § 1, at 2 (as amended through May 12, 1988), available at http://www.secinfo.com/dsvRq.986.d.htm.

175. See Donald E. Graham, The Gray Lady's Virtue, Wall Street Journal, Apr. 23, 2007, at A17 (arguing that a news business should not prioritize profits over journalistic excellence and integrity).

176. See Polly LaBarre, Leap of Faith, Fast Company, June 2007, at 97 (profiling Nau, Inc.)....

and socially responsible the firm should be, how shareholder profits (and other stakeholder interests) should balance such considerations, and how to achieve a desired level of sustainability and social responsibility—would likewise enjoy business-judgment-rule protection from shareholder derivative suits. While this deference admittedly saps some of these provisions' force, it also should keep activist-shareholder derivative suits to their current levels....

Time will tell whether this new paradigm for corporate governance takes hold and proves successful....

Dana Brakman Reiser, *Benefit Corporations— A Sustainable Form of Organization?**

Founders of social enterprises believe profits and social good can be produced in tandem and wish to form organizations that will pursue these dual missions. They will, however, encounter obstacles to articulating and enforcing such dual missions if they adopt either a traditional nonprofit or for-profit form of organization. Nonprofit forms bar profit distribution and for-profit forms will create practical, if not legal, pressure to favor profit maximization over social good when the two come into conflict. And these two imperatives will certainly, at times, conflict. If more profit could always be obtained by pursuing social good, traditional for-profits would produce the optimal level of social goods, charities would be swimming in resources, or both. Social entrepreneurs believe social good can be produced along with profits and desire hybrid forms of organization to smooth a single enterprise's path to realizing both goals.

A mounting number of jurisdictions have attempted to meet this demand by enabling new hybrid organizational forms. These include the low-profit limited liability company ("L3C") available in nine U.S. states and the community interest company ("CIC") available in the United Kingdom. In addition, "B Corp" is a private certification available to U.S. for-profits that demonstrate their commitment to a dual mission of making profits and promoting social good. Qualifying entities can license the B Corp mark to market themselves to consumers, investors, and others.... A handful of states have enacted statutes enabling "benefit corporations" in the past two years, and several more are considering similar legislation.[8] The benefit corporation form differs from the L3C, CIC, and B Corp in several respects, especially in its use of third-party standard-setting organizations to vet the social good bona fides of potential incorporators. This Article evaluates whether the innovations in the benefit corporation form can meet the goals social entrepreneurs have for hybrid organizational forms, ultimately concluding it will fall short.

---

* Originally published in 46 Wake Forest Law Review 591 (2011). Reprinted with permission.

8. See ... B Lab, Benefit Corporation Legislation, Certified B Corp., http://www.bcorporation.net/ public policy (providing updated counts of states adopting and considering benefit corporation legislation).

... [C]ompanies have been able to obtain private certification as a "B Corp" since 2006. B Corps must provide in their formative documents that fiduciaries must consider the impact of their decisions on various nonshareholder constituencies, including the environment and the local, state, and national economy. A private nonprofit organization, B Lab, vets aspiring B Corps to confirm that these governance structures have been established and conducts an extensive survey to determine how well an applicant uses "the power of business to solve social and environmental problems." Those applicants meeting B Lab's standards may license the B Corp mark and are subject to audit by B Lab on an ongoing basis. B Lab, of course, cannot confer a legal form on an organization. By varying governance structures and conveying information about conforming entities, however, B Corp status appeals to social enterprises in a manner similar to official hybrid forms.

In 2010, Maryland became the first state to establish a "benefit corporation" form of organization....[20] This new form blends both state enabling legislation and a third-party certification system. [Arizona, Arkansas, California, Colorado, Connecticut, Delaware, the District of Columbia, Florida, Hawaii, Idaho, Illinois, Indiana, Louisiana, Massachusetts, Minnesota, Montana, Nebraska, Nevada, New Hampshire, New Jersey, New York, Oregon, Pennsylvania, Rhode Island, South Carolina, Tennessee, Utah, Vermont, Virginia, and West Virginia] have since followed suit and benefit corporation legislation has also been introduced in numerous other states.[22] ...

Separate Statute

The benefit corporation concept has thus far been enacted only under special statutory authorization, separate and apart from the adopting jurisdiction's standard corporate legislation.... Perhaps proceeding with a special statute eases legislative adoption, but the special statute approach also ties in with the statutes' recurring theme of avoiding infiltration of general corporation law by benefit corporation norms. Yet, this walling-off does not go both ways. When benefit corporation statutes are silent, for-profit corporate statutory and decisional law will fill the gaps.

Although it exists under a separate statutory framework, "benefit corporation" status is available both to newly forming corporations that may use the form from their inception and to existing for-profit corporations that adopt benefit corporation form by amending their charters. The statutes use labeling and voting requirements to protect initial and existing shareholders from confusion. Upon adopting this status,

---

20. See Maryland Code Ann., Corps. & Ass'ns §§ 5-6C-01 to -08 (LexisNexis 2011)....

22. [As of 2016, legislatures in Alaska, Georgia, Iowa, Kentucky, Michigan, Ohio, and Oklahoma are considering similar legislation.] Legislation to permit a different kind of incorporated hybrid, the "flexible purpose corporation," has been [enacted] in California. A flexible purpose corporation would pursue profit and at least one charitable purpose or a purpose to pursue the interests of employees, suppliers, customers, creditors, community, society or the environment. See ... California Corp. Code § 2302(b)(2) (2011)). These purposes [must] be disclosed to the secretary of state, but not vetted by a third party as benefit corporation statutes contemplate....

charter documents, and in Maryland the stock certificates, must be clearly labeled or re-labeled to include the term "benefit corporation."

Those purchasing shares in the benefit corporation and inspecting its documents are thus placed on notice of the special nature of the corporation in question, if not specifically of the limits on what a benefit corporation may or may not do. Clearer labeling would be provided if the corporation's name were required to include the "benefit" term, as state law often demands inclusion of a designation of limited liability in other forms. In May 2011, Maryland added the requirement of a benefit legend into corporate names....

For an existing business corporation to reinvent itself as a benefit corporation, the statutes demand significant support for the change among shareholders. Charter amendments require a vote of at least two-thirds of the outstanding shareholders, with the request for a vote providing notice of the change.... Requiring specific notice and a statement of reasons provides greater information to shareholders whose interest may be transformed by the change to benefit corporation status. Similar notice and supermajority voting requirements apply if a business corporation merges with a benefit corporation. Notably, these requirements for opting into benefit corporation status apply to benefit corporations seeking to resume ordinary business corporation status as well.

Public Benefit

The main thrust of benefit corporation statutes is to require these entities to pursue purposes beyond profit-making. A benefit corporation must be formed for a "general public benefit," meaning a "material, positive impact on society and the environment."[34] Other than in the New Jersey statute, general public benefit is defined by measurement against a "third-party standard," and all statutes permit incorporators to also pursue more "specific public benefits." They include:

- Providing [low income or underserved] individuals or communities with beneficial products or services;
- Promoting economic opportunity for individuals or communities beyond the creation of jobs in the normal course of business;
- Preserving [or improving] the environment;
- Improving human health;
- Promoting the arts, sciences, or advancement of knowledge;
- Increasing the flow of capital to entities with a public benefit purpose; or [and]
- The accomplishment of any other particular [identifiable] benefit for society or the environment.[36]

The statutes provide little clarification of the hierarchy of purposes a benefit corporation will serve. Except in Virginia, the statutes do state that while a benefit cor-

34. [See, e.g.,] Maryland Code Ann., Corps. & Ass'ns §§5-6C-01(c), 5-6C-06(A) (LexisNexis 2011)....
36. [Id.] §5-6C-01(d) (bracketed language included in all but Maryland statute)....

poration may adopt purposes to pursue specific public benefits, these specific public benefits do not limit its obligation to pursue a general public benefit. However, general and specific public benefits may be articulated in addition to other purposes for which a corporation may be created, and these public benefits may, but need not, limit more traditional business purposes. Finally, the statutes all declare that the general or specific public benefits that benefit corporations pursue "are in the best interests of the corporation," seemingly conclusively. This provision alone might be used to trump potential shareholder claims that directors' decisions to pursue general or specific public benefits undermine the best interests of the corporation when they interfere with profit maximization or other business goals. The benefit corporation statutes, however, offer greater detail on how directors ought to make decisions and provide additional liability shields.

Directorial Obligations and Protections

Each statute explains the obligations of benefit corporation directors. They are required to consider the impact of their decisions on shareholders, employees of the corporation, subsidiaries and suppliers, "customers [to the extent they are] beneficiaries of the general or specific public benefit purposes of the benefit corporation," the community, society, and the local and global environment.[40] Some later-enacted statutes clarify that directors need not prioritize any particular person's or group's interests in their deliberations. Unless an individual benefit corporation elects to do so through a statement in its charter, directors may take action based on the effects of their decisions on any one of these groups or interests.

The intent of this language appears to be broadening the range of appropriate considerations in directorial decision making, in order to give directors discretion to make decisions favoring social mission achievement over profit-maximization. The statutes' permission for a director to also "consider any other pertinent factors or the interests of any other group that the director determines are appropriate to consider"[42] goes even further down this road. Moreover, in case this wide range of potential justifications for directorial decisions does not sufficiently comfort benefit corporation directors, the statutes also specifically provide directors of benefit corporations with immunity from liability for performance of their duties within the broad discretion described above and provide that no duty of such a director runs to the corporations' beneficiaries.

This language is clearly modeled on language from constituency statutes, also known as anti-takeover legislation. Such statutes permit directors to consider non-shareholder constituencies in weighing takeover offers and other decisions and have been criticized as simply giving directors cover to vote against control-shifting transactions and to take other actions in order to entrench themselves in their positions.[46]

---

40. [Id.] § 5-6C-07(a)(1)....

42. [Id.] § 5-6C-07(a)....

46. See, e.g., Frank H. Easterbrook & Daniel R. Fischel, The Economic Structure of Corporate Law 38 (1991) ("[A] manager told to serve two masters (a little for the equity holders, a little for the community) has been freed of both and is answerable to neither.")...

The broad discretion benefit corporation statutes accord to directors can likewise be faulted for giving directors unbridled discretion, with which they might pursue social good or might pursue foolish or self-serving practices.

Provisions in the later-enacted statutes suggest that their drafters may have had specific concerns about protecting benefit directors in the takeover context. These statutes require directors to consider "the short-term and long-term interests of the benefit corporation, including benefits that may accrue to the benefit corporation from its long-term plans and the possibility that these interests may be best served by the continued independence of the benefit corporation."[47] Thus, directors of benefit corporations appear protected from personal liability on claims that they have insufficiently produced public benefits or inadequately pursued profits for shareholders, whether in the context of ordinary business decisions or control transactions.

Third-Party Standard-Setters

The significant divergence between the corporate purposes and directorial obligations in business corporations and benefit corporations makes it vital that shareholders and others can differentiate the two. The crucible here is the issue of public benefit: only corporations pursuing a general (and perhaps also specific) public benefit can qualify as benefit corporations. Those that do not pursue a public benefit are excluded from the category. Rather than entrusting a government agency to make these initial determinations, the benefit corporation statutes delegate this responsibility to third-party standard-setters. All of the statutes anticipate that such third parties will make available standards "for defining, reporting, and assessing" the social and environmental performance of aspiring benefit corporations.[49] The statutes decline to provide even minimum content for such standards. In addition, they do not dictate how the standards should be applied, how often, or by whom.

Instead, the statutes simply mandate that standard-setters be independent and transparent. Sufficient independence is shown if the standard "is developed by a person [or entity] that is independent of the benefit corporation."[51] The Maryland statute offers no further definition of independence, but the later-enacted statutes define independence to exclude those with direct or indirect "material relationships" with the benefit corporation or its subsidiaries, including current or recent employment, familial relationships with executive officers, or direct or indirect ownership or management of five percent or more of the benefit corporation's equity.[52] For transparency to be sufficient, each statute requires the certifying party to make publicly available four types of information. Standard-setters must publicize "the factors considered when measuring the performance of a business, the relative weightings of those factors, and the identity of the persons who developed and control changes to the standard, and the process by which those changes were made."[54]

47. [See, e.g.,] N.J. Stat. Ann. § 14A:18-6(a)(6) (West 2011)....
49. [See, e.g.,] Maryland Code Ann., Corps. & Ass'ns § 5-6C-01(e) (LexisNexis 2011)....
51. [Id.] § 5-6C-01(e)(1) (bracketed language is only in Maryland statute)....
52. See N.J. Stat. Ann. § 14A:18-1 (West 2011)....
54. See Maryland Code Ann., Corps. & Ass'ns § 5-6C-01(e)(1)–(2) (LexisNexis 2011)....

B Lab has been deeply committed to and involved with the passage of benefit corporation statutes. Its survey and audit processes are fully documented online and thus appear to fit the transparency requirements, and B Lab will be independent of any unrelated potential incorporators. B Lab evaluates potential B corporations using the B Impact Assessment, which looks at issues of corporate accountability, employee policy, products' benefit to consumers, the company's relationship with its community, and its impact on the environment. The assessment contains a total of two-hundred points, and companies must score eighty points to be certified and granted access to the B Corp mark. B Lab also audits twenty percent of those companies who qualify for B Corp certification every two years.

Although the third-party standard-setter role seems tailor-made for B Lab, numerous existing standard-setters and entity-certification programs would also appear to qualify under the statutes.[61] Certifiers of fair labor practices consider social and, to some degree, environmental performance in their standards. They are transparent and would likely be independent in most cases. Certifiers of high environmental performance, such as those authorized to assess compliance with the ISO 14001 Environmental Management System standard, could likewise qualify as third-party standard-setters with a few changes. Even corporate governance advisory firms might be adjusted to fit the bill. As they are already beginning to offer advisory services to institutions and individuals seeking socially responsible investments, retooling to certify benefit corporations could likely be done with ease.

Likewise, current product-focused standard-setters could also enter the market to qualify benefit corporations. Consider Cradle to Cradle ("C2C"), a certification offered by McDonough Braungart Design Chemistry LLC ("MBDC"). C2C is a multi-attribute product label that is licensed to those meeting MBDC's criteria for Material Health, Material Reutilization, Renewable Energy Use, Water Stewardship, and Social Responsibility. C2C was not designed to vet aspiring benefit corporations. Rather, C2C is currently offered to products, such as the Method line of soap and cleaning products, rather than to entities. However, MBDC publicizes its standards for environmental and social performance (required only for the tiers of certification beyond "basic"), and is transparent regarding how the standards are weighted and the identity of those who develop and control changes to the standards. Thus, it could offer certification to potential benefit corporations. It is not yet clear whether the benefit corporation certification market will attract rating agencies, governance advisory firms, or existing product or entity certifiers. In any case, meeting the statutes' limited transparency and independence requirements will not be a significant barrier.

---

61. Indeed, the B Lab website itself offers a number of suggestions of other possible third-party standard-setters, including "Global Reporting Initiative ("GRI"), GreenSeal, Underwriters Laboratories ("UL"), ISO2600, [and] Green America," as well as a list of over one hundred raters on a referenced raters list. See B Lab, Benefit Corporation—Legal FAQs, Certified B Corp., http://www.bcorporation.net/resources/bcorp/documents/Benefit%20Corporation%20-%20Legal %20Provisions%20and%20 FAQ.pdf....

Enforcement

Whether or not B Lab is joined by other standard-setters, it is not the only body empowered to monitor and enforce the public benefit to which benefit corporations are devoted. The statutes also impose disclosure obligations upon benefit corporations, requiring them to provide annual benefit reports to their shareholders and to post them on their public websites. The statutes describe the contents of this report differently. Again, the Maryland statute is briefer than the later enactments, but all require timely benefit reports including elements of description and assessment. All benefit corporations must describe how they have pursued their general and specific public benefit purposes and any circumstances that hindered their ability to do so. Vermont's statute also demands that benefit corporations give a statement of actions they can take to improve performance in the future. Vermont, New Jersey, and Hawaii also require the report to disclose the names and addresses of a "benefit director" and optional "benefit officer," director compensation, a statement by the benefit director, and the names of anyone owning five percent or more of the corporation's stock. Assessment requires each benefit corporation to consider and report how well it performed in accordance with its third-party standard as compared with prior performance.

In addition to demanding publication, the New Jersey statute requires the report to be filed with the state Department of the Treasury, on penalty of forfeiture of benefit corporation status. Vermont's statute does not require filing, but demands that benefit corporations must submit the annual report for shareholder approval or rejection. The statute does not explain the consequences if the report is rejected. Hawaii's statute disavows any government involvement explicitly, mandating that the report state that "the sustainable business corporation and its activities are subject to the oversight of the board of the sustainable business corporation and are not subject to the direct oversight, regulation, or endorsement of any governmental body."

The positions of benefit director and benefit officer merit additional explanation. Vermont, New Jersey, and Hawaii require benefit corporations to name a benefit director and permit them to appoint a benefit officer. The benefit director must include in the annual report her own statement assessing whether the benefit corporation and its directors have acted in compliance with the benefit purposes of the corporation during the relevant period. If a benefit director opines that the benefit corporation has failed to meet the requirements of the law, she must describe these failures. In New Jersey and Vermont, benefit directors are immune from personal liability for their performance of these evaluative tasks, so long as they act in good faith and do not engage in intentional misconduct, knowing violations of law, or self-dealing. Unlike the benefit director, a benefit officer is optional in every enacting jurisdiction. If a benefit corporation chooses to select one (who may be the same person as the benefit director), the benefit officer "shall perform the duties in the management of the benefit corporation relating to the purpose of the corporation to create public benefit." Identifying at least one and perhaps two roles with clear responsibility for tracking and assessing public benefit provides additional monitoring and enforcement resources over mandated disclosure alone.

In addition, all benefit corporation statutes other than Maryland's, offer a special right of action often called a "benefit enforcement proceeding" to enforce the special duties of benefit corporation directors and officers and the public benefit purposes of the corporation. The statutes limit potential plaintiffs in benefit enforcement proceedings to shareholders entitled to bring derivative actions and, in some cases other groups, if specified in a corporation's charter. Thus, the additional proceeding does not expand standing to challenge conduct of benefit corporation fiduciaries, but does express support for an expanded range of inquiry in suits by traditional parties.

As yet, there is no case law addressing the obligations of benefit corporation fiduciaries, and the statutes do not speak to how courts should analyze such claims. One commentator argues that "the core duty of the benefit corporation can be defined as the duty to secure profits for the shareholders while considering the socially beneficial purposes of the corporation."[85] This seems a fair statement as far as it goes, but without greater legislative explanation or judicial interpretation, it remains difficult to provide guidance to fiduciaries in situations where profit and social benefit goals conflict.

Assessing the Benefit Corporation

... Fundamentally, founders and operators of social enterprises unsatisfied with traditional nonprofit or for-profit forms seek a type of organization that will legally establish their sense of a dual profit-making and social mission and enforce it over time. They would also like a hybrid form to expand the range of funding streams they can effectively access. Further, they seek to use the hybrid form as part of their effort to brand their social enterprises to enable them to market their products and services to consumers, business partners, and others as special and different from those offered by typical nonprofit charities and for-profit businesses. Many believe that achieving all or some combination of these three goals is the only way to make their endeavors sustainable....

1. The Benefit Corporation and Dual Mission Articulation

The benefit corporation statutes not only permit, but require, articulation of an expressly dual mission.... This express dual mission mandate contrasts starkly with traditional nonprofit forms, which prohibit entities from acting to pursue profits for owners. It also represents a significant change from for-profit forms in which some pursuit of social good is certainly within legal bounds, but significant sacrificing of profits to further social goals engenders real risks.

When one thinks more deeply about how a dual mission will be articulated in a benefit corporation, however, doubts emerge. The requirement of general public benefit is vague and undefined. The determination of whether a particular organization's goals pursue a general public benefit is left to an unregulated third-party

85. Marc J. Lane, Social Enterprise: Empowering Mission-Driven Entrepreneurs 128 (2011).

standard-setter. Moreover, the statutes provide no baseline or guidance for the standards these third parties should use to make this determination; they require only transparency and independence. If a standard-setter clearly and transparently sets low standards, it may qualify unrelated entities to form as benefit corporations just as would a standard-setter with higher standards, leaving the door open to greenwashing or even fraud. Perhaps transparency will enable consumers and investors to judge the mix of profit and social good individual benefit corporations serve based on which standard-setter is used. This, however, would require highly motivated consumers and investors to engage in significant research. At the moment, benefit corporations require only formal articulation of a dual mission, and oversight over the genuineness of these statements is lacking.

2. The Benefit Corporation and Dual Mission Enforcement

Third-party standard-setters, fiduciaries, and shareholders all play enforcement roles in the benefit corporation. Except in New Jersey, third-party standard-setters serve as initial gatekeepers; in order to qualify for benefit corporation status, an entity must meet the requirements of an independent third-party standard. As noted earlier, these standard-setters play this certification role bounded by neither standards nor oversight. Moreover, the role of the standard-setters themselves in ongoing enforcement is less clear. All of the statutes envision public benefit assessments in annual benefit reports will be made with reference to the third-party standard. But, none of the statutes specify whether or how standard-setters should be involved in vetting public-benefit provision after incorporation. Standard-setters may choose to engage in auditing or other monitoring functions to boost enforcement or they may consider their role complete when initial certification is granted or denied.

Shareholders are also involved at the initial adoption of benefit corporation status and on any exit from that status. Shareholders must be granted express notice of the change and must vote by a supermajority to approve it. These provisions may have been drafted to protect unsuspecting investors from being surprised by a benefit corporation's dual mission orientation. Yet, the notice and voting requirements apply in both directions. Thus, they also protect the benefit corporation and enforce its dual mission against termination without a strong consensus among shareholders.

Outside the context of transformation to fully for-profit status, though, the statutes offer little guidance to shareholders or fiduciaries on the thorny issue of how profit and social good should be balanced. They allow directors to forego profit maximization in favor of social good production or vice versa, but they do not instruct directors on how to exercise this broad discretion. Directors are not told to err on the side of social good in every decision, to pursue more profit than social good across the enterprise, or the opposite of either instruction. Rather, directors are merely instructed to consider the impact of every decision on nonshareholder constituencies. In addition, the statutes provide directors with a broad range of interests that they may act to benefit, and the role of benefit corporation director is constructed to be highly discretionary. Thus, the statutes impose no clear framework for directorial decision making. Without one, it is difficult to identify a metric by which shareholders might enforce fiduciaries' compliance with dual mission.

Shareholders of all benefit corporations retain the informational, voting, and litigation rights of ordinary shareholders. Any of these rights could, theoretically, be used to enforce dual mission. Benefit corporation shareholders may demand to inspect corporate books and records beyond the benefit report to determine how a particular mission conflict was resolved. They may vote out directors who fail to sufficiently pursue their favored balance of profits and mission. They may even sue directors for a failure to meet their special fiduciary obligations under the statute, and the later-enacted statutes also provide for the benefit enforcement proceeding.

Still, shareholders are unlikely to be assiduous and consistent enforcers. Their ability to obtain damages to redress faulty directorial decisions is significantly limited by ordinary fiduciary liability concepts like the business judgment rule and will be further frustrated by benefit directors' broad and unguided discretion and immunity. Moreover, benefit corporation shareholders have an additional reason not to engage in enforcement of dual mission—or at least a serious potential bias toward one-half of it. If a benefit corporation begins veering away from its dual mission to achieve greater profits, shareholders stand to gain financially from this decision. Thus, although many routes exist for shareholder enforcement, shareholders are uniquely hamstrung as enforcers in the benefit corporation context.

The statutes uniformly exclude other potential parties from engaging in enforcement through litigation. Beneficiaries and the public will not have standing to challenge actions by benefit corporation directors. This position resonates with the traditionally extremely limited standing to challenge actions by nonprofit corporate directors. This policy is justified as necessary in order to recruit directors, which are most often uncompensated, to serve on nonprofit boards. However, the nonprofit context provides for government enforcement by state attorneys general and, for exempt nonprofits, the IRS. There is no regulatory role for any public official in the benefit corporation.

Other hybrid forms of organization take very different stances on enforcement than the benefit corporation. The United Kingdom adopted public enforcement, launching a specialized CIC regulator in addition to allowing shareholder enforcement of dual mission. The regulator possesses broad authority to investigate, remove fiduciaries, and even terminate CICs found out of compliance.

L3Cs rely solely on private enforcement, and the contours of this enforcement remain somewhat unclear....

Like the benefit corporation, the B Corp retains the existing enforcement mechanisms of a for-profit corporation, including shareholder informational and voting rights as well as derivative suits. This private certification form, however, does not add benefit directors, benefit officers, or benefit enforcement proceedings found in some benefit corporation statutes. B Corp status also subjects adopters to potential audit by B Lab, which B Lab and other standard-setters may require for benefit corporations, but the statutes do not require by their terms.

3. The Benefit Corporation's Disclosure Model

The benefit corporation form relies significantly on disclosure, both to amplify dual mission articulation and to lubricate enforcement. The benefit report gives shareholders and the public an opportunity to view how the entity reacts to situations in which profit and social mission conflict. Of course, the benefit report need not address these questions specifically. It must only report on public benefits achieved and circumstances that have hindered public benefit production. The Vermont, New Jersey, and Hawaii statutes demand that benefit corporations provide somewhat greater information in their benefit reports. They also compel them to charge a benefit director with a monitoring role, including preparing an opinion of the entity's public benefit performance. The New Jersey and Vermont statutes also provide for potentially greater review of the annual report, demanding filing with a government agency and shareholder approval, respectively.

Whether these recipients of disclosure will actively enforce is not yet known. Empowering individuals required to engage activity in the process of creating and approving disclosures, however, may at least somewhat improve the likelihood that enforcement action will be taken based upon them.

In terms of disclosure, benefit corporations occupy a sort of middle ground between the situations of traditional nonprofit and for-profit entities....

Benefit corporations also require more disclosure on the question of social and profit-making activity than any other hybrid forms currently available in the U.S. L3C statutes require no disclosures beyond the annual reporting obligations derived from related LLC statutes, which include no requirement of reporting on the entity's furtherance of charitable and educational purposes. Investor-members in an L3C could certainly demand such reporting, but it is not statutorily mandated. The B Corp certification requires B Lab to have access to certified entities for potential audits but does not require any periodic disclosures to it, to investors, or to the public.

4. Expanding Funding Streams

The benefit corporation statutes do not speak expressly to the question of financing, but adopters of this form would certainly be ineligible to receive deductible contributions. Rather, benefit corporations can pursue the funding sources available to traditional for-profits. In this pursuit, the dual mission embedded in the form may or may not prove advantageous. The benefit corporation form seems likely to draw potential investors and lenders' attention to the dual mission of the organization. On the one hand, this may make those motivated purely by profit even more hesitant to invest or lend to a benefit corporation than to a for-profit social enterprise. On the other hand, it may attract potential investors or lenders who are interested in combining their financial contributions with a purchase of social good. Socially-motivated investors may be more willing to risk lower financial returns from a firm credibly committed to simultaneously pursuing profit and social good. While they might distrust the bona fides of a pure for-profit social enterprise, a benefit corporation statutorily committed to pursue public benefit could be more attractive.

In fact, both results might occur. Then, the question is whether the gain of attracting socially-motivated investors and lenders outweighs the cost of driving off purely-profit-motivated ones. This empirical question cannot yet be answered. Even assuming the gains would outweigh the costs, however, the potential gains are premised on the idea that the enforcement of dual mission is credible. The credibility of this claim comes back to enforcement and, as noted [above], enforcement in the benefit corporation remains uncertain....

5. Branding

The third reason founders and operators of social enterprises may find a hybrid form attractive is to help them to create a distinctive brand. The American Marketing Association defines a brand as "[a] name, term, design, symbol, or any other feature that identifies one seller's good or service as distinct from those of other sellers."[152] Social entrepreneurs wish to market their enterprises and their products to consumers, partners, and employees as meaningfully different from either traditional nonprofits or for-profits and view a hybrid form as one route to accomplish this goal.

... Whether the benefit corporation form can effectively function as such a brand, however, depends on whether it is a credible proxy for truly dual mission entities. The benefit corporation form will work as a brand only if it conveys relevant information to consumers, partners, and employees, demonstrating the value they will obtain from a relationship with the entity the brand denotes. These claims of value, and the benefit corporation's claims of differentiation from typical nonprofit and for-profit entities, also must be reliable. Consumers, partners, and employees interested in purchasing from, partnering with, or being employed by a dual mission entity will look for or be swayed by brands that demonstrate an entity can be trusted to pursue both profit and social good. This tracks, of course, back into the problems of dual mission articulation and enforcement addressed above.

The process of building the benefit corporation brand is at too early a stage to evaluate fully, though the uncertainties about enforcement of dual mission within the form create serious obstacles for its success. Of course, individual benefit corporations can certainly provide greater assurances of their dual mission bona fides, through shareholder agreements or other precommitment devices. By doing so, these individual benefit corporations may themselves become powerful brands. However, for the benefit corporation form of organization itself to function as a brand, it must convey this salient information on its own.

Finally, brands are weak unless and until they become familiar to their target audience. Even if an organizational form could reliably convey commitment and follow-through on dual mission, it can function as a strong brand only when enough entities adopt it and the brand's meaning becomes known in the marketplace. Standard-setters clearly have a stake in disseminating information about the benefit corporation brand and encouraging social enterprises to adopt it. This need to generate adoptions

---

152. *Dictionary*, American Marketing Ass'n, http://www.marketingpower.com/_layouts/Dictionary.aspx?dLetter=B....

seems, indeed, to explain B Lab's involvement in pursuing benefit corporation legislation in the various states. Thus far, there has been some publicity about benefit corporations, but few entities have adopted the form and little is known about how its future adopters will behave.

As is the case with expanding access to capital, other hybrid forms also face challenges similar to those of the benefit corporation in their drive to become effective brands. First, each form will need to prove an effective proxy for entities with clearly articulated and reliably enforced dual missions, issues addressed above. Second, each form will need to be adopted widely enough to spread knowledge of the brand to potential customers, partners, and employees. This job is already underway for each developing hybrid form. B Lab, of course, has a strong interest in creating awareness of the B Corp form and is actively pursuing this goal....

6. Sustainability

Finally, social entrepreneurs may also see a hybrid form as providing their enterprises with greater sustainability than traditional nonprofit or for-profit forms can offer. Of course, sustainability can mean many different things. When thinking about sustainable development, the UN Brundtland commission defined it as "meeting the needs of the present without compromising the ability of future generations to meet their own needs."[164] When researching sustainable corporations, one quickly runs across ideas like the triple bottom line (economic, social, and environmental outcomes) or the 3-P model (People, Profit, Planet).[165] These ideas clearly resonate with the fundamental ideas of a social enterprise, melding pursuit of profits with social good, often including environmental goals. But, the benefit corporation form is not there yet. This new hybrid form must allow social enterprises to articulate and enforce dual missions, to obtain greater access to capital, and to brand themselves to consumers and partners as distinct and special entities offering distinct and special products, in order to truly embody the sustainable corporation....

Antony Page & Robert A. Katz, *Is Social Enterprise the New Corporate Social Responsibility?**

The term "for-profit social enterprise" (or simply "social enterprise") refers to businesses with shareholder-owners that seek to address social problems by combining the dynamism of capitalized for-profit enterprise with the intentionally prosocial orientation of nonprofit organizations.... Some leading proponents of social enterprise seek to promote and facilitate social enterprise formation through business organizations law, most notably by supplying social entrepreneurs with new legal

164. United Nations Report of the World Commission on Environment and Development, available at http://www.un.org/documents/ga/res/42/ares42-187.htm.

165. See John Elkington, Cannibals With Forks: The Triple Bottom Line of 21st Century Business 20 (1998); Peter Fisk, People Planet Profit: How To Embrace Sustainability for Innovation and Business Growth 3 (2010).

* Originally published in 34 Seattle University Law Review 1351 (2011). Reprinted with permission.

forms designed specifically for social enterprises. The push for new forms reflects dissatisfaction with the seemingly binary nature of existing options—the for-profit corporation, which inclines controllers to increase shareholder wealth with little regard for the interests of nonshareholders and society at large, and the traditional charitable nonprofit organization, which primarily serves social purposes but has less access to capital and less leeway to compensate high-performing executives and employees....

L3Cs

The low-profit limited liability company or "L3C" was introduced in Vermont in April, 2008, and has since been adopted in [eight] other states.[65] A business organized as an L3C must pursue a charitable mission but can also distribute profits to its investors—although generating profit itself may not be a "significant" purpose.[66] Supporters of the L3C describe it as "the for-profit with a nonprofit soul," and claim that it "combines the best features of an LLC with the social conscience of a nonprofit."

The L3C is an expressly dual-purpose LLC driven primarily by tax considerations. An L3C must meet three requirements: first, the company must "significantly further[] the accomplishment of one or more charitable or educational purposes," and would not have been formed but for its relationship to the accomplishment of such purpose(s). Second, "[n]o significant purpose of the company is the production of income or the appreciation of property...." Lastly, the company must not be organized "to accomplish [any] political or legislative purposes...." Compliance with these three requirements qualifies the enterprise to accept "program-related investments" from charitable foundations, which under IRS regulations must be intended to further the foundation's charitable or educational purpose, and must not be intended to produce income or have a prohibited purpose (like lobbying).

Proponents of the L3C form envision that its controllers can leverage these program-related investments with private capital to achieve its social aims, which would also serve the investing foundation's purposes. On this model, investments in L3Cs would be structured in tranches: program-related investments would ideally take the riskiest position in the capital structure and receive no or lower returns, thereby lowering risk and increasing returns for other equity investors. The top tranche might be at the risk-adjusted market rate of return. There might also be a "mezzanine" tranche, designed for investors willing to accept a lower return because of their contribution to social welfare.

The L3C designation is intended to provide foundations with some assurances that a business will satisfy the tax law's criteria for program-related investments. To date, however, the IRS has not granted L3Cs any special privileges by virtue of the designation. Foundations thus still seek private letter rulings, and should perform

65. In addition to Vermont, Illinois, Louisiana, Maine, Michigan, North Carolina, Rhode Island, Utah, and Wyoming passed L3C legislation. [North Carolina has since repealed its L3C legislation, effective January 1, 2014.]

66. Vermont Statutes Annotated, title 11, § 3001(27)(B) (2011)....

appropriate diligence in order to comply with the treasury regulations regarding program-related investments.

Because the legislation implementing L3Cs has been minimal, proponents recommend protecting the L3C's social mission by contract in the operating agreement. This protection could take several forms. For example, LLC Class A members, intended for foundation investors, might have no right to distributions, but might have a "put," which is the right to have the company redeem their membership interests at a purchase price equivalent to the initial capital contribution. Members might also have a right of first refusal. Any member who wished to sell her membership interests must give the other members a right to buy those membership interests at a price equal to the lower of the offer she has already received or the fair market value of the membership interests, as determined by an independent appraiser. In addition, all members might have the right to veto the transfer through a unanimous consent provision. The manager could have more limited authority than in a conventional LLC, in that the members' consent could be required before the disposal of any of the LLC's assets beyond the ordinary course of business. Foundations, often sophisticated and well-advised, would protect an L3C's social mission by negotiating effective mission maintenance mechanisms.

Benefit Corporations

[The authors then described the Benefit Corporation form discussed in the previous excerpt.]

Community Interest Companies

Community Interest Companies (CICs) were introduced in the United Kingdom in 2005 by Tony Blair's government, and were designed expressly to meet the needs of social enterprise. CICs are companies intended to produce a community benefit by dedicating their assets and much of their profits to that purpose.

The two key legal features of CICs are a "community interest test" and "asset lock." The community interest test is relatively broad. "A company satisfies the community interest test if a reasonable person might consider that its activities are being carried on for the benefit of the community."[129] Political campaigning, however, is excluded. The organization also must not limit access to its benefits to too small a group. "Asset lock" is the term used for all provisions that ensure the CIC's assets and profits are used primarily for the benefit of the community and not for the excessive benefit of employees, contractors, or investors. Suppliers of goods and services may not be compensated beyond full market value. Thus, salaries "must not be disproportionately high in relation to [employees'] abilities and the services they perform." Investors may buy shares, but dividends are capped, both at a specific rate of return and as a percentage of profits that can be paid in aggregate dividends. At liquidation, shareholders are limited to receiving back the amount of their investment in the company. In essence, a CIC's shareholders are much more like holders of preferred stock.

---

129. The Community Interest Company Regulations, 2005, S.I. 1788 (U.K.), http://www.legislation.gov.uk/uksi/2005/1788/contents/made....

A CIC must also issue a "community interest company report" along with its annual financial filing. This report must address: "[1] how the company's activities have benefited the community; [2] what steps were taken to consult stakeholders and what was the outcome; [3] what payments were made to directors; [4] what assets were transferred other than for full consideration; [5] what dividends were paid; and [6] what performance-related interest was paid on loans or debentures."[136]

Enforcement is provided by a state regulator. The regulator may intervene if a CIC no longer meets the community interest test, and responses could include replacing the directors or managers, transferring assets, or winding up the CIC's operations. In essence, the regulator's role is analogous to states' attorneys' general supervision of charities.

Importantly, the CIC is intended to provide a brand identity for social enterprise, which could help lower its transaction costs. The government explained: "As the concept of social enterprise becomes more widely understood by the finance community, social entrepreneurs should find it easier to explain what they are doing and to get a competitive price for finance. Clear recognition of the CIC form will help this process."

Socially Responsible Corporations

Some progressives have proposed an organizational form that adopts some of the features of progressive corporate law, notably stakeholder representation. In particular, state legislators in Minnesota proposed legislation that would give businesses the option of incorporating as a "socially responsible" for-profit business corporation. Businesses choosing this designation would be required to allot 20% of their board for worker-elected representatives, and another 20% for board-selected directors to "represent and advocate for the public interest."[142] This proposal carries both the hallmarks of social enterprise, in that this is an optional form, and progressive corporate law, in that certain stakeholders are expressly privileged in a relatively uniform way across entities organized under this form.

Increasing the Number of Social Enterprises and Achieving Visions and Missions

Efforts to combine for-profit and nonprofit features and tendencies in a single structure can, to say the least, be problematic. States may, however, be able to promote social welfare by creating organizational forms that supply ready-made or off-the-rack means to solve or at least mitigate such problems. Most notably, they can reduce

136. Frequently Asked Question[s] for Funding Organisations, Community Interest Companies, 5 (Oct. 2009), www.cicregulator.gov.uk/guidance/Chapter%206%20-%20Feb%202010.pdf....

142. "The directors of a corporation ... must include directors whose role as directors includes representation of, and advocacy for, the interests of the corporation's employees and of the public interest." S. 510, 86th Leg., Reg. Sess. (Minn. 2009). "At least 20 percent of the corporation's directors must represent and advocate for the corporation's employees. These directors must be nominated and elected by the employees, through a process specified in the bylaws." Id. "At least 20 percent of the corporation's directors must represent and advocate for the public interest. These directors must be elected by the other board members, after seeking input from persons or groups representing the public interest." Id.

transaction costs for aspiring social entrepreneurs, provide them with conspicuous and inexpensive signals to potential supporters who share their social aims, shape preferences by enabling and encouraging prospective entrepreneurs to pursue broader social aims, and nudge controller and employee behavior in more other-regarding directions.

Transaction costs can be thought of as friction interfering with the free exchange of rights and obligations.[144] Transaction costs may include those costs incurred by searching for information about the transaction (e.g., which stock or house to buy), bargaining (e.g., the process of sorting offers and counteroffers in setting the price of a house), and policing and enforcing the agreement (e.g., suing the home buyer to complete the transaction in a falling real estate market).

New legal forms designed specifically for social enterprises could make it less costly for social entrepreneurs to launch such enterprises by manipulating the forms supplied by current organizational law. There would be fewer wheels for social entrepreneurs and their legal advisors to reinvent. As the forms become more common, there would be less need for the social entrepreneur to explain and bargain over standard provisions. Gradually, a market norm could emerge and become accepted. This virtuous spiral, at least with respect to transaction costs, might mirror the behavior of venture capitalists and angel investors in Silicon Valley. There, various standard market norms and organizational structures have become common, facilitating the efficient funding and development of start-ups, even if, when starting on a blank slate, other organizational structures might be more effective.

These new forms may cultivate and solidify more socially responsible norms within the firms that adopt them. Social norms are "customary rules of behavior that coordinate our interactions with others."[146] A common criticism of corporations is that through their norm of profit maximization, they encourage executives to make antisocial decisions and that, absent the corporation, the decision-maker would make more "ethical" decisions. In a nonprofit organization, the controllers and employees should feel less pressure to make decisions that maximize the entity's net earnings at society's expense. New organizational forms promise to promote social action more consistently than the conventional corporate form. For example, by altering decision-making procedures—say, by requiring controllers to consider how significant decisions would affect their mission and not simply profits—new forms could subtly alter controllers' agendas in more pro-social directions.

A third potential advantage of new forms is to increase the demand for the forms themselves and, with it, the supply of socially motivated entrepreneurial activity. The

---

144. *Black's Law Dictionary* defines a transaction cost as "a cost connected with a process transaction, such as a broker's commission, the time and effort expended to arrange a deal, or the cost involved in litigating a dispute." Black's Law Dictionary 398 (9th ed. 2009). Ronald Coase famously explored the problem with his discussion of the "costs of using the price mechanism" in his landmark article, *The Nature of the Firm*. R. H. Coase, The Nature of the Firm, 4 Economica 386, 390 (1937)....

146. H. Peyton Young, Social Norms, New Palgrave Dictionary of Economics Online, http://www.dictionaryofeconomics.com/article?id=pde2008_S000466&edition=current....

founder of a prospective business, when presented with an expanded array of organizational forms on the secretary of state's website or at her office, may find that the new form serves her social aspirations better than any of the longstanding options. Enacting the new form and making it readily available could serve to market the form itself.

A new organizational form could also serve a signaling or branding function toward potential customers. Some customers prefer, all things being equal, to trade with an organization that has a social mission rather than with a more conventional profit-maximizing corporation. Consumers who buy fair trade coffee, or Product (RED) may only be the tip of this particular iceberg.

There is admittedly some risk that social enterprises will divert resources from the nonprofit sector instead of attracting resources that would otherwise go to conventional for-profit corporations. There is also a risk that some social enterprises will prove to be wolves in sheep's clothing. In other words, they will derive benefits from signaling their social orientation but, absent an effective enforcement mechanism, will not actually be any better than conventional corporations. These risks may be worth taking. The social enterprise movement's optimistic hope is that not only will more socially responsible organizations be formed, but that these entities will also be more effective in achieving their social missions than the traditional nonprofits.

Lastly, as a practical matter, the enactment and provision of new forms designed for social enterprises seems less likely to arouse opposition than, say, legislation to advance progressive corporate law's agenda. A business's decision to adopt these forms is wholly voluntary as well as conspicuous to the business's potential investors, who can make decisions and adjust their expectations accordingly. The social enterprise movement's incremental approach to change through organizational law may therefore be politically more viable.

Joseph W. Yockey,
*Does Social Enterprise Law Matter?**

We know that benefit corporation laws are unnecessary to expand the discretion of a social enterprise's managers in the day-to-day running of the firm. [There are also] several reasons to be skeptical about how they approach accountability and enforcement, which would seem to harm their branding potential. Yet, if the benefit corporation form is negligible, why are states continuing to enact new benefit corporation statutes at an increasingly rapid pace? And what explains the many firms that keep adopting the form?

One answer is that perhaps these actors are mistaken. Entrepreneurs might be selecting the form based on false assumptions or a misreading of corporate fiduciary duties. The same goes for legislators. They might want to help social enterprises but could be getting it wrong by focusing on enabling statutes rather than, say, changes

* Originally published in 66 Alabama Law Review 767 (2015). Reprinted with permission.

to tax policy. Another possibility is that benefit corporation legislation is simply an attempt by lawyers and other professionals to create a new business form so they will have a new product to "sell." For example, B Lab lobbied to get versions of its Model Act passed in most of the states that now feature benefit corporation legislation. A cynic might note that B Lab also happens to be in a position to gain reputational benefits by providing firms with the assessment standards that the Model Act requires.

Any of these possibilities could be true. But there is also another plausible explanation: that many rational people know exactly what they are doing in promoting or adopting the benefit corporation form. After all, founders of benefit corporations were presumably guided by counsel when selecting the form. Furthermore, not every state has blindly followed B Lab's model, and the push for a new business form was largely organic within the social enterprise community. The question thus remains: what value do benefit corporation laws add in light of their apparent limitations?

... It's tempting to view benefit corporation laws as though they function just like traditional enabling statutes. However, much of the criticism surrounding them exposes a misunderstanding about the breadth of their design. Traditional corporate enabling statutes provide templates for specific business forms. Under the contractarian model, they are thought to lower transaction costs by providing managers and investors with default terms that reflect the likely hypothetical private bargain they would strike on their own.

Benefit corporation statutes also provide default rules for a corporate form but combine them with provisions that are more public or regulatory in nature. Some provisions are distinctly regulatory, like mandatory disclosure requirements, and others are quasi-regulatory, like mandatory assessments against third-party standards. These hybrid public/private characteristics make benefit corporation laws unique among corporate enabling statutes, which typically lack reporting or external engagement requirements like those found in the federal securities or environmental laws. Moreover, and most importantly for my purposes, they also call to mind several aspects of contemporary new governance theory.

What Is New Governance?

New governance defies easy definition but typically refers to a collection of ideas for governance where law serves as a launching point for a multi-dimensional approach to addressing complex social and economic challenges. Like the social enterprise movement itself, new governance seeks mainly to "harness private capacity to serve public goals."[154] It does so through two general strategies. First, recognizing that the state as a sole locus of rulemaking is usually one step behind private actors, new governance encourages dialogue and collaboration among multiple stakeholders—including firms, regulators, and professional groups—to develop meaningful tools for self-regulation. Throughout this process, the state is understood to act mainly as a facilitator rather than a top-down regulator. It provides a general legal framework by

154. Saule Omarova, Wall Street as Community of Fate, 159 University of Pennsylvania Law Review 411, 428 (2011).

virtue of its position and authority, but policy implementation is left to the people closest to the ground and who possess the most expertise on a given topic. Help in this regard comes when static rules give way to reflexive rules that allow for flexibility and adaptability in the face of new or changing phenomena.

Second, new governance principles of accountability often prioritize soft law in place of, or in addition to, hard law. For example, rather than rely solely on punitive sanctions to boost compliance, new governance emphasizes public-private partnerships, the importance of internalizing values within firms, and the development of industry standards and best practices to guide behavior. Similar strategies focus on harnessing both legal and market pressures to achieve policy goals—including reliance on mandatory disclosure requirements and third-party assessment programs—as well as regulatory principles that reflect insights from behavioral economics and the expressive powers of law.

Ultimately, as I will continue to unpack, new governance sees law as going beyond the enforcement of contract rights or the provision of default rules for business associations. Law becomes an important "coordinative mechanism" for creating a diverse array of policy solutions beyond the broadly contractual conception of the firm. Situating benefit corporation laws within this paradigm does not resolve every challenge facing dual-purpose firms, but it goes a long way toward explaining why [we should not abandon] the form.

Signals and Shocks

At the outset, looking at benefit corporation laws from the perspective of new governance offers a new way to think about their role in the market. For example, some maintain that benefit corporations statutes actually create a harmful dichotomy between "profit-only" corporations and "responsible" corporations. The argument is that, by resting on the false premise that managers of traditional corporations must prioritize profits above all else, the benefit corporation form undermines efforts to convince *all* corporate managers that CSR-driven activities are consistent with their fiduciary duties. Similarly, there is a fear that the form will prompt courts to redefine the obligations of corporate directors in traditional firms by adding a shareholder wealth maximization requirement where one does not currently apply. In either case, proponents of benefit corporation laws could be seen as acting contrary to their own interests by attempting to carve out their own statutory space.

But this perspective takes an overly narrow view of the qualities of the benefit corporation form. As Hoffman puts it, there is a difference between reducing unsustainability—the classic domain of CSR—and creating sustainability—the promise of social enterprise.[162] While it is true that managers of traditional corporations increasingly see sustainability and social impact as important strategic considerations, the worry is that this recognition is not translating into widespread positive change. Sustainability is still proving elusive, and, in many corners, there remains a "visceral

---

162. Andrew John Hoffman & John R. Ehrenfeld, The Fourth Wave, Sustainability and Change, Change and Sustainability (Rebecca Henderson et al. eds. 2013).

distrust" of traditional for-profit entities. Movements such as "Occupy Wall Street" and post-financial crisis populism reflect a continuing lack of faith in managers' ability to avoid excessive risk-taking. More broadly, sociologists find that many among the post-Baby Boom generations of entrepreneurs, investors, and consumers are idealistic, seek greater authenticity in their commitments, and desire to see corporations as instruments of change or reflections of their own values.

With these considerations in mind, a key lesson of new governance is that legal forms and structures can send important signals that help to form a consensus around particular norms. In the case of benefit corporation laws, they are meant to facilitate the formation of private social enterprises, which, in turn, are meant to promote the public good. They therefore reflect a legislative judgment about the desirability of firms that actively seek to solve social problems. Their reliance on an intertwining of public and private law characteristics also gives them something in common with classic public laws like the ones found in environmental or securities regulation: they reflect a public determination about how certain private actors should behave. And, like the laws in those fields, they rely heavily on disclosure and transparency rules to protect public interests and elicit public engagement.

The notion that benefit corporation laws make a statement about the social value of hybrid firms provides strong evidence for why so many entrepreneurs find them attractive. Under an expressive theory of law, one of the most important functions of law is to express beliefs about societal values. For example, anti-discrimination laws can be understood as expressing the view that racial discrimination is morally wrong. This message, and the social norm it conveys, can help shape individual behaviors and preferences independently of any separate punitive sanctions. In a similar vein, benefit corporations represent a potential shock to the system. Because laws send powerful signals about the importance of particular phenomena, the benefit corporation form can add value for a new wave of entrepreneurs simply by offering a systematic alternative to the old guard. The form offers something new, exciting, and unconventional to shake up the corporate landscape and displace "core beliefs" about the traditional corporate model. It goes beyond efforts to enact narrow reforms to existing corporate practice by offering a new corporate architecture that embodies the goal of generating positive impact within a profit-making framework.

Therefore, even if they are not legally necessary to accomplish what social enterprises desire, state-sponsored benefit corporation laws provide important information to the market that options like private certification cannot match. The state's backing lends legitimacy to the social enterprise movement, influences public expectations about the possibilities of dual-purpose firms, and provides an outlet with the force of law for firms to demonstrate their commitment to multiple bottom lines. It is plausible that these factors could, in the long run, change social attitudes about the importance of balancing social and economic concerns in all corporations. For now, they combine to raise the profile of hybrid firms and provide a window into what they value.

Self-Regulation and External Engagement

In keeping with the question of why an entrepreneur might want to organize her business as a benefit corporation, a second factor is the form's potential to drive a process of self-regulation within the social enterprise sector. The term "self-regulation" can refer to a wide range of activities, but I use it primarily in the way that scholars of new governance use it. Essentially, a new governance gloss on self-regulation posits that the state should allow private actors in specific industries or sectors to shape the standards and practices that govern their affairs. This idea came about as a way to manage market complexity. Unlike states, which suffer from several well-known structural, informational, and temporal limitations, private firms get a first-hand view of the underlying trends and obstacles they face on a daily basis. Self-regulation allows firms to take advantage of this "on the ground" knowledge to develop context-specific strategies for responding to new or changing circumstances.

Not only is this approach more flexible than traditional top-down rule-making, it can also be cheaper and more effective. For example, proponents of self-regulation stress that it often leads to greater levels of collaboration among firms, stakeholders, and policy groups on matters ranging from corporate best practices to market benchmarks and performance standards.[173] External engagement along these lines, in turn, has the "potential to foster shared values among industry actors, a stronger sense of participation in the process of rulemaking reflecting such common values, and voluntary compliance with the resulting rules."[174] This does not mean that there is no role for state involvement in self-regulation. However, by recasting its focus from enforcement to facilitation, the state's primary role becomes promoting collaborative policy development through tools such as legislative ambiguity, market-based certification or assessment requirements, and transparency rules that create additional market pressures for compliance.

In seeking to apply these principles to benefit corporations, we see first that social enterprise is nothing if not complex. The primary issues identified earlier relate to mission drift, the legacy problem, information asymmetry, agency costs, the difficulty of assessing social performance, and the governance challenge of managing competing stakeholder interests. These concerns make the task of lawmakers hoping to promote benefit corporations increasingly difficult. For benefit corporation legislation to facilitate growth, it must improve upon existing law and be both comprehensive and flexible enough to meet the needs of founders, investors, and other relevant stakeholders who occupy such a dynamic field. But the infancy of the social enterprise movement and the new combination of activities it entails means that few people can speak with certainty about what entrepreneurs or investors need to best protect

173. Omanova, supra note 154.
174. Id.

and advance their interests. Accordingly, rather than rely on static legislative pronouncements that cannot keep pace with this evolving sector, the complexity facing social enterprises suggests that a self-regulatory structure built around industry participation and reflexive policy development offers a valuable way forward.

Matters become slightly more complicated, though, when moving from the potential normative value of self-regulation to its practical execution. Fortunately, most benefit corporation laws feature several characteristics that ought to promote the type of self-regulatory regime I describe. One example relates to flexibility and ambiguity in key statutory provisions. While definitions of the stakeholder mandate and public benefit requirement are often criticized as vague and ambiguous, these attributes can go from a negative to a positive when the group targeted by a statute consists of many diverse actors who operate in dynamic environments. For instance, since every social enterprise features a unique stakeholder profile, a broad stakeholder mandate errs on the side of inclusion and flexibility to allow for context-specific approaches to governance. By the same token, when firms must engage with flexible legislative provisions it forces them to develop a more thorough understanding of legislative goals, industry trends, and their own circumstances if they are to avoid the paralysis that ambiguity might otherwise bring. Managers and employees must consider multiple perspectives, debate the meaning of broad terms, and reflect on myriad issues—all of which can trigger deeper knowledge and greater internalization of the values behind the standards and practices that emerge from their efforts to manage uncertainty.

Similarly, by instructing managers to balance stakeholder interests, benefit corporation laws raise awareness about issues that should inform their behavior. Stakeholder governance means little if there is no discussion about implementation. While it is possible that some managers might find a broad stakeholder mandate to be confusing or paralyzing, others will see it as a prompt to engage with corporate constituents to better determine how to incorporate their concerns into strategic decisions. This is an important strategy for all firms hoping to boost their legitimacy. Employees and stakeholders who feel included in the corporate decision-making process demonstrate higher levels of emotional investment and commitment to the firm's mission. They are more likely to accept and abide by organizational directives and norms, and to resist pressures to go against them, when they have a thorough understanding of the reasons behind them and feel they play a meaningful part in their development.

Other features of benefit corporation laws also come into clearer focus once we examine them from the perspective of self-regulation. The most obvious examples are mandatory disclosure and assessment requirements. The classic understanding of mandatory disclosure rules is that they mitigate information asymmetry. However, they also make it easier for market actors to monitor firm behavior and apply legal or market pressure when necessary to encourage compliance. On this theory, benefit corporations that fail to adhere to their public disclosure obligations should suffer reputational consequences that will hinder their ability to attract investors, talent, or consumers, thereby allowing their more compliant counterparts to use that distinction to their competitive advantage.

The benefit corporation's third-party assessment requirements are similarly outward facing, but they fulfill a slightly different role than mandatory disclosure. Success and failure are relatively easy to evaluate when profitability is the only metric for managers and investors to follow. However, different social enterprises produce different social outputs and weigh them against different financial goals. Social enterprise leaders agree that the movement's growth will depend on developing consistent, meaningful standards to measure and report social and financial performance in multiple contexts. There is a particular need for baseline and universal metrics to reduce information asymmetry so that all firms and investors can use the same tools, compare results, and revise tests as necessary for evaluative purposes.

As a result, benefit corporation statutes put the onus on the market to determine what it means for third-party standards to be "comprehensive, credible, and recognized for assessing social and environmental performance." This allows the relevant parties—including firms, investors, professional groups, and standard-setting organizations—to experiment and apply their own inputs when formulating standards to fit the changing needs of all social enterprises. The third-party evaluation process is thus best seen, not as a static framework, but as a way of moving toward a greater understanding of what the goals of social enterprise should be. The benefit corporation structure provides a way of deliberating and moving toward socially constructive action over time.

Building a Bridge to Self-Regulation

Collectively, the benefit corporation's self-regulatory characteristics offer a "structure through which private commercial exchange may be regulated for essentially public purposes" without any direct government oversight. The potential upside of this structure makes it easy to see why individual benefit corporations would engage with it. Self-regulation promises to temper concerns about transaction costs, mission drift, and information asymmetry by helping benefit corporations develop governance solutions for managing competing interests and encouraging them to put more higher-quality, social-enterprise-specific information into the market. These factors should provide a much-needed boost to the form's credibility among investors, consumers, and other groups.

And yet, despite the spirit of optimism that self-regulation often generates, there are a variety of issues that warrant further attention. The first is whether a new governance form of self-regulation will prove attractive or useful to every social enterprise that might be thinking of becoming a benefit corporation. The answer, I believe, is yes and no. In every sector, the active engagement of firms in the regulatory process can help overcome the limitations that traditional forms of top-down legislative rule-making present. For all firms, self-regulation is more responsive and flexible, and it shows great promise in leading to higher rates of compliance.

However, for present purposes, it seems likely that the social enterprises that stand to benefit the most from a self-regulatory process are those with broader social missions or less profit potential. With respect to firms at or near the hybrid ideal, such as Sanergy or Blue River, their social objectives are direct and market driven. There is little tension between profits and impact, and, in any case, mission drift is relatively easy to monitor. This likely explains why neither Sanergy nor Blue River has chosen to become a benefit corporation yet.

By contrast, as firms like Greyston Bakery—which has become a statutory benefit corporation—pursue broader social missions or missions that result in lower revenues, the governance challenge of managing heterogeneous interests among a potentially discordant group of shareholders and stakeholders takes on greater significance. The cost of capital will also likely increase as risk becomes harder to quantify, and agency problems will grow as individual shareholders lose their incentive to closely watch management. It is in these situations where self-regulation has been shown to have the most potential for helping to manage complexity.

But this leads to another, larger issue: even if they would benefit from self-regulation, can we necessarily expect social enterprises to use the benefit corporation form as their framework for doing so? Social enterprise is a diverse space, and becoming a benefit corporation is not cheap. Some firms might balk at adhering to its transparency and assessment requirements, particularly if they fear that competitors will skimp on compliance to save costs.[186] A similar but more general risk of self-regulation is that it will lead to cosmetic and self-serving standards, or that it will suffer from intractable free-rider problems. For example, one worry is that benefit corporations will use the form only as a vehicle for "cheap talk" or greenwashing. This concern highlights the fundamental challenge of giving firms more leeway and shared responsibility for finding policy solutions. Meaningful self-regulation depends on firms being willing to participate in a process that seeks to advance the collective good even if that means avoiding actions that might otherwise be in their individual self-interest. Is it safe to assume that this will happen in the case of benefit corporations?

... Most commentators agree that successful self-regulation can only occur in the shadow of the law. That is, for firms to meaningfully engage with it, the state must provide a formal legal framework that guides the self-regulatory process. One way states do this is by offering statutory provisions that "nudge" self-regulation forward. The benefit corporation's mandatory assessment and disclosure rules are two examples of this strategy. They both encourage external engagement and market-based collaboration by forcing firms to take an outward-facing view of their responsibilities.

---

186. Another potential objection is that much of what the benefit corporation form offers by way of self-regulation could arguably be handled through a private certifying regime rather than by statute. For example, some suggest that because social enterprise is evolving so quickly, it would be better to rely on private organizations like B Lab to drive the standard-setting process forward rather than give the job to less flexible state governments. Of course, arguably this is what states are already trying to do. By providing an initial framework that utilizes open-ended terminology rather than prescriptive rules, most benefit corporation laws leave the details of standard-setting and implementation to market actors.

Law can further assist self-regulation in another important respect. Similar to its expressive power, law establishes "focal points" that facilitate group interaction and influence collective behavior without resort to sanctions to induce compliance. This is another example of law's ability to minimize complexity and facilitate private ordering. Individuals often gravitate toward specific laws and the rules they embody because of law's perceived legitimacy and its ability to rise above other forms of expression. States that enact subject-specific laws thus help to guide behavior *ex ante* by signaling that certain outcomes are more preferable than others. Put another way, by making one outcome salient or "focal," legal rules "guide expectations toward that outcome" and create "self-fulfilling expectations that [the] outcome will occur."[192]

The idea of law as a focal point is relevant to social enterprise for several reasons. Even though firms might benefit from self-regulation and external engagement, the social enterprise space is so diverse that it may be difficult for collaboration to occur organically. However, widespread state sponsorship of benefit corporation legislation may direct social enterprises toward a desired starting point for structuring their behavior. Seeing benefit corporation laws as focal in this way does not mean they will dictate particular standards. Rather, they simply incentivize firms and stakeholders to participate in a self-regulatory process by providing a locus for networking that facilitates coordination, communication, and standards development. The laws help to attract social enterprises by pointing to a preferred organizational form, and, from there, their salience makes it more likely that firms will engage with each other since doing so is expected of them and supported by the coordinative framework that the law provides.

Furthermore, legal focal points can also focus the attention of other market actors, including consumers, NGOs, and stakeholders, toward pressuring firms to participate in self-regulatory activities. Though it occurs in a slightly different context, scholars often point to the creation of the Extractive Industry Transparency Initiative (EITI) as an example of this phenomenon. With the goal of improving government accountability and political stability in developing countries, the United Kingdom became a leader in the EITI in an effort to encourage all companies in the petroleum industry to disclose the payments they make to foreign governments. By doing so, the government was able to use the EITI as a focal point within the larger CSR space to marshal the support of NGOs and socially conscious institutional investors so that both groups could concentrate their efforts on pressuring firms to comply with the EITI's voluntary disclosure guidelines. This approach didn't solve every problem with illegal foreign payments, but it made it easier for a diverse group of values-based entities to accomplish a positive result.

... It's certainly possible that some firms will not buy in to the coordinating aspect of benefit corporation laws and may instead be drawn to alternative business forms. Only time and greater empirical study will tell. However, there is reason for optimism. The benefit corporation form continues to hold the most traction among state law-

192. Richard McAdams & Janice Nadler, Testing the Focal Point Theory of Legal Compliance, 2 Journal of Empirical Legal Studies 87 (2005).

makers and leading figures within the social enterprise sector. Publicity and industry leadership are two key conditions for creating strong legal focal points. Before founders will elect to organize as a benefit corporation, they will need to develop expectations about how the market will view the form and whether others will adopt and engage with it. Accordingly, the support of high-profile figures like Patagonia, Ben & Jerry's, and B Lab can convince social enterprises that the benefit corporation form is, or will become, the new market standard. When competent leaders express a preference in this way and then commit to it, their conduct influences others to do the same because of the added credibility that a leadership presence provides. In addition, given B Lab's longstanding history of promoting socially oriented investment and businesses, its role in shaping benefit corporation legislation should make the form appear more organic to the social enterprise community. This perception ought to engender greater support for and acceptance of it within that community.

Another important condition for incentivizing successful self-regulation and external engagement is a spirit of mutual dependence and cooperation within the relevant sector. Similar to the concept of building an industry "ecosystem" or "community of fate," the central idea is this: self-regulation has been shown to work best when firms within a specific sector or industry realize that their futures hinge largely on how well they interact with each other, their stakeholders, legislators, policy groups, and industry professionals. If firms believe that collaboration and the creation of a common normative framework are precursors for their collective survival, they are more likely to take the self-regulatory steps necessary to accomplish those results. Of course, this does not mean that firms will stop competing for funding, consumers, or talent. But along with competition, they must also come to appreciate that their relevance and impact depends on systemic action rather than the activities of one or two individual companies.

How do we know if such an ecosystem exists, or is likely to exist, for benefit corporations? The first clue is that many within the broader social enterprise space already speak of its importance. Among social entrepreneurs, many see themselves as part of a "movement" to achieve significant and lasting positive impact. The mentality they are part of something bigger than just one person or company should, in turn, prompt individual social enterprises to consider the benefits of taking steps to establish a self-regulatory framework.

A second factor in developing an ecosystem or community of fate mentality is the presence of industry interconnectedness and cooperation. Even though social enterprises come in different sizes and offer a wide variety of products and services, the sector exhibits a high degree of homogeneity and "intrasectoral" cooperation. Hoffman finds that social enterprises often "seek a leadership role in their industry," noting that, "while other companies seek to influence institutions to reduce regulations and external costs to protect their advantage, [social enterprises] seek to influence institutions to draw other companies into emulating them."[205] In these ways, social en-

205. Andrew J. Hoffman et al., Hybrid Organizations as Agents of Positive Social Change 15 (Oct. 2010).

terprises act as "institutional entrepreneurs; changing the rules of the game for all organizations ... [and] promoting practices that will eventually become established as industry norms that all must follow."[206] Many social enterprises also work with industry groups, government agencies, and other stakeholders to develop standards for sustainable production and industry practices. For example, in an effort to facilitate transparency and information sharing, Seventh Generation, a social enterprise that manufactures ecologically friendly cleaning products, now publicly discloses its product formulations so that competitors can learn from its advances. Other social enterprises interact extensively with their suppliers and communities to establish mutually beneficial arrangements on practices ranging from price and wage structures to employee training programs.

Corollary to its ability to create a focal point, the benefit corporation form offers a promising structure for facilitating such collective interaction. The form is a highly visible archetype within a complex space that provides common ground for firms and other market actors to coordinate their activities. Moreover, along with the examples set by leading benefit corporations, the form's explicit mandate to consider multiple interests should make cooperation more palatable. Firms that prioritize profits above other objectives often lack the incentive to share information with their competitors. In that case, first-movers will see their profits slip if information sharing allows others to easily replicate their techniques or strategies. However, by definition, the benefit corporation form means that profits are not the overriding organizational focus. Its hybrid nature thus creates more room for cooperation within a business model that still requires a degree of competition to be successful. Indeed, this is likely one reason why benefit corporations often cooperate to take advantage of group discounts and gain better access to service providers....

A final reason to be confident in the ability of the benefit corporation form to drive a meaningful process of self-regulation goes back to the form's expressive power. Specifically, an important step in addressing issues like mission drift, the legacy problem, and the corporate governance challenges facing hybrid firms is to recognize that, just as they send broader signals about values to the market, legal forms also influence internal corporate behavior and compliance. Individuals who associate with a social enterprise can come and go or alter their preferences. Yet since the people within an organization are the most significant determinants of its commitment to social mission, taking steps to ensure the "right" people (or their replacements) remain in place is crucial. When organizations are small, it may be enough if a small group of dedicated founders or controllers remains to describe the values and behaviors that are expected of all employees.[214] However, as firms grow and monitoring becomes

206. Id.

214. An alternative approach to managing mission drift, uncertainty, information asymmetry, and agency costs in a social enterprise is to keep the firm closely held. Doing so would allow founders to preserve control while minimizing the risk of activism from other shareholders. Monitoring and information costs are lowest when owners are few in number, share the same goals, and transact with each other on a regular basis. Consensus building becomes easier under these conditions. A similar

more difficult, they usually need to look beyond the influence of individual managers to address the company's overall culture.

With respect to the benefit corporation, organizational forms that reflect a specific ideological commitment influence internal culture and attitudes by signaling the values that should inform employee decision-making. Patagonia cited this belief as a motivating factor in its decision to become a benefit corporation. Its founder hopes to use the form as a framework to preserve the company's current culture of sustainability long after he departs. The founder of Plum Organics adds: "When [social enterprise] ideas become inscribed in your corporate bylaws [as part of being a benefit corporation], it becomes the compass of the company.... Every new employee that comes in to this company understands that we're a public benefit corporation."

Of course, much still depends on a firm's ability to educate employees on the importance of balancing social and economic goals and then rewarding them for doing so. But provisions like the benefit corporation's public benefit requirement or stakeholder governance mandate signal what actions are expected and reinforce the importance of taking the organization's core principles into account when acting on its behalf. The benefit corporation form thus provides a framework that managers and employees can turn to when facing difficult decisions such as whether to relocate, pay a bribe to ease customs duties, or distribute earnings rather than expand distribution capacity. Uncertainty is often unbearable, which is why many prefer the "clean" guidance that comes with the shareholder profit-maximization theory. However, by telling them, structurally, that profits are not the firm's overriding focus, a benefit corporation's managers and employees can filter their actions through that reference point in situations where they might be tempted to act in their self-interest at the expense of mission. This may give founders more confidence about encouraging compliance than leaving the job to internal guidelines that can easily change if there is no cohesive culture within the firm.

Finally, establishing a culture that leads to the internalization of values is easier when organizational goals match employees' personal beliefs and were important factors in drawing them to the enterprise. The benefit corporation's formal emphasis on dual objectives should attract socially minded employees by signaling that they will find a supportive structure in place if they join. In turn, when employees enter organizations that reflect their own values, they exhibit greater motivation to act consistently with those values. This dynamic provides them with a sense of autonomy, attachment, and identity that will enhance their feelings of responsibility and make compliance more likely.

---

strategy would be to rely primarily on debt rather than equity financing. However, not every social enterprise wants to be closely held. Founders with large ambitions, a desire to scale up quickly, or agendas that involve intensive research might find that reliance on personal wealth or a small group of investors hinders their ability to grow. Debt also has its limits. Most firms cannot survive on debt financing alone, and risk-averse lenders might be reluctant to fund social enterprise given that hybrid firms are still relatively new and present unfamiliar issues.

Lessons and Implications

While the infancy of the benefit corporation form makes it difficult to predict its full impact on the corporate landscape, social enterprises are becoming so popular that they need a normative structure to build around. I show above how the underlying dynamics of benefit corporation laws can advance this effort by virtue of their consistency with new governance ideas. They help observers move past a preoccupation with the discretion of corporate managers to serve a particular social goal in order to advance a more general framework for developing a corporate community disposed to care about social goals and equipped with self-regulatory tools to facilitate those goals. I will conclude by describing the practical lessons and implications that we can draw from this result, paying particular attention to issues of professionalization, corporate governance, legislative design, and education.

Facilitating legal and other professional involvement in the benefit corporation sector is of threshold importance if new governance strategies for self-regulation are to take hold. I say this for several reasons. First, lawyers who develop an expertise with a particular business form often go on to participate in a variety of networking activities. They teach continuing legal education programs, lobby state lawmakers, and participate in industry conferences and other outreach events. When professionals interact in these ways, no matter how informally, they spread and reinforce norms within the relevant industry on a national rather than just local basis.

Cooperation on issues like standards and best practices should then become easier as the players gain more familiarity with each other and come to understand what is expected of them. This is especially likely if an institutional group of actors working within the benefit corporation sector emerges to coordinate and "regularize" such interaction. Policy groups made up of representatives from business, government, NGOs, and academia often play a leadership role in prompting collaboration within a specialized industry by establishing workshops, training programs, and other systems for information sharing. A group like B Lab might be able to fill this role, but that would require a slight shift in its purpose. An "institutional intermediary" like the one I describe is "less about 'checking compliance with rules'" and more about fostering "professional accountability by pooling knowledge between members of an industry and 'developing a community of practice to sustain ... inquiry and learning.'"[227]

In addition to their role in shaping norms within the larger sector, attorneys and other professionals also have an important function to play in mitigating potential information asymmetry problems and designing corporate governance solutions. Traditional for-profit firms already operate within a well-developed ecosystem. Support from lawyers, consultants, and accountants who understand and offer services tailored to their needs is readily available. For social enterprises to solve previously neglected social problems through the application of sophisticated business strategies, they too will need the same type of infrastructure. A recent report on social enterprise from

227. [Briana Cummings, Benefit Corporations: How to Enforce a Mandate to Promote the Public Interest, 112 Columbia Law Review 578, 621–23 (2012).]

the Aspen Institute emphasizes that entrepreneurs, investors, and policymakers engaged in this sector must start to "speak the same language" and "harmonize" their activities in order for meaningful development to occur. The report adds that the creation of common funding vehicles, social assessment tools, and other examples of interoperability will "reduce redundancy, enhance competition for the best tools and solutions, increase market demand for infrastructure services, and align individual and incremental efforts toward a systematic solution."[230]

The newness and uniqueness of social enterprise makes achievement of these objectives a challenge, but recognition of their importance within the social enterprise community is a step in the right direction. Lawyers on the investor side can share information about what their clients need to feel secure, which, over time, should lead lawyers on the enterprise side to develop expectations and strategies for ameliorating their concerns. Parties on both sides should also start to understand what requests are seen as reasonable within the community, and how they can respond to specific demands for information or contractual rights. Shareholders will then obtain a better sense of what they are getting in their investment, and their attorneys can help convince them that tools are in place to mitigate concerns about mission drift or other problems. These developments should make deals simpler, faster, and cheaper by reducing the amount of due diligence required, and by leading to the creation of industry standards for benefit corporation financing.

Establishing a strong community of attorneys and professionals with benefit corporation expertise is also important for capital formation. On one hand, investor interest in the social enterprise sector is clearly growing. On the other, many founders claim that securing capital remains difficult despite having more options for finance. The non-traditional nature of a dual-purpose firm might scare away some investors who, rightfully or wrongfully, worry that socially oriented firms will only generate below-market rates of return. Similar issues can complicate efforts to obtain other forms of supplemental financing, like debt. These concerns leave many social enterprise startups with the daunting prospect of attracting the attention of a growing but still relatively small universe of socially oriented sources of private equity.

To help address this challenge, lawyers and other professionals can play an important "sorting" role in linking benefit corporations with potential investors. Over time, these professionals will start to become more familiar with the interests and demands of socially oriented firms and investors. They should then be able to help simplify the capital formation process by serving as go-betweens in matching suitable partners from within their network of contacts.

Many private equity investors rely on a network of lawyers, consultants, and accountants to help them locate and sort potential investments. Nurturing a similar dynamic within the benefit corporation community is vital. For example, venture capitalists ("VCs") and angel investors offer several unique advantages to social enterprise. First, both can be good sources of "patient" capital. One argument in favor

230. Aspen Institute, [Emerging Fourth Sector (2009).]

of the benefit corporation's stakeholder mandate is that without it, managers might ignore social impact due to shareholder pressure to focus on short-term profits. However, VCs and angels are often more willing to welcome longer-term business plans. Some find that patient capital is even *more* patient in social enterprise since the goal is creating social impact rather than immediate profit, and the former can be difficult to measure in the short-term. Angels in particular often share founders' non-financial objectives, and, since they invest their own money rather than that of a fund investor, are more likely to be comfortable investing for the warm glow and community benefits that social enterprises provide.

Second, VCs and angels are important sources of business expertise. Founders of social enterprises often have good ideas about solving social problems but little experience in running a company. Many will need professional managerial knowledge if they hope to attract customers and capital. VCs and angels with in-kind expertise can assist in this regard through their connections and personnel. Ibrahim also reports that many angels invest in startups because they miss the excitement of running a business and relish the chance to help new entrepreneurs. This explains why angels often invest at earlier stages than venture capitalists, as well as why they are more likely to fund smaller companies that VCs tend to avoid.[243]

VCs and angels are also well suited to invest in social enterprise because of their proficiency in guarding against information asymmetry and opportunism. VCs routinely negotiate complex contracts that provide them with considerable control and oversight in portfolio firms. Specific strategies include staged financing arrangements, the taking of convertible preferred stock, guaranteed seats on the board, and non-transferability provisions. For their part, angels typically obtain comparable protection through informal mechanisms that avoid the high transaction costs of negotiating comprehensive investment contracts. They do so first by taking common stock rather than the more complex preferred stock that VCs favor. Secondly, angels prefer to invest in companies where they know the industry. For instance, in social enterprise, many angels come from industries where hybrid firms are the most active. This experience provides them with an edge in judging a firm's prospects. Angels also offer the same expertise as VCs but usually take an even greater hands-on role with the firm. Their close relationship with management enables them to actively monitor for opportunism, mission drift, and other risks, in addition to simply helping the business grow.

The application of new governance ideas to benefit corporation laws also has implications for corporate governance practices. Fiduciary duties are fundamental to reducing the agency cost risks that come from the separation of ownership and control, but questions of duty often become more complex in benefit corporations because of their explicit dual purpose. Shareholders who worry that directors will be unable or unwilling to balance hybrid pursuits in the way they prefer will likely demand a discount in the price of equity or simply avoid investment.

243. [Darian Ibrahim, The (Not So) Puzzling Behavior of Angel Investors, 61 Vanderbilt Law Review 1405, 1416–18 (2008).]

As we've seen, self-regulatory strategies for managing the potential for competing, heterogeneous interests include the development of standards and best practices for governance. Going forward, a promising way to supplement these strategies involves a push for greater diversity on the board of directors. Homogeneous boards work well for firms with singular pursuits because directors who share the same viewpoints typically find it easier to reach a consensus. Thus, uniform boards might work well for benefit corporations that approach the hybrid ideal, although even in that case there remains a risk of "groupthink" and the suppression of debate and alternative ideas. The same is true for smaller benefit corporations that might have founders available to articulate a clear message about organizational goals.

Board composition takes on more significance for larger benefit corporations, as well as for those with social and economic goals that are more divisible. For these companies, board heterogeneity would augment available enforcement remedies by serving to keep the benefit corporation's multiple objectives in view at a structural level. Directors with an interest and expertise in a specific corporate pursuit (e.g. sustainability) are better able to affect the board's decision-making process by acting as a credible "moderating influence" during deliberations. A specialist on the board can help to ensure that specific issues like social mission feature in every high-level discussion about organizational objectives. She will have the ear of key executives and can apprise them of matters that bear on mission in the face of potential pressure to focus exclusively on profits.

Importantly, this strategy is not about dictating or guaranteeing specific outcomes. The broad discretion that the business judgment rule affords to directors means that their decisions will generally stand if the board is informed, acting in good faith, and free of a conflicted majority. Rather, the purpose of heterogeneity is to promote the consideration of multiple viewpoints during the *process* that leads to each outcome. The entire board sets corporate policy, but specialist directors are present to introduce specific interests into the discussion and guard against misunderstood messages. Several states already appear to recognize the advantage of this approach by requiring benefit corporations to appoint a "benefit director" to oversee issues relating to the pursuit of social benefits.

In addition to improving the quality of board deliberations, new governance research further shows that specialist directors or officers can play a useful role in coordinating external self-regulatory activities and then integrating them into internal corporate governance practices. For one, assigning someone the task of overseeing benefit issues and social assessment encourages her to become an expert in those areas. Individuals who are made responsible for tasks of high importance are more likely to exercise greater care and analytic rigor in performing them. Grappling with the uncertainty of the benefit corporation environment can also pave the way for the type of stakeholder collaboration and deep-seated knowledge discussed above. A director or officer in this role will then be in a position to apply that knowledge in developing firm policies and overseeing their implementation. She can also become a singular conduit for communicating a cohesive message about policy goals throughout the firm, as well as a point of contact for employees to share their granular knowledge about the challenges they face in the hybrid setting. When coupled with the information and standards that emerge from external engagement with stakeholders and peers, the resulting feedback loop should prove valuable in designing employee training programs and monitoring systems capable of mitigating mission drift. The end goal of this strategy is to embed the desired norms, culture, and expertise at every level of the firm so that the consideration of mission becomes part of standard operating procedure.

A third important aspect of new governance theory is its emphasis on responsive statutory revision. This suggests two key lessons for the design of benefit corporation statutes. The first concerns flexibility. By defining public benefit as requiring firms to follow a triple bottom line, many states undercut the benefits that legislative flexibility offers to the range of social enterprises. To remedy this problem, states should reframe the public benefit requirement in accord with comparable statutes that leave more room for experimentation. Delaware is the best example to follow. Eschewing a mandatory triple bottom line, Delaware's Public Benefit Corporation statute requires benefit corporations to identify the public benefits that they will promote and to operate in a responsible and sustainable manner. "Public benefits" are broadly defined as any positive effects, or the mitigation of negative effects, on persons, entities, communities, or interests of an artistic, charitable, cultural, economic, educational, environmental, literary, medical, religious, scientific, or technological nature. This definition puts social enterprises in the more flexible confines of the double bottom line. They are certainly free to focus on the environment in addition to social impact, if that is their specific mission or if that is how they or the market interprets sustainability, but neither is expressly dictated by statute.

Secondly, new governance's emphasis on self-regulation should not be confused with deregulation. For new governance strategies to operate successfully, the state must reserve enforcement power to encourage collaboration and minimize the risks of backsliding or free riding. Benefit corporation statutes frequently come under fire in this respect as a result of their lack of enforcement bite. Regardless of whether our focus is on industry standards or statutory mandates, market actors will demand that the benefit corporation form credibly commits individual firms to their dual social and economic pursuits. Firms must show that compliance with rules or standards is real and costly; otherwise, market actors will discount the value of the brand that comes from being a benefit corporation.

Similar themes appear in other situations. The non-distribution constraint that unites nonprofit law gives confidence to the market that managers cannot divert resources for personal gain. Similarly, because it is costly for firms to opt-in to the mandatory disclosure requirements of the federal securities laws, doing so credibly signals to investors that a company is honest and transparent. If the benefit corporation form likewise requires firms to take burdensome and meaningful steps that not every company is willing to take, that too will help market actors separate the wheat from the chaff when evaluating different social enterprises.

Proponents of benefit corporation legislation appear unwilling to introduce statutory asset locks or other constraints on financial distributions for fear of turning off would-be investors or triggering the inefficiencies that can plague nonprofits. But for this strategy to work, the transparency and accountability provisions found in benefit corporation laws must signal that compliance is costly and meaningful in a manner akin to what the constraint on distributions accomplishes in the nonprofit setting. The reason that the federal securities laws send credible signals is because disclosure is mandatory and burdensome. There are negative consequences for failure to comply. However, the benefit corporation laws to date do not include penalties for non-compliance. They leave enforcement to flawed and inefficient shareholder derivative procedures. As a result, benefit corporations are relatively free to ride on the coattails of well-meaning peer firms that thoroughly comply with statutory requirements and engage in the self-regulatory process that those requirements trigger. Firms in the former group can obtain some of the positive "aura" of being a benefit corporation without facing any real downside from practicing greenwashing or for playing fast-and-loose with the timing and content of the disclosures they provide.

Of course, market discipline and reputational sanctions should mitigate this failure to some extent. Benefit corporations that fail to comply with legal rules or industry standards may face challenges in attracting investors, talent, or consumers as their more compliant counterparts use that distinction to their advantage. "Good" benefit corporations can also hire social auditors to report on their pursuit of the double or triple bottom line and rely on the auditors' reputations for honesty as a separate signaling device. As helpful as these options might be, though, they will never offer the same credibility or signaling power of statutory requirements that allow for sanctions. Statutes that rely largely on self-regulatory strategies must provide firms with the assurance that their peers will engage with the collaborative and standard-setting processes that are built into the legislation. Mandatory requirements must actually be mandatory, and, given the challenges with shareholder monitoring, they must therefore present a risk of state-backed penalties for non-compliance.

In addition, states should also require an independent social audit rather than leave it to benefit corporations to provide their own assessments against a third-party standard. The recent rise of the social auditing industry has already led to a proliferation of social and environmental auditing standards developed through the type of multi-stakeholder collaboration that new governance envisions. An audit requirement in benefit corporation legislation would provide an additional boost to these efforts since more firms and investors will come to rely on them. Professional social auditors should also be more capable and efficient than firms acting independently given their experience and expertise in gathering, analyzing, and presenting social impact information.

Admittedly, shifting from an assessment model to one requiring an independent audit will introduce a new agent to the mix, the auditor, and thus raise agency costs. But the significance of this problem is often overstated. Auditors trade mainly on their reputations. They are not invested in the outcomes of their audits other than to show they are honest, competent, and fair. Auditors are not infallible, but this practical reality suggests they present a lower risk of cheating because they need to protect their reputations in the market. Another potential worry is that an audit requirement could raise costs in ways that will disproportionately affect smaller firms. However, many free social auditing services already exist, and, in any event, cost concerns must be weighed against the potential for an audit requirement to fuel the development of standards that will make benefit corporations more effective in achieving their social and economic goals.

William Cary Jones, the first Dean of the University of California, Berkeley, School of Law, described law as "a living principle ... in process of constant becoming."[270] Today, one of the most exciting things about applying new governance theory to benefit corporation legislation is the way in which both trends reflect a willingness to think creatively about traditional corporate law, norms, and behavior. However, for new governance ideas to firmly take root in this context, current and future market participants will need to develop the capacity to understand and apply them.

Fortunately, several important strides are already being made. I mentioned earlier how many leading business and law schools now feature specific courses and clinical opportunities in the social enterprise field. For example, Alicia Plerhoples directs a social enterprise clinic at Georgetown Law that provides students with hands-on experience in addressing the novel theoretical and practical issues that dual-purpose firms present. The next step is to integrate these approaches with the strategies of new governance that offer the most potential for bolstering the social enterprise sector. Thus, in addition to a strong emphasis on traditional topics like corporate finance, fiduciary duties, and shareholder litigation, students in law and business schools would also benefit from exposure to general problem-solving techniques, collaboration with parties from multiple disciplines, negotiation theory, and the formation of public-private partnerships. This does not mean that professional schools should abandon or neglect traditional skills and practices; rather, that they learn to integrate them with new governance ideals.

In fact, pedagogical approaches that incorporate new governance theory and its emphasis on collaborative problem-solving would arguably be more consistent with the responsibilities that many professionals now perform. To take the example of lawyers working in Silicon Valley, most no longer define their roles in terms of being either litigators or transactional attorneys. Instead, they describe themselves as "key players in an informal apparatus of socialization, coordination, and normalization that serves to avert potential disputes between members of the local business community."[271] If we extend this idea to professionals who represent social enterprises, many will need to work with a wide range of entrepreneurs who come from back-

270. Christopher Edley, Fiat Flux: Evolving Purposes and Ideals of the Great American Public Law School, 100 California Law Review 313 (2012).

271. [Mark Suchman & Mia Cahill, The Hired Gun as Facilitator, 21 Law & Social Inquiry 679 (1996).]

grounds in human rights, clean energy, education, medicine, and finance. Developing the capacity to collaborate and communicate with individuals from such diverse disciplines will be of central importance to adequately serving their interests.

Finally, beyond its relation to new governance theory, maintaining a strong focus on the benefit corporation in academic and professional circles has the potential to generate a subtle but significant shift in debates about corporate law. Benefit corporations, and social enterprises more generally, cannot solve every social problem. There will always be critical roles for nonprofits, government, and traditional corporations to play. However, discussions about CSR and the "proper" roles of nonprofits and government remain highly contentious. By contrast, conversations about social enterprises often take a constructive tone in keeping with the virtually universal support they receive from the right and the left. This dynamic is important. It calls to mind the concept of "bracketing," where the most intractable issues in an area are set to one side so that the focus can stay on matters of common agreement.

Using the benefit corporation as an archetype for social enterprise can perform a similar function. If actors who share a normative consensus come together to discuss how to support the benefit corporation form, the resulting dialogue may prompt them to re-conceptualize how they approach more controversial issues. The discussions that emerge could even render the form obsolete, if, for example, they reframe ideological disputes surrounding corporate purpose in ways that cause social entrepreneurs to feel less dependent on a separate statutory regime. In this way, founders and investors might come to see corporate law as reaching a point where distinctions between "regular" corporations and benefit corporations appear unthinkable—thanks in large part to the transformative power of social enterprise law.

Discussion Questions

1. Which business forms do you think best suit sustainable businesses?

2. Do you prefer the private certification model (B Corporations), the statutory avenues (from Oregon, from the Benefit Corporation states, from the L3C states), or neither (a customized corporation or LLC that departs from the statutory offerings)?

3. In at least the corporate forms, there remains the issue of the business judgment rule. If the business judgment rule protects management's disinterested, considered, good-faith business decisions, how can shareholders (or other stakeholders, if they have standing) challenge decisions they believe are too profit-focused (or not profit-focused enough)? Is there any way to allow such suits without unduly eroding efficiency and managerial authority?

4. Are you satisfied with the benefit corporation form's enforcement mechanisms? What, if any, alternatives would you suggest (keeping in mind your thoughts on the previous question)?

5. What do you think of proposals to expand standing in sustainable firms to non-shareholder stakeholders? To cap dividends? To put more pro-social and pro-environmental processes in place? *See* Steven Munch, "Improving the Benefit

Corporation: How Traditional Governance Mechanisms Can Enhance the Innovative New Business Form," 7 Northwestern Journal of Law & Social Policy 170 (2012).

6. If you managed a (privately certified) B Corporation, what considerations would you weigh in deciding whether to become a (statutory) benefit corporation, as well?

7. Visit the B Labs website at www.bcorporation.net and peruse the list of certified B Corporations. Do you recognize any of the businesses listed? Are there any in your area?

8. Are there any consumer benefits to being a B Corporation and displaying the B Corporation mark on one's products and advertisements? How could a B Corporation increase the visibility of its mark and enhance its value to certified businesses?

9. Do you think these new business forms advance or hinder sustainability overall?

Chapter 6

Sustainability and the Securities Laws

One means of encouraging sustainability in business is transparency: if a company discloses its financial, environmental, and social successes and challenges, it is more likely to have something positive to report. The readings in this chapter ask whether the securities laws currently require firms to make social responsibility disclosures, and whether the securities laws can or should require such disclosures. The chapter continues with a look at the voluntary social responsibility disclosures of a self-described progressive company most law students know well. The chapter concludes with a theoretical look at disclosure-oriented regulation and how it can work in tandem with traditional command-and-control laws to foster sustainability.

Thomas Joo, *Global Warming and the Management-Centered Corporation**

Unlike state corporate law, federal securities law deals primarily with disclosure. That is, it does not generally provide remedies for corporate *conduct,* but only for certain kinds of misleading or incomplete *information* companies may provide about their conduct. The primary cause of action under the securities laws has been implied by courts under section 10(b) of the 1934 Securities Exchange Act and SEC Rule 10b-5 promulgated thereunder. While the Rule prohibits untrue statements, as well as omissions, of "material fact," this does *not* mean corporations are required to disclose every fact that an investor might find material. Rather, it prohibits a misstatement or omission *only if* it is material. "Material" in this context is a term of art, as will be discussed below. Further, outside of certain specified financial disclosures, even a material omission is prohibited *only if* the omitted information is "necessary in order to make the statements made, in the light of the circumstances under which they were made, not misleading."[105] That is, merely withholding material information is not actionable unless it affects the accuracy of statements the corporation has made.

Securities law is narrowly designed and interpreted to protect investors *qua* investors. Those who would use securities law to address social-responsibility issues such as climate change must contend with this fact. For example, while it may seem obvious that climate change is a material issue, information is "material" in the context

---

* Originally published in 44 Wake Forest Law Review 671 (2009). Reprinted with permission.

105. Determination of Affiliates of Banks, 17 C.F.R. § 240.10b-5 (2008).

of securities fraud only if there is a "substantial likelihood that a reasonable shareholder would consider it important" in deciding whether to buy or sell.[106] The rule's applicability is further limited to misrepresentations or omissions made "in connection with the purchase or sale of [a] security." Courts have derived from this language a requirement that only a purchaser or seller of securities has standing to bring a securities fraud action under section 10b-5. Perhaps even more important for present purposes, a plaintiff in such an action must establish that a misrepresentation or omission caused her to suffer *economic* loss, which typically derives from distortions in the stock price caused by the misinformation. This requirement would be satisfied, for example, if a corporation's misrepresentation about its carbon impact caused its stock price to inflate *and* the plaintiff purchased at such inflated price *and* the revelation of the truth subsequently caused the price to fall *and* the plaintiff sold thereafter at a loss. All of these requirements must be satisfied; if, for example, the plaintiff sold before the stock price fell, or the stock price fell for some other reason, she would fail to establish causation and her lawsuit would fail. This focus on a plaintiff's investment loss shows that harm to the environment caused by the misrepresentation or omission is unlikely to be a relevant factor.

Like the harm required to support a cause of action, the mandated content of securities disclosures also reflects the law's focus on investment value over other harms. The SEC's Regulation S-K provides an integrated list of corporations' disclosure obligations under federal securities regulations. Most required disclosures pertain to specific, backward-looking quantitative data about a firm's finances. Unsurprisingly, the list includes no specific obligations to disclose a corporation's carbon footprint or other environmental impact. Item 303, entitled "Management Discussion and Analysis" ("MD&A"), imposes the most open-ended disclosure obligations. MD&A requires management to make certain narrative disclosures, many of which are *forward* looking. It requires management to, for example, "[i]dentify any known trends, or any known demands, commitments, events or uncertainties that will result in or that are reasonably likely to result in the [corporation's] liquidity increasing or decreasing in any material way" and to "describe any known trends or uncertainties that [the corporation] reasonably expects will have a material favorable or unfavorable impact on net sales or revenues ... [including] events that will cause a material change in the relationship between costs and revenues."[113]

... [A] 2003 [SEC] release states that MD&A requires companies to "identify and disclose known trends, events, demands, commitments and uncertainties that are *reasonably likely to have a material effect* on financial condition or operating performance."[116] This language must be read in the context of the regulation it interprets; that is, the 2003 release cannot have created an obligation to disclose *everything* that

106. Basic v. Levinson, 485 U.S. 224, 231 (1988)....

113. SEC Regulation S-K, 17 C.F.R. § 229.303(a)(1), (a)(3)(ii) (2008).

116. Commission Guidance Regarding Management's Discussion and Analysis of Financial Condition and Results of Operations, Securities Act Release No. 8350, Exchange Act Release No. 48,960, 68 Fed. Reg. 75,056, 75,057 (Dec. 29, 2003) (emphasis added).

might have a material effect, but only those things relevant to liquidity, revenues, costs, and other areas specifically required by MD&A. Moreover, as both the 2003 release and Item 303 itself state, the corporation need disclose only that which is *reasonably likely* to have a material effect on these areas, not everything that *might* have a material effect. [*In re Caterpillar*] does not seem to expand the meaning of MD&A significantly.[118] The Caterpillar corporation did not disclose the significant contribution its Brazilian subsidiary made to its overall earnings; nor did it disclose its advance knowledge that "sweeping economic reforms" were forthcoming in Brazil that would cut the earnings of the subsidiary and thus put a significant dent in overall earnings.

Thus, the SEC stated that the board had violated MD&A. The corporation failed to disclose known facts "reasonably likely" to "materially" reduce its earnings. While science is making it increasingly clear that greenhouse-gas emissions are environmentally destructive, and there is a possibility of future regulation, there are as yet no "reasonably likely" material consequences for that destruction (such as tort liability or regulatory fines) that would materially affect liquidity, revenues, or costs. Indeed, corporate activities routinely generate legal levels of socially costly negative externalities with no such material effects—externalities such as pollution, trash, illness, injuries, etc. While a company's carbon impact is certainly likely to affect *the environment*, it is a stretch to say such emissions are "reasonably likely to have a material effect" on the *company* under current law....

Caterpillar suggests that *if* a corporation had special knowledge of forthcoming greenhouse-gas regulations and those regulations were reasonably likely to have a material impact, then the corporation would have to disclose that knowledge and the extent of the expected exposure (which might include, for example, current levels of emissions, how critical they were to revenues and liquidity, as well as the expected cost of complying with the new regulations). But *Caterpillar* hardly seems to suggest that today's corporations would have to disclose the possibility that their greenhouse-gas emissions *could* someday be grounds for costs or liability of some unknown type. And since most investors can receive the same vague information from other sources, it is unclear what such disclosure would accomplish.

Indeed, MD&A may not even require a corporation to disclose its plans for dealing with carbon regulations after those regulations become known. A few years after *Caterpillar*, a federal district court held that a retailer did not violate MD&A by not disclosing its reliance on marketing plans that eventually failed ... One leading commentator thus argues that MD&A has only a very narrow purpose: not to disclose a corporation's plans, but "to pressure companies to give their shareholders advance warning of earnings downturns whenever possible."[123] This is of course consistent with the orthodox view that securities disclosure is narrowly focused on enabling investors to make the most profitable decisions and not on the dissemination of infor-

118. [In re Caterpillar, Inc., 50 S.E.C. 903 (1992).]

123. Paul G. Mahoney, Technology, Property Rights in Information, and Securities Regulation, 75 Washington University Law Quarterly 815, 821 (1997).

mation per se. Thus, it is unlikely that existing securities fraud law provides a cause of action against a corporation for failure to disclose information about its carbon impact. As noted above, disclosure about a corporation's carbon impact is unlikely to be required, and thus the materiality of an omission will be a moot point. Materiality would only be relevant if a corporation were to make an affirmative misrepresentation or were to fail to correct earlier statements that later became misleading. While carbon-impact information might be important to the buying and selling decisions of some, even many, environmentally concerned individuals, the legal standard is that of an objective "reasonable shareholder," who is presumed to invest in order to make money. Even in such a situation, the omissions or misstatements would have to be made in connection with a purchase or sale of securities, and only a person who actually bought or sold securities in reliance could bring suit.

To support a cause of action, the definition of "materiality" would have to be significantly broadened, or MD&A would have to be recast to require carbon-related information. But such reform seems far beyond the traditional scope of the securities laws. Securities law gives shareholders limited ability to make proposals and requests of management with respect to social concerns, but historically, it has not prescribed any specific disclosures of that kind. It seems much more realistic to look to other regulatory agencies, such as the EPA, for climate-related regulations, whether disclosure-related or substantive. Of course, environmental degradation potentially has a material effect on everyone, but for most corporations, it has no company-specific immediate effect of the type that might qualify as "material."

Cynthia A. Williams, *The Securities and Exchange Commission and Social Corporate Transparency**

I. Mandatory Disclosure under the Federal Securities Laws

The regulatory model of the Securities Act and of the Exchange Act emphasizes disclosure of specified information when a company issues securities. Public reporting companies traded on an exchange or over-the-counter are further required to disclose information on a regular basis thereafter. In essence, there are four categories of required disclosure: first, initial disclosure required under the Securities Act when new securities are issued to the public; second, "periodic reporting," required under the Exchange Act, which consists of disclosure when securities are registered and then quarterly and annually thereafter; third, proxy disclosure in conjunction with elections at the annual shareholders' meeting; and fourth, disclosure in conjunction with extraordinary corporate events such as a tender offer, merger, or sale of the business. Thus, under the securities regime, disclosure is a continuous process throughout the year.

... The instructions for developing each of the various types of disclosure documents are also now integrated into one omnibus regulation, Regulation S-K (or Regulation S-B for small businesses), which specifies precisely what information needs

* Originally published in 112 Harvard Law Review 1197 (1999). Reprinted with permission.

to be disclosed and in what format. Regulation S-K sets out five major categories of both narrative and financial information that corporations must disclose. These categories include information about the issuer's business; securities outstanding and to be issued; financial results of operations; directors and executive officers, including management compensation and security ownership by management; and the specifics of the stock issuance, where applicable (including information on the underwriting agreements and commissions). Within each category, Regulation S-K is extremely specific about what needs to be disclosed.

One needs to appreciate two points to understand the proposal being put forth here. First, while Regulation S-K identifies specific information to be disclosed, in many cases that information is further "filtered" through the screen of materiality. So, for instance, in describing the legal proceedings facing a company under Item 103, issuers are required to "[d]escribe briefly any material pending legal proceedings, other than ordinary routine litigation incidental to the business...." The instructions to Item 103 further (and helpfully) set out a materiality benchmark of 10% of the current assets of the issuer, except in an environmental proceeding against a government entity, in which case proceedings with the possibility of a $100,000 fine must be disclosed. When the regulation does not specifically provide a materiality benchmark, the general materiality standard prevails. Under this general standard, information is defined as material if there is a substantial likelihood that a reasonable investor would deem the information significant in the total mix of available information. Thus, Regulation S-K defines an issuer's disclosure obligations generally, as filtered through the "materiality" screen.

Second, Regulation S-K requires disclosure of both quantitative and nonquantitative information. Thus, the issuer must disclose general information about its business, the competitive risks facing the business, legal proceedings involving the company, the experience and background of management and potential conflicts of interest, the structure of the board of directors, the contractual relationship between the issuer and its underwriters, and so forth. Moreover, even when disclosing quantitative information, issuers are now required to provide a narrative analysis of their financial results, including discussions of trends, future risks, or contingencies that might affect those results....

II. Disclosure as a Regulatory Mechanism

On examination, Congress adopted mandatory disclosure in the federal securities laws to advance a number of distinct purposes. One of the major purposes of disclosure was to prevent fraud by corporate issuers and underwriters in the initial sale and subsequent trading of securities. Another purpose was to promote market efficiency so that the prices of securities would more accurately reflect the underlying values of the securities. In the case of section 14(a), Congress required disclosure of a broader range of information about management practices and policies to promote informed corporate suffrage, thereby strengthening the position of shareholders in the corporate governance relationship. Significantly, though, Congress also intended disclosure to play an additional role: disclosure was intended to affect corporate conduct. This conclusion is consistent with the intellectual derivation and legislative history of the acts, particularly the legislative history of the Securities Act, which most directly uses disclosure as its regulatory method.

A number of leading writers of the early 1900s—including Louis D. Brandeis, and Adolf A. Berle and Gardiner C. Means—championed disclosure as a regulatory method. For these writers, the purpose of disclosure was to bring to bear public pressure to change the actions and attitudes of corporate managers, bankers, and other insiders. These writers also believed disclosure would encourage corporate managers to exercise their power with a greater sense of fiduciary obligation, both toward shareholders and toward the public. The issues of primary concern to these writers were the concentration of economic power in the hands of a small group of bankers, corporate executives, and directors; management's lack of accountability to the company's shareholders; and the lack of public accountability or concern for the public among those wielding concentrated economic power. Disclosure was one regulatory method advocated to address each concern.

One such advocate of disclosure was Louis D. Brandeis, a progressive writer, "the People's Attorney,"[64] and ultimately an influential Supreme Court Justice. Justice Brandeis is credited with the most pithy expression of the value of disclosure: "Publicity is justly commended as a remedy for social and industrial diseases. Sunlight is said to be the best of disinfectants; electric light the most efficient policeman."[65] Brandeis was not directly involved in writing the securities laws because he was sitting on the Supreme Court by the early 1930s. Nonetheless, Brandeis had a great deal of influence on President Roosevelt's thinking about disclosure as the proper approach to securities regulation (Roosevelt had asked to be introduced to Brandeis soon after Roosevelt's election). Brandeis also strongly influenced the thinking of Felix Frankfurter, who oversaw the writing of the Securities Act and its passage through Congress.

As Professor Steve Thel has pointed out, disclosure was not an end in itself for Brandeis, but a means to an end—breaking up the untoward concentration of economic power in the hands of the "money monopoly."[69] ... Brandeis proposed disclosure as a remedy for [] problems such as excessive underwriter commissions, because he thought "if each investor knew the extent to which the security he buys from the banker is diluted by excessive underwritings, commissions and profits, there would be a strike of capital against these unjust exactions."[80] Brandeis put forth two rationales for disclosure of underwriters' commissions: to bring pressure to bear against unreasonable commissions through capital strikes, and to "aid the investor in judging of the safety

64. Richard M. Abrams, Introduction to Louis D. Brandeis, Other People's Money and How the Bankers Use It, vii, xvi–xvii (Harper Torchbooks 1967) (1914).

65. Id. at 62.

69. Steve Thel, The Original Conception of Section 10(b) of the Securities Exchange Act, 42 Stanford Law Review 385, 405–06, & n.90 (1990).

80. Brandeis, supra note 64, at 67.

of the investment."[81] Requiring disclosure of these potentially embarrassing fees could cause management to renegotiate them, or to abandon unnecessary financing entirely, which would reduce income to investment banks and ultimately reduce their economic power. Thus, the primary purpose that Brandeis articulated for disclosure as a regulatory device was to assert some measure of social and investor control over the economic concentration that he identified as a "social and industrial disease,"[82] while the secondary purpose was to permit investors to value securities accurately.

The second major contribution to the intellectual foundation of the securities acts was the publication by Adolf A. Berle and Gardiner C. Means in 1932 of *The Modern Corporation and Private Property*.[83] This book was a study of the changing nature of the ownership of corporate property within the American economy. It was written by Adolf A. Berle, a practicing lawyer and adjunct instructor at the Harvard Business School, and Gardiner C. Means, a Ph.D. student in economics at Harvard, both of whom relocated to Columbia University in 1927 to begin the research on which the book was based. Although Berle had a peripheral role in the actual drafting of the Securities Act and the Exchange Act, he was an important member of Roosevelt's "brain trust," and his ideas were pivotal in providing the intellectual foundation for securities regulation.

Berle and Means believed that mandatory disclosure would promote market efficiency in valuing securities. Yet, they discussed the concept of disclosure predominantly in the context of corporate power and a lack of accountability to shareholders and the public. Like Brandeis, Berle and Means recognized the increasing concentration of economic power in large corporations, writing that of the "over 300,000 non-financial corporations in the country in 1929[,] ... 200 of these, or less than seven-hundredths of one per cent, control[led] nearly half the corporate wealth." With this increased economic power came increased social power:

> The economic power in the hands of the few persons who control a giant corporation is a tremendous force which can harm or benefit a multitude of individuals, affect whole districts, shift the currents of trade, bring ruin to one community and prosperity to another. The organizations which they control have passed far beyond the realm of private enterprise—they have become more nearly social institutions.[89]

Berle and Means also recognized another aspect of the problem: as the number of shareholders of public companies increased, the ownership of large corporations became increasingly dispersed. At the same time, control became increasingly concentrated in the management, who for the most part owned very little of the company. Thus, there was a separation of ownership from control.

81. Id. at 69.

82. Id. at 62.

83. Adolf A. Berle Jr. & Gardiner C. Means, The Modern Corporation and Private Property (Harcourt, Brace & World 1967) (1932).

89. Id. at 46.

Berle and Means drew many implications from their observation about the separation of ownership from control. One implication was that as the "owners" increasingly could exert no control over nor assume responsibility for how their property was being run, the "controllers" could increasingly profit from actions that were not in the shareholders' interests. This divergence of interests between shareholders and managers, and potential lack of accountability to the shareholders, has preoccupied corporate law scholars ever since.

Yet Berle and Means were equally concerned about a potential lack of accountability to the public interest. As they stated the point, "[s]ize alone tends to give these giant corporations a social significance not attached to the smaller units of private enterprise.... New responsibilities towards the owners, the workers, the consumers, and the State thus rest upon the shoulders of those in control."[93] Thus, one theme that runs through Berle and Means's writing, and which some of the Exchange Act legislative history echoes, is that the men who exercised power over the large, publicly held corporations and banks were the "new princes," or the "economic autocrats," and that their "power in economic organization shall be subjected to the same tests of public benefit which have been applied in their turn to power otherwise."[94] As things stood at the time, Berle and Means were convinced that existing mechanisms of public accountability were insufficient to constrain large corporations.

Second, Berle and Means argued that the separation of ownership from control necessitated a shift in thinking about management's fiduciary duties, which Berle and Means construed to run to the corporation, and not to the shareholders individually. One implication of this view of management's fiduciary duties was that managers and directors could engage in what we now call insider trading because they were not held to have fiduciary duties (including to disclose material information) to the shareholders individually. Although, as Berle and Means recognized, most managers thought that insider trading was unethical, it was not illegal at the time. Based on this analysis, Berle and Means developed the argument that corporate powers must be understood to be held in trust for the shareholders, and managers must be understood to have fiduciary obligations to the shareholders as well as to the corporation. The idea of corporate powers being held in trust for the shareholders loudly echoes in the legislative history of the Securities Act and the Exchange Act.

Third, Berle and Means argued that the separation of ownership from control required a fundamental rethinking of the concepts of "property" and "ownership." If a person owns a small business or farm or other productive asset, that person has both a responsibility to develop that asset and an illiquid relationship to it. In contrast to prior types of ownership, stock ownership implies liquidity, at least in public corporations, in which the owners have traded control for liquidity. With stock ownership, all that modern stockholders own is "[a] set of legal rights that can hardly be en-

93. Id. at 7.
94. Id. at 310.

forced,"[104] and certain expectations of income and perhaps capital appreciation. Thus, Berle and Means argued, the functions of the stock market are to provide liquidity to stockholders, and to provide a system of appraising the value of what one owns.

Berle and Means then identified a number of problems affecting the ability of the markets to value securities accurately, including underwriters' engaging in behaviors specifically to avoid accountability for false statements and accountants' manipulating accounts to show false profits. Corporate issuers were also subject to inconsistent and inadequate legal obligations to disclose relevant facts to the markets. Berle and Means thought that problems with corporate managers' nondisclosure of information bearing on the accurate value of their company's securities were particularly acute when the managers were themselves trading in their company's stock, and could take advantage of inside information. Much of this part of Berle and Means's argument focused on the importance of developing a legal doctrine that directors and managers have fiduciary duties to the shareholders as well as to the corporation. Ultimately they concluded that the law applicable to the stock markets and economic theories about the markets' functions were in a rudimentary state of development, but that "[a]s far as can be observed now, the direction of thought appears to be towards preserving liquidity; buttressing the stock markets; and increasing their importance as a responsible financial mechanism."[110]

The final question Berle and Means addressed in their book was "in whose interests should the great quasi-public corporations (now representing such a large proportion of industrial wealth) be operated."[111] Applying traditional views of property to the "new situation" in which ownership was separated from control leads to a conclusion that the corporation must be run for the sole benefit of the shareholders. But Berle and Means challenged both that conclusion and the propriety of using traditional views of property to evaluate the claims of the new property, in part because owners had "surrendered" responsibility for the property. Thus, the new property disaggregated the bundle of rights traditionally associated with ownership. In part, Berle and Means based their conclusion that the corporation should not be operated solely for the benefit of shareholders on the "concentration of [corporate] power in the economic field comparable to the concentration of religious power in the mediaeval church or of political power in the national state,"[114] and the inevitable demands against any powerful organization that "the power shall be used for the benefit of all concerned."[115] That demand was just being put forth in America, Berle and Means believed, challenging "the men controlling the great economic organisms ... to accept responsibility for the well-being of those who are subject to the organization, whether workers, investors, or consumers."[116]

---

104. Id. at 252.
110. Id. at 290.
111. Id. at 293.
114. Id. at 309.
115. Id. at 310.
116. Id.

Berle and Means saw a number of ways that the "demand for responsible power" could be put forth. If, "without regard for the changed character of ownership," one accords the passive owner the same strict property rights that the law had traditionally accorded owners of active property, then:

> [T]he group in control of a corporation would be placed in a position of trusteeship in which it would be called on to operate or arrange for the operation of the corporation for the sole benefit of the security owners despite the fact that the latter have ceased to have power over or to accept responsibility for the active property in which they have an interest. Were this course followed, the bulk of American industry might soon be operated by trustees for the sole benefit of inactive and irresponsible security owners.[118]

Conversely, the view "apparently held by the great corporation lawyers and by certain students in the field" was that "corporate development has created a new set of relationships, giving to the groups in control powers which are absolute and not limited by any implied obligation with respect to their use."[119] Berle and Means thought that if these were the only alternatives, the first was the lesser of two evils. Yet they advocated a third possibility: that passive securities holders, by surrendering control and responsibility over their property, had also surrendered the right "that the corporation be operated in their sole interest," while the managers had put forth no compelling claim that they should be the beneficiary of the shareholders' reduced claims. Rather, "[n]either the claims of ownership nor those of control can stand against the paramount interests of the community.... It remains only for the claims of the community to be put forward with clarity and force."[122]

Certainly Congress did not adopt all of Berle and Means's views when it relied on their theory of the separation of ownership and control in adopting the Securities Act or the Exchange Act, or when it recognized the importance of disclosure to enable the markets to value securities accurately. Adolf Berle had suggested more direct approaches to President Roosevelt for ensuring corporate accountability, including federal incorporation, but Roosevelt rejected federal incorporation in favor of a disclosure-based approach drawn from Brandeis's and Frankfurter's ideas. Thus, it would be incorrect to argue that Berle and Means viewed disclosure primarily as a means to affect corporate conduct; Berle at least would have preferred using more interventionist means.

Yet, one aim of Berle and Means's project was to impose accountability on those who hold economic power, including accountability to the public. This aim contributed to the intellectual Zeitgeist in which the securities acts were passed, and Berle and Means's theme of corporate accountability to the public resounds in the legislative history. That history, as set out below, particularly emphasizes the views

118. Id. at 311.

119. Id.

122. Id. at 312.

that corporate managers hold power in trust, and that the "new" corporate managers, as "princes" or "economic autocrats," are properly subject to demands of public accountability.

Another person who was important in structuring the securities laws was Felix Frankfurter. Frankfurter was a professor at Harvard Law School at the time of Roosevelt's 1932 election, and ultimately assembled the drafting team that wrote the Securities Act of 1933. As Dean Seligman points out, Frankfurter's expertise was in administrative law, and so it was Frankfurter who argued for giving the SEC flexibility in its administration of the new laws. Moreover, it was Frankfurter who understood that the SEC's power over such matters as the accounting rules that companies would use to present their financial statements would ultimately be critical to the success of the securities laws.

Frankfurter, who was instrumental in shepherding the Securities Act through Congress, had been strongly influenced by Brandeis's ideas about the value of disclosure. Soon after the Securities Act was passed, Frankfurter wrote an article in Fortune magazine about the anticipated social and financial effects of the Act. Frankfurter was quite explicit that the purpose of disclosure was to affect the behavior of corporate managers, bankers, and accountants. In now celebrated language, Frankfurter wrote:

> The Securities Act is strong insofar as publicity is potent; it is weak insofar as publicity is not enough.... The existence of bonuses, of excessive commissions and salaries, of preferential lists and the like, may be all open secrets among the knowing, but the knowing are few. There is a shrinking quality to such transactions; to force the knowledge of them into the open is largely to restrain their happening. Many practices safely pursued in private lose their justification in public. Thus social standards newly defined gradually establish themselves as new business habits.[132]

In somewhat less celebrated language, Frankfurter also wrote of the Securities Act's promotion of business morals:

> The Securities Act embodies a wholly different conception of business morals. It aims to make it difficult for corporate managers to evade responsibility. Corporate officials and bankers will, it is hoped, hereafter not be "protected" through lawyers' skill in manipulating language. Real protection will reside, as it should, in competence and character.[133]

Frankfurter also discussed the investor protection rationale of disclosure: "Fair play at the start is most essential."[134] Thus, he stated, "[t]he information which must be furnished in the registration statement is intended to reveal facts essential to a fair

132. Felix Frankfurter, The Federal Securities Act: II, Fortune, Aug. 1933, at 55.

133. Id. at 111.

134. Id. at 54.

judgment upon the security offered."[135] For Frankfurter, then, affecting the "business morals" of the time was a major rationale for much of the required disclosure under the Securities Act, as was protecting investors from fraudulent sales by requiring financial disclosure, disclosure of underwriting arrangements, and disclosure of information about management....

V. Expanded Social Disclosure

Given the SEC's power to require proxy disclosure in the public interest, the remaining questions to consider are whether the SEC should require expanded social disclosure pursuant to that power, and what models it should use for such disclosure.

A. Categories of Social Disclosure

This Article has defined "social disclosure" broadly to include general information about what products a company sells, in what countries it does business, its employment and environmental records (both domestic and global), and specified information about a company's community and political effects in the United States and elsewhere. This proposal further recognizes that "social disclosure," as defined here, can be understood as composed of two different categories of information.

The first category is information that tracks compliance with a comprehensive array of statutes and international treaties. Since the 1960s, Congress has passed numerous federal statutes regulating corporate conduct. Such statutes include the Civil Rights Act of 1964, the Occupational Safety and Health Act, the Clean Water Act, the Safe Drinking Water Act, the Clean Air Act, the Consumer Product Safety Act, and the Foreign Corrupt Practices Act. These measures, among others, demonstrate some societal consensus (reflected in the terms of the statutes) about civil rights, consumer and environmental protection, and business ethics. One category of social disclosure, therefore, would be mandatory disclosure of companies' patterns of compliance with these (and other) statutes and international treaties that regulate corporate conduct.

The second category is information about corporate activity that is legal, though controversial. Examples of the second category abound, and include producing violent television programs or movies; selling military hardware, contraceptives, cigarettes, handguns, or Thunderbird whiskey; producing and distributing pornography; or investing in countries or regions such as Burma or Northern Ireland (where the company has not adopted the antidiscrimination principles of the MacBride Principles). Other examples include making "politicized" charitable contributions, downsizing employees (particularly laying off large numbers of employees when the business is profitable), moving production facilities offshore, or extending or denying domestic benefits to homosexual employees. A disclosure regime geared to elucidating these social practices could require disclosure of such information as the percentage of company income derived from controversial products such as military hardware, contraceptives and abortifacients, alcohol and tobacco; corporate practices such as downsizing and out-

---

135. Id. at 55.

sourcing; salary ratios within the corporation; labor compositions in the United States and elsewhere; pay scales, working conditions, and labor protections abroad; environmental practices abroad; and even the countries in which a company has production facilities.

B. The SEC and Expanded Social Disclosure

This discussion addresses three separate questions. First, assuming the investor qua economic person and using a strictly financial understanding of materiality, what arguments can be made for disclosure of information about compliance with the law? Second, still assuming a purely economic investor, what are the arguments that the SEC should require issuers to disclose social information beyond compliance with existing law? Third, relaxing the assumption about investors' characteristics to encompass the "social investor," what arguments can be made for social disclosure beyond that about compliance with existing law? (The term "social investor" typically describes either investors who screen investments to exclude investments in certain products, countries, or practices, or who actively seek to invest in certain companies because of the companies' environmental, labor, or community practices. The term is also used here to include investors who vote their proxies on shareholder proposals in accordance with similar social criteria.)

Before taking up the discussion, however, one short caveat is in order. The discussion has been separated into types of investors primarily for simplicity. It is unlikely that people are pure economic investors or pure social investors, however. Rather, different mixtures of economic and noneconomic preferences inform investors' views. Most "economic" investors would recoil from even extraordinarily profitable investments in slave-labor camps, for instance, were such things legal in another country, just as most "social" investors would recoil from investments that promised no return. These labels ought to be understood, then, as describing the relative priorities of investment preferences, with "social investors" giving higher priority to the social implications of a company's actions than do "economic investors."

1. Disclosure About Compliance with the Law

(a) Economic Investors. As discussed above, in its prior considerations of expanded social disclosure, the SEC ultimately concluded that people invest money to make money, and thus that investors are primarily interested in financially material information. The Advisory Committee on Corporate Disclosure reached a similar conclusion. As a result, the SEC decided to continue using financial materiality in weighing disclosure proposals.

The first conclusion, that people invest money to make money, is probably true for virtually all investors in the securities market; otherwise, people would just put excess money into bank accounts or stuff it under their mattresses and be done with it. The second conclusion, that investors are primarily interested in financially significant information, is probably true for most investors as well (although there may be significant disagreements about what information is "financially significant"). Yet to acknowledge these motivations is not to undermine the importance of disclosure of compliance with the law. Information about a management's pattern of compliance with domestic statutes and international treaties is financially significant information, and thus ought to be provided to shareholders as they prepare to vote in annual elections.

Domestic Statutes. Information about a company's compliance with domestic statutes is financially material because there may be negative economic consequences from the failure to comply with the law. Corporate employees' violations of the law may lead to private litigation, government litigation, loss of future government contracts, reputational injuries, follow-on consequences (including the loss of key employees), and various corollary effects such as institutional investor disinvestment, bond devaluations, and negative market consequences. These negative consequences can affect the current market value of one's investment and the company's future economic performance. Thus, information about management's compliance with the vast array of statutes applicable to any corporation's conduct is, at the core, financially material information. Moreover, because this information relates to future economic contingencies, disclosure in this area is likely to be particularly valued by economic investors.

Evidence that information about compliance with the law is material is found in the typical stock market reaction to a company's announcement of illegality: the stock price drops. To anyone who subscribes to some variant of the efficient capital markets hypothesis, stock market drops are an indication that the information about corporate illegality contained in such an announcement is significant information to investors in valuing the securities of the company. In other words, given the stock price effects that accompany most announcements of corporate illegality, one must conclude that information about corporate illegality—and its chiral partner, compliance with the law—is material information.

One response may be that disclosing information about illegal acts exposes the violations and thus increases the likelihood of an issuer's realizing those negative consequences. If so, is it really in the economic investors' interests to require disclosure of noncompliance? Perhaps yes, for at least two reasons. First, many (and perhaps most) violations will be discovered sooner or later, and whoever owns the issuers' stock at the time will pay the price. The violations will have already occurred and will have already created potential contingencies, thereby lowering the true value of the company, but the market will not have been able to discount the stock price properly because the violations were hidden. Required proxy disclosure of this material information would permit the market to discount more routinely and consistently for the potential consequences of illegality in its valuation of a company's stock, which advances the goals of both investor protection and market efficiency. Indeed, it is precisely this type of nonquantitative information about potential risks and contingencies that the accounting profession has suggested ought to be disclosed to the market more routinely.

Second, the argument that shareholders are harmed by disclosure, rather than by the underlying noncompliance, mistakes cause and effect. Although requiring disclosure could hasten liability, such a requirement could also encourage responsible managers to take effective steps to promote compliance with the law as a serious institutional goal. Indeed, such managers should have few concerns about disclosure because disclosing the company's record will, if anything, increase the market value of their company. Only companies' cavalier toward legal obligations would risk a higher cost of capital under this proposal. Additionally, given the inevitable time lag between proposed regulations and final regulations, companies with liability concerns would be on notice to put their houses in order before the disclosure obligation went into effect. Unless one assumes that stockholders simply do not care about compliance (a proposition that seems unlikely given the economic risks that noncompliance creates), information about such compliance is precisely the sort of information economically minded shareholders ought to know.

International Treaties. Under the Supremacy Clause of the Constitution, international treaties to which the United States is a signatory, upon approval by the Senate, become as much a part of this country's positive law as are congressionally enacted statutes. Yet, while international treaties provide causes of action to aggrieved individuals and provide penalties for noncompliance in some cases, for the most part they lack effective enforcement provisions. Thus, violations of the standards created by international treaties may not seem to harbor the same potential for future economic consequences as do violations of federal statutes.

Nonetheless, globalization of the economy is creating the clear—and unpredictable—potential that international conduct will produce domestic financial repercussions. As information about international labor practices, for instance, becomes more accessible and as firms further distinguish themselves through price and production values, compliance or noncompliance with international treaty provisions on labor rights can be expected to have more profound financial effects, particularly if consumers increasingly engage in purchasing or boycotting products on the basis of the firm's treaty compliance records. In addition, when federal, state, and local government officials travel abroad with leading executives of U.S. companies to promote business development, for instance, or engage in other business development activities, they will be likely to invite executives from companies with reputations as fair international players and good corporate citizens.

(b) Social and Economic Investors: Reflections on Management Integrity. Shareholders should have information on the overall pattern of management's compliance with applicable federal statutes for an additional reason: compliance with the law bears on management integrity and honesty, and ultimately on the quality of management generally. Management integrity may be of particular concern to social investors, but the honesty and integrity of management is information of potential interest to economic investors as well. Indeed, the SEC evaluated the materiality of management integrity from the perspective of the economic investor during the discussions about corporate accountability in the 1970s.

The SEC has never rescinded its 1974 Securities Act Release No. 5466, which stated that the integrity of management is material per se, and which defined compliance with the law as centrally indicative of management integrity. Moreover, in a number of proceedings, the SEC had taken the position that the integrity of management "is always a material factor" in an informed investment decision. Yet the SEC has not pressed the point in recent years. As a result, it is fair to say that the per se materiality of management integrity is currently in substantial doubt.

The proposition that management integrity is material is no less true today than when the SEC first articulated it, however, and the SEC should take this opportunity to reiterate its 1974 position on management integrity. The honesty of management and of the board is a critical factor in determining whether management is worthy of the shareholders' trust. Disclosure of management's pattern of compliance with applicable statutes and international treaties permits shareholders to judge this quality. Thus, this information is squarely within the proper purview of the shareholders in the corporate governance relationship.

2. Disclosure Beyond Compliance with the Law

(a) Economic Investors. Social investors are most obviously or directly interested in disclosure about corporate practices beyond that of compliance with the law, but economic investors have reason to be interested as well, particularly because today's social issue is tomorrow's financial issue. Ultimately, it is quite difficult to draw a meaningful distinction between a corporate "financial issue" and a corporate "social issue," because social, consumer, and investor trends with respect to the corporation's relationship with society can eventually affect a company's profitability, for good or ill.

Thus, firms enjoy positive economic consequences when a company's management does a good job in employment or environmental practices. A number of recent studies have shown that companies that "outperform their peers environmentally will also outperform them on the stock market," by between two and eight percentage points. Other studies have found positive stock market effects for companies that make particular efforts to hire a racially diverse workforce. These correlations between environmental or equal employment practices and a positive stock market effect do not establish causation; the stock market effects could simply be indications of good management more generally, so that companies that manage their potential environmental risks or their personnel issues intelligently may manage other aspects of the company's performance intelligently as well. This information about the quality of management is economically significant because it can relate to present and future stock market values, and it is thus information that an economically minded investor could find material.

Similarly, a company's global social and environmental practices may ultimately affect profitability. Given computers and the Internet, global stock markets, and twenty-four-hour-a-day cable news, the amount of information available to consumers in the United States about a company's activities abroad has expanded during this decade. Through the transmission of information, albeit episodic and incomplete, the actions of U.S. companies abroad are subject to scrutiny at home, with the potential for negative press, consumer effects, and government responses that could reduce profits. Global labor issues have become particularly salient to investors and consumers recently. Witness the public reaction to Nike's international labor policies, for instance, or the publicity surrounding the report that the line of clothes sold at Wal-Mart under the imprimatur of Kathie Lee Gifford was produced in Honduran sweatshops using child labor. Nike's earnings fell dramatically in 1998, at least in part as a result of the continuing negative publicity concerning the labor conditions in its overseas factories. Moreover, Congress responded to "the public outcry over child labor at offshore contractors for Nike Inc. and Wal-Mart Stores Inc." by adding a provision to the Fiscal Year 1998 Treasury Department Appropriations to indicate that merchandise manufactured with "forced or indentured child labor" may not be imported into the United States, and some enforcement actions have already been taken pursuant to that provision. Efforts such as the S.A. 8000 project—which seeks to create standards against which to evaluate manufacturers' and vendors' international labor practices, and a system of labeling to inform consumers of compliance—aim to develop and further harness consumer awareness of global labor issues. Should the S.A. 8000 project succeed, companies that do not comply with the S.A. 8000 standard may face further financial losses, as they will be unable to label or advertise their products as in compliance.

For these reasons, investors should be interested in information about a company's international practices. This investor interest should grow, because one thing we can predict with confidence is that globalization is going to become more, and not less, of a factor in the business and investment climate of the future.

(b) "Social" Investors. At the time of the NRDC proceedings, social investing was a thoroughly marginal phenomenon. The same cannot be said now. The recent growth in the social investor sector of the market has been dramatic: the number of mutual funds using social or environmental screens increased from 55 in 1995 to 144 in 1997 (which shows that there is a social investor market to tap), and the amount of money invested using social screens has been said to have increased from $639 billion to $1.185 trillion over the same period. Today, it is claimed that approximately 9% of assets under professional management in the United States are invested using social screening on the basis of products, countries, or management practices to avoid or to encourage.*

... [B]ecause people in the social investor sector of the market are using socially significant information to make investment decisions, that information is clearly material to them, irrespective of its economic implications. That is, a pool of investors is concerned with the environmental, labor, or social effects of corporate action (such as religious investors who might be concerned with sales of military hardware, contraceptives, or pornography). Thus, information on those topics and others is, by definition, significant in the "total mix" of available information to those investors. Some of this information is available for purchase from third party providers, but much of it is not. With a growing number of investors exhibiting a preference for

* [According to more recent numbers, "approximately $3.07 trillion out of $25.2 trillion invested in the U.S. investment marketplace" are invested according to sustainable or socially responsible criteria. See The Forum for Sustainable and Responsible Investment, Sustainable and Responsible Investing Facts, http://ussif.org/resources/sriguide/srifacts.cfm.]

corporate social accountability, variously defined, the SEC should act to provide those investors (and their advisors) with more readily accessible sources of consistent, comparable, high-quality information about corporate social effects, precisely as it has done with financial data.

Requiring proxy disclosure of socially significant information will advance the goal of investor protection for social investors. Currently the market is providing some information on companies' social effects, either information culled from companies' voluntary disclosure (very often in the companies' annual reports) or more often information developed by securities analysts who do the social screening for screened funds or other investment managers. There are, however, at least three problems with the current provision of socially significant corporate information: differential access to information between individual investors and market professionals; incomplete information; and information that is difficult to compare from company to company. Required disclosure of socially significant information by public reporting companies would address each of these problems....

C. Social Disclosure as a Mechanism to Promote Corporate Accountability

Although the social investment trend is relatively new and its ultimate impact is difficult to gauge, it seems unlikely that social investment per se will be able to influence what products are sold, in which countries a company does business, and what social and environmental effects U.S. companies create. In a diversified, efficient market, social investors withdrawing their capital from certain companies will not raise those companies' costs of capital, and thus will have little short-term financial impact on the companies. For each reluctant investor who sells shares of Phillip Morris because it is marketing tobacco products, there is a willing investor who buys shares of Phillip Morris because of or notwithstanding that it is marketing tobacco products, and so on.

Expanded social disclosure could be a mechanism to permit shareholders to impose greater accountability on the corporate exercise of power, nonetheless. This proposition assumes that the concerns about concentrated corporate power and accountability to the public good that animated Brandeis, Berle and Means, and Congress in the 1930s are still worthy of serious concern. If private corporations have contributed to society's problems, then it is fair to ask them to be accountable for those contributions: in the theory presented by this Article, they should be accountable simply to disclose to their shareholders the extent of the negative consequences of their pursuits. Thus, assuming the purpose of the private corporation is to produce needed goods and services for society and to create economic returns to be shared among shareholders (in the form of dividends), employees (in the form of wages), bondholders (in the form of interest payments), and the community and state (in the form of taxes), corporate accountability simply seeks an honest "social accounting" of the effects the corporation has had on society and on the environment in the process of creating those economic returns. Expanded social disclosure seeks to provide greater information to shareholders concerning these actions so that shareholders can determine the extent to which they approve of the trade-offs management has made between economic returns and social and environmental effects.

If it is true that managers "manage what they measure," then measuring social and environmental effects in a consistent, comparable way could act as an impetus for management to reduce those impacts that shareholders could interpret as negative. Perhaps there would be a "shrinking quality" to actions that managers would be willing to take in relative secrecy, but would not want to disclose to their shareholders or to have published on the front page of the New York Times. Required disclosure might also serve as an impetus for companies to do more expensive things for their communities, their employees, and the long-term welfare of the company, such as increased investment in education in the community or in employee training and development; enhanced employee flexibility in work hours and scheduling; or provision of on-site child care or elder care. Under expanded social disclosure, these actions would all appear in the "positive effects" column of the social accounting ledger, whereas currently they only show up in the "negative income" column of the financial accounting ledger.

Expanded social disclosure is not a panacea. But it may be one means to address a question of the first order of importance: how can we enjoy the obvious benefits of global capitalism while introducing constraints—respect for human rights, protection of individual autonomy, fairness in human relations, and environmental sensitivity—into otherwise "mindless" capital?

D. Criticisms of Expanded Social Disclosure

At least two criticisms of social disclosure have not yet been addressed in this Article: first, that such disclosure would interfere with the functioning of the market by introducing nonfinancial variables into people's investment decisions; and second, that it is beyond the authority of the SEC to require disclosure with the purpose of affecting the kinds of decisions corporate managers make.

The first criticism can be treated with relative dispatch because expanded social disclosure would support, rather than interfere with, the market. In a free market system, decisions in the market are construed as the expressions of the consumer preferences of fully autonomous, well-informed economic actors. Disclosure as a regulatory mechanism is important in such a system to support consumers' abilities to express intelligent preferences. The foods we buy, for instance, are now labeled both as to ingredients and as to calories, fats, carbohydrates, and so forth, so that consumers can express informed preferences for food with or without additives, with high versus low fat content, and the like.

Social investors also express consumer preferences about investing: preferences about companies' products, the countries in which they do business, and the social and environmental effects of their operations. In expressing those preferences, social investors are already using nonfinancial information to inform their preferences; the concern is that that nonfinancial information be accurate, complete, and comparable across companies. On a broad range of issues "beyond the law," the outcomes of various decisions with social implications could be clearly and simply disclosed in consistent, comparable formats, and with the possibility of securities liability for "puffery" or false claims. This disclosure would give social investors the information necessary to develop and express their social investment preferences intelligently. To require disclosure concerning these issues in systematic, comparable formats would not interfere with the free market, therefore, but rather would allow it to operate at a properly sophisticated level of preference formation and expression.

...The second likely argument against expanded social disclosure is that to require this disclosure would be beyond the power of the SEC, particularly if the purpose were, even implicitly, to affect the way corporations are being managed (such as what products they sell, in which countries they do business, or what social or environmental impacts they have). One response to this argument is that Congress enacted section 14 of the Exchange Act of 1934 with the purpose of increasing the knowledge and power of shareholders in the corporate governance relationship. The preceding discussion of the reasons for expanded social disclosure has emphasized the importance of this information to shareholders, both economic and social investors. And yet if one discusses expanded social disclosure as, in part, a mechanism to promote corporate accountability to the public the larger question remains: is that use of disclosure consistent with the SEC's public interest disclosure power under section 14(a)?

In large part, the response to this point has been developed earlier by recognizing two facts. First, Congress used disclosure in the securities laws partly to affect the way corporations were being managed, and to impose greater public accountability on corporate managers. Second, the SEC has promulgated disclosure requirements concerning the composition of a company's board of directors, its committee structure, and directors' records on attending meetings, again, to impose greater public accountability. Thus, expanded social disclosure, even if for the purpose of encouraging greater corporate accountability, is consistent with the SEC's statutory authority and its prior actions effectuating that authority....

VI. Models for Expanded Social Disclosure

This Article briefly concludes with some ideas on formats the SEC could use for social disclosure. Quite obviously, if the SEC were to decide to go forward with expanded social disclosure, it would develop the specific requirements in consultation with issuers, investors, securities analysts, and other interested parties. These suggestions are thus put forward simply as potential starting points for further thought and development. It is important to note that the accounting profession has been developing social audit procedures and disclosure formats since the late 1970s, with some success. The SEC could build upon those efforts in developing this expanded disclosure system.

A. General Overview

To implement expanded social disclosure, the SEC could require the following general categories of information to be disclosed in a company's annual proxy statement: first, product information; second, a list of the countries in which a company does business; third, information about domestic and international employment practices; fourth, information about domestic and international actions that affect the environment; fifth, information on domestic charitable contributions; and sixth, information on domestic and international political contributions. To maximize the availability of this information, issuers could be encouraged to make their social disclosure proxy reports available on the company's Web site....

This Article has recognized two categories of expanded social disclosure: disclosure of management's compliance with the law, and disclosure of corporate social policies that goes beyond information on compliance. Disclosure formats for each category of information are discussed briefly below.

B. Compliance with the Law

As a general matter, the SEC should require companies to discuss the company's efforts to comply with the law, including the relevant role, if any, of the board of directors. This information would include a description of the firm's compliance structure, which includes the departments and officers involved, the efforts made to train employees in their legal responsibilities, the efforts made to audit for compliance, and the handling of violations uncovered in those audits or otherwise. Then, to determine the specific compliance information that companies must disclose, the SEC would need to canvass federal and international law for the legal obligations of companies in various industries, and to determine appropriate disclosure formats by type of industry. Thus, the disclosure applicable to a chemical manufacturer would be different than that applicable to an insurance company or another participant in the financial services industry. With a conglomerate, the SEC could require the company to disclose separately the relevant information for each subsidiary or division of the company that produces above a certain threshold—say, 10%—of gross revenue or of net profits.

Some federal statutes already require companies of a certain size to submit compliance reports to the government on an annual basis. If the underlying statute has such a reporting requirement, the SEC's required disclosure could simply be an executive summary of the company's reports to the relevant federal agency, or the report itself, whichever is likely to be more informative to shareholders. Such a disclosure mandate has the virtue of being easy to implement, because companies already prepare this information and report it to the government. As technology advances, these reports could be made available on a company's Web page as well as in the SEC's EDGAR database.

One instance of an existing reporting mandate is the requirement that most companies with fifty or more employees prepare and file an annual report with the Equal Employment Opportunity Commission (the EEO-1 report), providing information on the number of women and minority group members employed, by job category. The SEC could require proxy disclosure of the EEO-1 reports, or it could require a separate report with similar data (and in a similar format, to reduce the burdens to reporting companies). In developing requirements for such disclosure, the SEC could look to England, where public reporting companies are required to disclose such employment data. Similarly, the Occupational Safety and Health Administration requires companies to report annually on their accident rates, per facility. The SEC could also require companies to disclose that report, aggregated at the division or company level, to shareholders in the annual proxy report.

Similarly, under the major federal environmental statutes, companies are required to report to the EPA about their environmental compliance, again on a facility-by-facility basis. The SEC could require an executive summary of this EPA data, on a company-wide basis, to be disclosed as part of the annual proxy statement. Alternatively, the SEC could promulgate disclosure regulations modeled on the Coalition for Environmentally Responsible Economies (CERES) reporting format. One part of the CERES report, entitled "Compliance," asks for the number of consent decrees, number of penalties, and total value of penalties that the company has paid or agreed to pay, for each of the prior five years, in nine specified categories of environmental statutes and regulations. Because the size of a company and the type of industry will likely affect the number of problems in the environmental area, this reporting format may not work well for intercompany comparisons. It would, however, work well to provide information on trends of compliance with the law at individual companies over time (in conjunction with more descriptive information on the results of the company's compliance audits, and how the company plans to correct any deficiencies that have been found). In addition, CERES has developed a reporting format concerning a company's substantive environmental effects that could facilitate intercompany comparisons and would be a good starting point from which the SEC could develop more extensive environmental disclosure. One of the values of using the CERES reporting format as a starting point is that a number of major manufacturing companies (including Sun Oil, Bethlehem Steel, General Motors, Polaroid, Coca-Cola, and ITT Industries) have endorsed the CERES principles and have experience reporting on their environmental impacts using the CERES reporting format.

For statutes that do not have a reporting requirement, the SEC will have to develop an "omnibus compliance report" format. This report could include a description of the procedures the company has in place to prevent and detect violations of the law, and results of the company's audits concerning compliance with specific laws. One type of social auditing, called a Compliance-with-Standard Report, consists of specifically identifying the legal standards that apply to the corporation in a broad range of areas and then reporting on fulfillment of these compliance obligations, and on plans for bringing noncompliant areas into compliance. Such a format would give shareholders the information necessary to evaluate management's compliance activities and integrity very precisely: in other words, it would hold management accountable to the shareholders and to the public to comply with the law.

C. Disclosure Beyond Compliance with the Law

Based on its public interest disclosure power, the SEC could also promulgate regulations requiring disclosure of information beyond compliance with the law, because ultimately these issues all relate to how the company is managed and what policies management is pursuing. Appendix A [of the article, omitted here] sets out such a proposal.

Alternatively, the SEC could seek statutory authorization from Congress to promulgate procedures that would allow shareholders to decide that a particular management issue warrants disclosure. Thus, if a significant minority (perhaps 20%) of a company's shareholders vote for disclosure of standard information on a particular topic, that vote could suffice to require the company to "opt in" to disclosure for the following year on that topic, at which time the shareholders could once again vote on the company's social disclosure. To effectuate this category of "optional disclosure," the SEC could promulgate a "pull-down menu" of potential social issues about which shareholders might want further information, and shareholders could vote on an annual basis for disclosure concerning the menu items that interested them. In effect, the SEC would use the corporate proxy system to develop objective information about the subjects a reasonable shareholder would find significant in the total mix of information (which assumes that the disclosure interests of a significant minority of shareholders should be recognized as "reasonable").

If the SEC itself promulgates disclosure requirements of information beyond compliance with the law, another possible approach is the S.A. ("Social Accountability") 8000 standard and audit procedures, which could serve as a useful starting point for designing this type of disclosure generally. Moreover, S.A. 8000 can serve as a good disclosure model for labor issues, just as the CERES reporting system can serve as a useful starting point for environmental issues. The S.A. 8000 standard is a "uniform, auditable standard for a third-party verification system" concerning labor practices, designed to be used across countries and industries. It sets out specific "social accountability requirements" for labor relationships (based on International Labor Organization (ILO) conventions) concerning the following issues: child labor, forced labor, health and safety, freedom of association and the right to collective bargaining, discrimination, disciplinary practices, working hours, compensation, and management systems. These standards, because they are based on ILO Conventions, tend to be broadly supported minimum standards for labor protection. The S.A. 8000 standards were written with the participation of members of the KPMG Accounting Firm, with the goal of producing standards that a third party auditing company could use as the basis for a social audit. Prior to the standards' release, the drafters of the S.A. 8000 standards conducted pilot audits in Mexico, Honduras, New York, and Pennsylvania. Thus, this model, too, provides the benefit of some issuer experience with using the standards as a basis for conducting social audits. Although the S.A. 8000 standards do not contemplate disclosure, a disclosure format could easily be grafted onto them. The disclosure could be Compliance-with-Standard disclosure, with narrative descriptions of specific areas not in compliance with the standards, the ways in which they were not in compliance, and the company's plans for bringing those areas into compliance. Similar types of disclosure could be developed for each of the other categories of social disclosure identified at the beginning of this section.

*Starbucks Corporation Fiscal 2014 Global Responsibility Report**

What is the role and responsibility of a for-profit public company?... We have always believed building a great, enduring company requires being performance-driven through the lens of humanity. I [Chairman and CEO Howard Schultz] am proud that Starbucks not only achieved another year of record financial performance in 2014, but we did so while doing more for our people and the communities we serve than at any time in our history. By staying true to our mission, values and guiding principles, I believe we've proven it is possible to build a world-class company with a conscience.

Over the next few years, our efforts will increasingly focus in three areas where we think we can have the biggest impact—building a future with farmers, pioneering green retail on a global scale, and creating pathways to opportunity for young people. With your input, we want to set ambitious goals, some of which we may not achieve. But I strongly believe that today, more than ever, companies such as Starbucks must lead, using their platforms and resources to create opportunities for their people, as well as for the communities they serve. We believe this is our role and responsibility....

Our report for fiscal 2014 focuses on our performance against the goals we set in 2008 in three key areas: ethical sourcing, environmental stewardship, and community investments.... In developing this report, we've covered topics and issues that are important to Starbucks and our stakeholders based on year-round engagement with and feedback from advocates and investors, and ... customer[s] and Starbucks partner[s] (employee[s]).... These efforts are complemented by industry and trend analysis conducted by strategic advisory firm SustainAbility and Edelman public relations, along with direct conversations with the many organizations with which we work. By ensuring both internal and external engagement is a critical component of how we do business, we help ensure our programs, policies, and the content of this report are material to our business and our stakeholders.

As with previous Global Responsibility reports, this year's report highlights the work we are doing in ethical sourcing, community investments and environmental stewardship. These areas are critical to our business and are also where we know we can and do have the greatest impact.... While our commitments are global, our reporting—with the exception of our coffee purchases—is focused largely on Starbucks U.S. and Canada company-operated retail stores and global supply chain operations. These operations, together with our coffee purchases, currently represent the most significant segment of Starbucks social, environmental and economic impacts based on percentage of revenue and number of stores covered....

Starbucks management is responsible for the preparation and integrity of the information reported for fiscal 2014. Through a system of internal controls, including a comprehensive verification process involving internal subject matter experts, we believe this information accurately represents our global responsibility activities and performance results for the fiscal year 2014. External verification is provided by [public accounting firm] Moss Adams LLP....

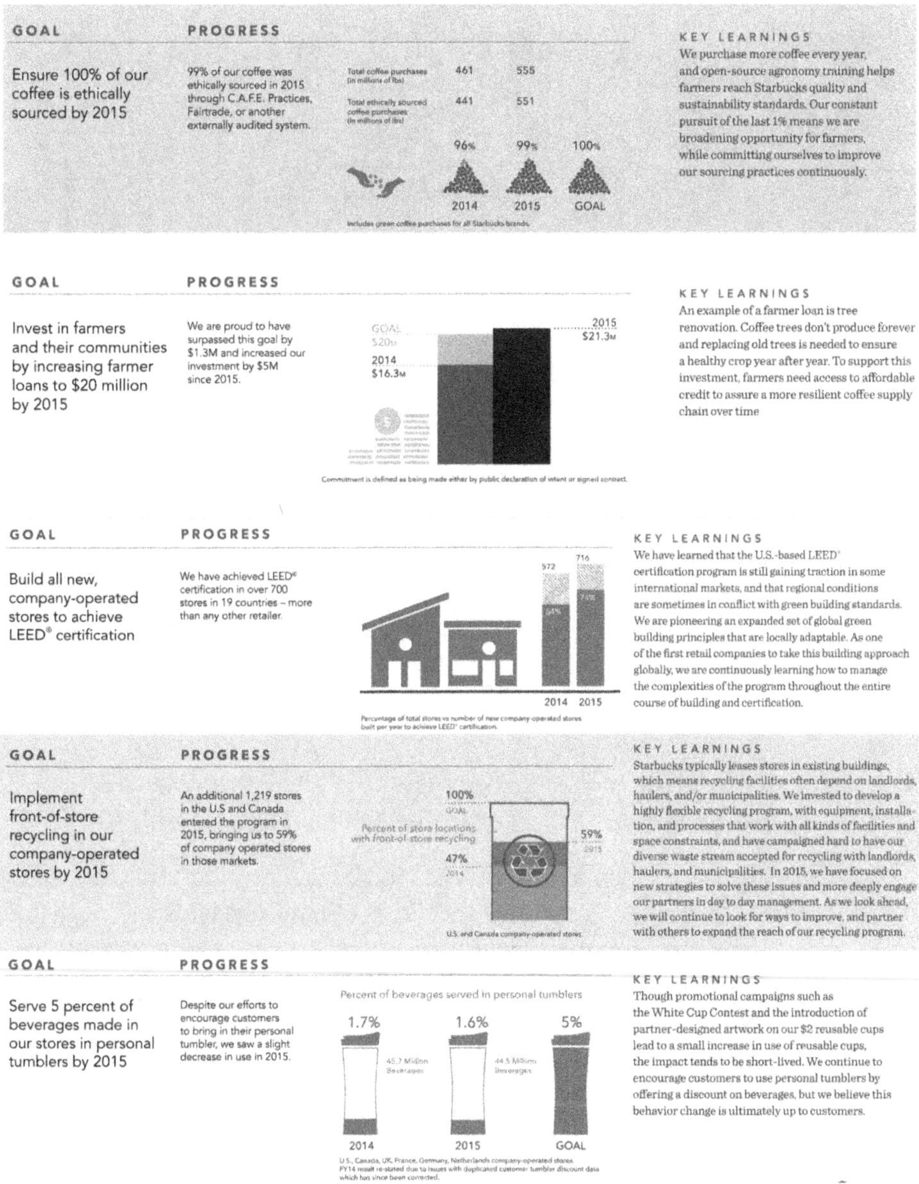

GOAL

Ensure 100% of our coffee is ethically sourced by 2015

PROGRESS

99% of our coffee was ethically sourced in 2015 through C.A.F.E. Practices, Fairtrade, or another externally audited system.

KEY LEARNINGS

We purchase more coffee every year, and open-source agronomy training helps farmers reach Starbucks quality and sustainability standards. Our constant pursuit of the last 1% means we are broadening opportunity for farmers, while committing ourselves to improve our sourcing practices continuously.

GOAL

Invest in farmers and their communities by increasing farmer loans to $20 million by 2015

PROGRESS

We are proud to have surpassed this goal by $1.3M and increased our investment by $5M since 2015.

KEY LEARNINGS

An example of a farmer loan is tree renovation. Coffee trees don't produce forever and replacing old trees is needed to ensure a healthy crop year after year. To support this investment, farmers need access to affordable credit to assure a more resilient coffee supply chain over time

GOAL

Build all new, company-operated stores to achieve LEED® certification

PROGRESS

We have achieved LEED® certification in over 700 stores in 19 countries – more than any other retailer.

KEY LEARNINGS

We have learned that the U.S.-based LEED® certification program is still gaining traction in some international markets, and that regional conditions are sometimes in conflict with green building standards. We are pioneering an expanded set of global green building principles that are locally adaptable. As one of the first retail companies to take this building approach globally, we are continuously learning how to manage the complexities of the program throughout the entire course of building and certification.

GOAL

Implement front-of-store recycling in our company-operated stores by 2015

PROGRESS

An additional 1,219 stores in the U.S and Canada entered the program in 2015, bringing us to 59% of company operated stores in those markets.

KEY LEARNINGS

Starbucks typically leases stores in existing buildings, which means recycling facilities often depend on landlords, haulers, and/or municipalities. We invested to develop a highly flexible recycling program, with equipment, installation, and processes that work with all kinds of facilities and space constraints, and have campaigned hard to have our diverse waste stream accepted for recycling with landlords, haulers, and municipalities. In 2015, we have focused on new strategies to solve these issues and more deeply engage our partners in day to day management. As we look ahead, we will continue to look for ways to improve, and partner with others to expand the reach of our recycling program.

GOAL

Serve 5 percent of beverages made in our stores in personal tumblers by 2015

PROGRESS

Despite our efforts to encourage customers to bring in their personal tumbler, we saw a slight decrease in use in 2015.

KEY LEARNINGS

Though promotional campaigns such as the White Cup Contest and the introduction of partner-designed artwork on our $2 reusable cups lead to a small increase in use of reusable cups, the impact tends to be short-lived. We continue to encourage customers to use personal tumblers by offering a discount on beverages, but we believe this behavior change is ultimately up to customers.

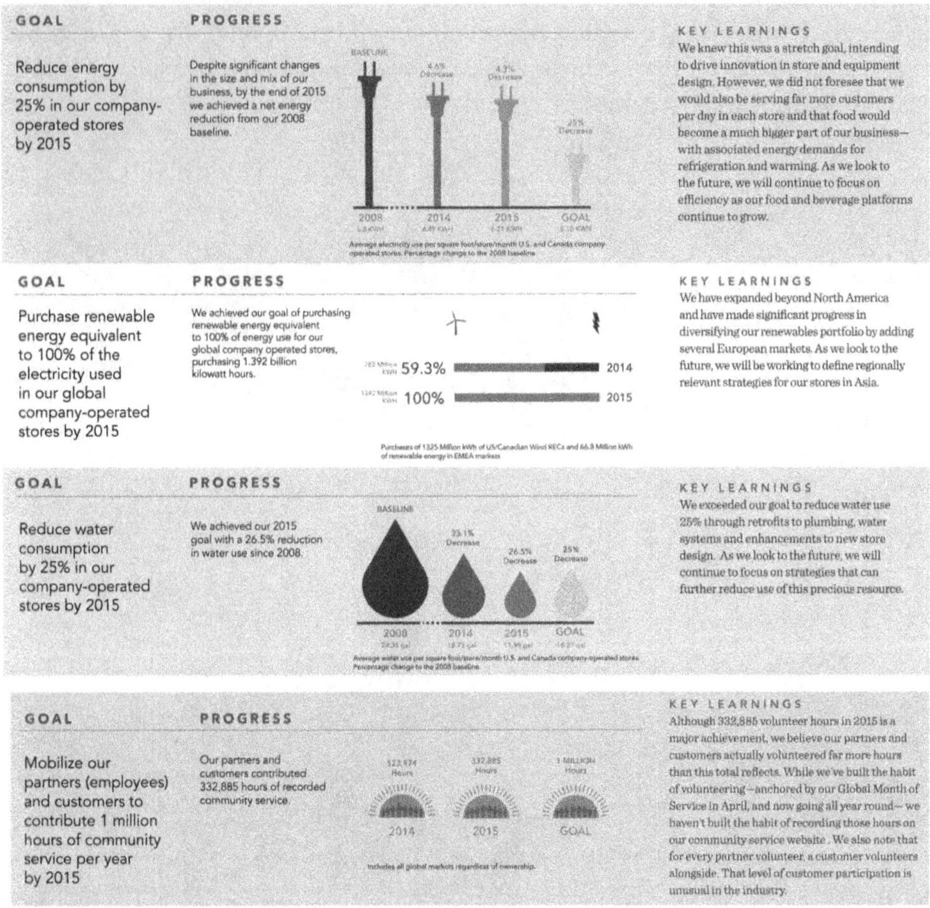

Dennis D. Hirsch, *Green Business and the Importance of Reflexive Law: What Michael Porter Didn't Say**

... As coined by the German social theorist Gunther Teubner, the term reflexive law refers to law that fosters self-regulation.[24] It consists of legal standards and regulatory policies that push private firms to: (1) internalize social goals (e.g., environmental performance goals) and adopt them as their own, and (2) creatively self-manage their operations so as better to achieve these goals. Reflexive laws do not mandate specific technologies like traditional regulation. Nor do they require particular environmental results like outcome-based rules. Instead, they use tools such as information disclosure, stakeholder involvement, and planning requirements to motivate companies to undertake their own, self-directed improvement efforts, while leaving it up to the firms to determine both the means of pollution reduction and the ultimate environmental outcomes.

---

* Originally published in 62 Administrative Law Review 1063 (2010). Reprinted with permission.

24. See Gunther Teubner, Substantive and Reflexive Elements in Modern Law, 17 Law & Society Review 239, 275 (1983).

[For example, t]he Emergency Planning and Community Right to Know Act requires facilities that use toxic substances to report annually the amount of such substances they have released or transferred off-site. Each year, the Environmental Protection Agency (EPA) compiles this information and publishes the Toxics Release Inventory (TRI), which ranks companies by the amount of toxic substances they released.[32] News reporters and environmental groups put together additional rankings by industry, state, and zip code.[33] No company wants to appear near the top of these lists. The TRI rankings accordingly provide a substantial incentive for firms to reduce their use, transfer, and release of toxic substances. Studies credit TRI with causing a 45% drop in toxic releases between 1988 and 1998. The TRI does not push facilities to adopt particular technologies, as traditional regulation would do; nor does it mandate a specific environmental result, as outcome-based regulation would do. Instead, it uses information disclosure to create incentives that lead firms themselves to decide to reduce their toxic emissions and to manage their operations to this end. The TRI is thus a law that promotes self-regulation. It is a reflexive law....

Encouraging Industry to Internalize Environmental Norms

Reflexive law encourages industry to internalize environmental norms in two primary ways: information-based strategies and communication-based strategies.

Information-based strategies require firms to collect and disseminate information about their environmental performance. The TRI, described above, is an example of this type of regulation. Such disclosure empowers stakeholders to bring pressure on industry through purchasing decisions, media campaigns, and other actions. It also serves to educate those who work in industry about the environmental impacts of their own actions and so appeals to their moral commitments as social beings. The combined effect should be to get industry to take more seriously, and seek to reduce, its impacts on the environment and human health. It should "lead to environmentally beneficial changes in organizational behavior as a result of influences and interactions generated by consumption of ... information by public stakeholders." Information-based strategies for getting firms to internalize environmental norms fall into three subcategories: those that, like TRI, collect and disseminate negative information about firms' environmental impacts and so make them want to do better; those that collect and disseminate positive information about the companies' environmental performance and thereby use a carrot, rather than a stick, to encourage improvement; and those that disclose other types of relevant information, such as descriptions of green business success stories.

Reflexive law also seeks to promote the internalization of environmental norms by enhancing communication between stakeholders and the industries that affect them.

32. See TRI Explorer: Introduction, Envtl. Prot. Agency, http://www.epa.gov/triexplorer/ introduction.htm. [The] TRI Explorer is a tool that can be used to construct rankings.

33. For example, Green Media Toolshed uses the Toxics Release Inventory (TRI) data to build its Scorecard website that allows users to construct "a detailed report on chemicals being released from any of 20,000 industrial facilities, or a summary report for any area in the country and Scorecard spotlights the top polluters in the U.S., and ranks states and counties by pollutant releases." ...

As mentioned above, systems theory predicts that part of the problem is the lack of communication between the broader society and industry and that part of the solution, accordingly, involves breaking into industry's own discourse—its norms, values, and language—so that it can better hear, and ultimately incorporate, others' perspectives on its actions. Communication-based initiatives seek to facilitate this. For example, the government might require industry to reach out to and meet with stakeholders to demonstrate that it has given due consideration to their input regarding environmental management. Alternatively, the government might issue a public challenge to a given industry sector to improve its environmental performance, thereby stimulating dialogue and media attention on the topic. In these ways and others, government officials become the "structural engineers of communicative systems." The information-based strategy connects to the communication-based one, since well-informed stakeholders will be more motivated to communicate with industry and more persuasive when they attempt to make their case. It is worth noting that neither information-based nor communication-based strategies prescribe specific environmental outcomes. They do, however, enable stakeholders to express their desires to industry and press it to align its norms and behaviors with their own. In Teubner's terms, law's role shifts from prescribing specific behaviors or environmental outcomes to "coordinating" the objectives of different sectors of a highly complex and differentiated society....

Once information-based and communication-based strategies have gotten firms to understand and internalize environmental norms and objectives, the next step is to get them to reflect on their own environmental performance and manage their operations to bring them more into line with these values.

Here, reflexive law's primary modus operandi is procedural. It requires or encourages firms to engage in planning and decisionmaking procedures through which they reflect on and manage their environmental performance. For example, some states require facilities to engage in pollution prevention planning as a condition of permit issuance. Others provide incentives for such behaviors or technical assistance to facilitate them. Laws like these do not prescribe specific control technologies or pollution levels. Instead, they require or encourage firms to undertake planning and decisionmaking steps. The law accepts the environmental outcomes that emerge from these processes.

In sum, reflexive law seeks to get firms to internalize environmental norms and objectives, reflect on where they stand with respect to them, and manage their operations to perform better....

Discussion Questions

1. What is the purpose of securities disclosure? Does this suggest that securities-driven corporate social responsibility reforms will be ineffective, as Joo seems to suggest?

2. Is the Management Discussion and Analysis ("MD&A") requirement—that companies disclose known trends, events, demands, commitments, and uncertainties that are *reasonably likely to have a material effect* on the financial condition of the

company—too vague to apply to sustainability concepts? If so, how could the MD&A standard be rewritten to compel disclosure of corporate social responsibility?

3. In 2010, the SEC issued an interpretative release relating to climate change, indicating that certain climate-change-related matters may need to be disclosed under existing securities laws and regulations. See Commission Guidance Regarding Disclosure Related to Climate Change, Release Nos. 33-9106, 34-61469, available at 75 Federal Register 6,290 (Feb. 8, 2010). According to the release, existing as well as pending laws, regulations, and treaties relating to climate change may have a material impact on a company's finances. (Imagine the impact a carbon tax might have on a business and ask yourself whether a reasonable investor in that business might want to know the extent of that possible impact.) The release also notes that legal, technological, political, and scientific developments regarding climate change, and physical changes brought about by climate change, may likewise materially affect a company's financial condition and thus require disclosure. Do you agree with the SEC that the interpretative release is merely an application of existing securities laws or do you think the SEC made new rules here? How does the release affect Joo's analysis of the SEC's *Caterpillar* decision?

4. The SEC is currently considering new and different disclosure requirements, including "sustainability matters" on the theory that they "are of increasing significance to voting and investment decisions." See SEC Concept Release, No. 33-10064, Business and Financial Disclosure Required by Regulation S-K, 81 Fed. Reg. 23915 (Apr. 13, 2016). Do you agree with the SEC's premise?

5. What reform measures does Williams suggest to encourage sustainable and socially responsible corporate behaviors? What is the likelihood of such reforms coming to pass?

6. Why did the drafters of the securities laws think disclosure would be more effective than, say, fiduciary duties, in regulating corporate behavior? Do these reasons apply with equal force to social responsibility and sustainability disclosures?

7. Williams distinguishes between "economic investors" and "social investors." Does this distinction make sense if sustainable practices on the whole help a firm's financial bottom line?

8. What are the pros and cons of expanded social disclosure? Are there better ways to make corporations accountable?

9. Many companies voluntarily engage in some form of social responsibility reporting. In fact, in 2010 all but four of the Fortune 50 did so. Why do you think voluntary reporting is so prevalent? Unfortunately, these reports tend to use various formats and are, as a result, often difficult to compare with one another. The Global Reporting Initiative Sustainability Reporting Guidelines (the successor to the CERES format Williams mentions, now in their third revision) offer some standardization, and firms may be coalescing around them.

10. Visit the website of a company you think is likely to publish a corporate responsibility report. Does it have one? Are you surprised at its contents? Now visit the website of a company you think is unlikely to have one. Does it? If it does, are you surprised at its contents?

11. Do you think Starbucks is "cherry-picking" only positive information to report? Do you think other businesses making similar disclosures engage in this sort of behavior? Do you think investors are likely to be fooled by corporate efforts to "greenwash" social and environmental impacts?

12. In describing its goals and progress, the Starbucks report refers to LEED-certified buildings and C.A.F.E. Practices for sourcing coffee beans. The latter (which stands for "Coffee and Farmer Equity") is a Starbucks-developed set of guidelines, as opposed to the third-party "Fair Trade" standard you may have seen adorning other brands of coffee and chocolate. Why do you think Starbucks developed its own equity standard? Is it trustworthy? Do you think Starbucks customers trust it?

13. Starbucks has a senior vice president of global responsibility who oversees its social responsibility efforts. Other firms employ chief sustainability officers on par with the chief executive officer and other "c level" executives. Do you think such a role is helpful, vital, or unnecessary? Does it depend on the firm?

14. Requiring or pressuring firms to make social and environmental disclosures is a form of reflexive law. (The stakeholder assessment proposal described above in Chapter 3 is another.) What are some problems with reflexive law strategies? How could they be improved?

Chapter 7

Sustainable Investing

Earlier chapters asked whether corporate managers may, may not, or must engage in sustainable business practices given their fiduciary obligations to the firm. This chapter addresses the investment version of this question: whether financial institutions may not, or must practice socially responsible investing ("SRI") by considering environmental, social, and good governance ("ESG") factors in making investment decisions. Fiduciary duties apply here as well, although they derive from trust law, differ slightly from corporate-law fiduciary duties, and in the United States are a function of various state and federal statutes and the common law.

The first excerpt presents background on these issues, detailing and critiquing arguments in favor of SRI from one of the world's leading law firms. The second reading canvasses the various rationales frequently offered in support of SRI, ultimately finds them lacking, and formulates a new rationale for the practice. The third reading updates the literature about whether SRI in fact sacrifices returns or enhances them. In other words, just how strong is the so-called "business case" for SRI?

Joakim Sandberg, *Socially Responsible Investment and Fiduciary Duty*[*]

Socially responsible investment (SRI) can be taken to refer to the practice of integrating social, ethical and/or environmental considerations—sometimes referred to as "environmental, social and governance" (ESG) considerations—into one's financial investment process. Whereas conventional or mainstream investment focuses solely upon financial risk and return, SRI thus includes social or environmental goals or constraints as well as more conventional financial criteria in decisions over whether to, e.g., acquire, hold or dispose of a particular investment. This practice has received increased attention over the last couple of decades—according to some recent estimates, the total amount of investments with an explicit social or environmental profile is currently as much as $2.71 trillion in the U.S. and €2.665 trillion in Europe. The factor which many commentators think will determine whether SRI can grow further than this, however, is whether it is a viable form of investment for institutional investors. Institutional investors are organisations which invest and financially manage large pools of other people's money—for instance pension funds, banks, insurance companies and other kinds of financial trusts.

---

* Originally published in 101 Journal of Business Ethics 143 (2011). Reprinted with permission.

Institutional investors are really the major players in the world's financial markets: They control over 84% of total shareholdings in the U.K., for instance, and over 61% in the U.S.—where they also stand for over 80% of all share trades. Quite obviously, if a lot of institutional investors could be persuaded to invest according to social or environmental guidelines, the SRI movement could become an important force for corporate social responsibility worldwide. A critical point of controversy in this context, however, is whether taking ESG considerations into account really is legally permitted for institutional investors. Being a form of trusts, institutional investors by law have so-called fiduciary duties towards their beneficiaries—that is, they are generally required to manage their funds in the best interest of the underlying owners or ultimate recipients of these funds. And many institutional investors argue that there is a conflict between their duties to their beneficiaries and the idea of taking ESG considerations into account. While they personally may care about many social, ethical and environmental issues, some say for example that their fiduciary duties disallow them from attending to personal biases. Others argue that their duty to beneficiaries simply is to maximise the profits on their investments, and this is then thought to rule out the integration of ESG concerns.

The traditional position among business lawyers and legal scholars has been that this view is correct.[1] My central focus in this article, however, is a report commissioned by the United Nations Environment Programme's Finance Initiative to the law firm Freshfields Bruckhaus Deringer in 2005, which has come to be known simply as the "Freshfields report" and has given rise to considerable optimism among those in favour of SRI as a viable alternative for institutional investors. According to the authors of the Freshfields report, taking ESG considerations into account may not only be legally acceptable for institutional investors under certain circumstances, but it is actually legally obligatory on many occasions.[2] The Freshfields report has been called "the single most effective document for promoting the integration of environmental, social and governance (ESG) issues into institutional investment" and its conclusions are nearly universally accepted by proponents of the SRI movement.

The present article aims to put the arguments of the Freshfields report into some further both empirical and critical perspective and consider whether they indeed call for considerable optimism about the prospects for SRI on the part of institutional investors....

The fiduciary duties of institutional investors

"Fiduciary" comes from a Latin verb meaning "to trust" and, hence, "fiduciary duties" is the common term for the duties which trustees—e.g., pension funds—have towards their beneficiaries—e.g. present and future retirement pensioners. It should

1. See, e.g., ... John H. Langbein & Richard A. Posner, Social Investing and the Law of Trusts, 79 Michigan Law Review 72 (1980).

2. Freshfields Bruckhaus Deringer, A Legal Framework for the Integration of Environmental, Social and Governance Issues into Institutional Investment (2005), [available at http://www.unepfi.org/fileadmin/documents/freshfields_legal_resp_20051123.pdf].

be noted from the start that the extent to which these duties are legally defined, how they are legally defined, and then how they are understood in practice and what specific requirements they impose on investment institutions, varies a great deal between different countries and also different types of institutions.... To a fair degree, however, it seems that most countries, both common and civil law jurisdictions, impose a roughly similar set of core responsibilities on institutional investors, which they have exactly in virtue of being trustees of other people's money. For reasons of brevity, I will continue to refer to these as the fiduciary duties of institutional investors.

The core fiduciary duties imposed on institutional investors in most countries could be said to consist in the following two tenets: (A) Trustees are to manage their funds in the interests of the ultimate beneficiaries, and not in their own self-interest. This is sometimes stated more generally as the duty to act in accordance with the purpose of the trust and, to be fair, some trusts may have terms which give trustees a somewhat different purpose. In the standard case, however, as with e.g. pension funds and mutual funds, the purpose of the trust is typically taken to be to provide financial benefits for the beneficiaries. Furthermore, (B) trustees are to exercise due care and prudence when managing their funds. This is generally referred to as the "prudent man rule" or "prudent investor rule" in some jurisdictions, and could be taken to be the part of the fiduciary duties of institutional investors issuing more concrete action-guidance. The duty to exercise due care and prudence is typically taken to imply that trustees should, e.g., seek adequate information before making investment decisions, consult with expertise if they are not financial experts themselves, and carefully weigh the expected returns of particular investments against both expected risk and how they fit in with the rest of the overall portfolio.

Whether the fiduciary duties of institutional investors are compatible with purposively taking ESG concerns into account has been the subject of intense debate, really since the dawn of the SRI movement.... Now, it may be noted that some rather high-profile institutional investors frequently are referred to as pioneers in this movement for instance, the California Public Employees' Retirement System (CalPERS) and the New York Teachers Retirement System in the U.S., and the Universities Superannuation Scheme (USS) in the U.K. Hence there are some institutional investors, then, which seem to think that SRI is compatible with fiduciary duty. However this is far from the received view. A vast amount of institutional investors around the world interpret the legislation surrounding fiduciary duty as precluding them from doing anything else than seeking maximum returns on investments. In a recent survey among American pension fund trustees, for example, as many as 45% of respondents indicated that considerations of fiduciary duty were their main reason for not engaging more actively in SRI.

The traditional position among business lawyers and legal scholars, as noted at the outset, has tended to be that this view basically is correct. After all, the two tenets above seem to combine into the idea that trustees are to act prudently in the financial interest of their beneficiaries. This is then, rather straightforwardly, thought to preclude institutional investors from taking non-financial considerations into account in their investment decisions and to sacrifice returns for social or environmental goals. According to the classic and oft-cited commentary of the Chicago law professors Langbein and Posner, e.g., "[t]he duty of prudent investing ... reinforces the duty of loyalty in forbidding the trustee to invest for any other object than the highest return consistent with the preferred level of portfolio risk" and, were fiduciaries to take ESG considerations into account, "both the duty of loyalty and the prudent man rule would be violated."[3]

To once and for all establish whether the traditional position on this matter really is correct, the Asset Management Working Group of UNEP commissioned ... the Freshfields report.... The striking feature of the report, however, is its contention that the traditional position on the incompatibility of these responsibilities and SRI is fundamentally mistaken. The report suggests that the fiduciary duties of institutional investors are consistent with taking ESG concerns into account in many situations and, what is more, it is sometimes obligatory to take such concerns into account.

The Freshfields report's arguments

The general argument of the Freshfields report is that profit maximisation never has been a part of the fiduciary duties of institutional investors in any country. In countries like the U.K. and U.S., the idea that fiduciary duty requires profit maximisation is suggested to stem from a common but superficial reading of certain central court decisions.... Whereas the purpose of the trust certainly should be respected, which most often will mean that the overriding goal should be to provide financial benefits for the beneficiaries, as long as institutional investors exercise their investment powers carefully and fairly they are not required to maximise profits with complete disregard of all other factors.... The report thus argues that institutional investors have some discretion in deciding what it means to exercise due care and prudence, and sometimes this may include taking ESG concerns into account.

In contrast with the traditional view, the report more specifically presents three sorts of circumstances where it is argued that taking ESG concerns into account is either permissible or, in fact, obligatory for institutional investors. (1) First of all, choosing investments on the basis of their ESG characteristics is argued to be permissible when deciding between investments with exactly similar financial characteristics. That is, if the financial prospects of investing in either company A or company B are found to be exactly on a par, the report argues that choosing company A over company B for ESG reasons is compatible with the duty of having the financial interests of the beneficiaries as one's overriding goal. (2) Secondly, taking ESG concerns into account is argued to be obligatory when such concerns are financially relevant—that is, when a certain company's or industry's ESG performance reasonably can be expected to have an impact on its financial performance or valuation. The report suggests that this quite generally would be the case, and so a duty to take ESG

3. Langbein & Posner, supra note 1, at 98.

considerations into account is thought to follow directly from the duty to seek adequate information before making investment decisions noted above. (3) Finally, choosing investments on the basis of their ESG performance is argued to be obligatory when it is reasonable to think that this actually would be supported unanimously by the beneficiaries....

It seems fair to say that the Freshfields report has been met with considerable enthusiasm among proponents of the SRI movement.... [Institutional investment expert] Jim Hawley is reported to have said that "[t]he report is extraordinarily significant for a number of reasons: first, it essentially flip-flops the conventional wisdom on fiduciary duty, completely turning it on its head, [and s]econd, the fact this report was prepared by Freshfields—the third largest law firm in the world ... carries huge clout." ... [A]ccording to a report prepared for the U.S. Environmental Protection Agency, "the Freshfields report marked a turning point in the debate on fiduciary duty and ESG investments" and it "remains the most authoritative study to this point on the legal context in which ESG investing does or does not take place in most advanced capital markets around the world." Finally, according to a Canadian public committee on the environment and the economy, the Freshfields report "essentially put this question [of fiduciary duty versus SRI] to rest."

In July 2009, UNEP FI published another report, officially labelled as a follow up to the Freshfields report and appropriately named "Fiduciary II."[4] ... [I]ts authors solemnly acknowledge that "the law regarding fiduciary duty has changed very little in the years since the Freshfields Report." ...

I certainly agree that the Freshfields report indicates grounds for some optimism on the issue of SRI versus fiduciary duty. However, I will now suggest that much of the extreme praise noted above is greatly exaggerated. Even though the report persuasively supports the contention that taking some ESG considerations into account sometimes can be compatible with fiduciary duty, a rather basic and legitimate question seems to be exactly what level of devotion to ESG issues it allows for. In the following three sections, I will go through the three central arguments of the Freshfields report and discuss this issue more carefully, and in the section following that, I will note a dimension of this issue not addressed by the authors of the Freshfields report.

ESG considerations as tie-breakers

... [A] first argument for the compatibility between fiduciary duty and SRI is that ESG considerations may be considered as tie-breakers between investments with similar financial characteristics.... That is, in situations where trustees conclude that the financial characteristics of two or more investments are exactly on a par, the argument suggests that they are permitted to decide which one to pursue by reference to whatever social or environmental concern they may have.... The obvious question

4. United Nations Environment Programme Finance Initiative, Fiduciary Responsibility: Legal and Practical Aspects of Integrating Environmental, Social and Governance Issues into Institutional Investment (2009) [available at http://www.unepfi.org/fileadmin/documents/fiduciaryII.pdf].

in relation to this first argument, however, is exactly how often trustees will be able to give effect to such an agenda—that is, how likely it is that trustees will find themselves in situations where the financial characteristics of two or more investments are exactly on a par.

... Given that trustees adequately analyse their investment opportunities according to modern portfolio theory, Rosy Thornton—an expert on trust law—suggests that it would be outright "inconceivable" that they would find themselves in a situation where the financial characteristics of two investments are exactly the same. "Not only is it extremely improbable that the complex measures used to estimate expected return and variance will produce two identical sets of values," she suggests, "but it must be remembered that these assets are not being considered in isolation but in relation to an existing portfolio. Therefore the trustees should be comparing not only the expected return and variance of the two assets themselves, but also the covariance between those assets and the rest of the holdings within the portfolio. When this factor is taken into account, it becomes inconceivable that there would be no legitimate investment ground upon which to distinguish between the two assets."[5] These are clear words indeed and, if this interpretation of the law is correct, the Freshfields report's appeal to the possibility of integrating ESG considerations as tie-breakers indeed would seem to be seriously misleading.

Perhaps Thornton's view could be said to be too legalistic—one may, for instance, ultimately want empirical evidence on to what extent CalPERS and USS manage to live up to (at least the spirit of) modern portfolio theory and fiduciary law. And perhaps Thornton's interpretation of the law also is somewhat strict—it may be noted that some countries' legal standards explicitly give a bit further leeway in the present context. In a decision from Maryland Court of Appeals..., for instance, the court suggested that investors have not transgressed their duty of loyalty as long as the costs of considering the social consequences of investment decisions are de minimis[6]—and this obviously goes further than the tie-breaker clause. Taking these considerations into account, I suggest that it probably is exaggerated to say that it is entirely "inconceivable" that investors will find themselves in situations where the financial characteristics of two or more investments are equal in the sense encoded in the law. Nonetheless, I contend that it at least would seem rather unlikely that they will find themselves in such situations—at least that they will do so very often. Even though no one is perfect, investors with adequate skills in modern financial analysis can be expected to be able to judge which of two investments suits their portfolio best in most situations. The likelihood that they will find themselves in a situation where non-financial tie-breakers can come in, then, is relatively slim.

5. Rosy Thornton, Ethical Investments: A Case of Disjointed Thinking, 67 Cambridge Law Journal 396 (2008).

6. Freshfields Report, supra note 2, at 111 (citing Board of Trustees v. Mayor of Baltimore City, 562 A.2d 720 (Md. 1989), cert. denied, 493 U.S. 1093 (1990)).

Thornton wishes to add a further problem here. Even if some trustee, perhaps because of lack of information or just lack of financial analysis skills, indeed were to judge that two investments seemed to present the exact same financial opportunities, she suggests that the recommendations of modern portfolio theory are not exhausted. After all, the investments may still differ in terms of hidden (or underlying) risk and so the prudent choice may be to simply invest in both of them in order to spread this hidden risk. I do not wish to put too much emphasis on this last point, in order to give the Freshfields report's interpretation of the law the benefit of the doubt. In conclusion, however, I take the above considerations to suggest that the report's first argument for the compatibility between fiduciary duty and SRI leaves only limited room for institutional investors to take ESG considerations into account.

The financial relevance of ESG factors

[T]he authors of the Freshfields report ... put a lot more emphasis on their second argument. The report quite straightforwardly states that: "In our view, decision-makers are required to have regard (at some level) to ESG considerations *in every decision they make.* This is because there is a body of credible evidence demonstrating that such considerations often have a role to play in the proper analysis of investment value." (emphasis added) The second argument, then, is that the ESG performance of companies quite generally has an impact on the financial performance (or valuation) of these companies and, for this reason, a duty to take ESG considerations into account is thought to follow directly from the duty to seek adequate financial information before making investment decisions. Taking ESG considerations into account is not only permitted for institutional investors according to this argument, but it is actually required.

Scrutinising the great amount of praise given to the Freshfields report more closely, it seems fair to say that it is this second argument which the majority of commentators applaud and/or support most intensively. Now curiously, the only real example of when ESG performance affects financial performance given in the Freshfields report is the case of climate change. The report says in a note: "Climate change is an obvious example of an environmental consideration that is recognised as affecting value. Following the recent release of a report by Mercer Investment Consulting noting the financial impact that climate change has already had on companies' costs, revenues, assets and liabilities, the U.K. Carbon Trust expressed the view that 'Pension fund trustees have a duty to address the financial risk posed by climate change when making investment decisions.'" Fiduciary II is equally unable to present further examples, besides the case of climate change, of when ESG considerations are financially relevant. However, could this kind of thinking be generalised to cover all ESG considerations?

It should be noted that the issue of the possible financial relevance of ESG considerations has been the subject of an enormous amount of studies over the last couple of decades—indeed, UNEP FI itself has published a number of studies and summaries on this issue. In a [2007] meta-analysis of previous research in the area, probably the most ambitious one to date, Margolis et al. compared a total of 192 statements in as many as 167 previous studies on the link between what they call corporate social performance (CSP) and corporate financial performance (CFP). The result of their analysis is that the overall link seems 'positive but small.'[7] However, what is most interesting in the present context is the enormous spread of results discovered in the analysis. Of all 167 previous studies, 58% found no statistically significant relationship between CSP and CFP, 27% found a positive relationship and 2% a negative relationship.*

... [W]here does this leave the Freshfields report's second argument? I conclude that if institutional investors only are justified in taking ESG considerations into account when they are financially relevant, this could at best be a very contingent support for their adoption of SRI practices....

There is actually a further problem with justifying SRI from an appeal to the financial relevance of ESG considerations. Arguably, not only companies but also social investors sometimes want to take social or ethical concerns into account exactly for social or ethical reasons. One such situation in particular seems to be when a certain company or industry is performing extremely poorly along some ESG dimension, but there is no economic disadvantage to such behaviour in the foreseeable future. A genuinely social investor would plausibly want to avoid investing in, or perhaps attempt to reform, this company or industry—part of the reasoning behind the whole SRI movement, after all, is that SRI as such could be a force for penalising poor ESG performance. However, since there is no reason to think that these particular cases of such performance will have any financial relevance in the foreseeable future, such behaviour would seem to be ruled out by the present line of argument. The SRI of institutional investors could only be reactive and never truly proactive, then, if they only are justified in taking ESG considerations into account when they are financially relevant.

Richardson makes a similar observation. In his terminology, the current legislative framework surrounding fiduciary duty only supports "business case SRI" and not "ethical SRI." And even though institutional investors to some degree are allowed (or even obliged) to take ESG considerations into account, then, he suggests that the focus on "business case SRI" does not call for very much optimism. He writes:

> The notion that environmental care and business success can be compatible is, of course, not inconceivable. The danger is how the optimism behind this synergy can become a pretext for standard business practices. A huge gap between a financial materiality model of SRI and an ecologically sustainable economy persists. That model does not guarantee cessation of resource depletion and environmental damage, because current financial metrics cannot reflect all environmental values. Moreover, a potent business case continues

---

7. Joshua D. Margolis et al., Does It Pay to Be Good? A Meta-Analysis and Redirection of Research on the Relationship Between Corporate Social and Financial Performance [available at http://www.hks.harvard.edu/m-rcbg/papers/seminars/margolis_november_07.pdf].

* [Subsequent studies, including those discussed below in the Gary excerpt, show a stronger positive correlation between financial and social performance.—Eds.]

> for many environmentally tragic practices, such as the vacuuming of the oceans of marine life and the unabated oil fields exploitation despite looming climate change.[8]

The issue of the financial relevance of ESG concerns is an interesting one, and it will most probably continue to be the most widely researched issue in relation to SRI in academia. I have said nothing here which should be taken to mean that it is absolutely futile to continue trying to establish a (positive) link between CSP and CFP. I have suggested, however, that it seems overly optimistic to build one's case for why SRI is compatible with the fiduciary duties of institutional investors on an appeal to financial relevance alone and, therefore, also the second argument of the Freshfields report seems to leave limited room for SRI among institutional investors. Could an appeal to the non-financial interests of beneficiaries perhaps be more fruitful?

Finding a consensus among beneficiaries

According to the Freshfields report, ... "a decision-maker may integrate ESG considerations into an investment decision to give effect to the views of the beneficiaries in relation to matters beyond financial return. Courts in the U.K. have recognised that trusts such as charities are entitled to exclude investments that conflict with their values and that the concept of beneficiaries' 'best interests' under a general pension trust may extend beyond their financial interests to include their 'views on moral and social matters.' In a similar way, U.S. law permits investments to be excluded where the beneficiaries so consent." According to the third argument of the Freshfields report, then, as long as the beneficiaries so consent, institutional investors are perfectly allowed to take ESG considerations into account in their investment decisions. Indeed, it is argued that doing so sometimes may obligatory—that is, not taking ESG considerations into account may be a breach of the fiduciary duty of trustees when this is the will of the beneficiaries.

However, exactly how should the appeal to the "will of the beneficiaries" be spelled out? According to the report, the general rule is that taking a certain ESG concern into account only is permissible when you know that all beneficiaries consent to doing so—"[a] decision-maker who chooses to exclude an investment or category of investments on this basis will need to be able to point to a consensus amongst the beneficiaries in support of the exclusion." Now, it is acknowledged that determining what all beneficiaries want seldom will be practically feasible. In the absence of such knowledge, the report suggests that trustees may use certain well-established social conventions as a kind of proxies for the will of the beneficiaries. "Whilst there is little guidance directly on point," the report says, "it can ... be argued that even in the absence of ... express consensus, there will be a class of investments that a decision-maker is entitled to avoid on the grounds that their ESG characteristics are likely to make them so repugnant to beneficiaries that they should not be invested in, regardless

8. Benjamin J. Richardson, Socially Responsible Investment Law: Regulating the Unseen Polluters 383 (2008); see also Benjamin J. Richardson, Keeping Ethical Investment Ethical: Regulatory Issues for Investing in Sustainability 87 Journal of Business Ethics 555 (2009).

of the financial return that they are expected to bring. It is not possible to define the parameters of this class, but it might include investments that are linked to clear breaches of widely recognised norms, such as conventions on the elimination of child labour."

Do these suggestions entail a stronger support for SRI for institutional investors than the previous two arguments? Unfortunately, although the report's general line of reasoning in connection with this argument is inspiring, I do not think it does....

[W]hile the report acknowledges certain practical problems in identifying a consensus among beneficiaries, it seems to assume that a consensus actually exists (or at least can exist) on at least some ESG issues. I suggest, however, that this idea has more than practical problems—indeed, I think it is extremely unlikely that there is a single ESG issue on which all beneficiaries can agree.

... [A] relatively popular research topic in relation to SRI has been the psychological profile of individual social investors and their views on various issues related to SRI. A couple of studies have inquired directly into what ESG issues social investors are most concerned about, for instance, and one found that sales to military purchasers, tobacco and gambling were popular issues, whereas another found that environmental issues and labour relations were most important. According to the authors of the first study, some of the variation in what ESG areas different social investors have strong feelings about could be explained further by dividing them into certain subgroups—for instance, the "sin stock" group, the "human rights/pacifist" group and the "post industrial" group. A couple of other studies have inquired into what investment strategies social investors prefer and one study found considerable support for the kind of investment strategies currently used by so-called ethical funds, although a consistent minority supported more progressive investment strategies. Another study, however, found that social investors were genuinely conflicted when it comes to having to choose one investment strategy over another, and even gave contradictory answers to differently formulated questions about this.

A number of studies ... have shown that people exhibiting certain "pro-social" or "green" attitudes are more likely to invest in SRI vehicles than others, but that many actually choose SRI for the financial returns as well. Quite interestingly, one study showed that over 50% of social investors seem to accept that SRI comes with a cost and would not sell their SRI vehicles even if they substantially underperformed the market....

A lot of further research certainly needs to be done in this area. However, what is interesting in the present context is the incredibly diverse picture of social investors that is beginning to emerge. As far as we presently know, there is simply no such thing as what "typical" social investors care about or want.... [If] there is so much heterogeneity ... among social investors, it seems obvious that there will be enormous heterogeneity in terms of what ESG issues beneficiaries care about—at least for the most common types of institutional investors (e.g. insurance companies and pension funds).

[T]he report [also] suggests that trustees may use certain well-established social conventions as a kind of proxies for the will of the beneficiaries. I think this suggestion is very interesting, but I am not sure whether it really solves anything in the present context. Indeed, it may be noted that it gives rise to a number of problems on its own.

First of all, there is obviously a tension between this idea and the direct appeal to a consensus among beneficiaries. Even though certain social conventions, most obviously national laws and international treaties, to a large extent are the result of democratic processes, this should in no way be taken to mean that exactly everyone agrees with them. Even on the issue of child labour, one may note that some people (and, indeed, some academics) think that giving the children of destitute families jobs at least is better than letting them starve. If the appeal to a consensus among beneficiaries is taken at face value, however, all it seems to take in order for a lack of consensus to persist is that one person disagrees....

Just as the appeal to financial relevance, then, the appeal to social conventions can at best give rather contingent support for the inclusion of SRI by institutional investors. And these arguments actually share a further flaw. It may be noted that international treaties generally are the result of long and complicated political processes, and something similar seems to be true also of other kinds of widely recognised social conventions. That is, it takes a lot of time, awareness and discussion among the general public before anything like a social convention could be said to be in place. However, once again, then, the SRI of institutional investors could only be reactive and never truly proactive—that is, institutional investors are only allowed to take certain ESG concerns into account once the desirability of this has become widely recognised in society. I take it that this conclusion should be regarded in a negative light in the present context. After all, an important driving force of the SRI movement as such is the idea that social investors actually can be a part of the creation of new social conventions, and in changing the way people generally tend to think....

Concluding discussion

The aim of the present article has been to put the arguments of the Freshfields report into some further both empirical and critical perspective. My general argument has been that while the understanding of fiduciary duty outlined by the Freshfields report seems to allow institutional investors to at least sometimes take some ESG considerations into account, the support it gives for SRI is notably contingent and, furthermore, it rules out exactly the kind of SRI which proponents of social responsibility and environmental sustainability should hold in highest regard: proactive cases and socially effective investment strategies. When put into some further perspective, then, I have suggested that—contrary to what most proponents of the SRI movement suggest—the Freshfields report does not call for very much optimism. And if SRI is to become an important force for corporate social responsibility through its adoption by institutional investors, I believe that legal reform is needed....

Benjamin J. Richardson, *Socially Responsible Investing for Sustainability: Overcoming Its Incomplete and Conflicting Rationales**

The following sections examine the major theoretical rationales behind SRI, beginning with the oldest rationale, the complicity-based doctrine. The discussion illustrates the changing pretext for SRI and the increasing attempt to refashion SRI into an investment practice compatible with institutional investors' financial goals and legal responsibilities.

Complicity-Based Doctrine

"Complicity" is sometimes cited as the touchstone for attributing responsibility to investors or companies for social harm, and it informs the SRI policy of the Norwegian Government Pension Fund-Global (NGPF-G), the world's largest sovereign wealth fund. The notion of complicity has considerable legal and ethical heritage,† and its legal connotations have been enumerated most clearly in the area of aiding international crimes and violating human rights.[23] Complicity essentially means indirect involvement by actors in abusive conduct where another party commits the actual harm. It has been a formative ethical doctrine for some SRI practitioners because investing in companies can lead to one being regarded as an accessory or accomplice to their misdeeds. The complicity doctrine can also be understood in terms of the *methods* of SRI, it being associated most commonly with divestment from problematic entities that one wishes to eschew association with.

When Norway sought to develop SRI regulations for the NGPF-G, it appointed a committee of experts to advise on the appropriate normative framework. The committee rationalized "ethical investment" (its preferred phrase) primarily on the ground that the NGPF-G should avoid complicity in gross or systematic breaches of ethical norms relating to human rights and the environment:

> the Committee considers, in principle, that owning shares or bonds in a company that can be expected to commit gross unethical actions may be regarded as complicity in these actions. The reason for this is that such investments are directly intended to achieve returns from the company, that a permanent connection is thus established between the ... Fund and the company, and that the question of whether or not to invest in a company is a matter of free choice.[24]

The committee elaborated that the substantive moral criteria to judge such "gross unethical actions" should be informed by international agreements on environmental

* Originally published in 2 Transnational Environmental Law 311 (2013). Reprinted with permission.

† [The author earlier traces SRI back to 18th Century American Quakers.—Eds.]

23. John Ruggie, Business and Human Rights: Mapping International Standards of Responsibility and Accountability for Corporate Acts, U.N. Doc. A/HRC/4/35, U.N. General Assembly, Feb. 19, 2007.

24. Norwegian Ministry of Finance, The Report from the Graver Committee § 2.2 (2003).

protection and human rights that Norway supports. It reasoned that while most international obligations apply only to states, companies may aggravate or facilitate violations committed by states, and the NGPF-G might subsequently contribute to companies' misconduct through its stock ownership. While excluding companies from the NGPF-G might influence their behaviour, the committee focused on refusing investment as a means of *avoiding* the Fund's own complicity in ethically problematic activities in addition to any influence achieved by engagement and dialogue with corporate managers.

Legally-binding regulations (misleadingly labelled as "Guidelines") inspired by the above considerations were adopted for the NGPF-G in late 2004 and revised in 2010, with a Council on Ethics concurrently appointed to evaluate potential investments for compliance. The SRI Guidelines specify exclusion of companies related to enumerated products such as tobacco and certain military weapons. The Guidelines also direct exclusion in a secondary category relating to corporate conduct that the Ministry of Finance, on the advice of the Council, believes is "an unacceptable risk that the company contributes to or is responsible for." Such conduct includes:

a) serious or systematic human rights violations, such as murder, torture, deprivation of liberty, forced labour, the worst forms of child labour and other child exploitation;

b) serious violations of the rights of individuals in situations of war or conflict;

c) severe environmental damage;

d) gross corruption;

e) other particularly serious violations of fundamental ethical norms.

Within these categories, which already pitch a high threshold for offending conduct, the "aim is to target [the] worst case[s]." Consequently, some unethical behaviour will be overlooked.

The Norwegian fund's approach is a form of deontological ethics, as also found in older traditions of ethical investing associated with faith-based investors. Deontological ethics judges the morality of our actions in specific features of the acts themselves, regardless of their consequences. One strand of this ethics is the divine command doctrine, associated with morally absolutist stances taken by religious groups. Another deontological approach is Immanuel Kant's theory that morality rests on inherent moral duties discoverable by rational people. Kant believed that through reasoning, rational individuals would reach the same conclusions, providing an objective and universal morality. Natural law theory is yet another variant of the deontological tradition, emphasizing law's inculcation with fundamental moral norms. These ethical approaches can inform SRI that calls for respect for universal, "fundamental" human rights or avoidance of support for "sinful" activities such as gaming or alcohol businesses. This style of SRI is not overtly intended to change the behaviour of shunned companies as an explicit goal, although arguably, like other SRI behaviour, it is implicitly trying to sway the companies in question if only by depriving them of needed capital.

Although the NGPF-G and faith-based investors are renowned for some of the most principled approaches to SRI, the complicity doctrine is not an adequate normative rationale for SRI and cannot comprehensively define the parameters of investor responsibility for sustainability. First, complicity has a negative orientation, focusing on avoiding association with actors who are perpetrating harms, rather than encouraging investment portfolios that prioritize sustainability. Avoiding companies that waste the environment leaves untouched the need to *promote* positive practices. A second deficiency is that complicity places the threshold for divestment or other investor sanctions too high, requiring *gross* violation of human rights or *severe* environmental damage, for example; but much injustice or ecological degradation arises incrementally from actions or omissions that, viewed in isolation, might seem trivial. As Judith Lichtenberg explains, harm is "essentially aggregative: there is nothing intrinsically harmful to the environment or other people in burning fossil fuels; the harms depend on the joint effects of many people's action."[33]

Third, complicity may be a problematic ethical standard for a culturally and morally diverse world in which investors have divergent views about "what is right." For example, the moral absolutism of divine command provides no guidance when moral imperatives clash: some social investors categorically oppose investing in nuclear power while some might believe this form of energy is a climate-friendly alternative to fossil fuels. Moral judgements in Kantian theory are also problematic to defend. As the theory focuses on the reasons behind actions rather than on actions themselves, it can be hard to universalize moral axioms without knowing the motivating reason underlying someone else's action.

A further concern with the complicity doctrine is its conceptual confusion and imprecision regarding the degree of knowledge or assistance necessary to trigger consequences. Notions of "impact" and "influence" are not easily measurable. "Complicity," as a legal concept, can attribute liability to actors in various situations ranging from direct complicity (where one knowingly assists another in committing a legal violation) to beneficial complicity (where one benefits directly from the violation committed by someone else). Thus, at one pole, an actor might be condemned as being complicit for providing practical assistance or encouraging others to commit the harm; at another extreme, merely deriving a benefit from another's human rights abuse or environmental crime might suffice. Clearly demarcating the requisite degree of proximity between investors and the resulting harm to trigger moral or legal responsibility is fraught with challenges. Christopher Kutz suggests that "[g]iven the complex intertwining of capital in a globalized world, it is inevitable that any investment decision would link one to wrongdoing in some form."[35] From a legal perspective, such a "link" can sometimes be established only tenuously, because the chain of causation between the investment

33. Judith Lichtenberg, Negative Duties, Positive Duties, and the "New Harms," 20 Ethics 557, 568 (2010).

35. Christopher Kutz, Responsibility Beyond the Law?, in Human Rights, Corporate Complicity and Disinvestment 64, 74 (Gro Nystuen et al. eds. 2011).

and the resulting harm may be weak. Thus, some scholars of criminal law and human rights law invite abandoning the complicity doctrine.

Although complicity is not a comprehensive rationale for SRI and can only capture a few, particularly salient environmental issues, it has garnered some influence in financial markets through the related concept of "reputational risks" to those associated with problematic businesses. For example, the Australian ANZ bank denied a loan worth AUD $2 billion to ... a forestry company wishing to build a pulp mill in Tasmania, apparently due to reputational concern associated with the project's grave environmental impact. The SRI industry is also pioneering more nuanced methods to quantify the economic value of environmental and social performance to a company's brand name, in order to help investors factor such performance into their decision-making. Reputational value can be significant. Robert Eccles summarizes that "studies have found that only twenty-five percent of a company's market value can be attributed to accounting book value, with the remaining seventy-five percent based on an assessment of value created by intangibles, such as strategy, product innovation, people and customer loyalty."[38] Yet, reputational risk to companies or their financiers is not a proxy for all underlying societal concerns, and most investors will only respond to the usually more limited "financial materiality" of the reputational risk, rather than its unadulterated ethical significance.

Leverage-Based Responsibility

A second commonly advanced rationale for SRI is that it provides a means for investors to *improve* the social and environmental performance of companies and the economy at large. This rationale hinges on the belief that social investors should use their available leverage to influence the behaviour of targeted companies. As Wood explains, "[t]he kernel of a leverage-based approach is the proposition that, in some circumstances [an entity] has a responsibility to exercise its leverage over actors with whom it has relationships in an effort to improve that state of affairs."[39] Thus, rather than basing the morality of investing on any intrinsic goodness or wrongness by deference to human reasoning or divine will, this teleological approach to SRI judges morality by the *consequences* of investors' actions. Where an investor can influence a company to do good or to avoid harm, these positive consequences behooves it to invest ethically. This approach has influenced SRI most notably in the South African divestment campaign of the 1970s and 1980s that aimed to topple the apartheid regime. Some commentators believe that the teleological approach can offer a robust framework for SRI by enabling "a clear, simple and direct link ... between harmful corporate behaviour and the moral reasons for opposing it."[41] This rationale of SRI is increasingly associated with corporate engagement, a method by which social in-

38. Robert G. Eccles, Enhanced Business Reporting Consortium Releases Framework to Promote Greater Transparency in Corporate Reporting, The Free Library, Oct. 18, 2005.

39. Stepan Wood, An Argument for Leverage-Based Business Responsibility for Human Rights, 22 Business Ethics Quarterly 63 (2012).

41. William Ransome & Charles Sampford, Ethics and Socially Responsible Investment: A Philosophical Approach 72 (2010).

vestors use their leverage as shareholders or financiers to foster dialogue with companies in the hope of changing their practices and policies.

An important challenge for this SRI rationale is setting credible thresholds and parameters for when investors should seek to exert influence. Most obviously, ethical responsibility can arise where investors have an impact on corporate environmental behaviour established by a causal connection, as when a bank provides a substantial loan for a major development project. Here, the nexus between the actions of the financier and the funded project is clear, and responsibility for taking remedial action (including withholding finance or imposing environmental conditions on the loan, as well as lender liability for any residual ecological damage) should be proportionate to the financier's degree of contribution.

A wider penumbra of responsibility is suggested by some commentators when an economic entity sits within a "sphere-of-influence." This idea is developed cleverly by Stepan Wood[42] and Lene Bomann-Larsen and Oddny Wiggen;[43] they emphasize the diffuse web of relationships that a business or other economic actor may have with associated companies, customers, local communities and other parties. Thus, a financier or investor might share responsibility not because of any specific contributory behaviour, but because of its omissions and failure to exercise leverage over others when it should have and could have made a difference. This wider view of leverage-based responsibility appears in the preamble of the U.N. Global Compact of 2000, and the draft U.N. Norms on the Responsibilities of Transnational Corporations, proposed in 2003. However, the sphere-of-influence yardstick was later rejected by John Ruggie, Special Representative of the U.N. Secretary-General for business and human rights, who argued that it represents "a useful metaphor for companies in thinking about their human rights impacts" outside their own organizational boundaries, but "a more rigorous approach is required to define the specific parameters of [their] responsibility to respect human rights"[46] and it might lead to companies' performing roles that should be played by states. By contrast, the sphere-of-influence yardstick is acknowledged in the International Organization for Standardization's (ISO) recent 26000 guidance on corporate social responsibility.

By this approach, therefore, SRI's rationale stems from the potential of some financial actors to wield positive influence and leverage to promote social and environmental "returns" to society. The expectation arises most directly when a financier has a material connection to a business (e.g., ownership of its securities), where the business itself can make a difference to its environmental and social behaviour through operational changes, and the cost to the financial institution of acting responsibly, such as through corporate engagement, is reasonably affordable. Leverage-based re-

42. Wood, supra note 39.

43. Lene Bomann-Larsen & Oddny Wiggen, eds., Responsibility in World Business: Managing Harmful Side-effects of Corporate Activity (2004).

46. John Ruggie, Protect, Respect and Remedy: A Framework for Business and Human Rights, U.N. Doc. A/HRC/8/5, April 7, 2008, at 19.

sponsibility to invest sustainably is thus not an absolute and open-ended standard, but rather, is qualified depending on the specific context and circumstances.

As for the complicity rationale for SRI, leverage-based responsibility can only push SRI so far. The theory is attractive and persuasive in regard to regular business corporations, but less applicable to financial institutions and markets. First, it does not provide a compelling rationale for investors to take action when they lack leverage or influence. Even if a financier cannot sway a specific company, it may still be in its long-term financial self-interest to take account of environmental impacts such as climate change.... Second, in many financial transactions it would be impossible to satisfy the criterion of a "material connection" or lesser threshold of a "web of influence;" the array of relationships between corporations and the financial sector is immense and diverse. The financial ties are tenuous and fleeting, such as in a large pension fund in which "the average traded firm ... [is] just one stock in large diversified portfolios."[48] Investors participate in financial markets through many layers and chains of intermediaries, and even the very largest actors, such as sovereign wealth funds like the NGPF-G, typically own only a wee fraction of the total shares issued by an individual company. Relatedly, much incremental and occasional environmental harm cannot be captured by a leverage-based standard of responsibility, because individual contributions to consequences are not easily ascertained or quantified. Such circumstances require more nuanced judgements of culpability. Thus, while investors' collective influence may be significant, that of an individual fund in relation to any specific company is typically greatly diluted and difficult to discern. As with complicity, rationalizing SRI on its basis to leverage positive consequences can fail to capture many dimensions relevant to the sustainability of the financial economy at large.

Furthermore, as a matter of current practice to overcome, most financial institutions would baulk at the suggestion that they have a responsibility to exercise leverage. Even among social investors, most disavow any pretence of being surrogate regulators, as they do not view themselves as qualified, capable or authorized to police the market. Only a minority of deeply ethical investors, such as those associated with religious and activist groups, would regard their mission as including civilization of the market. The rest of the financial industry largely views itself as mostly just passively tied to its clients and borrowers, and not meant to meddle in their policies and operational practices unless those policies and practices overtly jeopardize the industry's financial interests. Thus, social investors face formidable challenges in impressing upon the financial sector a responsibility to govern the market for sustainability more broadly.

The Universal Owner (UO) Thesis

The UO thesis, proposed by Robert Monks and Nell Minnow[50] and elaborated by

48. Gordon Clark & Eric Knight, Implications of the U.K. Companies Act 2006 for Institutional Investors and the Market for Corporate Social Responsibility, 11 University of Pennsylvania Journal of Business Law, 256, 266 (2009).

50. Robert Monks & Neil Minnow, Corporate Governance (1995).

James Hawley and Andrew Williams,[51] is both a descriptive proposition about how some institutional investors already behave and a normative theory about how they all should. It implies that large institutional investors are sufficiently diversified in the economy that they should be motivated to curb environmental pollution and other harmful externalities. Global banks holding substantial and diverse lending portfolios may also be considered to have such "universal" characteristics. Hawley and Williams explain:

> [b]ecause of their widely diversified portfolios universal owners effectively own the economy as a whole by owning a small portion of almost every company with marketable equity. As such, the portfolios' performance—hence their ability to provide for beneficiaries—depends more on the overall health of the economy than on the fortunes of any particular company.[52]

Because the UO approach posits that the portfolios of the biggest financial institutions are of such a size that they effectively "own the economy," their fiduciary mandate to safeguard their assets is effectively a mandate to safeguard the economy by being attentive to social and environmental costs and benefits. These investors should be self-interested in the health and sustainability of the entire economy because they "have no interest in abetting behaviour by any one company that yields a short-term boost while threatening harm to the economic system as a whole."[53] As their investment portfolios are closely tied to the overall health of the economy, universal investors should be concerned about any ecological impacts that might erode financial returns. The related notion of the "civic investor" is advanced by Franck Amalric in his characterization of pension funds' structural interest in caring about environmental externalities.[54]

Expressed differently, the UO or civic investor thesis suggests a way to resolve, in the context of financial markets, the generic collective action paradox ... where seemingly rational choices for individuals are irrational for society collectively. In contrast to lone investors with incentives to exploit market failures for personal gain, which ultimately leaves all worse off as the externalities accumulate, UOs should be motivated to act in the interests of all.

A few institutional investors acknowledge the UO thesis explicitly as a rationale for their SRI practices. The British Universities Superannuation Scheme (USS) declares "its role as a Universal Investor. Here, the Fund has an interest in minimizing externalities and market failures (e.g. pollution or weak corporate governance controls) that would affect economic performance." Also, the policy of the French Pension Reserve Funds ... explains that the "performance of investments does not depend only on the impact of the financial and extra-financial strategy of the companies, but also

---

51. ... James Hawley & Andrew Williams, The Universal Owner's Role in Sustainable Economic Development, 9 Corporate Environmental Strategy 284 (2002).

52. Id. at 286.

53. Stephen Davis, Jon Lukomnik & David Pitt-Watson, The New Capitalists: How Citizen Investors Are Reshaping the Corporate Agenda 18 (2006).

54. Franck Amalric, Pension Funds, Corporate Responsibility and Sustainability, 59 Ecological Economics 440 (2006).

on the impacts that they generate for the industry in which they operate or for the whole economy." Thus, the French fund believes "[a]n analysis of these externalities, positive or negative, and therefore of the environmental and social sustainability of corporate strategies and their implications for the community, is necessary."

In practice, some institutional funds appear to be implementing this "universal" approach, investing positively in social and environmental initiatives while seeking to bolster their portfolio returns. The California Public Employees Retirement System (CalPERS) has recently invested U.S. $800 million in infrastructure projects, and the Teachers Insurance and Annuity Association—College Retirement Equities Fund (TIAA-CREF) has contributed U.S. $50 million to Good Energies Inc. for energy efficiency projects. The NGPF-G has also initiated a positive investment program to deliver environmental or social returns in addition to financial returns, and has published an "expectations" document regarding companies' management of risk factors relating to climate change. However, such examples do not represent how most financial institutions invest, and the extraordinary growth of financial markets in recent decades has coincided with a significant decline in the health of the global biosphere.

The UO thesis has some conceptual weaknesses that suggest that such a shift in investor practice is no assurance that the environmental footprint of the financial sector would materially improve. First, the thesis cannot explain how environmental externalities in aggregate may become internalized in the economy. Many externalities, such as disappearance of species or toxics in the food chain, can occur without manifesting any discernible economic cost, at least not in the near-term. Some noble attempts have been made to quantify such economic costs; a study by two U.N. bodies in 2008 calculated the cost of the major types of ecological externalities caused by the world's largest 3,000 companies at U.S. $2.15 trillion. Another report prepared for the U.N. evaluated the price of environmental damage worldwide to which the companies in a representative investment portfolio contribute, and estimated these in 2008 to be U.S. $6.6 trillion or 11 per cent of global gross domestic product (GDP). The report expects such costs to grow to U.S. $28.6 trillion (18 per cent of projected global GDP) by 2050. However, it is misleading to extrapolate that "a large proportion of these externalities were internalized by firms owned by universal investors, actively reducing the value of other firms in the portfolio."

While an economy-wide investor might be willing to scrutinize the externalities of individual companies, the economy as a whole does not necessarily internalize all those costs. Markets lack an internal mechanism to constrain the economy's total resource use or pollution load within biosphere limits. While many investors are surely aware that climate change is both a serious environmental and economic problem, they struggle to coordinate their activities to limit investment in fossil fuel industries or other sources of global environmental pressure in a competitive market. (Such coordination typically requires governmental intervention, such as through a carbon cap-and-trade scheme.) Also, some environmental values are too remote temporally or spatially for markets to recognize. In any event, any UO would presumably not be interested in externalities proportional to their impact on social welfare, but rather, only in those corresponding to their adverse effect on the prosperity of the economic assets the fund holds. Thus, we cannot assume that investors view the current health of the economy as a whole as a proxy for the long-term health of the biosphere.

Further criticisms of the UO thesis or its assumptions can be made. One is that financiers commonly focus on the credit risks of individual borrowers or the financial risks of a specific security. While investors design diversified portfolios to minimize overall financial risks, they tend to evaluate assets on a case-by-case basis (especially in the case of project financing loans). Thus, constraints arise when institutions have characteristics of UOs but rely on one-off or narrowly framed analytical techniques in evaluating financial transactions. Another criticism derives from the management of investment portfolios. The portfolio of large institutional investors is commonly dispersed over several asset management companies, possibly resulting in each portfolio being narrower than the original "universal" portfolio (e.g., because they focus on a specific geographic region or industry sector). Moreover, as portfolio management is commonly delegated to specialist fund managers hired on limited-term performance contracts, pressures for short-term or opportunistic investing intensify. Finally, the argument that UOs invest responsibly because they are accountable to a broad investor base is questionable. While institutional intermediaries have given mass society a stake in the financial markets, these funds do not represent all stakeholders in society, especially the poor or unemployed, and they do not represent future generations. In sum, it is unpersuasive to proclaim that simply because an investor with an economy-wide portfolio is potentially exposed to an array of externalities, that that investor will or should thereby "internalize" those costs in its financial decisions....

An Alternate SRI Rationale and Fiduciary Standard for Long-Term Investing

If SRI is to thrive and become more influential in the market, it must more cogently articulate the symbiotic relationship between the sustainability of the economy and those who invest in it. Because ecological systems function over indefinite time horizons, valuing the future is essential. It is not good enough simply to eschew companies that morally offend (as in the complicity doctrine) or seek to change their behaviour only when an individual investor has influence (as in leverage-based responsibility). These approaches leave unaddressed the importance of promoting sustainable development and fail to consider how a fund's beneficiaries may benefit in the long term from a socially responsible stance even if the fund cannot change the behaviour of others today.

The UO thesis better recognizes the financial materiality of environmental and social issues compared to other SRI rationales, but it has some limitations, including its focus on very large institutional funds (rather than investors generally), its emphasis on the spatial, economy-wide scale of investing (rather than its temporal scale over the long term) and its failure to take seriously the need to address systemic market failures to safeguard the environment. While proponents of the UO thesis certainly refer to the importance of investors taking a long-term perspective, they do not elaborate how such a perspective can be achieved and the barriers to overcome. The UO thesis captures the long-term orientation mainly indirectly as a criterion for managing costly externalities, though the challenges to overcoming the discounting of future costs and benefits and other market failures are largely glossed over. Tellingly, the SRI industry's most widely ratified code of conduct designed explicitly for universal owners, the 2006 UNPRI, omits any reference to a "long term" approach in its key six principles even though the UNPRI preamble declares that institutional investors "have a duty to act in the best long-term interests of [their] beneficiaries."[102]

Investing for the long term provides a conceptually clearer benchmark for financial institutions. It provides a better assurance for taking into account environmental externalities because such costs may be latent and often do not fully manifest for many years. A long-term approach also requires an emphasis on both avoiding harm and promoting good. A far-sighted outlook can also mitigate impatience and thus foster more careful and diligent decision-making. And it is not always necessary to define ex ante the temporal period covered by "long term;" the sustainability paradigm mitigates the perceptual barriers people face in valuing the future over some indeterminate time frame or conceptualizing the needs of posterity. Its focus is maintaining core ecological services and functions *now*, and keeping depletion of renewable resources within sustainable harvest rates. Part of that sustainability agenda also requires greater understanding of the past in order to save the future. If sustainability is merely measured against the state of the environment today, it may fail to assure enduring ecological health given so much previous pollution and resource depletion. In framing baseline conditions to guide investing for the long term, it is thus important also to have a program of positive investment for restoration and rehabilitation of damaged landscapes.

On the other hand, social issues such as respect for human rights and poverty alleviation, which are also issues for some social investors, are not as easily accommodated within the financial tools and metrics of financial markets and are perhaps better addressed through more traditional legal approaches.... In any event, ensuring that development respects ecological parameters should, in turn, improve social welfare and respect for human rights. Many unabated environmental problems such as pollution can engender social injustices when the poor or marginalized bear the brunt of the harm.

Though there are incipient tendencies in the SRI industry towards this temporal shift to long-term sustainability—evident in the establishment of prescient investor groups such as the U.K.-based Marathon Club and the French-based Long-Term Investors Club—significant barriers to marathon investing remain.... Planning over decades defies the normal outlook of most investors and, indeed, is beyond most types of institutions or individuals. Short-termism and impatience is rife in global financial markets. The fetishistic focus on short-term performance may involve in-

102. UNPRI, The Six Principles, available at http://www.unpri.org/about-pri/the-six-principles/.

flating current profits at the expense of the long-term health of a fund or firm, or using short-term trading tactics that ignore the underlying value of businesses. One potent indicator of short-termism is the high turnover of corporate securities; the average holding period for shares listed on the New York Stock Exchange has plunged from about seven years in the 1940s to just over five years in 1970 and down to six months in 2009. Significantly, these trends towards short-termism have generally coincided with the growth of institutional investing, directly contrary to the expectations of the UO thesis. These impatient investors may suffer financially over the long term through "decreasing market efficiency, reducing investment returns, and impeding efforts to strengthen corporate governance." Such findings are in addition to the costly depletion in natural capital that may not be fully accounted for until many decades.

The challenge is to elaborate the conceptual and legal framework and practical tools to guide and operationalize investing with a long-term outlook. The current divergence between the business and ethical case for sustainability is a significant impediment for SRI practice, but mainly one in the short term; with enough time, they should converge. Shifting the market towards an enlightened, long-term focus can be substantiated by the sustainability paradigm, a framework for indefinitely safeguarding ecological integrity and a healthy biosphere. A substantial body of norms and procedures on sustainability has evolved in the area of environmental law and policy that could help inform its application to the financial economy. For example, the legal concept of the precautionary principle could help with the appraisal of economic activities that pose uncertain risks but potentially irreparable environmental harm. But additional specific measures are needed that are tailored to financial markets and the fiduciary law context.

The SRI industry and legal reformers must focus on procedural standards rather than disciplining rigid adherence to specific performance outcomes, because a sustainable investment portfolio depends on many variables and contexts. In legal terms, the pathway to inculcate this new direction is through the prudent investing standard of fiduciary and trusts law, which is informed mainly by the collective market practice rather than legislative prescription. So far, that market has egregiously herded investors towards a limited range of unimaginative practices out of fear of being seen as unorthodox and thus risking liability. As Keith Johnston and Frank de Graaf explain, "what functioned as a 'prudent expert' fiduciary standard 30 years ago has become more of a 'lemming standard' that increases the severity of booms and busts and discourages adoption of improved practices that are not yet used by peers."[112] A different market convention that underpins a more socially responsible view of "prudent" investing is needed. Essentially, "prudence" must mean extensive environmental due diligence, appropriate valuation of future costs and benefits, and more selectivity in

112. Keith Johnston & Frank de Graaf, Modernizing Pension Fund Legal Standards in the 21st Century, Network for Sustainable Financial Markets, Consultation Paper No. 2, February 2009, available at: http://www.oecd.org/corporate/ca/corporategovernanceprinciples/42670725.pdf.

the composition of investment portfolios, with a view to long-term financial performance and sustainability.

In turn, a reformulated notion of prudent investing can help disarm concerns that SRI does not directly and materially benefit financial beneficiaries.... Fiduciary law already recognizes that the duty of loyalty owed to beneficiaries does not exclude providing collateral benefits to others, such as would be the case in the promotion of sustainable development: the standard is usually framed to act in their *best* interests, as against their *sole* interests. The underlying fiduciary and trust law standard of prudent investing can also, to some extent, evolve flexibly in response to the ensuing shift in the best practice conventions of the market. As the American Law Institute's authoritative restatements on trusts law enjoin: "[t]rust investment law should reflect and accommodate current knowledge and concepts. It should *avoid* repeating the mistake of *freezing its rules against future learning and developments.*"[114] As it becomes recognized that prudence requires investing in sustainability, fiduciary law in turn can reinforce the collective market practice. Yet, given the entrenched market attitudes and practices that militate against such change, legislative intervention to codify and clarify the parameters of fiduciary responsibility is probably necessary in order to behoove fund managers and trustees to practice SRI. For instance, legislation governing pension funds could stipulate that fiduciary responsibility must be measured not merely against near financial returns but also weighted to take account of best environmental practices.

Several specific building blocks to creating this new fiduciary ethos of prudent investing should be introduced. First, there must be far greater SRI research into the economic value of ecological services and resources, and public-private partnerships to sponsor such research must be forged to counter the risk of industry-bias. Second, financial accounting and reporting must use appropriate discount rates that do not undervalue long-term environmental costs and benefits, and such information should be incorporated into the valuation of financial assets. Third, decision-making within the financial industry must be more transparent and inclusive to enable new perspectives. Revised investment protocols that steer markets towards the long term should be developed in collaboration with other societal stakeholders such as environmental organizations, trade unions and the state. Some emerging collaborative investor networks that operate transnationally that could be harnessed for this purpose are UNEP-FI, as noted earlier in this article, and CERES (Coalition for Environmentally Responsible Economies). Such initiatives would strengthen the putative "global administrative law" character of SRI standards and protocols, which are important in order to compensate for the deficits in the reach of national fiduciary law beyond state borders. The voice of non-investor groups must be included in order to ensure that public interest considerations are incorporated. Fourth, governments should manipulate the economic incentives for acting in the long term, such as through taxes

114. American Law Institute (ALI), Restatement (Third) of Trusts § 227 (1992) (my emphasis).

on short trading in corporate securities and capital gains tax deductions for patient investors. And fifth, public sector financial institutions such as sovereign wealth funds (SWFs) should show leadership in forging new SRI approaches that emphasize the long term through positive investment in sustainable development. In a transnational economy, SWFs ... are best placed to revamp their SRI legal mandates to play this leadership role. Helpfully, the foregoing strategies do not require rigid prescriptive judgments on what a sustainable future looks like, but provide tools to nudge investors towards it.

The main task to resolve within fiduciary law would be how to judge whether a financial trustee has behaved appropriately when the impacts of today's decisions may not become apparent for many decades. In other words, how can we judge now whether a fund is acting correctly over the long term? One response would be for fiduciary law to enshrine prophylactic rules such as duties to consult, undertake research and make informed decisions that are likely to be conducive to long term investing. In other words, compliance with fiduciary finance law would be demonstrated by adherence to procedural standards of due diligence. This would help overcome the problems ... about how to quantify the relationship between investing socially and beneficiaries' financial interests.

The foregoing recommended shift towards long term and patient investing would not necessarily entail jettisoning entirely the other rationales for SRI canvassed in this article. Indeed, the long-term outlook could provide an additional layer to them, with each rationale guiding more specific and nuanced investor action, such as eschewing investments that may be ecologically sustainable but nonetheless still morally questionable for a given individual who does not wish to be "complicit." However, the existing rationales could not necessarily always stand untouched from the perspective of promoting sustainability. Concerning the UO thesis, which has the narrowest conceptual distance to the approach advocated in this article because it also recognizes the financial materiality of environmental performance, it is not good enough simply to advocate long-term investing when the UO thesis assumes that institutional investors are and will remain broadly diversified across the entire economy (as "universal" investors). Instead, a long-term investor may need to shun some sector sectors, thereby becoming a "sectoral" investor who focuses on supporting a narrower range of sustainable and responsible businesses. Many fossil fuel industries, for example, might have no place in the portfolio of a sustainability-focused investor.

In sum, the foregoing argument sketches an alternate rationale and amended legal framework for SRI that arguably is more isomorphic with the environmental sustainability agenda. Moving in this direction, however, requires an equally critically assessment of the limitations of the existing rationales for SRI, as this article sets forth. The UO thesis is an important innovation in making SRI more relevant to the environmental challenges facing the global economy, offering a more comprehensive approach to such challenges than that of other SRI rationales. However, the thesis has structural limitations that are best overcome by adopting a clearer temporal orientation to SRI coupled with supportive fiduciary and procedural reforms to governance of investing.

Susan Gary, *Values and Value: University Endowments, Fiduciary Duties, and ESG Investing*[*]

Ever since the interest in SRI began, researchers have wondered whether a decision to use SRI in building a portfolio will lead to lower returns for the portfolio.... Two themes emerge from a review of recent research. First, in the majority of portfolios under study the use of SRI strategies has had a neutral or positive effect on returns. Second, the use of ESG investing as a strategy, in contrast with screening, may improve returns. The studies refute the old idea that [SRI] necessarily leads to underperformance. Before turning to the empirical studies, this section reviews the now out-of-date concerns about diversification.

Diversification and Modern Portfolio Theory

... [T]he prudent investor standard adopted in [the Uniform Prudent Investor Act] is based on the concepts of modern portfolio theory, and modern portfolio theory emphasizes the importance of diversification as a way to reduce risk in the portfolio. Any restriction on the universe of potentially available stocks could reduce the risk-adjusted return of the portfolio. The use of negative screens,[†] a common strategy in the early development of SRI, limits the universe of available stocks, so some commentators have argued that the restriction necessarily results in costs to the portfolio.

... Andreas Hoepner analyzed portfolio diversification in connection with the use of ESG criteria and found that although using negative screens reduces the number of stocks available, a firm's ESG rating reduces its specific risk and therefore improves portfolio diversification by reducing specific stock risk.[154] Hoepner found that negative screening produced a diversification penalty, but best-in-class screening produced a diversification bonus.

Renneboog, ter Horst, and Zhang studied the question of diversification by measuring net selectivity. They found that the SRI and non-SRI funds did not differ significantly in net selectivity, and therefore did not differ in costs of diversification. They noted that this finding is consistent with "the classic view that a well-diversified portfolio does not require a large number of stocks...."[158] Comparing SRI funds with each other, the authors found that returns increased with the number of screens—more screens led to better returns. The authors conclude: "This finding supports the hypothesis that SRI criteria help fund managers to pick stocks."[160]

---

* Originally published in 42 Journal of College and University Law 247 (2016).

† ["Negative screening" involves removing or "screening out" poor-ESG investments from consideration; an alternative method ("positive" or "affirmative screening") entails considering only investments with strong ESG records.—Eds.]

154. Andreas Hoepner, Portfolio Diversification and Environmental, Social or Governance Criteria: Must Responsible Investments Really Be Poorly Diversified? (2010).

158. Luc Renneboog, Jenke ter Horst, & Chendi Zhang, The Price of Ethics: Evidence from Socially Responsible Mutual Funds 20 (May 1, 2007), available at http://ssrn.com/abstract=985265.

160. Id. at 25.

There Must Be a Cost

In a 2007 article, Dylan Minor observes: "according to fundamental economic principles, there must be a net *financial* cost to SRI."[161] He then analyzes SRI and non-SRI funds against three principles: (1) supply and demand, (2) portfolio theory's emphasis on diversification,[163] and (3) externalities.[164] Minor's conclusion, after testing these principles, is that the cost that "must" occur cannot be seen. He finds no statistically significant difference between the SRI and non-SRI funds. He then says that perhaps the cost does not appear because SRI managers are superior to non-SRI managers, and that superior performance compensates for higher management fees. He suggests that the superior results for the SRI managers could come from working with a more narrowly defined universe of stocks, because the narrowing may allow SRI managers to find value in stocks overlooked by "the masses." Thus, limiting diversification may have contributed to better performance. He does not identify as a possible reason for better performance by the SRI managers the idea that the externalities that SRI managers consider help them make better choices....

Another article by authors who assume there must be a cost to SRI due to economic principles has gotten attention in connection with discussions about fossil-fuel divestment. Mark Kritzman and Timothy Adler used a Monte Carlo simulation to find a cost to a portfolio when a percentage of otherwise available stocks are randomly excluded.[171] The problem with Kritzman and Adler's methodology is that their simulation does not simulate the way an SRI fund actually works.

Kritzman and Adler explain that their simulation only applies to non-actively managed funds, [but as] Adam Kanzer, the Managing Director and General Counsel of Domini Social Investments, points out ... all SRI funds are actively managed.[173] Decisions about which stocks to include or exclude are not made randomly, as in [a Monte Carlo] simulation. In some cases, a fund might exclude all stocks in a particular sector, for example tobacco stocks or oil and gas stocks, but in that case the fund manager would then construct the portfolio with that information in mind. Further,

---

161. Dylan B. Minor, Finding the Financial Cost of Socially Responsible Investing, 18 Journal of Investing 55 (2007). The full sentence reads: "This study's purpose is to show while there may be no net total cost (i.e., financial and social costs and benefits) with SRI, according to fundamental economic principles, there must be a net financial cost to SRI." Id. at 54.

163. ... Portfolio theory says that constrained choices should result in a diversification cost.

164. ... Externalities include non-financial criteria like environmental events and corporate social performance. Id. at 63.

171. [Timothy Adler & Mark Kritzman, The Cost of Socially Responsible Investing, 35 Journal of Portfolio Management 52 (2008).] Monte Carlo simulations are used in finance to model the probability of different outcomes based on random variables....

173. [Adam M. Kanzer, Exposing False Claims about Socially Responsible Investing: A Response to Adler and Kritzman 2 (Jun. 4, 2013), available at http://www.advisorperspectives.com/newsletters13/Exposing_False_Claims_about_Socially_Responsible_Investing.php] ("All forms of social investment are forms of active management, because SRI involves a process of principled decision-making. Even passively managed SRI funds track indices that are themselves actively managed (compare, for example, the management of the MSCI KLD 400 Social Index with the Russell 3000). Truly passive SRI is a contradiction in terms.")....

economic as well as social or environmental reasons may be part of the decision to screen a category of stocks. Kanzer writes, "Each of these decisions [in selecting stocks to include or exclude], often driven by moral concerns, carries a set of financial implications. One fails to see this by viewing the world through the distorting lens of so-called good and bad companies."[175]

... SRI as currently practiced is complex and involves careful analysis of both financial and extra-financial factors. ESG investing as a strategy focuses on factors that may have financial consequences for a company but may not be reflected in the company's market value and therefore may improve returns for investors. The simulation might have the most relevance in connection with divestment, which removes stocks on a list from an existing portfolio. However, divestment does not remove stocks randomly, and any analysis of the consequences of divestment would need to examine the industry subject to removal. Divestment of fossil-fuel stocks might have different financial results than divestment of tobacco stocks. Further, other decisions for that portfolio will be made based on the knowledge of which stocks were removed, so the portfolio can be adjusted accordingly (and not randomly)....

Why ESG Factors Have Financial Consequences

A question in considering whether the use of ESG factors will improve performance is whether the environmental, social, and governance information that will affect a company's performance is already reflected in the company's financial data. If the market and the financial indicators already reflect all of the potential social and environmental benefits that could affect the company, the ESG factors will contribute no additional information. Under some circumstances, consideration of ESG factors may lead to that information. The two hypotheticals that follow provide examples of the types of information that might not be included in the financial indicators.

Assume that Company A uses international suppliers that keep costs down by allowing employees to work long hours under unsafe conditions. The suppliers have had no dramatic problems, and the supply chain has never been broken. Company B uses suppliers that conform to production standards it imposes. Factories are safe and employees work under conditions that minimize on-the-job accidents. Company B has also faced no dramatic problems. Company B may have a slightly higher cost for the goods produced by its suppliers, and that information could make Company B's financial data look slightly less favorable than Company A's data. What the data will not reflect is the possibility that a catastrophic fire in a factory used by one of Company A's suppliers could kill hundreds of workers. The repercussions for Company A could include a break in the supply chain, loss of consumer goodwill if the company is linked to the supplier, and even a consumer boycott. The financial impact on Company A could be significant, but current financial data probably does not reveal that risk. The risk is a long-term risk, and merely a risk, not a certainty, but in a process that purports to evaluate financial risk, the risk to Company A may be missing if the evaluator uses only traditional financial data.

175. Id. at 4.

Adam Kanzer explains the reason that SRI/ESG information should improve analysis as follows:

> The core financial performance claim for SRI is that corporate value depends upon numerous relationships, including those with employees, customers, communities and the natural environment. Companies that manage these relationships well should prosper in the long run, and those that damage them will face obstacles to their long-term success.[183]

ESG factors relate to a company's long-term value, and will have a greater impact when viewed on a long-term basis. Short-term financial strategies are less likely to benefit from ESG analysis, but an investor concerned about long-term value may benefit from an investment strategy that incorporates an ESG analysis....

Research on SRI and ESG Performance

Various academic and financial industry studies have attempted to understand whether different types of SRI strategies have a negative, positive, or neutral effect on portfolios.... Two generalizations follow from a review of the studies. First, the use of ESG factors in analyzing stocks independently or in building portfolios may improve investment results. Second, the performance of SRI funds compared with non-SRI funds has been, in most cases, neutral or positive. Few of the studies show negative results when comparing SRI funds with non-SRI funds, and none of the empirical studies support the idea that SRI necessarily leads to lower returns.

While some studies found outperformance using ESG factors and comparison of fund performance with benchmarks provides information about the performance of the fund, any attempts to draw conclusions must be done carefully. The difference in performance between an SRI fund and a conventional fund may relate to any of a number of variables, including the skill of the fund manager, investment style, time period, and decisions about when to be in cash and when to be in the market. Thus, the difference may not be caused by the decision to invest based on an SRI policy. Another caution is that some of the studies focus on the strength of the companies in the study rather than on current returns to investors. That is, a determination of out-performance may not translate into immediate benefits to investors. However, the long-term strength of companies may benefit investors over the long-term by reducing risk.

... A [2012] meta-study published by the Climate Change Investment Research division of Deutsche Bank found that companies with high ratings in CSR and ESG overperformed in corporate financial performance.[196] The study examined more than 100 academic studies of responsible investing, 56 research papers, two literature reviews, and four meta-studies. The report categorized the studies based on CSR, ESG (and E, S, and G separately), and SRI, and then looked for a correlation between

183. Kanzer, supra note [173], at 3....

196. Deutsche Bank Group, Sustainable Investing/Establishing Long-Term Value and Performance (2012).

scores in those three categories and the cost of capital (equity or debt), corporate financial performance (both market based returns and accounting measures), and fund returns for funds based on these factors (most funds were SRI). The report is useful both because of the large number of studies included in the research and because the analysis differentiated between different investment strategies.

For securities, the Deutsche Bank report found "overwhelming evidence" that companies with high ratings for CSR and ESG have a lower cost of capital, both debt and equity. The study found "compelling evidence" that high ratings in either category correlated with overperformance in corporate financial performance. The correlations for SRI securities were weaker, but more studies found a positive or neutral correlation between high SRI ratings and overperformance in corporate financial performance than negative. With respect to fund performance, most studies were neutral or mixed. The report found no studies that reported underperformance at either the security or fund level.

A prior meta-study, conducted by the United Nations Environmental Program Financial Initiative (UNEP-FI) and [the consulting firm] Mercer, examined 20 academic studies and 10 broker studies that examined the link between ESG factors and investment performance.[204] Most studies found the use of ESG factors led to neutral or positive results. The UNEP-FI and Mercer report characterizes the academic studies based on the type of responsible investing strategy studied. Fifteen of the studies focused on screening, three on activism, one on ESG integration, and one was described as ESG/screening. Of the studies that focused on screening, two showed a positive relationship between ESG and performance, six were neutral (with one neutral-positive and one neutral-negative), and three were negative. One activism-focused study was neutral and all the other strategies showed positive results. Thus, only three of the 20 studies found a negative relationship and all of those were studies that analyzed [negative] screening as a strategy.

Of the 10 broker studies discussed in the UNEP-FI report, half were thematic in nature and the other half used some form of quantitative analysis. Although the authors of the thematic studies all discussed positive effects of ESG factors on performance, because no quantitative tests were conducted, the meta-study reported these five studies as "neutral." Of the other studies, three were positive and two were neutral. Only one study examined screening as a strategy, and it reached a neutral result.

An international study found that consideration of CSR in stock selection neither strengthens nor weakens portfolios.[211] Christophe Revelli of the KEDGE Business School in Marseilles, France, and Jean-Laurent Viviani of the Université de Rennes 1 examined 85 studies and 190 experiments to test the relationship between SRI and

---

204. Asset Management Working Group of the United Nations Environment Programme Finance Initiative & Mercer, Demystifying Responsible Investment Performance (Oct. 2007), available at http://www.unepfi.org/fileadmin/documents/Demystifying_Responsible_Investment_Performance_01.pdf.

211. See Christophe Revelli & Jean-Laurent Viviani, Financial Performance of Socially Responsible Investing (SRI): What Have We Learned? A Meta-Analysis, 24 Business Ethics: A European Review 158, 161 (Apr. 2015)....

financial performance while also analyzing researcher methodologies with respect to dimensions of SRI. They found that differences between the studies they examined resulted from the differences in the dimensions studied. The authors conclude that CSR does not result in stronger or weaker returns compared with conventional investments. They suggest that because SRI does not increase costs, investors can invest in SRI funds without financial sacrifice while addressing the investors' social, environmental, and ethical concerns.

A 2007 study analyzed SRI funds around the world to test the authors' hypothesis that investors pay a price for SRI screening.[216] The authors studied the risk and return characteristics of SRI mutual funds, grouped in the following regions: the U.S., the U.K., Europe (other than the U.K.), and "the Rest of the World," and compared them with conventional (non-SRI) benchmarks from the U.S. and the U.K. Confirming the authors' hypothesis in part, the study found that SRI funds in Europe and Asia-Pacific countries underperformed benchmarks on average 5% per year. In contrast, however, in the U.S. and the U.K. the returns of SRI and non-SRI funds were not statistically different. The finding of underperformance in Europe supports the hypothesis "that ethical considerations influence the stock prices and that ethical firms are overpriced by the market" but only in certain countries.[221] The study did not differentiate by type of SRI strategy, so it is possible that differences in strategies may have led to differences in results.

In a 15-year study, Robert G. Eccles, Ioannis Ioannou, and George Serafeim analyzed the governance and organizational structure and financial performance of 180 U.S. companies.[222] Half of the companies had "voluntarily integrated social and environmental issues in their business models and daily operations"[223] by 1993 and half had few or no sustainability policies. The companies in the first group were dubbed High Sustainability companies and those in the second group were Low Sustainability companies.

The researchers matched and then compared companies in the two groups so they could "shed light on the organizational and performance implications of integrating social and environmental issues into a company's strategy and business model through the adoption of corporate policies."[226] Among other organizational findings, High Sustainability companies were more likely to create a process to engage stakeholders in identifying risks and opportunities, to be long-term oriented, and to measure and disclose more non-financial data. The researchers found that High Sustainability companies outperformed Low Sustainability companies in both stock market performance and accounting performance. Further, the market underestimated the future profitability of the High Sustainability companies compared to the other group.

---

216. See Renneboog et al., supra note [158].

221. Id. at 13.

222. Robert G. Eccles, Ioannis Ioannou, & George Serafeim, The Impact of Corporate Sustainability on Organizational Processes and Performance (Mar. 1, 2013), available at http://ssrn.com/abstract=1507874.

223. Id. at 2.

226. Id. at 3.

In June 2015, Cambridge Associates and the Global Impact Investing Network (GIIN) announced that they had collaborated to create the Impact Investing Benchmark. The new benchmark gathers data from 51 private equity and venture capital funds with a range of social objectives. The funds operate across sectors, target both risk-adjusted market rate returns and social impact objectives, are available to institutional rather than individual investors, and were launched from 1998 to 2010....

[An analysis of] the funds in the benchmark found the returns of funds launched from 1998 to 2004 in line with or better than returns of non-impact investing funds.[234] More recently launched impact-investing funds trailed their non-impact investing comparators, but the report suggests that the returns for the impact investing funds were largely unrealized at the time of the analysis. Emerging market impact investing funds raised from 1998 to 2004 outperformed their comparators 15.5% to 7.6%, while later funds lagged behind their non-impact investing peers. Many smaller impact-investing funds, defined as those raising less than $100 million, outperformed their smaller non-impact investing counterparts, especially the older funds.

The new benchmark will become more useful as the sample size and available data grow, and the report notes that definitive conclusions on performance would be premature, but the report observes: "Despite a perception among some investors that impact investing necessitates a concessionary return, the Impact Investing Benchmark has exhibited strong performance in several of the vintage years studied."[238] The report also notes that the findings support the view that manager selection and due diligence are key to superior returns and risk management, in impact investing just as much as in non-impact investing.

Other studies generally have found either neutral or positive effects of ESG factors on investment performance....

After reviewing these recent studies, it is interesting to reflect on an article published in 1997, in the early years of SRI expansion after the end of the anti-apartheid divestment period.[254] Lloyd Kurtz reviewed the available literature but explained that only a few studies existed at that time. At the outset of his paper he notes three "apparent contradictions:"

> First, despite apparently unavoidable diversification costs, the universe of SRI stocks does not appear to have systematically underperformed the market portfolio in recent years, on either a nominal or risk-adjusted basis....
>
> Second, some management science studies have found that factors monitored by social investors, such as environmental policies, employee relations, and R&D spending, could be associated with positive abnormal returns. The results are mixed, however....

---

234. See Amit Bouri et al., Introducing the Impact Investing Benchmark (2015), available at http://www.thegiin.org/binary-data/Introducing_the_Impact_Investing_Benchmark.pdf.

238. Id. at 19.

254. See [Lloyd Kurtz, No Effect or No Net Effect? Studies on Socially Responsible Investing, 6 Journal of Investing 37, 39–40 (Winter 1997)].

> The third contradiction is born of the first two. Money managers who have handled both screened and unscreened accounts for many years report that, over time, the performance of these accounts does not differ materially.[256]

The studies discussed in this section have helped to explain the contradictions. SRI strategies do not result in "unavoidable diversification costs" and SRI strategies, in particular ESG investing, can improve financial investment results....

Discussion Questions

1. Sandberg writes that the "financial relevance" argument for SRI is very limited, citing a lukewarm 2007 meta-study of earlier studies. Does the more recent Gary excerpt cast doubt on his conclusion? If so, is the Freshfields report saying a lot when it states that fiduciaries must consider ESG factors insofar as they are financially relevant?

2. Do the studies showing the business case for SRI (and sustainable business) surprise you? After all, manufacturing efficiency, conservation efforts, and climate-change risk management seem to all make business as well as environmental sense, do they not?

3. Despite the Freshfields report, many financial institutions still ignore ESG considerations. Why do you think this is the case? Fiduciary II (the follow-up report, five years after Freshfields) blames "cultural impediments to SRI"—for instance, lagging social norms. What, if anything, can be done to advance social norms about SRI?

4. What about "ethical" as opposed to "business case" SRI? If by definition there is no financial argument for purely ethical SRI, the Freshfields report leaves us with tie-breaker scenarios, which should be very rare, and situations where the fund's beneficiaries direct, or would direct, fiduciaries to practice SRI tenets.

5. How often do you think individual investors would direct their money to be managed in a socially responsible way? Sandberg notes the total amount of SRI in the U.S. is more than $2.71 trillion. Why do you think some investors choose SRI?

6. Would you invest in a "green" mutual fund if it made no difference in your financial return? How about if it meant sacrificing some amount of financial performance? Do you ever purchase a more expensive product or service because it is more environmentally or socially conscious?

7. Sandberg concludes that "legal reform is needed." Do you agree, or do you believe the market will sufficiently encourage SRI on its own? If you agree with Sandberg, what sorts of legal reforms do you recommend?

8. After his discussion of SRI rationales, Richardson proposes that the prudent investor standard incorporate a long-term view of the firm as well as environmental considerations. Do you agree?

9. Are you swayed by all of the studies analyzing the "business case" for SRI? If so, do you believe fiduciaries of non-SRI funds may or should incorporate ESG considerations into their investment strategies?

---

256. Id. at 37.

Chapter 8

Sustainability and Contract

Contract law is based on the basic principle of private law that individual parties autonomously and freely decide what their respective obligations will be. While the contracting parties usually bargain in their own best interests, they may find that supporting sustainable environmental and social practices is good for the economic bottom line. As the first article points out, a corporation may decide to "self-regulate" and draft a corporate code, make warranties to its customers, or submit to third-party certification. Companies may also impose sustainable business requirements on their suppliers, as the second article illustrates with Wal-Mart and other major multinational companies. Businesses often are fearful of new legislation and regulations, as well as lawsuits, and thus may engage in "good neighbor" agreements (or negotiated agreements with the regulator or with the community) to ward off lawsuits or pre-empt the legislation regulation, as the third reading explores. Finally, when a natural resource is scarce, it may be imperative for businesses to enter into voluntary agreements with each other to restrict the harmful activity and ensure that the flow of business revenue continues from the protected resource. When reading this chapter, consider all the types of agreements (mergers and acquisitions, bank loans, insurance, etc.) that could play a role in encouraging sustainable business practices.

Carola Glinski, *Corporate Codes of Conduct: Moral or Legal Obligation?*[*]

There are a considerable number and variety of self-regulatory instruments. Some were initiated by national or supranational institutions,[1] some were negotiated with non-governmental organizations (NGOs) or trade unions, and others have been unilaterally adopted by individual enterprises, groups of enterprises or by business associations.

With a view to the relationship between CSR [corporate social responsibility] and the law, one can find two extreme positions. The long-standing opinion among business, NGOs and also many lawyers is that codes of conduct and other self-regulatory instruments create moral obligations at best but have no legal effect whatsoever. At

---

* Excerpted from The New Corporate Accountability: Corporate Social Responsibility and the Law (Doreen McBarnet, Aurora Voiculescu & Tom Campbell eds. 2007).

1. See, e.g., the Global Compact initiative by Kofi Annan, unglobalcompact.org; the EC Commission's communication on Corporate Social Responsibility, 346 (2002).

other end of the spectrum, some academics have developed rather generalizing ideas of legal pluralism which might lead—very generally speaking—to the recognition of self-regulation of the different social sectors (e.g. the business sector) as a source of law that is as valid a source law as formal national or international law.[2] [This excerpt] focuses on already possible private law effects of corporate self-regulation in order to bridge, at least to a certain extent, the legal gap public law leaves....

In essence, two types of corporate self-regulation can be distinguished: *published* codes of conduct, guidelines or agreements on the one hand; and *internal* regulation in contracts, management handbooks or simply through the internal organization by multinational enterprises of their environmental and safety management on the other hand.

... Published self-regulation usually aims at market effects. Typical examples are codes of conduct, social and environmental reports, and labels and messages transported in advertisements. They are used as marketing tools, designed to build confidence for improving a corporation's reputation and market share. This is particularly true for private regulation of social and environmental standards for production in, or trade with, developing countries. Nevertheless, companies can be surprised to find that they are held to the promises they made in voluntary codes or other public statements, as happened to Nike.[3]

Relevant legal effects can be based on the legal protection of the addressees' legitimate expectations in the compliance with these self-regulatory instruments in contract law, as well as in the law of misleading advertisement that forms part of the law of unfair competition.

Two potential legal effects must be distinguished. First, public statements on one's own environmental conduct in low-standard countries, in whichever form, can of course be binding on the author of such statements. Second, widely publicized codes of conduct may be able to set a standard with an effect that goes beyond their immediate signatories. This means that they may be able to set a standard that all traders or producers of the same line of business must comply with unless they indicate otherwise. Thus, they may have an external effect on third parties that have not been involved in the regulatory process or that have not agreed to the code of conduct.

Defining one's own behavior: setting individual standards

There cannot be any doubt that a corporation is allowed to make binding promises concerning its own behavior by establishing or signing a (corporate) code of conduct. To varying extents, all legal orders recognize the protection of confidence in promises.

2. See in particular the contributions [of Gunther] Teubner....

3. [See Kasky v. Nike, Inc., 45 P.3d 243 (Cal. 2002), cert. granted, 539 U.S. 654 (2003), where activist plaintiffs sued Nike under California's false-advertising law regarding assertions the company made about its labor practices.]

Where, in a business context, one party attracts confidence by another party, the other party must be protected by law. The key element consists of a (self-)binding behavior that makes the impression of being serious. Sociological research into codes of conduct and other self-regulatory instruments has revealed that they all use the language of promises. Otherwise they fail in their intention to gain, or regain, reputation. The only crux, in particular with advertising messages, can lie in their vagueness. However, even from vague statements, or promises, one can extract a binding minimum content. Another issue is that codes of conduct sometimes explicitly declare not to be binding, and there appears to be wide belief that promises in codes of conduct can be invalidated in such a way. However, declarations on the non-binding character of a statement are inconsistent with the expectations the statement aims to create otherwise. Thus, they can only destroy the addressee's expectations if they are as visible and as prominent as the confidence-building features.

The recognition and support of self-regulatory instruments by official authorities, such as the UN Global Compact logo, increases public trust further. Also, discrepancy in expertise and knowledge between the producer and the consumer makes the consumer more dependent on the producer's information, so that his/her trust in the producer's statements deserves even more protection. Besides, ethical consumption is the only way in which people can take influence on production patterns in low-standard countries.

Contracts of Sale

In the first place, binding promises can be introduced into a contract. Contract law is based on the principle of party autonomy that allows the contracting parties to determine freely their mutual obligations according to their own needs. The consent of the parties is to be assessed objectively. Although the contracting parties usually pursue their own interest, this does—of course—not exclude altruistic intentions and expectations, which equally deserve the protection afforded by contract law. A typical example would be the purchase of a 'fair trade' product.

Nevertheless, former German sales law, and also the sales law of other countries, was fairly restrictive in recognizing the binding effect of such promises, in particular where they were not made by the seller but by the producer and where they did not relate to the physical properties of goods but only to production patterns.

These deficiencies can and must be overcome by interpreting the EC sales law provisions on the conformity of a good with the contract (and their national implementations) in such a way that the conformity requirement includes all the qualities that determine the value of a product. According to Article 2(2)(d) of the Consumer Sales Directive 100/44/EC ... the concept of conformity extends not only to product-related characteristics of the goods in question, such as their toxicity, but also to the circumstances under which they were produced. Especially where the price of the ethically produced goods is higher than the price of goods produced otherwise, the specific production patterns are usually decisive for the purchase. The only reservation to be made is that public statements must relate to the 'specific characteristics' of a good.

The emphasis is on the term 'specific.' This means that public statements must relate to facts that can be proven, which is usually the case with labeling or codes of conduct but not necessarily with advertising spots, although a fact content can usually be extracted from any statement on social or environmental performance.[5]

Sales law, therefore, offers the consumer or the trading partner the opportunity to enforce promises that are related to the circumstances of the production. This can be of particular relevance if it comes to mass protests against specific producers that have been identified to act against their public statements, as in the case of the anti-Nike movement. Furthermore, consumer associations may sue for injunctions, stopping sellers from selling goods that are not in conformity with the producers' public statements without correcting these statements.

Michael P. Vandenbergh, *The New Wal-Mart Effect: The Role of Private Contracting in Global Governance**

[M]ore than half of the largest firms in eight retail and industrial sectors impose environmental requirements on their domestic and foreign suppliers. This contracting ... reduces externalities by translating a complex mix of social, economic, and legal incentives for environmental protection into private contractual requirements....

Unilateral firm standard setting often involves standards tailored to the particular operations of the adopting firm, or to the particular pressures of the firm's customers, investors, or employees. An example is the set of environmental standards imposed on suppliers by General Electric. GE began including environmental, health, and safety terms in its supplier contracts in 1997. Although the standards themselves are not publicly available, based on public comments by GE managers, the standards appear to be GE-specific standards and may have been adopted before many of the collective standards were finalized. In addition, GE does not rely on external auditors to monitor suppliers but conducts audits using its own employees....

Private standards, whether collectively or unilaterally generated, influence firm environmental behavior in exporting countries through contracts between importing and exporting firms, and through internal implementation when a [multinational corporation] operates in the exporting and importing countries. This Article focuses on the former....

Supply Agreements

The nature and extent of environmental terms in cross-border supply agreements are difficult to evaluate empirically. Few public sources exist of these supply agreements, corporate disclosure is often not required, and the literature on environmental supply-chain contracting typically makes only anecdotal mention of the extent of the

5. [The author's description of German sales law largely comports with sales law in the United States. See, e.g., UCC § 2-313 (express warranties); James J. White & Robert S. Summers, Uniform Commercial Code (5th ed. 2000).—Eds.]

* Originally published in 54 UCLA Law Review 913 (2007). Reprinted with permission.

contracting. Nevertheless, analyses of the publicly released policies and statements of firms in several sectors, and of supply agreements filed with the SEC, suggest that environmental supply-chain contracting requirements are widespread and may be an important source of global private environmental governance.

An analysis of the publicly available environmental policies and statements of firms in eight sectors confirms that a large number of firms impose environmental requirements on their suppliers and that these requirements often extend to suppliers in developing countries. To examine the extent of these environmental requirements, and to provide a basis for evaluating both the incentives for firms to adopt environmental supply-chain contracting requirements and their likely influence on suppliers, the sectors included in the analysis below include firms that are likely to have global supply chains. For each sector, the analysis examines the top ten firms in the sector (either by U.S. or by global sales) as identified by Hoovers, a Dun & Bradstreet affiliate. The study identifies supply-chain contracting by examining public disclosures of environmental supply-chain requirements.

To evaluate the breadth of supply-chain contracting and to provide insights into the incentives that induce firms to impose supply-chain requirements, the analysis includes sectors comprised of large retail firms, mixed retail and industrial firms, and nonretail industrial firms. Three sectors are comprised principally of firms that have retail operations in developed countries and do little or no manufacturing (the discount and variety retail, home improvement and hardware retail, and office products retail sectors), two sectors are comprised principally of firms that have both retail and industrial operations (the automobile manufacturing and personal computers sectors), and three sectors are comprised principally of firms that do not have retail operations (lumber and wood production, aluminum production, and industrial machinery and equipment manufacturing).

The top ten firms in the discount and variety retail sector in the United States are Wal-Mart, Kroger, Costco Wholesale, Target, Walgreens, Albertsons, Safeway, CVS, Ahold USA, and Loblaw. The top ten firms in the sector have a combined total of approximately $697 billion in annual sales. Of the ten largest firms, half (representing $495 billion in sales) state that they impose environmental requirements on suppliers. The remaining firms (with $202 billion in sales) do not indicate whether they impose environmental standards on suppliers.

Wal-Mart is the largest firm in the sector, with $315 billion in annual sales worldwide, 1.2 million employees in the United States and 600,000 in other countries, and 60,000 suppliers. The potential for Wal-Mart to influence firms in developing countries is vast. For example, Wal-Mart imports roughly $15 billion in goods from China annually. Wal-Mart also has been the subject of NGO-led protests regarding a variety of environmental, health, safety, and labor issues, and recently began adopting a number of new policies. In 2006, Wal-Mart announced that it was "educating" suppliers about packaging reduction and other sustainability measures and was doubling its selection of organic products. In addition, it announced plans to purchase wild-caught fish for its North American market only from fisheries certified by the MSC

[Marine Stewardship Council]. The company will purchase fish only from MSC-certified suppliers and will give noncertified suppliers a three-to five-year grace period to develop programs for certification. Wal-Mart's position as the largest seller of groceries in the United States, and a major seller of wild-caught fish, has generated ripple effects throughout the grocery and fishing industries.

The largest of the other firms in the sector that state that they impose environmental requirements on suppliers is Costco Wholesale ($60 billion in sales), which requires suppliers to comply with local environmental laws. Costco also "strongly encourages" suppliers to adopt "above and beyond goals" regarding hazardous materials handling and pollution control if not required by local laws. Target ($53 billion) and Albertsons ($40 billion) require their suppliers to comply with the environmental laws of the host country. Ahold ($37 billion) imposes standards on suppliers of fish and coffee.

The largest of the remaining five firms that do not disclose whether they impose environmental standards on suppliers is Kroger ($61 billion in sales), which is the second largest firm in the sector and the second largest seller of groceries behind Wal-Mart. In addition, Walgreens ($42 billion), Safeway ($38 billion), CVS ($37 billion), and Loblaw ($24 billion) do not disclose whether they impose standards on suppliers.

The home improvement and hardware retail sector had sales of roughly $291 billion in 2005. Home Depot and Lowe's control more than a third of the U.S. market. The top ten companies in the United States in this sector, representing over $178 billion in sales, are Home Depot ($81 billion), Lowe's ($43 billion), Wolseley ($20 billion), CCA Global ($9 billion), Menard ($7 billion), Sherwin-Williams ($7 billion), Stock Building Supply ($4 billion), 84 Lumber ($3 billion), Ace Hardware ($3 billion), and Do it Best (sales figures unavailable).

The two largest firms in the sector, Home Depot and Lowe's, impose environmental requirements on their suppliers. Two of the other firms, Wolseley and Stock Building Supply, also appear to do so, although their disclosures are somewhat ambiguous. In the aggregate, these four firms comprise $152 billion in sales, or 85 percent of all sales by the top ten, and 52 percent of all sales in the sector. Firms that do not disclose whether they impose environmental requirements are CCA Global Partners, Menard, Sherwin-Williams, Ace Hardware, Do It Best, and 84 Lumber.

Home Depot is perhaps the best-known example in the sector of a firm that imposes environmental contracting requirements on suppliers. Home Depot has roughly 2000 stores generating annual sales of approximately $82 billion. Home Depot responded to roughly six hundred protests by Rainforest Action Network by agreeing to purchase as much FSC-certified wood as it can locate. Lowe's, which has 1250 stores generating $43 billion in sales, apparently followed suit after a meeting with, and two phone calls from, NGO representatives.

The ten largest firms in the United States by sales in the office products retail and distribution sector are Staples, Office Depot, OfficeMax, Unisource, IKON, United Stationers, Corporate Express, S.P. Richards, School Specialty, and Global Imaging

Systems. The sector has more than $300 billion in annual sales in the United States, and the top ten firms account for $61 billion in sales. The three top firms are Staples ($16 billion in sales), Office Depot ($14 billion), and Office Max ($9 billion). Environmental groups have targeted all three of these firms with boycotts or public relations campaigns directed at inducing the firms to adopt stronger environmental protection practices. The two largest of these firms, Staples and Office Depot, representing $30 billion or almost 50 percent of the sales of the top ten firms, state that they impose environmental requirements on their suppliers. The other firms in this sector do not disclose whether they impose environmental requirements on their suppliers.

The ten largest automobile manufacturing firms in the world are General Motors, Toyota, DaimlerChrysler, Ford, Volkswagen, Nissan, Honda, Peugeot, Fiat, and Renault. The automobile manufacturing sector, including suppliers, accounted for more than 13 percent of all global exports by manufacturers in 2003. Of the ten largest automobile manufacturers, six impose some form of environmental requirements on their suppliers (General Motors, DaimlerChrysler, Toyota, Ford, Nissan, and Fiat), and one has stated plans to do so in 2007 (Renault). These seven firms account for $910 billion in sales, or 77 percent of the sales for the top ten firms in the automobile manufacturing sector.

The major automobile manufacturers headquartered in the United States impose a variety of environmental requirements on their suppliers, whether domestic or foreign. General Motors required first-tier suppliers to achieve ISO 14001 certification by the end of 2002. DaimlerChrysler does not yet require ISO 14001 compliance by all suppliers but anticipates doing so. It does require its suppliers to comply with host country environmental laws and "encourages them to pursue proactive environmentally responsible practices." Ford Motor Company required that its first-tier suppliers achieve ISO 14001 certification by 2003 and has stated that "[s]uppliers that did not meet the deadline [for ISO 14001] are not eligible for Q1 status, which is a prerequisite for ... future Ford business. We also encourage our suppliers to extend the benefits of improved environmental performance by implementing similar requirements for environmental management systems in their own supply base."

Several automobile manufacturers headquartered in Japan have imposed environmental management and performance standards on their suppliers. For example, Toyota has adopted environmental requirements for its suppliers that include ISO 14001 certification, compliance with the law of the host country (although it is unclear if this applies only in North America), and a ban on approximately 450 substances. Although Nissan indicates that it requested rather than required ISO 14001 certification of its suppliers by March 2005, it asserts that 95 percent of its suppliers gained certification with ISO 14001 or Japanese Eco Action 21 by that date, suggesting that the request functioned as a requirement. Although Honda encourages ISO 14001 certification by its suppliers, it is unclear if it requires ISO 14001 adoption or certification.

The approaches taken by the European automobile manufacturers vary but are generally less extensive than those imposed by Japanese and U.S. automakers. Volkswagen and Peugeot do not assert that they impose ISO 14001 or other environmental requirements on their suppliers. Fiat appears to require ISO 14001 certification but only of suppliers that are large companies. Renault does not indicate whether it currently imposes any environmental standards on suppliers but states that it intends to do so by 2007.

The top ten firms in the personal computers sector in the United States had global sales of roughly $336 billion in 2005. The top ten firms in the sector are Hewlett-Packard ($87 billion in sales), Sony ($64 billion), Dell ($56 billion), Toshiba ($54 billion), NEC ($41 billion), Apple Computer ($14 billion), Acer ($7 billion), Fujitsu Siemens Computers ($6 billion), Gateway ($4 billion), and Lenovo ($3 billion). Hewlett-Packard and Dell account for roughly half of the personal computer market in the United States.

The seven largest firms in the sector (Hewlett-Packard, Sony, Dell, Toshiba, NEC, Apple Computer, and Acer), accounting for $323 billion or 96 percent of sales, all impose environmental performance requirements on their suppliers and most impose law compliance requirements. Two (Sony and Acer) also require environmental management systems (EMSs), and two (Hewlett-Packard and Toshiba) prefer suppliers who adopt EMSs.

In addition, several of these firms have not only announced environmental procurement requirements but also have imposed explicit contract terms on their suppliers. An example is Hewlett-Packard, which has adopted the Electronic Industry Code of Conduct (EICC), along with other firms in the personal computers and related sectors such as Celestica, Cisco, Dell, Flextronics, Foxconn, IBM, Intel, Jabil, Lucent, Microsoft, Sanmina SCI, Seagate, and Sony. The EICC requires firms that adopt it to impose standards only on next-tier suppliers, but it encourages participants to "regard the code as a total supply chain initiative." Hewlett-Packard not only has implemented specifications for suppliers but has required suppliers to execute an agreement that supplements supply contracts. The three smallest firms in the personal computers sector (Fujitsu Siemens Computers, Gateway, and Lenovo), accounting for 5 percent of sales, do not disclose whether they impose environmental requirements on suppliers.

In addition to these ten firms in the personal computers sector, several other companies that make computers or other electronic products as part or all of their business have imposed environmental terms on their suppliers. For example, in 2004 IBM adopted supplier conduct principles that require suppliers to comply with minimum environmental, labor, health, and safety requirements. The firm adopted the principles after adverse publicity arising from a 2002 NGO report on the disposal of electronic waste in Pakistan, India, and China, and a 2004 report on working conditions in facilities operated by suppliers to IBM and other computer makers.

The top ten U.S. firms in the lumber, wood production, and timber operations sector had combined sales of more than $91 billion in 2005. These top ten firms by 2005 sales are: International Paper ($24 billion), Weyerhaeuser ($23 billion), Georgia-Pacific ($20 billion in 2004 sales), OfficeMax ($9 billion), MeadWestvaco ($6 billion), Bowater ($3 billion), Louisiana-Pacific ($3 billion), Universal Forest Products ($3 billion in 2004 sales), Potlatch ($1 billion), and Sweetheart (recently acquired by Solo Cup, whose 2004 sales were $2 billion).

The timber industry has been the subject of sustained pressure by NGOs, and six of the seven largest firms in the sector state that they impose some type of environmental requirements on their suppliers. All six impose SFI and law compliance requirements on their timber suppliers. Potlatch, the ninth largest firm in the sector, states that it strives to impose FSC standards on suppliers. Together, these seven firms account for $80 billion in sales, or 88 percent of the sales by the top ten firms in the sector. Three firms do not disclose whether they impose standards on their suppliers (Office Max, Universal Forest Products, and Sweetheart/Solo Cup). These three firms are the fourth, eighth, and tenth largest firms in the sector, respectively.

The aluminum production sector includes firms whose principal business is aluminum production and other firms for which aluminum production is a small component of the business. The largest firms in the world whose principle business is aluminum production by sales are Alcoa ($30 billion), Norsk Hydro ($25 billion), Alcan ($20 billion), and Nippon Light Metal ($5 billion). Of these four firms, none discloses that it imposes environmental requirements on its suppliers.

The top ten firms in the industrial machinery and equipment manufacturing sector had sales of roughly $211 billion in 2005. According to Hoovers, the top ten firms in this sector worldwide are United Technologies ($47 billion in sales), Caterpillar ($41 billion), Mitsubishi Heavy Industries ($24 billion), John Deere ($22 billion), ABB ($22 billion), MAN Aktiengesellschaft ($17 billion), Komatsu ($14 billion), Illinois Tool Works ($13 billion), CNH Global ($12 billion), and Parker Hannifin ($9 billion). Of these ten firms, seven state that they impose some type of environmental requirements on their suppliers and three do not. The seven firms account for $154 billion, or 73 percent, of the $211 billion in sales by the top ten firms in the sector.

The seven firms that impose environmental requirements on their suppliers—United Technologies, Mitsubishi Heavy Industries, John Deere, ABB, MAN Group, Komatsu, and Illinois Tool Works—vary in size and in the type of requirements imposed. United Technologies began to impose environmental standards on some suppliers in 2005, although the content of the requirements is unclear.

Mitsubishi Heavy Industries also imposes environmental standards on suppliers, although again the content is unclear. John Deere imposes environmental law compliance requirements. ABB requires ISO 14001 certification. MAN Group imposes environmental law compliance and EMS [Environmental Management System] requirements on its suppliers. Komatsu requires that suppliers attain ISO 14001 certification or an equivalent by 2008. Illinois Tool Works requires environmental compliance of its suppliers.

As mentioned above, three of the ten firms in this sector do not state whether they impose environmental standards on their suppliers. The three are Caterpillar, CNH Global, and Parker Hannifin. These three are ranked second, ninth, and tenth, respectively, in sales among the top ten firms in the sector.

Although no publicly accessible database exists for material supply agreements entered into by firms that are not publicly traded in the United States, publicly held firms in the United States are required to file copies of material agreements with the SEC, and the SEC makes them available in an electronic database. An analysis of the supply, acquisition, and credit agreements filed with the SEC during the fourth quarter of 2001 identified a smaller number of supply agreements (52) than acquisition (314) or credit agreements (514). Publicly traded firms may file fewer supply agreements with the SEC because any one supply agreement is only occasionally likely to be material, and thus most supply agreements are not subject to SEC filing requirements. Of the supply agreements filed with the SEC during this period, 21 percent (11 of 52) included environmental provisions.

These supply agreements include several types of environmental provisions of importance for the evaluation of supply-chain contracting as a means of private governance: (1) environmental performance (a requirement to meet an environmental standard even if not required by host country environmental laws); (2) law compliance (a requirement to comply with host country environmental laws); and (3) a requirement to adopt an EMS: any of these agreements included other environmental provisions: Examples include provisions for indemnification, private dispute resolution, post-closing monitoring rights, and reporting environmental matters to the other contracting party.

The existence of these nongovernmental incentives for positive environmental behavior on the global level is suggested by the widespread adoption of the Equator Principles, which often apply to projects that are likely to receive only limited regulatory oversight by the developing countries in which many of the projects will be constructed. The Equator Principles have been adopted by forty-one of the largest private banks, representing roughly $125 billion or 74 percent of the $170 billion in global project finance lending.[122]

Acquisition and Credit Agreements

The potential influence of the global market for corporate transactions on firms in exporting countries is huge. In any given year, many firms purchase all or part of the assets of other firms located solely in other countries or with operations in other countries. In 2001, the total value of cross-border corporate mergers and acquisitions was $594 billion. The global credit market also has the potential for similar influence. For example, according to a recent report, the total value of global project finance lending, which only comprises a part of the global credit market, is $170 billion.

Although no comprehensive assessment has been conducted of the environmental provisions in acquisition and credit agreements involving firms in developed and developing countries, an assessment of the contracts with environmental provisions in the United States provides one indication of what may be occurring on the global level. As discussed above, the SEC requires publicly traded firms to file material agreements,

122. [See http://www.equator-principles.com.]

and it makes those agreements publicly available in an electronic database. A recent assessment concluded that more than 70 percent of the acquisition and credit agreements filed in the fourth quarter of 2001 with the SEC have environmental terms....

Insurance Agreements

Insurance markets also have substantial potential to influence firm environmental behavior in global settings where the firm behavior may be beyond the effective reach of national and international environmental laws. Although an empirical analysis of the extent and influence of insurance contracting on the environmental behavior of firms is beyond the scope of this Article, there are indications that insurance contracting may have important effects. For example, Ronald Mitchell examined the effects of insurance and other requirements on oil tanker discharges of ballast tanks, the largest—although not the most dramatic—source of oil pollution from ships. Mitchell found that although firms largely failed to comply with an international treaty placing limits on ballast discharges, far higher levels of compliance were achieved under a requirement to adopt maritime oil pollution control technology. A factor in the higher compliance levels was the greater ability of classification societies and insurance companies to add the technology-based standards to existing private monitoring programs. In the case of oil tanker discharges, insurance contracting served as a means of enforcing a public international law requirement. Insurers also may be important monitors and enforcers of contractual requirements that regulate firm environmental behaviors not subject to formal legal requirements. The role of global insurance contracting in influencing firm environmental behavior is an area that is ripe for additional research.

Private Contracting as Global Private Governance

... To be effective, the private governance agreements must meet several conditions: (1) widespread adoption in the form of incorporation into procurement policies or into terms in procurement contracts; (2) standards that have content adequate to achieve environmental protection objectives; and (3) adequate implementation of the standards by suppliers.

The data presented above suggest that environmental procurement standards have been adopted by a large number of firms in sectors whose suppliers have the potential to create enormous environmental damage. Firms in seven of the eight sectors studied impose environmental requirements on their suppliers. Of the seventy-four firms included in the study across all eight sectors, 53 percent impose environmental supply-chain requirements. The extent of supply-chain contracting is even more impressive when examined from the perspective of total sales. Of the $2.8 trillion in total sales represented by the seventy-four firms in the study, firms that impose environmental supply-chain requirements account for $2.2 trillion, or more than 78 percent of the total. In short, environmental supply-chain contracting is remarkably widespread among the firms in the sectors studied. Although the firms in this study do not necessarily impose environmental requirements on all of their suppliers or on all goods supplied, the magnitude of the environmental supply-chain contracting identified by the study suggests the potential for substantial impact on the environmental behavior of hundreds of thousands of suppliers around the world.

In turn, there is reason to believe that this private environmental contracting extends private standards to a meaningful swath of several threatened environmental resources. As discussed above, a substantial amount of commerce is conducted pursuant to private environmental contracts, and private standards exist for a variety of important natural resources potentially affected by that commerce. For example, roughly 7 percent of the world's forests are covered by some type of certification program. Similarly, thirty-six of the world's fisheries are covered by MSC certification or are under assessment for such certification.

Although the breadth of the sectors with firms that have adopted environmental supply-chain contracting requirements is impressive, the depth of the requirements is less impressive: There is little indication that many of the requirements penetrate beyond first-tier suppliers. Collectively set standards typically do not require imposition on second- or third-tier suppliers for certification. In addition, although some firms recommend that their first-tier suppliers require second-tier suppliers to abide by environmental requirements, it is unclear whether any firm has required second- or third-tier supplier compliance. To the extent environmental damage arises from second- or third-tier suppliers, many of the standards adopted to date will have little or no impact. This limitation is potentially profound. For example, China is expected to extract $100 billion in natural resources from South America over the next decade, in large part to support its production of consumer products for developed countries.

In addition, Errol Meidinger has noted that the FSC forestry standards are more frequently adopted by suppliers in developed as opposed to developing countries, suggesting that the forestry standards may not be affecting many of the most vulnerable forests. It is unclear whether this developed/developing country dichotomy also exists for other types of standards and supply chains in other business sectors, although there are several indications that environmental supply-chain contracting is occurring with exporting firms in developing countries.[139]

The data also provide insights into firms' incentives to impose environmental requirements on suppliers. The concept of a social license to operate suggests that firms face not only pure legal and economic incentives to behave in a particular way, but also incentives to engender a favorable view of the firm and favorable treatment by customers, shareholders, employees, and the communities in which they operate. In the absence of a favorable view of the firm among this broad group of stakeholders, the firm may be subject to a variety of negative effects, including new regulatory requirements, obstacles to obtaining permits or zoning changes, reduced sales, investors who refuse to buy its shares, reduced employee morale, and community opposition ranging from protests to tort litigation. Although this study does not provide a basis for quantitative analysis of firm incentives, the data presented

139. [Errol Meidinger, The Administrative Law of Global Private-Public Regulation: The Case of Forestry, 17 European Journal of International Law 47 (2006)].

above are consistent with the concept of a social license to operate. Several patterns emerge that provide intriguing indications of the complex mix of social, economic, and legal influences that affect adoption of environmental supply-chain contracting requirements.

At the outset, consumer pressure, whether created by or merely expressed by NGOs, appears to be an important incentive for firms to adopt supply-chain environmental requirements. It is not possible to evaluate fully which firms were targeted by NGOs, but many of the firms examined in the study adopted environmental contracting requirements after NGO public information campaigns or boycotts. Prominent examples of such firms include Wal-Mart, Home Depot, and Staples. Similarly, NGOs targeted many of the banks that ultimately adopted the Equator Principles.

Another possible indication of the role of consumer pressure is that the larger firms in each sector appear to be more likely than the smaller firms to impose environmental requirements. In fact, the largest firm in seven of the eight sectors studied has adopted some form of environmental supply-chain requirements. In most sectors, the largest firms also have been the ones targeted by NGOs. Interestingly, although standard adoption is more uneven among smaller firms, it appears to occur even in the absence of intense NGO pressure. In some cases, smaller firms appear to follow the lead of larger firms. For example, Wal-Mart's adoption of environmental supply-chain contracting appears to have induced other firms in its sector to follow suit. Similarly, although Home Depot adopted its environmental supply-chain requirements only after hundreds of protests by environmental groups, after Home Depot adopted its requirements, allegedly only two phone calls were required to induce its next largest competitor, Lowe's, to follow suit.

Another indication of the role of consumer pressure is that many of the firms in the five sectors that rely on retail sales, including the firms in the retail and mixed retail and industrial sectors, impose environmental requirements on suppliers. Fifty percent of the firms in these five sectors impose environmental supply-chain requirements, and these firms account for 78 percent of the sales among the top ten firms in their sectors. In addition, the industrial sector with the highest percentage of environmental supply-chain requirements by sales (85 percent), lumber and wood production, is also a sector that has high visibility with consumers and that has been the subject of intense NGO pressure.

At the same time, the consumer incentives explanation is far from complete. Although one might expect retail firms and mixed retail and industrial firms to be more vulnerable to consumer pressure and therefore to be more likely to impose environmental requirements on suppliers than industrial firms, the pattern is unclear. For example, although none of the firms in the aluminum production sector state that they impose environmental requirements on suppliers, seven of the top ten firms in the industrial machinery and equipment manufacturing sector (accounting for 73 percent of sales) impose these requirements. In terms of total sales, 72 percent of the total sales in the three retail sectors are by firms that have established environmental supply-chain requirements, as opposed to 81 percent by the firms in the two mixed retail and industrials sectors, and 64 percent by the firms in the three industrial sectors. In short, environmental supply-chain contracting is surprisingly common among industrial firms if consumer pressure is the only important influence on firms.

Other factors that comprise the social license to operate also may be influential. Socially responsible investment (SRI) firms may be pressuring firms in all sectors, although if SRI firm pressure is an important influence, it is unclear why standard adoption is more common among large firms than small firms. The social and personal norms of firm managers and other employees also may affect adoption of environmental supply-chain requirements. These norms may influence decisionmaking directly—for example, a chief executive officer may feel a sense of obligation to reduce the environmental harms caused by the firm and its suppliers—or they may induce a firm to act to avoid the pecuniary costs of adverse effects on employee morale. Again, however, if employee norms and morale are important influences, the relationship with firm size is unclear.

The desire to avoid future government regulation may be consistent with the observed pattern of NGO protests (which may heighten perceived risks of government regulation) and with the adoption of environmental supply-chain contracting by large as opposed to small firms. Yet the desire to avoid future government regulation also falls short as a complete explanation. Many of the importing firms that have adopted environmental supply-chain requirements have adopted requirements, such as law compliance by suppliers in developing countries, that are unlikely to have a meaningful effect on the future regulatory landscape in the developed countries in which the importing firms operate. Similarly, many firms that have imposed environmental supply-chain requirements have done so regarding subjects that are unlikely to be the subject of government regulation in the foreseeable future.

Two pure economic incentives are consistent with the prevalence of large firm adoption of environmental supply-chain requirements. The first is the incentive to assure investors of the supply of raw materials. Large firms may have a sufficiently large demand for raw materials or other goods such that their demand can threaten the long-term availability of some natural resources. As a result, large firms may have incentives to induce suppliers to engage in more environmentally sound practices to assure investors that supplies are sustainable. Wal-Mart confronted this concern regarding the long-term supply of wild-caught fish before deciding to require MSC certification for its North American retail outlets. Asian pulp and paper firms also have confronted these issues regarding whether they have adequate supplies of pulp wood over the time horizons of interest to their investors.

The second economic incentive that is consistent with large firm adoption of environmental supply-chain contracting requirements is the incentive to raise rivals' costs. Large firms may buy sufficiently large quantities of goods that suppliers invest in expensive infrastructure (for example, fishing nets designed to avoid by-catch or to generate sustainable yields) to be in a position to sell to the large firms. To cover these investments, the suppliers then may raise the prices of their goods not only to buyers with environmental supply-chain requirements, but to all buyers. By increasing the price of goods to all buyers, the large firm may reduce the competitive disadvantage it would otherwise face by insisting on more expensive environmental performance by its suppliers.

In sum, although the mix of social, economic, and legal influences is complex, the incentives are sufficient for a surprisingly large number of firms to impose environmental contracting requirements on their suppliers. This new Wal-Mart effect already includes firms with over $2 trillion in aggregate global sales and tens of thousands of suppliers. . . .

After standard adoption, the next critical issue is whether the content of the standards being adopted is sufficient—assuming adequate implementation—to achieve meaningful improvements in environmental conditions. The environmental standards adopted by the firms discussed above can be grouped into three types in terms of their prospects for improving the environmental behavior of suppliers: (1) environmental performance requirements that are independent of or exceed the legal requirements imposed by the exporting firm's host country (for example, FSC wood certification, MSC fish certification, or prohibitions on the use of hazardous materials that are not banned in the host country); (2) requirements to comply with the laws of the host country; and (3) adoption of EMS standards that do not include specific environmental performance standards (such as ISO 14001). . . .

Many firms require only compliance with the laws of the host country. These requirements are likely to lead to meaningful improvements in environmental protection if the host country has adequate but underenforced environmental regulations and if the importing firm monitors and enforces the supplier's regulatory compliance. If the regulations are inadequate, compliance with them may make little difference. Similarly, although in theory the importing firm can enforce a law compliance provision directly, it is much easier to evaluate whether government enforcement actions have been taken than to monitor actual compliance. As a result, even if a country has adequate standards, if its enforcement is lax an importing firm may have difficulty assessing its supplier's law compliance.

Some firms have required that their suppliers adopt an EMS, rather than requiring that they meet environmental performance or law compliance standards. Many EMSs require rigorous systems for the management of environmental matters, and these systems may result in reductions in the environmental harms arising from a firm's operations. At the same time, EMSs generally do not require reductions in a firm's total environmental emissions or harms. For example, ISO 14001 requires firms to set environmental goals for their operations and to make continual improvements, but a firm may comply with the ISO 14001 requirements by setting its goals at very low levels and by making only minimal improvements. Perhaps even more important, if firms set their environmental goals in the form of reductions in environmental emissions per unit of production rather than reductions in total emissions, they can meet their environmental goals in periods of increased production yet have greater total emissions.

The standards thus vary greatly in the extent to which they are likely to generate improvements in the environmental behavior of suppliers. Twenty-four of the seventy-four firms in the study have adopted environmental performance standards, which hold out the prospect of environmental improvements even if the exporting countries' laws are lax. Twenty-two firms require law compliance, which may lead to environmental improvements if public laws are adequate and if private enforcement supplements public enforcement. If the underlying standards or private enforcement are lax, however, the improvements may be negligible. Finally, twelve firms impose EMS requirements. The effect of EMS requirements on firm environmental behavior is unclear.

The effect of environmental supply-chain requirements on firm behavior is a function not only of the standards adopted, but also of whether they are implemented. Although no systematic study has been conducted of the extent to which suppliers have implemented environmental supply-chain requirements, there are a number of indications of the implementation status in several sectors. As to environmental performance requirements, Meidinger concluded that the forest certification programs are "having some effect on forestry practices" and are having some effect on forest policy more generally.[170] The MSC certification program has extended to nineteen fisheries and may extend to dozens more in the near future, although the effect of MSC certification on the sustainable production of fish has yet to be demonstrated. As to law compliance requirements, Petra Christmann and Glenn Taylor found an association between those Chinese firms that have a large proportion of exports and environmental law compliance. They also found an association between firms that have a large proportion of exports to developed countries and environmental law compliance.[171]

As to supplier requirements for the adoption of environmental management systems, Prakash and Potoski, in the study discussed above, concluded that countries whose firms trade with countries that have higher levels of ISO 14001 certification also have higher levels of certification.[172] In short, firms in importing countries appear to be inducing ISO 14001 adoption by firms in exporting countries. Anecdotal information also suggests that suppliers respond to buyer EMS requirements. For example, Ford Motor Company has stated that in response to its ISO 14001 certification requirements, "[b]y mid-2005, 99.5% of Q1 production suppliers had ISO 14001 certification."[173] Similarly, Nissan recently reported 95 percent ISO 14001 adoption among its suppliers. Of course, for EMS requirements to improve environmental conditions, the EMSs themselves must lead to better environmental performance. As

170. Meidinger, supra note [139], at 77.

171. [Petra Christmann & Glen Taylor, Globalization and the Environment: Determinants of Firm Self-Regulation in China, 32 Journal of International Business Studies 439, 450–52 (2001).]

172. [Aseem Prakash & Matthew Potoski, Racing to the Bottom? Trade, Environmental Governance, and ISO 14001, 50 American Journal of Political Science 350, 351–52 (2005).]

173. [Ford Motor Company, Sustainability Report 2004/05: Suppliers, http://www.ford.com/en/company/about/sustainability/report/relSuppliers.htm (last visited Feb. 15, 2007).]

discussed above, it is unclear at this point whether adoption of EMSs actually leads to improved environmental performance.

In the final analysis, for supply-chain contracting to function as an important part of the global environmental governance regime, a broad and deep number of firms must implement standards that will make meaningful improvements in their suppliers' environmental performance. The data discussed above suggest that environmental supply-chain contracting is becoming remarkably widespread. At the same time, the extent of the standard adoption, the content of standards adopted, and the extent of implementation all have potentially serious shortcomings....

Tory H. Lewis, *Managing Manure: Using Good Neighbor Agreements to Regulate Pollution from Agricultural Production**

Contract law offers an alternative method of environmental regulation that successfully promotes sustainable agriculture. By negotiating contracts known as good neighbor agreements ("GNAs"), farmers and local community members can work cooperatively to make farm operations more transparent and environmentally friendly while simultaneously protecting farmers from potential nuisance suits. These agreements, which require self-regulation and public participation, are arguably the best response to the shortcomings of environmental law. After hundreds of years of nuisance law and twenty-five years of command-and-control regulations, agricultural law is ready for a more innovative means of environmental regulation, which comes in the form of GNAs.

Agriculture Requires an Alternative Method of Environmental Regulation

Both common law deterrence mechanisms and regulatory schemes administered by the EPA have benefits and shortcomings. In an effort to combine the approaches to reach an optimal method of environmental regulation, Harvard Law School professor Steve Shavell proposes four factors to consider when choosing whether to apply ex ante statutes and regulations or ex post nuisance actions to cope with a pollution problem.[164] A comparison of the relative amount of knowledge possessed by the regulators and private parties, a polluter's capacity to pay damages, the likelihood of a nuisance suit, and administrative costs should determine which approach is optimal, according to Shavell. For instance, if the regulator possesses more knowledge on the issue than private parties and a nuisance suit is unlikely, then the regulator should sanction the polluter for noncompliance. On the other hand, if administrative costs of enforcing environmental regulations are high and a suit is likely, the agency should permit private individuals to regulate the pollution by filing a nuisance claim.

Even with these factors in mind, these approaches still fail to achieve the optimal balance between regulating the environment effectively and promoting sustainable

---

* Originally published in 61 Vanderbilt Law Review 1555 (2008). Reprinted with permission.

164. [Steven Shavell, Liability for Harm Versus Regulation of Safety, 13 Journal of Legal Studies 357, 358 (1984).]

agriculture. Tort remedies afford farmers few defenses and are difficult to apply in the pollution context because the environmental harms resulting from agricultural production are spread diffusely over a large area. And regulatory regimes that punish polluters by taxing away their benefits from polluting cannot regulate the constant changes in agricultural production effectively. Notwithstanding Shavell's theory, agricultural production requires agriculturists and environmentalists to consider an alternative to the common law and statutory regulation of farm waste.

As an alternative to command-and-control regulatory schemes and common law remedies, a number of industrial facilities across the country have implemented voluntary self-compliance methods to curb pollution and mend relationships with communities. A good neighbor agreement is one method of self-compliance that has been used by large-scale industrial polluters since the 1980s. It is a legally binding agreement negotiated between the stakeholders and industry. The violating industry "agrees to reduce or eliminate pollution risks to the surrounding community." By adapting the concept to the agriculture industry, parties can use these agreements to promote sustainable agriculture and resolve disputes between farmers and neighbors.

Using Self-Compliance and Public Participation to Regulate Pollution

As society seeks an alternative to common law and statutory approaches to environmental regulation, American corporations have adopted a variety of self-compliance programs, indicating that businesses view environmental protection as obligatory rather than optional. In addition, communities have become more active in the regulatory process, using both informal and formal approaches to regulate local polluters. Examples of these approaches include informally picketing in front of polluting companies that fail to adopt stringent environmental standards and formally requiring municipal governments to assess environmental impact statements before granting operating permits to polluters.

Self-compliance programs, which take a variety of forms, have the potential to benefit both the businesses that adopt them and the environment they aim to protect. One common method of self-compliance is the environmental audit, which evaluates a firm's compliance with federal and state regulations and is included in the company's overall environmental management program. To conduct an audit, a firm either hires an independent auditing team or, through the use of its own employees, collects information regarding pollution reduction technology and emissions. When an auditor finds the firm compliant, the firm is heralded as environmentally friendly and benefits from the positive publicity. When an audit reveals noncompliance, however, legal liability becomes a serious risk. Audits are generally less candid than they should be because management wants to protect the firm from such risks. As a result, some states are calling for a self-evaluation privilege that would protect documents and communications collected in the audit and limit the liability to which a firm could be subject for noncompliance. Other states believe the audit information should be discoverable, however, and the uncertainty of liability alone may deter firms from auditing themselves.

In the alternative, a number of communities have become more involved in the environmental regulation of local polluters. Communities sometimes use informal regulations to force polluting firms to comply with community-generated standards. While an informal approach provides communities with a measure of flexibility as to the standards they employ, the penalties that communities may impose on a violator (such as picketing and boycotts) can be costly and disruptive. Furthermore, communities that use only informal methods are at a disadvantage because they do not have sufficient access to information about a polluter's emissions, production processes, or environmental policies.

The Emergency Planning and Community Right to Know Act,[180] a federal initiative that provides local citizens with information about nearby hazardous chemicals and establishes a planning and response program for emergency situations, has assisted some communities by guaranteeing them access to information available in an online database called a toxic release inventory ("TRI"). Unfortunately, the information in the database is organized poorly and is difficult to sift through. Furthermore, the database is only useful if citizens have Internet access, which may inhibit a substantial number of interested parties from using the information. Thus far, only firms that have a high level of emissions and are of a certain size develop TRIs regularly; TRIs are not required for small firms like the average farm.

Communities also have developed more formal methods for local environmental regulation. A community group may conduct an assessment and formulate an impact statement of how it believes the community will be affected if a particular firm either moves into the community or expands its existing operation. City commissions in some municipalities must take into account the firm's impact statement and hold public hearings before granting the firm a permit to expand or build in the area. Likewise, citizens may form community working-groups, comprised solely of local residents, to evaluate upcoming proposals or facilities located within the community. The groups provide notice to the community of upcoming meetings and discussions and present their opinions on the issues raised.

In addition to targeting polluters directly, the public can participate in the EPA's development of environmental regulations that impact local communities. Although regulatory development generally includes a notice-and-comment period for communities to vocalize their concerns, a presumption in favor of the agency's report makes it difficult to amend the agency's planned course of action through comments alone. Furthermore, local community members and farmers do not track every regulation the EPA develops and probably would not submit comments in response to such regulations. As a result of the shortcomings of this requirement, other methods have been used to encourage public participation.

For instance, the EPA may arrange a regulatory negotiation that involves the regulators, regulated parties, and interested parties in rulemaking by encouraging cooperation and problem solving. Although the negotiations allow community groups

180. 42 U.S.C. § 11023(j)....

to be directly involved in the process, the groups that generally participate are well-organized special interest groups rather than local citizens and neighbors who have a variety of concerns with emissions. Furthermore, the negotiations can be very costly since the participants must hire technical experts who can verify their arguments. While regulatory negotiation is a step in the right direction, it may be prohibitively time consuming and expensive for concerned community members and farmers.

Citizen advisory groups are even more representative of the public participation methods than negotiations. Under this method, the sponsoring agency chooses citizens directly affected by the regulations to serve on an advisory board. The advisory board investigates the issue and recommends solutions. Because the board's decisions are not binding, however, the members of the board may have little power to effect change.

Concern with environmental injustice has also improved public participation in environmental rulemaking. Environmental injustice occurs when poor communities disproportionately bear the burdens of environmental hazards. The problem results in part because private citizens do not believe that they have real power to affect environmental decisionmaking. In fact, most major agency decisions are made prior to any public hearings or other solicited public participation, and historically, community groups have made little difference in environmental policies. As a result, communities are not inclined to participate in environmental decisionmaking. In 1994, President Clinton signed an executive order requiring each federal agency to make environmental justice part of its mission. Even so, without equal access to information, communities cannot negotiate on a level playing field with the agencies, industry leaders, and experts.

Good Neighbor Agreements: Merging Public Participation and Self-Compliance

Good neighbor agreements incorporate aspects of public participation and self-compliance into a cohesive method of pollution regulation. These agreements are based on the theory that "citizens and workers should view corporations as neighbors and apply similar standards of behavior to them." Therefore, corporations should not "endanger the lives of the people with whom they share land, water and air." Rather, by developing GNAs, private citizens can hold firms accountable for their contribution to environmental degradation. Since the phrase was first coined in the 1980s, GNAs have evolved into sophisticated tools for environmental regulation. Originally, GNAs granted community groups an informal right to inspect local industries. In the early 1990s, an environmental watchdog group developed the "Minnesota model" for GNAs, which reduced nonbinding emissions goals to writing.[204] Today, most GNAs in the United States are legally enforceable. The terms are always in writing and list the requisite standards that the private firms must meet.

Both local citizens and participating firms benefit from GNAs. The agreements allow citizens to participate in firms' environmental inspections, assessments, planning,

204. [Sanford Lewis & Diance Henkels, Good Neighbor Agreements: A Tool for Environmental and Social Justice, 23 Social Justice Journal 4, 4 (1996).]

and decisionmaking. Community stakeholders work directly with the industry to create solutions for the environmental problems at hand. Firms are enticed to enter GNAs in order to establish positive relationships with local government and employees. A firm's public image affects its ability to obtain loyal workers, the rate at which it is taxed locally (as determined by city officials), and the regulations the community chooses to impose on its operations. GNAs often include provisions by which a firm agrees to provide information to the local community beyond that required by law, reduce emissions below legal requirements, or provide local subsidies to support public health clinics or parks. Because both industries and private citizens seek to benefit from the agreements, parties successfully negotiate GNAs when the relationship between the stakeholders is balanced.

Several major principles work to establish the balanced relationship between a local industry and community stakeholders. These include: (1) ensuring a right of access to information for all parties involved; (2) encouraging stakeholder initiative to work with the polluting firm to develop a GNA; (3) sharing control among all the stakeholders in the participation process; (4) securing parity in decisionmaking; (5) hiring independent experts; and (6) creating an enforceable, holistic agreement that provides shared benefits and includes standards for best management practices.

Equal access to information is, essentially, the key to GNA success. Primarily, stakeholder audits ensure this equal access. Audits provide opportunities for local stakeholders to inspect facilities themselves or oversee an auditing group that performs the inspection. The firm gives stakeholders a right of access to industry documentation on key activities that affect the environment. Equal access generates consensus, and as a result, each stakeholder benefits from the shared information.

In addition to acquiring information, stakeholders must be active in their negotiations. A GNA is not signed until every participant agrees to the terms of the contract; unless parties seek compromise, stalemates can result, destroying a GNA's chance of success. Because of this, it may be helpful to hire independent experts to "bolster the bargaining positions of stakeholders on technical matters." Parties to the agreement should work collaboratively so the terms of the final approved GNA will benefit everyone involved.

Although the total number of these agreements is unclear, there are at least several dozen in the United States today with substantial potential for more. Most often, GNAs are linked to a permit process or serve as settlement agreements in the aftermath of an industrial accident. For instance, the Chevron Refinery in Richmond, California, agreed to a GNA with the West County Toxics Coalition, Communities for a Better Environment, and People Do! in response to CAA violations in 1992. When the refinery sought a state air quality permit for additional manufacturing, the permit was challenged, which led to the GNA negotiations. In exchange for the permit, Chevron agreed to install leakless valves, refuse pollution credits for emissions reductions, and contribute five million dollars over five years to local communities. Likewise, the City of Philadelphia and the Sun Oil Company negotiated the Sun Oil Agreement, a GNA enacted in 1997 to settle a lawsuit that a community group brought against the firm.

The agreement required Sun Oil to invest five million dollars to improve its refinery and reduce emissions. In addition, the firm was obligated to plant trees, construct a bike trail, and fund environmental education programs in the community. Both the Sun Oil and Chevron agreements resulted from the companies' efforts to avoid further litigation and compensate the community for past pollution.

A firm may also be inspired to sign a GNA if it faces the threat of litigation. In 2000, the Stillwater Mining Company in Billings, Montana, agreed to a GNA that addressed environmental concerns after the mine sought permits for expansion and was threatened with potential lawsuits from the community. The mine agreed to establish a mechanism for communication with the community, allow the Northern Plains Resource Council (a citizens' group) to participate in company decisions, and minimize adverse environmental impacts on the community in exchange for minimal future litigation. Because the firm realized the possible consequences of litigation, it was motivated to negotiate with the Resource Council. The threat of litigation, as well as other concerns, motivates firms to negotiate GNAs and has led to an increase in the number of these agreements in recent years.

When it comes to reducing environmental degradation caused by agricultural production, contracting offers several key advantages over traditional regulatory methods. First and foremost, contract law allows the parties to consider both economically quantifiable and non-quantifiable costs and benefits in the agreement. An agricultural operation may provide a number of benefits to society, like ensuring food security, maintaining open spaces, and preserving an image of idealized agrarian life that plays an important psychological function in American communities. These social benefits are not often, if ever, quantifiable, and are therefore undervalued by nuisance law and command-and-control regulations. In developing the terms of a GNA, a farmer provides information regarding the social and economic costs and benefits of his farm, which gives the community group access to more information than it would have otherwise. Because contract law permits the parties to bring to the table any number of factors for consideration, the contracting parties can ensure that agricultural operations are adequately valued in the final agreement.

In addition to ensuring greater accuracy in valuing farm practices, contracting also protects the public image of farmers and farm operations by encouraging open dialogue between communities and farmers. Farmers who voluntarily provide community groups with information about their operations and vow to maintain environmentally sound practices are viewed as competent environmental stewards. The public also views the farming industry more favorably when producers run their operations with a measure of transparency. Such transparency ensures that a producer remains accountable for fulfilling the terms of the agreement because the community may hold him liable if he breaches the GNA. The parties' relationship is a symbiotic one in which the farmer relies on the community group to hold him accountable, and the community group relies on the farmer to provide access to key information. The opportunity to protect their farms' images and social value through contract law incentivizes agriculturists to enter GNAs.

As with other industries, the agricultural industry mandates certain prerequisites that must be met for a GNA to regulate agricultural emissions effectively. First, the polluter must be motivated to negotiate an agreement. Generally, this motivation arises as a result of a "triggering event." If the polluter is a CAFO [Concentrated Animal Feeding Operation], the triggering events are identical to those in other industries: applications for permits or settlements from suits filed for violating federal or state environmental regulations. On the other hand, where the source of the contamination is, for instance, runoff from a large number of small farms, permits are not required and federal regulatory law generally does not apply. The triggering event in this case may instead be a neighboring landowner's filing or threat to file a nuisance suit against the producer. In this way, nuisance law supports an effective and efficient contractual method of regulation. Of course, like corporate firms, farmers also may be motivated by a desire to cultivate positive relationships with the community. Even so, it is unlikely that farmers will recognize the gravity of the environmental situation and the level of community concern unless citizens have the opportunity to voice those concerns first.

Members of the local community also must be organized and able to present a coherent message in order for negotiations to succeed. Citizens' groups should meet with the agricultural polluter to delineate the issues to resolve and identify additional stakeholders to involve in the process. Agriculture is part of the culture of many small communities, so in the early stages of the negotiations, stakeholders likely will present a wide array of opinions and possible solutions to the pollution problems caused by agriculture. Such divergence of opinion may result in the formation of multiple citizens' groups reflecting varying levels of concern with the environmental threats caused by agricultural emissions.

A GNA should be very detailed, prescribing the exact standards applied and remedies available under the agreement if either party breaches. To constitute a valid contract, both parties must bargain for favorable terms in the agreement. The parties may opt to include pollution prevention efforts that are methods-based, standards-based, or a combination of the two. Methods-based terms focus on the agricultural practices that farmers should implement to protect air, water, and soil. Such methods include carbon sequestering, buffering, constructing efficient irrigation systems, composting, and disposing of animal waste carefully. In contrast, standards-based terms include maximum emissions or discharge levels ["TMDLs"] for point source pollution and the TMDLs (below the national standards) of pollutants permitted in any stream running through or near the agricultural operation. For point source discharge, the agreement may allocate a portion of the proposed maximum daily load to each source; such allocations will not, however, reduce non-point source discharge.

In addition, the citizens' group also must negotiate for access to information on environmental quality. The final agreement may require the farmer to perform regular soil and water testing or submit annual reports to the citizens' group that describe environmental practices on the property. Because most farms are not open to the public, the parties should agree upon an independent auditor who can visit the property regularly to observe the producer's environmental practices. An independent auditor who has a thorough understanding of the agriculture industry could provide objective assessments of agricultural practices. Use of an independent auditor also would protect the farmer from any negative reactions that a community member might have to established agricultural practices. Regardless of the method adopted, the citizens' group should consider the type and amount of information needed and include a provision in the agreement granting itself access to that information.

Farmers also must bargain for consideration in the agreements. In a GNA, the farmer's consideration probably would include a binding arbitration clause preventing the contracting stakeholders from filing nuisance suits against the farmer in the future. The agreement may also grant the producer a much-needed easement, buffer, or other property right conveyable between private landowners. In addition, CAFOs may commit to the agreement to receive permits for production or expansion of existing operations under the CWA or to escape further penalties for failure to comply with environmental regulations.

If any party fails to meet the terms of the agreement, the non-breaching party has a valid breach of contract claim. Although a GNA does not have to be written in order to be binding, a non-breaching party will find it considerably easier to provide evidence of the breach if the terms of the agreement are in writing and signed by the breaching party. The breaching party may allege all of the defenses common to contract law. For instance, if the nonoccurrence of a particular event was a basic assumption upon which the agreement was made and the event occurred, the breaching party may be able to claim impossibility or impracticability as a defense. This defense can only apply, however, if none of the contracting parties are at fault or assumed the risk that the event might occur. If, for example, a farmer were alleged to have breached the GNA by failing to bring a stream's TMDLs into compliance with the standards set forth in the agreement, a court might find that compliance was impracticable if a company later built a factory next to the farm and discharged effluent into the stream, greatly affecting the stream's TMDLs and preventing the farmer from complying with the agreement.

Similarly, a contracting party may also raise the defenses of mistake or misrepresentation if appropriate. A mutual mistake occurs when both parties make a mistake regarding a basic, material assumption of the contract at the time the contract was formed. As a result, the contract is voidable by the adversely affected party. Misrepresentation, on the other hand, occurs when a party makes a fraudulent and material statement not in accord with the facts; if the hearer is justified in relying on such facts, he or she can recover damages. Where environmental standards are concerned, instances of mistake or misrepresentation could be consequences of GNAs. If, for instance, a farmer agrees to lower the level of E. coli in a local stream by fifty percent, only to discover later that, at the time the contract was formed, the E. coli bacteria count was zero, the provision would be voidable for mutual mistake.

When the breaching party is unable to present a valid defense, the court will award the non-breaching party damages. Generally, the remedy for a breach of contract is expectation damages, a form of compensatory relief that makes the non-breaching party ex post whole by putting him in the position he would have been in if the contract had been fulfilled. Expectation damages consist of: direct damages, which compensate for the loss of value of the subject matter of the contract; incidental damages, which are the costs of obtaining substitute performance; and consequential damages, or losses that flow from the breach. Because it may be impossible for a court to value, for instance, the cost to a citizens' group of polluted water or poor air quality, the court may be persuaded to award restitution or reliance damages instead. Like the damages that may be awarded in a nuisance suit, the type and amount of relief for breach of contract is difficult to predict. So, parties should negotiate the provisions of a GNA carefully, considering every likely outcome of the contract and protecting themselves from liability.

Although GNAs have the capacity to serve a much-needed regulatory function, there are two pragmatic concerns with the systemic use of these voluntary agreements. First, a primary maxim of contract theory is that a contract binds only the parties to the agreement. A party cannot enforce a contract against one who refuses to assent to the terms of the agreement. Therefore, even if a GNA between a farmer and local citizens' group protects the farmer from future nuisance actions from the members of that group, a neighbor who is not a party to the contract may still file a nuisance claim against the farmer. To provide the greatest incentive for a farmer to negotiate a GNA, community members would do well to convince any and all neighbors with a legitimate claim against the farmer to surrender their rights under common law by signing the agreement. Conversely, a farmer must recognize that such agreements will not categorically protect him from tort liability. The "stubborn" neighbor (who refuses to be a party to the agreement) or "new" neighbor (who moves into the area after the agreement is formed) may file a nuisance claim if he suffers harm.

In addition to the parties to the agreement, the remedies available are also a source of concern. To remedy a breach of contract, and absent binding arbitration or negotiation, the non-breaching party must engage in the very act that GNAs are designed to avoid: litigation. Just as nuisance suits require time and money, contract disputes also necessitate considerable expenditures. From the farmer's perspective, it would seem circular to consider GNAs an escape from nuisance claims if enforcing such agreements only resulted in similar contract claims. In most situations, parties could avoid litigation entirely by including a binding arbitration clause in the agreement. Such a clause would reassure farmers who are concerned that signing a GNA that might result in litigation and costly court proceedings.

Discussion Questions

1. Ethical codes are required under the Sarbanes-Oxley Act. Do you think most company codes have enough specificity to trigger corporate liability, as the Glinski excerpt suggests? There have been cases where corporate codes have set forth stricter standards than state law and customers have successfully sued. For example, one retail store had a code that required that shoplifters should not be apprehended on the premises by security guards but should be pursued only after their license plate numbers

were obtained. When a customer was apprehended on the spot, in accordance with state law, the court held that there was a violation of the specific company code.

2. Do you agree with Glinski's thesis that self-regulatory instruments in contract law (as well as in the law of misleading advertising) have "relevant legal effects"?

3. Glinski points out that industry groups may also set forth specific environmental standards that businesses in that industry must follow. Examples include the International Organization for Standardization (ISO) 14001 environmental management standard; the Forest Stewardship Council (FSC), Sustainable Forestry Initiative (SFI), and Pan-European Forest Certification Council (PEFC) forestry standards; the Marine Stewardship Council (MSC) fisheries standards; and the Equator Principles for environmental assessment in project finance lending.

4. Do you think that private contracting is a more effective avenue for sustainability promotion than governmental regulation? Does your answer change when production takes place abroad, in nations that may have inadequate environmental policies or ineffective enforcement capabilities?

5. A wide range of agreements could affect a firm's environmental behavior, including supply agreements, merger and acquisition agreements, credit agreements, and insurance agreements.* Vandenbergh mostly focuses on supply agreements; how could further research assess the environmental impact of other agreement types?

6. Vandenbergh highlights several industries and some of the largest companies in each. How do these industries compare? In which industries do private supply contracts have the most impact?

7. Do you find something inconsistent about searching the globe for cheap labor and reduced regulation but requiring suppliers to abide by strict U.S. standards of practice?

8. Do you think GNAs are better or worse than traditional regulatory law?

9. What do you think are the biggest challenges with GNAs?

---

* Musician Jack Johnson's concert rider requires venues to recycle, install energy-efficient light bulbs, purchase carbon offsets, and provide bike valets. "'You hear all these horror stories of people's riders requesting one color of M&Ms or super fancy champagne,' the 40-year-old singer recently told *The Huffington Post*. 'We just figured, all right, let's be demanding with these, because we know they're not going to switch back to those energy-draining bulbs once the show is over.'" Carla Herreria, Concerts Create a Huge Amount of Waste, and Jack Johnson Is Tackling It Head On, Huffington Post, Mar. 29, 2016.

Chapter 9

Sustainability and Taxation

One of the key issues that federal and state governments face is how and whether to subsidize or penalize certain business behaviors through the taxation system. The first part of this chapter deals with environmental taxation. The lead article sets forth the theoretical basis for environmental taxation and compares each theory to environmental goals, tax rates, and use of revenues. The second article takes one of these theories and advocates for stronger environmental taxes. The third assesses the current state of environmental taxation on the federal level in the United States. This is followed by a fourth article that discusses the merits of a carbon tax versus a cap-and-trade system.

The second part of this chapter examines tax expenditures or tax incentives. The first article in this part discusses how current fiscal policy impedes sustainable practices by promoting environmental harms or creating uncertainties. We next have a general overview of the U.S. tax incentive system and an example of our tax expenditure budget. This is followed by a series of excerpts that highlight (1) when the tax system encourages bad practices, such as for advertisement, (2) when the tax system has ineffective tax policies, such as with nuclear power, and (3) how the tax system has passed effective tax subsidies for renewable energy, such as for wind. The chapter ends with a chart (by industry sector) of the good and bad environmental tax policies and suggestions for reform.

When reading this chapter ask yourself whether the United States is instituting adequate environmental taxes necessary for corporations to internalize their external costs of pollution on the environment, and what changes need to be made in the U.S. tax incentive system to be less harmful to the environment and more effective in encouraging sustainable business practices.

Part I: Environmental Taxation

Janet E. Milne, *Environmental Taxation: Why Theory Matters**

Although economics provides the conceptual linchpin of environmental taxation, a number of different economic theories have been espoused to support the use of

* Originally published in 1 Critical Issues in Environmental Taxation (Janet E. Milne et al. eds., 2003). Reprinted with permission of Oxford University Press.

environmental taxation: the theory of internalization of external costs, the polluter pays principle, the theory of least cost abatement, and the double dividend theory. Each theory takes a different conceptual approach that has different implications for the design of environmental tax instruments.

The following analysis explores the differences among these economic theories and the implications of those differences for the theoretical design of environmental taxes. It briefly introduces the economic theories and discusses how each of the theories influences, in theory, three elements of an environmental tax: the identification of the environmental goal the tax is serving, the formula that underlies the tax rate, and the decision about how government will use the revenues that the tax generates. The analysis reviews these questions from a purely theoretical perspective, admittedly putting aside the practical issues involved in actually implementing theory in the real world of empirical limitations and political obstacles.

1. Economic Theories Underlying Environmental Taxation

The most prevalent economic theories underlying environmental taxation each have their own unique characteristics. Although each may achieve the result of changing behavior by raising the tax cost of the targeted product or activity, each is premised on its own, distinct economic rationale. The following is a brief discussion of these rationales.

1.1 Pigouvian theory

Environmental taxation traces its genesis to the Pigouvian theory that taxes can internalize external costs. Early in the 20th century, Arthur Cecil Pigou introduced the notion that government should use taxation to equalize the private and social net costs in instances where the private producers are imposing costs on others. In the environmental realm, these Pigouvian taxes in theory can impose on entities the costs of the marginal uncompensated environmental damage to society generated by the entities' activities, thereby fully internalizing to those entities the costs that otherwise would be externalized to society. This approach is based on Pigou's premise that equalization of the private and social costs will increase what he referred to as the national dividend and, therefore, increase economic welfare to an optimal level. Thus, the Pigouvian rationale for environmental taxation—that the full internalization of external environmental costs will maximize welfare—is a theory of economic efficiency that derives from the proper allocation of costs between entities engaging in pollution and victims of that pollution in society at large.

1.2 The polluter pays principle

A second economic theory is the polluter pays principle, a concept officially adopted by the Organisation for Economic Co-operation and Development (OECD), the European Community and the signatories to the Rio Declaration that has evolved in meaning over the course of 30 years but the contours of which remain somewhat amorphous. Unlike the Pigouvian theory, which is limited to taxation, this principle can be implemented through regulatory controls, taxation, liability regimes and permit trading systems, but the focus of this article is on the applicability of the principle to environmental taxes....

Like the Pigouvian theory, the polluter pays principle is fundamentally concerned with the issue of cost allocation: the polluter should be the entity to pay. From an economic perspective, however, the question remains as to what economic theory drives this determination to allocate cost to the polluter. Why is cost allocation important? The answer to this question may vary depending upon the point in time in the evolution of the principle, the institution espousing the principle, the words one chooses to emphasize in any given formulation of the principle and the legal instrument being used to execute the principle. However, two economic rationales seem to emerge as themes. One ... is that the allocation of costs to the polluter will avoid trade distortions. The other is that the allocation of costs to the polluter will yield greater economic efficiency....

The polluter pays principle implements its goal of avoiding trade distortions by preventing government subsidies of environmental compliance costs that would give the entities in one country a competitive trade advantage over entities in another country. By placing the costs of pollution control and prevention on the polluter, the principle also achieves an efficiency goal. Allocating the costs to the polluter makes the polluter more aware of the consequences of using scarce environmental resources and, as a result, can induce more rational, economically efficient decisions about the use of those resources. It creates an economic incentive to consider environmental consequences.

A key issue in defining the polluter pays principle for economic purposes is the determination of the costs that are being allocated to the polluter. The polluter pays—but for what? The answer to this question has not been uniform and ranges from (1) the costs of pollution prevention and control, (2) the costs of pollution prevention and control, plus the cost of restoration of damage that is not prevented, and (3) the full internalization of pollution costs, including the costs of prevention, control and restoration plus the costs of any residual environmental damage that society incurs as a result of less-than-full prevention and restoration. Full internalization would bring the polluter pays principle in line with the Pigouvian theory....

When the polluter pays principle is used, however, to allocate costs of pollution from society to the polluter, then taxation can play a role in implementing the principle. The tax itself becomes the governmental measure used to achieve some degree of environmental protection, and it serves as the mechanism for allocating environmental costs to the polluter. The tax approach varies from the regulatory and liability approaches because not all of the polluters will reduce their pollution. The polluter will either engage in the polluting activity and pay the cost by paying the tax, or the polluter will find a way to avoid the pollution and, therefore, avoid the tax. By avoiding the tax, the polluter is till assuming the cost of pollution prevention. This allocation of costs through the tax can implement the efficiency rationale by making forms more aware of the economic consequences of using scarce environmental resources and the cost of environmental consequences. However, this allocation is consistent with the trade rationale only if one assumes a broad reading of that rationale.

The Pigouvian theory and the polluter pays principle at a fundamental level both involve the policy choice between whether the price of products and activities should include environmental costs and whether these costs should be borne by the society at large. In other words, they address the allocation of costs between the private and public (governmental or not-governmental) sectors. They are driven by the question, "Who should pay?" The reason for asking this question, however, can be different for each theory, creating a different flavor to the economic justification for each theory. The Pigouvian theory is concerned with who should pay because it is trying to maximize total economic welfare by accurately assigning external costs to products and activities. The polluter pays principle, on the other hand, is concerned with preventing trade distortions and achieving efficiencies that are incentives but do not necessarily fully internalize cost....

1.3 Least cost abatement

A third economic theory behind environmental taxation is that taxation is an economically efficient means of addressing environmental issues because, compared with governmental regulation, it may provide the least cost approach to solving environmental problems. Under this theory, environmental taxation creates an economic incentive for some entities to change their behavior in environmentally advantageous and economically efficient ways that, in the aggregate, will produce the desired degree of change in behavior among firms overall. By not requiring all entities to change their behavior regardless of cost effectiveness, this approach can yield the desired degree of environmental protection at lower economic cost than regulatory mandates. Hence, it achieves "least cost abatement." This approach is driven by the question, "Is an environmental tax the most economically efficient means of achieving a specific environmental goal that otherwise would be obtained through regulation?" The tax is regulatory is the sense that it attempts to achieve an environmental goal that otherwise would be pursued by regulation but to achieve that goal in a more economically efficient manner.

This efficiency rationale is different from the efficiency rationales underlying the Pigouvian theory and the polluter pays principle. It focuses on the efficiency of the instrument relative to other instruments, while the other two focus on the efficiencies in result created by imposing costs on the entity. Note, however, that the theories are not necessarily mutually exclusive. For example, environmental taxes that are consistent with the polluter pays principle may also be beneficial because they achieve least cost abatement.

1.4 The double dividend theory

A fourth, and final, theory is the double dividend theory that environmental taxation implemented in a revenue-neutral fashion potentially can yield both reductions in pollution and reductions in other economically inefficient taxes. The environmental tax will yield the first dividend of environmental protection, but the revenues generated by the tax can then be used to reduce other, more inefficient taxes, producing the second dividend of the economic benefits that result for increased tax efficiency. This approach, which assumes the enactment of an environmental tax based on some independent economic theory, is driven not only by the theory motivating the environmental tax buy also by the question, "How should the revenues from environmental taxes be allocated?" Its uniqueness (the economic efficiencies resulting from recycling the revenues produced by the environmental tax) lies in its focus on the second dividend....

2. The Effect of Theory on the Environmental Goal

Advocates of environmental taxation state that taxation can be used to achieve environmental protection, but the various economic theories for environmental taxation yield different articulations of the environmental goal that can be achieved under each theory.

2.1 The Pigouvian theory

The Pigouvian theory is not based on the achievement of any specific environmental goal keyed to a certain level of change in behavior. By fully internalizing external costs of environmental damage, it will change prices in a manner that presumably will affect behavior of firms, the consumers to whom firms pass on the cost and possibly the victims of the environmental damage. The specific degree of change in behavior, however, does not drive the design of the tax; the tax instead is driven primarily by the decision that society's costs of environmental damage should be reflected in the prices of the activities or products that produce those costs. Specific environmental results are secondary to the economic goal of increasing economic welfare by properly allocating costs.

2.2 The polluter pays principle

Under the polluter pays principle, the polluter pays—but for what level of environmental protection? Under either the trade or the efficiency rationale for the polluter pays principle, the environmental goal is usually an explicit goal set by public authorities. Government must identify the pollution (or pollution abatement) for which the polluter will be held accountable and, therefore, must pay....

It is important to note that when environmental taxation, not regulation or a liability regime, is used as the instrument for achieving a specific environmental goal, the assumption is that not every entity will respond to the tax in the same way. Some may choose to pollute and pay the tax; others may choose to avoid the polluting activity and the tax. Consequently, the statement of the explicit environmental goal for an environmental tax based on the polluter pays principle cannot assume uniform results on an entity-by-entity basis. The explicit goal will be based on the aggregate environmental performance achieved by all entities after imposition of the tax. As a result, the goal will be stated in terms of the overall level of desired improvement rather than as across-the-board level of improvement.

2.3 Least cost abatement

The theory of least cost abatement should have a very clearly defined environmental goal that drives the regulatory environmental tax. When it relies on this theory, the government is trying to determine how to achieve a specific environmental standard at least cost to the private sector. The starting point in this instance is the decision about what level of abatement is desired, and all other decisions flow from that determination. In this respect, least cost abatement is similar to a polluter pays tax that does not fully internalize costs.

2.4 Double dividend theory

Finally, the double dividend theory assumes that an environmental tax will generate an environmental benefit. Consequently, the determination of whether the environmental tax is linked to a clearly defined environmental goal will depend on which of the theories above is used to design the environmental tax. As indicated above, this analysis assumes that a Pigouvian tax would be the starting point for the double dividend theory, in which case the government would not have a specific environmental goal. However, to the extent that the double dividend theory is used to support environmental tax reform in a broader sense, where full internalization is not the goal, the environmental tax could be a polluter pays tax or a least cost abatement tax. In that case, the environmental goal would be more specific.

Thus, the different economic theories yield very different statements of the environmental goal. The way in which any given policymaker resolves this dilemma will depend on his or her conclusions about the significance of the need to achieve a specifically identified environmental goal for environmental reasons, given the particular environmental problem at hand, and his or her views about the significance of a specific goal to the conduct of a sound policy debate over the use of the environmental tax instrument in any given situation.

3. The Effect of Theory on the Tax Rate

The tax rates used to implement each of the economic theories similarly flow directly from the fundamental nature of each theory. When one activity or commodity is taxed, the theories can produce different tax rates, yet each can be called an "environmental tax."

3.1 The Pigouvian theory

The Pigouvian principle seeks to internalize the external costs. Consequently, it sets the tax rate according to the net marginal external environmental costs of the environmentally damaging activity or product—in other words, the marginal costs of the environmental damage to society that exceed the private costs that have already been paid by the private sector. This tax rate will internalize the full external costs, so the taxpayer will fully compensate society for the costs of pollution.

3.2 The polluter pays principle

The tax rate for a polluter pays tax depends upon how one approaches the question: the polluter pays—for what? The definition of the actual costs that the principle is expecting the polluter to pay through an environmental tax will determine the formula for the tax rate.... Thus, if the tax is designed to allocate the costs of pollution prevention and control, one can either use a tax rate keyed to specific marginal pollution and control costs and achieve a lower environmental goal, or one can use a higher tax rate that will achieve the desired aggregate behavioral result and argue that the allocation of prevention and control costs means the allocation of any tax costs required to meet a specific goal. Which interpretation one chooses will significantly affect the environmental result and the design of the tax rate.

3.3 Least cost abatement

The least cost abatement principle sets the tax rate according to the level that will yield the desired amount of change in behavior. Like the determination of a tax rate that could be used to implement the polluter pays principle, this calculation will take into account the prevention and control costs that an entity is likely to incur if it changes behavior. It will set the rate high enough to ensure that the tax yields the desired aggregate change in behavior.

3.4 Double dividend theory

Finally, the double dividend theory often uses the Pigouvian approach as a starting point for setting the tax rate. The economists who create models of the double dividend theory usually begin with the premise that the first dividend is achieved through internalization of external costs under the Pigouvian model, and then they modify the Pigouvian assumptions to recognize economic ramifications of using the tax revenues for tax relief that may achieve the second dividend. However, if the double dividend theory is being used in a looser sense to support a non-Pigouvian tax, then the tax could be based on the other rationales discussed above and the tax rate would be designed accordingly.

4. The Effect of Theory on the Use of the Revenue

The choice of theory also has a significant effect on the freedom to determine how the revenue from the environmental tax will be used.

4.1 The Pigouvian theory

Under the Pigouvian theory, the tax internalizes the external cost so that the product or activity reflects the actual environmental cost, but do the revenues resulting for the tax need to be dedicated to the environmental problem? Pigou did not explicitly address this issue, but some of his text suggests dedication of the revenues. When Pigou proposed using taxation to equalize marginal private and social costs, he cited an example to illustrate why the revenues should be used to compensate third parties for the costs that otherwise would have been uncompensated. He explained that a British tax on gasoline and drivers' licenses represented a "very incomplete and partial" application of his principle because the revenues were used to build new road improvements rather than to fund ordinary maintenance to repair damage caused by the motorists. Thus, his discussion seems to suggest that the government can dedicate the revenues to the governmental repair of the actual damage linked to the activity that generates the tax, rather than expenditure for new purposes or distribution to the victims.

4.2 The polluter pays principle

Under the polluter pays principle, the polluter pays—but into which governmental account? A polluter pays tax is incurred only when the polluter engages in a polluting activity, but does the categorization of the tax as a "polluter pays tax" means that the revenues should be dedicated to the environmental problem associated with the tax, or is government free to use the revenues as it wishes? Views on this question are mixed.

4.3 Least cost abatement

The least cost abatement theory attaches no strings to the revenue stream. Merely inducing a desired degree of change in behavior more cost-effectively than regulation fulfills the purpose of the tax, so the manner in which government uses the revenues is not relevant. Government has the freedom to use the new funds to increase spending for any purpose or to reduce other tax burdens.

4.4 Double dividend theory

Finally, the double dividend theory should only be linked to an environmental tax that does not require that the revenues be dedicated to a particular purpose. The fundamental premise of the double dividend theory is that the environmental tax will generate revenues that can be used to reduce some other existing tax burden that is economically inefficient. Consequently, it can be linked with a Pigouvian tax or a polluter pays tax, if neither is interpreted as requiring the dedication of revenues, or a least cost abatement tax, which never requires dedication of the revenues....

However, if the polluter pays principle is interpreted to mean the full-internalization of external costs in the tax context, then a polluter pays tax and a Pigouvian tax become very similar. Moreover, if the polluter pays principle fully internalizes costs and neither a Pigouvian tax nor a polluter pays tax require dedication of the revenues, then either type of tax could be used to create a double dividend, effectively allowing the three theories (Pigouvian, polluter pays and double dividend) to yield one type of tax. Thus, the theoretical questions that remain unsettled but very significant are: What does the polluter pays principle mean in the context of environmental taxation? What costs does it allocate? Does it require dedication of the revenues? And does the Pigouvian theory require dedication of the revenues? The resolution of these questions will have a significant influence on the theoretical design of environmental taxes and the articulation of the goal the tax is intended to achieve.

[The following chart summarizes these different theories of environmental taxation:]

Differences among the Economic Theories of Environmental Taxation

Economic Theory	Fundamental Concern	Environmental Goal	Tax Rate	Use of Revenue
Pigouvian theory	Private/societal allocation of external costs	Optimal welfare	Marginal costs of damage	Dedicated? Or open-ended?
Polluter pays principle	Private/ governmental or societal allocation of environmental costs to: • Prevent subsidies to avoid international trade distortions • Encourage efficient use of scarce environmental resources by allocating: – prevention and control costs; – restoration costs; or – full external costs	Explicit environmental goal unless full internalization of costs	• Tax not applicable to preventing direct governmental subsidies. • To allocate costs: – For prevention and control costs, marginal costs of abating pollution or price increase required to achieve desired degree of change in aggregate behavior – For restoration, marginal restoration costs – For full external costs, marginal costs of damage	Open-ended under economic rationale, unless purpose is restoration or ethical/ equitable rationale requires dedication
Least cost abatement theory	Cost-effective instrument for achieving specific environmental goal	Explicit environmental goal	Price increase required to achieve desired degree of aggregate change in behavior	Open-ended
Double dividend theory	Improved efficiency in tax system	• Optimal welfare if Pigouvian tax • Explicit environmental goal if non-Pirouvian	• Marginal cost of damage as starting point if Pigouvian-based • One of the above if not Pigouvian-based	Dedicated to offsetting tax relief

David Malin Roodman, *Environmental Taxes: Adopting a "Polluter Pays" Principle**

Among the greatest failings of tax codes is that they barely penalize activities that do economic harm, e.g., pollution, while heavily taxing ones that do economic good, including work and investment. Indeed, more than any other shortcoming in the world's fiscal policies—more than the high subsidies for destructive activities, the low subsidies for relatively benign ones, and the low capture rates on natural windfalls—this lopsidedness is what makes fiscal policies so destructive to human health and the environment today.

The question too rarely asked about taxes is: What are the best things to tax? The obvious answer is that societies should start by taxing things of which they want less (like resource waste), not more (e.g., employment). Benjamin Franklin observed that taxation is as inevitable as death. But there is freedom in what to tax, so why should tax codes discourage job creation, for example, any more than necessary if other parts of government are striving to stimulate it? Why should not taxes discourage pollution, especially since large bureaucracies are already being funded—with tax dollars—to do the same thing? The idea that people should bear responsibility for the harm that they do others is the cornerstone of most moral and legal codes. Yet it is remarkably absent from the world's tax codes.

Remedying that absence is the single most important step that policymakers can take in conforming fiscal policy to environmental principles. Only taxes can bring consumers and businesses face to face with the full costs of the environmental harm that they cause, and only when they face those costs can they realistically be expected to make choices that also make sense for society.

Famed British economist Arthur Cecil Pigou was the first to advocate taxes on environmental harm. In his 1920 classic, *The Economics of Welfare*, he pointed to the hidden costs of smoke pouring from factories and fireplaces in Manchester. Costs of extra laundry cleaning, artificial lighting necessitated by darkened air, and repairs to corroded buildings had been estimated at £290,000 per year (about $10 million at today's prices). As a result, a steelmaker might have made £100 worth of steel with a furnaceful of coal and done £200 in damage in the process—a gain for the company, but a net loss for the city. In effect, pollution victims were subsidizing pollution causers, and making society as a whole poorer.

Modern parallels abound. Fertilizer and manure from farms in the American heartland drain, along with industrial effluents, into the Mississippi River and from there to the Gulf of Mexico, where they produce an oxygen-depleted "dead zone" the size of New Jersey, in which few fish survive and no shrimper can thrive. Ozone pollution, particularly from cars, sends 50,000 people to the hospital each year in the Washington D.C. area. And for every dollar spent extracting natural gas in one Malaysian project, roughly another dollar of harm is imposed on future generations by depriving them of cheap energy at a time when it will be scarcer.

---

* Originally published in 11 Journal of International Taxation 34 (2000). Reprinted with permission.

In all of these situations, it is inconceivable that the winners and the losers—who number in the millions or are not even born yet—could resolve the problems on their own, through courts, or over the bargaining table. The solution to such problems, Pigou argued, is for governments to intervene, by using taxes to make people who create environmental problems absorb the costs of the harm that they do. Then when they tally up the costs and benefits of environmental harm for themselves, they would have to take society's interests into account....

The limits of regulations. Pigou's sensible prescription became received wisdom within economics, but most of the bricks in the environmental policy edifice built during the last 30 years have been fired from the stuff of regulations, not taxes. To be sure, regulations have scored important successes. In Western Europe, for example, regulators can point to a 47% reduction in sulfur emissions between 1970 and 1993, due substantially to rules requiring scrubbers in coal plants. In the U.S., tightened tailpipe emissions standards for new cars and light trucks made catalytic converters universal over the same time span, cutting nitrogen oxide emissions 6%, carbon monoxide 33%, and volatile organic compounds 54%, all despite a 44% increase in driving.

Nevertheless, regulations are increasingly being pushed beyond their limits. Because they often focus on means rather than ends—for example, by prescribing the use of particular kinds of water filters—they tend to discourage innovation. And though they often work well when there is a front-runner solution (such as catalytic converters for cars), they tend to break down in the face of complexity. A joint study by the U.S. Environmental Protection Agency (EPA) and Amoco Corporation documented one telling absurdity at the oil company's Yorktown, Virginia, refinery. Regulations required Amoco to spend $31 million on a wastewater treatment plant to stop airborne emissions of benzene, a carcinogen. Meanwhile, the rules failed to cover benzene emissions from a nearby loading dock—emissions that could have been reduced as much for just $6 million....

Environmental taxes. The growing use of environmental taxes is one response to that plea. One of the best and earliest examples is the system of water pollution taxes in the Netherlands. Since 1970, gradually rising charges on emissions of organic material and heavy metals into canals, rivers, and lakes have spurred companies to cut emissions, without dictating how. Between 1976 and the mid-1990s, emissions of cadmium, chromium, copper, lead, mercury, nickel, and zinc into waters managed by regional governments (which adopted the charges earliest) plummeted 72%–99%—primarily because of the charges, according to statistical analyses.

The Dutch example illustrates the strengths of environmental taxes at their best. Companies that could prevent pollution most cheaply presumably did so most. Firms also would have passed part of the taxes on to their customers through higher prices, causing them to switch to less pollution-intensive products. And demand for pollution control equipment has spurred Dutch manufacturers to develop better models, triggering innovations that regulators could never have planned, lowering costs, and turning the country into a global leader in the market. The taxes have in effect sought the path of least economic resistance, i.e., of least cost, in cleaning up the country's waters.

Tax shifting. As revenues from environmental taxes and permit auctions rise, other taxes can fall. Since the total tax burden would not rise with this seesaw-like tax change, the cost for economies overall would probably be quite small or nil, and that is before counting the economic benefits of a healthier environment.

The economic and rhetorical appeal of tax shifting—"taxing bads, not goods"—began to dawn on West European environmentalists in the 1970s. In 1975, for example, Norwegian economist Agnar Sandmo argued in the Swedish Journal of Economics that an "optimal" revenue code would make substantial use of Pigouvian taxes in order to pass the costs of pollution back to polluters and reduce the need for other taxes. In the mid-1980s, analysts in the German-speaking world began to discuss in less abstract terms the idea of taxing energy rather than wages to fund social security. A few years later, the prominent German environmentalist Ernst Ulrich von Weizscker seized on the idea of tax shifting. Von Weizscker's name (his father a well-known physicist and philosopher, his uncle the president of Germany) brought almost instant legitimacy to the proposal. His 1992 book, *Ecological Tax Reform*, became a best-seller among environmentalists and dramatically raised the profile of the tax-shifting concept in Western Europe.

But though the proposals appeared in German-speaking countries, they were implemented elsewhere, especially to the north. One of the world's most environmentally proactive nations, Sweden, became the first to take up the idea in 1991. The government took $2.4 billion from new taxes on carbon and sulfur dioxide emissions, equal to 1.9% of all tax revenues, and used it to cut income taxes. As concern grew over unemployment in Western Europe, further shifts in the mid-1990s in Denmark, Finland, the Netherlands, Spain, and the U.K focused more on cutting wage taxes.

Huge revenue potential. Since environmental tax and permit auctions work by raising revenues comparable to economic damage done, their revenue potential is similarly huge. The damage estimate for Germany, for instance, equals 58% of tax revenues there; those for Sweden and the U.S. exceed public revenues. In practice, taxes would raise much less than this suggests, since taxing environmental damage will reduce the amount that occurs. And especially once taxes reached their final rates—in some instances, well into the next century—revenues might decline with time. In counterpoint, conventional taxes on work and investment could fall at first but might eventually have to rise again. Since taxes have long fluctuated at this slow tempo, the adjustment stresses would not be high by historical standards.

Tax shift. The Stanford Energy Modeling Forum results suggest that carbon taxes or permit auctions could eventually supply about 15% of government revenues worldwide. Cutting environmentally harmful subsidies 90% could free up another $600 billion, or an additional 8% of current revenues. The remaining subsidy funds could be targeted at truly deserving recipients, from developers of clean technologies to low-income people who have trouble paying the energy taxes on their utility bills. Land taxes and resource royalties could generate another $900 billion each year, or 12% of total revenues. Taxes on wages and profits would therefore need to supply only some 65% of that $7.5 trillion revenue pie, nearly a one-third cut from today's 93%. In many countries, income and profits taxes (or sales or payroll taxes) could be eliminated. The changes would stimulate economic development even as they guided it toward environmental sustainability.

Environmental Taxes: Practical Limits and Potential

The main planks of environmental fiscal reform—cutting payments to polluters, capturing more resource rents, judiciously subsidizing environmental protection, taxing environmental harm, and cutting conventional taxes—can be powerful tools precisely because they are designed according to incisive principles. Those who harm society should be taxed rather than subsidized. Human labor and entrepreneurship should be taxed less, and exploitation of nature should be taxed more.

Taken to their fullest, taxes that "make the polluter pay" will engineer nothing less than another industrial revolution. They will change how things are made, where people live, and how they travel, in order to rebalance economy and environment. Precisely because environmental taxes can change so much, they must be investigated most carefully.

Will environmental taxes work? One blunt objection to environmental taxation is that it will not work, or at least not nearly as well as environmental regulations. A general response to that assertion, by J. Andrew Hoerner, a tax analyst at the Center for a Sustainable Economy in Washington D.C., is that environmental taxes can in fact work better than conventional regulations, since they are often administered by revenue-collection agencies. These bodies typically have more enforcement authority and personnel than environmental regulatory agencies, which are often hobbled by underfunding in rich and poor countries alike. And lax enforcement compromises even the best laws.

Nevertheless, there is no question that however elegant environmental taxes are in theory, and however enforceable, they rarely work so neatly in practice. For one thing, taxing pollution or resource depletion requires measuring it, which is not always easy. There are no affordable technologies, for instance, for tracking automobile emissions of carbon monoxide and smog-causing nitrogen oxides and hydrocarbons. Even if there were, setting taxes perfectly according to the economics textbooks would require knowing exactly how much damage the chemicals will do at a given time, and that depends on how many other cars are around, the temperature and humidity of the air, the number of people breathing the air, and the health effects of the pollutants. Estimating these variables with precision would require sophisticated mathematical models and impossibly detailed knowledge of local car-use patterns, smog chemistry, and human biology.

Blending market, regulatory forces. As a result, like government trust-busters that intervene in the market in order to make it work better, environmental policymakers would often do best to summon regulations and other policies to the aid of market-based approaches. The taxes can even fund some of these steps. The Swedish government credits a drop in fertilizer use during the 1980s to both the taxes on fertilizer sales and to education programs, funded by the new revenues, that raised farmers' awareness of the financial and environmental costs of fertilizer overuse.

No guaranteed response. Having chosen practical tax bases, policymakers then run into another problem: even when meaningful tax signals can be sent, there is no guarantee that consumers and businesses will respond. But experience with gasoline taxes in industrial countries offers hope. The U.S. has by far the lowest gasoline taxes: in Europe, [high] taxes push pump prices two to four times higher than in the U.S.

Of course, many factors shape people's decisions about what size cars to buy and how much to drive them, including population density and convenience of public transit. But the influence of gas price is obvious to any visitor to the U.S. where gas is cheap, minivans and sport utility vehicles roam the roads in droves....

Homo sapiens is clearly only distantly related to H. economicus, the mythical species that populates most of the economics literature. H. economicus knows every product and every price and is driven only by profit maximization and material accumulation. Real people, by contrast, miss large opportunities to save money. Efficiency standards adopted in the U.S. during the last ten years, for instance, on refrigerators, fluorescent lights, and other appliances have increased the average efficiency of new models sharply by pushing inefficient ones off the market and forcing companies to innovate ... That consumers and companies did not switch to the money-saving models on their own shows that although people respond to market signals, they do not do so nearly as nimbly as economists tend to wish.

The general lesson is that making the industrial economy operate efficiently within environmental limits will require integrating environmental taxes with other kinds of policies, using the strengths of each to compensate for the weaknesses of the other. If governments of especially sprawl-afflicted countries such as the U.S. and Australia want motor fuel tax hikes to work well, and fairly, they need to give people better alternatives to driving. They will need to spend more on mass transit, as much of Western Europe already does, and rewrite zoning laws to foster neighborhoods that more closely mix schools, homes, and shops. Together, these changes can lure people from behind the wheel and onto sidewalks, bike paths, or bus lines. Meanwhile, to the extent that government policies force people to drive, and to the extent that people already drive efficient cars, taxing gas will not so much discourage gas use as punish it.

When are market approaches useful? On balance, the question of practical import is not whether market approaches work, but when they are useful. Whenever environmental goals can be expressed in significant part in a single number—how many tons of benzene should be permitted into an airshed each year, how much water pumped from an aquifer, how many hectares developed—and whenever actual pollution or depletion rates can be estimated, market mechanisms offer a way to protect the environment while exploiting the market's flexibility.

State innovations. Some of the most innovative environmental tax and permit systems to date have been developed by state governments in the U.S. Arizona instituted one of the world's few groundwater depletion tax regimes in 1991. New Jersey has used permits to add flexibility to its plan to protect the Pinelands, a 445,000-hectare region of wildlife habitat, berry farms, and small towns under strong development pressure. After extensive consultations with residents, the state set limits on building density in designated forest, farm, and town zones. Since the state believed that the character of the region was threatened not just by the rising number of buildings, but also their dispersion across the landscape, it then established a trading system to facilitate more concentrated development in existing town centers. Developers in designated growth areas can exceed local construction limits if they buy credits from landowners in other areas that agree to build less than they could....

Janet E. Milne, *Environmental Taxation in the United States: The Long View**

Market-based economic instruments generally fall into two categories—price signals (tax-based price signals and environmental user fees or charges) and property-based regimes (most notably permit trading regimes). These two categories operate very differently, given the price and property distinction. The price signals involve one-on-one transactions between the private sector player—the taxpayer or fee-payer, on the one hand, and the government, on the other hand. The payment to the government or, in the case of tax expenditures, the claim of a tax benefit from the government is the operative mechanism. In the case of property-based regimes such as permit trading, multiple parties can be involved. The government issues permits (the property-like interests it has created) to match the desired level of permitted pollution for any given year. Players acquire the permits, and they may sell the permits or keep them. Transactions then proceed until the permits in effect are returned to the government at the end of the year to match the polluters' allowed levels of emissions. Environmental taxes and permit regimes may co-exist, as has happened with U.S. control of ozone-depleting chemicals where both an environmental tax and a trading regime applied to the same chemicals. Figure 1 highlights the role of market-based tax instruments in relation to other market-based approaches....

Figure 1: An Overview of Economic Instruments for Environmental Protection Highlighting the Role of Taxation

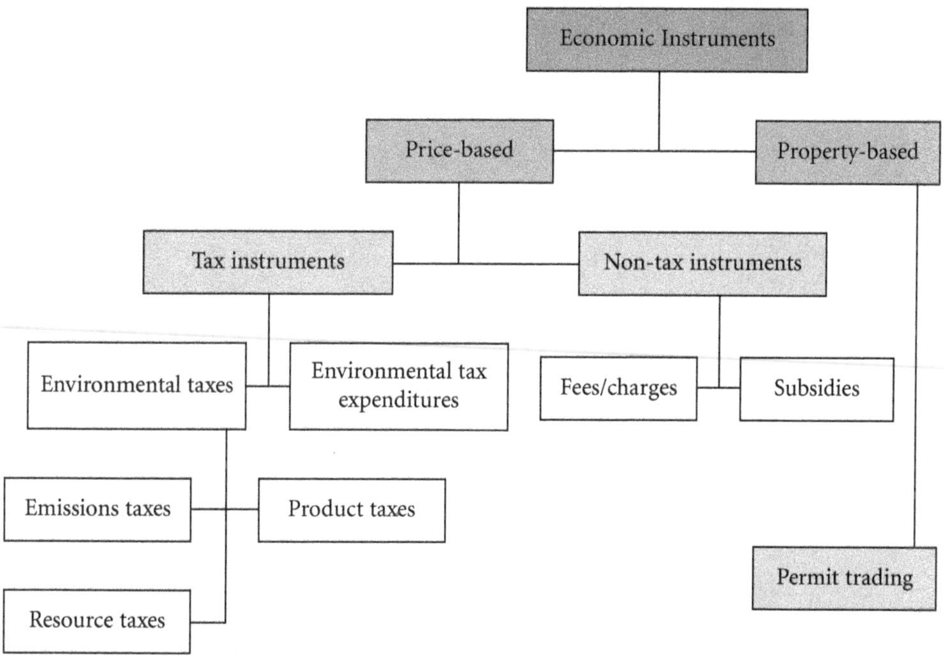

* Originally published in 15 Lewis & Clark Law Review 417 (2011). Reprinted with permission.

Figure 2 provides a visual picture of the distinction between environmental tax reform and environmental fiscal reform and the role of tax instruments in each. The placement of environmental tax expenditures on the fiscal reform side rather than the tax reform side reflects the fact that the literature on environmental tax reform focuses on the tax-shifting concept, using environmental taxes to reduce other tax burdens. Discussions of environmental fiscal reform, however, also often overlook the role of environmental tax expenditures, leaving it somewhat intellectually homeless. Placement of environmental tax expenditures within environmental fiscal reform seems appropriate, given its broader focus on subsidies and the larger fiscal picture.

Figure 2: The Relationship between Environmental Tax Reform and Environmental Fiscal Reform

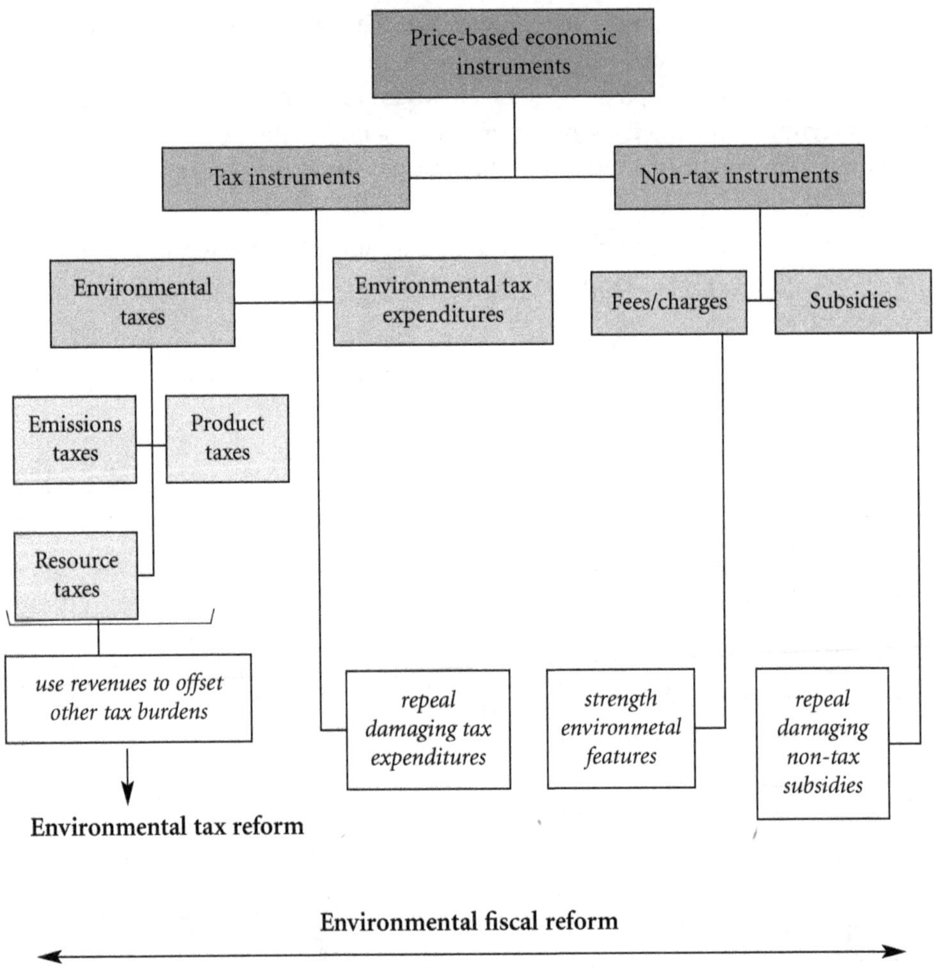

Design Features of Environmental Taxes— The Tax Base and Tax Rate

The basic design components of environmental taxes are quite simple and are common to most taxes:

Tax Base x Tax Rate = Tax Revenue.

The *raison d'être* of environmental taxes lies in their environmental goal, and the choice of the tax base and tax rate reflect that goal, as can the use of the revenue. Like other taxes, however, the design details of environmental taxes are also shaped by traditional tax policy considerations, such as their economic impact, equity and administrative feasibility, and by calculations of political feasibility. The design features of two U.S. environmental taxes and President Clinton's proposed energy tax illustrate how policy and political considerations affect the choice of the tax base and tax rate....

The federal excise tax on ozone-depleting chemicals offers a positive example of design features of an environmental tax. It was enacted to help address the problem of emissions of ozone-depleting chemicals that erode the stratospheric ozone layer and leave the earth more vulnerable to ultraviolet radiation. Under the international Montreal Protocol, countries agreed to phase out the use of key ozone-depleting chemicals, and the U.S. tax supplements U.S. obligations under the Protocol.

The tax neatly correlates the tax base and the tax rate to the environmental problem. The tax base consists of 20 chemicals known to have ozone-depleting characteristics. By the same token, the tax base rightly excludes chemicals that will be entirely consumed in the manufacture of another chemical (feedstocks) and therefore will never be released into the atmosphere. The tax rate varies according to the ozone-depleting potential of each chemical. An annual increasing base tax rate is multiplied by the ozone-depleting factor for each chemical, using factors established in the international Montreal Protocol. For example, CFC-11 has an ozone-depleting factor of 1.0 whereas Halon-1301 has a factor of 10.0, causing the tax on the more potent Halon-1301 to be ten times greater. Thus, the tax base and the tax rate link directly with the chemicals' potential to damage the environment.

From an administrative feasibility perspective, the tax was logically imposed on the manufacturers, producers and importers of the chemicals at the time of their sale or use. This upstream taxable event facilitates the collection of the tax and yet is consistent with the environmental assumption that most non-feedstock ozone-depleting chemicals ultimately will be released into the atmosphere at some point in the life of the final products. Placing the collection point at the more environmentally precise point of emission would not have been administratively feasible. In a finessing detail, the annual increases in the tax rate apply to chemicals that have already passed the collection point but are still being held for the manufacture of future products (a tax on floor stocks).

The tax's design was also shaped by economic considerations, in particular the effect on competitiveness of U.S. industries. As indicated above, the tax base includes imported chemicals, and it also extends to imported products that contain or were made using ozone-depleting chemicals, thereby imposing a border tax adjustment that puts

U.S.-manufactured chemicals and products on equal economic footing with imports. According to one study, the tax on imported products represented about $40 million dollars, or 11 percent of the revenue, in 1993, indicating that the border tax adjustment on products containing the chemicals was a significant feature of the tax. Regulations implementing the tax on imported chemicals and products offer a very useful example of the how to address the details of a border tax adjustment, such as how to account for subsequent uses that are exempt and how to determine the amount of ozone-depleting chemicals associated with imported products. This border tax adjustment is consistent with tax's environmental rationale, although the same cannot be said of the partial exemption for exports of U.S.-manufactured ozone-depleting chemicals.

The tax has generated an interesting, undesired, but perhaps not unforeseeable consequence relevant to the administrative feasibility of the tax and its border tax adjustment. The combination of the substantial tax and the Montreal Protocol's phase-out requirements created an incentive to smuggle ozone-depleting chemicals into the United States from countries subject to more liberal phase-out rules and no tax. As a result, the government has brought charges based in part on multi-million dollar tax evasions. Thus, the question of administrative feasibility can extend beyond the normal auditing procedures, which may be inevitable when dealing with high tax rates and non-harmonized international markets.

The federal excise tax on gas-guzzling vehicles similarly employs an environmentally logical tax base and tax rate, but it contains design features that reduce its environmental effectiveness and serve as warnings to future tax writers. Although the tax was enacted in 1978 in response to concerns about reliance on imported oil following the Oil Embargo, its existence today is directly relevant to the environmental problems caused by carbon dioxide and other emissions from motor vehicles' combustion of gasoline, including climate change.

The tax applies to automobiles based on their fuel economy, which is a significant factor contributing to the level of emissions, and the tax rate appropriately increases as fuel economy decreases. The tax rate starts at $1,000 for vehicles with fuel economy less than 22.5 but more than 21.5 miles per gallon, and it rises with each one-mile decrease in fuel economy until it reaches $7,700 for vehicles with fuel economy less than 12.5 miles per gallon. In terms of administrative feasibility, the tax is imposed on the manufacturer at time of sale, but to preserve the environmental awareness and behavioral impact of the tax, dealers must place a notice about the tax on the sticker price for the car.

The environmental effectiveness of the tax, however, has been eroded significantly by the fact that it does not apply to "non-passenger vehicles," a term that now encompasses sport utility vehicles (SUVs). Part of the original 1978 law, this exemption was created long before SUVs were contemplated as a common choice for everyday travel, but the failure to amend the law to adjust to new circumstances has significantly undercut its force as an environmental instrument. In addition, the tax rates have not been increased since 1990, nor have the fuel economy thresholds been changed since 1978. If an environmental tax is intended to serve a long-term environmental purpose, the tax rate should be indexed for inflation or adjusted periodically to preserve its incentive effect and policymakers should consider adjustments to the definitions and thresholds that determine the tax base ...

The Revenue Issue

The revenue-raising function of taxes is axiomatic. Taxes exist to provide government with the revenue it needs to provide its government services. Environmental taxes will raise revenue, but policymakers must decide whether the environmental features of the tax primarily lie in the tax base and tax rate, freeing some or all of the revenues for non-environmental purposes, or whether the environmental character of the tax arises in whole or part from the way in which its revenues are used. The decision about how to use the revenue from an environmental tax can be reduced to three basic choices or some combination thereof:

- dedicating the revenue to the environmental problem;
- using the revenues for some other governmental purpose, such as deficit reduction or increased spending (including the possibility of using revenue to address the equity and economic impacts of the tax); or
- using the revenues to reduce other tax burdens to achieve significant tax reform, often on a revenue-neutral basis.

To date, the United States has chosen the first two options but pending proposals illustrate how the third might be designed.

Three Superfund taxes serve as leading examples of taxes that generate their environmental impact primarily through the use of their revenues. The tax base for each is somewhat associated with the environmental problem, but absent dedication of the revenue, it would be more difficult to classify the Superfund taxes as strong environmental taxes. Note, however, that dedication of revenue to the environmental problem need not necessarily suggest that a tax is not an independently strong environmental tax. In some instances, policymakers may choose to devote the revenues to the environmental problem to achieve enhanced or accelerated results.

The Superfund taxes were created to provide financing for the Superfund, a federal trust fund. Part of a regulatory liability regime that requires operators or owners to be responsible for remediation of hazardous waste sites, the Superfund provides the federal government with funds to clean up abandoned sites. One Superfund tax imposed an excise tax on 42 chemicals sold by manufacturers or imported into the United States, with tax rates varying by chemical from $0.22 to $4.87 per ton, and a border tax adjustment for imported taxable substances. The second tax applied to crude oil and imported petroleum products at the rate $0.097 per barrel. The third took a different approach, taxing corporations at a rate of 0.12 percent of their modified alternative minimum taxable income over $2 million. By statute, the taxes expired at the end of 1995, and efforts to reinstate them have been intertwined with difficult negotiations over the associated, ongoing liability regime for hazardous waste sites.

The design of the Superfund taxes does not provide the tight correlation between the tax base and the resulting pollution evident in the tax on ozone-depleting chemicals. The taxed chemicals and products and the taxable income cannot be traced directly to specific hazardous waste sites but rather served as a rough "guilt by association" proxy. In addition, the relatively low levels of tax were unlikely to significantly influence behavior. The stronger environmental identity of the taxes instead derived from the dedication of their $19 billion cumulative revenue stream to cleaning up contaminated sites. Supplemented by recoveries from responsible parties, the taxes generated almost two-thirds of the Superfund's revenue through 1995. Thus, the dedication of the revenue to environmental purposes gave heft to their environmental nature....

The BP Deepwater Horizon oil spill in the Gulf of Mexico in 2010 highlights the role of the tax on petroleum that funds the Oil Spill Liability Trust Fund. The tax is too low to generate a significant behavioral impact, but its revenues significantly enhance environmental protection. The Oil Pollution Act of 1990 created a legal liability regime for parties responsible for oil spills, requiring them to pay for removal costs and damages up to certain levels, and the Oil Spill Liability Trust Fund serves as a backstop source of relief. Financed by an 8-cent-per-barrel tax on crude oil produced in the United States and petroleum products imported into the United States, the Trust Fund serves in effect as an industry-funded risk pool. The Trust Fund pays for the government's emergency costs for removing the oil, providing it with the ability to respond quickly without waiting for appropriations. It also finances the assessment of damage to natural resources, the preparation and implementation of restoration plans, and the costs of economic and natural resource damages that the responsible parties do not pay due to legal limits on their liability or their inability to pay.

The Oil Spill Liability Trust Fund played a crucial role in responding to the Gulf oil spill. Although the responsible parties are ultimately liable for all removal costs for spills from offshore facilities, the federal government is able to draw upon the Trust Fund to pay for the costs of its emergency response and then seek reimbursement from the responsible parties. As of September 15, 2010, the National Pollution Funds Center, which administers the Trust Fund, had billed the responsible parties for $518.4 million in expenses, of which BP had paid $389.9 million with one recent bill still pending. If the Coast Guard and other federal agencies had not been able to draw on the fund, they could have been hard-pressed to find the resources on short notice to cover the cost of the massive, immediate response. At the same time, the magnitude of the BP spill illustrates the Trust Fund's limits. Congress had to pass legislation authorizing special advances from the Fund. In addition, the Trust Fund's $1 billion-per-incident cap on payments for removal costs, damage assessments and uncompensated damages would have severely limited relief if BP had not voluntarily assumed responsibility beyond the level of its legal responsibility. Nevertheless, the tax plays a significant environmental role through the use of its revenues.

If dedication of the revenue is not an essential part of the environmental role of the tax, government can use the revenue for other purposes. Those purposes can provide independent and often important opportunities and momentum for environmental taxes, as illustrated by U.S. efforts to reduce the deficit in the late 1980s and early 1990s.

Nancy E. Shurtz, *Carbon Pricing Initiatives in Western North America: A Blueprint for Global Climate Change Policy**

A heated battle currently is being fought as to whether a cap-and-trade or a carbon tax will be better to solve our climate change problem. Many commentators and authors of law reviews have advocated that a cap-and-trade is better, whereas many others have argued that a carbon tax is best. My thesis is that both carbon taxes and cap-and-trade should be used on the local and regional level, particularly for Canada and the U.S., two of the largest contributors to climate change and two of the biggest beneficiaries of climate change. If designed properly, these market mechanisms can work together and be effective....

Most economists prefer carbon taxes. According to most economists, price instruments, such as carbon taxes, can be expected to be more efficient and effective than quantity instruments, such as tradable allowances. Economists favor taxes because "they provide the clearest price signal, unencumbered by factors like baselines, allowance allocation, and use of credits." Price instruments are thought to perform better under uncertainty, to raise valuable revenues and to avoid transaction costs. Economists say a viable market for tradable pollution rights can rarely exist unless the government makes the right decision and clears all market barriers to free trade. Furthermore, tradable allowances may lead to environmental hot spots in low-income communities and diminish the pressure on emitting companies to make technological changes to restrict GHG emissions.

On the other hand, most environmentalists and politicians favor cap-and-trade. Environmentalists want a certain cap on emissions to assure environmental benefits. Politicians hate taxes and have even signed pledges not to raise them. Furthermore, cap-and-trade systems allow politicians to allocate original allowances to favored constituents.

Business groups can go either way. Businesses usually like a certain price so they can accurately determine their profit and calculate whether they can pass on the increased cost to their consumers. Cost certainty "enables business to plan ahead, secure in the knowledge that raising the tax rate beyond any automatic adjustment, which can be planned for, requires another vote" in the legislature. Nonpolluting companies might support a carbon tax if they do not pollute and the revenues from the tax will reduce their corporate tax. Of course, if the exiting industry can be grandfathered into the cap-and-trade without paying for the initial allowance, they would favor the cap-and-trade. In addition, business groups that can sharply reduce their emissions will prefer cap-and-trade as they can profit from selling their excess allowances to others. Lastly, Wall Street would also most likely support cap-and-trade as "hefty fees" can be charged "for arranging trades in allowances and futures trading."

---

* Originally published in 7 San Diego Journal of Climate & Energy Law 61 (2016). Reprinted with permission.

...Both the carbon tax and the cap-and-trade are market-based mechanisms so both can encourage cost-effective technological innovation. Both can be superior to the regulatory approach, which specifically mandates emissions, tends to be complicated, and is slow to be fully implemented. In addition, these mechanisms can be better than tax incentives for renewable energy as they "incentivize efficiency improvements, reduction in energy use, and fuel switching from higher-to-lower emissions fuels." Since greenhouse gas emissions occur throughout the world, a market-based instrument, such as cap-and-trade, when linked with other countries, could prove the best approach to solve the climate change problem. Nevertheless, both of these market mechanisms can work together and be administered, politically feasible, revenue generating, efficient, equitable, and effective.

1. Administrability

Whether a carbon tax or cap-and-trade system is adopted at the regional or national level, the administrability issues are similar. Thus, both can be effectively designed with a broad base, a low cap/or high tax, and few exemptions. Both carbon taxes and cap-and-trade schemes can be imposed "upstream" or "downstream." Upstream measures usually hit emissions from fossil fuel production (oil, coal and natural gas), such as refineries and power plants. Such a system could be effective because it would ensure that all sources of carbon dioxide at the point entering the economy are covered and would impact fewer entities than downstream. The upstream approach also reduces complexity because it covers large sources. Downstream would work better locally as it hits consumption, such as motor vehicle drivers, electricity users, and arguably all sectors of the economy emitting heat. However, this might impact political feasibility as it more directly affects the consumer. In addition, the broader range of sources could make administration more complex, because of the necessity to increase the monitoring.

In general, a cap-and-trade tends to be more administratively complex. First, a baseline must be set to establish an emissions cap and this might be inaccurate. If this is set too high, than the system will be ineffective in reducing carbon emissions. If the cap is set too low, the costs to the emitters will be too high and make carbon allowances more expensive on the market. Once a cap is set, a mechanism must be instituted to determine how allowances will be created and distributed. Free allowances will benefit the current industries or polluters and no money will be raised. In the alternative, a charge can be made for the allowance or the allowance can be auctioned off. Third, the trading in allowances must be established, creating a market for purchases and sales. Fourth, monitoring of the trading must occur, to prevent fraud and punish violators. Fifth, to prevent cost uncertainty banking and borrowing need to be established. Banking will allow a holder to save its allowances for use in the future. Borrowing allows the holder to emit now and pay back later by emitting less. However, these very mechanisms can prevent the desired certainty of benefit. Sixth, offsets must be established for carbon sequestration. Offsets allow the emitter to invest in forest conservation and other projects that absorb carbon. Finally, to be internationally effective, the cap-and-trade program needs to be coordinated with other cap-and-

Comparison of Cap-and-Trade and Carbon Tax

Cap-and-Trade	Carbon Tax
Upstream/downstream Set level of emissions Determine quantity of allowances Determine allocation of allowances (free/fee/auction) Create a market Monitor emissions Monitor market Banking, borrowing, credits and offsets	Upstream/downstream Set tax Determine exemptions Determine credits Monitor emissions

trade regimes and carbon tax systems. Often, it is difficult, both politically and design-wise, to coordinate with other systems.

For a carbon tax, one must decide whether to tax upstream or downstream, then set a tax rate, decide on any exemptions or credits, and monitor. Unlike cap-and-trade, carbon taxes can be enforced by existing revenue departments. Thus, carbon taxes are generally simpler than the cap-and-trade regime, but do not work as well on the international level.

Cap-and-trade programs take a long time to get passed and implemented, whereas a carbon tax can be enacted and enforced practically overnight. Most cap-and-trade bills are long and complicated, whereas carbon tax proposals are shorter and simpler. The longer the text the more likely it will not be understood—and the greater possibly of loopholes.

Allowances under cap-and-trade raise interesting securities, tax, and international trade issues. Securities issues arise with the regulation of futures trading in allowances. Tax issues arise when allowances are free, upon trading and selling of allowances, and when banking borrowing and offsets are involved. World Trade Organization compliance issues also arise with cap-and-trade. Carbon taxes, on the other hand, do not raise securities or tax issues and do not pose international trade problem because it can be collected on imports and rebated on exports and not imposed on domestic production.

2. Political Feasibility

At the local level, just as at the federal level, differences arise between the traditional values of Republicans and Democrats. In general, Republicans are reluctant to pass a tax, so a cap-and-and trade regime is probably more politically feasible. The public might also not like a tax, although a cap-and-trade will also result in higher gas and electric bills. In general, polls have shown that citizens have a "strong public resistance to new taxes." Since a tax is more transparent, it is more likely to have citizen complaints. For example, a July 2014 poll showed that taxpayers in California would not support the cap-and-trade if their gas and electric bills would go up. On the other hand, the British Columbia carbon tax has had sustained popularity even with the recession and several administrations.

It is possible that a cap-and-trade may be more politically acceptable because the U.S. has already experienced a very successful permit system under the Acid Rain Program, implemented under the Clean Air Act Amendments of 1990. This program offered a successful model in the trading system of sulfur dioxide and nitrogen oxide—pollutants that cause acid rain and smog. This success at the federal level could translate into a more politically feasible regional cap-and-trade system.

A cap-and-trade is probably more consistent with pre-existing government environmental regulations. The new EPA rules under the CPP specifically cover "market-based trading programs." Although nothing in the plan mentions carbon taxes, EPA officials have mentioned that local carbon taxes would be acceptable. However, cap-and-trade can "more easily dovetail with similar existing and proposed regimes" in other regions. Thus, cap-and-trade can be regionally connected. Commentators have favored cap-and-trade for a similar reason in the international realm.

There is also a difference in political economy between a cap-and-trade and a carbon tax. The legislative, administrative, and budgetary considerations for a tax can be quite different. Taxes are passed in the legislature by a finance, not an energy or environment committee, and are administered by the department of revenue. In addition, different requirements exist for how the funds are distributed. These differences were illustrated by the recent cases challenging the California cap-and-trade regime. In August 2013, the courts held the cap-and-trade system was a fee and not a tax. As the court said, a tax has to be passed by supermajority of the California state legislature, a voting requirement in the state constitution. Fees only need a majority in the state agency authorized in the statute. Here, the state's landmark carbon dioxide legislation of 2006 was passed by a simple majority and granted power to the Air Resources Board to establish the cap-and-trade regime. The court also points out another difference—revenue from taxes can be spent on anything, such as rebates to the poor, whereas a fee must go into programs closely aligned with the fee itself. Because the purpose of the California cap-and-trade is to reduce GHG, the fees from the auctions of the permits must go into the Greenhouse Gas Reduction Fund. Thus, California has struggled to make the cap-and-trade system equitable....

3. Revenue Generation

Both carbon tax and cap-and-trade can generate revenue—in money from selling permits and with funds raised from carbon taxes. However, if the initial permits are given away and not auctioned, then no money will be generated. A carbon tax, however, will always result in revenue.... However, the use of the revenue can determine the impact on efficacy, economic growth and equity. To accomplish efficacy, the revenues should go to fund research into low-emission technologies or recycled into green practices, or to mass transit, research and development, carbon sequestration, and other greenhouse-gas reducing efforts. To promote economic growth, economists often favor a reduction in capital taxes or reduction in deficits. To ensure equity, the money should be used to "shift the tax" burden off labor or sales taxes, lessen the tax on small businesses and low-income taxpayers, or used for lump sum rebates or refundable credits to poor households....

4. Efficiency or Economic Growth

One of the biggest issues with a carbon tax is the impact on business and industry. The companies that will suffer the most from a carbon fee or tax are those in cement, chemicals, car manufacturing, iron and steel, aluminum, mining and oil. If the cost of doing business goes up for these industries, they could move to other jurisdictions. This so-called "leakage" can have an adverse impact on the economy and employment of the state or region. However, to eliminate this negative economic effect, the carbon systems can exempt industries (allocate free permits to them) and/or use the revenue to reduce their taxes.

The rate of the carbon tax or the cap set on the cap-and-trade will impact the criteria of efficiency or economic growth. In general, the higher the rate of carbon tax or lower the emissions cap, the more adverse impact on the economy. For example, the Congressional Budget Office estimates that in order to decrease CO2 levels by 20% below 1990 levels, a $250 per ton tax would be needed. However, if even a $50 per metric ton tax is imposed, estimates are that U.S. gross national product will decline by as much as $146 billion. With a moderate carbon tax of $20 or $30, economic studies in several European Countries, British Columbia, and Oregon have all shown no significant adverse impact on the economy.

Where the revenue from the carbon tax or cap-and-trade is directed or earmarked will also impact the criteria of efficiency or economic growth. One study concluded that using pollution tax revenues to lower other distortionary tax burdens can even improve economic performance, and no decline in GNP would result. A study by the Economic Policy Institute even concluded that over 2 million jobs could be created over the next twenty years with a fifty percent reduction in U.S. carbon emissions under alternative market approaches. Other economic studies have shown that the most economically efficient use of the tax revenue would be to cut taxes on capital, followed by reducing payroll taxes and that recycling the revenues with lump-sum rebates to lower-income households would have the worst economic efficiency outcomes.

5. Equity or Incidence

The incidence, and thus the equity, of the carbon tax or cap-and-trade will also depend on how much revenue is generated and how the revenue is used. Both mechanisms will increase the energy costs to consumers and thus could have some inequitable impacts on lower-income taxpayers. An American Enterprise Institute paper estimates that a tax of $15 per ton of carbon dioxide emitted would increase the cost of a gallon of gas by 24 cents and the price of coal-fired electricity by $1.63 per kilowatt-hour. The Congressional Budget office estimates a 15% cut in emissions would cost the poorest households an additional $677 a year in current dollars. Other studies also demonstrate that low-income households spend greater percentage of their income on energy and that the distribution of the tax revenues from a carbon tax can make the tax less regressive. If the consumer can substitute public transportation for driving then the carbon mechanism will have less of an adverse impact. However, electricity tends to be inelastic and could have a larger impact on the consumer. At least a carbon tax guarantees revenue that can be used to alleviate the burden on the poor, whereas there is no such guarantee when the cap-and-trade constitutes a fee.

6. Efficacy

Scientists say that emissions of greenhouse gasses must be cut by at least 60% to stabilize global warming. Limiting the average global temperature rise to less than 2°C "is commonly regarded as a prerequisite to avoid dangerous climate change." The investment needed, however, in the energy sector alone, to accomplish this objective is "estimated to be US $910 billion per annum during 2010–2050." ... In terms of efficacy, the key difference between a carbon tax and a cap-and-trade is that a cap-and-trade places a cap on emissions so there is what is called "benefit certainty," whereas carbon taxes set an exact price on emissions or a cap on the costs of abatement, so there is "cost certainty." The benefit certainty of the cap, however, is not an advantage if the cap us not set accurately. This is the "Achilles heel" of the cap-and-trade system. Once the price is set, it may not be effective, as the market (such as low gas prices) might depress the price. Furthermore, changing the cap might be difficult—unless of course, it is somehow phased-in incrementally over the years in the initial legislation.

The only way to prevent cost uncertainty in a cap-and-trade is to have safety valve mechanisms. If the market price allowances become too high, businesses can receive or purchase at a fixed price additional allowance at a set price from the government. If the cap amount "begins to seriously hurt business and the price allowances spikes," the cap can be lowered. These mechanisms, however, frustrate the efficacy or benefit of the cap-and-trade.

Similarly, a carbon tax cannot guarantee a certain benefit, it can just set a price. Again, the tax rate may not be effective to impact behavior. If the tax is set too low, it will not cause a reduction in carbon consumption and if the tax is set too high, it may have adverse equity or economic repercussions. Like cap-and-trade, the rates can be increased over time with a phase-in. Arguably, the tax could be set to accomplish the benefit desired. However, exemptions can also make the tax ineffective, and credits can be given to carbon sequestration projects and other projects that reduce greenhouse gas emissions, but dilute the price signal. In the end, carbon taxes, like cap-and-trade, leave environmental outcomes uncertain.

Even if the revenues from the tax or cap-and-trade program go back and are 100% reinvested in lower-carbon alternatives, such as renewable energy, or into energy efficiency, "the efficacy of those projects is similarly uncertain." And any revenue used in this way would not be available to mitigate the regressive impacts of such policies. In the end, there is no authoritative evidence that putting a price on carbon (either through a carbon tax or a cap-and-trade regime) by themselves will effectively reduce emissions.

[In conclusion, b]oth carbon tax and cap-and-trade systems can be designed to be effective. Both can have strict cost-containment mechanisms: setting a stringent cap, including all economic sources of emissions, covering all heat-trapping gas emission, and excluding loopholes. Allowances can be auctioned off and revenue used for the public good. Although emissions have been reduced by these market mechanisms, they have not been reduced enough. A cap-and-trade program is thus alone "not sufficient to meet the challenges of climate change." Therefore, we need local carbon taxes in addition to regional level cap-and-trade, but other policies are also needed. We should require utilities to provide a greater percentage of their electricity from renewable energy sources, require automakers and producers of appliances to increase performance standards, and mandate stronger energy efficiency for new and existing buildings. In addition, policies should be established to create positive tax incentives for good behavior. We should promote conservation, encourage smart growth, and provide incentives for investment in low-carbon or renewable technologies. Lastly, we need to eliminate the bad policies, such as the removal of fossil fuel subsidies, at the federal level and the perverse corporate welfare subsidies at the local level. A comprehensive approach is what is needed to solve our climate change crisis.

Discussion Questions for Part I

1. Milne espouses four theories to justify environmental taxation. How does the "Pigouvian" theory differ from the "polluters pay principle"? Which theory is broader? How do they approach the allocation of costs issue? How are these two theories different from the least cost abatement theory? How is the efficiency rationale different? Are the theories mutually exclusive?

2. Which of the two economic rationales for allocating cost under the polluters pay principle make more sense to you?

3. What are the different kinds of costs that could be internalized? Should *all* of these costs be internalized by the company? How do the theories disagree in this regard?

4. What is the "double dividend" theory and how would this theory work if the environmental tax successfully stopped the polluting behavior? Does the theory incorporate the basic tenet that polluters must pay the costs of their pollution? Is it different from the other theories only in the use of the revenue?

5. Are there any clear views on how the revenue is to be used or what costs should be abated under each of the theories Milne discusses? How can environmental taxes be passed if these questions are unclear? How important is theory in this regard?

6. Which theory do you think is best from a practical, political, and equitable point of view?

7. How does the tax approach vary from the regulatory, marketable permit, or liability approaches?

8. According to Roodman, the worst fiscal policies are not bad or ineffective tax incentives, but the failure to adopt comprehensive environmental taxation. What does he suggest we tax?

9. Arthur Cecil Pigou, in his 1920 classic, *The Economics of Welfare*, was the first to promote the "polluters-must-pay" principle by advocating taxes on companies that

pollute. What are some examples where the costs of the environmental harm are not borne (or internalized) by the polluting company but by the general public?

10. What are some examples of successful and unsuccessful regulation? Can you think of an example of a successful environmental tax?

11. What does Roodman mean by "tax shifting"? Would it ever be possible to raise enough revenue through environmental taxes if these taxes become successful in discouraging the bad behavior? Would that depend on the elasticity of the activity or product being taxed?

12. What are the limits or potential problems of environmental taxation? What are the practical, equity, and economic ramifications of comprehensive environmental tax reform?

13. What does Roodman suggest is the best approach? For example, what might be the best approach in the transportation area?

14. Both the federal and state governments can use income, excise, and even estate tax to accomplish environmental objectives. In addition, states can use property taxation. With such diverse taxing mechanisms, how can these different jurisdictions work together to accomplish important environmental objectives?

15. Assess the ozone depletion tax from a practical, effectiveness, and international perspective.

16. What was the major flaw in the gas guzzler tax? Does it work better than the CAFE (miles per gallon) standards?

17. Milne points out three ways to use environmental tax revenue. What has the United States adopted? Do you agree with this approach?

18. The United States is behind other countries in the use of environmental taxation. For example, most of Europe has high taxes on fuel. France and Germany tax water pollution, the Netherlands has a high tax on dumping lead and other pollutants into waters. Sweden has adopted a carbon tax (and a SO2 tax). Why do you think this is?

20. Shurtz points out the various stakeholders and the tax policy criteria in the carbon tax versus cap-and-trade debate. Is one mechanism better than the other or, as Shurtz argues, should we have linked regional and international cap-and-trade in addition to local carbon taxes?

21. What do you think about auctioning off as opposed to giving carbon allowances away for free? According to several authors, granting free allowances would be both inefficient and inequitable: inefficient because higher consumer prices would result under either scenario, and inequitable because free allocation would benefit wealthy corporations and their stockholders. See Alan D. Viard, "Don't Give Away the Cap-and-Trade Permits!," 123 Tax Notes, 613, 617–18 (May 4, 2009).

22. Do you agree that cap-and-trade is more administratively complex than a tax? With a carbon tax, a rate must first be determined, then taxes must be collected

and tax cheats pursued. Does the recent financial meltdown make you wary of market trading?

23. Who would, and who should, bear the financial burden of carbon taxing or capping and trading? One study indicated that 85 percent of the burden will fall on consumers. *See* A. Lans Bovenberg & Lawrence H. Goulder, "Neutralizing the Adverse Industry Impacts of CO Abatement Policies: What Does it Cost?," in Behavioral and Distributional Effects of Environmental Policy 45–85 (Carlo Carraco & Gilbert E. Metcalf, eds., 2001).

24. What should be done with carbon-tax (or permit-auction) revenues? Should they be used, as Mann suggests, to offset payroll taxes (and thereby reduce disincentives to work)? Reduce personal or corporate tax rates? Address distributional issues by compensating the public according to income levels? Balance the budget or pay down the national debt? Create a fund for environmental protection or renewable-energy research?

25. One of the arguments in favor of instituting a cap-and-trade system on the national level is that we already have successful air-pollution abatement trading systems in place in the California Cap-and-Trade System and in the Northeast Regional Greenhouse Gas Initiative. If we want to curb carbon emissions on an international level, would a carbon tax system be better? One author has suggested cross-border regional plans—one for the United States, Canada, and Mexico (i.e., the NAFTA region), another for Southeast Asia, and a third for Southern Africa—that would eventually be integrated into a single global market. See Nicholas A. Robinson, "Hedging Against Wider Collapse: Lessons from the 'Meltdowns,'" in Critical Issues in Environmental Taxation 625, 654 (Lin-Heng et al. eds., 2009).

26. President Obama moved away from the carbon tax/cap-and-trade legislation because of the difficulty of getting these initiatives passed in the majority Republican Congress. Instead, the Obama administration focused on the Environmental Protection Agency's initiatives (through the Clean Power Plan for fuel-fired electric plants) to treat greenhouse gas emissions as pollution under the Clean Air Act. What is the best approach here? What do you think the Trump administration will do?

Part II: Tax Subsidies

Marilyn A. Brown and Sharon (Jess) Chandler, *Governing Confusion: How Statutes, Fiscal Policy, and Regulation Impede Clean Energy Technologies**

The United States shares with many other countries the goal of the United Nations Framework Convention on Climate Change "to achieve ... stabilization of greenhouse gas concentrations in the atmosphere at a level that would prevent dangerous an-

* Originally published in 19 Stanford Law & Policy Review 472 (2008). Reprinted with permission.

thropogenic interference with the climate system." The critical role of new technologies in achieving this goal is underscored by the fact that most anthropogenic greenhouse gases (GHGs) emitted over the next century will come from equipment and infrastructure that has not yet been built. As a result, new technologies and fuels have the potential to transform the nation's energy system while meeting climate change as well as energy security and other goals .... [Unfortunately many fiscal barriers exist] to the commercialization and deployment of clean energy technologies ...

Fiscal barriers are impediments related to taxation and public revenue and debt policies promulgated by governments that impact markets in which a clean energy technology is expected to compete. They can take many forms such as tax incentives and penalties, liability insurance, leases, land rights-of-way, waste disposal, and guarantees to mitigate project financing or fuel price risk. While fiscal policies are imposed in pursuit of the public good, they can become impediments to innovation and competition, and they can be unfavorable to clean energy technologies. In addition, fluctuating and variable tax incentives as well as the possibility of future tax penalties related to GHG emissions all contribute to fiscal uncertainty, which can undermine marketplace efficiency.

A. Unfavorable Fiscal Policies

Fiscal policies can be used to encourage investment in a particular technology area or to overcome market failures. However, technologies and goals can change quicker than fiscal policy, leading to outdated fiscal instruments, which then incentivize undesired behaviors or technologies. A variety of tax subsidies, differential taxation across capital and operating expenses, unfavorable tariffs, and utility pricing policies illustrate this phenomenon.

1. Tax Subsidies

Existing tax subsidies can act as barriers to the commercialization and deployment of GHG-reducing technologies. For example, subsidies for conventional fuels, both implicit and explicit, can significantly lower final energy prices, putting alternative energy options at a competitive disadvantage unless they enjoy an equally large tax assistance.

The transportation sector offers examples of policies that provide tax advantages for conventional energy sources and encourage high levels of energy consumption:

- The IRS provides business deductions for the purchase of large light trucks (> 6000 lbs) that amount to a tax break—encouraging the purchase of large light trucks when they may not be needed....
- The gas-guzzler tax on cars (but not on light trucks) has discouraged the purchase of gas-guzzling luxury cars while providing no discouragement for the purchase of gas-guzzling trucks.

Examples in the realm of energy resource development include oil depletion allowances, which allow owners to claim a depletion deduction for loss of their reserves. Specifically, oil and gas wells can claim cost depletion and in some cases, percentage depletion. Also, government support for research on the production of liquid fuels from coal and the production of petroleum from shale oil and tar sands can appear as barriers to low-carbon alternative fuels. If successful, this research would promote the continued use of high-GHG transportation fuels. These fiscal incentives exemplify the problem of conflicting social goals. They exist because of the public desire to promote U.S. oil independence and energy security, but they conflict with the goal of stabilizing greenhouse gas concentrations in the atmosphere.

2. Unequal Taxation of Capital and Operating Expenses

Tax policies that encourage operating expenses and penalize capital expenses serve to slow capital stock turnover, preclude technological change, and result in the over-consumption of energy products and the over-production of GHG emissions. Examples of this issue are evident in industry, buildings, and energy supply.

In American industry, the current federal tax code discourages capital investments in general, as opposed to direct expensing of energy costs. In addition, the federal tax code forces firms to depreciate energy efficiency investments over a longer period of time than many other investments (e.g., only five years for a new data center). This is partly because energy-efficient products have long depreciable lives, such as fifteen years for a new motor or a new industrial boiler. Interestingly, a new back-up generator would be depreciated over three years while a new combined heat and power (CHP) system would be depreciated over twenty years. The CHP system would provide both reliability and energy efficiency while the back-up generator provides reliability at the expense of energy efficiency and clean air. This is another case of legislation lagging behind (and inhibiting) technological progress. Federal depreciation schedules were put into place more than two decades ago as part of the IRS Tax Reform Act of 1986, and they have not kept up with technological innovations. Modification of depreciation schedules would remove a significant barrier to industrial efficiency investments, but it would require legislative action.

Similarly, as buildings are capital expenses, these fiscal policies retard buildings turnover in all sectors. United States tax rules require capital costs for commercial buildings and other investments to be depreciated over many years, whereas operating costs can be fully deducted from taxable income. Since efficient technologies typically cost more than standard equipment on a first-cost basis, this tax code penalizes efficiency.

In the electricity supply market, Jenkins et al. have shown that projects with high capital-versus-expense ratios have higher tax burdens.[19] Interestingly, this is a market in which a mix of capital-intensive and expense-intensive technologies competes. For example, wind and nuclear plants have proportionately high projected capital costs in 2015 while natural gas combined cycle and coal plants have proportionately high fuel (i.e. operating) costs.

---

19. Alec Jenkins, Richard Chapman & Hugh Reilly, Tax Barriers To Four Renewable Electric Generation Technologies (1999), available at http://www.energy.ca.gov/papers/CEC-999-1996-003.

Reducing the demand for electricity by improving the efficiency of energy use is the least-cost way to deliver new energy services. Because its capital-to-operating ratio is particularly low, energy efficiency is fiscally disadvantaged as an electricity "resource." The problem is that capital and operating costs receive different tax treatment, and these differences result in unequal tax loads between projects built using different technologies. Jenkins et al. compared the tax loads associated with constructing and owning eight different renewable power plants with the tax load of constructing and owning a natural gas-fired generation plant. The researchers found that all but one of the eight renewable projects carried the higher tax burdens under the tax codes as they existed when the 1999 study took place. Whether or not this remains true today is unclear given the expanded incentives provided for renewable energy in the recent Energy Policy Act (EPAct) and other fiscal policy changes. Assuming capital-intensive technologies still have a differentially higher tax burden than expense-intensive technologies in the electricity generation market, the competitiveness of both renewable and nuclear technologies is reduced as a result.

Many states have similarly uneven sales tax treatment of capital-versus-operating expenses. For instance, most states charge sales tax on residential energy-saving devices but not on residential fuels and electricity. Recognizing this disparity, several states now offer periodic sales tax moratoria for the purchase of Energy Star® appliances. Georgia, Florida, and Virginia have adopted temporary (three- and five-day) sales tax holidays for certain energy-efficient products, and Connecticut has an eighteen-month tax holiday on home weatherization products. Similar holidays are being considered by Illinois, New York, Pennsylvania, Rhode Island, and Vermont.

Clean energy innovations diffuse slowly through the economy in many cases because of the long lifetime of existing productive capital stock, and because of the major investment in hardware and infrastructure that is required for significant market penetration. Power plants may operate for forty or fifty years, commercial buildings last even longer, while, on average, heavy trucks are driven for twenty-eight years and cars for seventeen years ... To quicken the pace of change, stock turnover must be accelerated by removal of policies that slow capital investments. Policy options for accelerating turnover include taxing consumption instead of income and decreasing taxes on income from capital investments....

The long-lived energy infrastructure systems of highways, buildings, power plants, and transmission lines are distinct from the shorter lifespan of most energy end-use products. This infrastructure longevity contributes to the "lock-in" of incumbent technologies. Companies must take into consideration the risks involved with adopting a new technology, the payback period of a technology, and the appropriate discount rate and transaction costs. Newer, relatively expensive technologies have longer payback periods and represent a greater risk. Thus, "lock-in" not only slows technological change in general but also tends to skew it toward suboptimal choices.

Given that the slow rate of capital stock turnover in many industries has been identified as a key barrier to the introduction of a new generation of carbon mitigation technologies, tax reforms that lower the tax burden of energy construction projects relative to energy consumption activities warrant consideration.

3. Unfavorable Tariffs

Tariffs imposed by the government can present a barrier to clean energy technologies. The following examples draw from the markets for alternative fuels and electric power.

The import tariff for ethanol is an example of a policy that raises the cost of ethanol blends produced by domestic refineries. The market for fuel ethanol is heavily dependent on incentives and regulation. In 1980, the United States Congress allowed for a secondary tariff on imported ethanol to promote energy independence; this duty, since 1983 (phased in over three years), has been set at the same level as the tax credit given to gasoline blenders and is currently 14.27 cents per liter (54 cents per gallon). In addition, the United States government provides the domestic ethanol industry with 51 cents per gallon, and EPAct 2005 requires refineries to use 4 billion gallons of ethanol in 2007, climbing to 7.5 billion gallons in 2012. With the refineries choosing to phase out MTBE in 2007, the demand for ethanol is even greater than expected, and it is not clear if the domestic supply will be able to meet the growing demand. The import tariff prevents refineries from buying ethanol from wherever it is cheapest on the global market, as from Brazil where ethanol production from sugarcane costs are forty to fifty percent less than United States ethanol production from corn.

Independent System Operators (ISOs) also can create tariffs that bar new technologies. These tariffs are effectively connection (market entry) charges although they are not called as such. For example, small generators hoping to connect to the grid in the mid-Atlantic area must undergo a review at a cost of $10,000 to the generator before being allowed to tap into the ISO-PJM (Pennsylvania, New Jersey, Maryland) interconnection. Other tariffs levied by individual utilities on customers include standby charges, buyback rates, and uplift fees.

4. Utility Pricing Policies

Unfavorable electricity pricing policies and rate recovery mechanisms present obstacles for an array of clean energy technologies; these include the regulated rate structure, lack of time-of-use pricing, and imbalance penalties. The origin of many of these policies is often based on historically long-standing practices that have been incrementally modified over years of regulatory oversight....

B. Ineffective Fiscal Policies

Some fiscal policies simply do not meet their intended objective or are at cross-purposes with their stated goal of stimulating the deployment of clean energy technologies. Tax credits for clean energy investments that cannot be claimed and property taxes that encourage deforestation are cases in point.

Several tax credits passed in legislation cannot be claimed by the targeted markets and therefore fail to achieve the anticipated market penetration of energy-efficient devices and systems. For instance:

- In 2005, Energy Policy Act authorized a tax credit for fuel cells ($1,000/kW or 30 percent of the total cost, whichever is less), effective January 1, 2006. However, by the middle of 2007, the IRS had "yet to establish guidelines that would clarify the eligibility criteria and spell out procedures for claiming the credit." Companies had to spend large amounts of money with consultants to figure out how to use the tax credit. Yet the credit expired at the end of 2007. Planning cannot be done cost-effectively around two-year tax programs.
- Several of the tax credits for individuals have limited value because of the Alternative Minimum Tax (AMT), which sets a floor for tax liability and can prevent those subject to the AMT from claiming credits. Examples include the tax credits for hybrid electric vehicles and residential photovoltaic systems. Similarly, more and more of the large industry tax credits are becoming less of a viable strategy because of the AMT. Many large companies already qualify for the AMT, so the tax code is not moving industry any further along. "The Energy Policy Act of 1992 provided independent domestic oil developers with relief from AMT, but did not do so for renewable generation or energy efficiency technologies."
- The maximum business credit deduction has also reached eligible thresholds for many companies. The IRS code requires that in any tax year a company may not reduce its payable taxes by more than fifty percent. Firms can carry unused credits over for five years, but many are still maxed out even with this rollover provision. These companies qualify for more tax credits than they can use, so the credits are often not being fully used. Piling on more tax credits is not effective. When considering EPAct 2005 tax credits, the American Council for an Energy Efficient Economy reduced the expectation by at least a third because they expect that at least a third of the firms will not be able to use them.

Ineffective fiscal policies are not just the purview of the federal government; they also exist at the state and local levels. Of particular importance to the viability of biomass as a renewable resource for transportation fuels, electricity, and chemicals is the tax treatment of farmland and forests. Many states have property tax laws that provide incentives for landowners to develop their forestland rather than leave the forest standing. These development incentives are found when forestlands are taxed based on their location (ad valorem), or are not exempted from taxation when the forests are conserved. Almost all states tax property based on ad valorem values while only four offer exemptions for forestlands. These local land values, and corresponding taxes, may rise due to urban sprawl or other drivers of new residential or commercial building in an area, but the value of the timber stand tends not to increase accordingly. A transition in the ownership structure of forests from vertically integrated forest products companies to investment trusts or investment management organizations is also occurring largely due to the double taxation of harvested timber resources. This fiscally driven shift in land ownership may also contribute to reductions in forestland as investment firms search for the "highest-value or best-use" of property. Future cellulosic ethanol production across the country depends upon the maintenance of forest resources and the landowner-to-timber-industry infrastructure.

C. Fiscal Uncertainty

Policies that subsidize energy technologies on an inconsistent and sporadic basis do not motivate rational market behavior. Similarly, future uncertainty related to penalties for GHG emissions also distorts investment options.

1. Fiscal Incentives

Fluctuating and sporadic fiscal incentives lead to uncertainty as well as abandonment of initiatives before their potential can be realized. This is particularly the case for capital-intensive improvements and technologies that require a large investment for an uncertain return.

One example of this is the renewable production tax credit (PTC), which provides a tax credit for each kilowatt hour of electricity generated by qualified technologies. These tax credits were initially made available for the first ten years of operation for all qualifying plants that entered service from 1992 through mid-1999. The subsidy was later extended to 2001, then to 2003, and again with EPAct 2005 to the end of 2007. In 2006, the provisions were extended for an additional two years, ending seven years of on-again/off-again subsidies. Because planning and permitting for new wind turbines takes about two years, expirations of the PTC contribute to investment downturns even if reauthorized shortly afterwards. [An omitted figure] shows how PTC reauthorization stimulates market activity, and how PTC expiration is promptly followed by declines in capacity additions.

The tax credit has created a seller's market resulting in increased competition for the wind production capacity, which is currently sold out into 2008, raising prices due to "supply and demand" by roughly fifty percent to $1600/KW today. Further, with the sporadic tax credits, production is geared to the short-term, which is not necessarily the most efficient—focusing on an accelerated timetable instead of optimizing production over the long-run by, for instance, investing in longer-term facility needs, systems, and personnel training.

State or local production incentives, similar to the federal PTC, are available in at least five states, adding another layer of geographic diversity and inconsistency. The variability across states for incentives and programs for renewable energy and energy efficiency can be seen using the Databases for State Incentives for Renewables and Efficiency (DSIRE) web data application.

2. Fiscal Penalties

Investors must often choose between certain financial gains and uncertain financial penalties when looking at options for the future. When possible taxation or costs for GHG emissions is unknown, investors may choose to delay adoption of clean energy technologies while their tax treatment is being debated. A clear example of this is the market for CO2 storage and sequestration, but it also occurs in other climate change technology areas. For instance, Chad Holliday, the CEO of DuPont, told Thomas

Friedman that he is reluctant to expand the corporate investment in ethanol because he cannot anticipate what the price of ethanol will be:

> What are the regulations going to be? Is the ethanol subsidy going to be reduced? Will we put a tax on oil to keep ethanol competitive? If I know that, it gives me a price target to go after. Without that, I don't know what the market is and my shareholders don't know how to value what I am doing.

Long-term financial uncertainties are particularly relevant to projects that involve carbon sequestration, where issues of liability over the full duration of the project are largely unresolved. During the operational phase of CO2 storage projects, financial responsibility and liability reside with either the owner of the CO2 and/or the operator of the storage facility. In the long-term, the turnover of responsible parties poses risk and uncertainty to investors and stakeholders. Success may require the establishment of government bonds or trust funds, privately-backed insurance funds, or public-private partnerships. Until such long-term risk management strategies are established through public-private dialogue, the financial uncertainties will hold back carbon capture and storage (CCS) projects.

Office of Management and Budget, *2015 Budget of the United States Government**

[Stanley S. Surrey helped institute the Tax Expenditure budget in 1967 when he was Assistant Secretary for Tax Policy at the Treasury Department. Tax expenditures are defined in the Congressional Budget Act of 1971 as the estimated revenue losses attributable to various tax exclusions, deductions, credits, exemptions, deferrals, and preferential tax rates. These provisions reduce the tax liability of either the individual or business (or both). What is the difference between an exclusion, an exception, a deduction, and a credit? Note that most of the tax expenditure items in the energy section of the table below are in the form of credits. What is the difference between a refundable and non-refundable credit?

The Office of Tax Analysis in the Treasury Department, the Congressional Joint Committee on Taxation, and the Office of Management and Budget (OMB) estimate tax expenditures. Examine the portion of the budget relating to "Energy," "Natural Resources/Environment," and "Agriculture" and see if you can estimate the revenue loss from all the subsidies. Do you think the direct subsidies for energy are more or less than the tax subsidies?]

* Available at https://www.whitehouse.gov/sites/default/files/omb/budget/fy2015/assets/budget.pdf.

Estimates of Title Income Tax Expenditures

Total from corporations and individuals (in millions of dollars)

ENERGY	2013	2014	2015	2016	2017	2018	2019	2015–2019
Expensing of exploration and development of costs, fuels	500	510	510	590	600	550	520	2,770
Excess of percentage over cost depletion, fuels	530	670	780	920	1,070	1,230	1,390	5,390
Alternative fuel production credit	10	0	0	0	0	0	0	0
Exception from passive loss limitation for working interests	20	20	20	20	20	20	20	100
Capital gains treatment of royalties on coal	90	80	90	110	120	120	130	57-
Exclusion of interest on energy facility bonds	20	30	30	30	30	30	30	150
Energy production credit [1]	1,650	2,370	3,000	3,330	3,370	3,210	3,130	16,040
Energy investment credit [1]	1,950	1,840	1,470	1,380	850	220	-20	3,900
Alcohol fuel credits [2]	40	10	10	0	0	0	0	10
Biodiesel and small agri-biodiesel producer tax credits [3]	20	20	0	0	0	0	0	0
Tax credits for clean-fuel burning vehicles	270	440	670	680	650	400	150	2,550
Exclusion of utility conversion subsidies	340	340	340	340	320	320	320	1,640
Credit for holding clean renewable energy bonds	70	70	70	70	70	70	70	350
Deferral of gain from disposition of transmission property to implement FERC restructuring policy	—	-60	-220	-220	-200	-170	-140	-950
Credit for investment in clean coal facilities	180	200	140	40	20	-10	-10	180
Temporary 50% expensing for equipment used in the refining of liquid fuels	600	-100	-700	-830	-870	-800	-660	-3,860

ENERGY								
Amortize all geological and geophysical expenditures over 2 years	100	110	130	130	120	100	100	580
Allowance of deduction for certain energy efficient commercial building property	70	40	20	0	0	-20	-20	-20
Credit for construction of new energy efficient homes	150	120	60	20	0	0	0	80
Credit for energy efficiency improvements to existing homes	610	0	0	0	0	0	0	0
Credit for energy efficient appliances	150	130	120	100	0	0	0	220
Credit for residential energy efficient property	960	1,060	1,170	1,300	540	0	0	3,010
Qualified energy conservation bonds	20	30	30	30	30	30	30	150
Advanced Energy Property Credit	210	110	90	0	0	-10	-10	70
Advanced nuclear power production credit	—	0	0	0	210	470	590	1,270

NATURAL RESOURCES AND ENVIRONMENT								
Expensing of exploration and development costs, nonfuel minerals	50	50	50	60	60	60	60	290
Excess of percentage over cost depletion, nonfuel minerals	580	590	590	600	610	620	640	3,060
Exclusion of interest on bonds for water, sewage, and hazardous waste facilities	450	490	560	630	690	730	790	3,400
Capital gains treatment of certain timber income	90	80	90	110	120	120	130	570
Expensing of multiperiod timber growing costs	280	300	300	320	330	340	360	1,650
Tax incentives for preservation of historic structures	570	580	600	610	620	630	640	3,100
Industrial CO2 capture and sequestration tax credit	80	80	80	130	250	120	0	580
Deduction for endangered species recovery expenditures	20	20	20	30	30	30	30	140

AGRICULTURE	2013	2014	2015	2016	2017	2018	2019	2015–2019
Expensing of certain capital outlays	90	100	100	110	110	120	120	560
Expensing of certain multiperiod production costs	140	140	140	140	150	150	160	740
Treatment of loans forgiven of solvent farmers	40	40	40	40	40	40	40	200
Capital gains treatment of certain income	920	800	920	1,060	1,160	1,230	1,280	5,650
Income averaging for farmers	130	130	130	140	140	140	140	5,650
Deferral of gain on sale of farm refiners	20	20	20	20	20	20	20	100
Expensing of reforestration expenditures	70	70	70	80	80	90	100	420

Notes:

[1] Firms can tax an energy grant in lieu of the energy production credit or the energy investment credit for facilities placed in service in 2009 and 2010 whose construction commenced in 2009 and 2010. The effect of the grant on outlays (in millions) is as follows: 2013 $8,080; 2014 $4,710; 2015 $2,520; 2016 $1,580; 2017 $330; 2018 $0; and 2019 $0.

[2] In addition, the alcohol fuel credit results in a reduction in excise tax receipts (in millions) as follows: 2013 $10; 2014 $0; 2015 $0; 2016 $0; 2017 $0; 2018 $0; and 2019 $0. The alternative fuel mixture credit results in a reduction in excise tax receipts (in millions of dollars) as follows: 2013 $350; 2014 $200; 2015 $0; 2016 $0; 2017 $0; 2018 $0; 2019 $0.

[3] In addition, the biodiesel producer tax credit results in a reduction in excise tax receipts (in millions) as follows: 2013 $1,600; 2014 $610; 2015 $0; 2016 $0; 2017 $0; 2018 $0; and 2019 $0.

Mona Hymel, *Consumerism, Advertising and Tax Policy**

One significant force stimulating us to consume is massive advertising. In turn, a significant force stimulating businesses to advertise is the tax benefit afforded advertisers. Advertisements feed American buying and consumption habits, inundating us with "must have," throw-away products. With the average American devoting almost three years of his or her life to watching television commercials, television ad campaigns spearhead the charge. Children, the most vulnerable television watchers, are a primary advertising target with the average child viewing about forty-thousand television commercials a year. In fact, advertisers annually spend over $1 billion on ads directed only towards U.S. children. By age twenty, a typical child, who has viewed over one million commercials, has been thoroughly initiated into our consumer culture. What's more, advertisers have every incentive to increase their advertising budgets. Advertising pays off: Americans buy advertised products at alarming rates. A recent documentary on consumption noted that, on average, Americans spend only forty minutes a week playing with their children, while they shop at least six hours per week. Sadly, the products amassed not only are not making us happier, the consumption has a devastating impact on our environment. Ultimately, it will destroy the ability of our natural resources to restore themselves.

A problem of this scope requires national attention and demands action on the part of policymakers to create awareness and to design solutions to curb consumption. A better understanding of the forces that drive us to consume will assist policymakers in their attempts to find solutions to change these high consumption levels....

[T]ax policies contribute to the shape of our collective culture. For example, the current preferential tax treatment of advertising costs encourages firms to invest in advertising. Advertising encourages us to participate in the consumer society—a message sent implicitly by the federal government by virtue of advertising's favored tax treatment. The tax preference facilitates the exchange of advertising, suggesting that the government views the exchange as having social value....

When we test advertising against traditional tax policy criteria, in addition to the social science research, a strong case for change emerges. [The author proceeds to examine advertising from the point of view of equity, efficiency, practicality, and politics.]

In considering over-consumption problems, any tax proposal should instill the value of conservation as it pertains to use of the "commons." Thus, we should consider taxing activities that corrode the public good. For example, a national policy of resource conservation could be incorporated through the use of excise taxes, which are designed to incorporate externalities not accounted for in the market. Other proposals

* Originally published in 20 Virginia Tax Review 347 (2000). Reprinted with permission.

would operate to eliminate existing distortions or provide incentives within the context of the current income tax.

To discourage actions that corrode the public good, income tax policies should subsidize neither wasteful consumption nor environmentally harmful consumption. Rather, tax policy should burden wasteful and environmentally harmful consumption, particularly consumption of natural resources, virgin materials, and goods and services that pose environmental risks. To this end, tax subsidies for inefficient and environmentally harmful activities should end, while tax penalties should be imposed on destructive consumption. Tax policy should, of course, be neutral, or even favorable, toward consumption of basic necessities, such as food, clothing and shelter. Thus, the tax proposals designed to discourage consumption in this article depart from tax reform proposals advocating that we abandon the federal income tax in favor of a personal consumption tax. While existing reform proposals tax consumption as defined by traditional economics, the sale of any good or service, the proposals in this article seek to tax consumption defined by reference to its environmental consequences....

For example, part of improving sustainability might include shifting the tax burden off of labor and capital through taxes on environmental bads. In the United States, the tax burden on labor is, on average, 30% considering income and payroll taxes. Alan Durning concludes that this burden pushes the economy toward natural resource use and away from labor.[74] As a result, Durning claims that the cost of things like medical care and education are over priced because of high taxes on capital and labor. Thus, he claims that a tax shift onto environmental bads will improve the economic efficiency through increased jobs and wages. We must, therefore, reexamine our current practice of using tax policy mainly to stimulate economic growth without taking into account environmental considerations....

Consumption Problems

Consumption in the United States consists of two general and overlapping problems—high consumption and environmentally destructive consumption. The combination of high consumption levels (referring to volume) and environmentally destructive consumption (referring to toxicity) threaten the U.S. resource base. The volume of material goods and services consumed in the United States is higher than ever before. As our population grows, our high levels of consumption begin to exceed available resources resulting in a negative environmental impact. For example, the use of wood, not harmful per se, becomes harmful when we harvest forests to the point at which we severely damage the natural ecosystem. Similarly, when nontoxic garbage grows to such an extent that we cannot afford to put it anywhere, it becomes a problem. Today's lifestyles insure that we engage in high volume consumption. Two

74. See [Alan Thein Durning & Youram Bauman, Tax Shift: How to Improve the Economy, Improve the Environment, and Get the Tax Man off Our Backs] 10 (1998)....

cars, two (or more) television sets, long commutes to work, and "shop til you drop" are the norm. The average resident of an industrialized country, like the United States, consumes three times as much water, ten times as much energy, and nineteen times as much aluminum as someone in a developing country. High consumption rates have enormous environmental consequences.

Environmentally destructive (or toxic) consumption occurs when our use of a material, even in small amounts, is toxic or has other harmful environmental consequences. Examples include the release of dioxins and chlorofluorocarbons into the atmosphere. The consumer life-style staples, like the automobile, a high-fat diet, throwaway goods and packaging, and air-conditioning, are produced at a great environmental cost. Enormous and continuous quantities of energy, chemicals, metals and paper are needed to sustain our way of life. These four commodities are the most damaging to the Earth to produce. In the United States, these industries top the industry-by-industry rankings for energy intensity and toxic emissions. Furthermore, they head the most-wanted lists for polluting the air with sulfur and nitrogen oxides, particulates and volatile organic compounds. Two of our most environmentally destructive consumption activities are the use of nonrenewable fossil fuels and the creation of toxic by-products. The fuels burned by industrialized countries discharge approximately three-fourths of the sulfur and nitrogen oxides that cause acid rain. Over 96% of the world's radioactive waste is generated by atomic power plants. Almost 90% of the chlorofluorocarbons responsible for depleting the ozone are released from air conditioners, aerosol sprays and factories. Thus, the U.S. resource base is threatened by both the high volume of all resource consumption and the high volume consumption of toxic materials.... [W]e exceed our carrying capacity when consumption levels reach the point so as to threaten the viability of our resource base.

U.S. energy consumption (both toxic and high in volume) may well be the factor determining whether the United States has exceeded—or when it will exceed—its carrying capacity. The consensus is that the demand for energy will continue to increase. Studies indicate that demand will increase in the range of 34% to 44% by 2010 and 54% to 98% by 2020. While most of this rise in demand centers in developing parts of the world, America's dependence on foreign oil insures that we, too shall feel the effect of increased worldwide demand. Moreover, in the absence of specific policies to alter market incentives, most new energy production is likely to come from fossil fuels. Renewable energy sources, such as solar, wind and farm-grown energy crops will likely provide only 2% to 4% of global energy supplies in the near future.

In addition to the stress such energy demands will place on U.S. lifestyles, these trends will cause increased air pollution and emissions of greenhouse gases globally, as well as regionally. Emissions of carbon dioxide from industrial activity increased 38% between 1970 and 1990 and are predicted to rise an additional 30% to 40% by 2010. Scientist, in increasing numbers, believe that as a result of increasing greenhouse gas emissions, the Earth's mean temperature will increase, a phenomena [sic] commonly referred to as "global warming." Atmospheric scientists are extremely concerned that if these emissions continue unchecked, the Earth's delicate atmospheric balance will be damaged in disastrous and irreparable ways. The United States, currently the largest source of industrial emissions of carbon dioxide, will likely be responsible for producing the lion's share of these emissions. Energy strategies and practices worldwide must change significantly, if only to stabilize greenhouse gas emissions. Such reductions, however, can occur only through more efficient use of existing energy supplies and movement to non-fossil energy sources. Moreover, the movement to non-fossil fuel energy sources and more efficient use of energy supplies must be stimulated by policies that encourage this change....

Current environmental protection mechanisms fail to take into account consumption or levels of consumption. As one commentator explains, "conventional environmental protection policies merely seek to mitigate the impact of industry as it meets the demand for what it offers."[142] Even market mechanisms, such as incentives or penalties, can impact demand, but fail to directly discourage consumption. At most, consumption is discouraged only for those who cannot afford goods whose prices reflect internalized environmental costs. "Green consumerism" also fails to condemn overall consumption levels and may even mislead consumers into believing that "green consumption" has no negative impact on the environment. All consumption uses available resources and, thus, has some impact on the carrying capacity equation. As such, *all* consumption is suspect. Therefore, policies that promote reducing *all* consumption will be important in any successful strategy to alleviate stress on the environment. Likewise, policies that promote reducing consumption *per se* will not succeed without a change in the current consumer mentality....

This next section analyzes various options for reform. By looking at advertising in a broader way, not only in terms of traditional tax policy criteria, the basis for reform and the solutions crafted can incorporate those values that many complain the tax system has lost.

Legislative Proposals to Limit Advertising Deductions

When crafting new policies, policymakers should articulate the goals they are trying to achieve. In reviewing the problematic aspects of advertising discussed in this article, the following stand out as priorities to be incorporated in any legislative proposal. First, Congress should increase awareness of over-consumption problems in the United States and advertising's role in encouraging consumption and consumerism. Second, as part of recognizing advertising's detrimental effects, legislation should reduce the incentives to advertise, and ultimately, lead to a reduction in overall advertising and consumption in the United States. Third, if the tax system

142. [Bradley A. Harsch, Consumerism and Environmental Policy: Moving Past Consumer Culture, 26 Ecology Law Quarterly 543, 572 (1999)].

is the vehicle for legislation, any proposals should be consistent with fundamental tax principles. Finally, any revenues generated from the proposals recommended should be earmarked to further the goal of reducing the negative aspects of advertising and over-consumption....

The data on investments in advertising suggests that preferential tax treatment has significantly encouraged advertising activities. Furthermore, the enactment of section 197 likely contributes to the attractiveness of advertising investments. Before Congress enacted section 197, purchased intangibles, such as goodwill, had to be capitalized, and, in most cases, were not amortizable. Section 197 considerably improved the tax treatment of purchased intangibles by allowing amortization, and one recent study suggests that corporate acquisition activity is now routinely planned around utilization of section 197's tax benefits. The combined effect—immediate deductions for the cost of self-created intangibles (like advertising that creates goodwill), and the tax benefits now afforded purchased intangibles (like goodwill created through advertising), adds up to a significant tax subsidy and thus, a huge incentive for businesses to invest in these types of assets. Furthermore, the type of advertising investments that reap the most tax rewards are those that result in long-term benefits—the most virulent in terms of promoting consumption....

A number of commentators who have considered the negative social impacts of massive advertising argue that the tax deduction for advertising should be eliminated and that advertising revenues be subjected to an additional penalty tax. Such proposals make clear that the federal government recognizes the negative impact of advertising on society. Recognition of a problem by the federal government sends a powerful message. When the government indicates that it supports decreased consumption, it creates a multiplying effect. Furthermore, significant revenue could be raised and used to further the goals of conservation.

In *The Overspent American*, Juliet Schor advocates using taxes to combat consumerism problems. A central tenet of Shor's description of consumerism in the United States is that competitive consumption creates a "prisoner's dilemma." Overall well-being could be improved if competitive incentives were reduced and individual behavior harmonized. Schor claims: "If the Jones could be induced not to upgrade their car or house or whatever, then the Smiths wouldn't have to either, and both would be happier."[549] ...

Schor's suggestion to eliminate the tax deduction for advertising costs is similar in design and impact to the proposals denying tax deductions for alcohol or tobacco advertising. Schor's propels would increase awareness of consumerism and advertising's impact. Denying the tax deduction for advertising would increase its cost, and therefore discourage some advertising/consumption. Her proposals would also raise revenue and be relatively simple in operation. By completely eliminating the tax deduction

549. [Juliet Schor, The Overspent American: Upscaling, Downshifting and the New Consumer 163 (1997).]

for advertising, however, advertising becomes significantly disadvantaged as compared to other economically similar investments. Complete elimination would certainly deter investment in advertising, but it would also create perverse incentives to characterize advertising as some more tax-favored asset. Furthermore, to the extent that some advertising does serve the function of informing consumers, complete elimination is arguably unfair to those businesses who are not engaging in the targeted socially undesirable behavior.

Professor Edwin Baker, a well-known media scholar, has also proposed that Congress tax advertising. Baker opposes advertising because he believes it "results in censorship, skews content, contributes to inequality and impairs media competition."[555] Baker would impose a tax on a business' advertising revenues.... Because of his concerns, he then advocates that tax revenues generated from his proposals be returned to education and to the press, for the purpose of subsidizing readers.... He argues that such a scheme diminishes advertisers' control over media content. By subsidizing advertisers through tax deductions, the federal government indirectly supports advertiser control of the media, and thus, the lack of a free press. In a similar vein, Ronald Collins, Co-founder, Center for the Study of Commercialism, advocates the creation of incentives that would motivate advertisers to make their commercial purposes better known. He contends that tax deductions for advertising expenditures not clearly and continuously identified as advertisement or commercial should be denied. He would also deny deductions for advertising expenditures made in connection with influencing or controlling editorial content in the print and broadcast media. Another commentator suggested that commercials be taxed progressively based on their length and frequency. The longer and more frequent the commercial, the higher the tax....[561]

Alan S. Lederman, *How Powerful Is the Nuclear Reactor Income Tax Credit?**

The Section 45J credit is available during each year of the eight-year period beginning on the date the reactor is originally placed in service. As discussed below, the Section 45J credit is up to $125 million per year per reactor times the number of gigawatts (GW) of "nameplace capacity" of that reactor. The "nameplate capacity" of a reactor is its maximum rated output, which may be expressed in GW per hour, and is usually indicated on a nameplate physically attached to the reactor.

Thus, over an eight-year period, the total credits are up to $125 million per year times eight years, or $1 billion, times the GW of nameplate capacity. [For] reactors ... between 1.117 GW and 1.700 GW of nameplate capacity, the maximum total credits per reactor are between $1.117 billion and $1.7 billion.

555. [Edwin C. Baker, Advertising and a Democratic Press 83 (1994).]
561. [Roy F. Fox, Harvesting Minds: How TV Commercials Control Kids 162 (1996).]
* Originally published in 114 Journal of Taxation 100 (February 2011), ThomsonReuters/WG&L.

The otherwise available credit is subject to reduction, however, based on such factors as an allocation of a 6 GW national limitation to all credit-eligible reactors, low utilization of the specific reactor's nameplate capacity, and increases in the national reference price of reactor-generated electricity ....

Unfortunately, ... the Section 45J credit does not necessarily reduce the magnitude of many financial risks that have historically vexed nuclear energy. Among the tremendous obstacles to new reactor construction have been:

1. The financial risks associated with uncertainties as to construction costs and the time to obtain licenses.
2. The absence of a solution to handling radioactive waste.
3. Concerns about safety of the production process.
4. Fears relating to terrorism and proliferation.

Even contemporary commentators that are not necessarily opposed to new reactor construction view these problems as continuing and serious.

Section 45J credits are at best, only a modest minority of the total estimated construction costs of a reactor. Some government estimates of construction costs are between \$5 billion and \$10 billion per reactor, and some private estimates are higher. At a \$10 billion per reactor cost, an annual Section 45J credit of, say, \$76 million per year represents merely 0.76% per year times eight years, with is about 6% of construction costs.

While the exact impact of the Section 45J credit on the net-present-value return of an equity investor would depend on such other items as the amount of capital contributed by the investor, allocations of credits and distribution of cash flow to the investors, and the risk-adjusted discount rate, an overall after-tax Section 45J credit annual return for eight years of 0.76% of projected construction costs does not seem likely by itself to attract sufficient equity capital to make an otherwise non-financeable reactor financeable.

Tax-credit-oriented structures used for syndicating wind farms in the pre-construction phase, for example, may not be commercially viable for reactor development.

The amount of the Section 45J credit does not increase as the construction costs of the reactor increase. Similarly, the Section 45J credit is plagued by other risks that have historically materialized against planned reactors, such as delays or ultimate abandonment of construction.... The Section 45J credit is not immune from concerns relating to inability to properly store nuclear waste, to safety of the reactor process, or terrorism.... The Section 45J credit similarly is not immune from business risks relating to insufficient market demand for the rector's electricity.... A phase-out of the Section 45J credit due to increase in electricity prices would not necessarily be offset by a corresponding increase in the taxpayer's own after-tax profitability....

Thus, although tax practitioners will wish to undertake their due diligence and confirm their client investors' rights to the Section 45J credits if the reactor under construction is timely commenced and place in service, it seems doubtful that Section 45J would itself entice an investor to contribute sufficient funds to bridge the gap between a financeable and non-financeable project.

Viva Hammer, *Alternative Energy Gets a Second Wind**

Wind energy provides only about 2 percent of the total electricity production in the United States, but it provides more than half the total production from renewable sources and almost 40 percent of the total new energy generating capacity in the country. By the end of 2008, the United States had added enough new wind energy capacity to make it the world leader in wind energy production. In 2008 alone, U.S. wind energy capacity increased by 50 percent. In 2009 more than 10,000 megawatts (MW) of new wind energy capacity was added, and as of the first quarter of 2010, more than 35,600 MW of wind energy capacity was operating in the United States, enough to power almost 10 million homes. None of this blossoming of activity would have been possible without the federal government's careful tending in the form of the PTC.

Wind energy projects are less costly than other types of renewable energy projects because of lower installation costs and operating efficiency. Nevertheless, they require large initial financial outlays and many fallow years before turning a profit. The largest costs associated with developing a wind energy project are the costs of building a facility and connecting it to an electricity grid. In a cost comparison performed by the federal government's Energy Information Administration, a wind facility's capital cost is estimated to be \$130.5/megawatt hour (MWh), while a coal plant's capital cost is \$69.2/MWh and a natural gas plant's capital cost is \$22.9/MWh. However, a wind facility requires only \$10.4/MWh to operate and manage, while a coal plant requires \$27.7/MWh and a natural gas plant requires \$56.6/MWh....

Mechanics of Section 45

Section 45 provides a production tax credit for each kilowatt-hour of electricity produced by the taxpayer from a "qualified energy resource" at a "qualified facility" that is sold to an unrelated person during a tax year. The PTC, which is 2.2 cents per kilowatt-hour for wind energy, is available for a 10-year period beginning on the date on which the facility is placed in service. Wind is a qualified energy resource, and a facility using wind to produce electricity is a qualified facility as long as it was placed in service after December 31, 1993, and before January 1, 2013. Also, in Rev. Rul. 94-31, the IRS ruled that for wind energy, each wind turbine together with its tower and supporting pad is a separate qualified facility.

---

* Originally published in 129 Tax Notes 895 (2010). Reprinted with permission.

The PTC is tied to production, rather than investment, to ensure that only facilities actually contributing energy to the grid will benefit from the tax credit. The PTC also requires that the electricity produced by a qualified facility be "sold by the taxpayer to an unrelated person during the taxable year." A facility that generates electricity from wind that is not sold, is sold to a related person, or is used for the producer's own electrical needs, will not qualify for the PTC. The rationale for this requirement is not explicitly stated but likely was included to address sales of electricity between related parties made solely in order to claim the PTC, because of Congress's concern with the abuse of tax credits under the previous investment tax credit regime.

Another requirement of the PTC is that the energy be "produced by the taxpayer." Thus, a person must own the energy facility in some capacity in order to claim the tax credits. Section 45(e)(3) provides that, "in the case of a facility in which more than 1 person has an ownership interest, except to the extent provided in regulations prescribed by the Secretary, production from the facility shall be allocated among such persons in proportion to their respective ownership interests in the gross sales from such facility." In the case of a wind farm owned by a limited liability company that has more than one member and is taxed as a partnership for federal income tax purposes, the project is considered owned by the partnership. The net income from the sale of the electricity is allocated to the partners in accordance with the partnership tax rules. The requirement that the taxpayer own the energy facility precludes the use of sale-leasebacks or inverted lease structures, structures available to recipients of the section 48 ITC, for example, because they are not limited by this ownership requirement.

Interestingly, under a provision enacted in ARRA, a wind energy developer can elect to claim a 30 percent ITC in lieu of the PTC beginning in 2009. A developer that makes such an election can engage in a sale-leaseback or inverted lease structure. In light of Congress's concern with tax shelter abuse under the original 10 percent ITC for wind, it appears that Congress has overcome (or forgotten) that worry by providing a bigger ITC benefit than that available under prior law....

Based on Congress's practice for nearly 10 years, presumably that PTC will continue to be extended, although it may undergo changes. For example, a present-value cap of 35 percent of cost on the PTC was proposed in the House version of the Emergency Economic Stabilization Act of 2008. The cap was not included in the final version of that act, but such a cap could become part of future legislation.

Another factor that already has affected the wind industry and further emphasizes the need for more creative federal incentives is state-level Renewable Portfolio Standards (RPSs). An RPS generally obligates electricity supply companies to produce a specified fraction of their electricity from renewable energy sources and provides mechanisms that are permitted to achieve compliance, such as renewable energy credits. Currently, 29 states and the District of Columbia have an RPS.

Federal incentives, such as the PTC, have helped the renewable energy industry and especially the wind industry grow and prosper. The PTC's chief deficiency is that it fails to stimulate use of alternative energy when fossil fuel prices fall below a certain level. The wind industry has pressed for legislation on federal RPS, which would decrease the wind industry's dependence on high electricity and fossil fuel prices by requiring a specified amount of energy to be produced from renewable sources. The House has passed legislation that includes a federal RPS, but the Senate has not put the issue to vote. The wind industry sees the enactment of a federal RPS as crucial to its long-term future, and indeed to the future of the renewable industry as a whole. That legislation would further secure the status of the wind industry as an indispensable part of America's energy future.

Nancy Shurtz, *Carbon Pricing Initiatives in Western North America: A Blueprint for Global Climate Change Policy**

Sector	The Bad	The Good	Reform
Energy	Coal-fired Oil-fired	Renewable: Wind, solar, hydroelectric, geothermal Energy conservation Increasing efficiency Reducing waste	Reduce or eliminate the current oil, gas and coal subsidies. • Percentage depletion • Intangible drilling cost • Enhanced oil recovery credits Pass new energy law extending and adding tax incentives • Extend and modify the renewable energy production tax credit; • Extend and modify the solar energy and fuel-cell investment tax credit; • Remove the caps on credits for residential solar property and residential fuel-cell property; • Create a tax credit for plug-in hybrid vehicles; • Create a credit for cellulosic alcohol production; • Extend the credit for biodiesel production; • Extend and increase the credit for alternative refueling stations; • Eliminate the "SUV loophole," which allows business to claim a tax break for buying less-efficient heavy vehicles; and • Create renewable energy bonds for public power providers and electric cooperatives

* Originally published in 7 San Diego Journal of Climate & Energy Law 61 (2016). Reprinted with permission.

Sector	The Bad	The Good	Reform
Forestry	Clear-cutting Logging Soil erosion Nonsustainable forest practices	Preserve existing forests Increase carbon sequestration by planting new forests Increase wildlife habitat and biodiversity Prevent soil erosion Improve watershed management Harvest forests sustainably Preserve spiritual respite and scenic beauty for humans	Eliminating below-cost timber sales and other subsidies on public lands End preferential timber-tax treatment • Capital gains for timber sales • Expanding timber production Continue incentives for conservation and reforestation Allow tax credits for carbon sequestration
Industry	Low energy efficiency Non or low recyclable content	High energy High recyclable content	Limit the advertising deduction Eliminate policies favoring debt and consumption Tax packaging, waste and non-biodegradable products. Impose pollution tax on SO_2 NO, noise, air and water pollution
Agriculture	Erosion of wetlands Nitrogen fertilizer High transportation costs Eutrophication	Organic farming Local production Sustainable farming	Eliminate or reduce bad tax incentives • Capital intensive subsidies • Capital gains preferences on sale of cattle • Cash method for farmers Impose tax on fertilizer
Transportation	Fuel-inefficient cars Airplane travel Parking	Fuel-efficient cars Public transportation Walking, biking	Eliminate the tax preferences for commuting • Tax the parking provided by the employer • Reduce expensing of light trucks (SUVs) • Eliminate light truck exception to tax-guzzler tax Continue to promote hybrids and electric cars and car pooling Increase gasoline tax

Sector	The Bad	The Good	Reform
Housing	Urban sprawl Large new and /or inefficient homes in open areas Erosion of wetlands Low energy/ Inefficient appliances	High-density housing Renovated homes Energy efficient homes High energy-efficient appliances	Limit mortgage interest deduction on low-energy efficient or large homes Disallow mortgage deduction on vacation homes Tax inefficient appliances
Population	Over population Over consumption	Limit population Limit consumption	Limit dependency exemption Eliminate or limit per-child credit Tax consumption (VAT or national sales tax)

Discussion Questions for Part II

1. Do you agree with Brown and Chandler's assessment that fiscal barriers like tariffs and utility pricing policies impede the commercialization and deployment of clean energy technologies?

2. Brown and Chandler believe that tax legislation lags behind technological change. What are some examples of tax subsidies that incentivize undesired behaviors or technologies? Why should these subsidies be eliminated?

3. How does the federal tax system penalize capital expenditures and encourage over-consumption of energy products in industry, buildings, and energy supply? Should the tax code lower the tax burden of energy construction projects rather than encouraging energy consumption activities? What is the "lock-in" effect and how does it contribute to incumbent technologies?

4. What are some examples of ineffective tax policies—those that cannot be claimed or encourage environmentally damaging behaviors? What is the AMT and how does it impede transparency?

5. How do tax policies contribute to fiscal uncertainty and how does this undermine marketplace efficiency?

6. Do Brown and Chandler provide any remedy to the financial uncertainties posed by tax policy? What are these and do you have any other recommendations for change?

7. Would Brown and Chandler think the current tax subsidies for green energy (solar panels, wind, etc.) are examples of good fiscal policy?

8. Take another look at the 2015 United States Tax Expenditure Budget. Tax expenditures operate like direct expenditures, but do not go through the direct appro-

priations process each year. Do you think tax expenditures should have the same scrutiny as the regular budget?

9. Do you agree with Hymel's assessment of American overconsumption? How important do you think advertising is to our consumption level? Can you think of a better way to reduce overconsumption? Should consumers play a more direct role?

10. Hymel suggests several ways the tax code can be modified to curb consumption. Do her policies curb the bad behaviors as well as tax the bad behaviors? Do her policies encourage the good behaviors, like conservation? Currently the federal code allows for deductions for conservation easements of property during life or at death. What about eliminating a sales tax on the purchase of used products?

11. Like nuclear power, wind requires large capital outlays. What is the cost of wind compared to more traditional energy, such as coal and gas?

12. What is Hammer's assessment of the Section 45 Production Tax Credit? Examine the Tax Expenditure Budget—how much more is being lost to the treasury by subsidizing this credit? How does that compare to other items in the budget?

13. Study the Shurtz chart on good and bad tax policies by sector. Do you agree with her on what reform measures are needed? What other business practices (reducing methane and other GHG emissions, etc.) do you think should be curtailed? How could the tax code be used for this?

Chapter 10

Sustainability, Torts, and (

An important issue of corporate social and environmental responsibility is the liability (or punishment) of businesses for the damage caused by their tortious or criminal activities. Businesses may find themselves in court if they cause significant harm to the environment or public health, engage in deceptive or misleading conduct, or repeatedly violate the law. The first reading in the chapter describes the new corporate accountability that results from tort actions, setting forth the elements that must be present and whether a "safe-harbor" can ever exist. The second reading deals with limited liability issues and suggests a control-based alternative to shareholder liability. The third reading distinguishes tort from environmental regulation, concluding that both are necessary. A short article raises tort issues about oil spills. Finally, a reading addresses when criminal liability should arise from environmental misbehavior. As you read this chapter consider what the tort and criminal law (and penalties) should be to encourage sustainable business practices.

Carola Glinski,
*Corporate Social Responsibility and the Law**

Technical standardisation in tort law

Technical self-regulation may aim at harmonisation in order to facilitate economic transactions, at informing the profession, or at providing guidance to employees or subsidiaries in order to improve their performance and to prevent damages. However, it may also aim at creating legal effects by establishing a legally 'safe harbour' for those who comply with the private rules. Technical self-regulation mainly comes in the form of private norms adopted by one or more corporations, the usual or actual practice of one or more corporations, or measures that are recognised as necessary by one or a number of corporations.

In legal terms, it might define the required standard of due diligence in classical fault-based tort law. In very general terms that would mean (1) if the conduct was not in line with the relevant technical norm, there would be a strong presumption of negligence and (2) vice versa, if the conduct was in line with the relevant technical norm, there would be a presumption of due diligence and therefore against negligence

* Excerpted from Corporate Codes of Conduct: Moral or Legal Obligation?, in The New Corporate Accountability: Corporate Social Responsibility and the Law (Doreen McBarret, Aurora Voiculescu & Tom Campbell eds. 2007).

ough damage was caused. Such a standardisation effect has already been dis-ed controversially with a view to semi-private technical norms adopted by recog-ised standardisation organisations or institutes such as the Deutsches Institut für Normung eV (DIN), the British Standards Institution (BSI), the Comité Européen de Normalisation (CEN), and the International Organisation for Standardisation (ISO). These presumptions may either form part of substantive law or merely impact on the burden of proof. In contrast, it is common ground that technical norms do not have an immediate binding effect in tort law.

Clearly, the legally required standard of due diligence is a normative standard not an empirical one. Therefore, it cannot simply be related to a custom or a common practice as it might be unacceptably lax. Instead, its concretisation has to lead to the correct determination of the one legally required conduct in a particular situation, taking account of the two main purposes of tort law. One purpose is the compensation of the victim, which in fact means the allocation of damages, the other purpose is the prevention of damage, a purpose of ever increasing importance especially in the field of environmental liability. For the prevention of damage, it is essential that the standard of due diligence is technically or substantially correct, a question that can be answered best by experts. In contrast, the decision on the allocation of damages—which means the determination of the required conduct, the compliance with which exempts from liability—is a question that has to reflect the public interest. It is a question of societal values, for example of the individual freedom to act or public interest in economic development versus the protection of health and safety or the environment.

Still, it is worth considering the tort law consequences of technical self-regulation. Below the legal effect of defining a 'safe harbour' there are two other legal effects one should be aware of: the setting of individual standards of diligence; and the setting of generally applicable minimum standards of diligence.

Individual standard of diligence

Corporations can be held liable if they violate their own (internal) technical norms or deviate from the usual conduct that they have recognised as necessary. This is true even if their own individual standards exceed what is legally required in general. Here the private rules or usual conduct of a corporation are used (by law) in order to establish an individually higher standard of diligence.

The reason is that tort law liability was traditionally based on individual fault. This has changed insofar as (more) objective standards of negligence have evolved. This objective standard, however, merely has the purpose of introducing a minimum standard, thereby raising the diligence required from those who lack certain abilities. This is in line with the increasingly important purpose of prevention. In contrast, the objective approach has not lowered the diligence requirements for those who have special knowledge and abilities.

Strictly speaking, this is not an issue of standardisation at all, since here private regulation or practice does not take effect on other producers (outsiders) but is only binding on the respective corporation. Therefore, there is no reason for further legitimacy considerations. This is different with the following effects, where private regulation may have a real standardising effect that it is binding on outsiders.

Baseline or minimum standard the non-compliance of which attracts liability

Beyond this individual effect, private regulation by (a certain variety of) corporations defines the minimum standard, the breach of which constitutes liability. Private regulation here includes the common practice as well as the measures recognised as necessary—no matter whether it is based on an agreement between corporations, or simply exercised or (internally) regulated in parallel. Outsiders—that is, producers who do not adhere to the relevant practice or rule—are bound by this minimum standard defined by the practice or regulation of others as well.

This essentially stems from the tort law requirement of negligence, according to which damage must be predictable and avoidable. Here, the individual ability to recognise and avoid damage is replaced by the respective abilities within a certain line of business or category of producers. The binding effect on outsiders is a (legitimate) consequence of the legal decision in favour of objective standards. This objective approach is also reflected by the term 'duty of care'.

All measures to prevent damage that are usually applied in practice or that are deemed adequate by the relevant category of producers must be regarded as measures that the members of the same profession or business can recognise and take. Notably, this determination of the minimum standard does not disallow producers to take different measures as long as they achieve the same level of safety. With a view to semi-private technical norms Falke and Schepel have observed a growing international consensus that 'compliance with standards is a necessary but not necessarily sufficient condition for the exemption of liability in tort.'[70] An illustrative example from English law is the case of *Ward v. Ritz Hotel.* The balustrade of the hotel's balcony was lower than the relevant British norm and a guest fell down and was injured. Whereas the judge in the first instance denied the relevance of a breach of an institutionalised norm for establishing negligence, the majority of the Court of Appeal held that the failure to comply with the relevant technical norm constituted negligence.

This legal effect of a minimum standard of due diligence has, however, some prerequisites. First of all, the private rule or practice must be established or followed by a representative variety of corporations. In contrast, a great number of adhering corporations is not necessary since the relevant criterion is not consent but the general ability within the relevant category of producers, or peer group (*Verkehrskreis*), to recognise and follow the rule.

The second prerequisite is the correct determination of the peer group. In the context of an industrialised country, the relevant peer group is the respective line of business that is also usually subjected to the same public law requirements. This may be

70. [1 Harm Schepel & Josef Falke, Legal Aspects of Standardisation in the Member States of the EC and EFTA 257 (2000)].

different in a developing country where the domestic producers at a low level of environmental and safety standards meet producers that are subsidiaries of and controlled by multinational corporations. Under such circumstances, the relevant category of producers cannot simply be identical with the line of business but has to take into consideration other criteria such as technological know-how, (environmental and safety) management abilities, access to technology and financial resources. Consequently, this approach leads to different standards within the same line of business, where sophisticated producers — in particular, subsidiaries of multinationals — have to adhere to the higher standard of their peer group.

With such a consideration of different peer groups that forms part of tort law, it is also possible to level out — at least with the legal consequences of tort law — the different protection standards globally. These different tort law requirements on different categories of producers in the same line of business should not be in breach of international law — and in particular of the principle of national treatment that is usually enshrined in investment agreements — so long as the nationality of the producer or his link with a foreign investor as such are not relevant criteria.

In contrast, the final legal effect of a 'safe harbour' may be the one actually intended by corporations. By producing their own (technical) codes or norms, corporations may hope that courts refer to these self-regulatory requirements when determining the correct standard of lawful conduct, the compliance with which exempts the producer causing damage from liability. As a consequence, the victims and/or the general public (would) have to bear the costs of the damage. Ironically, corporations may find that this type of binding effect proves elusive.

This standard of a safe harbour is usually higher than or at least as high as the baseline or the minimum standard but — in principle — not necessarily the highest state of the art. Obviously, third persons (the victims) and the public interest (e.g., in environmental protection, public safety or simply in avoiding public costs of remedying the damage) are directly concerned by any regulation with regard to a safe harbour. Therefore, private regulation of a safe harbour would not only presuppose the substantive correctness of the standard derived from 'ideal expertise' but also a fair and representative procedure to ensure the reflection of the public interest.

As a first consequence, technical self-regulation by corporations *unilaterally*, although relevant for defining an individual or an objective minimum standard, lacks the legitimacy to define a safe harbour for producers to the disadvantage of third persons or the general public, as there are no safeguards for their substantial correctness (although they may in fact reflect the state of the art) or for the reflection of the public interest.

However, a number of tort law-specific objections must be raised against *multilateral* technical regulation as well. To start with, the existence of an 'ideal' committee that really reflects the 'ideal expertise' and the public interest is not very likely, as the oft-mentioned shortcomings of ISO, CEN and DIN demonstrate, where — despite all precautions — the producers and users of technology dominate the standardisation process, simply because of their superior knowledge and their resources.

But there are further important reasons why a safe harbour cannot be established. Also, environmental liability law—that is, liability for damages caused by industrial installations—follows a (worldwide) trend towards strict liability. In principle, fault-based liability in these circumstances is a relict anyway. In order to be in line with this tendency towards strict liability, the standard of due diligence required by fault-based tort law should reasonably reflect the highest state of the art that can be answered by the 'ideal expert'. Any safe harbour below appears inadequate.

Legitimacy considerations also prevent private regulation from establishing a safe harbour in tort law. If a private committee, no matter how pluralistic, could determine a standard of due diligence below the highest state of the art, it would decide that in the case of compliance with this lower standard the victims have to bear their damage without any compensation. Thus, a private committee would be allowed to place a special burden on a group of persons (the future victims) that cannot be identified in advance and that cannot therefore be included in the decision-making process proportionately to their potential suffering. This is a problem that—for tort law—cannot be solved by requirements of fair procedure. Importantly, future victims of industrial accidents usually have no choice as to whether or not they expose themselves to the risk of uncompensated damage. Moreover, a private committee has no alternative compensatory mechanisms available.

Therefore, the general exclusion of liability for certain conduct below the highest state of the art can only be decided by a democratically legitimated legislator, and it should then be accompanied by an insurance solution. Political reasons for such a decision may be the wish to attract (risk) technology, or to offer an incentive to establish some reasonable standard at all, in particular where—like in low standard countries—there is no adequate public law regulation on the subject matter.

Therefore, tort law does not really give room for the determination of a safe harbour, no matter whether it is by a corporate code of conduct, by the ideal pluralistic committee or by semi-private institutionalised norms. In principle, due diligence in environmental liability requires diligence at the highest state of the art. A general decision in favour of an exclusion of liability for conduct below the highest state of the art can only be decided upon by a democratically legitimated legislator. Apart from this, the justification for not meeting the highest state of the art in the individual case can only be decided by the civil courts. In exceptional cases it may, for example, be acceptable not to apply the highest standard of safety where the costs incurred are grossly disproportionate to the preventive effect of the measure or to the severity of the damage. This task necessitates the weighing of the respective interests of the producer and the victim in order to achieve justice in the individual case, although the decision may be influenced by societal values on the correct allocation of damages.

The same result can be found in literature and case law from other member states of the European Community (concerning semi-private institutionalised technical norms). Falke and Schepel observe that in tort law, 'non-compliance is of greater legal significance than compliance with standards' and compliance 'leads to scarcely more than a mere indication of fulfilling duties of care (at all).' For example, in the 'ice hockey case' a spectator was injured by a puck that flew over the board. Although the height of the board was in compliance with the relevant German standard, the German Bundesgerichtshof regarded this norm as generally too low. The court held that 'they (the technical norms) do not always determine the ultimate care that can be expected in a particular case and do not discharge the judge from his duty to take account of the safety interests of potential victims himself.'

Nina A. Mendelson, *A Control-Based Approach to Shareholder Liability for Corporate Torts*[*]

There is little disagreement that limited shareholder liability for corporate torts can encourage socially costly corporate activity—risky activity selected because the corporation and its shareholders do not bear all the expected costs of the activity. While the size of this externality remains to be quantified, individuals engaging in risky business enterprises are regularly advised to create corporations precisely for the purpose of shielding their assets, and corporations engaging in risky activities are advised to create subsidiaries for the same purpose. Federal government settlement guidelines for civil enforcement actions have explicitly assumed that a corporate defendant's "ability to pay" a government claim generally should be determined without counting shareholder or parent company assets. Even given the very limited opportunities for "piercing the corporate veil," thousands of corporate tort victims have spent money litigating, trying to obtain compensation from shareholders in cases where corporate assets and insurance may be inadequate to cover injury costs.

Commentary on limited liability for corporate torts falls into two major camps. Some defend limited liability rules against all comers.[6] Others propose to abandon it altogether in the case of tort and statutory violations and substitute a scheme of unlimited shareholder liability divided among shareholders pro rata.[7]

Both groups, however, focus on the corporation as the unit. Inexplicably, neither regime seems to account fully for qualitative differences among shareholders. Shareholders may have varying access to information and ability to influence management decisions, and controlling shareholders may have special opportunities to benefit from corporate activity. A shareholder liability regime's consequences can differ significantly by shareholder. Take limited liability's articulated benefit of reducing information costs. A limited liability regime might indeed save significant costs for a shareholder with only a tiny proportion of a corporation's shares and limited access to information. By contrast, when the shareholder is a parent corporation or a shareholder that otherwise can control corporate affairs, information costs savings may be less significant—or lacking altogether.

---

* Originally published in 102 Columbia Law Review 1203 (2002). Reprinted with permission.

6. See, e.g., Frank H. Easterbrook & Daniel R. Fischel, The Economic Structure of Corporate Law 41–44 (1991)....

7. See, e.g., [Henry Hansmann & Reinier Kraakman, Toward Unlimited Shareholder Liability for Corporate Torts, 100 Yale Law Journal 1879, 1880 (1991)]....

The moral hazard created by limited liability for a corporation to overinvest in excessively risky activity also depends on shareholder characteristics. For example, a controlling shareholder will be more able to influence a corporation to take excessive risks because the shareholder will be better able to curb the effects of managerial risk aversion. Further, a controlling shareholder likely will be more inclined to favor risky corporate projects because of a general ability to reap a share of corporate benefits in excess of a pro rata share. Consequently, the presence of a controlling shareholder likely will prompt a corporation to externalize more costs than if the corporation's equity is diffusely held by many very small shareholders. However, neither the limited liability regime nor the pro rata regime adequately accounts for the differences in incentives and transaction costs that can face different shareholders in a single corporation.

In contrast, a control-based liability regime would focus vicarious liability for corporate torts and tort-like statutory violations only on the shareholder with the capacity to control the corporation. When liability exceeds corporate assets, a shareholder with the capacity to control would be fully responsible for corporate torts or statutory violations. A control-based regime would thereby respond to the greater incentive for excessive risk taking resulting from the presence of a controlling shareholder. It also would address a potential shortcoming of the pro rata unlimited liability regime: the prospect that its incentives for controlling shareholders might be inadequate to deter excessive corporate risk taking. At the same time, because it would not treat shareholders identically, a control-based liability regime could preserve potential efficiencies created by limited liability for truly small shareholders, such as reductions in transaction costs. A control-based liability regime is not free from disadvantages. It could overdeter some socially beneficial activities that cannot be insured, and the application of a more flexible liability standard could generate transaction costs compared with a detailed ex ante rule. Definitively resolving the relative size of these effects requires further empirical investigation into issues such as the value of control and the location and significance of transaction costs. Nonetheless, because a control-based liability regime more explicitly responds to differences among shareholders and appears most likely to compel corporations to internalize the costs of their risky activities, it deserves serious consideration.

A control-based liability regime deserves such consideration for pragmatic reasons as well. Implementing it would be comparatively straightforward. Of course, retaining the status quo is generally easiest—but that would also require retaining the undiluted moral hazard of limited liability. However, compared with a pro rata liability regime, a control-based liability regime could be more easily adopted. Congress or state legislatures could pass statutes imposing such a regime, and courts could also implement it by simply building on the common law rules of veil piercing.

The Efficiency Justification for Limited Liability

The primary justification for limited liability for corporate torts is efficiency-based: Limited liability not only encourages investment in socially beneficial activities, but, by addressing market imperfections, it encourages an efficient level of investment. For limited liability in tort, the argument is that limited liability efficiently facilitates economic investment in two ways: (1) by reducing information costs, thereby facilitating the efficient separation of "capital" from "skill"; and (2) by correcting risk aversion among shareholders.

The Basic Moral Hazard Problem

At least with respect to risky activities for which tort victims might seek to obtain legal recourse, limited liability presents an opportunity to avoid paying the appropriately-sized tort judgment. A corporation may be created or operated in a way that renders it "judgment-proof"—having only nominal assets available to pay a tort judgment. Or, a corporation simply may have inadequate assets available to fully cover its responsibility. And once the corporate assets are exhausted, the shareholder typically has no personal responsibility for the judgment except under quite limited circumstances—when the corporate veil can be pierced or when the shareholder's own conduct violates the law.

Consequently, corporate managers may select overly risky projects more often than is socially optimal. As a matter of economic theory, a shareholder will favor increases in risky activity as long as the anticipated marginal benefit to the shareholder from an increase in risky activity (for example, the present value of increase in expected dividends from corporate income) exceeds the anticipated marginal loss (present value of reduction in expected dividends or share price from costs of the activity, liability judgments, and the like), up until the point where the marginal benefit and marginal loss from an incremental increase in risky activity are equal. Under limited liability rules, the shareholder's total losses are capped at the value of the shareholder's potential lost equity. Thus, such risky projects may appeal to the shareholder even though they may be socially costly.

Further, as between two projects with equal benefit, each of which presents, say, a 10% risk of some liability that exceeds the corporation's assets, the shareholder will be indifferent between them, even though one might be more socially costly than the other. Suppose now the two projects are characterized by different potential benefits. Because the corporation will bear the project's costs only up to the amount of total corporate assets, rather than bearing full costs, the shareholder will prefer the project with a greater potential benefit, even if the net social benefit is smaller.

More generally, limited liability reduces the shareholder's incentive to gather and process information regarding a subsidiary's potentially hazardous activities, even when the shareholder is in a position of control or for other reasons can cheaply acquire that information. Consequently, even a risk-averse shareholder may make fewer attempts to encourage management to obtain more insurance, take more precautions, or avoid the risky activity altogether. Thus the costs of excessively risky corporate decisions for which shareholders bear no responsibility (because corporate assets have been exhausted) are shifted to third parties, including tort victims, the environment, and the community, as well as other "involuntary creditors" to which the corporation is liable.

This moral hazard has a number of consequences. The easy availability and effectiveness of limited liability in protecting the corporation's shareholders or parents will lead companies to select corporate restructuring as a means of managing the risk presented by hazardous corporate activities. Restructuring is essentially an investment in transaction costs.

Because corporations can limit liability by forming subsidiaries, the corporate tendency will be to divert investment from other, more efficient risk management strategies. For example, a corporation will be less likely to purchase adequate insurance or otherwise allocate risk through contracts. Further, a corporation may invest less in directly reducing the risks of its hazardous activities—say, by changing technologies or adding additional safeguards. With respect to environmentally hazardous activities, for example, because application of limited liability could be as, or more, effective in reducing potential environmental liability as investing in pollution-reducing technology, corporations whose managers decide to engage in environmentally risky activities often will direct their resources to creating a new corporate layer.

For example, in one case, a company engaged in oil transport incorporated separate subsidiaries, each of which owned a number of barges that transported oil on Lake Champlain. The companies had identical officers and directors, and the subsidiaries remitted profits to the parent by way of dividends. The parent had substantial involvement in subsidiary operations. Poor barge operation led to a number of spills on Lake Champlain. The spills resulted from employees continuing to pump oil into the water after encountering a leak, employee failures to cap pipelines, and disregard of navigation agreements.[127] The limited liability doctrine apparently encouraged resources to be devoted to corporate restructuring as a way to minimize environmental liability. Instead, the parent should have invested (or encouraged the subsidiary to invest) in training barge employees regarding appropriate measures to avoid oil spills.

Preferred Risks Under Limited Liability

The tendency toward excessive risk taking under limited liability will be skewed toward risky activities that present the risk of large losses. For example, suppose a parent company with a subsidiary owning $2 million in assets compares a choice of two risky projects for the subsidiary. One presents a 1% risk of a $10 million loss in the next year; the other presents a 25% risk of a $400,000 loss in the next year. With unlimited liability for a parent corporation, and assuming that the corporation is risk neutral, these choices might well be evaluated equally: Expected loss would equal risk of loss times projected loss. With limited liability, however, the preferred project is clearly the first one—the small risk of a large loss—since the parent corporation will not bear the full costs in case the gamble fails. The company is simultaneously less likely to purchase adequate insurance to cover the risk.

As among excessively risky projects, corporations will be more inclined to select those with a relatively delayed realization of expected costs. Projects where the risky activity leads to a latent injury—one not immediately detectable, such as pollution or cancer—will be preferred. Projects with costs that cannot be imposed without a

127. These facts are taken from *United States v. Ira S. Bushey & Sons, Inc.*, 363 F. Supp. 110 (D. Vt. 1973).

judgment in a court of law (e.g., common law tort litigation) will be preferred to projects with costs that can be imposed more quickly (say, through administrative fines). This is so even if the delayed costs have the same present value as if they were imposed today (if, for example, a court judgment rendered later were to include interest). If there is delay, a corporation and its shareholders can more easily separate corporate assets from the risky corporate activity. For example, the corporation is more likely to have sufficient time to distribute dividends to shareholders. Once the payments are made, a tort victim generally cannot gain access to those funds unless the corporate veil is pierced.

While some have argued that tort victims may be indirectly protected from excessive corporate risk taking by contractual creditors that will insist on a showing that the corporation is maintaining adequate operating reserves, the judgment values of tort suits still may greatly exceed available capital, leaving victims unprotected.

Tort judgment statistics suggest that the largest risks may involve defective products, toxic substances, and environmental injuries. In the case of environmental risks, the combination of "small risk/large loss" and "delayed cost realization" is typical. First, environmental losses tend to be delayed because the injuries to human health and the environment of particular substances may take years to manifest themselves. Second, once an environmental injury has occurred, cleaning it up or restoring the natural environment can be very expensive due to technological difficulty. Third, the process of enforcing environmental liabilities—especially large ones—is likely to take place years after the original conduct that created the environmental injury. Moreover, as a practical matter, legal action to address environmental harm faces significant obstacles. Lack of scientific knowledge often presents an obstacle to discovering environmental damage and to documenting such damage in court. Fourth, the probability of liability is reduced because environmental enforcement is predominantly pursued by federal, state, or municipal government entities. Liabilities are frequently large, but many violations are not pursued. For example, in fiscal year 1997, the EPA obtained, on average, a penalty of over $700,000 in Clean Water Act settlements, in addition to the costs of action to abate the violation, but the total number of such judicial settlements was only thirty-five.[138] One estimate is that between 18% and 27% of "major" facilities holding such permits (a total of 7000, at that time), were in significant noncompliance with their permits. In the hazardous waste context, as well, the EPA has taken enforcement action at only a fraction of the hazardous waste sites that warrant cleanup under its standards.

As noted, the presence of large liabilities is also likely to be marked in areas such as new product development, pharmaceuticals, and other areas presenting health and environmental risks. For example, the cost of damages from asbestosis alone amounted

138. Office of Enforcement and Compliance Assurance, EPA, EPA-300-R-98-003, Enforcement and Compliance Assurance Accomplishments Report FY 1997, at A1–A2 (1998).

to $1.2 billion by 1986 and is expected to exceed $31.7 billion. Current cases involving the separation of treads on Firestone tires used on Ford Explorers are expected to exceed hundreds of millions of dollars. Whether investment in corporate activities presenting these risks can be seen as "excessive" depends in part on whether the liability costs are likely to be paid. In some of the preceding examples, companies did pay liability costs. Nonetheless, the scale of these liabilities suggests that even large companies could take "excessive" risks (i.e., risks likely to be externalized).

A Control-Based Shareholder Liability Regime

In general, legal structures and rules fail to fully address the problems flowing from limited liability. Moreover, the justifications for limited liability are largely confined to the case of the small, passive shareholder with no ability to control corporate direction. Meanwhile, the advantages of limited liability can be substantial for controlling shareholders.

A control-based regime would respond to these concerns. Such a regime would impose liability for a corporation's torts or statutory violations on a shareholder (including a corporate parent) when the shareholder has the "capacity to control" the corporation by virtue of ownership. To the extent more than one shareholder can be said to possess the "capacity to control," each would be jointly liable, with a right of contribution. Such a change could be accomplished by a liberalization of the common law rule of veil piercing or through a statutory modification of the rules of vicarious liability.

The rule would not impose responsibility on the shareholder that holds only a small percentage of shares. For the individual who purchased two hundred shares of General Motors on the open market, limited liability would remain a feature of the investment. Nor would the rule impose responsibility on the pension fund with a small percentage of shares.

How could one tell if a particular shareholder possessed the "capacity to control" a corporation? A shareholder would be responsible if it possessed significant ownership and if it exercised "actual control" over a corporation's activities by virtue of that ownership. Exercise of "actual control" over even some aspects of corporate operations would be relevant to the question of whether the shareholder possessed the "capacity to control" the risky activity, even if the actual control was unrelated to the operations that resulted in a tort or statutory violation. The exercise of actual control by virtue of ownership suggests the ability to control the corporation in other respects, either by involvement in the selection of the corporation's board of directors, the exercise of authority over significant asset sales, or participation in other major corporate decisions.

For example, in *In re Pollution Abatement Services*, which dealt with a close corporation's liability for discharging refuse into and storing thousands of drums of chemicals on the banks of a creek, the two (of four total) shareholders that ran the corporation's day-to-day operations would have had vicarious responsibility under a control-based regime for the costs of cleaning up the chemicals if the shareholders had possessed potential control by virtue of their ownership.[284] Such vicarious liability would have been in addition to whatever direct responsibility the shareholders might have had by virtue of their own actions. In [*State Department of Environmental Protection v. Ventron Corp.*,*] for example, where the subsidiary's mercury processing operations substantially polluted a waterway, such a rule would have resulted in vicarious environmental liability for the parent company, which owned 100% of the subsidiary and which elected its own officers to the subsidiary's board of directors, where the board met monthly and knew the details of daily operations.

In addition to imposing liability on shareholders exercising actual control over a corporation by virtue of ownership, a "capacity to control" regime also would impose vicarious liability for a corporation's torts and statutory violations on those possessing potential control by virtue of ownership in the corporation. A potentially controlling shareholder's attempt to maintain a more passive role would not shield it from liability for risky corporate activity.

A majority shareholder clearly would qualify as possessing potential control by virtue of ownership. For shareholders holding less than a majority of the outstanding shares, whether the shareholder has the "capacity to control" the corporation would have to be decided based on the facts of the individual case.

The American Law Institute takes the position that a controlling influence should be assumed where there is ownership and/or possession of the power to vote more than 25% of the corporation's shares. The SEC has publicly noted the "widely held belief that the ownership of 20% voting power in a widely held company in most instances constitutes control." However, the question whether a particular shareholder has the capacity to "direct ... the management and policies of a [corporation]" could in some cases be an issue requiring expert testimony.

Whether a particular minority shareholder has the capacity to control the corporation might depend on the total value of the corporation and consequently the value of the shareholder's holdings; whether there is a majority shareholder; the relationship between the minority shareholder and that shareholder or other minority shareholders; or the relationship between that shareholder's board representatives and those of the other shareholders. Evidence that the shareholder has asserted a significant role in corporate organization also might be relevant, although that alone would not be sufficient to find that the shareholder possessed the capacity to control by virtue of ownership. For example, a socially conscious shareholder with 0.1% of ownership that influences a corporate decision through advocacy at an annual meeting would not have the capacity to control by virtue of ownership. Similarly, suppose a pension fund with 8% of a company's shares affects—through advocacy or as a "swing vote"—the election of a corporate director. Because the capacity to control signifies the con-

284. In re Pollution Abatement Services, 763 F.2d 133, 135 (2d Cir. 1985).

* [468 A.2d 150, 155 (N.J. 1983).]

sistent ability to exert control over the corporation by virtue of ownership, such activity would not make a shareholder one with a "capacity to control."

Christopher H. Schroeder, *Lost in the Translation: What Environmental Regulation Does That Tort Cannot Duplicate**

Environmental regulation differs from tort in three critical respects—one procedural, one remedial and one substantive—which prevent the one from replacing the other. With respect to process, environmental regulation determines levels of environmental quality through public processes and collective choices, rather than as the aggregation of a series of private decisions. With respect to remedies, environmental regulation seeks prevention rather than cure. With respect to substance, the levels of environmental quality that our current environmental regulatory system embodies cannot be achieved under current tort standards, because the collectively chosen levels differ from the cost-beneficial levels of environmental quality tort is geared to achieve.

Proponents of tort over environmental regulation routinely criticize regulation for its highly centralized structure of command-and-control, which micro-manages how individual pollution sources must behave. They contrast this with tort's decentralized structure, which is responsive to local variations and able to take advantage of local knowledge. It can hardly be denied that environmental regulation as practiced under many American environmental statutes remains heavily oriented toward a command-and-control style of implementation. Command-and-control, however, is but one type of environmental regulation. For example, environmental statutes may be implemented, and increasingly are implemented, through regulatory structures emphasizing market-based or incentive-based regimes, whereby allowable emissions are traded among sources. These and other such regimes give individual sources much more flexibility, insofar as they can trade "rights to pollute" among themselves, thereby in principle achieving least-cost means of pollution reduction.

So there is more than one way to implement environmental standards via regulatory systems. Taking command-and-control as paradigmatic of all such regulation, and then making invidious comparisons between it and tort, deflects attention toward non-essential differences between the two regimes and obscures truly basic structural differences between them. The first such basic difference relates to the processes through which desired levels of environmental quality are established. A regulatory regime establishes the amount of environmental degradation legally permitted through a collective or public decision-making process, whereas tort law establishes that amount through a private law process of judicial application of general principles to particular cases. Tort law still applies community or collective norms, often under a rubric of "unreasonableness." Those norms, though, are spelled out through an it-

---

* Originally published in 41 Washburn Law Journal 583 (2002). Reprinted with permission.

erative process of individualized litigation, not through an intentional decision of some public entity.

The key to this distinction is the public versus private identification of environmental quality levels, not the fact that private actors sue each other in the private case instead of using administrative or legislative procedures in the public case. Private litigation might well be used to supplement or supplant a public enforcement scheme that operates through bureaucracies, inspectors, administrative compliance orders, administrative law judges and the like. The citizen suit provisions that can be found in almost all pollution related statutes are intended to do just this. Citizen suits, however, are limited to enforcing standards established by the regulatory process. Private litigation that uses statutory or regulatory violations as negligence *per se* can also supplement public enforcement. There are many things to be said in connection with the possibilities of private versus public enforcement of the public standards, but such forms of litigation do not set those standards.

The decision to replace a collective decision regarding environmental standards with private ones is itself going to be a collective decision, and one that will require some justification to the public, which will be relinquishing a significant authority. Two types of arguments might be made in favor of such a change. First, one's theory of rights, responsibilities and governance might argue for resolving environmental disputes solely by private parties to a lawsuit. Such an argument would not rely upon any description of the physical or environmental consequences of litigation. Rather, individual outcomes to litigation would be justified solely on the basis of a claim that the correct procedures for resolving it had been followed, whatever the outcome might be. In contrast, a second kind of argument for substituting tort for regulation does rely on consequences. One might claim that the consequences of tort law will approximate the environmental quality levels that the collective desires or should appropriately be seeking. Decentralizing dispute resolution would in that case be justified as a means to a collectively congenial end. Tort law might have this pleasing consequence, furthermore, even if the underlying motivations and ends of tort law itself were in significant respects autonomous from influence by the collective selection of desired results.

The first type of argument does not work. Many of our concerns are exacerbated precisely because the interests taken into account in private transactions affecting the environment are too narrow to encompass all that people value. There are significant externalities involved in disputes over environmental quality, externalities that can be spatial, temporal or value-based. Spatial externalities arise when the actions of the parties involved in a private transaction have physical effects on the interests of persons remote from the site of the transaction. Temporal externalities involve the implications of actions affecting the environment on future generations. Value-based externalities involve the wide variety of interests implicated by non-anthropocentric ethical systems, such as those positing that animals and even ecosystems are entitled to respect in their own right. These values deserve a "place at the table" when actions that significantly affect them are taken. The internal structure of the tort system, however, requires only that the interests of the parties before the court be respected, thus leaving it up to the beneficence of the parties to raise the concerns of the unrepresented, assuming the court would permit them to do so. That beneficence will often substitute inadequately for more inclusive structures, such as public ones. Therefore, the structure of the tort system supplies an argument in favor of public mechanisms, not private ones, to deal with environmental issues that implicate many interests.

That being so, the case for supplanting regulation with tort will have to place great weight on arguments of the second type. This type of argument asserts that the tort system, whatever its internal features, produces results sufficiently close to what the collective wants so that it possesses a comparative superiority to alternative regulatory systems.

To evaluate such a claim, we need a picture of the results the tort system is likely to produce. One can begin to assess the environmental consequences of large-scale reliance on tort by first determining what our tort system is trying to accomplish in general. Once we have grasped the general ends or objectives of the tort system, we can then see what the pursuit of those objectives in the environmental area would produce, first as a theoretical matter and then as the anticipated results of any practical efforts to put those objectives into practice.

In trying to understand the objectives of tort, we are met immediately with a substantial obstacle: The objectives of tort are the subject of a long-running debate that shows no signs of resolving itself any time soon. The debate centers on two competing theories, deterrence and corrective justice, each of which has variations. Deterrence theory, frequently building on the Judge Learned Hand definition of negligence in *United States v. Carroll Towing Co.*,[7] understands tort law to be aimed at preventing those harms whose costs of precaution are less than the anticipated cost of the harm. Corrective justice theories understand tort as the redress of injury due to the culpable action of the defendant. As a form of rectificatory justice, corrective justice theories support liability even if it could be shown that liability had absolutely no deterrent effect at all.

An outsider to the debate between deterrence and corrective justice would be justified in concluding that this is a contest neither side can win. For one thing, a number of features of tort doctrine are consistent with either theory. Were this not the case, one side would have triumphed long ago. While such doctrines are inconclusive in choosing between deterrence and corrective justice, other doctrines do seem more easily explained by one—and hence more of an embarrassment to the other. Unfortunately, however, these other features do not uniformly favor one side. Pegging dam-

7. ... Under *Carroll Towing*, an action is unreasonable if the costs of injury discounted by the probability of injury occurring exceed the costs of prevention. United States v. Carroll Towing Co., 159 F.2d 169 (2d Cir. 1947). See also Richard A. Posner, A Theory of Negligence, 1 Journal of Legal Studies 29, 32 (1972) (explicating in deterrence theory of negligence and citing *Carroll Towing* as "adumbrating ... an economic meaning of negligence.").

ages to actual loss rather than expected loss fits corrective justice theory nicely, but makes less sense from a deterrence perspective. Holding liable persons who caused a harm likewise comports with corrective justice, whereas deterrence theory wants to impose liability on the best risk avoider, who may be someone else entirely. On the other hand, corrective justice theory has real difficulties justifying the vicarious liability of an employer for torts of an employee, whereas this doctrine has a straightforward deterrence rationale.

Looking to what judges write when they author significant tort opinions proves no more helpful in resolving the dispute between deterrence and corrective justice. Judicial decisions seldom if ever reveal what the judge understands the objectives of tort law to be. In *Sindell v. Abbott Laboratories,*[12] for example, the California Supreme Court applied a novel "market share" theory of liability to the 200 or so manufacturers of diethylstilbesterol (DES), holding each of them liable for a share of plaintiff's injuries proportionate to their market share of the product during the period of exposure. Holding the manufacturers liable in the circumstances of *Sindell* constituted a significant innovation in California tort doctrine at the time. One might have thought that the court would justify such an innovation by explaining how market share liability furthers the fundamental purposes of tort, thereby revealing what it took those fundamental purposes to be. The opinion does nothing of the sort. In fashioning its approach, the court's only succinct statement of an end or objective of tort law is the principle that "as between an innocent plaintiff and negligent defendants, the latter should bear the cost of the injury," a principle that could have its roots in either deterrence or corrective justice.

Sindell is by no means unusual. Judicial decisions in tort frequently rest upon such intermediate principles, ones that are consistent with both deterrence and corrective justice. They rely, in other words, on incompletely theorized doctrine, and do not reach for higher principles than necessary to decide the case before them.

Gary Schwartz has made a very strong case that the best explanation of tort law may be a mixed theory, combining aspects of deterrence and corrective justice.[16] His tentative suggestion is "that tort law imposes or assigns liability for proper deterrence reasons unless this result is not compatible with the criterion of corrective justice." The peace-agreement efforts of Professor Schwartz notwithstanding, the debate between corrective justice and deterrence shows every sign of continuing, and judicial opinions show no sign of fully revealing a deep explanatory rationale for tort law. So for the foreseeable future, those wishing to consider replacing regulation with tort will be impaired by uncertainty over the ends or objectives of the tort regime.

Suppose, however, that for the sake of argument one were to adopt the deterrence theory as the best rationale for tort law, and hence the best assumption on which to base a prediction concerning the likely consequences of a tort regime for environmental

12. 607 P.2d 924 (Cal. 1980).

16. [Gary T. Schwartz, Mixed Theories of Tort Law: Affirming Both Deterrence and Corrective Justice, 75 Texas Law Review 1801, 1801 (1997)]

quality disputes. Many advocates of replacing regulation with tort favor just such a deterrence approach to tort. So adopting an assumption friendly to their point of view is a way to put the case for tort in the best light.

The goal of much modern environmental regulation is to prevent harm to the environment before it occurs, with an implementation structure that includes prior approvals, permits that embody standards to be met, and the monitoring of compliance, all with that goal in mind. Modern environmental regulation announces to risk takers the legally enforceable levels of risk or harm. Unlike tort, environmental regulation does not even contemplate compensation of victims, the remedy that is essential to tort's ex post operation, but its increasing reliance on criminal and civil liability for fines and jail time for responsible corporate officers and others can get the attention of risk takers better than tort can. Permit requirements translate rules and regulations into risk taker specific terms as they frequently do and administrative agencies exist to provide further guidance. Environmental regulation does not ask risk takers to appraise their own risks, thus reducing the problem of over-optimism. Because the regulation is ex ante, it does not depend on detection of harm caused (which might be years down the road), but instead depends on detection of present violations. While such detection also can be difficult, it will be less so than the detection tort requires. In sum, the compliance signal regulation sends to risk takers faces much less interference or static than does tort's deterrence signal, as the following discussion elucidates.

The deterrence theory of tort states its objective as the prevention of harm, just like environmental regulation. Unlike regulation, though, tort has an operational structure designed to function ex post, after harm has occurred. Its objective of preventing acts from occurring that can be judged to be inefficient or unreasonable is one that it must accomplish through implementation and enforcement structures that operate after the fact. For such a system to deter, it must be able to send a signal to parties regarding their future behavior, but to send that signal it must have a case of prior harm to decide.

There are some limited exceptions to tort's ex post operation, but they do not significantly change the ex post nature of that regime. Equity courts did and courts still do recognize a cause of action for anticipatory nuisance, brought prior to harm occurring. Plaintiffs have most frequently sought to bring this type of action, though, in efforts to enjoin conflicting land uses prior to the landowner commencing with the land use, where the extent of the harm that the land use would eventually cause is highly predictable. Where harm is more speculative, even though it might be more likely than not, courts are reluctant to intervene before the fact. The requirement that harm must be imminent and practically certain before an injunction will lie substantially impairs the usefulness of the anticipatory injunction.

The limited circumstances in which injunctions will lie fail to cover many types of cases in which people today worry about environmental risks. Consequently, for many environmental risks the ability of tort to prevent harm will depend entirely on the success of its deterrent effect, which must inevitably be an indirect effect of the signal or message that the tort system sends. It is not enough that tort cases send a message, either. That message must be heard, understood and acted upon before deterrence succeeds. These downstream components to the mechanism of deterrence depend upon individuals, incentive structures and institutions that tort cannot affect directly.

Considerable disagreement surrounds the issue of whether tort law deters. Advocates of deterrence theories with a law-and-economics emphasis are often fairly blithe in asserting that it does. The empirical evidence regarding the deterrent impact of tort law, however, is in some respects quite inconclusive, as Peter Cane has written in his contribution to the Ahrens Seminar.[26]

Several findings from the empirical research on deterrence are more conclusive than others. Many studies of the deterrent, effect of liability rules focus on whether or not plant managers, doctors, landowners and others are aware of liability rules and make changes to their behavior in response to the prospect of liability. Evidence confirms that they often do make changes. When Gary Schwartz looked at the question of whether or not tort law really deters by examining available studies in a number of areas, including workers' injuries, medical malpractice, motorist liability, products liability and others, he concluded that "tort law provides something significant by way of deterrence."[27]

There is however, more to be said. Predicting the consequences of tort's deterrence signal—and hence its impact on environmental quality at the point in time that the public desires, before harm occurs—requires more precision than is provided by the blunt conclusion that people react ex ante to the prospect of liability. The question is do they react in a predictable and satisfactory way. The deterrence theory of tort aspires to eliminate only undesirable behavior, defined against a standard of efficiency or unreasonableness, and it predicts that this level of deterrence will be what is observed.

On whether or not this prediction is borne out in practice, the empirical evidence is also fairly compelling, and it is negative evidence. When it comes to achieving the level of risk reduction predicted by the deterrence models, tort law is "not as effective as economic models suggest."

A number of features of the larger institutional ecology within which the tort deterrence signal must be sent and acted upon help explain why risk-creators do not respond to the prospect of tort liability by eliminating all of the undesirable behavior.

- Risk takers tend to be more optimistic about the success of their enterprises than warranted. They systematically underestimate the harm-causing features of their businesses, resulting in taking fewer precautions than disinterested appraisal of the risks would suggest.

---

26. Peter Cane, Rethinking the Relationship Between Tort Law and Environmental Regulation, 41 Washburn Law Journal 427, 447 (2002).

27. Gary T. Schwartz, Reality in the Economic Analysis of Law: Does Tort Law Really Deter?, 42 UCLA Law Review 377, 443–44 (1994).

- Chances of detection can be small. Because the signal sent by the prospect of liability will be discounted by the probability of being held liable, this produces underdeterrence.
- Managers of corporations can have shorter time horizons (discount the future more heavily) than required to motivate proper evaluation of future environmental harms, because they will not be with the corporation indefinitely, or because they prefer short-term profitability in order to ward off takeovers due to shareholder dissatisfaction. For long-latency risks, this can lead to under deterrence.
- The causal effects of a risk can be masked by background causes of the harm. This adds to the detection problem and also leads risk takers to think they might avoid liability altogether.
- Harm can be diffuse and relatively small per victim, creating the possibility that transactions costs and free rider problems will make litigation difficult, so that risk takers would discount the chance of a lawsuit actually being brought.
- The limited liability protections of the corporate form cap the amount of liability to which corporations can actually be exposed. This also caps the strength of the deterrence signal received by risk takers. "Bet the company" gambles will be insufficiently deterred if the net worth of the company is less than the expected harm to the environment.

These imperfections in the transmission mechanisms that deterrence signals must necessarily use suggest reasons why those signals will not have their desired effect. The imperfections, furthermore, are particularly noticeable in cases of environmental risks, to such an extent that Troyen Brennan, himself an advocate of increased environmental tort litigation, concludes that the "[e]mpirical evidence suggests that environmental torts suits currently send a weak deterrent signal."[31] Compound these real imperfections with the highly imperfect understanding of them by judges and juries, and the idea that the size of the signal could be modulated to compensate, so as to achieve the correct level of deterrence, becomes rather implausible.

In contrast to tort's ex post structure, the preventive, ex ante orientation toward environmental quality levels is a fundamental attribute of the modern environmental regulatory regime. The basic architecture of that regime came into being in a remarkably short period of time, between 1969 to 1976, when a broad environmental movement helped sweep our core environmental statutes onto the pages of the United States Code. Looking back on the history of that movement, we can locate reasons for why these laws have the ex ante orientation that they do.

Now, even assuming that tort operated in exactly the way that an idealized law-and-economics analysis portrays, a tort regime would still produce enormously different results from the levels of environmental quality the current regulatory regime seeks to achieve. Environmental legislation regularly establishes standards different from

31. Troyen A. Brennan, Environmental Torts, 46 Vanderbilt Law Review 1, 6 (1993).

those chosen by cost-benefit considerations, standards aimed at protecting public health as much as possible within the limits of technical and economic feasibility.

Ethyl Corp. v. EPA illustrates how different these standards are. In that contest over the EPA's decision to phase down the lead content in gasoline, Judge Wilkey's dissent convincingly shows that the EPA lacked the evidence necessary to prevail under common law tort standards in an action against gasoline manufacturers.[40] Proof of the damaging health effects of airborne lead was too inconclusive. For one thing, blood lead levels were the actual objects of public health concern, not the airborne lead levels. Yet the correct way to translate inhaled lead quantities into quantities in the blood was not firmly established. For another, the population was exposed to lead through a variety of sources, and it was difficult to pinpoint the contribution that airborne lead made to blood lead levels. In addition, the levels of blood lead that the EPA was attempting to achieve through its regulation were below those at which studies had convincingly shown adverse health effects. Instead, they reflected the Center for Disease Control's designation of the level of public health concern, the level at which parents were urged to take preventive or precautionary measures to reduce the lead exposure of their children.

A tort law regime would not have sustained the agency action in *Ethyl Corp.* Indeed, it would not matter whether one were pursuing a deterrence or corrective justice theory of tort, because the agency would have failed to establish cause-in-fact, a bedrock requirement of both. Under a tort regime, Ethyl Corporation would have been given no deterrent signal from prior tort cases, nor would it have been specifically deterred in a lawsuit involving it directly.

The EPA proceeded to regulate lead in gasoline anyway, and years later it became possible that a tort standard might have been met. Two factors changed. First, new medical evidence subsequently demonstrated adverse health effects at and below the EPA's target levels for blood lead. Second, the connection between the lead in gasoline and blood lead levels was conclusively demonstrated by a near perfect correlation between declining lead content and epidemiological reports showing declining blood lead levels. It bears note, however, that this latter finding was only made possible by the EPA's preventive action, because it was the ordered phase-down of lead content in gasoline that provided the basis for studying the correlation between it and blood lead levels.

The regulation of criteria air pollutants under the Clean Air Act provides another illustration of the difference between a standard enacted by public choice and a cost-benefit standard. In selecting a health-based standard for the control of the criteria air pollutants, Congress intentionally chose to preclude the consideration of compliance costs, and thus to make it a near certainty that standard-setting for these ubiquitous pollutants would not adhere to cost-benefit principles. If the calculations of industry petitioners are credible, it is very difficult to make a national cost-benefit case for the latest reduction in permissible levels of ozone. It would be quite impossible

40. Ethyl Corp. v. EPA, 541 F.2d 1, 94–97 (D.C. Cir. 1976).

to make such a case on the more localized level at which tort litigation occurs, where every separate compliance measure could be the subject of litigation, even using the EPA's more favorable economic estimates. Under a tort regime, air quality standards would be different.

Ethyl Corp and the criteria air pollutant standards illustrate the final point of this Section regarding the choice between tort and regulation. The modern regulatory system adopts important elements of a constraint-based view of environmental quality that would be lost if one were to switch to a tort regime.

There are, then, three important and deep points of contrast between tort and regulation. Environmental regulation operates ex ante in an explicit and direct way. Tort operates ex post, and has ex ante effects indirectly and then only in an attenuated form. Environmental regulation makes choices about appropriate levels of environmental quality through public processes, and views those choices as constraints on private action. Tort makes choices about appropriate levels of environmental quality through private, individual decisions, and those decisions tend to treat environmental quality as an ordinary commodity whose level should coincide with a cost-benefit determination.

Tort Law and Environmental Risks

There are certain types of environmental harms that are objects of public concern and yet largely evade the tort system because of the doctrinal restrictions of the tort regime. Tort will not be able to address these situations well. On the other hand, there is a paradigm case of harm that tort is relatively well equipped to address. The more the features of an environmental risk resemble the features of the paradigm case of harm or injury tort was originally developed to handle, the better tort is in addressing the environmental risk. Contrariwise, as the features of an environmental risk deviate from the paradigm, the harder it is for tort to address those risks absent wholesale restructuring of tort doctrine.

The paradigm tort case involves a single plaintiff suing a single defendant for a well-documented and significant harm. This is frequently called a bipolar structure, and Ernest Weinrib is correct in asserting that it is the implicit model that the core of tort doctrine assumes.[43] Among those core doctrines of tort is the principle that the plaintiff bears the burden of demonstrating by a preponderance of the evidence that the defendant was the cause-in-fact of her harm. Of course, civil litigation forms in general, and tort in particular, are themselves flexible instruments, and it is totally familiar that tort suits can involve numerous plaintiffs and defendants. Tort acquires this flexibility by augmenting basic doctrine with supplemental provisions to deal with the complications involved, including doctrines distinguishing several from joint and several liability, doctrines of contribution and apportionment, rules regulating joinder of plaintiffs, procedures and standards for creating and maintaining class actions and the like.

43. [Ernest Weinrib, Legal Formalism: On the Immanent Rationality of Law, 97 Yale Law Journal 950, 981 (1988); Ernest Weinrib, Causation and Wrongdoing, 63 Chicago-Kent Law Review 407, 448 (1983).]

In developing the supplemental doctrines necessary to move beyond the bipolar case, so as to deal with harms as they actually arise in the world around us, one fundamental feature of tort has remained constant. Tort innovations have scarcely changed the cause-in-fact requirement. When the harm context implicates a number of defendants, the plaintiff is always faced with the burden of showing that the cause-in-fact of her harm came from within the totality of the defendants' actions, and almost always cannot recover any amount from a defendant unless she can demonstrate that an action of that specific defendant at least contributed to her harm. In part to relieve some of the pressure modern cases put on the cause-in-fact requirement, tort has innovated within damages doctrine, recognizing a right of recovery for costs such as medical monitoring or cancerphobia. These techniques provide some measure of relief for plaintiffs who have been exposed to potential harm by the otherwise actionable conduct of the defendant by finding a way to characterize a harmful effect that the defendant has caused.

One classification scheme with which to characterize environmental risks can be generated by distinguishing between those that involve single versus numerous parties. On the defendant's side, the source of the plaintiff's harm can emanate from numerous sources—increased lead levels from auto pollution is an example. On the plaintiff's side, the harm that defendants cause can be spread over a wider and wider geographical area, potentially implicating more and more people. Acid rain or global warming are good examples. We can visualize the possible plaintiff-defendant arrangements with the help of the [table below].

		EFFECTS	
		Concentrated	Diffuse
ORIGINS	Concentrated	Trespass; "old" nuisances; "signature" toxic harm	Tall stack air pollution; non-signature toxic emissions
	Diffuse	Contaminated groundwater; Superfund site	Criteria air pollutants; non-signature toxic emissions

The origins (defendants) and the effects (plaintiffs) of environmental harm actually vary along a continuum, but the Table marks out the ideal types, and this serves a useful illustrative purpose.

First, note that the bipolar paradigm, in the upper left hand box, fits some modern environmental risks as well as older types of tort situations. A particular toxic emission can come from a concentrated set of sources *and* the toxic substance can be the predominant source of a particular type of harm, as for instance asbestos is with respect to mesothelioma. Here we have a "signature" tort. In such a case, there will often be a straight causal link from a downstream case of mesothelioma back to one or a few sources. Long latency periods confound problems of proof, to be sure, but the case fits the idealized bipolar model fairly well.

Cases in the upper right, those with diffuse effects from concentrated origins, face some doctrinal difficulties in tort. The fundamental one arises in situations where harm falls broadly on a large group and any individual harm does not rise above a threshold necessary to constitute an actionable injury. In that case, the sources of the harm may be causing harm that in the aggregate justifies intervention, but no one will be able to litigate. Even if this doctrinal threshold is passed, plaintiffs with small injuries face daunting and unattractive transaction costs of litigation. While class action devices can ameliorate some of the transaction costs problem, cases of only moderate individual injury remain difficult to bring.

Lower left cases, concentrated effects from diffuse origins, present different doctrinal problems, especially ones having to do with the cause-in-fact requirement. Joint and several liability can provide plaintiffs with one way around an individualized cause-in-fact showing; this has the practical effect of shifting the burden onto the defendants to figure out a way to apportion the plaintiff's loss among themselves, or for individual defendants to disprove a causal connection between their acts and the plaintiff's harm. The range of cases to which joint and several liability applies is under continual pressure from defendants claiming it to be unfair.

Cases in the lower right, diffuse effects from diffuse origins, pose the greatest challenges for tort. Ozone, for example, is produced from precursors that themselves originate from numerous sources, including stationary and mobile sources, both local and remote. Plaintiffs having asthma attacks face insurmountable difficulties in identifying and bringing into court enough defendants sufficient even to capture a bare majority of the human origins of causes of asthma attacks, let alone the entire group of responsible sources. Sustaining the burden of showing that plaintiff's harm resulted from the actions of the defendants will thus prove quite difficult. Compounding the problem of absent defendants is the fact that asthma attacks can be caused by factors other than manmade elevated ozone. The manmade causes of asthma attacks may actually be a small enough fraction of total expected asthma attacks that the plaintiff could not prevail on cause-in-fact even if she had 100 percent of the human origins of ozone present as defendants.

Background rates of injury can make toxic cases instances of diffuse effects as well. Seeing how requires a little elaboration, because from the ex post perspective of tort, a suit for injury of the type expected from toxic exposure would wait until harm had occurred. At that point, the case would look like a case of concentrated effects, and hence one that tort might at least in some halting way handle. The difficulty is that in a case in which the effects caused by the manmade risks remain hidden within a slightly elevated background rate, we cannot tell whether a given case of harm originates in something done by the defendant(s) or in some other causes, including natural ones. Because the tort is non-signature, we cannot trace any harm back to any specific human origin, so the effects of defendants' risky behavior will remain spread out among the entire exposed population as risk exposure, rather than as identifiable concentrated harm. When the contribution of the defendant to the total expected incidence of harm is significant but small, it will be possible to say that the defendant more likely than not caused *some* harm, but impossible to say *which* harm. This concatenation of elements has led some commentators to urge a cause of action for having exposed people to risk. So far, however, the common law tort system has remained quite resistant to such an innovations.

Cases in this final category of environmental risks, then, are likely to remain impervious to the doctrines of tort. Yet such risks diffuse effects from diffuse origins—are among some of the most important objects of regulatory attention today. In cases such as these, shifting from regulation to tort would be tantamount to abandoning efforts to reduce the prevalence or magnitude of such risks.

John P. Manard, Jr., Patrick O'Hara, Kelly R. Blackwood, *Katrina's Tort Litigation: An Imperfect Storm**

The most conventional tort suits are those involving damages from oil spills. While it is not every day that a hurricane causes a spill or that oil floats into homes on floodwaters, oil spills often generate tort suits. More than twenty class action lawsuits have been filed in federal court in the Eastern District of Louisiana against Murphy Oil USA and related entities. All suits seek to recover damages from oil spilled from an eighty-five thousand-barrel oil tank operated by Murphy Oil in Meraux, Louisiana, in St. Bernard Parish—an area particularly hard hit by the Katrina storm surge. Murphy Oil reports that some twenty-five thousand barrels of oil spilled from the tank. The plaintiffs assert liability under theories of negligence, strict liability, and absolute liability, and seek to recover for damages to property, mental anguish, emotional distress, and diminution in property value. Certain of the suits also allege liability under the Oil Pollution Act of 1990 (OPA), 33 U.S.C. § 2701 *et seq.*, which, in addition to property damages, provides for recovery of revenue losses relating to property damage, loss of subsistence use of natural resources, and lost profits or earning capacity relating to property damage.

Other lawsuits have been filed against Shell Pipeline and against other oil and gas operators in Plaquemines Parish, south of New Orleans, for separate oil spills. These lawsuits assert similar claims based in negligence and under OPA. Additionally, a class action lawsuit on behalf of all commercial fishermen who depend upon waterways, now contaminated, for their livelihood has been filed against Shell Pipeline, Chevron, and other oil and gas operators for oil spills at seven separate facilities in southeastern Louisiana, downriver from New Orleans.

In much of the litigation over spills, negligence and OPA appear to be the likely battlegrounds. Tort reformers in the 1990s successfully lobbied to amend portions of the Louisiana Civil Code that recognized civil law strict liability concepts. Prior to 1996, strict liability applied to things in one's garde (custody) and for damages caused to neighbors by one's use of his or her property. The Civil Code now imposes

---

* Originally published in 20 Natural Resources & Environment 31 (Spring 2006).

liability only upon a showing that the person knew or, in the exercise of reasonable care, should have known of the vice or defect in the thing, and that the damage could have been prevented by the exercise of reasonable care. As part of the same tort reform package, absolute liability for ultrahazardous activities specifically was limited to pile-driving or blasting with explosives. Without the benefit of strict or absolute liability standards, plaintiffs must establish defendants' negligence. In Louisiana, this follows a duty-risk analysis, and requires a plaintiff to prove that: (1) the defendant had a duty, (2) the defendant breached that duty, (3) the defendant's conduct was the cause-in-fact of plaintiff's injury, (4) the defendant's conduct was the legal cause of plaintiff's injury, and (5) the plaintiff suffered actual damages.

Louisiana recognizes act of God as a defense to tort liability where a defendant proves that the injury is due directly and exclusively to natural causes without human intervention, and that no negligent behavior by defendant contributed to the accident. Louisiana courts have found hurricanes to be acts of God as recently as Hurricanes Georges (1998) and Lilly (2002). Plaintiffs attempt to avoid the defense by arguing that the act of God was not the sole cause of their injury; that is, that the defendant's negligent conduct contributed to the damages. Plaintiffs likely will focus on the many oil, gas, and chemical manufacturing and processing facilities in the area that are subject to extensive state and federal environmental regulations. Louisiana also recognizes the doctrine of res ipsa loquitur, which allows an inference of negligence when facts and circumstances demonstrate that the only fair and reasonable explanation is that the accident would not have resulted absent a defendant's breach of duty. The survival of nearby tanks and pipelines under similar or worse storm conditions could play a role in arguments that res ipsa loquitur should be applied.

A recent line of cases puts another chink in the act of God defense armor. Two Louisiana appellate courts have held in past hurricane-related cases that despite a successful act of God defense, a defendant is not protected against claims for the cost of removing its property from wherever it came to rest after the storm. One case involved a tree falling on a neighbor's house. The second involved a barge swept away from its mooring and deposited on the plaintiff's marshland property 1,000 feet from the nearest waterway. Neither plaintiff challenged the trial court's ruling that the act of God defense precluded liability for their property damages. However, in both cases, the appellate court agreed with the plaintiffs that, regardless of fault (or lack thereof), the defendants were liable for the cost of removing their tree or barge from the plaintiffs' property. The act of God defense, therefore, does not entitle a defendant to abandon property swept away by a hurricane.

Additionally, claims under OPA may prove attractive to plaintiffs. OPA established a strict liability scheme similar to that found in CERCLA.* The owner or operator of a vessel or onshore facility from which a discharge of oil into navigable waters has occurred (responsible party) is liable for the cost of removing the oil, cleaning up

---

* [The Comprehensive Environmental Response, Compensation, and Liability Act of 1980, 42 U.S.C. § 9601 et seq.—Eds.]

contamination, property damages, natural resource damages, and certain lost use/profit damages. Liability for the owner of an onshore facility is limited to $350 million per incident. Fault is not an element, although a responsible party may escape liability if the discharge was solely the fault of a third-party or caused by an act of God. As under the Clean Water Act (CWA) and CERCLA, this act of God defense is more restrictive than the common law concept of act of God. OPA requires that the natural phenomenon must be exceptional, inevitable, and unresistible. There is little jurisprudence interpreting the act of God defense under OPA, although courts interpreting that defense under CERCLA and the CWA view the defense narrowly. Federal courts have reasoned in CERCLA litigation that a hurricane striking a hurricane-prone area during hurricane season does not qualify as an act of God because it is not "unanticipated."

One additional point is the scope of recoverable damages. Louisiana law permits punitive damages only under limited circumstances where expressly authorized by statute. No Louisiana exemplary damage statute applies here. Beginning in 1984, Louisiana recognized a cause of action for exemplary damages based on the reckless and wanton handling of hazardous substances. However, that statute was repealed in 1996 and it is unlikely that exemplary damages will be a factor in any Louisiana hurricane litigation.

David M. Uhlmann, *Environmental Crime Comes of Age: The Evolution of Criminal Enforcement in the Environmental Regulatory Scheme**

The Rivers and Harbors Act of 1899 often is considered the first environmental criminal statute because it contains strict liability provisions that make it a misdemeanor to discharge refuse into navigable waters of the United States without a permit. When Congress passed the Rivers and Harbors Act, however, it was far more concerned with preventing interference with interstate commerce than environmental protection. For practical purposes, the environmental crimes program in the United States dates to the development of the modern environmental regulatory system during the 1970s, and amendments to the environmental laws during the 1980s, which upgraded criminal violations of the environmental laws from misdemeanors to felonies.

The enactment and amendment of the federal Clean Air Act, the Clean Water Act, the Comprehensive Environmental Response, Compensation, and Liability Act of 1980 ("CERCLA"), and the Resource Conservation and Recovery Act of 1976 ("RCRA") during the 1970s and 1980s brought more than the birth of the environmental crimes program in the United States. For the first time, storage or disposal of hazardous waste without a permit or the discharge of pollutants into waters of the United States without a permit was a felony under federal law. Waste management practices that had been legal for decades, and which were standard operating procedures for busi-

* Originally published in 2009 Utah Law Review 1223. Reprinted with permission.

nesses across America, suddenly could give rise to felony prosecution if committed "knowingly" by corporations and their employees.

As a result, the 1980s brought a series of "firsts" for environmental criminal enforcement: the first felony prosecutions under each of the major environmental laws, the first knowing endangerment cases, and the first jail sentences imposed for environmental crime under the federal sentencing guidelines. In the 1990s, the "firsts" continued as indictments and then trials occurred in federal judicial districts where there had never been environmental crimes prosecutions.

The development of the environmental crimes program involved significant growing pains as federal prosecutors and Environmental Protection Agency ("EPA") criminal investigators struggled to define their respective roles, and Congress investigated claims that political appointees at the Justice Department were interfering with environmental prosecutions. As those issues subsided, judges, defense attorneys, and academics raised questions about the role of criminal enforcement under the environmental laws.

Some critics questioned whether criminal enforcement was appropriate for violations of statutes and regulations that often are mind-numbingly complex.[7] Others raised concerns that the mental state requirements for environmental crimes were minimal and bordered on strict liability,[8] particularly when corporate officials were prosecuted under the "responsible corporate officer" doctrine for environmental crimes.[9] Advocates of criminal enforcement responded that the exercise of prosecutorial discretion would filter out cases that were too technical or where evidence of criminal intent was weak.[10] Nonetheless, commentators protested that the criminal provisions of the environmental laws were too broad, and that Congress had delegated too much authority to prosecutors to decide which environmental violations were criminal.[11]

A common theme of the complaints raised during the 1980s and 1990s about environmental prosecutions was the absence of a meaningful basis for determining what makes an environmental case criminal. In most instances, the act requirement for a

7. See Kevin A. Gaynor et al., Environmental Criminal Prosecutions: Simple Fixes for a Flawed System, 3 Villanova Environmental Law Journal 1, 25–27 (1992); Timothy Lynch, Polluting Our Principles: Environmental Prosecutions and the Bill of Rights, 15 Temple Environmental Law & Technology Journal 161, 165–71, 177–83 (1996).

8. See John C. Coffee, Jr., Does "Unlawful" Mean "Criminal": Reflections on the Disappearing Tort/Crime Distinction in American Law, 71 Boston University Law Review 193, 210–13 (1991); R. Christopher Locke, Environmental Crimes: The Absence of "Intent" and the Complexities of Compliance, 16 Columbia Journal of Environmental Law 311, 320–21 (1991).

9. See Michael C. Ford, Reconciling Environmental Liability Standards After Iverson and Bestfoods, 30 Environment Reporter 229, 231–33 (1999); Keith A. Onsdorff & James M. Mesnard, The Responsible Corporate Officer Doctrine in RCRA Criminal Enforcement: What You Don't Know Can Hurt You, 22 Environmental Law Reporter 10099, 10102–04 (1992).

10. Kathleen F. Brickey, The Rhetoric of Environmental Crime: Culpability, Discretion, and Structural Reform, 84 Iowa Law Review 115, 125–35 (1998).

11. Richard J. Lazarus, Meeting the Demand of Integration in the Evolution of Environmental Law: Reforming Environmental Criminal Law, 83 Georgetown Law Journal 2407, 2487 (1995)....

criminal prosecution under the environmental laws involves the same conduct that could give rise to civil or administrative enforcement. In terms of statutory elements, the only additional proof required in a criminal prosecution is that the defendant acted with the requisite mental state, which many critics argued was a minimal showing. In all other respects, the same conduct could give rise to criminal, civil, or administrative enforcement, all at the whim of the investigating agency or prosecuting office.

In the last decade, the environmental crimes program has thrived. The number of environmental prosecutors grew during the Bush administration, even as other environmental protection efforts faltered, and a consensus emerged that significant environmental violations may warrant criminal enforcement. As with other regulatory schemes, criminal enforcement of environmental violations promotes compliance and deters violations because it is more difficult for companies to treat criminal prosecutions as a "cost of doing business." Corporations that are criminally prosecuted may lose lucrative government contracts and incur damage to their public (and commercial) images, in addition to paying criminal fines, serving probationary terms, and facing other sanctions.[17] Corporate officials can be criminally prosecuted and face possible incarceration, which may provide a greater deterrent than the threat of either criminal or civil fines imposed against the corporation. Yet despite the potential benefits of criminal enforcement, the historical criticism of environmental prosecution occasionally resurfaces, and the question of what makes an environmental case criminal remains unanswered.

The Criminalization of Environmental Violations and the "Act" Requirement

A threshold concern about criminalization is that individuals may lack sufficient notice that their conduct is prohibited, especially during the years immediately following the creation of "new" crimes. These fairness issues had the potential to be particularly significant for environmental crime because Congress simultaneously authorized a new environmental regulatory scheme and established criminal sanctions for violations of those new regulations. The underlying regulations were not promulgated until after notice and comment from the regulated community, however, and significant criminal enforcement did not occur until environmental crimes became felonies in the 1980s, a decade after enactment of the environmental laws.

A more fundamental concern about criminalization is that it may extend the criminal law beyond its proper role. Long before the 1970s, scholars debated the dangers of "overcriminalization."[26] Some scholars argued that undue reliance on criminal prohibitions undermines the legitimacy of the criminal sanction by reducing, if not elim-

17. See, e.g., 33 U.S.C. § 1368(a) (2006) (prohibiting federal agencies from entering contracts with any person convicted of a criminal violation under the Clean Water Act until the administrator certifies that the condition giving rise to the violation has been corrected).

26. See Henry M. Hart, Jr., The Aims of the Criminal Law, 23 Law & Contemporary Problems 401, 415–25 (1958); Sanford H. Kadish, Some Observations on the Use of Criminal Sanctions in Enforcing Economic Regulations, 30 University of Chicago Law Review 423, 435–49 (1963); Francis Bowes Sayre, Public Welfare Offenses, 33 Columbia Law Review 55, 78–88 (1933).

inating, its moral underpinning. They posited that the criminal law only should be invoked for morally reprehensible conduct. Other scholars, including sociologists, countered that the criminal law provides techniques to achieve social ends, not necessarily dependent upon prevailing notions of morality.[29] In addition, to the extent that moral considerations are relevant, they argued that moral culpability and blameworthiness evolve over time within communities.

Since the 1970s, the overcriminalization debate has continued, fueled by the expansion of the regulatory state and the fact that Congress has been quick to create criminal laws in response to temporary social or political upheaval. To some extent, the overcriminalization debate now involves more than different perspectives about the role of morality in the criminal law; the discussion also reflects conflicting views about the role of the federal government and the exercise of its regulatory authority. It therefore is not surprising that environmental crime is cited as an example of overcriminalization. Critics of the expansion of federal criminal law describe environmental violations as *malum prohibitum* (a prohibited wrong), as opposed to *malum in se* (inherently wrongful), because the conduct had been legal before the 1970s. They claim that environmental laws subject "otherwise law-abiding" citizens to criminal prosecution for morally neutral conduct.

A more nuanced view is that environmental crimes do not fit easily within the common law distinctions between conduct that is *malum in se* and *malum prohibitum*, in part because a wide range of conduct is considered environmental crime. Pollution offenses, particularly those that result in harm to the environment and/or public health, may have been *malum in se* from their inception. Congress enacted the environmental laws at a time of significant environmental degradation and widespread concern about pollution prevention. It therefore could be argued that by the 1970s ecological concerns already had altered historical notions about the wrongfulness of pollution. In other words, pollution may have been morally wrong even before Congress made some pollution illegal.

In contrast, paperwork offenses such as recordkeeping or failure to report violations might be characterized as *malum prohibitum*. There was no underlying duty to keep records or report discharges until Congress passed the environmental laws. Yet even when a violation of the law is *malum prohibitum*, the conduct is still wrongful *(malum)* and, inasmuch as the violation involves disobedience of the law, the crime has moral content. In addition, *malum prohibitum* environmental offenses may involve regulations that are as essential to effective environmental protection as those implicated by environmental offenses that are *malum in se*. For example, some reporting obligations enable the government to make permitting decisions with the benefit of complete information about sources of pollution activity; others enable the government to respond quickly to cleanup spills. Absent compliance with those reporting obligations, the government might be limited in its ability to prevent harmful pollution.

---

29. See Harry V. Ball & Lawrence M. Friedman, The Use of Criminal Sanctions in the Enforcement of Economic Legislation: A Sociological View, 17 Stanford Law Review 197, 210–14 (1965).

Moreover, overcriminalization arguments about environmental crime do not account for the significant sociological changes that have occurred since the 1970s. In the nearly forty years since Congress enacted the environmental laws, an extensive waste management industry has developed. Environmental compliance has become a professional field. Climate change and the deterioration of the global environment have become pressing national and international concerns. In the process, a new generation has come of age, and a new set of societal norms has emerged, both emphasizing the need for greater stewardship of the environment and internalizing the notion that pollution is inherently wrong.

A separate concern about criminal enforcement under the environmental laws involves the complexity of the underlying statutory and regulatory systems. Environmental regulations consume multiple volumes of the Code of Federal Regulations and hundreds (if not thousands) of parts and subparts of those volumes. Critics of environmental criminal enforcement often quote a former EPA Assistant Administrator for the Office of Solid Waste and Emergency Response who stated, "RCRA is a regulatory cuckoo land of definition.... I believe we have five people in the Agency who understand what 'hazardous waste' is."[40] Indeed, although RCRA is one of the more difficult environmental regulatory programs, it is by no means the only environmental statute with complex implementing regulations.

Mental State Requirements for Environmental Crime and the Responsible Corporate Officer Doctrine

The number of environmental criminal cases surged after Congress amended the environmental laws during the 1980s and increased even more dramatically after Congress passed the Pollution Prevention Act of 1990, which required the EPA to hire 200 criminal investigators. In the ensuing years, many criminal prosecutions involved litigation over the knowledge requirements for environmental crime. Courts frequently described the question as determining how far down the sentence the word "knowingly" traveled. For example, RCRA imposes criminal penalties on any person who "knowingly treats, stores, or disposes of any hazardous waste identified or listed under this subchapter—(A) without a permit under this subchapter...." As a matter of statutory construction, reviewing courts framed the question as one of syntax: which words did "knowingly" modify? Similar questions were raised in cases prosecuted under the Clean Air Act and the Clean Water Act.

Although characterized as an issue of statutory construction, the question in cases addressing the mental state requirements for environmental crime was whether the government was required to prove knowledge of the law. Prosecutors argued that knowledge of the facts was sufficient. They cited the time-honored maxim that "ignorance of the law is no defense" and argued that the principle carried greater weight where deleterious or hazardous substances are involved. Defense counsel countered that the knowingly requirement would be meaningless if it did not also include knowl-

40. See, e.g., United States v. White, 766 F. Supp. 873, 882 (E.D. Wash. 1991) (quoting former EPA Assistant Administrator Don R. Clay).

edge of the governing legal requirements, particularly in cases where defendants were charged with knowing violation of permit limits. They asserted that a defendant who had a permit authorizing discharges could not be criminally prosecuted for permit violations unless she knew the permit was violated.

The courts overwhelmingly sided with the government. In RCRA cases, the government only was required to show that a defendant knew the material that was transported, treated, stored, or disposed of improperly had a substantial "potential to be harmful to others or the environment."[67] The government was not required to prove that the defendant knew the material met the legal definition of hazardous waste. In Clean Air Act cases involving asbestos renovation and demolition, the government was required to show that the defendant knew that asbestos was being removed and the methods used to remove it; the government was not required to show that the defendant knew the legal requirements that governed asbestos removal. Similarly, in Clean Water Act cases, the government was required to prove that the defendant knew what was being discharged, although knowledge of the law was not required.

The unifying theme of the appellate court decisions considering mental state requirements for environmental crime was that the government must prove knowledge of the facts but not knowledge of the law. The Supreme Court subsequently made clear in a firearms case that the appellate courts were construing knowledge consistent with the general approach of the criminal law.[72] The Court explained that the term "knowingly" does not involve a culpable state of mind or knowledge of the law because individuals are presumed to know the legal requirements that govern their actions. The term "knowingly" "merely requires proof of knowledge of the facts that constitute the offense" (in contrast to willfulness, which requires "that the defendant acted with an evil meaning mind, that is, that he acted with knowledge that his conduct was unlawful").

Other federal regulatory crimes, including food and drug, antitrust, and securities violations, also impose criminal liability using a knowingly standard.[75] Still, there are legitimate questions that can be raised about the appropriateness of a mental state standard for environmental crime that does not require knowledge of regulatory requirements. If much of environmental law is technical and complex, a defendant might reasonably but erroneously believe her conduct was lawful. Such misunderstandings might be particularly likely with new regulatory programs or when the government changes its interpretation of the governing law. Yet mistake of law is not a defense for environmental crime.

---

67. United States v. Laughlin, 10 F.3d 961, 965, 967 (2d Cir. 1993).

72. Bryan v. United States, 524 U.S. 184 (1998).

75. Two exceptions, closely related to environmental crime, are prosecutions under the hazardous material transportation and worker safety laws. See Hazardous Materials Transportation Act of 1975, 49 U.S.C. §5101–5128 (2006), and the Occupational Safety and Health Act of 1970, 29 U.S.C. §§651–78 (2006).

The Responsible Corporate Officer Doctrine

Congress included responsible corporate officers in the definition of "person" under the Clean Water Act and the Clean Air Act. The responsible corporate officer doctrine originated in two Supreme Court cases involving violations of the food and drug laws, *United States v. Dotterweich*[87] and *United States v. Park.*[88] In *Dotterweich,* the Court upheld a strict liability misdemeanor conviction of a corporate official "standing in responsible relation to a public danger." The Court recognized there might be circumstances where injustice could result from a strict liability prosecution but declined to limit the reach of its holding, relying instead on "the good sense of prosecutors, the wise guidance of trial judges, and the ultimate judgment of juries...." In *Park*, the Court further extrapolated its holding in *Dotterweich,* explaining it would be appropriate to hold "criminally accountable the persons whose failure to exercise the authority and supervisory responsibility reposed in them by the business organization resulted in the violation" and that the law "imposes not only a positive duty to seek out and remedy violations when they occur but also, and primarily, a duty to implement measures that will insure that violations will not occur."

The inclusion of the responsible corporate officer doctrine in the Clean Air Act and Clean Water Act has prompted concern that individuals could commit felony violations of the environmental laws without knowledge of the underlying facts. Under this argument, a corporate official could be convicted of a felony and sentenced to a multiyear jail sentence based on status alone (e.g., a responsible relation to the violation). Nor does reliance on the good judgment of prosecutors (and judges and juries) provide much comfort to critics of the doctrine. Criminal prosecution can be personally and professionally devastating, even if the result is exoneration.

The responsible corporate officer doctrine expands the definition of persons who can be criminally prosecuted; it holds that corporate officials, who stand in a responsible relationship to a violation, can be prosecuted for their failure to prevent the violation. The doctrine imposes a duty to act on responsible corporate officials, thereby eliminating the direct act requirement and creating liability for a failure to act.

Significantly, however, the responsible corporate officer doctrine does not dispense with the underlying mental state requirements. The felony provisions of the environmental laws require that the defendant act knowingly. As a result, the holdings of *Dotterweich* and *Park,* which involved strict liability offenses, must be adapted to reflect the higher mental state for environmental crimes, which require proof of knowledge. For those violations, a responsible corporate officer can only be found guilty if she (1) knows the conduct is occurring, (2) has the authority to prevent the conduct from occurring, and (3) fails to prevent the conduct. Except in a case of

87. 320 U.S. 277, 281–84 (1943).
88. 421 U.S. 658, 679 (1975).

willful blindness, even a responsible corporate officer cannot be found liable for her failure if she lacks knowledge of the facts.

There are challenges inherent in determining what facts a defendant must know in a prosecution for environmental crime. Those questions would carry over into a prosecution based on the responsible corporate officer doctrine, since the knowledge requirements would be the same. As a result, to prove that a responsible corporate officer "knows the conduct is occurring," the government must show that she knows all nonjurisdictional facts. Absent that knowledge, a prosecution under the responsible corporate officer doctrine would expand criminal liability unfairly, just as it would in a case that did not involve use of the doctrine.

Nonetheless, critics of the responsible corporate officer doctrine miss the mark when they argue that the doctrine allows conviction based on status alone, without proof of knowledge. They attack a strict liability straw man from the statutes construed in *Dotterweich* and *Park* and erroneously conclude that Congress eliminated the knowingly requirement for environmental crime. When the responsible officer doctrine is properly understood as imposing a duty to act, it is clear that corporate officials cannot be prosecuted based on status alone. Instead, the responsible corporate officer doctrine serves the broader goals of environmental protection and deterrence of violations by ensuring that corporate officials with authority over environmental compliance cannot ignore violations they know are occurring and have the ability to prevent.

What Makes an Environmental Case Criminal

This section describes four categories of environmental violations that may be appropriate for criminal sanctions and therefore should be the focus of the government's criminal enforcement efforts.

1. Cases Involving Significant Harm or Risk of Harm to the Environment or Public Health

The first category of cases that may be appropriate for criminal enforcement is violations involving significant harm or risk of harm to the environment or public health. Congress included knowing endangerment provisions in RCRA, the Clean Water Act, and the Clean Air Act, thereby acknowledging the significance of cases involving harm or risk of harm to public health. As a matter of prosecutorial discretion, the government considers criminal prosecution in most cases that involve significant harm or risk of harm to the environment.

The classic example of a case that was criminal because of the gravity of the harm involved was the prosecution of the Exxon Valdez oil spill. No one would argue that Exxon Shipping Company intended to release hundreds of thousands of gallons of crude oil into Prince William Sound. The United States nonetheless prosecuted Exxon because there was evidence that the company was negligent in its crew supervision and the resulting harm was so substantial.

From a public health standpoint, there are even more examples of cases that were criminally prosecuted because of the deaths and injuries that occurred. The United

States recently prosecuted British Petroleum for Clean Air Act violations at a Texas refinery that resulted in fifteen deaths.[117] W.R. Grace Corp. was prosecuted, although eventually acquitted, for Clean Air Act knowing endangerment after hundreds of people died of asbestos-related diseases in Libby, Montana.[118] Perhaps not surprisingly, the longest jail sentences for environmental crime have occurred in cases where there were significant injuries or public health risks. In *United States v. Elias*, a federal district court judge sentenced the defendant to seventeen years in prison for sending his workers into a tank of cyanide waste, which left one of the employees severely and permanently brain-damaged.[119] In *United States v. Salvagno*,[120] the defendants were sentenced to twenty-five years and nineteen years in prison after conducting improper asbestos removal at hundreds of buildings in New York State.

Few dispute the appropriateness of criminal prosecution in cases that involve significant environmental and public health effects. The EPA devotes the first section of its memorandum regarding the exercise of investigative discretion to cases involving significant environmental harm. Even critics of criminal enforcement concede that cases involving significant harm or risk of harm may be appropriate for criminal prosecution. When a violation puts the environment or public health at risk, the goals of the environmental protection laws are undermined, and there are significant societal costs.

Ironically, cases involving significant harm or risk of harm may raise the greatest danger of prosecutorial overreaching. When an environmental catastrophe occurs or a violation puts lives at risk, there is a natural tendency to seek the most severe sanction possible. The government receives a more sympathetic hearing about any legal issues that arise, and convictions are easier to obtain and affirm on appeal. Yet, without sufficient evidence of wrongdoing, neither the desire for retribution nor the jury appeal of cases involving harm justifies criminal prosecution.

Investigators and prosecutors should be expected to look for more than simply the harm or risk involved when determining whether to pursue criminal charges. After all, with the exception of knowing endangerment, neither harm nor risk of harm is an element the government must prove. As a result, while cases involving harm or risk are appropriate to consider for possible criminal enforcement, the government should prosecute only when there is evidence that the violations charged caused the harm (and not simply that violations occurred that had minimal, if any, causal relationship to the harm). Likewise, the government should emphasize cases where the defendant was aware of the risks associated with the misconduct (or willfully blind to those facts). By limiting criminal prosecutions to violations that caused the harm and to defendants who knew or should have known about the risks involved, the government will avoid opportunistic prosecutions based solely on the desire for retribution.

---

117. United States v. BP Products North America, Inc., 610 F. Supp. 2d 655, 660 (S.D. Tex. 2009).

118. United States v. W.R. Grace, 504 F.3d 745, 749–51 (9th Cir. 2007).

119. United States v. Elias, 269 F.3d 1003, 1007–09 (9th Cir. 2001).

120. United States v. Salvagno, 2009 WL 2634655, at *1 (2d Cir. Aug. 29, 2009)....

2. *Cases Involving Deceptive or Misleading Conduct*

The second category of cases that may warrant criminal enforcement is violations involving deceptive or misleading conduct. RCRA, the Clean Water Act, and the Clean Air Act all include false-statement provisions and make it a crime to fail to submit required reports to the EPA and the states. The Clean Water Act, which depends upon honest self-reporting of permitted discharges, also criminalizes tampering or rendering inaccurate a Clean Water Act monitoring method. CERCLA contains one criminal provision: a failure to report crime.

Cases involving deceptive or misleading conduct also are charged under the general criminal provisions found in Title 18 of the United States Code. Title 18 includes conspiracy, fraud, false statements, concealment, obstruction of justice, and perjury. Prosecutors frequently include Title 18 charges, along with environmental charges, to highlight traditional badges of criminality. By emphasizing Title 18 charges, prosecutors emphasize the aspect of the violations that traditionally justifies criminal enforcement (false statements, concealment, obstruction of justice, fraud) and utilize charges that are most familiar (and therefore acceptable) to federal district court judges.

Classic examples of violations involving deceptive and misleading conduct are midnight dumping, hidden discharge pipes, tampering with required samples, and falsification of required reports. For example, in *United States v. Sinskey*,[129] two individuals were convicted for conduct that included the repeated falsification of monthly reports required under the Clean Water Act, which did not disclose any permit violations even though the facility was discharging at levels greater than permit limits. The falsification occurred alongside efforts to manipulate the discharges and selective sampling to make it appear that the facility was meeting its permit limits, which the government charged as a separate violation (rendering inaccurate a Clean Water Act monitoring method).

More recently, environmental crimes prosecutors have charged conspiracies to defraud the United States and obstruction of justice when a pattern of deceptive conduct frustrated efforts of the EPA and the states to ensure compliance with the environmental laws. Perhaps the best example is the multi-district prosecution of McWane, Inc., for environmental and worker safety violations at five facilities across the United States. All but one of the cases involved efforts to deceive government regulators (and the fifth involved a worker death).[132]

Whether charged as violations of false statement provisions of the environmental laws, under Title 18, or as a pattern of misconduct, the theory of criminality remains the same in cases involving deceptive conduct. Fair and effective administration of the environmental laws, like other regulatory programs, cannot occur if the government does not have complete and accurate information about compliance from the

129. 119 F.3d 712, 714 (8th Cir. 1997).

132. See ... David Barstow, Guilty Verdict in New Jersey Worker-Safety Trial, N.Y. Times, Apr. 27, 2006, at A22.

regulated community. No factor is more decisive than lying in making a criminal case out of what might otherwise be a civil matter.

3. Cases Involving Facilities that Operate Outside the Regulatory System

The third category of cases where criminal prosecution may be appropriate involves facilities that operate completely outside the regulatory system. RCRA, the Clean Water Act, and the Clean Air Act (after the 1990 amendments) include permitting requirements. A facility that treats, stores, or disposes of hazardous waste must obtain a RCRA permit. A company that discharges waste into waters of the United States must obtain a Clean Water Act permit. A refinery that releases benzene must comply with the benzene [standards] under the Clean Air Act.

In myriad ways, the environmental laws impose regulatory obligations on facilities across America. To understand and meet regulatory requirements, companies must make a significant financial commitment to regulatory compliance. In addition, under many of the environmental statutes, the government's ability to provide adequate environmental protection depends upon its ability to identify all sources of pollution. For example, the government's ability to ensure that air quality standards are met depends upon accurate information about sources and quantities of pollution that affect air quality.

Companies that operate outside the regulatory system may be appropriate targets of criminal prosecution for three reasons. First, they are flouting their legal obligations and doing so in a system that depends upon regulated facilities to self-identify and seek appropriate permits. Second, their conduct undermines the goal of environmental protection by frustrating the government's ability to monitor and control all sources of pollution. Third, they would otherwise have a significant competitive advantage over companies that make the requisite (and costly) commitment to environmental compliance.

The argument for considering criminal enforcement against facilities that operate outside the regulatory system does not mean all such violations warrant criminal enforcement. The exercise of prosecutorial discretion, while always essential, may carry particular significance in this category because not every failure to participate in the regulatory system carries equal weight. Much as prosecutors have historically avoided criminal prosecution in more ambiguous areas of environmental law, they should ensure that the criminal sanction is reserved for cases where the failure to meet regulatory requirements has the potential to undermine environmental protection and does not involve technical requirements.

4. Cases Involving Repetitive Violations

The fourth category of cases that may warrant criminal prosecution is repetitive violations. EPA and state regulators often begin enforcement efforts with a notice of violations or pursue other administrative remedies prior to seeking judicial relief (civil or criminal). Whether a preference for counseling is appropriate for violation of environmental and public health requirements might be disputed by some environmental groups. On the other hand, some business organizations might suggest that environmental regulators are too heavy handed about pursuing civil or criminal enforcement.

Without resolving the normative question about whether the government should emphasize compliance assurance or enforcement, it seems reasonable to suggest that repeated noncompliance may warrant enforcement. If the noncompliance undermines environmental protection or continues after civil enforcement action, criminal prosecution may be appropriate.

A classic example of a case involving repetitive violations was the prosecution of *United States v. Williams.*[138] The defendant, who operated a drum manufacturing facility, received numerous notices of violation over a period of more than ten years from state and federal officials. Eventually, he had accumulated 30,000 drums in a residential neighborhood, several thousand of which were full or partially full. After a $1.5 million Superfund cleanup action, the United States prosecuted Williams criminally for illegal storage and disposal of hazardous waste, and he was convicted and sentenced to forty-six months imprisonment.

While there is little dispute about prosecution for repetitive violations in cases like *Williams,* it is worth noting that there are at least two areas where the prosecution of repetitive violations has resulted in discord: wetlands violations and chronic noncompliance by public entities. Wetlands prosecutions are among the most controversial criminal cases ever brought by the United States. Perhaps the contentiousness of the criminal wetlands prosecutions simply reflects disagreement about the appropriate scope of Clean Water Act jurisdiction and the impact of wetlands regulation on property rights. But there is no disputing the fact that criminal enforcement has occurred, in most instances, only after the unpermitted filling of wetlands continued after repeated warnings and civil violations. Likewise, there is disagreement even within the environmental enforcement community about whether public entities should be prosecuted criminally. The United States has brought civil enforcement actions against major cities including Atlanta, Detroit, and Los Angeles, but rarely has pursued criminal cases, even when civil lawsuits do not result in compliance.

Although wetlands cases present difficult jurisdictional issues, and prudential concerns may counsel against prosecution of public entities, repetitive violations generally warrant consideration for criminal enforcement. At some point, a facility that repeatedly violates its permit, even if those violations are disclosed, arguably is no more lawful than a facility that does not obtain a permit or lies about its permit compliance. Moreover, continued non-compliance raises the same issues for environmental protection and for fairness to law-abiding competitors that arise when a facility operates outside the regulatory system. In this area, the government would better deter violations if it prosecuted more aggressively.

---

138. 195 F.3d 823 (6th Cir. 1999).

Discussion Questions

1. Glinski points to two purposes of tort law: (1) the prevention of damage, and (2) the compensation of the victim. How are these different? Do you think one is more important than the other?

2. When should "safe harbors" exist in tort law? Can you give some examples?

3. How would Mendelson's control-based liability regime be different from current veil-piercing law? Do you think it would be an improvement?

4. Would Mendelson's proposal affect corporate officers and the board of directors, as they arguably "control" the corporation?

5. How does tort law differ from environmental regulation from a structural point of view? Is the public decision-making process going to be a better deterrence mechanism than the private law process?

6. How do the regulations under the Clean Air Act illustrate the differences between the public-choice and the cost-benefit approach?

7. How does the oil spill case against Shell Pipeline differ from the BP-Deepwater Horizon oil spill of 2010?

8. What is the difference between negligence and strict liability in tort law? Are there any defenses to strict liability?

9. How do you show negligence when a spill is caused by an act of God?

10. What sanctions can be imposed on corporations that violate environmental criminal laws? If you cannot put corporations in jail, will corporations be properly deterred from their activity?

11. How does the debate on "overcriminalization" invoke both the role of morality and the role of government?

12. Identify five threats to ecosystems resulting from corporate activities. Do you think the firms should be penalized for such activities? If so, how and why?

Chapter 11

Sustainability and Work Law

One way to make corporations more sustainable is to broaden the group of stakeholders in the decision-making process. The first article examines a number of strategies to increase the role of employees in corporate governance. The second reading applies the concept of political responsibility to labor conditions in the global apparel industry. The last reading asks why sustainability seems to value environmental resources more than human resources. It then looks at ways in which businesses can improve employee health and well-being and whether those efforts, like their environmental counterparts, are good for the financial bottom line. In reading this chapter, think about the intersection of sustainability, work law, and employment practices.

Brett H. McDonnell, *Strategies for an Employee Role in Corporate Governance**

One way to make U.S. corporations more sustainable is to broaden the group of stakeholders whose interests are considered in making decisions. One of the most important groups of stakeholders is corporate employees, both because their own stake is critical to their well-being and because employees may value the interests of other stakeholders more than corporate shareholders or managers do. Yet, corporate law does nothing to encourage any role for employees in corporate governance. Corporate law focuses on just three groups within the corporation: shareholders, directors, and officers....

Employees and Sustainability

Why look to corporate governance as a way to promote sustainability? Why not instead focus on legal changes that force or encourage companies to behave more sustainably? Such external approaches have serious limits. First, it would be quite difficult, and highly intrusive, to write laws that adequately constrain or price all external effects of corporate actions. Second, even if the laws were fully adequate in principle, they are likely to be under-enforced; therefore, enforcement depends on corporate actors to voluntarily comply. Third, corporations built to ruthlessly pursue profit are likely to capture the political system and prevent many needed laws from ever being passed. Thus, an external legal strategy needs to be supplemented by efforts to make corporations internally consider their effects on the environment and society.

---

* Originally published in 46 Wake Forest Law Review 429 (2011). Reprinted with permission.

308

Yet, any approach that looks to changes in corporate governance as a strategy for promoting sustainability faces serious objections from the conventional economic picture of the firm. Markets should push firms to efficiently use available resources, and corporate governance itself should be adapted to minimize transaction costs. How can changes in governance improve the markets? Part of the answer is that if, as just suggested, the law has not forced prices to internalize all relevant externalities, then we may want corporate decisionmakers to voluntarily choose to internalize those externalities. But doing so, by definition, requires accepting a lower financial surplus than would otherwise be available. Is it plausible that changes in governance can induce companies to do that?

I see two broad ways in which stakeholder theories of corporate governance hope to address this challenge. First, they hope that giving more power to parties with environmentally friendly preferences will induce companies to be more "green." But there are two major limits to that answer. One must explain why shareholder-focused companies will not take on such green-friendly actions themselves, if such actions will induce stakeholders to associate with the company more cheaply. The answer to this is that, presumably, companies that give some real power to other stakeholders are able to more credibly commit to promoting their interests, and hence can better earn their commitment and loyalty. The other, more severe limit is that it would appear that most members of the major stakeholder groups, at least in the current state of human culture, are only willing to go a modest distance in accepting lowered economic returns in a trade-off for better environmental performance.

A more promising reason arises for believing corporate governance can help if one believes that many, indeed most, current companies have large amounts of waste in their performance—as suggested by X-efficiency theory.[9] If this is so (as I suspect it is, although that is a major debate), then there may well be room for improving the environmental impact of companies without lowering the stakeholder's economic returns. For addressing global warming, more efficient energy use by companies is a very promising area. Even if one believes this possibility exists, one must still explain why involving stakeholders in governance may help improve X-efficiency. I suggest here why that may be so in the case of employees.

The relationship between employees and sustainability depends in part on the notoriously slippery concept of "sustainability." ... Of greatest importance to a discussion of sustainability is how employee involvement might change the external impacts of corporations, particularly their impact on the environment—the third bottom line. Since environmental laws do not go far enough on their own to force businesses to internalize all the effects they have on the environment, we want internal decision makers to take into account—above and beyond any legal requirements—the environmental effect of their company's actions. My claim: involving employees in cor-

---

9. See generally Harvey Leibenstein, Allocative Efficiency v. 'X-Efficiency', 56 American Economic Review 392 (1966) (explaining the theory of X-efficiency[, which posits that firms under conditions of less-than-perfect information and competition will fail to maximize their efficiency]).

porate decision making will cause companies to more fully internalize such environmental effects.

Are there any good reasons to believe that claim? I think there are a few, although it remains an open empirical question with little systematic evidence of which I am aware. One reason goes back to the first bottom line, inefficient use of energy and other natural resources may be widespread, and employees may have much useful knowledge about that waste. For another, many environmental externalities mainly affect communities near the place of work. Compare the interest of employees with such local effects versus the interests of shareholders in a public corporation, shareholders in a closely held corporation, and top managers. Employees work in the affected area and live nearby. They are thus likely to feel the effects of environmental harm themselves and would like to avoid such harm. Shareholders in a public corporation, on the other hand, do not live nearby and are thus not as likely to feel the effects of environmental harm. Shareholders in a closely held corporation are more likely to be as locally rooted as their employees. However, such shareholders have a greater personal economic stake in a corporation's profit than employees do, making them care less about goals other than profit maximization. Managers are as likely to work and live locally as employees, hence they might be as prone to consider environmental effects as employees if they are not motivated to pursue shareholder interests, although it is possible that high level corporate managers are likely to be more physically mobile in their careers than lower level employees, possibly dissipating their interest in the welfare of the local community.

Employee involvement could also change the norms felt by corporate decision makers. A telling critique of the shareholder primacy model is that it induces shareholders and managers to adopt a simple measure of maximizing shareholder wealth as the sole criterion for judging corporate success. This is true even for managers who in their personal lives may care a lot about the environment: at work, they feel morally obliged to look after shareholders and the bottom line first. In corporations that focus significantly on responding to the ideas and preferences of their own employees, those employees are less likely than shareholders or managers to focus on a narrow norm of achieving a high stock price.

Strategies for Increasing Employee Involvement

There are many possible strategies for encouraging businesses to take greater account of the interests of their employees. I group those strategies into seven clusters and briefly delineate and discuss them here.

Laws other than business association law. One can try to protect the interests of employees through other areas of the law. General contract law, agency law, and especially employment law, are widely used to protect employees. This gives individual employees a certain set of rights: either rights dictated for all employees of a certain kind within a legal jurisdiction, or rights negotiated between a company and its employees. If a company violates one of these rights, employees may be able to sue in court to protect their rights or seek remedies from an administrative agency.

Encourage officer or board power. American corporate law focuses on three main groups: shareholders, directors, and officers. Employees play little part. There is an ongoing power struggle between shareholders and managers (as well as directors and officers) over what legal powers a public corporation's shareholders have and what legal powers they ought to have. To encourage greater attention to the interests of employees while operating within this traditional focus of corporate governance, one must side with one or two of these nonemployee groups and hope that one's preferred group will tend to act in the interests of employees. Some scholars favorable to the interests of employees have argued for siding with corporate officers and directors over siding with shareholders, hoping that inside managers—who are themselves a kind of employee, after all—will choose to side with the employees with whom they work instead of the more abstract and distant interests of shareholders.

Encourage shareholder power. Perhaps employees share more common interests with shareholders than managers. It may be that both would be hurt by self-dealing if managers are left too unaccountable. Shareholder interests may be brought closer to the interests of employees since most of the leading institutional shareholder activists are union or public employee pension funds. Indeed, some have even termed the growing clout of such funds "pension fund socialism."

Support unions. Historically, the leading way in which employees have found a voice in a large number of companies was through unions. Unions have been in decline for decades and have become quite a small part of the private sector in the United States. But millions of employees still belong to unions, and labor law reform and revised unionization strategy could increase the rate of unionization. Both legal reform and internal reform of unions could also encourage unions to focus on more than just pay and benefits, thus using unions to increase employee voice over a variety of decisions.

Promote means to give employees voice within corporations. There are many ways to give employees more voice within corporations. At the highest level, employees could elect some directors. A step below that, Germany provides the example of work councils at the plant level that give employees a voice on a variety of issues. Employees could have nonbinding votes on particular issues, or employee opinion on some matters could be surveyed. Employees could be given a voice on a variety of issues. Thus, one can classify possible laws along three axes: the level within a corporation at which employees have a voice, the scope of decisions over which they have a voice, and the degree or kind of voice they have over a particular matter.

Laws can be more or less aggressive in how they encourage any of those measures. A law might require all corporations to provide a particular measure. Or, a law might make a measure the default rule but allow corporations to opt out—and the law may choose how difficult opting out will be. The state can subsidize a preferred measure with direct payments or tax preferences. Or the law can simply permit—without affirmatively encouraging—some forms of employee voice. Assuming the law allows a given form of voice, proponents need not focus attention on legal reform—they can instead focus on attempting to persuade individual corporations to adopt the measure, or forming new corporations that do.

When one considers both the large variety of possible forms of employee voice within a corporation and the large number of ways to encourage any particular form, this fifth category of strategy covers a very large range of options.

Promote other legal forms of business association. Despite the wide range of legal options just discussed, and the great flexibility of U.S. corporate law, legal support for employee involvement in corporate governance will always be a foreign graft within corporate law. Corporate law is designed for shareholders to elect boards that are responsible for running the company; accordingly, employees are simply absent from the law's core DNA.

Employee advocates, thus, may want to pursue other legal forms of business association. The worker cooperative is the most obvious form. Flexible forms like the limited liability company ("LLC") might be more easily adaptable than corporations to the goals of employee advocates. Additionally, social responsibility advocates are currently exploring a variety of new legal forms that reflect their interests.

Promote changes in corporate culture and norms. One staple of a certain strand of organizational behavior and management improvement literature is that the corporate culture ought to promote employee engagement. This strategy does not require any sort of legal change. Rather, it seeks to promote change company-by-company through affecting the norms of managerial behavior. The management literature frequently makes the point that a corporate culture in which employees feel engaged offers many benefits to a corporation. However, there is at least some reason to be skeptical that this literature is just a "fad for the millennium."

This list of seven categories of strategies addressing the interests of employees is not exhaustive, and each category is itself broad and contains a range of options. Still, I hope it provides some useful organization in thinking through the best strategies.

Criteria for Choosing Among Strategies

Before evaluating the attractiveness of these strategies, we must first consider what criteria to use in making those evaluations. Considering a wide range of factors makes comparisons more ambiguous, as inevitably some strategies will appear superior according to some criteria but inferior according to others. Nonetheless, all the criteria considered matter and it won't do to simply ignore them for simplicity's sake.

We must think about the strategy's probability of success and also how much good it would accomplish if successful. The latter can be divided into several factors—the triple bottom line. We care about the net economic surplus (somewhat narrowly conceived in money terms) generated within companies, and also about the well-being (more broadly conceived) of employees themselves. Beyond this, we care about the externalities that companies generate, and in particular about their effects on the environment. Aggregating these different predicted effects is, of course, hard—and there is no objective, neutral, and authoritative way to do so.

Probability of a strategy's success can also be divided into uncertainty concerning the chances the strategy will actually succeed in creating the intended employee involvement, and uncertainty about the effect that involvement would have if it were achieved. For instance, consider a law intended to increase unionization. There is uncertainty about how much of an increase in unionization any given law would achieve. There is also uncertainty as to how increased unionization, if it were (somewhat miraculously) achieved, would affect company output, employee satisfaction, and the environment.

Political feasibility is a crucial consideration in evaluating the probability of success. One aim is to find strategies that are self-perpetuating and generative—not only can one see a path for initial political success, but also such a success can create support for future, more ambitious initiatives. One should, however, be careful about using political infeasibility to weed out a strategy too quickly. What seems hard to imagine now may become imaginable in the future; indeed, academic exercises can sometimes crucially shape future ideas about what is possible and attractive. As Keynes said:

> Practical men, who believe themselves to be quite exempt from any intellectual influences, are usually the slaves of some defunct economist. Madmen in authority, who hear voices in the air, are distilling their frenzy from some academic scribbler of a few years back. I am sure that the power of vested interests is vastly exaggerated compared with the gradual encroachment of ideas.[56]

A final element to consider in evaluating strategies is short-run versus long-run effects and probabilities. Some strategies (especially the first three in our list) are likely to pay off more quickly than others. Other things being equal, these strategies are favored. But presumably in a discussion of how to promote sustainability we should apply a low-discount rate and not overly handicap strategies likely to pay off only in the longer run, since creating businesses and an economy that are functional for the long haul is, after all, the defining focus of our task.

Choosing Among Strategies

... *Laws other than business association law.* Probability of success depends upon what types of legal change one contemplates. Employers will fight changes that impose significant constraints on their ability to treat employees as they choose. But modest changes in this area are probably one of the most politically viable among the strategies under consideration. Employment law has seen a great deal of change in recent decades, in both legislation and in courts, which suggests that this is an area in which movement is possible.

However, the potential gains from changes here may be quite limited. There are presumably a variety of reforms available that could improve employee welfare. There are very few reforms that could do so while simultaneously improving net output as well (always a problem—after all, if such easy changes were out there, why would companies not already be acting accordingly?). But for our purposes here, the biggest problem with strategies that focus on changing judicially or administratively enforceable individual rights is that they don't increase collective employee involvement in decision making. Instead, they focus on employees as individuals with rights, not as

56. John Maynard Keynes, The General Theory of Employment, Interest, and Money 383 (1936).

a group that could help influence company behavior. Thus, these laws do not help us use employees to directly improve the way businesses affect the environment and other external constituencies. The strategy nonetheless remains valuable insofar as it can improve the lot of employees without sacrificing (too much) in economic productivity, but it is of less interest for a conversation focused on sustainability.

Encourage officer or board power. The next two strategies do not aim to increase employee involvement directly, but rather they help employees by promoting another group in corporate governance. The big advantage of both of these strategies is that they have quite a good chance of political success. The ongoing struggle between boards and shareholders is close and heavily fought—and both sides could win many battles. Deciding to throw the weight of persons and organizations that favor employees to one side or the other could very well tip the balance of power.

Which side should employee advocates favor? Shareholder power may lead to short-termism or cost-cutting measures that may hurt employees. Directors and officers that are not subject to excessive pressure from shareholders may better balance the interests of all corporate constituencies, including the employees, the environment, and the broader community. Note that directors and officers may often side with employees, but not with the environment or community. After all, keeping employees happy and productive can more readily be reconciled with the interests of a company and its shareholders than protecting the environment above and beyond what the law requires. If one believes that employees will tend to favor community interests, then that is a real disadvantage of pursuing employee interests indirectly rather than by directly increasing employee involvement. Moreover, siding with managers does little to increase the political power of employees and hence does little to expand the long-run picture of what is feasible.

Encourage shareholder power. Employee advocates could instead side with shareholders. Doing so may both constrain self-dealing within particular corporations and reduce the power of the managerial class within society and politics as a whole. Employees themselves are also increasingly important as shareholders, both through pension plans and through 401(k)s and similar holdings. In choosing between this pro-shareholder strategy and the previous pro-management strategy, note that unions themselves (or at least the pension funds that they manage) have chosen shareholders over managers as their allies, with union funds playing a leading role in contemporary shareholder activism. Of course, from the perspective of those who put shareholder interests first, this union role in shareholder activism is problematic, but it is a good thing from my perspective.

But again, as with the previous strategy, it may be that the persons put in power by shareholder activism, with the help of unions, may tend to favor employee interests but not environmental or other community interests. This strategy does not give employees themselves more power, but only more power to another group (shareholders) that may side with employees on some issues but not others. Again too, this strategy does little to directly empower employees politically and hence does little to expand the long-run set of possibilities available.

Support unions. This strategy has the great advantage of having achieved real success in the past. Unions were instrumental in helping to improve wages and working conditions and giving employees some degree of voice within many companies (although the matters subject to collective bargaining have been more limited than a sustainable corporation advocate would probably want to see). It is disputed to what extent, if any, this came at the expense of economic productivity. Just as importantly, when unions were powerful, they had great political power, and that power made many other kinds of progressive reforms and policies more achievable. Unions are not always natural advocates of the kind of policies that those concerned with sustainability prefer—strong environmental laws, for instance, may create concerns about lost jobs. Still, increased unionization would generally help put more progressive politicians in power, which on the whole would increase the range of politically feasible options for improving sustainability. And unions may even sometimes support environmental regulation itself.

The greatest defect of this strategy is also political. Unionization levels have decreased for so long that it does not seem likely that the United States will ever approach the levels seen in the first few decades after World War II. The weakness of unions is self-reinforcing, as companies successfully fight legal changes to make union organizing easier. Moreover, unionization is harder than it once was because of the changing nature of employment, including both the move from factories to service industries and the increasingly weak ties between employees and their companies.

Promote means to give employees voice within corporations. This strategy includes many variations, and thus it is hard to apply my criteria. But this strategy is unlikely to have large payoffs in the short run. The versions of this strategy that involve large legal changes that would strongly encourage or mandate significant employee involvement are politically quite unlikely to succeed, while versions that involve smaller legal changes or a focus on organizing within particular existing or new firms may face less resistance, but will also bring about less widespread change in the short run.

On the other hand, the longer-run prospects for this strategy are more promising. More modest legal changes in the short-run may set the stage for bigger changes in the long-run. Experiments at individual companies may highlight successful approaches that eventually spread widely. A series of small-scale successes over time may help build political support for bigger and bolder experiments.

Promote other legal forms of business association. This strategy also appears more promising for the long run. States are unlikely to adopt drastically new statutes en masse, and even if they did, there are enough obstacles to highly innovative organizational forms that such forms will not be quickly adopted. One might point to LLCs as a contrary example. But LLCs drew heavily upon existing experience with corporations and forms of partnerships and were not as radical as, say, worker co-ops. The LLC suggests that organizational change through new forms of business association is a promising strategy, but the organizational change is most likely to succeed if it is evolutionary rather than revolutionary. Rather than leaping immediately to widespread adoption of a form that gives employees strong elements of control, success is more likely with a procession of innovations that gradually and incrementally extend employee involvement.

Promote changes in corporate culture and norms. Changes in corporate cultures and norms can be accomplished without legal change. Changes can occur incrementally and can build upon themselves. Norm entrepreneurs can champion new norms, and if they are lucky they can create bandwagon effects leading to cascading change. The business school and management literature on empowering employees may represent such a norm cascade. But I would not hold my breath just yet as that literature is notoriously subject to fads, and employees should often be rightly skeptical of managers who come bearing gifts of alleged empowerment....

Iris Marion Young, *Responsibility and Global Labor Justice**

Many of the goods sold by some of the most high-profile retailers in the United States, Canada, and the United Kingdom, Japan and Germany are made in small factories far away in the Philippines, Sri Lanka, Guatemala, and other countries whose governments offer tax and other incentives to foreign investors. Others are manufactured in small production facilities in the United States employing immigrants. The American or Japanese brand name companies rarely operate the factories themselves, but rather place highly specified orders with other companies, who themselves often contract out the work to local entrepreneurs. Education and publicity about conditions under which much apparel sold in affluent countries is made in less developed countries has led to awareness that similar conditions in often illegally operating apparel manufacturing facilities exist in many cities closer to home—in Chicago, Los Angeles or New York, for example. The arguments I make here about responsibility apply to relations between strangers in the same country or city as much as transnationally. They are part of a connected global apparel industry system that produces both. In this paper I nevertheless concentrate the argument on transnational connection, because many people question that responsibility extends so far.

It is not hyperbole to label these factories "sweatshops." The vast majority of garment workers worldwide are women, often young women, who are readily accessible and relatively pliant from the employers' point of view. Shifts are commonly at least ten hours, six days a week, and forced overtime is common. Factories usually have strict rules, which often include restrictions on talking and going to the bathroom, and supervisors are often abusive as a matter of policy. Working conditions are often dangerous, with poorly ventilated, overheated spaces and little protective equipment. Women workers often suffer sexual harassment or verbal abuse. Workers who protest their exploitation or attempt to organize unions are typically intimidated, beaten, or fired. Wages for these workers are often below the local legal minimum wage, and even when they are not, the wages fall below what the workers need for subsistence.

---

* Originally published in 12 Journal of Political Philosophy 365 (2004). Reprinted with permission.

Health benefits and pension plans are a fantastic dream, and there is no job security. Indeed, workers are often defined as temporary workers just so their employers can legally escape the requirements of labor laws. According to a report from the International Labor Organization, dozens of millions of workers worldwide toil under such conditions.[1] ...

The most common model of assigning responsibility [for the injustice these workers suffer] derives from legal reasoning to find guilt or fault for a harm. Under the fault model, one assigns responsibility to particular agents whose actions can be shown as causally connected to the circumstances for which responsibility is sought. This agent can be a collective entity, such as a corporation, but when it is that entity can be treated as a single agent for the purposes of assigning responsibility. The actions found causally connected to the circumstances are shown to be voluntary. If a candidate for responsibility can successfully show that their causal relation to circumstances was not voluntary, that they were coerced or otherwise did not evince free choice, then their responsibility is usually mitigated if not dissolved. When these conditions do exist, however, it is appropriate to blame the agents for the harmful circumstances. A concept of strict liability departs from a fault or blame model in that it holds a person liable for an action that caused a harm even if they did not intend the outcome, or holds a person or institution liable for a harm caused by someone under their command. I include both fault liability and strict liability in the liability model of responsibility, because they share other features that I will use to distinguish this model from the model of political responsibility. The liability model is primarily backward-looking in its purpose; it reviews the history of events in order to assign responsibility, often for the sake of exacting punishment or compensation. Assigning responsibility to some agents, on this model, finally, usually also has the function of absolving other agents who might have been candidates for fault. To find this person or group of persons guilty of a crime usually implies that others who were accused are not guilty.

Because their decisions and actions are the immediate and repeated cause of factory conditions, the owners and managers of these factories are certainly the prime candidate for blame if these conditions violate minimal standards of decency and human rights. Local firms that directly buy from these enterprises, who presumably are the most likely to know about such violations, probably should also be held responsible. When confronted with accusations that they wrongly exploit and oppress their workers, however, some of these agents are likely to try to mitigate their responsibility by appeal to factors outside their control. They may claim that they have little choice about the wages they pay, and cannot afford to give workers time off or invest in

1. For an account of working conditions, see Ellen Israel Rosen, Making Sweatshops: The Globalization of the U.S. Apparel Industry (Berkeley: University of California Press, 2002), ch. 2; Edna Bonacich and Richard P. Appelbaum, Behind the Label: Inequality of Los Angeles Apparel Industry (Berkeley: University of California Press, 2002), esp. ch. 6; Naomi Klein, No Logo (New York: Picador, 1999), esp. ch. 9.

better ventilation and equipment. They operate in a highly competitive environment, they say, where other operators constantly try to undercut them. They can stay in business only by selling goods at or below the prices of worldwide competitors, and they can do that only by keeping labor and other production costs to a minimum. Apparel dealers who sell to American wholesalers are looking for the best deal, and they will take their business elsewhere if these employers raise their prices. Surely it cannot be better for the workers that they have no job at all, these employers are likely to claim.

Such an appeal to mitigating circumstances can only go so far, of course. No employer can legitimately excuse making people work sixteen-hour days, refusing them bathroom breaks, or beating them, as necessary for keeping the costs of production competitive. Nevertheless, there is a good measure of truth to the claim that these employers themselves operate under considerable constraints. Many of these factories do operate on the edge of solvency, in a highly competitive environment. Under such circumstances of anarchistic competition, labor rights advocates might turn to the states in whose jurisdictions the factories operate.

A typical justification for state-enforced labor standards appeals to the need to maintain a level playing field among competitors. If there is a human rights floor below which wages and working conditions should not be allowed to fall, the state is the proper agent to guarantee such a floor through regulation. In this way those employers who wish to be decent to workers need not fear being undersold by more unscrupulous employers.

Certainly, the states in which sweatshops operate must be blamed for allowing them to exist. Many of these state agencies are inept and corrupt, and often enough some of their officials directly profit from the system that exploits their poor compatriots. As the movement uncovers sweatshops in the United States and other states with supposedly high labor standards and good enforcement processes, it should certainly blame these agencies for not doing their jobs.

Some states not unreasonably say, however, that they themselves are under severe constraints that prevent them from improving working conditions. Many governments of less developed countries have indirectly encouraged these very practices by constituting special export processing zones whose factories are exempt from taxation and regulation that apply to other enterprises in the country. We desperately need investment and jobs, they say. To get them we are forced to compete with other poor states to promote a "favorable" investment climate, which includes low taxes and minimal regulation. To avoid or pay down balance of trade deficits they need companies that produce for export. They have never had a strong enough public sector properly to monitor and enforce compliance with their regulations, and it is difficult to create one with their low tax base. Their bureaucrats and inspectors are overworked and underpaid themselves, and thus easily succumb to bribe offers. Pressures for reduced public spending by international financial institutions such as the International Monetary Fund have further weakened public sector capacity....

International Justice

Activists' claims that university administrators, corporate executives, students and consumers in Europe and North America have responsibilities toward workers in faraway lands excite controversy partly because they presuppose a strong notion of moral responsibility between agents in different nations and political communities. Many people reject the idea of such transnational responsibilities, believing that the requirement to rectify injustice toward others extends only to those who live within the same political jurisdiction and/or share a sense of common national membership. Are there grounds for the assumption that some obligations of justice extend globally and that therefore better-off people in some parts of the world have responsibilities toward globally worse-off people wherever they are? I will build on arguments of Onora O'Neill and Thomas Pogge that there are.

Onora O'Neill argues that the scope of an agent's moral obligation extends to all those whom the agent assumes in conducting his or her activity. Each of us acts according to interests and goals we set within the frame of specific institutions and practices, within which we know others act. Our actions are partly based on the actions of others, insofar as we depend on them to carry out certain tasks, and/or insofar as our general knowledge of what other people are doing enable us to formulate expectations and predictions about events and institutional outcomes that affect us or condition our actions. In today's world of globalized markets, interdependent states, rapid and dense communication, the scope of the actors we implicitly assume in many of our actions is often global. The social relations that connect us to others are not restricted to nation-state borders. Our actions are conditioned by and contribute to the institutions that affect distant others, and their actions contribute to the operation of institutions that affect us. Because our actions assume these others as a condition of our own actions, O'Neill argues, we have made practical moral commitments to them by virtue of our actions.

While it is not possible to trace how each person's actions produce specific effects on others, because there are too many mediating actions and events, we have obligations to those who condition and enable our actions, as they do on us. There is an asymmetry in these obligations, however O'Neill argues, insofar as some people are rendered more vulnerable to coercion, domination or deprivation by the institutional relations. While everyone in the system of structural and institutional relations stands in circumstances of justice that give them obligations with respect to all others, those institutionally and materially situated to be able to do more to affect the conditions of vulnerability have greater obligations.[7]

Important for O'Neill's analysis and the use I want to make out of it, these presuppositions of activity need not to be present to an agent's consciousness in order to hold as assumptions. These relationships are objective. Although most of us are often unaware of or indifferent to the situation of those whose activities condition our own options

7. Onora O'Neill, Faces of Hunger (London: Allen and Unwin, 1985); Towards Justice and Virtue (Cambridge: Cambridge University Press, 1996), p. 99....

for actions, this does not erase the potential obligations we have toward these others. It is not uncommon for agents to deny the connection to others their actions assume, but such efforts at bad faith are pragmatically inconsistent. If I implicitly depend on anonymous others to fulfill their roles or occupy these statuses as I conduct my business, I cannot deny this connection if they should make claims upon me to redress injustices they claim to suffer in the institutions we inhabit together. Moral critique of both individuals and institutions consists to a significant extent in bringing to consciousness the assumptions about others that agents make in their activities, and exposing the inconsistency between these assumptions and the denials of connection.

This method of discovering responsibility to others applies easily to the context of apparel purchase. When I buy a sweatshirt or a pair of shoes, my action presupposes the actions of all the persons connected with the process that transforms raw materials into clothes and brings them to my local store. When I look for low-priced clothes, I presuppose the actions of those who make decisions to minimize costs of production, decisions like failing to equip garment factories with smoke detectors and sprinklers. On O'Neill's account, because I am connected to all these people through my consumer actions, I have obligations of justice toward them. I cannot escape these obligations by claiming that I have not participated in design of the relations of production and distribution, nor by saying that I do not know where or who all these people are. I know that there are others elsewhere, that I am connected with them in these institutions and processes, and that especially workers in these processes are vulnerable to harm from employers and others. My first responsibility may be to acquire more specific knowledge. As I will discuss shortly, I share responsibility with the many others who also contribute by their actions to the processes that connect us. Just because I cannot disentangle my particular actions from the complex process in which some people are made particularly vulnerable to deprivation or domination, to identify which specific actions of mine affect which specific individuals in particular ways, I have a relation of responsibility to the process itself.

Charles Beitz and Thomas Pogge also offer accounts of the bases of a claim that people within one nation-state have responsibilities of justice toward many people in other nation-states. People in relatively affluent countries act within a transnational system of interdependence and dense economic interaction, which has systemic consequences for the relative privilege and disadvantage that people experience in different parts of the world or within particular locales. The grounds of moral responsibility lie neither in political structures of the nation-state nor in people's awareness and affirmation of a connection to others, but in the objective systemic institutional relations in which they dwell together with distance to others. Pogge in particular argues that persons who live in more affluent industrial parts of the world act within a common institutional scheme with persons who live in less industrialized parts of the world....[9]

9. Thomas Pogge, "A universalistic approach to international justice," Internationale Gerechtigkeit und Interpretation, ed. Giuseppe Zaccaria (Munchen: WT Verlag, 2002), Section 2.1; ed. Charles Beitz, Political Theory and International Relations (Princeton: Princeton University Press, 1979).

To summarize so far, these philosophers theorize a complex set of structural relations across the globe which condition the material circumstances and possibilities for action of most of the world's people. Reciprocal obligations of justice obtain between most if not all of these people not simply because they are human nor because they live under the same political constitution, but because they all depend to some degree on schemes of social cooperation which they presuppose in making their own plans or to which the contribute by their actions. Within this global "basic structure," however, some people have significantly more power than others, not only over the conditions of their own lives, but also over decisions and processes that affect others. Within the structures, furthermore, some people occupy positions of privilege while others are relatively or absolutely deprived....

Political Responsibility

I have argued that local owners and managers of factories with superexploitative working conditions should be held responsible for those conditions. Their actions causally contribute most directly towards the workers' situation, and they should be blamed for it. I have also argued, however, that workers, owners and even the nation-states that have jurisdiction over them are embedded in transnational economic structures which connect individuals and institutions in faraway corporate boardrooms and retail outlets to them. These structural conditions provide incentives for setting up and buying from manufacturing operations that violate worker rights. Blaming and punishing a few factory owners, while often appropriate, does not remedy the general problem so long as that incentive structure is in place and sanction is not routine. These economic structures constrain the options of owners and managers in the less developed countries, and implicate many others in the world in the processes that produce those constraints. Because of these connections, activists claim that consumers, corporate executives, university administrators and others in Europe, North America, Japan and other relatively well-off places have responsibilities toward the working conditions of apparel factories in South Asia, Latin America and elsewhere.

This claim only makes sense, I suggested earlier, if the faraway consumers, executives, and administrations bear responsibility in a different sense from the owners and managers of the factories. Earlier I said that the owners and managers are responsible for working conditions in the sense of liability. The liability model of responsibility is sought with specific actions of particular agents. In this sense the liability model individualizes even when the agent it identifies is a corporate entity. The liability model is backward-looking; it seeks to lay blame for harms that have occurred, often for sake of exacting punishment or compensation. The many agents whom O'Neill or Pogge would identify as connected with the transnational institutions and structures that help bring sweatshop conditions about have responsibilities for harmful or unjust conditions in a different sense, which I call *political responsibility*....

Jeffrey Pfeffer, *Building Sustainable Organizations: The Human Factor**

... Virtually all of the [management literature] focused on sustainability [is] primarily concerned with the effects of organizations on the physical as contrasted with the social environment. Even when there is concern with the social effects of organizational activities, these concerns are mostly directed to the consequences of economic development and resource exploitation for the viability of indigenous cultures rather than the consequences of management practices for every individual's health and well-being and the richness of social life assessed by participation in civic activities.

Environmental sustainability is important and nothing [here] should be taken to imply that this is not the case. Nonetheless, this emphasis on the natural environment raises an interesting research question: Why are polar bears, for instance, or even milk jugs more important than people, not only in terms of research attention, but also as a focus of company initiatives?

In 2008, Doug McMillon, the CEO of Sam's Club, a division of Wal-Mart, expounded on the innovation in milk jugs and the fact that his company had introduced a new jug that was able to increase the shelf life of milk, reduce the cost between 10 and 20 cents, and eliminate more than 10,000 delivery trips, thereby conserving energy. In 2005, Lee Scott, Wal-Mart's CEO, made the first speech in the company's history broadcast to all of its associates. In that speech, also made available to Wal-Mart's 60,000 suppliers, Scott committed the company to the goals of being 100% supplied by renewable energy, creating zero waste, and selling products that sustain resources and the environment. Meanwhile, Wal-Mart paid its employees almost 15% less than other large retailers, and because of the lower pay, its employees made greater use of public health and welfare programs. In 2005, 46% of Wal-Mart employees' children were either uninsured or on Medicaid, a state program to provide medical care to low-income people. Compared to Costco, Wal-Mart offered fewer medical and other benefits although these lower costs did not result in higher profits per employee.

Wal-Mart's relative emphasis on the physical environment over people is far from unusual. British Petroleum, a company that touts its environmental credentials in its advertising and other presentations, was one of the first major oil companies to devote significant investment to alternative energy, and at one point wanted BP to also stand for "beyond petroleum." Apparently less concerned about its people, the company paid a record fine of $87 million for an explosion in its Texas City, Texas refinery that killed 15 workers. The fine penalized not just the explosion but also the results of a subsequent investigation that found numerous safety violations and a failure to correct those deficiencies even after the fatal explosion.†

---

* Originally published in Academy of Management Perspectives 34–45 (February 2010). Reprinted with permission.

† [This article went to press shortly before the April 2010 Deepwater Horizon explosion and oil spill in the Gulf of Mexico.—Eds.]

Even as businesses have appointed "eco-managers" to oversee company efforts to become more energy efficient and environmentally conscious, and even as companies track and publicly report carbon emissions from their activities, one would be hard pressed to find similar efforts focused on employees. Just as there is concern for protecting natural resources, there could be a similar level of concern for protecting human resources. For example, there has been no groundswell of reporting on employee physical and mental health and wellness, even though that might be an interesting and informative indicator of what companies are doing about the sustainability of their people. This lack of concern is puzzling given that health-care costs, which as noted below are related in part to what companies do in the workplace, are an enormous problem in the United States and throughout the industrialized world.

In this paper, I want to first make the case for broadening our dependent variables in management research from a focus on profitability and other indicators of firm performance, such as shareholder return and productivity on the one hand and environmental sustainability practices and social responsibility on the other, to also include organizational effects on employee health and mortality. Being a socially responsible business ought to encompass the effect of management practices on employee physical and psychological well-being. Indeed, there is a large epidemiological and public health literature that suggests there may be important organizational effects on human health and life span. The available evidence suggests that there is a good likelihood of finding some interesting research results if we continue to expand our understanding of the connections between organizational practices and human well-being.

Then I want to open up the question as to why employee health has received relatively short shrift in considerations of organizational effects on the environment and the implications of such effects for sustainability. In so doing, I argue that an ideology of the primacy of markets and shareholder interests and the associated idea that market outcomes are fair and just, with sentient individuals making informed choices, may help explain the constrained focus of our research attention. The paper concludes with some implications for building a research focus on human sustainability.

Broadening Our Dependent Variables: Organizational Effects on Employee Mortality and Morbidity

In the assessment and evaluation of countries and other political units, measures of population health (e.g., infant mortality and life span) are frequently used as indicators of societal effectiveness and the level of country development.... Indeed, Marmot explicitly argued that "health functions as a kind of social accountant. If health suffers, it tells us that human needs are not being met."[1] Similarly, Gakidou,

1. Michael Marmot, The Status Syndrome: How Social Standing Affects Our Health and Longevity 247 (2004)

Murray, and Frenk wrote that "health is an intrinsic component of well-being,"[2] and the economist Deaton also noted that "health is a component of well-being."[3]

What is true for countries or other political units is also true for organizations. The health status of the work force is a particularly relevant indicator of human sustainability and well-being because there is evidence that many organizational decisions about how they reward and manage their employees have profound effects on human health and mortality. A few of the many ways company decisions affect the health and welfare of their people follow.

The Provision of Health Insurance. In the United States, in contrast to every other advanced industrialized country, access to health insurance—and, as a consequence, access to health care for working-age people who are not so poor as to be covered by increasingly limited social welfare programs—depends on whether or not one's employer voluntarily chooses to offer medical insurance as a benefit. Approximately half of the U.S. population today receives health insurance through an employer, and the evidence shows that the proportion of employers offering health insurance has declined while the amount employees pay for their coverage has increased....

These employer decisions about offering health insurance and the cost to employees, something that can also affect access, are consequential because there is a great deal of evidence showing that having health insurance affects health status.... Having health insurance also affects people's economic well-being, because medical bills are a large contributor to personal bankruptcy.... When employers decide to drop or curtail medical coverage, there are health and economic well-being consequences for their people.

In addition to providing, or not providing, health insurance, some employers have recently begun implementing health and wellness programs for their employees, which can also have important effects on health. Because most large employers are self-insured, any savings from better employee health and reduced medical expenditures flow directly to company profits. An evaluation of one such program at GlaxoSmithKline covering more than 6,000 employees continuously employed from 1996 to 2000 reported an increased use of stress reduction techniques, more eating of fruits and vegetables, and an average cost savings of $613 per participant, largely because of reduced disability expenses.[4]

The Effects of Layoffs.... Research has shown that layoffs are very harmful to the physical and mental health of those laid off. There is consistent evidence that job loss is a significant predictor of reported symptoms of psychological disorders. Being laid off increases the likelihood of an individual engaging in violent behavior by some

2. Emmanuela E. Gakidou et al., Defining and Measuring Health Inequality: An Approach Based on the Distribution of Health Expectancy, 78 Bulletin of the World Health Organization 42, 42 (2000).

3. Angus Deaton, Health, Inequality, and Economic Development 41 Journal of Economic Literature 113, 115 (2003).

4. Gregg M. Stave et al., Quantifiable Impact of the Contract for Health and Wellness, 45 Journal of Occupational and Environmental Medicine 109 (2003).

600%. One study reported that job displacement increased the death rate of those laid off by about 17% during the following 20 years, so that someone laid off at age 40 would be expected to live 1.5 fewer years than someone not laid off. A study of plant closings conducted in Sweden, a country with a relatively generous social safety net, nonetheless found that mortality risk increased 44% in the four years following job loss. A New Zealand study reported that unemployed 25-to-64-year-olds had more than twice the odds of committing suicide, which helps explain the cause of the increased mortality following layoffs.... And downsizing is associated with negative changes in work behavior, increased smoking, less spousal support, and twice the rate of absence from work because of sickness.

Work Hours and Work-Family Conflict.... Americans work longer hours than workers in most European countries and now exceed the working hours of even Japanese. A report by the National Institute for Occupational Safety and Health summarized the extensive evidence on the harmful effects of long working hours and shift work on people's health-related behaviors as well as on on-the-job injuries and employees' health status.

There is a reasonably extensive body of evidence connecting work hours to poor health outcomes.... Long work hours [also] increase the likelihood of people facing a conflict between work and family responsibilities. Work-family conflict is a form of stress and has been found to influence health and health-related behaviors.... Depending on the type and degree of work-family conflict and the particular disorder being investigated, employees were between 2 and 30 times more likely to experience a significant mental health problem if they experienced work-family conflict compared to people who did not.

Work Stress and the Consequences of Job Design.... [J]ob design has important psychological consequences—for instance, for motivation—as the large literature on job design attests. Job design also has important effects on people's physical well-being. One important dimension of job design is the amount of control people have over their work. High job demands that people cannot control, because they have little or no discretion over the pace and content of their work, coupled with work that is socially isolating, produce job stress. Marmot and colleagues have done extensive studies on the effects of job stress, emanating from an absence of control over one's work, on health outcomes ranging from metabolic syndrome to cardiovascular disease and mortality.[5] Using both retrospective and prospective panel studies, Marmot reported large effects of job stress on mortality and morbidity....

Inequality. The ... literature [shows a] connection between inequalities in health outcomes and inequality in individual attributes ranging from income to education.... It is not just the case that people with more income, higher education, and better jobs are more likely to enjoy better health and live longer lives—although that is clearly the case. Some argue that there is an effect of inequality, particularly income

5. Tarani Chandola et al., Chronic Stress at Work and the Metabolic Syndrome, British Medical Journal (2006); Marmot, supra note 1.

inequality, on the average health status of a population. Lynch et al. argued that income inequality in the United States in the 1990s caused as much loss of life as the combined mortality resulting from lung cancer, diabetes, motor vehicle crashes, homicide, and AIDS combined.[6] Although the effect of inequality on average health outcomes remains a contested issue, there is growing concern about inequality in health outcomes within societies and increasing research attention to the causes and consequences of a number of forms of health-relevant inequality.

The research and policy link to organization studies is clear: Many, although certainly not all, of the inequalities in social systems that result in inequalities in health are produced in and by organizations. Because most people work for organizations rather than being self-employed, income inequality is produced in part by decisions taken inside employers about how much wage dispersion to have, both within and across organizational levels, and who and what types of people will obtain higher and lower level positions and incomes. The organizations literature has a number of studies exploring the effects of wage dispersion on various outcomes ranging from satisfaction to indicators of organizational performance. The importance of inequality for health suggests two important extensions to this line of research: first, including health outcomes as a dependent variable in studies of the consequences of wage dispersion, and, second, renewing efforts to understand the factors that create greater or lesser inequalities in income, power, job responsibilities, time pressure, and other such dimensions inside organizations. If inequality is consequential for health, we need to better understand how that relationship operates inside organizations and what factors produce inequality in the first place.

The forgoing is only a partial review of a large epidemiological literature that potentially ties organizational decisions to health outcomes. There seems to be overwhelming evidence that organizational decisions about whether to offer health insurance and choices about layoffs, work hours, job design, and the degree of inequality created by wage structures have profound effects on employee physical and mental health and even people's life-spans. There are other aspects of the work environment that are also likely to be important and might productively be studied, including whether or not people have paid sick days, the amount of vacation they receive and take, and the emotional climate of the workplace, including whether or not there is bullying and verbal abuse. If we want to understand employee psychological and physical well-being and if we want to assess the effects of management decisions on people, health outcomes would seem to be one productive focus of research attention. That's because organizational effects on psychological well-being frequently manifest themselves in people's health status, as, for instance, in the effect of socioeconomic status on physical health as operating through its effect on negative emotions. Moreover, health care costs are important both to companies and to society.

---

6. John W. Lynch et al., Income Inequality, Psychosocial Environment and Health: Comparisons Across Wealthy Nations 358 Lancet 194 (2001).

Why Does Human Well-Being Receive Relatively Short Shrift?

Given the profound effects of organizations and work arrangements on the psychological and physical well-being of the people who work in them and the growing interest in sustainability, it is interesting that the human dimension of sustainability remains largely in the background. In both social psychology and economics, there is increasing research attention to happiness as an important dependent variable in and of itself. And as already noted, health is considered an important indicator of well-being for both individuals and societies.

However, in the management literature, the focus on a somewhat related topic, job satisfaction has evolved over time to largely although not exclusively consider the connection between job satisfaction and turnover—which is costly to the firm—and also the relationship between job satisfaction or its conceptual cousin, employee engagement, and customer service and other dimensions of organizational performance. Although there is obviously a large and important literature on work-family conflict and its consequences, once again a focus of at least some significant fraction of this literature is on the consequences of such conflict for organizational well-being, as reflected in absenteeism, sickness, turnover, and job performance.

This is not to say there is no interest in social responsibility and people for their own sake, but in the management literature, such concerns are often, although not invariably, coupled with their connection to profits, costs, or productivity. This is scarcely the first time this point has been made. Walsh, Weber, and Margolis have noted that while the Academy of Management was founded to deal with society's objectives and the public interest along with organizational economic performance, over time the field "has pursued society's economic objectives much more than it has its social ones."[7] ...

There are undoubtedly many reasons that the physical environment has received more emphasis than have people. One possibility is that the consequences of organizational actions on the physical environment are frequently much more visible and, therefore, salient. You can see the icebergs melting, polar bears stranded, forests cut down, mountaintops reshaped by mining, and experience first-hand the dirty air and water that can come from company economic activities that impose externalities. Reduced life expectancy and poorer physical and mental health status are more hidden from view. Even the occasional and well-publicized act of employee or ex-employee violence has multiple causes and is often seen as aberrant behavior outside of the control and responsibility of the employer.

Another explanation for the relative attention to physical versus human sustainability is the differential actions taken to make sustainability salient. Organizations and groups focused on improving the physical environment have taken actions to increase the visibility of what companies do—reporting on carbon emissions and measures of environmental compliance, for instance, and trying to ensure that these

7. James P. Walsh et al., Social Issues and Management: Our Lost Cause Found, 29 Journal of Management 859 (2003).

reports generate news coverage. Partly as a result of this public attention, laws have been passed in numerous countries mandating environmental compliance to various standards and requiring assessments of environmental impact before certain forms of economic development can take place. These laws, at a minimum, ensure the availability of more data to assess physical environmental effects. And while between 1980 and 2006 there was a 62.3% increase in the number of U.S. federal staff dealing with the environment, during that same period there was a *decrease* of 34.5% in staff in agencies overseeing the workplace. These changes in federal staffing oversight also provide some indication of shifting social priorities and alterations in the focus of public policy attention.

One lesson for those interested in human sustainability is that developing a consistent set of measures or indicators of the construct, gathering data on them, and publicizing such data might provide more impetus for focusing on the human sustainability implications of what organizations do. Another implication is that federal and state regulation and oversight matter—both for the substantive effect and as a signal of what society values.

Both environmental and social sustainability confront one similar issue: the belief that the sole goal of companies should be to maximize profits and the idea that "markets work well to reach optimal use of scarce resources"[8] so that markets should generally be left unimpeded. Davis has provided an account of the rise of shareholder (as contrasted with stakeholder) capitalism and the associated primacy of economic criteria in business and public decision-making as well as noting the growing importance of the market-like aspects of many domains of life ranging from housing to employment.[9] Because all forms of sustainability contravene both the idea of economic performance above all else and the inviolability of markets, much more research is needed to understand the waxing and waning of managerial ideas and ideology....

Another factor that may explain the difference between environmental and human sustainability derives from the different actors in the two systems and the presumption of choice. Few would argue that trees "choose" to be cut down, that the air or water decides to be dirty, or that polar bears make decisions that result in disappearance of food and habitat. Therefore, there is an implicit assumption that people must act on behalf of the environment, threatened species of both plants and animals, and possibly even indigenous populations because these entities can't act on their own behalf. Employees, however, have choices, and exercise their choices in a labor market in which they compete for jobs and employers compete for talent. Presumably if they don't like the conditions of their jobs, including the degree of inequality, the amount of stress, or the absence of health insurance, employees can decide to work elsewhere.

8. Stefan Ambec & Paul Lanoie, Does It Pay to be Green? A Systematic Overview, 33 Academy of Management Perspectives 45 (2008).

9. Gerald F. Davis, Managed by the Markets: How Finance Re-Shaped America (2009); Gerald F. Davis, The Rise and Fall of Finance and the End of the Society of Organizations, 23 Academy of Management Perspectives 27 (2008).

At the limit, if the conditions of work are really life-threatening, as the evidence shows, employees can choose unemployment over ill health and/or premature death.

Ideas about market outcomes being fair—even if they sometimes aren't—the primacy of markets, and the fact that people are capable of making choices—even if such choices are constrained and socially influenced—lead naturally to a very different approach to human sustainability. Threatened plants and animals and the natural world need protection, but sentient humans making free choices in competitive markets can, and should, fend for themselves. This line of argument, coupled with the finding that profitable companies are believed to be more ethical than unprofitable ones[10]—as one way of justifying their profitability and as an example of the tendency to attribute good qualities to an entity that is successful—lead to greater reluctance to find human sustainability problematic and requiring intervention.

Although I have highlighted two factors—visibility of consequences and ideology—as helping to account for the relative emphasis on environmental as contrasted with human sustainability, there are undoubtedly many other factors at work. The fundamental message is that we need to understand what subjects receive attention and why, as well as the beliefs and values that form the foundation for our theorizing—not just for the topic of sustainability but for many others, as well. The evidence suggests that these are important and underexplored issues.

What If We Took Human Sustainability Seriously: A Research Agenda

... [O]ne of the major issues addressed by research on environmental sustainability has been whether or not adopting sustainability practices imposes net costs on companies, thereby eroding their competitiveness, or whether the benefits of being "green" more than outweigh any costs incurred. Completely parallel questions and issues confront a focus on human sustainability. First, just as in the case of environmental pollution, companies that do not provide health insurance, lay people off, pay inadequate wages, and that have working arrangements that stress and overwork their people also impose externalities that others pay for even as they save on their own costs. That's because some portion of the extra costs of increased physical and psychological illness fall on the broader health system through, for instance, increased use of public health and emergency room facilities. Second, just as green companies enjoy reputational benefits that help in brand building and product differentiation, so, too, we might expect that companies with better records of human sustainability might enjoy benefits in attracting and retaining employees and also in building a reputation that could attract additional consumer demand. Therefore, whether or not it pays to be a company that offers a system high in human sustainability, and how the various costs and benefits balance and under what conditions, would be an important focus for research.

There are some data that suggest that human sustainability may pay off for companies. Each year the Great Place to Work Institute, in conjunction with *Fortune*, pub-

10. John T. Jost et al., Fair Market Ideology: Its Cognitive-Motivational Underpinnings, 25 Research in Organizational Behavior 53 (2003).

lishes a list of the best places to work. Most of those places are noted for their provision of good working conditions and benefits, including vacations, sick days, health insurance, training, and jobs that provide people autonomy and challenge. The Institute's website shows data indicating that companies on the list consistently outperform benchmark indices over varying periods of time, indicating that, at least as measured by stock market performance, it is good to be a great place to work. How and why these returns accrue remains to be explored in more detail. But it is quite likely that, just as in the case of environmental sustainability, human sustainability pays. Indeed, the literature on the positive effects of employee-centered management practices is extensive.[11] If so, that raises a third question: If it does pay to be green, whether "green" is assessed in environmental or human terms, or both, then why is it so difficult to get companies to adopt practices consistent with sustainability?

Another implication of the research cited may help to explain one of the paradoxes of the U.S. healthcare system—why it costs so much even as it does not deliver measurable health benefits, as assessed by indicators ranging from infant mortality to life expectancy to survival rates for various serious illnesses, that are no better than many other industrialized countries. Once again, there are undoubtedly many answers to this important question. But one possibility is this: If health status is importantly affected by what happens to people on the job, the relatively poor health-care outcomes in the U.S. might result from a laissez faire labor market that leaves even the provision of paid sick days and paid vacation at the discretion of employers.... Exploring whether those variations also account for variations in health-care outcomes and costs would be fruitful.

Wilper et al. estimated there were more than 44,000 excess deaths annually because people lack health insurance.[12] Some, although not all, of the absence of health insurance results from employer decisions. If one added to the portion of these deaths resulting from employer actions the mortality coming from layoffs, company-generated inequalities in income and control over work, and all the other factors briefly reviewed in this article, the resulting number would be both interesting and important. It might possibly spark some serious effort to prevent deaths from employer decisions. There is already a great deal of focus on individual choices such as diet and exercise. A focus on the role of the employer in individual health status would round out the picture.

There is no reason why building sustainable companies should focus just on the physical and not the social environment. It is not just the natural world that is at risk from harmful business practices. We should care as much about people as we do about polar bears—or the environmental savings from using better milk jugs—and also understand the causes and consequences of how we focus our research and policy attention.

---

11. E.g., Brian E. Becker & Mark A. Huselid, High Performance Systems and Firm Performance: A Synthesis of Research and Managerial Implications, 16 Research in Personnel and Human Resources Management 53 (1998).

12. Andrew Wilper et al., Health Insurance and Mortality in U.S. Adults, American Journal of Public Health 99 (2009).

Discussion Questions

1. McDonnell discusses how employee involvement might change corporate environmental practices. What about changes in the treatment of employees themselves?

2. Which of McDonnell's strategies do you think have the highest probability of success in the short run? In the long run?

3. How do you balance the criteria McDonnell sets forth in deciding on the best strategy?

4. Other commentators have argued that corporate boards should owe fiduciary duties to employees. See, e.g., Marleen O'Connor, "Labor's Role in the American Corporate Governance Structure," 22 Comparative Labor Law & Policy Journal 97 (2000). What are some benefits and problems with this position?

5. How does Young's political responsibility model differ from the liability (fault) model? Under the traditional fault model (which also incorporates the concept of strict liability), are corporations seen as the most responsible party? Why or why not?

6. Individual purchase decisions, as well as organized boycotts, may be effective ways of exercising political responsibility. Do you have any objections to the concept of political responsibility?

7. Are there better ways to effect change around social injustice issues?

8. How does Young apply the concepts of political responsibilities to labor conditions in the global apparel industry?

9. Young focuses on labor conditions in the apparel industry; can you think of any other industry whose practices are also unfair to workers? Could Young's political responsibility theory be applied in these other contexts?

10. Do you agree with Pfeffer's argument that "human sustainability" gets short shrift? How should we go about improving human sustainability—leave matters to the markets, regulate private employment more, improve social safety nets for the unemployed, or something else?

Chapter 12

Sustainability and Internatio

Nations, not corporations, are the traditional subjects of international law; international law for the most part leaves it to nations to regulate the businesses that operate within their borders. That said, various sources of international law establish norms and standards by which transnational corporations (TNCs) are expected to abide. These include the Universal Declaration of Human Rights and guidelines specifically addressed toward multinational enterprises' activities. The first reading in this chapter discusses these and other "soft laws" and the place TNCs occupy in international law. The second reading details the rise and fall of the United Nations' attempt to create binding international law obligations on TNCs; the effort ultimately failed, and the excerpt offers possible explanations for this result. The third reading turns to trade and "hard" international law obligations under the General Agreement on Tariffs and Trade and the World Trade Organization and makes recommendations for their improvement.

David Kinley & Junko Tadaki, *From Talk to Walk: The Emergence of Human Rights Responsibilities for Corporations at International Law**

It must be acknowledged at the outset that foreign direct investment injected by TNCs into developed and developing countries alike can and does bring jobs, capital, and technology, and thereby protects and promotes the rights to work and to adequate living standards, along with such derivative rights as health, education, housing, and even political freedoms. That said, it is equally certain that human rights abuses by TNCs do occur, and do so frequently in the sphere of economic, social, and cultural rights. Many TNCs, including Nike and The Gap, have been accused of violating their workers' rights to just and favorable conditions of work by paying unfair and inadequate wages, requiring unreasonable overtime, and providing unsafe working conditions. Furthermore, there is ample evidence of the involvement of TNCs in suppressing trade unions and thereby denying workers the right to organize. It has been alleged, for instance, that Coca-Cola in Colombia and Phillips-Van Heusen in Guatemala have been associated with, or are directly responsible for, the systematic intimidation, torture, kidnapping, unlawful detention, and murder of trade-unionist employees by paramilitaries operating as both of these corporations' agents. TNCs

* Originally published in 44 Virginia Journal of International Law 931 (2004). Reprinted with permission.

in the extractive industries have caused environmental disasters, threatening the right to adequate food and the right to an adequate standard of living. Royal Dutch/Shell's oil production in Nigeria, and BHP Billiton's copper mining in Papua New Guinea, for example, seriously damaged the environment and the livelihood of peoples in local communities, which depended on fishing and farming.

Such instances of corporate responsibility for, or complicity in, human rights abuses are increasingly widely publicized, especially by non-governmental organizations (NGOs) using the immediacy of global communications. Mounting activism by NGOs, workers and consumers in developed countries in the form of protests, product boycotts, and selective purchasing has forced many TNCs to accept some level of human rights responsibility by adopting internal codes of conduct. A growing industry of social auditing now uses these codes, as well as independently devised ones such as SA8000 and the Fair Labor Association's Workplace Code of Conduct, as standards against which to assess a corporation's achievements and failures in human rights and environmental protection.

What is still largely invisible in this picture is the matter of the legal accountability of TNCs, and in particular international legal accountability. To be sure, there is an established corpus of domestic legal regulation of corporate activities that affect human rights, including in such areas as criminal law, anti-discrimination, health and safety at work, environmental protection, and labor rights. [At the time of this article's publication there was also a] body of extraterritorial domestic jurisprudence that focuse[d] on the human rights implications of actions taken by corporations overseas.*

At international law, however, the corporate form is barely recognized, still less directly bound, whether with respect to human rights or any other field. There is no transnational regime of human rights law governing the transnational activities of corporations. TNCs have been able to operate in a legal vacuum because international human rights law imposes no direct legal obligations on TNCs. The orthodox vision of international human rights law generally binds only states because it is principally designed to protect individuals from the excesses of state power. Thus, where infringements are caused by abuse of private power, it is still the state that will be held vicariously liable at international law, if any legal entity is to be held liable at all. Despite egregious human rights abuses committed by non-state actors, international law generally, and human rights law in particular, is still undergoing the conceptual and structural evolution required to address their accountability.

Transnational Corporations and International Human Rights: Law, Practice, and Liability

The invisibility of TNCs' accountability at the international level, especially under international human rights law, has arisen from the combined consequences of two factors. The first is the fact that historically, international human rights law has de-

* [That body of law—premised on the extra-territorial application of the U.S. Alien Tort Claims Act—is now largely defunct following the United States Supreme Court's decision in Kiobel v. Royal Dutch Petroleum Co., 113 S. Ct. 1659 (2013).—Eds.]

veloped as a tool to protect individuals from the arbitrary use of power by states, not corporations or other private entities. To the extent that international human rights law does embrace non-state actors, it does so very largely by way of holding states indirectly liable for the direct infringements of others, including corporations. Typically, this comes in the form of a fundamental treaty duty imposed on a state to ensure to all within its jurisdiction the rights contained in that instrument. Though such a vicarious route to liability may seem unnecessarily circuitous, it is not altogether illogical. To a significant degree, international human rights law relies on domestic law implementing its provisions, not only with respect to a state's own actual or potential violations of individual rights (vertical application), but also, importantly, with respect to actions between private actors (horizontal application). Where such horizontal application of domestic law is found wanting, calls for direct regulation under international law may be heard. This leads us to the second factor. Corporations law traditionally has been almost exclusively a domestic matter. The human rights responsibilities of corporations under domestic law are not usually couched in corporations or commercial laws themselves, but in separate anti-discrimination, workplace health and safety, and labor laws. Moreover, except in certain exceptional circumstances discussed below, these domestic human rights laws are designed to operate intra-territorially only.

As a result, the extraterritorial operations of TNCs—the very feature that defines them—are substantially regulated neither by international nor domestic (home state) laws with respect to their impact on human rights. Domestic regulation by host states is, of course, theoretically possible. However, in many states, especially developing ones, such regulation may be heavily compromised by the economic considerations of the host state's unbalanced relationships with TNCs....

TNCs in International Law

TNCs traditionally have not been recognized as "subjects" of international law. The creation or adaptation of international regulatory regimes that impose human rights responsibilities upon corporations therefore appears to require a radical departure from the structure of international legal orthodoxy, which views non-state actors as mere objects of international law. Before such human rights duties can be imposed on TNCs, they must be recognized in international law as subjects of, or at least "participants in," international law, capable of bearing international legal duties. In other words, they must possess international legal personality.... In principle, ... there is nothing to prevent states from accepting TNCs as subjects of international law....

[H]owever, it is neither necessary nor desirable for TNCs to possess full legal personality on a par with states.... It is sufficient, rather, that TNCs have limited rights and responsibilities, such as the right to sue and be sued, the ability to assert a right, and the acceptance of legal responsibility in judicial forums, but not have the status of a party to intergovernmental forums or international instruments. Not only would this constitute a sound base upon which to build a regime of direct human rights responsibilities at international law, but it would also preserve the primacy of states on the international plane.

The extent to which TNCs already possess an international legal status may be ascertained by enquiring whether TNCs have any existing rights or duties under international law. There is, in fact, ample evidence that TNCs do possess international rights and duties, and, with respect to their rights, the capacity to enforce them. TNCs have traditionally been given rights under foreign investment law, particularly in relation to expropriation, compensation, and non-discriminatory national treatment relative to domestic firms. TNCs also have direct duties under some multilateral conventions. For example, both the International Convention on Civil Liability for Oil Pollution Damage and the Convention on Civil Liability for Damage Resulting from Activities Dangerous to the Environment directly impose liability on legal persons including corporations....

TNCs are also empowered to enforce their rights. For example, a treaty created under the World Bank enables corporations to submit disputes to binding arbitration by the International Center for the Settlement of Investment Disputes. And under NAFTA, corporations are able to seek recompense, spectacularly, from foreign governments for breach of their right to unhindered, cross-border trade through the Agreement's private dispute-settlement mechanism. There are many other tribunals that allow corporations to bring claims, including the Seabed Dispute Chamber, the Iran-United States Claims Tribunals, and the United Nations Claims Commission, to name a few. Evidently, therefore, as even this brief survey makes clear, it is possible to invest in TNCs sufficient international legal personality to bear obligations, as much as to exercise their rights.

Human Rights Duties of TNCs:
The Current Scope at International Law

The Universal Declaration of Human Rights (UDHR) is most often spoken about as a potential legal source of corporate human rights responsibilities. The Preamble's oft-quoted provision that "every individual and every organ of society ... shall strive" to promote respect for human rights and to secure their recognition and observance, has been interpreted by Louis Henkin as excluding "no one, no company, no market, no cyberspace."[64] Although it is difficult to avoid the conclusion that the provision expresses no more than an aspiration to "strive" to promote respect for human rights, rather than to impose a binding legal obligation, there is stronger language in the body of the text of the UDHR itself. Article 29 specifies that "[e]veryone [including non-state actors] has duties to the community," and article 30 prohibits "any State, group or person" from engaging in any activity or performing any act aimed at the destruction of any of the rights and freedoms in the Declaration. This combination can be read as constituting a statement of non-state actors' duties not to deny or violate the human rights of others. But, even if this reading is accepted, the nature of the duties is unclear. The UDHR is a declaration, and thus is non-binding. Although it is widely accepted that some provisions in the UDHR have become customary international law, it is uncertain whether articles 29 and 30 have acquired such status.

64. Louis Henkin, The Universal Declaration at 50 and the Challenge of Global Markets, 25 Brooklyn Journal of International Law 17, 25 (1999).

In the absence of binding effects, therefore, the duties that the UDHR imposes on TNCs may amount to ethical duties at best. Thus, in terms of international law, the UDHR may be the "most fragile basis on which to construct a doctrine of individual duties to respect human rights," and by extension, a most uncertain ground to bind corporations.

It is true that greater certainty either way in this regard would have been possible had the drafters of the UDHR had corporations specifically in mind, but they did not. International instruments or initiatives that do specifically contemplate corporations will therefore have to speak more directly to them and also be expressly tailored to their activities. To date, however, the only examples of such tailoring are soft law, non-binding agreements, and voluntary codes of conduct.

Soft Law Human Rights Responsibilities of TNCs

Since the 1970s a number of intergovernmental organizations have formulated voluntary guidelines, declarations, and codes of conduct aimed at regulating TNCs' activities. These include, notably, the Organization of Economic Cooperation and Development (OECD) and the International Labor Organization (ILO). Although, typically, these guidelines are not directed at corporations themselves (rather, they are directed at states whose task it is to apply them to the corporations within their jurisdiction), and they are not in any case binding on signatory states, the OECD and ILO instruments are the only such guidelines that contain implementation mechanisms specifically enabling corporate behavior to be scrutinized.

The OECD's 1976 Guidelines for Multinational Enterprises (as revised in 2000) recommend that enterprises "[r]espect the human rights of those affected by their activities consistent with the host government's international obligations and commitments."* Specifically, they recommend that enterprises contribute to policies of non-discrimination with respect to employment, to the effective abolition of child labor, and to the elimination of all forms of forced or compulsory labor.

The ILO's 1977 Tripartite Declaration of Principles Concerning Multinational Enterprises and Social Policy is addressed to governments of member states, employers' and workers' organizations, and corporations (including, of course, TNCs) operating in their territories. The Declaration urges parties to respect the UDHR and the corresponding international covenants, as well as a number of core labor-related rights.†

From the point of view of the regulation of human rights abuses by TNCs, the implementation mechanisms of the OECD Guidelines and the ILO Declaration can hardly be considered intrusive on states or corporations. Quite apart from the fact that they are non-binding, the monitoring bodies do not function as judicial or quasi-judicial bodies, but rather their roles are limited to clarification of the interpretation of the instruments. They do not make specific findings of misconduct by individual

* [The most recent text of the OECD Guidelines can be found online at http://www.oecd.org/daf/inv/mne/48004323.pdf.—Eds.]

† [The entire text of the ILO Tripartite Declaration can be found online at http://www.ilo.org/empent/Publications/WCMS_094386/lang—en/index.htm.—Eds.]

companies and their identities are kept confidential, thereby shielding them from public scrutiny and potential embarrassment. Furthermore, while the Guidelines and the Declaration encourage TNCs to respect internationally recognized human rights norms, they simultaneously uphold the primacy of national law. Thus, they can do nothing to prevent host states from adopting lax labor and environmental standards, and TNCs cannot be condemned for taking advantage of such standards.

The UN Global Compact is another soft law instrument directed at TNCs. Though it is not strictly a code of conduct, its object is to encourage businesses to "embrace and enact" nine core principles relating to respect for human rights, labor rights, and protection of the environment, both through their individual corporate practices and by supporting complementary public policy initiatives.* However, again, the lack of independent monitoring and enforcement via sanctions highlights the limited ambition, and therefore, impact, of this initiative in providing protection against corporate abuse of human rights. It is true that the UN expressly acknowledges that it has neither the mandate nor the capacity to monitor and verify corporate practices. Yet, there is some concern as to the credibility of the Global Compact given that it is quite possible for TNCs to continue to violate human rights while enjoying the status of signatory to the Global Compact. At the end of the day, the Global Compact is little more than an instrument of rhetoric. It has indeed raised awareness of the issues involved, both within the corporate world and the UN itself, which is an important first step, but it is no more than that.

Reviewing the soft law instruments of the OECD, the ILO, and the UN's Global Compact, one might conclude that in practice they have achieved little of substance, due largely to their non-binding nature and the lack of meaningful implementation mechanisms. But they have at least demonstrated an increased willingness on the part of certain multilateral institutions to formulate some human rights standards against which the conduct of TNCs can be measured. Moreover, some commentators raise the possibility that such soft-law initiatives may be elevated to hard-law through the formation of customary international law. Hans Baade, for example, argues that the follow-up procedures of the OECD Guidelines constitute the requisite state practice because its monitoring body—the Committee on International Investment and Multinational Enterprises (CIIME)—is composed of the delegates of the member states.[81] However, decisions of the CIIME are largely ignored at the national level, and only three labor cases were brought in the 1990s. The weak implementation of the OECD Guidelines seems, at the moment, to point to an absence of common and consistent state practice and opinio juris necessary to constitute a custom. Thus, while they may be transformed into a hard-law instrument in the future, the Guidelines do not yet provide an authoritative source of TNCs' international duties. The position is somewhat the same for the ILO's Declaration, and even more distant with respect to the Global Compact.

---

* [The Global Compact's (now ten) core principles can be found online at http://www.unglobalcompact.org/what-is-gc/mission/principles.—Eds.]

81. Hans W. Baade, The Legal Effects of Codes of Conduct for Multinational Enterprises, in Legal Problems of Codes of Conduct for Multinational Enterprises 3, 13 (Norbert Horn ed., 1980)....

So, while it is desirable to promulgate more effective international legal standards applicable to TNCs, it will be a complex, time-consuming process in a world of diverse interests. It is almost inevitable that there will be delay before the law can properly respond to human rights abuses by TNCs, in which case there will be victims left without legal redress in the interim.

The Impact of Soft-law

The broader social, economic, and commercial contexts within which international initiatives have emerged have been crucial to their current shape, both in the sense of what they have and have not achieved, especially with respect to their impact on private actors. Even more importantly for the purposes of this article, is the continuing development of private, soft-law initiatives directed toward private actions in these contexts that will likely influence the future shape of international human rights regulation of TNCs.

The notion of corporate social responsibility (CSR) ... has now entered the lexicons of social, political, commercial, and legal discourse. The notion finds expression in the spreading instance of CSR directorships or managers, not only in TNCs, but also in NGOs, such as Human Rights Watch and Amnesty International. One would be hard-pressed to find any major corporation today that did not make some claim to abiding by a code of conduct that comprised, at least in part, adherence to human rights standards. Indeed, more often than not, such adherence to codes is trumpeted by major corporations. The escalating demands for corporations to be more socially responsible, made by NGOs, community groups, trade unions, and consumers in developed countries, have been prompted in part by the inertia of international human rights law in tackling the problems posed by TNCs. The traditional corporate response has been that human rights are concerns of states and international bodies such as the UN, not private actors such as corporations. Their ultimate responsibility, it is argued, is owed to their shareholders, whose overwhelming (if not only) concern is with profit maximization. Certainly, this attitude is still prevalent, but increasing exposure of human rights infringements by corporations has clearly signaled to businesses that alongside other reasons, it may well be in their commercial interest to rethink their actions and policies in terms of their social impact. Thus, on the negative side, a tarnished brand image and loss of consumer goodwill is not good for business on the positive side, corporate respect for human rights will not only engender goodwill, but will eventually contribute to a stable, rule-based society in host states, which in turn promotes the smoother and more profitable operation of business.

Many TNCs accede to private initiatives that urge greater corporate compliance with international human rights standards or to develop their own internal codes of conduct. Prominent among the former category are the forerunners of the trend—the Sullivan Principles (a U.S.-based initiative that targeted corporations working in apartheid South Africa) and the MacBride Principles (which encouraged affirmative action employment programs in Northern Ireland). More recent initiatives in this category include the U.S. Apparel Industry Partnership's Workplace Code of Conduct, SA 8000, and WRAP (the last two being administered by bodies which accredit auditors to perform social audits on corporations for compliance with their respective program's standards). Examples of individual corporate codes of conduct abound, but they include in particular those corporations with high-profile brand images to protect, such as Adidas, Nike, The Gap, Reebok, and Levi Strauss & Co., and those within the extractive industries sector, such as Royal Dutch Shell, BP, and Rio Tinto, because the bulk of their operations is often in developing countries.

Although the contents of individual corporate codes differ significantly, labor and environmental issues are most frequently addressed. The codes also vary in terms of the degree of detail, ranging from brief, general principles to comprehensive guidelines. Some codes even expressly support an international human rights instrument. For example, Rio Tinto's code upholds the UDHR and states that the Rio Tinto Group "seek[s] to have international standards upheld and to avoid situations that could be interpreted as condoning human rights abuses." Even accepting that this falls far short of a declaration that the company is bound by international human rights law, it nonetheless begs to be explained what such guidance means for TNCs in practice.

The proliferation of corporate codes of conduct—which have led some to lament an already incipient feeling of "code fatigue"—has attracted considerable discussion and debate as to their practical effect in combating human rights abuses by corporations. Are such codes merely paying lip service to their stated objects, or do they constitute concrete steps towards lasting human rights protection? On top of the overarching difficulty of the general absence of enforceability mechanisms for codes, the most significant and contentious concerns center on the myriad of problems associated with the monitoring of corporate compliance with the codes: what, if any, auditing process exists? If there is one, who undertakes the audit and how independent are they? To what extent are the results open to public scrutiny? How do they measure compliance in practice, or is it measured at all? What remedies are available for breaches of the code? How does one take account of variances in local circumstances between countries, especially, for example, when local laws conflict with code standards? How does one deal with differences or inconsistencies between codes? How far down the supply chain can responsibility be attributed and measured? And, to what extent are all stakeholders—employees, trade unions, local communities, governments, and relevant NGOs—involved in the process?

Much of the considerable debate over codes of conduct revolves around these questions. At base, the principal concerns are with the voluntary, self-regulatory nature of these codes and their capacity to bring any meaningful pressure to bear on corporations. To put it bluntly, it might be asked whether the fact that codes are generally not backed by law is fatal to any aspirations they might have to influencing corporate behavior. There are two ways to address this question. One is to point out that it is not entirely true to say that such codes are utterly unenforceable in law. The other is to argue, that even without express legal form, codes might nonetheless contribute to establishing norms that are recognized as quasi-binding, and which may in fact lead to their legal incarnation.

With respect to the former approach, there are, as Halina Ward notes,[103] at least three means by which "voluntary codes" may be clothed in legal garb. First, corporate or industry-sector codes "can shape the standards of care that are legally expected of businesses" in their dealings with employees, suppliers, local communities, and government through their incorporation into employment, supplier, or agency contracts. Thus, for example, a South African diamond mining industry code that provides warranties against so-called "conflict diamonds" was included in a settlement agreement made subject to a U.S. court's approval. Contractual agreements forged by way of collective bargaining between corporations and employees that are based on aspects of a code will also have a legalizing effect on the codes. Second, standards expressed in certain industry codes can be adopted by regulatory agencies as reporting requirements, and as these bodies are invested with the legal authority of enforcement, an ability to bind is effectively bestowed on the code indirectly. This is the case, for example, with superannuation legislation in the United Kingdom, Australia, Belgium, and Germany; mandatory annual disclosure and reporting requirements for the largest corporations under French corporations law; and the adoption by the JSE Securities Exchange South Africa of a "Code of Corporate Practices and Conduct" that requires all publicly listed corporations to disclose non-financial information in accordance with the Global Reporting Initiative Sustainability Reporting Guidelines. And third, proclamations made by corporations of standards that they claim to abide by are capable of constituting grounds upon which claims of misrepresentation, false, or misleading conduct can be made. The watershed case of *Kasky v. Nike* illustrates how corporate codes might be used in this way. In *Kasky* it was asserted that Nike's public statements about good labor conditions in its Asian factories amounted to false advertising in contravention of California's consumer protection laws and the Federal Trade Commission Act. The case was in fact settled on September 12, 2003, a few months after the Supreme Court of the United States dismissed the petition for certiorari as improvidently granted. Thereby, in not deciding the question of whether Nike's statements were constitutionally protected free speech, the Supreme Court left standing the Supreme Court of California's conclusion that Nike's statements were in fact "commercial speech" and therefore subject to the limitations under that state's unfair competition law.

Besides these limited instances of codes having legal backing, codes do possess a non-legal, norm-making capacity that can both effect corporate behavior and form a basis for future legal regulation. This is the second approach to the question of the legal enforcement of codes mentioned above.

It has been suggested in this respect that the proliferation of codes may lead to the creation of new legal standards for TNCs. Such an argument is underpinned by a "bottom-up" view of international law, whereby it is held that state behavior may be

103. See Halina Ward, Legal Issues in Corporate Citizenship 6–7 (Feb. 2003), available at http://www.iied.org/docs/cred/legalissues_corporate.pdf.

shaped by "the relationship of states to the domestic and transnational social context in which they are embedded." Under this analysis, informal social norms established and applied by non-state actors inter se are capable of shaping the behavior of states, and hence of inter-state institutions. As a result, conclusions can be drawn about legal standards on the basis of compelling trends in social behavior, rather than behavior deduced from legal standards. Jennifer Johnson postulates that if TNCs concertedly implement human rights standards through market practice, domestic values supporting such standards could arise.[114] Assuming domestic law responds to these values, the human rights standards in the market will invite legislative support. If the standards are extensively implemented within certain domestic regimes, collective pressure will grow for their implementation at the international level and thereby to all, or many, other states. In this way, public and private laws "converge," reshaping the creation and formation of international law.

... Suggestions that the expansion of codes as a regulatory form of corporate behavior might constitute a "second human rights revolution," shifting human rights responsibilities from states to private actors, are certainly overblown, but the movement has had some significant impact on the perspectives and practices of corporations. With regard to the whole question of the role and impact of soft-law initiatives in this area, it can be said by way of interim conclusion that their significance at present lies more in their potential rather than extant power to shape corporate behavior. This is not to damn with faint praise. In reality such potential offers an important path forward. What our brief study here reveals is that though each of the legal and non-legal (or quasi-legal) components of soft-law is significant in its own right, they are inextricably interlinked. The continuing tendency to discuss the issues along the lines of the regulatory/voluntary divide that the two parts are supposed to represent is a distraction, and if we are to make the most of the potential before us then we must, as Halina Ward counsels, focus on the "discussion of new legislation or regulation as a response to contested CSR issues."[121] For it is in the solidifying of soft-law into hard law (whether domestic or international) that the whole codes of conduct movement will realize its greatest effect.

The Human Rights Responsibilities of TNCs

Notwithstanding the fact that the proliferation of corporate codes of conduct and other private initiatives might lead to the bolstering of international legal human rights standards for TNCs, there remain the twin questions of how TNCs' liability arises and what their substantive duties might be. Although some TNCs are considered to be more powerful than many states and some perform many of the tasks usually expected of governments, it cannot be simply assumed that TNCs should have the

114. [See Jennifer L. Johnson, Public-Private-Public Convergence: How the Private Actor Can Shape Public International Labor Standards, 24 Brooklyn Journal of International Law 347–48 (1998).]

121. Ward, supra note 103, at 1.

same human rights duties as states. As private entities, TNCs are designed to serve the primary economic purpose of profit maximization, not to assume broad-based welfare functions. Merely to extend the duties of states with respect to human rights to business enterprises, therefore, is to ignore the differences between the nature and functions of states and corporations.

An especially significant difference in this respect relates to the question of jurisdiction. Under international human rights law, a state is deemed to have a measure of responsibility for the human rights-impacting actions of all actors within its jurisdiction—that is, even those of private (non-state) actors—on the basis that the state has, at least in theory, the constitutional authority to legislate and regulate such actions to ensure their compliance with its international obligations. But how far, it may be asked, can any analogous jurisdictional claim be made with respect to corporations? To what extent might corporations legitimately be held responsible for the human rights infringements of their subsidiaries, agents, suppliers, and buyers? There are no easy answers to these persistently difficult "supply chain" questions in terms either of operational practice or legal regulation....

The Conceptual Framework of Human Rights Duties

The disaggregation of the human rights duties of states is undoubtedly a complex business; the same task with respect to non-state entities, and corporations in particular, is even more challenging. Conceptual schemas and practical propositions as to how to identify and attribute duties generally range variously from Wesley Newcomb Hohfeld's seminal work,[130] to the InterAction Council's controversial 1997 proposal for the establishment of "A Universal Declaration of Human Responsibilities."[131] Of course, none of these is complete, and gaps abound. Conspicuously absent in all of them is any established structure within which to frame the specific international human rights legal duties of TNCs.

At the most general level of this question of the appropriate conceptual architecture, it can be said that there is a single overarching objective of international human rights law—that is, to protect human rights. Three more specific obligations flow from that objective: to prevent human rights abuses; to provide means and mechanisms for human rights compliance; and to promote the understanding, appreciation, and application of human rights standards. There are, of course, many dimensions to this matrix that affect the manner, form, and practical impact of the human rights duties that flow from it, but in the present context, the most important of these is the question of whether the duty applies with respect to the duty-bearer's own conduct (what we call a "self-reflexive" duty), or the conduct of others with whom the duty-

130. Wesley Newcomb Hohfeld, Fundamental Legal Conceptions as Applied in Judicial Reasoning (1919).

131. InterAction Council, A Universal Declaration of Human Responsibilities (Sept. 1, 1997), available at http://www.interactioncouncil.org/udhr/declaration/udhr.doc.

bearer might have dealings or over which it might have some control or influence (what we call a "third-party" duty).

This binary structure is especially important in the context of our concern to articulate the international human rights duties that are, or might be, placed on corporations. It cuts across all three sub-categories of obligations identified above and serves to highlight the key questions that must be answered. There are both self-reflexive and third-party dimensions to the duty to prevent human rights abuses (that is, by the TNC itself, and by other parties with which it is associated); to the duty to provide the means of protection (that is, through in-house standards, facilities and procedures, and through the provision of such services outside the corporation where they are otherwise absent); and to the duty to promote the cause of human rights (that is, by advocacy, persuasion, and by example throughout the corporation's ambit of power and authority).

It can be supposed that in so far as human rights duties are self-reflexive, the proposition that corporations are so bound is relatively unproblematic, requiring principally that the corporations refrain from interfering with the enjoyment of human rights by adopting preventive strategies to curb and scrutinize their own actions. This is a minimum duty to "do no harm" to all those with whom TNCs have contact. All other things being equal, the greater the proximity of the TNCs to human rights bearers, the greater will be the duties of the TNCs towards them. Thus, TNCs would owe the greatest duties to those within their "spheres of activity and influence," such as workers, consumers, and members of a local community. Alongside this, TNCs must also have the obligation not to be complicit in human rights abuses committed by others with whom they are working. For example, in joint ventures between TNCs and national (or provincial) governments, the corporation may be complicit by actively participating or knowingly assisting its partner in violating human rights when it provides financial or material assistance to security forces to protect its investments, where it knows (or should know) that the security personnel are likely to commit human rights abuses.

In contrast, the matters within the scope of third-party responsibility and the nature of the entities that might fall within the category of third party are much more difficult to establish. How far beyond the duty not to directly violate human rights in their everyday commercial activities ought the base requirement to protect human rights oblige TNCs to take action to prevent their violation by others? On the face of it, it might appear unjustified or inappropriate to impose on TNCs the obligation to police the conduct of the state as well as other private entities within the territories that they operate, even if it is supposed that they have the resources to do so. Such an obligation would appear to lie wholly within the province of governments, even if the jurisprudence on the nature and extent of these indirect, third-party responsibilities of the state is as yet undeveloped. However, it can be argued that TNCs do have duties to prevent human rights abuses in certain circumstances where they maintain close connections with potential victims or potential perpetrators, and where TNCs are in a position to influence the level of enjoyment of human rights. For instance, TNCs' proximity to their employees suggests that TNCs should have a duty to take reasonable steps to protect the employees from human rights violations committed by the state. TNCs should also have a duty to ensure that their business partners, whether subsidiaries, subcontractors, suppliers, joint venture partners, or others with whom they work do not violate human rights. This duty is particularly strong where the contractual relationships throughout the supply chain allow some room for the TNCs to exert significant influence over the conduct of their business partners. The TNCs' obligation to protect human rights is perhaps greatest where they act as de facto governments and exercise control over the territories in which they operate. In such situations, they effectively step into the shoes of governments and should be required to fulfill duties more akin to those of states.

Related to such duties to prevent third-party violations of human rights are the two questions concerning the extent to which TNCs ought (i) to be required to provide means for protection where others have not, and (ii) to actively lobby others to better protect human rights. Both of these are essentially public functions, apparently going beyond what might be considered the core responsibilities of TNCs. However, the private exercise of public power is nothing new to TNCs, especially given the extent of privatization and corporatization of public utilities and services in the industrialized world over the past twenty years or so, and more recently, with equal vigor, in developing countries. What is more, TNCs are clearly able to use their considerable economic leverage (especially where they are operating in developing countries) to effect public and private conditions that are favorable to their enterprise. It may be the case that one readily associates the duty of providing the appropriate means for actively securing human rights (especially economic and social rights), as well as the duty of providing compliance with human rights, with the activities of the state. And to the extent that these activities fulfill this duty, then it can be said both that they cannot be transposed onto TNCs, and on strong democratic grounds, ought not to be so transferred. But there is simply no reason why TNCs should not be obliged to take steps along the lines of these typical governmental functions to provide for and to promote human rights, when such steps are within their power and jurisdiction. Thus, for example, TNCs in developing countries can be expected to help in the human rights training of state-based security personnel, and to provide health care and even education for workers and their families where none is accessible or would otherwise not be provided by the state. The improvement of the overall human rights situation of the population may indeed be ... a central purpose of government, but we would add that TNCs not only can, but must, provide collateral and sometimes crucial collateral support to that end.

Substantive Human Rights Duties of TNCs

The international human rights obligations of TNCs must, as we have already said, necessarily be narrower than those of states. But they are not to be minimal, or non-existent. They will substantially comprise the general self-reflexive obligation not to interfere with the enjoyment of human rights, but TNCs must also be required, to some extent, to positively provide means for human rights attainment and to promote third-party compliance with, and provision for, human rights guarantees. In terms of a practical frame of reference of what duties international human rights law might impose upon TNCs, the substantive dimensions of such duties are likely initially to be somewhat confined, given the primary focus of international human rights law on states. Some human rights norms may be directly applicable to TNCs, while others can be reformulated to suit the corporate circumstance. For example, the appropriate perspective on the right to education might be that which requires TNCs to abolish or curtail child labor and to provide financial assistance or alternative employment arrangements to children so that they could return to school. Similarly, the right to social security might require TNCs to make pension contributions and provide maternity pay. There are, however, certain international human rights duties which, no matter what perspective is adopted, are inappropriate, if not practically impossible, to place on TNCs. This is likely the case, for example, with protecting the right to asylum, the right to take part in government, and the right to a nationality, and certainly the case with many rights concerning criminal defendants, such as the presumption of innocence, freedom from arbitrary arrest, and the right to be brought promptly to trial. These rights fall squarely within the proper province of states' responsibilities for maintaining public order and ensuring a fair trial.

TNCs are private actors acting on a global stage, and the very fact of their private form sets them apart from states. As legal persons, TNCs have legal rights, including in certain circumstances and under certain jurisdictions, human rights. To the extent that TNCs have such rights under either domestic or international law, they must be balanced against the rights of others. This clearly differs from the situation of the state. As a duty-bound protector of human rights, the state has few countervailing legal rights, and no human rights, that it might call in aid against the rights-claims of private legal persons. Corporations, on the other hand, do possess such private legal rights. Thus, for example, as Ratner suggests, a TNC breaking into anyone's home to wiretap conversations or intercept mail under suspicion of their theft of company property would violate the right against arbitrary or unlawful interference with privacy, family, home, or correspondence, not least because the means are disproportionate to the ends.[158] However, TNCs would likely not be violating employees' human rights by screening their work emails for inappropriate or illegal use. What actions do and do not constitute human rights infringements are not, of course, always so clear-cut as in this pair of examples. In any event, it must be accepted that as private entities, TNCs do legitimately possess greater scope than states to pursue their self-interest.

In delineating certain essential, minimum categories of international human rights duties that may be appropriately placed on TNCs, we have separated our consideration of such rights into two basic categories: "core rights" and "direct impact rights," with each being further divided into particular rights. With respect to core rights, we address a set of fundamental rights that comprise the right to life, liberty, and physical integrity, mindful of the need to balance rights-claims of corporations and individuals as outlined above. These rights are less likely to attract the complexities of such counterbalancing, because their protection from infringement by TNCs is as necessary as

158. [Stephen R. Ratner, Corporations and Human Rights: A Theory of Responsibility 111 Yale Law Journal 443, 514 (2001).]

their protection from infringement by states. Under direct impact rights, we consider the human rights duties of TNCs associated with those individuals, groups, and communities who are most directly affected by the TNCs' actions—namely, employees, their families, and members of local communities. From the rights-holders perspective, the very proximity and immediacy of the rights in this category mark them out as deserving of particular attention, but these rights are also those that TNCs are most ready to concede are to some extent their responsibility to protect. The rights of concern here are labor rights, environmental rights, and peculiarly, though significantly given the propensity for TNCs to operate in remote and/or developing countries, the rights of indigenous peoples.

International human rights laws safeguard rights to life, liberty, and physical integrity by prohibiting actions that are injurious to the inherent dignity and security of the human being. Such actions include war crimes, genocide, crimes against humanity, arbitrary killing, torture, and other cruel, inhuman, or degrading treatment or punishment. While at international law the duties not to engage in such criminal acts are not directly imposed on corporations (though they may be with respect to their officers and/or employees), they can be and are imposed indirectly, by way of states passing on their obligations through national law and policy....

In most cases, these duties would focus on the matter of corporate complicity because businesses are more likely to be complicit (with their state partner) in the commission of war crimes, genocide, and crimes against humanity, rather than directly to commit those crimes themselves. Thus, for example, where coffee companies stored arms and equipment used by those who carried out the genocide in Rwanda in 1994, there are grounds to claim their complicity in the crime. Equally, there are grounds for arguing that Deutsche Bank was complicit in the Holocaust, on the basis that it financed the construction of Auschwitz despite knowing of its intended use.... TNCs should have the obligation to avoid complicity in supplying products or services or providing financial or other material support, when they are aware that such conduct would further the design to commit war crimes, genocide, and crimes against humanity.

The right to life is one of the most fundamental human rights, from which no derogation by states is permitted even in times of public emergency. It is recognized in most international instruments, such as the UDHR and the ICCPR [the International Covenant on Civil and Political Rights], as well as in regional instruments, including the European Convention, the American Convention, and the African Charter. In addition to these treaties, the right to life is recognized as a customary international right, and may well have achieved the status of jus cogens, and thus, a peremptory norm, which cannot be abrogated. Similarly, freedom from torture and other cruel, inhuman, or degrading treatment or punishment (collectively "freedom from torture") is a non-derogable right, protected not only by the ICCPR, the Convention against Torture (CAT), and the UDHR, but also by customary international law and through its status as a jus cogens norm.

Given the "universally recognized and relatively concrete" status of the rights to life and freedom from torture, it is appropriate to impose on TNCs the obligation to respect these rights. Indeed, abundant evidence of TNCs' activities that threaten physical integrity and security of persons clearly points to the need to make this obligation stick. One of the most direct and clearest ways in which TNCs affect the enjoyment of the rights to life and freedom from torture arises from their engagement of security personnel who are likely to commit such crimes against the person. Drawing upon our obligation framework above, the self-reflexive duty of corporations to respect these rights in this context would be to ensure that their own security personnel exercise restraint and caution in a manner consistent with relevant international standards, such as the UN Code of Conduct for Law Enforcement Officials or the UN Basic Principles on the Use of Force and Firearms by Law Enforcement Officials, which lay down strict limitations on when force and firearms can be used. The implications of such an approach have been the subject of specific consideration under a joint initiative of the U.S. and U.K. governments, resulting in the U.S./U.K. Voluntary Principles on Security and Human Rights ("the Voluntary Principles"). Thus, it is reasoned that TNCs ought to develop policies regarding ethical conduct that meet the applicable international standards, and that they adequately train security personnel accordingly.

Alongside this self-reflexive duty to refrain from directly infringing the right to life, TNCs also have a third-party duty to guard against such infringements by others with whom TNCs are associated. This may mean, for example, that where TNCs employ or provide equipment to public or private security forces, they must consider the risk of human rights abuses, assessed against any relevant previous engagement and whether the security staff concerned have had any previous involvement in human rights violations or are likely to in the future. Indeed, such a classic example of private actors performing public (normally state) functions adds strongly to the argument for insisting upon their compliance with international human rights standards. Thus, generally speaking, TNCs should be required to take all appropriate measures to mitigate any foreseeable negative consequences. Where TNCs employ public or private security forces, there arises either the third-party or self-reflexive duty to prevent human rights abuses by the contracted security forces, depending on whether the security personnel are directly or indirectly employed by the TNC. Where they directly employ security personnel, TNCs should be able to incorporate these principles in their contracts and ensure that these employees observe the principles. Contracts could also include the term that the contract can be terminated where there is credible evidence of contravention of the principles by the public or private security personnel. Furthermore, TNCs should support efforts by governments to provide human rights training as well as aid them in establishing adequate monitoring systems, in order to facilitate investigations into allegations of abusive or unlawful acts by security personnel.

By virtue of their particular position as employers, TNCs' policies and practices have the most immediate impact on the enjoyment of labor rights. The critical need to formulate labor standards is reflected in the fact that the majority of existing international initiatives attempt to address TNCs' responsibility to respect labor rights more than any other set of rights. The minimum duties of TNCs in relation to labor rights should be grounded on "core" labor rights, as expressed in Article 2 of the ILO Declaration on Fundamental Principles and Rights at Work, and expanded on by the eight fundamental ILO Conventions. These core labor rights consist of the freedom of association, the right to organize and bargain collectively, and the prohibitions against discrimination, bonded and forced labor, and child labor.

There are, however, a number of factors that must be addressed in any attempt to implement TNCs' obligations regarding labor rights. Perhaps the most important of these is the fact that such attempts are sometimes resisted by those they aim to protect—namely, workers in developing countries. Most often, however, the opposition comes from governments of developing countries, who claim to fear a loss of the competitive advantage they supposedly derive from cheap labor costs and who perceive the imposition of labor standards as a disguise for protectionism of industrial countries. This is a complex and difficult issue. Some empirical studies show that observance of the core labor rights would not significantly reduce the competitive advantage of cheap labor. Further, respecting the rights of workers, particularly in relation to health and welfare issues, may lead to enhanced proficiency and increased productivity, and hence attract more foreign investment. What cannot be denied is that in the long run, educated and healthy workers are vital for economic development, which in turn creates stable business environments. The key challenge is, of course, determining how to establish and maintain such benign conditions for workers, for, in reality, the mechanisms that provide, or can provide, such conditions operate beyond the workplace and even the immediate local community to include national and often international agencies. However, the fundamental tenet of our argument remains that economic development does not necessarily require a tradeoff in human rights. Therefore, it follows that developing countries should not myopically block the imposition of duties on TNCs to respect labor rights. Any comparative advantage derived as a result of violations of core labor standards cannot be promoted as a legitimate advantage that developing countries should be able to enjoy. The concept of comparative advantage, in other words, while focusing on economic efficiency, must also have regard to social ramifications if it is to be considered an appropriate doctrinal principle in promoting economic development.

Where the imposition of international labor standards is opposed by those who argue that it would hurt the very workers they are designed to help, it is often on the basis that such conditions might put them out of work. Nicholas Kristof and Sheryl WuDunn observe that developing country workers often claim that the simplest way to help them is to buy more from sweatshops, not less, because sweatshops offer an escape (albeit a precarious one) from their poverty.[197] Premature unilateral implementation of core labor standards can have devastating consequences on workers because it may result in immediate termination of their employment, leaving them without any alternative means of earning an income. What must be appreciated here

197. Nicholas D. Kristof & Sheryl WuDunn, Two Cheers for Sweatshops, N.Y. Times, Sept. 24, 2000, § 6 (Magazine), at 70.

is the importance of exercising a great degree of sensitivity in determining methods of implementing TNCs' duties to respect labor rights so that such duties are not seen merely as an imperialistic exportation of a Western construct. To this end, TNCs should be required to implement core labor rights with "a relativist sensibility," which necessarily entails entering into dialogue with the workers in developing countries. TNCs must increase consultation with workers and adopt implementation methods that focus on actual consequences to them, rather than unilaterally imposing universalist norms of the developed world....

Pini Pavel Miretski and Sascha-Dominik Bachmann, *The UN Norms on the Responsibility of Transnational Corporations and Other Business Enterprises with Regard to Human Rights: A Requiem**

After endorsing the 2011 "Guiding Principles for Business and Human Rights," the Office of the UN High Commissioner for Human Rights issued a press release announcing that

> in an unprecedented step, the United Nations Human Rights Council has endorsed a new set of Guiding Principles for Business and Human Rights designed to provide—*for the first time*—a global standard for preventing and addressing the risk of adverse impacts on human rights linked to business activity.[2]

While such a categorisation may be debatable, there remains little disagreement over the importance of such an endorsement by the UN Human Rights Council. The Secretary-General's Special Representative for Business and Human Rights (hereinafter SRSG), Professor John Ruggie, declared that "[t]he Council's endorsement establishes the Guiding Principles as the authoritative global reference point for business and human rights." ...

In 1998 the Working Group on the Working Methods and Activities of Transnational Corporations was established by a Sub-Commission of the UN Commission on Human Rights. Its mandate was to make recommendations and proposals concerning the working methods and activities of transnational corporations (TNCs), in order to ensure that these correlate with the economic and social objectives of their host countries and promote human rights. The final detailed document, and its commentary, were approved in August 2003 by the Sub-Commission. The document was named the *Norms on the Responsibilities of Transnational Corporations and Other Business Enterprises with Regard to Human Rights* (hereinafter *Norms*).[9] The *Norms* were far-reaching and included a duty for TNCs to impose human rights obligations upon states, even if states failed to ratify the human rights instruments establishing these duties.

---

* Originally published in 17 Deakin Law Review 5 (2012). Reprinted with permission.

2. ... [F]or the full text of the Guiding Principles, see [http://www.ohchr.org/Documents/Publications/GuidingPrinciplesBusinessHR_EN.pdf].

9. [For the full text of the Norms, see http://www1.umn.edu/humanrts/links/norms-Aug2003.html.—Eds.]

The draft *Norms* represented a significant departure from the prevailing practice among international organisations when dealing with the often difficult relationship between business and human rights: that of voluntary compliance. The *Norms* were designed to constitute a "non-voluntary," comprehensive framework, creating direct obligations for TNCs and supplemented by a rigid enforcement mechanism including the monitoring by non-state actors (NGOs and TNCs themselves). The document was prepared in accordance with the mandate that the Working Group received and was in line with the background reports upon which it was supposed to structure its work. Many scholars hailed the document as the groundbreaking initiative that might succeed, for the first time, in ending corporate abuses of human rights.

Such explicit support for the *Norms* was accompanied by often fierce opposition from various states and the majority of the business community. Such opposition arose from the moment the *Norms* were formally introduced as a discussion paper after their approval by the Sub-Commission. Most states expressed strong reservations, emphasising their determination not to depart from the traditional framework of international law, which stresses the central and pivotal role of the state as a legal subject of public international law.

The *Norms* were eventually abandoned in 2005 and the task of regulating transnational corporate accountability was transferred to other UN organs. This article discusses possible reasons why the *Norms* failed to be approved by the UN Commission on Human Rights. This discussion is necessary to help us understand the difficulties involved in creating "hard law" obligations governing TNCs with regard to human rights within the wider framework of international law. It is crucial to understand the possible motives as well as the underlying rationale which led first to the adoption and then the rapid abandoning of the *Norms*. The discussion will also shed light on the future of indirect, vague voluntarism, as well as on our prospects of finding alternative solutions to the problems addressed by the *Norms*.

The *Norms* were defined by one of their drafters as a "non-voluntary set of norms binding upon corporations." Deva expressed the importance of the *Norms* in the observation that they constituted a shift in paradigms "that have to date dominated the discourse of corporate social responsibility" and have caused ineffective regulation of corporate conduct, resulting in abuses of human rights.[17] The *Norms* were defined by their authors largely as a restatement of existing obligations of TNCs in respect to human rights under international law. However, some of the obligations in the *Norms* were a teleological manifestation of an ongoing "progressive development" of the existing principles of international law.

Perhaps their main novelty, and possibly the main reason for the subsequent controversy over the *Norms*, was the fact that the obligations were to be imposed directly on TNCs, rather than states being requested or required to implement legislation to

17. See [Surya Deva, UN's Human Rights Norms for Transnational Corporations and Other Business Enterprises: An Imperfect Step in the Right Direction, 10 ILSA Journal of International & Comparative Law 493, 497 (2004).]

regulate the actions of the TNCs within their jurisdiction. While most of the rules in the *Norms* represented obligations already recognised within the existing frameworks of international law, in the vast majority of cases they are imposed only indirectly on TNCs, through the intermediary of the states. Baxi further argues that the *Norms* reflected duties that applied to states and that may not be automatically transposed to apply to TNCs. In that respect he believes that while the *Norms* may have embodied a good vision of *de lege ferenda*, or the law to which we may aspire, they did not reflect *lex lata*, or positive existing law.[20]

This article identifies three reasons which most likely led to the eventual abandoning of the draft *Norms* by the UN Commission on Human Rights: Firstly, the fact that a large part of the *Norms* constituted a further development of existing international norms, rather than actual codification of existing international law, enabled critics of the *Norms* to argue their incompatibility, as legal analogies, with otherwise positivist foundations of international law. Secondly, the fact that the *Norms* assigned an important legal role to TNCs ... rather than to the traditional addressees of international law, the states, was problematic. The construction of the TNCs as addressees blurred the distinction between international public and private legal frameworks, and thus undermined the central role of states as international law subjects. Finally, inherent contradictions within the *Norms* themselves and a vagueness in their overall nature and applicability helped to foster opposition against their adoption....

Legislative Context and Relevance of the Norms

The *Norms* aimed at "maximizing the good that companies do while eliminating the abuses they commit."[22] Their rationale was to establish (and enforce) a balance between corporate business behaviour and human rights. Such a balance would acknowledge the positive role corporations can play in regard to economic development and overall prosperity, while preventing the occurrence of corporate human rights violations. One of its drafters, Professor Weissbrodt, argued that grave human rights abuses by corporations occur in a variety of business situations and consequently need to be regulated at the supranational level.[24]

As pointed out by Kinley and Chambers, the 1990s saw widening concerns with respect to increased violations of human rights by TNCs. These violations were occurring against a background of an increased liberalisation of international trade rules, the increase of foreign direct investment in developing and emerging economies as well as the growing power and influence of MNCs and TNCs.[25] ... The UN Sub-Commission on the Promotion and Protection of Human Rights (hereinafter Sub-Commission) recognised the possibility of MNCs aiding and abetting human rights

20. Upendra Baxi, Market Fundamentalisms: Business Ethics at the Altar of Human Rights 5 Human Rights Law Review 1, 14 (2005).

22. [David Weissbrodt, Business and Human Rights, 74 Cincinnati Law Review 55, 58 (2005).]

24. [Id. at 56–58.]

25. [David Kinley & Rachel Chambers, The UN Human Rights Norms for Corporations: The Private Implications of Public International Law, 6 Human Rights Law Review 447, 457 (2006).]

violations and hence being indirectly liable for them. It voiced "significant concerns about the conduct of transnational corporations and other businesses."

Weissbrodt believed that international law in general, and international human rights law (IHRL) in particular, focused on protecting the individual from violations by governments, rather than from violations by other actors. Weissbrodt also thought that, while new groups of non-state actors are becoming subject to liability through the operation of various sub-fields of international law, TNCs and businesses in general remained largely unaffected by these developments. While some international legal documents may be interpreted as applying to corporations, most of them have applied to the TNCs only indirectly. However, such indirect regulation did not prevent abuses of human rights by businesses and therefore several international efforts to create frameworks of direct obligations on TNCs were made. These attempts included the unsuccessful attempts to establish a UN Code of Conduct for Transnational Corporations, the OECD Guidelines for Multinational Enterprises, the ILO Tripartite Declaration of Principles Concerning Multinational Enterprises and the Global Compact initiative.

The new *Norms* seemed at last to remedy the lack of accountability of corporations. Scholars were referring to the *Norms*, after their final drafting and their eventual disappearance from the agenda of the UN, as the "most promising human rights norms for TNCs to date."[31] The German government described the *Norms* as a "useful contribution to the ongoing debate on ways and means of integrating business enterprises in the international endeavours to promote and protect human rights and sustainable development." The drafting initiative was supported by many NGOs. Furthermore, several transnational businesses, which participated in the "Initiative for Respect" and the "Ethical Globalisation Initiative," volunteered to participate in the "pilot project" for the *Norms*, as part of their wider commitment to human rights.

The *Norms* drew heavily from existing human rights documents and it seems that their overall aim was to fill a void in the existing frameworks of international law, by providing a single, comprehensive and constituting set of human rights norms with binding effect for all corporations. They were designed to serve as an accessible legal document which could be applied even by non-experts in international human rights law, particularly corporate directors....

Progressive Development, Novelties and Shortfalls of the Norms

The *Norms* were, in many ways, setting new legal standards regarding corporate human rights responsibilities. Although reflecting and drawing from already existing human rights obligations, the *Norms* incorporated notions of progressive development and novel conceptions of human rights protection. The *Norms* attempted to establish direct responsibility of TNCs for human rights violations, utilising existing frameworks of international law. They aimed to establish an explicit duty for TNCs to promote human rights from "top to bottom," even in respect of corporations registered in

31. [See, e.g., Deva, supra note 17, at 497; Weissbrodt, supra note 22, at 55.]

non-state parties. These norms were designed to constitute a "non-voluntary" framework, which was far more codified than any voluntary framework, but which fell short of being mandatory, constituting "soft law" instead of "hard law." This [section] will discuss these novelties and contradictions.

The Preamble of the *Norms* essentially reiterated the fundamental character of Corporate Social Responsibility as a means to promote and protect human rights. The *Norms* were basically a furtherance of human rights principles already set down in the Universal Declaration on Human Rights of 1948.... As part of the attempt to characterise the *Norms* as a mere codification of already established principles of customary international law, rather than a progressive development of such legal principles, the Preamble contained an open, non-exhaustive list of the international treaties and conventions which established the legal basis for TNCs' obligations in the area of human rights. Some of them arguably even reached the level of jus cogens. In Baxi's view, this raised the problem of intelligibility, as not everyone among those affected by corporate violations of human rights—nor among the CEOs in the business community—is familiar with the full range of human rights instruments referred to in the *Norms*.[56] Consequently, the Preamble of the Norms not only served as an introduction to the main document, but also explained the core substance of the *Norms*.

The operative part of the *Norms* was divided into seven main categories. It presented a comprehensive list of human rights obligations relevant to TNCs. The *Norms* did not set down so called "negative" duties (whereby TNCs should refrain from violating human rights), but rather introduced as a "positive" duty for TNCs the obligation to promote and ensure respect for human rights....

Under "General Obligations" in Part A of the *Norms* were listed the following responsibilities: the duty of due diligence to ensure that business activities do not directly or indirectly contribute to human rights abuses; the duty to ensure that corporations do not benefit from such abuses; the duty to refrain from undermining efforts to promote human rights; the duty of a corporation to use its influence to promote human rights; the obligation to assess the human rights impact of the corporation; and the overall responsibility to avoid complicity in human rights abuses.

These obligations are significant and affected the entire document. Article 1 recognised states as the traditional holders of the primary responsibilities

> to promote, secure the fulfilment of, respect, ensure respect of and protect human rights recognized in international as well as national law, including ensuring that transnational corporations and other business enterprises respect human rights.

The *Norms*' overall impact, however, would have been more radical than Article 1 suggests: they essentially relegated states to the background in the attempt to protect human rights in the transnational business context. TNCs would have been forced

56. ... [T]he text of the *Norms* refers to at least 56 previous human rights instruments. Baxi, supra note 20, at 3–6....

to operate against the interests of a state in order to comply with the "greater, internationally-derived good" of transnational human rights compliance.[63]

The primacy of the role given to corporations, and its lack of definition in the *Norms* led to significant reservations being expressed against such—perceived—"demotion" of states. Baxi argued that there are several possible interpretations of the term "primary responsibility" which would significantly influence the scope of the role of the states and their obligations according to the *Norms*.[64] The United States Council for International Business criticised the *Norms* for the fact that they "represent a fundamental shift in responsibility for protecting human rights—from governments to private actors, including companies—effectively privatizing the enforcement of human rights laws."[65] This critique was aimed at the very nature of the *Norms*. They were intended to improve human rights protection in cases where states failed to act, thereby widening the scope of applicability of international human rights law by including situations where corporations have de facto greater influence than that of the states.

> Within their respective spheres of activity and influence, transnational corporations and other business enterprises have the obligation to promote, secure the fulfilment of, respect, ensure respect of and protect human rights recognized in international as well as national law, including the rights and interests of indigenous peoples and other vulnerable groups.

The [official c]ommentary on the *Norms* ... clarified that the *Norms* should apply regardless of the state in which TNCs operated, and what the level of human rights protection in the respective state was.

The *Norms* laid down, as specific rules and obligations for corporations, the duty to protect the right to equal opportunity and non-discriminatory treatment, the right to security of persons, labour rights of workers, the right of fair remuneration, the respect for national sovereignty and human rights, obligations relating to consumer protection (which were uniquely designed for TNCs) and, finally, obligations with regard to environmental protection.

Of particular interest is Part E of the *Norms*, in which TNCs were identified as possible multipliers for the development of a global business society bound to the rule of law, transparency, accountability and sustainable development, and in which the peoples' civil, political, economic and cultural rights were realised. This was an innovation in three main respects. Firstly, instead of limiting TNCs' obligations to civil and political rights only, the *Norms* included both civil rights and collective social, economic and cultural rights of the second and third generations of human rights. Secondly, as mentioned above, this imposed positive obligations upon TNCs....

---

63. [Larry Catá Backer, Multinational Corporations, Transnational Law: The United Nations Norms on the Responsibilities of Transnational Corporations as Harbinger of Corporate Responsibility in International Law, 37 Columbia Human Rights Law Review 287, 373 (2006).]

64. ... Baxi, supra note 20, at 9–10.

65. [Carlos M. Vázquez, Direct vs. Indirect Obligations of Corporations under International Law, 43 Columbia Journal of Transnational Law 927, 929 (2005).]

Thirdly, TNCs were expected to respect and promote even the rights of those individuals who were affected only indirectly by their activities.

Part H dealt with the general provisions concerning implementation of the *Norms.* Deva distinguished between direct and indirect aspects of implementation of the *Norms* as defined there. TNCs were expected to both internalise the culture of the *Norms*, as well as being subjected to periodic monitoring and verification by different bodies. Indirectly, the *Norms* were to be promoted through amendment by the states of their national legal frameworks, which would ensure that TNCs implemented the *Norms.*[72] Backer claimed that, through the general provisions, the *Norms* exploited the flexibility of private lawmaking to maximise the efficiency of implementation, without the interference of state actors.[73]

The final part of the *Norms*, Part I provided various definitions required for the interpretation of the *Norms.* Of particular importance was the definition of the term "transnational corporation," which was kept deliberately broad and referred to an "economic entity operating in more than one country or a cluster of economic entities operating in two or more countries—whatever their legal form, whether in their home country or country of activity, and whether taken individually or collectively." This definition was to be read in conjunction with the definition of "other business entities," which was drawn up to "ensure that transnational corporations could not change their identity ... and therefore avoid the draft *Norms*," and potentially included nearly all existent business entities to date. The terms "human rights" and "international human rights" were also defined widely for the purposes of the *Norms.* The terms included

> civil, cultural, economic, political and social rights, as set forth in the International Bill of Human Rights and other human rights treaties, as well as the right to development and rights recognized by international humanitarian law, international refugee law, international labour law, and other relevant instruments adopted within the United Nations system.

This definition allowed the inclusion of human rights norms and standards of different levels and generations. While some of the norms listed in the document had universal legal effect, others were norms of positive character existent only between parties to certain agreements. Some were even norms with no general legal effect and as such of nonbinding "soft law" effect.

It seems that a discrepancy existed between the major issues discussed while drafting the *Norms* and the issues which were the basis for the later criticism of the *Norms.* There were five main features of the *Norms* which were widely discussed during the drafting process.

72. Deva, supra note [17], at 514–18.

73. [Backer, supra note 63, at 334.]

The first was the scope of application of the *Norms* and the decision to define the term "transnational corporations" to include all types of business entities. Weissbrodt emphasised that, while most media attention focused on the misdeeds of major corporations, applying human rights standards only to large TNCs could have been considered discriminatory. Moreover, the drafters considered it difficult to define the term TNC in such a way as not to allow corporate lawyers to restructure the corporation in a way that would prevent these standards being applied to this corporation.[78]

Secondly, because the drafters of the *Norms* believed that the principles should be respected by all businesses, and in order to avoid distinctions between the standards applied to domestic and transnational corporations, they applied the *Norms* to all corporations, while minimizing the need for implementation of the rules by small "mom and pop" shops. Thirdly, the drafters of the *Norms* decided on an approach according to which the power and the influence of a corporation should be matched by the appropriate level of responsibility.

Fourthly, the *Norms* were designed to constitute the most comprehensive and human rights-focused document applying transnational rules to businesses up to that time. Finally, the *Norms* were designed to have a special non-voluntary character. While the *Norms* did not amount to an "international treaty," according to their drafters, the drafters described the *Norms* as a "soft-law" restatement of the principles applicable to corporations. Such principles were derived from international treaties and customary international law.

Another novelty of the *Norms* was their use of a binding "shall" language, instead of the previously accepted "should" terminology.

Out of the issues mentioned above, only the all-inclusive and the non-voluntary character of the *Norms* were mentioned by the opponents of the *Norms*. The criticism of the *Norms* was focused mostly on (1) the transition of responsibility from states to TNCs and the associated alteration of the traditional framework of international law; (2) the imposition on TNCs of responsibility for the actions of other actors; and (3) the perceived excessive legalism of the document on the one hand and its vagueness on the other.

The *Norms* related to TNCs as entities with distinct social, cultural, civil and political rights and duties. The *Norms* did not treat TNCs only as legal entities whose function is limited to the economic sphere and whose activities must be regulated in order for the entity to remain active in this sphere. Backer asserted that the *Norms* treated corporations as "virtual State actors" for the purposes of many normative requirements.[84] They bypassed the medium of the state, in order to create a direct link between international law and TNCs. In doing so they made the TNCs important

78. Weissbrodt, supra note [22], at 65–66; see also Baxi, supra note 20, 6–9.

84. Backer, supra note [63], at 371....

actors in promoting human rights, mainly in the developing countries, but also in the developed countries that refused to adopt certain human rights norms.

Several aspects of the *Norms* are worthy of a deeper analysis. The *Norms* drew from previous human rights instruments the obligations relevant to TNCs and other business entities and applied them directly to the corporations. At the same time they reemphasised the primary and the overarching responsibility of the states. Kinley and Chambers identified four points where the *Norms* diverged from traditional human rights documents.

Firstly, unlike other human rights instruments, the *Norms* revolved around the duty-bearers, to which the different rules apply, rather than focusing on a single set of rights (civil, political, and economic) or rights holders (women, children, racial groups).[87] The focus of the *Norms* on duty-bearers, rather than on a specific set of rights also caused them to be indeterminate about the exact scope of the specific rights, applicable to the TNCs.

Secondly, the notion of a "sphere of influence," and thus responsibility, derived from the corporate social responsibility (CSR) movement. This aspect of the *Norms* has also been criticised for not being clear enough, and being ambiguous about the question of whether the entire supply chain of the corporation lies within its "sphere of activity and influence."[89]

Thirdly, the *Norms* sought to establish new enforcement mechanisms applicable to non-state actors, and to make non-state actors the promoters of these norms and mechanisms when entering into contractual relationships with their business partners.[90] The subject of enforcement was a key issue addressed by the *Norms*. TNCs were to be subject to "periodic monitoring and verification by United Nations and other international and national mechanisms already in existence or yet to be created regarding the application of the *Norms*." Vázquez further claimed that states would be reluctant to create and maintain institutions, established under the *Norms*, as this would limit their own sovereign powers. Furthermore, he suggested that legal norms were less likely to be observed by non-state actors in the absence of effective enforcement mechanisms carrying sanctions.[94] Another alleged shortcoming of this mechanism was its unintended anti-democratic character: an allegation based on the fact that the *Norms* had been drafted by subject matter experts and were not subject to further scrutiny by the (affected) states.

This outcome could have been the result of the influence of NGOs on the drafting process. Yet another perceived shortfall of this mechanism was its supposed lack of enforcement available in case of violations. However, this shortcoming was only al-

87. Kinley & Chambers, supra note [25], at 452.

89. [Id.]

90. [Id. at 452–53.]

94. Vázquez, supra note [65], at 954–55.

leged. In fact, there was a rigid enforcement mechanism which obligated the TNCs to have business relations only with TNCs that adhered to the *Norms*. Another element of implementation was the duty of the TNCs to provide "prompt, effective and adequate reparations to those persons, entities and communities" that had been adversely affected by failure to comply with the *Norms*.

Fourthly, the *Norms* added to the traditional list of human rights and fundamental freedoms other rights associated with consumer protection, the environment and issues of corruption. Kinley and Chambers observed that this development was sensible as violations of the dominant norms in these areas may lead to violations of other, more basic human rights, such as the right to life and may deny populations their economic, social and cultural rights and other basic and widely accepted rights such as the right to health and the right to development.[101]

One of the advantages of the *Norms* was the range of their possible impact. By virtue of their non-voluntary nature they had, as an instrument of regulation, the potential to overcome the so-called "free-rider" dilemma of many TNCs. By contrast, the adoption by TNCs of voluntary programmes for the protection of human rights would disadvantage them economically against their competitors in the market, who did not take similar actions. Backer also argued that the support for the *Norms* by both important sectors of civil society and by the international law establishment was evidence for the evolving of transnational law, an evolution which has produced "a mechanics of interplay between national, international, public, and private law systems in allocating and competing for regulatory power."[103]

The Norms—An Appraisal

... Backer identified and analysed the two main types of response to the *Norms*. The "public sector oriented" participants, a term which mainly refers to academics and NGOs, supported this instrument for being an advance over existing voluntary standards by providing a single comprehensive regime which drew an appropriate balance between the obligations of states and those of companies with respect to human rights. They claimed that the *Norms* provided also a template for state compliance with human rights along with a system of restorative remedies for individuals supervised by a supra-national organisation. The second group, "private sector" or "market oriented" participants, emphasised the extreme radicalism of the *Norms*—the mandatory approach; the presumption that private economic entities were more, rather than less, likely to promote human rights and development; the lack of a legal basis for imposing obligations on TNCs under international law, particularly in light of the vagueness and questionable legal effect of some of the norms mentioned in the document.[104] The second group was the more influential one, and it was the one that eventually determined the future of the *Norms*.

101. Kinley & Chambers, supra note [25], at 472–74.

103. Backer, supra note [63], at 288.

104. Backer, supra note [63], at 356–57....

We shall first examine the responses of the business sector. Despite the fact that the majority in the business community—mainly the business chambers and industry organisations—rejected the *Norms*, some favoured the application of the *Norms* and even volunteered as test participants in an implementation of the *Norms*. On the other hand, parts of the business community claimed that compliance with human rights law should be by choice and should occur only to the extent needed by the business community. They also argued that nation states, rather than the UN, should enforce human rights. The International Chamber of Commerce and the International Organisation of Employers issued a joint statement opposing the *Norms* and their "legalistic approach." At the same time the US Council for International Business opposed the *Norms* through criticising their vagueness. Senior Vice President Deal, claimed that the *Norms* created a "legal no man's land."[106] He argued that because the document did not distinguish between binding and non-binding human rights obligations (since some of its principles were drawn from non-binding human rights instruments) it blurred the line between voluntary and mandatory corporate compliance, thus making "corporate compliance virtually impossible." ...

Under the *Norms*, the duties of the TNCs were to increase not just directly, but indirectly as well. Not only might the *Norms* have placed a legal liability upon a corporation which colluded with a state in the commission of human rights violations, but they also stipulated the duty of a TNC to "impose" human rights obligations upon states, even if these states refused to ratify the human rights instruments involved. Backer claimed that this reflected the use of mechanisms of so called "low level" international governance, meaning international governance that arises "at the level of private law in the municipal systems of sovereign states," which has been a contested issue in the field of international relations.[110] As Deva observed, the *Norms* were probably too focused on stressing the importance of the universality of human rights, while ignoring both operational standards and the realities of human rights protection in the context of corporate business realities, and regional and cultural differences.[111]

Perhaps, the best characterisation of the approach adopted by the *Norms* was reflected in the eleventh paragraph of its Preamble:

> Noting that transnational corporations and other business enterprises have the capacity to foster economic well-being, development, technological improvement and wealth as well as the capacity to cause harmful impacts on the human rights and lives of individuals through their core business practices and operations, including employment practices, environmental policies,

---

106. The extreme criticism of the *Norms* by these bodies is of particular interest, in light of the fact that they were invited to participate and did participate to some extent, in the drafting process of the Norms. Weissbrodt, supra note [22], at 70.

110. Backer, supra note [63], at 334.

111. Deva, supra note [17], at 511–13.

> relationships with suppliers and consumers, interactions with Governments and other activities....

According to some commentators, the second part of this paragraph and the extended scope of responsibility of TNCs for the activities of other participants in the business chain, such as suppliers, partners, joint ventures and even governments, was one of the most problematic aspects of the *Norms*. The business community criticised the *Norms* and referred to the benefits of corporate business activities in terms of economic growth and stability as well as its own commitment to voluntary self regulation in the few cases where human rights violations were happening. John Cridland, Deputy Director-General of the Confederation of British Industries was quoted to have said, "[t]hat leaves business having to blow the whistle on something that aims to subject firms to criticism and liability for abusing human rights. It is quite wrong to suggest that firms are generally involved in widespread abuse of human rights—where is the evidence?"[114]

Another major concern for many corporations was the matter of reparations that the companies would be liable to pay, in accordance with the *Norms*. This was particularly worrisome, because, as mentioned above, TNCs might have been liable not only for the direct actions of the corporation itself, but for the ill-deeds of their suppliers, joint venturers and other groups, including governments, from whose activities they as corporations might have benefited.

Campagna argued that the main reason for the general opposition of the business community to the *Norms* was not some perceived flaws in the text of the *Norms*. Rather, it was a substantial flaw in the thinking of business leaders when faced with the prospect of applying international human rights standards to business strategies. She alleged that businesses viewed the need for adherence to IHRL solely as a management issue, whereas, in her opinion, only the question of whether to comply with IHRL constituted a management issue. The more essential question of general human rights compliance resembled a legal issue which should not be left to the discretion of businesses alone to decide.[117] The *Norms* therefore represented a major deviation from the self-regulation approach which was more widely accepted and preferred when relations between business and human rights needed to be governed.

Backer regarded the *Norms* as going even further—altering the foundations of corporate regulation by actually transforming the authority to regulate TNCs. The drastic change in the definition of stakeholders that was embedded in the *Norms* altered the foundations of corporate governance and regulation. Backer's view was that human rights under the *Norms* would enter municipal legal systems and international law not from above as part of prescribed international treaty law, but rather

114. Kinley & Chambers, supra note [25], at 448–49.

117. [Julie Campagna, United Nations Norms on the Responsibilities of Transnational Corporations and Other Business Enterprises with Regard to Human Rights: The International Community Asserts Binding Law on the Global Rule Makers, 37 John Marshall Law Review 1205, 1229 (2004).]

from below through private law governing business relations, which would then establish binding rules which in turn would become new customary international law.[119]

The far-reaching character of the *Norms* drew significant opposition from various states as well. Most states expressed strong reservations, emphasising the undesired departure from the traditional framework of international law, and stressing the central role of the state as an actor under international law. Backer further pointed out that many states indicated that they would be unwilling to accept any legal regime which had the potential to threaten their monopoly of power to adopt and implement international norms within their territory.

Developing states were concerned that the *Norms* favoured the implementation of human rights standards in their state territory by means of corporate authority rather than state control. Another concern was that the *Norms* could reduce incentives for some TNCs to expand their operations into developing states, due to considerations based on the extended liability standard explained above. Such a disincentive to corporate engagement, as well as investment, would have the potential to harm the economic development of these host states....

Western states voiced concern that shifting responsibility for the implementation of human rights standards to corporations would dilute the primary responsibility of states as legislators of international law. The United Kingdom argued for a framework containing "a universally accepted collation and clarification of the minimum standards of behaviour expected of companies with regard to human rights." The Australian Government held the firm view that legal responsibility for the implementation of international human rights standards rests primarily with those States who are party to the standards, not individual businesses. Businesses are obliged to comply with the laws of the countries in which they operate.

The Canadian Government recognised that "companies have an important role to play in the promotion and protection of human rights," but emphasised the primary role of the states in this matter. It also expressed several concerns regarding the Norms—mainly that they purported to extend existing human rights obligations of states to TNCs; entrusted enforcement mechanisms, which may become ineffective, to non-state actors, which in turn could assist states in avoiding their human rights obligations; and changed the existing framework of obligations within the framework of international law. The United States went even further by claiming that the *Norms* were not based on existing legal frameworks, that they were "doomed from the outset" and that the international community should rather focus on assisting states to implement their human rights obligations and enforce national law. Moreover, they claimed that the *Norms* represented a significant divergence from the existing frameworks of international law by attempting to impose duties and obligations on non-state actors, while these were applicable solely to states.

119. Backer, supra note [63], at 357–58.

There was also some anxiety that the *Norms* would make TNCs both a subject and a source of international law, thus obliterating traditional boundaries of international law. Of particular interest was the response of the United States, which began by reiterating the US position that the *Norms* have no status—legal or otherwise. Not only was this exercise beyond the mandate of the Sub-Commission—but it was undertaken wholly without consideration for the views of the States.

The United States also refuted the claim that TNCs were responsible for widespread human rights abuses in countries where they operate, claiming that such abuses were the result of "action or inaction of States." The United States further alleged that the international community should focus on promoting and enforcing the rule of law by governments and not on "a drafting exercise geared toward creating 'norms' out of whole cloth."

These adverse views seriously impacted on the views of other UN Member States when the *Norms* were considered for adoption by the Commission at its 60th session in 2004. Further work on the *Norms* was consequently put on hold. Later, the [Office of the High Commissioner of Human Rights] issued a statement thanking the Sub-Commission for drafting the *Norms*, confirming the overall importance of the subject, and at the same time clarifying that the draft proposal had no legal status, and therefore the Sub-Commission should not perform any monitoring functions regarding the *Norms*. Subsequently, the *Norms* were effectively abandoned by the Commission on Human Rights in its 61st session in 2005....

In their present form, the *Norms* have no binding force in international law. The Sub-Commission which drafted the *Norms* was not mandated to create binding new international law. At present, there is no international treaty which incorporates the *Norms*, nor is there evidence of any evolving state practice indicating the development of customary international law to that effect.... However, already existing principles of customary international law which were restated in the *Norms* retain their force as independent principles of international law.

... On a normative level, [however,] the *Norms* may turn out to be (at least) a partial success. Despite the failure of not having become binding law, the *Norms* created a significant impact on stakeholders at the non-state level. Investment institutions began applying the *Norms* to persuade companies to improve their social responsibility; NGOs began using the *Norms* as a basis for their advocacy of corporate social responsibility; companies have expressed general support for the *Norms*, while others even began "road-testing" the *Norms*. Perhaps, after all, the *Norms* are fulfilling the role designed for them, even if they were not adopted officially.... Rule suggested that the *Norms* were designed to stimulate societal change rather than to become a binding legal document, and that they should therefore be read as relating to an ideal structure of *de lege ferenda* regarding the connection between business and human rights.[157]....

157. [Troy Rule, Using Norms to Change International Law: UN Human Rights Laws Sneaking in Through the Back Door, 5 Chicago Journal of International Law 325, 332 (2004).]

Paulette L. Stenzel, *Why and How the World Trade Organization Must Promote Environmental Protection**

At the August 2001 annual meeting of the Academy of Legal Studies in Business, members of a panel discussed the [World Trade Organization's] obligations with respect to environment, labor, and consumer protection. In response to the proposition that the WTO should act to protect the environment, one professor wondered whether the WTO can be held responsible for these concerns, or if environmental protection should be left to individual countries. Another professor suggested that if the WTO were given power over matters such as environmental protection and worker's rights, the WTO would acquire the powers of a quasi-world government.

This section responds to those concerns. First, the WTO must be held responsible for environmental damage, because such damage is inextricably linked to increased trade. Even if the WTO's powers do not appear to be far-reaching, the environmental effects of its work are far-reaching. Second, there is precedent for such responsibility through application of the tenets of Corporate Social Responsibility (CSR), a movement that advocates holding businesses responsible for alleviating social ills. The WTO has a responsibility to discourage and clean up environmental damage because it facilitates that damage.

The WTO's operations are relatively small in terms of personnel and budget. As of 2001, it had 550 employees and an annual budget of $90 million. Additionally, its legal powers are limited. Enforcement of the decisions of the WTO's dispute resolution bodies depends primarily on the willingness of its members to abide by those decisions. For example, two dispute panels ruled that U.S. embargoes on tuna violated [the General Agreement on Tariffs and Trade] or GATT, yet the United States failed to adopt the reports and did not follow the panels' recommendations. In a dispute related to the importation of bananas, the WTO found EU practices to be discriminatory, yet the EU refused to comply with the ruling. Similarly, when the WTO found the EU's ban on hormone-treated beef to be invalid, the EU failed to lift its ban and the United States imposed sanctions. "... [T]he non-compliance of the losing party in each instance may seriously undermine the effectiveness of the WTO's dispute resolution process."

On the other hand, from the viewpoint of many members of the public, the WTO wields tremendous powers. For example, reports described the mood at recent protests: "'God is dead. The WTO replaced it,' read one banner, underlining a widespread view that the Geneva-based trade body is invisible but all-powerful."

To call the WTO "all powerful" is an exaggeration, but the WTO does exercise significant powers as it promotes and controls trade, and that trade has led to major environmental problems. Global trade and the environmental effects of that trade are inextricably linked. "[T]he rebuttal to unfettered free trade policies argues that

* Originally published in 13 Duke Environmental Law & Policy Forum 1 (2002). Reprinted with permission.

trade cannot be isolated from the social and environmental milieu in which it occurs." Because our governments have given the WTO significant powers over trade, they must also hold the WTO responsible for the environmental effects of its actions.

The WTO has some powers to protect the environment through Article XX of the GATT and agreements adding to the GATT. Under the Uruguay Round Agreement on the Application of Sanitary and Phytosanitary Measures (SPS) and the Agreement on Technical Barriers to Trade (TBT), it is possible for a WTO member to maintain regulations necessary to protect life and health and protect exhaustible natural resources, but it must overcome numerous hurdles before it may do so.

Beyond the provisions of the GATT, the WTO has taken a few steps to show its concern for the environment. For example, in 1995, it established a Committee on Trade and the Environment (CTE). The CTE serves as a forum for discussion on trade and the environment, however it does not set forth environmental standards. In addition, at the fourth Ministerial, plans were made for a new round of negotiations that set the stage for the discussion of sustainable development and the pursuit of trade and environmental objectives. The agenda will be addressed over three years of negotiations that are scheduled to end by 2005. Negotiators have been directed to focus on environmentally related topics including the following:

- Reduction or elimination of harmful subsidies in fisheries;
- Reduction of export subsidies in agriculture; and
- Improved market access for environmental goods and services.

Additionally, the role of the Committee on Trade and Environment was strengthened. WTO members agreed to enhance cooperation between the WTO and the secretariats of multilateral environmental agreements (MEAs) and to explore relationships between such agreements. However, this is not necessarily a "step forward." The new provision exempts any country not a signatory to an MEA. For example, the United States has not ratified the Kyoto Protocol (global warming). Therefore, it would not be bound by the WTO's recognition of trade provisions in the agreement.

Ultimately, the GATT does not have a mandate to protect the environment. As one author states: "The silence of the WTO and GATT treaty is deafening on the matter of environmental standards." But this void is not necessarily a "defect" in the eyes of corporations, WTO officials, and WTO members (or their leaders, at any rate). As one law professor observes: "The WTO is not a global government with the power to order new environmental or labor laws.... We cannot make the WTO into the organization that will deal with all the problems that elected, national governments struggle with every day."[162]

Nevertheless, the WTO does have de facto power over the environment, as the extensive negative effects of trade on the environment reveal. The fact that the WTO's economic policies have major environmental effects provides a compelling reason

162. James Salzman, Seattle's Legal Legacy and Environmental Reviews of Trade Agreements, 31 Environmental Law 501, 516 (2001).

for the WTO to take responsibility for environmental problems. In the long term, the WTO and the corporations affected by its operations will benefit if they take this responsibility. As one author states: "[T]he economic system will fail if the ecological system is not well managed."[163]

[Furthermore, t]here is precedent for holding a non-governmental organization responsible for the social consequences of its actions. It comes from the public movement to promote Corporate Social Responsibility (CSR). CSR recognizes the power of corporations in the global economy and suggests that corporations should be held accountable for the effects of their activities in non-financial areas, such as environmental protection. Corporations are asked to be more transparent in communicating their business practices and activities and to accept social responsibility for the effects of their activities.

Writings on CSR were published as early as the 1950s and 1960s. The early writings emphasized the collapse of laissez-faire and described a movement toward a system in which businesses would recognize their obligation to do more than merely obey the law while producing goods and services at a profit. It was not without opponents, of course. The most well known was the economist Milton Friedman, who published a book and a widely cited New York Times article in defense of laissez-faire. Nevertheless, by the 1970s and 1980s, with the support of many respected scholars, CSR was becoming an accepted rule of operation for many corporations. Scholars Lee Preston and James Post articulated two key themes to be examined as a business tries to determine its responsibilities to society: (1) the scope of the social duties of the business, and (2) the criteria for assessing a business's involvement with society. A corporation's social duties should be directly or indirectly related to the function of the corporation. Thus, an automobile manufacturer should be responsible for the effects of air pollution and the safety of those who ride in its automobiles.[168] But it should not be held responsible for general societal concerns such as the need for low-income housing. With respect to the criteria for assessment, Preston and Post asserted that the scope of social duties is based on public policy. Public policy includes the "spirit" of the law as well as societal values and commitments that are a part of that "spirit." This concept of public policy and social responsibility means that CSR provides "a guide for managerial behavior more objective than individual moral or ethical insights and more general than the literal texts of statutes and regulations."

Today, many corporations engage in behavior guided by concepts of CSR, especially in the area of environmental law. For example, Interface Americas, Inc., a carpet manufacturer, has recently introduced biodegradable carpet products derived from corn and recycled soda bottles. Patagonia uses recycled soda bottles in its production of an innovative fleece material used to produce outerwear for cold climates. The 3M Corporation is one of the world's most renowned socially responsible corporations. It removed tobacco advertisements from company-owned billboards to show its sup-

163. [Eric A. Davidson, You Can't Eat GNP: Economics as if Ecology Mattered 8 (2000).]

168. [Lee E. Preston & James E. Post, Private Management and Public Policy 9–10 (1975).]

port for health programs. It also pulled Scotchgard, one of its most popular products, from its product line when tests showed that trace amounts of chlorofluorocarbons from the product could be found in the bodies of some employees and customers. Although the chemicals had not been banned by a government regulatory agency, the company pulled the product from the market and searched for a safer, water-based version of the product. Thus, its actions took a cautious approach to a hazard, opting for a proactive rather than a reactive approach to possible harm.

Various organizations promote CSR principles. For example the Coalition for Environmentally Responsible Economies (CERES) asserts that corporations have a responsibility to protect the environment. This responsibility is described in a list of ten principles: Protection of the Biosphere, Sustainable Use of Natural Resources, Reduction and Disposal of Wastes, Energy Conservation, Risk Reduction, Safe Products and Services, Environmental Restoration, Informing the Public, Management Commitment, and Audits and Reports. The CERES principles establish "an environmental ethic with criteria by which investors and others can assess the environmental performance of companies." Adoption of the CERES principles is on a purely voluntary basis and, between 1989 and 1997, only about fifty companies chose to adopt them. There are several reasons why so few companies adopted the principles. Business leaders fear that ambiguous language in the principles might lead to litigation. They also object to the mandatory self-disclosure systems of CERES. Nevertheless, CERES paved the way for other sets of voluntary standards.

For example, the International Organization for Standardization (ISO) is an influential, non-governmental, worldwide federation involved in standardization of industrial practices. In 1996, the ISO issued the ISO 14000 Series Environmental Management Standards. The series has been adopted by thousands of companies around the world. A company can be certified under one of the Series's standards labeled "ISO 14001." To be certified under ISO 14001, a company must:

1. Create an Environmental Management System (EMS);
2. Demonstrate that it is in compliance with the environmental statutes and regulations of countries in which it does business; and
3. Demonstrate its commitment to continuous improvement in environmental protection and pollution prevention.

Implementation of an EMS under ISO 14001 encourages managers and employees to go beyond the dictates of law and consider environmental issues throughout the company's operations. The ISO 14000 Series standards are receiving significant amounts of attention from business managers and their legal and economic advisors, and it is said that the standards may be a "watershed in the annals of environmental regulation." Thousands of companies are certified under ISO 14001, and thousands more are seeking certification. Those companies come from both developed and developing countries. Business managers view the ISO 14000 series as a market-driven approach to environmental protection that provides an alternative to "command and control" regulation by government. Therefore, the standards are of significant interest to business organizations and their legal representatives; environmental groups and their members; and governments, their agencies, and their officials.

By gaining certification pursuant to ISO 14001 and similar voluntary programs, corporations are accepting their responsibility to protect the environment. Similarly, the WTO must accept responsibility for environmental protection. It should do so for several interrelated reasons. First, environmental problems are created when industrialization increases. The WTO's trade rules and policies promote increased industrialization. Second, the WTO exercises a great deal of power as it promotes and regulates trade throughout the world. It should exercise that power in a socially responsible manner. Just as CSR does not purport to require businesses to address all social ills, neither is the WTO being asked to address all social ills. Environmental NGOs and others are asking the WTO to address those social ills directly or indirectly resulting from its own activities. This is what is asked of corporations under CSR principles. Third, the WTO promotes the interests of corporations. Many of those corporations have adopted CSR by choosing to accept social responsibility for environmental problems related to their business operations. Therefore, by accepting responsibility for the environmental harm resulting from its policies, the WTO would be following the lead of environmentally responsible companies such as 3M Corporation, Patagonia, and others. Fourth, the WTO's members are governments. Governments traditionally have accepted responsibility for the social welfare of their citizens. Governments should not be allowed to hide behind the facade of a trade organization to escape from responsibility toward their citizens.

CSR demands that corporations be more transparent in communicating their business practices and activities. It also demands that they accept social responsibility for the effects of their activities. Similarly, the WTO should be more transparent in its activities and accept social responsibility for the effects of its rules and policies. If the WTO accepts that responsibility, it will not be converted into a quasi-world government. Rather, it will be acknowledging that it has a responsibility to protect the public from the harms that result from the major trade-related powers it already exercises.

How the WTO Must Change

Although the WTO is not a democracy, it must use democratic practices in order to be able to respond to various groups of citizens affected by its actions. The WTO must seek, facilitate, and listen to many voices....

To begin, it is important to acknowledge that the WTO's current stance is not anti-environmental. Rather, the WTO simply does not view environmental protection as part of its mission. On its web page, the WTO states, "[I]t's not the WTO's job to set the international rules for environmental protection. That's the task of the environmental agencies and conventions."

If it wishes to function efficiently and avoid massive protests such as those in Seattle and Genoa, the WTO must adopt new policies and implement practices designed to protect the environment. This fact is evidenced by the difficulties other international organizations have faced in their efforts to conduct business in the face of substantial opposition. For example, in the late 1990s, the Organization for Economic Cooperation and Development (OECD) had been working on a multilateral agreement on investment (MAI) for over three years when negotiations were brought to a halt by a storm of protest. Those opposing the MAI included a coalition of 600 organizations including the Sierra Club, Amnesty International, the United Steelworkers of America, the Ontario Public Interest Research Group, and the Third World Network (based in Malaysia). The organizations protested due to their fear that environmental degradation and human rights violations would occur as a result of the treaty. In the end, the treaty was put on hold. Similarly, the WTO's 1999 meeting in Seattle was halted due to protests.

Following protests against the MAI, one commentator said, "The lesson for the economic elites is that the days of negotiating behind closed doors are over and gone; future international institutions must be created with a wider base of participation." Similarly, the WTO must abandon its history of secrecy and lack of transparency and open its operations and decision-making process to the public. But it must also go beyond simply releasing information. The WTO's leaders must seek out information about the potential environmental effects of increased trade, and they must consider a variety of perspectives, including those of developing countries, poor communities, and environmental groups....

NAFTA provides an example of how environmental needs in the late twentieth century were considered during negotiations for an international trade agreement. While NAFTA was under consideration, environmentalists lobbied members of the U.S. Congress heavily and successfully. Before NAFTA could be passed, President Bill Clinton was forced to negotiate an environmental side agreement. When its provisions were finalized in 1993, NAFTA represented a turning point in international law because it explicitly recognized that trade and environmental policy were inextricably linked. The process through which the agreement was approved shows that environmentalists can have a major influence on trade negotiations....

Reform will be difficult because the WTO has not shown a willingness to assume responsibility for environmental protection.... Environmentalists assert that the WTO needs to incorporate democratic processes; the WTO does not believe it needs to do so.

If the WTO is going to protect the environment, it must consider the needs of nations and citizens around the world, not just the interests of industrialized countries or the big businesses that dominate governmental decision-making in those countries. The WTO must implement processes and projects that will enable a wide cross-section of citizens, organizations, and governments to voice their needs and concerns. As it does so, it must also recognize that leaders of developing counties do not necessarily represent the needs of their citizens who suffer when the natural resources of their country are depleted and their environment is polluted. For example, in Qatar at the WTO's fourth Ministerial, leaders of developing countries opposed initiatives supported by U.S.-based labor and environmental NGOs. The NGOs argued that trade sanctions should be imposed on countries that fail to recognize standards for workers' rights and environmental protection. Yet, India and other developing nations objected to demands for environmental provisions....

It may seem patronizing to suggest that NGOs can better represent the needs of citizens in developing countries than do leaders of these countries. Yet, the position simply recognizes economic and political realities. Due to economic pressures, especially from businesses, governments may choose to overlook the environmental and health consequences of their policies. Therefore, it is important for the WTO to hear and consider the contributions of environmentalists and other NGOs.

Moreover, processes modeled after those used by democratic governments require more than just opening the WTO to multiple voices. The WTO needs actively to seek information about environmental problems, and it must listen to the concerns of citizens from a variety of backgrounds. As of 1994, only three people in a GATT staff of more than 200 were assigned to environmental matters. This is a grossly inadequate commitment of resources for an organization that should be listening actively to discussions related to climate change, ozone layer protection, biodiversity, forest management, and other environmental effects caused by trade....

Environmental NGOs work with elected officials, bureaucrats, and employees of corporations; raise money and sponsor various environmental projects; campaign and organize public protests; promote media coverage of environmental issues; litigate and promote the implementation of environmental law; exchange and disseminate information; undertake original research; acquire and manage wildlife habitats; and generate local community involvement in environmental protection. At the international level, environmental NGOs act as information brokers and as whistleblowers; promote democracy by ensuring that the views of their members are heard during treaty deliberations; highlight and challenge failed domestic policies; provide models for government programs; and build international coalitions.

The extensive activities and experience of environmental NGOs should render them eligible to make important contributions to WTO discussions regarding environmental issues. In the absence of a global governmental authority empowered to protect the environment, and in view of the WTO's lack of expertise, the input of environmental NGOs is sorely needed.

In addition..., the WTO should also actively facilitate environmental education for citizens around the world. Education is at the heart of democracy. As Thomas Jefferson said, "[I]f we think [the people are] not enlightened enough to exercise their control with a wholesome discretion, the remedy is not to take it from them, but to inform their discretion." In the United States, this philosophy is reflected in numerous statutes and regulations. For example, the need for information and education is at the heart of laws like the Community Right to Know Act, the Worker Right to Know Act, and the Right to Act. The WTO can help people gain access to important environmental information by promoting eco-labeling programs and laws, such as the EU law that requires labeling of products that contain genetically modified soybeans or corn. The WTO took an initial step through its CTE report, which concluded that eco-labels "can be effective instruments of environmental policy to encourage the development of an environmentally-conscious consumer public." However, the WTO must do more than simply announce that eco-labeling can be an effective instrument. It needs actively to promote labeling programs and help educate people so they can understand the information conveyed on such labels. "People are empowered by information, and provided that at least some semblance of democratic institutions exist[s], informed people will demand responsiveness from their government." With information, citizens will be in a better position to provide informed recommendations to their own governments and to the WTO.

One of the most basic steps the WTO must take, should it choose to combat environmental degradation stemming from global trade, is to fund a staff that would deal exclusively with these issues. In addition, the WTO should provide direct funding for specific projects. These programs should include educational curriculums, environmental impact studies with respect to WTO policies and rules, and research into environmentally sustainable business.

WTO members might free up money to contribute to such programming by ending their subsidies in agriculture and fishing which assist individual industries but lead to environmental harms. Another possible funding source is the "Tobin" tax. This tax would be imposed on foreign currency transactions. Funds raised from this tax would be used to provide funds for sustainable development projects in poor countries. Simultaneously, it would reduce the volume of short-term cross-border financial flows that can be destabilizing for poor countries. Support for the Tobin tax, which was first proposed about thirty years ago, is growing around the world. Attac, a group that supports the tax, has over 30,000 paid members across Europe. French Prime Minister Lionel Jospin supported it during his 2001–2002 campaign for the French presidency, and Germany's chancellor, Gerhard Schroder, has indicated an interest in the tax.

In addition..., the WTO must develop new policies recognizing the legitimacy and importance of environmental protection. It must also create new rules implementing those policies. The WTO must use these rules in ways that prevent downward harmonization of environmental laws and a "race to the bottom" in enforcement of those laws. Several examples of potential WTO actions are outlined in the following discussion.

At the outset, the WTO should recognize the value of the "precautionary principle" and adopt new rules allowing it to be implemented by WTO members in situations involving scientific uncertainty and environmental protection. For example, the precautionary principle is used by the European Union in response to genetic modification; EU nations can exclude genetically modified organisms (GMOs) from their markets, citing the precautionary principle. By contrast, in cases involving growth hormones and GMOs, WTO rules have forced countries to prove that hormones or GMOs are harmful to human beings before the country may restrict the import of products containing them. The EU continues to defend its stance on GMOs in spite of WTO rulings against it. At the fourth Ministerial of the WTO, the EU argued that

WTO rules should be altered to allow countries to restrict entry of GMOs without breaking WTO trade rules.

To understand the potential impact of adopting the EU's proposal, further explanation and examination of the precautionary principle is needed. The principle is not a straightforward concept or tool that can be adopted and implemented through a simple declaration or the adoption of a single rule. Rather, the precautionary principle is one intended to guide decision makers in a variety of contexts by encouraging, or perhaps even obligating them "to consider the likely harmful effects of their activities on the environment before they pursue those activities."

... [T]he EU [followed the precautionary principle] in its regulation of GMOs. However, as Professor John Applegate ... explains, the United States has not followed the EU in applying the precautionary principle to the regulation of GMOs. The United States "regards genetic technology as having enormous potential benefits and relatively minor, or at most manageable, risks." Accordingly, it takes a product-specific approach to regulating GMOs, considering guidelines for each product individually. Thus, the United States places the burden of proof on a party that wishes to ban GMOs. The EU, on the other hand, focuses on the dangers of GMO technology from a more general perspective. "It is the process, not the final product that matters."[246] "This view counsels regulation that forbids GMOs or at least applies strict screening tests and other controls to all GM products."[247]

The United States has traditionally required that a party using dangerous substances or conducting hazardous activities pay for any harms caused by those activities or their products. The approach is reactive rather than proactive. With few exceptions, United States policy places the burden of proving the existence of an environmental risk and the magnitude of the risk on the party proposing regulation.

The WTO currently takes a similar approach. In general, the GATT is interpreted to require WTO members to regulate individual products instead of concentrating on the processes used to produce the products. In cases involving new technology, significant questions about potential harm are often raised, but these questions are not addressed if evidence is insufficient to evaluate the risk of harm. In such cases, the WTO should allow members to rely on the precautionary principle when imposing temporary bans on technologies or products. If the WTO employed the precautionary principle, the burden of proof would be shifted to manufacturers and they, rather than the EU, would have to demonstrate the product's safety. The EU should not have to prove the risks attendant to use of GMOs with "scientific certainty" when such information is much more accessible to the manufacturers of GMOs. In view of the complex studies that will be needed to gain greater knowledge and certainty regarding the harms that could result from GMOs, the WTO should allow members to proceed cautiously.

---

246. [John S. Applegate, The Prometheus Principle: Using the Precautionary Principle to Harmonize the Regulation of Genetically Modified Organisms, 9 Indiana Journal of Global Legal Studies 207, 230 2001).]

247. Id. at 208.

This proposal for an interim shift in the burden of proof, of course, requires a fundamental change in the way the WTO and individual countries approach new technologies and the related scientific uncertainty. The United States and the WTO deal with new innovations using a traditional risk analysis process: that which cannot be quantified is not included in the analysis. The traditional risk assessment model attempts to calculate the mathematical likelihood that new technology will harm the public. Therefore, even if it appears that a new technology may present significant risks to the public's health or safety, it can be approved for the market because the party wishing to ban it has not had time to gather the data necessary to demonstrate its harmful effects. At the present, we insist on proof of harm before we act. "The problem very often is that long before the science does come in, the harm has come in, the harm has already been done."

By contrast, under the precautionary principle, a shift in the burden of proof would allow precautionary action to be taken to prevent harm to the environment and public health before it occurs. This approach does not mean that the EU and other countries should be allowed to ban GMOs (or other potentially harmful substances) indefinitely, without further examination. However, the EU should not be required to accept imports of GM food and wait for decades to see if it causes cancer, immune system deficiencies, or other serious health effects. In return for the right to exercise precaution, the EU should be required to conduct continuing studies in a good faith effort to determine any potential harms and the causal links between consumption of GM food and alleged effects. Results of continuing studies by the EU (and by its opponents such as the United States) should be reviewed at several year intervals to evaluate the current state of knowledge about technology's risks. At some point, sufficient information may be gathered to justify a permanent ban on GMOs. Alternatively, new information may be sufficient to determine what degree of safety would need to be established to lift a ban instated under the precautionary principle.

In addition to allowing for use of the precautionary principle, WTO rules should be amended to permit process-related measures designed in good faith to protect the environment.... The WTO currently bars member states from "considering social, environmental, and justice issues when deciding what and from whom to buy." This mandate is a direct prohibition on process-related measures and should be changed. In disputes [involving tuna fishing and dolphins], the WTO has exercised its power to promote trade in ways that thwarted members' attempts to protect the environment. Instead, WTO dispute resolution panels should find ways to uphold members' laws designed to protect the environment. Ultimately, this approach will benefit businesses, too. "Although environmental protection measures could, in the short run, inhibit trade to some extent, conservation of the environment may be the best way to ensure the continued existence of the resources upon which trade depends."

The fact that [Environmental Trade Measures (ETMs)] by individual countries can be an effective means for protecting endangered species is illustrated in events related to the Tuna/Dolphin dispute. Both before and after the WTO issued rulings in the case, the United States and other countries took significant steps to protect dolphins. With the help of the United States, the Inter-American Tropical Tuna Commission (IATTC) developed a dolphin protection program. It included research on dolphin release methods and workshops to disseminate the information. It required an international observer on every tuna-fishing vessel and established an international review panel of government, industry, and environmental representatives. The program was highly successful; every country and every vessel in the region participated, realizing 100% compliance, while fishers' catch and profits remained high. As a result of the program, dolphin mortality fell dramatically from 1986 to 1994.

During this period, U.S. canneries and distributors imposed their own "embargo" that remains in effect as of 2002. The canneries and distributors require that absolutely no "dolphin-encirclement" with nets occur in order to earn a "dolphin-safe" label on the tuna produced; the requirement holds even if dolphins were encircled but released unharmed. U.S. consumers are very aware of the "dolphin-safe" label and it appears on virtually all packaged tuna. The sad irony is that the alternative methods to dolphin-encirclement kill young tuna and other species, including endangered sea turtles.

Meanwhile, through the IATTC program, methods were developed to use the purse-seine nets and release dolphins, thus reducing dolphin deaths below limits permitted by the U.S. Marine Mammal Protection Act. In other words, when skippers are educated about release practices and proper gear is used, the purse-seine nets can be used in ways that protect dolphins within limits required by the U.S. law. The outcome in this example leads to a clear conclusion: ETMs can be both necessary and effective. The GATT needs to be interpreted (or amended) to ensure the use of ETMs in efforts to protect endangered species and the environment.

As a further measure to promote environmental protection through its policies, the WTO should support the fair trade movement. This movement encourages companies to import and sell products that are produced in ways that protect workers' rights and the environment. The movement is a global effort that seeks "to help small producer groups and farmers in the developing world to fight exploitation and to trade on more advantageous terms." Fair trade organizations help farmers and other producers to sell their products directly to retailers, thus bypassing the "middlemen" and returning more profits to the producers. The most commonly cited criteria for fair trade are derived from the Fair Trade Federation (FTF). Among other conditions, membership in the FTF requires the use of environmentally sustainable practices and the provision of safe and healthy workplace conditions. Additionally, farmers who adhere to environmentally friendly practices are often paid a premium by their customers for their efforts.

Unfortunately, WTO rules state that "goods [are not] subject to statutory labeling requirements or differentiated on the basis of how they are produced." This policy conflicts directly with the goals and mechanisms of the fair trade movement. Moreover, the WTO has recently considered adopting trade regulations that would find fair trade initiatives violative of its non-discrimination rules. To the contrary, the WTO should adopt rules specifying that such initiatives are exempt from WTO non-discrimination rules.

In additional efforts to promote environmental protection, the WTO must discourage subsidies that lead to environmental degradation. For example, the United States and other nations have suggested that fishing subsidies be eliminated. Such subsidies add up to as much as $14–20 billion annually and have led to an overcapacity in the world's fishing fleet and depleted resources in the world's fisheries. "The subsidies are one reason that all of the key ocean fisheries are now below sustainable levels. Some of their most valuable species, such as cod and haddock in the North Atlantic, have been driven to near commercial extinction—that is to such scarcity that industries based on them have either collapsed or turned to other species." Ranching and coal mining are additional examples of subsidized industries that harm the environment.

Subsidies for agriculture must also be examined. Some of the divisive issues brought before the Third and Fourth Ministerials of the WTO were related to agricultural protection. Since 1948, GATT (now administered by the WTO) has cut industrial tariffs to an average of less than 5 percent, but agricultural tariffs were still averaging 50% as of late 2001. According to a Toronto-based environmental organization, in Canada "the federal and provincial governments contributed $3.55 in subsidies for every $1 earned by Canadian farmers." Europeans are the strongest opponents of lowered tariffs, particularly the French, who fear their small farms will suffer from competition brought by U.S. agribusinesses. Other countries providing substantial support for agriculture include Japan, Korea, Switzerland, Norway, and some developing countries.

Farmers are both producers of food and stewards of the land, the front-line protectors of our ecology. But government policies and subsidy incentives that reward intensive production encourage farmers to use processes that destroy land, deplete water resources and ultimately threaten rural communities. Ironically, then, farm subsidies have been dismantling the very systems they were designed to preserve. One rationale often cited in favor of subsidies is that they will protect small farmers. However, that is not true in many cases. "In the United States, a third of government agriculture payments go to the wealthiest five percent of farms...."

The amount of money involved in subsidies is overwhelming. A 1998 study from Oxford University calculated that annual worldwide government subsidies reached a total of over $2 trillion (U.S.) including, for example, $390 to $520 billion for agriculture, $110 billion for fossil fuels and nuclear energy, and $220 billion for water. During the upcoming round of talks scheduled as a result of the fourth Ministerial, the WTO must consider the effects of subsidies as it reviews the Agreement on Agriculture adopted as a part of the 1994 version of the GATT.

Finally, in working to promote environmental protection the WTO must exercise caution before adopting rules that only facially appear to be environmentally friendly. For example, at the fourth Ministerial, the WTO adopted Article 31(iii) calling for "the reduction, or as appropriate, elimination of tariff and non-tariff barriers to environmental goods and services." Environmentalists argue that this proposal poses a threat to the world's freshwater resources if water is considered a "service" or a "good." Water is not currently listed under the General Agreement on Trade in Services (GATS) as an environmental service. However, the United States, Canada, and other countries have pushed for its inclusion. This is, of course, a serious concern to environmentalists. Moreover, it appears that under the GATT water is a "good." Therefore, the new language would make it illegal to restrict the export of bulk water for commercial purposes. This outcome frustrates environmentalists and human rights activists who argue that water should not be "privatized" and sold to transnational water companies that, in turn, profit from the sale of water and wastewater treatment. In other words, the WTO provisions could actually prevent a country from protecting its water as a public service and human right because such protection could be held by the WTO to be a "non-tariff" trade barrier in violation of the GATT. Fears that water may be sold to multinationals who can afford it, to the detriment of the poor in developing countries, are based on experience. For example, the World Development Movement states, "[W]ater privatization in Puerto Rico has meant that poor communities have gone without water while US military bases and tourist resorts enjoy an unlimited supply." An important cautionary tool to guard against such results is the incorporation of information and perspectives contributed by many parties.

In summary, the WTO must enlarge its vision to include environmental protection within its mission.... This article has examined several options, but many others can and should be considered.

Discussion Questions

1. What role do soft law instruments play in the socially responsible behavior of corporations? Do these instruments rely on transparency, public accountability, and/or self-regulation to be effective?

2. Social responsibility can take not only an economic, but social, environmental, and ethical dimensions as well. How do soft law instruments incorporate these principles into their guidelines? Can you think of any type of activity that is not covered?

3. What U.S. (or other domestic) laws could be used to sue TNCs for their infringement of human rights to health, education, housing, and a clean and healthy environment (and protection from cultural denigration)? Given the general unavailability of the U.S. Alien Tort Claims Act, can domestic legislation or corporate codes of conduct help in this area?

4. What are the international human rights duties of TNCs imposed by customary international law, treaty, obligations, or other guidelines or compacts? How effective are these instruments?

5. What can we learn from the demise of the UN Norms so that the next effort to make multinational enterprises more socially responsible does not suffer the same fate? Should any next effort attempt to impose obligations on TNCs directly, as the Norms sought to do, or should reformers concentrate their focus on soft law instruments?

6. How does the WTO contribute to the triple bottom line and the principles of sustainable development? What does Stenzel suggest needs to be done to promote these principles?

7. Do the readings in this chapter give you hope for the future of TNCs' social responsibilities? Are there other ways, outside of international law, to constrain TNCs' undesirable international behavior?

8. Find a country that seems to have a successful national policy for sustainability. How do its policies compare to those of the United States?

Chapter 13

Sustainability, Bankruptcy, a Commercial Law

Sustainability becomes an issue when businesses go bankrupt and pass the costs of environmental cleanup on to the company's creditors and the public. In this chapter we start with the mining industry, where bankruptcy has been a common business practice. Next we explore the general principles of bankruptcy and apply those principles to a hypothetical bankruptcy of British Petroleum. We then consider a proposal to create a new class of priority claims under commercial law for loans to improve environmental practices. When reading this chapter, consider how to ensure that environmental costs are borne by the appropriate parties and whether commercial, bankruptcy, or other laws should be changed to accomplish this result.

Jared Diamond, *Collapse: How Societies Choose to Fail or Succeed* *Big Businesses and the Environment: Hardrock Mining Operations**

... Let's now turn to the hardrock mining industry. (That term refers to mines that excavate ores from which to extract metals, as opposed to mines that excavate coal.) The industry is currently the leading toxic polluter in the U.S., responsible for nearly half of reported industrial pollution. Of western U.S. rivers, nearly half have sections of their headwaters polluted by mining. In most of the U.S. the hardrock mining industry is now declining towards extinction, largely because of its own misdeeds. Environmental groups have for the most part not taken the trouble to learn essential facts about the hardrock mining industry, and declined to participate in an initially promising international initiative that the industry commenced in 1998 to change its behavior.

These and other features of the hardrock mining industry's current status are initially puzzling, because the industry seems superficially so like the oil and gas industry ... and also like the coal industry. Don't all three industries involve extracting non-renewable resources for the ground? Yes, they do, but they have nevertheless unfolded differently, for three reasons: different economics and technology, different attitudes within the industry itself, and different attitudes of the public and government towards the industry.

---

* Excerpted from Jared Diamond, Collapse: How Societies Choose to Fail or Succeed 452–463 (2005), copyright © 2005 by Jared Diamond. Used with permission of Viking Books, an imprint of Penguin Publishing Group, a division of Penguin Random House LLC.

ne environmental problems caused by hardrock mining are of several types. One ıvolves disturbance of land surface by digging it up. This problem especially affects surface mines and open-pit mines, where the ore lies near the surface and is reached by scraping away the earth over it. In contrast, no one now extracts oil by digging the surface off of an entire oil formation; instead, oil companies typically disturb only a small surface area sufficient to drill a well to tap down into the oil formation. Similarly, there are some mines at which the ore body does not lie near the surface but deep underground, and at which tunnels and waste piles disturbing only a small surface area are dug down to the ore body.

Further environmental problems caused by hardrock mining involve water pollution by metals themselves, processing chemicals, acid drainage, and sediment. Metals and metal-like elements in the ore itself—especially copper, cadmium, lead, mercury, zinc, arsenic, antimony, and selenium—are toxic and prone to cause trouble by ending up in nearby streams and water tables as a result of mining operations. A notorious example was a wave of cases of bone disease caused by cadmium discharged into Japan's Jinzu River from a lead and zinc mine. Quite a few of the chemicals used in mining—such as cyanide, mercury, sulfuric acid, and nitrate produced from dynamite—are also toxic. More recently, it has become appreciated that acid draining out of sulfide-containing ores exposed to water and air through mining causes serious water pollution and leaches out metals. Sediment transported out of mines in runoff water may be harmful to aquatic life, for instance by covering up fish spawning beds. In addition to those types of pollution, the mere consumption of water by many mines is high enough to be significant.

The remaining environmental problem concerns where to dump all the dirt and wastes dug up in the course of mining, consisting of four components: the "overburden" (dirt scraped away to get down to the ore); waste rock found to contain too little mineral to be of economic value; tailings, the ground-up residue of ore after its minerals have been extracted; and the residues of heap-leach pads after mineral extraction. The latter two types of residue are generally left in the tailing impoundment or pad respectively, while the overburden and waste rock are left in dumps. Depending on the laws in the particular country where the mine is located, the methods of disposing of tailings (a slurry of water and solids) involves either dumping them into a river or ocean, piling them up on land, or (most often) piling them up behind a dam. Unfortunately, tailings dams fail in a surprisingly high percentage of cases: they are often designed with insufficient strength (to save money), they are often constructed cheaply from wastes themselves instead of from concrete, and they are built over extended periods so that their condition must be monitored constantly and can't be subjected to a final inspection declaring them completed and safe. On the average around the world each year, there is one big accident involving a tailings dam. The largest such accident in the U.S. was West Virginia's Buffalo Creek disaster of 1972, which killed 125 people.

Several of these environmental problems are illustrated by the status of the four most valuable mines on New Guinea and neighboring islands, where I do my fieldwork. The copper mine at Panguna on Papua New Guinea's Bougainville Island was formerly the country's largest enterprise and biggest earner of foreign exchange, and one of the largest copper mines in the world. It dumped its tailings directly into a tributary of the Jaba River, thereby creating monumental environmental impacts. When the government failed to resolve that situation and associated political and social problems, Bougainville's inhabitants revolted, triggering a civil war that cost thousands of lives and nearly tore apart the nation of Papua New Guinea. Fifteen years after the war's outbreak, peace has still not been fully restored on Bougainville. The Panguna mine was of course closed down, has no prospect of reopening, and the owners and lenders (including the Bank of America, U.S. Export-Import Bank, and Australian and Japanese subscribers and lenders) lost their investment. That history provided a reason why Chevron worked so closely with local landowners at the Kutubu oil fields to gain their acceptance.

The gold mine on Lihir Island dumps its tailings into the ocean via a deep pipe (a method viewed by environmentalists as highly damaging), and the owners claim that this is not harmful. Whatever the effects of that one mine on marine life around Lihir Island, the world would have a major problem if many other mines similarly dumped their tailings into the ocean. The Ok Tedi copper mine on the mainland of New Guinea did construct a tailings dam, but experts who reviewed its design before construction warned that the dam would fail soon. It did fail within a few months, so that 200,000 tons of mine tailings and wastes are now discharged each day into the Ok Tedi River and have destroyed its fishery. From the Ok Tedi the water flows directly into New Guinea's largest river with its most valuable fishery, the Fly River, where suspended sediment concentrations have now increased five-fold, resulting in flooding, deposition of mine wastes on the river's floodplain, and killing of floodplain vegetation over an area of 200 square miles so far. In addition, a barge carrying barrels of cyanide for the mine up the Fly River sank, and the barrels have gradually been corroding and releasing their cyanide into the river. In 2001 BHP, the world's fourth largest mining company, which operated the Ok Tedi mine, sought to close it, explaining, "Ok Tedi is not compatible with our environmental values, and the company should never have been involved." However, because the mine accounts for 20% of Papua New Guinea's total exports, the government arranged for the mine to be kept open while permitting BHP to withdraw. Finally, the Grasberg-Ertsberg copper and gold mine of Indonesian New Guinea, a huge open-pit operation that is Indonesia's most valuable mine, dumps its tailings directly in the Mimika River, whence they reach the shallow Arafura Sea between New Guinea and Australia. Along with the Ok Tedi mine and another gold mine in New Guinea, the Grasberg-Ertsberg mine in one of only three large mines in the world that is currently being operated by an international company and that disposes of its wastes into a river.

The prevalent policy of mining companies towards environmental damage is to clean up and restore the mined area only after the mine has shut down, rather than follow the coal mining industry's practice of reclaiming the area as mining proceeds; the hardrock mining industry opposes that strategy. Companies assume that what is called "walkaway" restoration will be adequate: i.e., that cleanup and restoration will incur minimal costs, will go on for only 2 to 12 years after mine closure (whereupon the company can walk away from the site with no further obligations), and will involve nothing more than resloping of disturbed areas to prevent erosion, applying a growth medium like salvaged topsoil to stimulate revegetation, and treating water flowing out of the mine site for a few years. In reality, this inexpensive walkaway strategy has never sufficed for any major modern mine and regularly leaves water quality standards violated. It is instead necessary to cover and revegetate all areas that could be sources of acid drainage, and to capture and treat polluted groundwater and surface water flowing out of the site for as long as the water remains polluted, which often means forever. The actual direct and indirect costs of cleanup and restoration have typically proved to be 1.5 to 2 times mining industry walkaway estimates for mines without acid drainage, and 10 times those estimates for mines with acid drainage. The biggest uncertainty in those costs is whether the mine will produce acid drainage, a problem recognized only recently at copper mines though appreciated earlier at other mines, and almost never predicted accurately in advance.

Hardrock mining companies facing cleanup costs frequently avoid those costs by declaring bankruptcy and transferring their assets to other corporations controlled by the same individuals. One such example is Montana's Zortman-Landusky gold mine … developed by Pegasus Gold Inc., a Canadian company. When opened in 1979, it was the first large-scale open-pit cyanide heap-leach gold mine in the U.S., and the largest gold mine in Montana. The mine proceeded to cause a long series of cyanide leaks, spills, and acid drainage, abetted by the fact that neither the federal government nor the Montana state government required the company to test for acid drainage. By 1992, state inspectors had established that the mine was contaminating streams with heavy metals and acid. In 1995 Pegasus Gold agreed to pay \$36 million to settle all law suits by the federal government, state of Montana, and local Indian tribes. Finally, in 1998, at a time when less than 15% of the mine site had undergone any surface reclamation, Pegasus Gold's board of directors voted themselves more than \$5 million in bonuses, transferred Pegasus's remaining profitable assets to the new company of Apollo Gold that they created, and thereupon declared Pegasus Gold bankrupt. (Like most mine directors, those of Pegasus Gold did not live downstream watershed of the Zortman-Landusky mine, and they thus exemplified elites insulated from the consequences of their actions.…) The state and federal governments then adopted a plan of surface reclamation to cost \$52 million, of which \$30 million would come from the \$36 million payment by Pegasus while \$22 million would be paid by U.S. taxpayers. However, that surface reclamation plan still does not include the expense of water treatment in perpetuity, which will cost taxpayers much more. It turns out that five out of the 13 recent major hardrock mines in Montana, four of them (including the Zortman-Landusky mine) open-pit heap-leach cyanide mines will require water treatment forever, thereby increasing their closure and reclamation costs by up to 100 times previous estimates.

A bankruptcy more expensive to taxpayers was that of another Canadian-owned heap-leach gold mine in the U.S. Galactic Resources' Summittville Mine in a mountainous area of Colorado receiving over 32 feet of snow annually. In 1992, eight years after the state of Colorado has issued an operating permit to Galactic Resources, the company declared bankruptcy and closed the mine on less than a week's notice, leaving a large local tax bill unpaid, laying off its employees, stopping essential environmental maintenance, and abandoning the site. A few months later, after the start of the winter snowfalls, the heap-leach system overflowed, sterilizing an 18-mile of stretch of the Alamosa River with cyanide. It was then discovered that the state of Colorado had required a financial guarantee of only $4,500,000 from Galactic Resources as a condition for issuing the operating permit, but that the cleanup would cost $180,000,000. After the government had extracted another $28,000,000 as part of the bankruptcy settlement, taxpayers were left to pay $147,500,000 through the Environmental Protection Agency.

As a result of such experience, American states and the federal government eventually began to require hardrock mining companies to guarantee in advance some form of financial assurance that enough money would be available for cleanup and restoration, in case the mining company itself refused or proved financially unable to pay for the cleanup. Unfortunately, those assurance costs are typically based on a cleanup cost estimate made by the mining company itself, because government regulatory bodies lack the time, knowledge, and detailed mine engineering plans necessary to make such an estimate for themselves. In the many cases where mining companies have not cleaned up and the government has been forced to fall back on that assurance, the actual cleanup costs have proved to be up to 100 times the mining company estimate. That's not surprising, because the estimate was provided by the company, which regularly underestimates because it has no financial incentive or government regulatory pressure to estimate the amount fully. The assurance is provided in one of three forms: cash equivalents or a letter of credit, the safest form; a bond that the mining company obtains from an insurance company in return for an annual premium; and a "self-guarantee," meaning that the mining company pledges in good faith that it will clean up and that its assets stand behind its pledge. However, frequent breaking of such pledges has shown self-guarantees to be meaningless, and they are now no longer accepted for mines on federal land, but they still account for most assurance in Arizona and Nevada, the American states most friendly to the mining industry.*

U.S. taxpayers currently face a liability of up to $12 billion to clean up and restore hardrock mines. Why is our liability too large, when governments have supposedly been requiring financial assurance of cleanup costs? Parts of the difficulty are the just-mentioned ones of assurance costs being underestimated by the mining companies, and the two states with the biggest taxpayer liabilities (Arizona and Nevada) accepting company self-guarantees and not requiring insurance bonds. Even where an

* [Self-bonding remains common in the coal industry. See Interstate Mining Compact Commission, Self-Bonding Survey (2014), available at http://imcc.isa.us/Self%20Bonding%20Survey.pdf.—Eds.]

underfunded but real insurance company bond exists, taxpayers face further costs for reasons that will be familiar to any of us who have tried to collect from our insurance company for a large loss in a home fire.... Of the mines posing the 10 biggest taxpayer liabilities in the U.S. (adding up to about half of the total of up to $12 billion), two are owned by a mining company on the verge of bankruptcy (ASARCO, accounting for about $1 billion), six others are owned by companies that have proved especially recalcitrant at meeting their obligations, only two are owned by less recalcitrant companies, and all 10 may be acid-generating and may require water treatment for a long time or forever.

Not surprisingly, as a result of taxpayers' being left to foot bills, there has been a backlash of anti-mining public sentiment in Montana and some other states. The future of hardrock mining in the U.S. is bleak, except for gold mines in underregulated Nevada and platinum/palladium mines in Montana.... Only one-quarter as many American college undergraduates (a mere 578 students in the whole U.S.) are preparing for careers in mining as in 1938, despite the explosive growth of the total college population in the intervening years. Since 1995, public opposition in the U.S. has been increasingly successful in blocking mine proposals, and the mining industry can no longer count on lobbyists and friendly legislators to do its bidding. The hardrock mining industry is the prime example of a business whose short-term favoring of its own interests over those of the public proved in the long-term self-defeating and have been driving the industry into extinction.

This sad outcome is initially surprising. Like the oil industry, the hardrock mining industry too stands to benefit from clean environmental policies, through lower labor costs (less turnover and absenteeism) resulting from higher job satisfaction, lower health costs, cheaper bank loans and insurance policies, and the relative cheapness of installing state-of-the-art clean technology at a project's outset as compared to having to retrofit old technology as environmental standards become more stringent. How could the hardrock mining industry have adopted such self-defeating behavior, especially when the oil industry and the coal mining industry facing apparently similar problems have not driven themselves towards extinction? The answer has to do with the three sets of factors ...: economics, mining industry attitudes, and society's attitudes....

[Economics] Economic factors that make environmental cleanup costs less bearable to the hardrock mining industry than to the oil industry (or even the coal industry) include lower profit margins, more unpredictable profits, higher cleanup costs, more insidious and long-lasting pollution problems, less ability to pass on those costs to consumers, less capital with which to absorb those costs, and a different labor force....

[Corporate Culture] Those economic disincentives are exacerbated by the attitudes and corporate culture that have become traditional within the hardrock mining industry. In the history of the U.S., and analogously also in South Africa and Australia, the government promoted mining as a tool to encourage settlement of the West. Hence the mining industry evolved in the U.S. with an inflated sense of entitlement, a belief that it is above the rules, and view of itself as the West's salvation—thereby illustrating the problem of values that have outlived their usefulness, as discussed in the preceding chapter....

[Society] The third factor underlying mining industry environmental practices, besides economics and corporate attitudes, is the attitudes of our government and society, which permit the industry to continue with its own attitudes. The basic federal law governing mining in the U.S. is still the General Mining Act passed in 1872. It provides massive subsidies to mining companies, such as a billion dollars per year of royalty-free minerals from publicly owned lands, unlimited use of public lands for dumping mine wastes in some cases, and other subsidies costing taxpayers a quarter of a billion dollars per year. The detailed rules adopted by the federal government in 1980, termed the "3809 rules," did not require mining companies to provide financial assurance of cleanup costs, and did not adequately define reclamation and closure. In the year 2000 the outgoing Clinton administration proposed mining regulations that achieved both of those goals while also eliminating corporate self-guarantees of financial assurance. But in October 2001 a proposal by the incoming Bush administration eliminated almost all of those proposals except for continuing to require financial assurance, a requirement that would in any case be meaningless without a definition of the reclamation and cleanup costs to be covered by financial assurance.

It is rare that our society has effectively held the mining industry responsible for damages. Laws, regulatory policies, and the political will to chase mining scofflaws have been absent. For a long time the Montana state government was notorious for its deference to mining lobbyists, and the Arizona and Nevada state governments still are. For example, the state of New Mexico estimated reclamation costs for the Chino copper mine of Phelps-Dodge Corporation at $780 million, but then decreased that estimate to $391 million under political pressure from Phelps-Dodge. When our American public and governments demand so little of the mining industry, why should we be surprised that the industry itself volunteers little?

Jackie Gardina, *What if BP Were to File for Bankruptcy?**

Corporate polluters have walked away from billions of dollars in clean-up costs and BP is in a position to do the same. Environmental catastrophes come with enormous price tags and often take decades to resolve. In theory, the responsible parties, like BP and the other corporations involved in the Gulf oil spill, are responsible for paying for all environmental costs. But when corporate polluters file for bankruptcy all bets are off—they can abandon contaminated properties, ignore clean-up obligations, leave innocent victims of corporate negligence or malfeasance with no real

* Unpublished manuscript, on file with editors. Reprinted with permission.

remedy and result in taxpayer money being used to repair the damage. It's all perfectly legal and that needs to change.

The problem is very real and stakes are high for the American taxpayer. A bankruptcy judge recently ordered Lyondell Chemical Co. to pay $103 million to clean up an 80-mile stretch of the Kalamazoo River that it admittedly polluted with PCBs, a cancer-causing agent, even though the government had estimated the costs at $1 billion. The judge overseeing Marcal Paper Mills Inc.'s reorganization rejected the government's $946 million claim and approved a settlement under which the debtor was required to pay just $1.5 million to clean up a Superfund site outside Newark, New Jersey. And the true costs of the GM and Chrysler bailout will not be known until we calculate the amount of the environmental clean-up costs discharged in the underlying bankruptcies and left to be borne by the public.

Bankruptcy not only allows corporations to reduce their clean-up costs, it can also eliminate all present and future liabilities related to the environmental catastrophe. What if, like the herring in Prince William Sound, the fisheries never come back, and BP declares bankruptcy? How much could the fishing industry expect to recover under existing law? Not much. Any private entity or individual affected by the damage—from economic injury to wrongful death claims—must file in the bankruptcy court and frequently receive damages that are severely discounted, often just pennies on the dollar. A vast majority of the Gulf region's fishing and tourism industries have essentially ground to a halt, the long term effect of the chemical dispersants are unknown, and the public health effects of the oil spill are still being debated. Yet if BP were to file for bankruptcy, those most directly affected by the oil spill will likely be forced to accept settlements far lower than their proven damages.

The government has fallen woefully short in ensuring that corporate polluters are held accountable. A 2005 GAO report found that the EPA had failed to use existing authority to ensure that bankrupt businesses met their cleanup obligations, putting the U.S. taxpayer at significant risk. According to the report, the EPA had not required financial assurances, had not obtained tax refund offsets, and had failed to secure liens to ensure payment. But the existing authorities are not a cure-all in the wake of corporate bankruptcies. Yet Congress has done little to address the problem. While several bills have been introduced into Congress to demand polluter financial accountability, only Senator Cantwell's bill, Cleanup Assurance and Polluter Accountability Act (CAPA), even addressed the bankruptcy issue. Unfortunately, it failed to garner support and died in committee.

The Bankruptcy Code creates a gaping loophole through the polluter pay principle that is the foundation of our environmental laws. The government can shrink that gap by using the tools currently available to ensure polluter accountability and Congress needs to act by giving certain environmental clean-up costs priority in the bankruptcy system and to make it more difficult for corporate polluters to discharge their environmental obligations. Under current law, the corporations involved in the Gulf oil spill could simply file for bankruptcy and shed many of their long-term commitments to ensure the Gulf coast and its residents are made whole.

Environmental Obligations in Bankruptcy: An Overview of Conflicting Policies

"During the 1930s, it was said that Germany's situation was serious but not hopeless. Of Austria, it was said the situation was hopeless but not serious. The present treatment of environmental obligations in bankruptcy is serious *and* hopeless."[1] The goals of bankruptcy are in direct conflict with the goals of environmental law. The purpose of environmental remedial statutes, such as the Oil Pollution Act (OPA) and the Comprehensive Environmental Response, Compensation, and Liability Act (CERCLA) is to promote clean-up by those most responsible for the contamination—the oft-cited "polluter pays" principle. Once the responsible party or parties are identified, liability is strict, joint and several.[2] In contrast, Congress' primary goal in enacting the Bankruptcy Code was a debtor's fresh start. With few exceptions, bankruptcy law discharges debts to bolster a debtor's fresh start or successful reorganization. Liability evaporates for pennies on the dollar. It is not possible to make debtors pay for cleanup *and* give debtors a fresh start.

Courts continue to produce a mishmash of case law. Some opinions reflect the gravitational pull of bankruptcy. Others orbit around the sun protecting the environment and enforcement of environmental laws. All courts bolster their conclusions by referring the two Supreme Court pronouncements in the area, *Ohio v. Kovacs*[3] and *Midlantic National Bank v. New Jersey Department of Environmental Protection*.[4] Courts revisit and reexamine these opinions much like "the ancient priests studying the entrails of goats." *Kovacs* and *Midlantic* have meant different things to different courts. It is not a pretty picture.

The interface of environmental cleanup laws and federal bankruptcy statutes is never tidy; jurisprudentially it is somewhat grubby.... [CERCLA] seek[s] to protect public health and the environment by facilitating cleanup of environmental contamination and imposing costs on the parties responsible for the pollution. [Bankruptcy law was] designed to give debtors a fresh start by discharging as many debts as possible. The tension between these fundamental aspects of our nation's policy is profound.

1. Ingrid Michelson Hillinger & Michael G. Hillinger, Environmental Affairs in Bankruptcy, 2004 ABI Law Review, 332, 333 (2004).

2. It is important to recognize that environmental laws exist at every level in the United States: federal, state, and local. The type of obligation imposed upon the debtor varies significantly from one environmental statute to another and even from section to section within a particular statutory environmental system. In addition to statutory liability under environmental laws, causes of actions based on nuisance or tort may apply. While most environmental obligations in bankruptcy cases arise out of major federal or state environmental acts, more and more causes of action are being brought by individuals and groups of individuals who were injured by the debtor's improper environmental activities.

3. 469 U.S. 274 (1985).

4. 474 U.S. 4 (1986).

Unfortunately, the exact scope of the problem is unknown. Information on the number of bankruptcies involving environmental liabilities is very limited. While the bankruptcy courts collect data on the number of bankruptcy filings each year, neither the courts, the Environmental Protection Agency, nor private providers of business data collect information on how many of these businesses have environmental liabilities. For example, between January 1, 2009, and September 30, 2010, over 103,000 businesses filed for bankruptcy; yet we have no information on how many of these bankruptcies involved environmental obligations, let alone the total amount discharged. Anecdotal evidence suggests that while the numbers of bankruptcies involving environmental liabilities may be small as compared to the total number of filings, the amount of obligations discharged in these bankruptcies is significant.

A Bankruptcy Primer

Bankruptcy is essentially about the relationship between creditors and debtors. Assuming a debt exists, bankruptcy law establishes *if*, *when*, and *how much* a creditor will get paid. In addition to the debtor's fresh start, bankruptcy attempts to ensure the ratable distribution of the debtor's scarce resources. If the debtor's assets are less than its debts, by definition every creditor will not be paid in full. Bankruptcy helps answer the question to whom should a debtor's scarce assets be allocated—the debtor or its creditors, and if its creditors, to which ones, and in what order. The Bankruptcy Code relies on certain substantive rights created outside of bankruptcy to help determine the *priority* of creditors' claims. Priority, in the bankruptcy context, simply refers to which creditor is at the head of line for purposes of payment.

Once a debtor files for bankruptcy, all property in which it has a legal or equitable interest becomes property of the estate. This pool of assets represents the resources from which the creditors will be paid. Not all creditors are created equal, however. In bankruptcy, a properly secured creditor is going to obtain the value of the property securing the debt. If there are any assets remaining after the satisfaction of secured claims, a distribution will be made to holders of unsecured claims. In most instances, however, there is little left to satisfy the claims of unsecured creditors.

One might assume that since equitable distribution of the debtor's assets is a fundamental goal of bankruptcy law, all unsecured creditors would share equally or "pro rata" in the debtor's assets. One would be wrong. The Bankruptcy Code creates priorities among unsecured creditors, mandating in § 507 that some be paid before others. In most cases the debtor's assets are insufficient to pay all the claims, so having a priority claim is extremely valuable. Section 507(a)(1) through (a)(10) sets out categories of unsecured claims that have priority over general unsecured claims.[5] Not

5. The list contains 9 priority claims with some specific limitations: (1) domestic support obligations; (2) administrative expenses for "the actual and necessary costs of preserving the estate"; (3) involuntary gap claims; (4) claims for wages, salaries, or commissions earned 180 days before the filing date; (5) unsecured claims for contributions to an employee benefit plan arising from services performed 180 days before the filing date; (6) specific unsecured claims related to farming and fishing; (7) allowed unsecured claims related to deposits for property never provided; (8) allowed unsecured claims of governmental units for particular tax obligations; (9) allowed unsecured claims for any

only do these ten categories of unsecured claims come ahead of general unsecured claims, but within the nine categories of claims the order established by section 507(a) is absolute; that is all section 507(a)(1) claims must be paid in full before section 507(a)(2) claims receive anything. One way to think about this distributional scheme is to consider a series of nine buckets representing the nine categories of priority claims. The buckets are situated one above the other and the distribution of funds to these creditors begins by pouring funds into the first bucket. When the first bucket is full, any additional funds overflow into the second bucket, and so on down the line. In the final analysis, if a creditor isn't secured, it at least wants to have § 507 priority and preferably first in line. In the absence of a secured interest in the debtor's property or a priority claim, a creditor is considered a general unsecured creditor and it will receive a pro rata distribution of the remaining estate assets.

The Bankruptcy Code does contain a number of exceptions to discharge. A corporate debtor, however, has far fewer exceptions to discharge than an individual debtor. For example, an individual debtor cannot discharge a debt "to the extent that debt is for a fine, penalty, or forfeiture payable to and for the benefit of a governmental unit, and is not compensation for actual pecuniary loss." Congress did not place the same burden on a corporation's fresh start. In practice this means that a corporate debtor can walk away from certain debts that an individual debtor cannot.

Environmental Obligations in Bankruptcy

Understanding how environmental obligations are treated in bankruptcy is critical to engaging in appropriate pre-bankruptcy planning. Once a debtor files for bankruptcy, there is little room to maneuver. Courts tend to interpret the Code to ensure the debtor's fresh start and the ratable distribution of the debtor's assets amongst creditors. Attorneys must understand the complexities of the bankruptcy system to ensure that they take proper precautionary measures before a bankruptcy is filed and to protect their client's interests once a petition is filed.

As noted earlier, when a debtor files for bankruptcy an estate is created. The estate is compromised of all property in which the debtor has a legal or equitable interest. If the debtor lacks an interest in the property at the commencement of the case, then it does not become property of the estate, is not subject to the automatic stay, and cannot be a part of the general distribution to creditors. In the environmental context, courts have found that debtors lack an interest in some financial assurance instruments such as letters of credit, irrevocable trusts, third party insurance proceeds, and certain bonds. Entities with claims on such instruments can access the proceeds without going through the bankruptcy process.

Only an entity or individual with a "claim" against the debtor is a creditor in the underlying bankruptcy. Two important questions emerge when considering whether a claim exists. First does it meet the definition of "claim"; and second when did the claim "arise"? Claim is broadly defined as a right to payment or a "right to an equitable

---

commitment by the debtor to a FDI regulatory agency; and (10) allowed claims for death and personal injury as a result of an alcohol related accident.

remedy for breach of performance if such breach gives rise to a right to payment." The question of whether an obligation of the debtor represents a right to payment, thereby qualifying as a claim, has important consequences. If the obligation is not a claim, then the entity has no right to participate in the bankruptcy distribution and the obligation is not "discharged" in bankruptcy. Moreover, the entity is not subject to the Code's automatic stay, allowing it to enforce its rights outside the bankruptcy proceeding. Courts have construed certain injunctive remedies in the environmental context to be outside the definition of claim because they cannot be converted to a right to payment.

When the "claim" arose also has great significance. According to the Code, the confirmation of a plan under Chapter 11 "discharges the debtor from any debt that arose *before* the date of such confirmation...." If a claim arises after confirmation, then the creditor is not subject to the bankruptcy discharge injunction and can pursue the debtor for full payment. In the environmental context, there are several possible moments when a claim may arise:

1. Upon release or threatened release of the hazardous substance.
2. When the debtor did the act that caused the pollution.
3. When the debtor incurred the response costs.
4. When the creditor knew or should have known of the potential obligation.
5. When the parties had some type of relationship; or
6. Some combination of these factors.

Courts have considered each of these key moments but have come up with inconsistent results. Unfortunately, environmental claims are not easily categorized as occurring at one moment in time. How should a court treat existing but undiscovered damages? What about ongoing pollution?

A creditor can attempt to argue that either it does not have a claim in the underlying bankruptcy or its claim arose after plan confirmation. It is important to note that a creditor only wants to argue that it does not have a claim if the debtor files for reorganization under Chapter 11. Reorganization assumes the debtor will emerge from bankruptcy and be available to pay the outstanding debt. If the debtor files for Chapter 7 (or its Chapter 11 is converted to a Chapter 7) then the corporation ceases to exist and it will be unavailable to meet its outstanding obligations.

As the previous discussion reveals, a secured creditor is guaranteed the value of the property that secures the debt. Some federal and state laws permit government units to obtain liens against the polluter's property. For example, the Massachusetts legislature created a so-called "super lien" statute that is triggered when a polluter incurs a debt to the Commonwealth based on clean-up costs. It allows the government's lien to trump all prior liens thereby circumventing the "first in time first in right" priority system.[6] Congress also provided for a federal lien under CERLCA. The

6. Mass. Gen. Laws ch. 21, § 13.

lien, however, is not "super lien" and is subject to all prior valid liens. Nonetheless, it is possible for the federal government to be a "secured creditor" under CERCLA.

Section 507(a)(2) mandates that all claims that are the "actual necessary costs and expenses of preserving the estate" are given priority status. The Supreme Court has interpreted this to include damages incurred by the estate itself. For example, if a debtor violates environmental laws *post petition*—that is after it files for bankruptcy—then the clean-up costs and any fines and penalties related to that violation are an administrative expense. Timing is everything. Courts have also used 28 U.S.C. § 959(b) to require the debtor's estate to expend money, labeled an administrative expense, to comply with state environmental laws. Section 959(b) provides that a trustee "shall manage and operate the property in his possession ... according to the requirements of the valid laws of the State in which such property is situated." In the absence of a properly secured interest in the debtor's property, an administrative expense provides the best opportunity for satisfaction of a creditor's claim.

The vast majority of environmental creditors are general unsecured creditors. General unsecured creditors received a pro rata distribution of the assets remaining in the estate after the secured creditors and the administrative expenses are paid. The hardest hit creditors are usually individuals who are not in a position to negotiate voluntary perfected security interest in the debtor's assets or obtain and execute a court judgment before the debtor filed for bankruptcy. Victims of toxic torts, such as [those in] the Asarco and W.R. Grace bankruptcies, have little leverage in the bankruptcy and often receive pennies on the dollar.

Possible Solutions

Creditors have a number of tools available to them under non-bankruptcy laws. To the extent possible, creditors should require financial assurances in which the debtor lacks a legal or equitable interest; obtain and perfect voluntary security interests in unencumbered assets; act on the availability of statutory liens; and quickly execute on court judgments or consent decrees. A 2005 GAO Report concluded that the EPA had failed to require financial assurances or acquire liens as allowed by statute, placing the public fisc at greater risk.

There are certainly a variety of local, state, and federal laws that lack a mandate or even permission to obtain financial assurances or security interests in the event of the polluter's financial distress. Laws could be amended to include such a requirement. The New Jersey Spill Compensation and Control Act is an example of such a comprehensive statute. It allows the state to obtain a lien against all the debtor's property, not just the property subject to a clean-up order. Statutory protections such as these will only work if they are properly executed, however. Some state officials express reluctance to obtain liens both because of the transaction costs and the stress it places on the polluter. A financially stressed polluter will have difficulty obtaining financing if it lacks unencumbered property.

There are several amendments to the Code that would, in some respects, prevent debtors with environmental obligations from shedding those debts in bankruptcy.

[First, the Code could p]revent debtors from discharging some or all environmental obligations[, but this would interfere] with a debtor's fresh start and may make a successful reorganization unlikely. [Second, the Code could p]rovide certain environmental debts, like some tax obligations, with priority status[, but] in practice, the environmental obligation[s are] paid by the unsecured creditor[s], not the debtor. [And third, Congress could e]nact the Clean-up Assurance and Polluter Accountability Act (CAPA) (S. 452)[which] would authorize a trustee in bankruptcy proceedings to avoid any transfer of a debtor's interest in an asset made during the 10 years before the bankruptcy petition is filed if: (1) the debtor had environmental liability under CERCLA; and (2) the debtor made such transfer with intent to hinder, delay, or defraud any person with respect to such liability.[7] [The Act would] only affect a small number of bankruptcies [however, and it would be] difficult [for trustees] to establish the necessary intent.

When it comes to the conflict between bankruptcy policy and environmental policy, bankruptcy judges choose a debtor's fresh start, the successful reorganization of a corporation, and the ratable distribution of the estate assets over the polluter pays principle. Bankruptcy judges often must interpret gray areas of the law and find equitable solutions. Many of the first cases involving environmental obligations were decided in the mid-1980s when CERCLA first imposed significant costs and corporations sought to shed their new CERCLA obligations in bankruptcy. Courts continue to rely on these early cases even though the legal and scientific landscape has changed dramatically. Bankruptcy judges should revisit some of these early cases and ask whether the court struck the right balance. A review of cases from 1980–2005 shows that bankruptcy judges are beginning to struggle more with the underlying environmental principles, but there is no evidence of significant shift towards the polluter-pays goal of environmental law.

Who Pays for the Gulf Coast Recovery if BP Were to File Bankruptcy?

The answer to the question presented is complex and depends on a number of factors unknown at this time. Creditors in a hypothetical BP [Exploration and Petroleum ("BPEP")] bankruptcy are in a unique position because of the Trust Agreement [entered into between the United States and] BPEP. In the vast majority of bankruptcies involving environmental obligations there is no trust agreement to ensure payment of environmental damages. In the absence of a Trust, the general unsecured creditors and the American taxpayer assume the burden for clean-up obligations. That may be the case here as well.

Who is the debtor? Although BP, p.l.c. has been the public relations face of the oil spill, it is not legally liable for the damages. BP Exploration and Petroleum (BPEP), a [BP] subsidiary, has been identified as the responsible party. If BPEP were to file

7. The Act contains a number of other requirements unrelated to the Bankruptcy Code [as well]....

bankruptcy, the damages owed as a result of the oil spill would be subject to the Bankruptcy Code and relevant non-bankruptcy law.

Who are the potential creditors? Federal agencies (from the EPA to the IRS), state agencies, local governments, PRPs (other potentially responsible parties, i.e., Transocean), businesses (i.e., suppliers, vendors, banks, lessors/lessees) affected by spill (i.e., [incurring] economic losses), individuals ([with] i.e., employment discrimination or breach of contract [claims]) affected by spill (i.e., [with] economic or health and safety claims).

What are the bases for potential claims? Claims under federal laws including OPA, CWA, CERCLA, Endangered Species Act, Marine Mammals Protection Act, Migratory Bird Treaty Act, OSHA, Refuse Act, Federal securities law, Jones Act, Death on the High Seas Act, Longshore and Harbor Workers Compensation Act, Outer Continental Shelf Lands Act, state laws (of Florida, Louisiana, Alabama, Mississippi, and Texas), and common law claims.

Does the Trust set up between BPEP become property of the estate? As you may remember, BP agreed to set up a Trust and claims processing facility to pay damages resulting from the spill, including final judgments or settlements that occur outside the process. The Grantor is BPEP (not BP, p.l.c.) and it has agreed to deposit $20 billion dollars into an irrevocable trust. The Trust documents require that the BPEP contribute $5 billion dollars by the end of 2010 and then $1.25 billion every quarter until the end of 2013.

At the time a debtor files for bankruptcy any property that the debtor has a legal or equitable interest in becomes "property of the estate." Article II, § E provides that any assets remaining in the Trust Fund shall revert to the BPEP upon termination of the Trust. Based on this language, BPEP appears to have an equitable interest in the Trust Fund and that interest (the right to the remaining assets) would become property of the estate. But the trust assets themselves would arguably not be property of the estate. This places creditors who have claims related to the oil spill in a unique position compared to other corporate bankruptcies involving environmental obligations.

Is BPEP required to continue funding the Trust if it files for bankruptcy? As stated above, BPEP has until the end of 2013 to fully fund the Trust. What happens if it files for bankruptcy before all payments have been made? In short, BPEP would not be allowed to meet its obligations under the agreement and the Trustees would not be able to enforce the agreement outside the bankruptcy process.

There are two possibilities to ensure the Trust obtains additional funds. First, in the Trust agreement, BPEP agreed to secure its obligations through a "first priority perfected security interest in production payments pertaining to the Grantor's U.S. oil and natural gas production." In the event the production payments fell below the amount still owed, BPEP agreed to assign a perfected security interest in additional property. The Trustees were given the power and the responsibility to negotiate the necessary security interests. If the perfected security interest were properly obtained, then it is possible that some or all of BPEP's obligations under the agreement are secured. If not, then the agreement is simply a "promise to pay" and it would be treated as a general unsecured debt in the bankruptcy context. Second, BP North America Corporation, Inc. (another subsidiary of BP, p.l.c.) has been identified as a responsible party based on its Guarantor status under the Oil Pollution Act. BP North America has guaranteed BPEP's payment of damages under the Act up to $150 million.

What happens if the Trust is exhausted, not fully funded, or a claim is not covered by the Trust? Assuming the Oil Spill Liability Trust Fund is available claimants could attempt to obtain payment through that fund. The Fund cannot be used to pay for costs, damages, or injuries that are not covered by the OPA and the Clean Water Act. Otherwise, the vast majority of creditors will be general, unsecured creditors paid with assets remaining after secured creditors and administrative expenses are fully paid.

Outside of the Trust document, will the costs associated with the spill, including fines and penalties, be given priority or special consideration in bankruptcy? It is important to note that the Trust agreement explicitly states it cannot be used to pay for fines and penalties associated with the damage. There is nothing in the Bankruptcy Code that accords debts arising from environmental issues special status. Moreover, fines and penalties are not treated differently than other debts. Although to the extent the fine or penalty was assessed against the estate (that is it is the result of conduct that occurred after the bankruptcy petition was filed) it will be treated as an administrative expense. The Gulf States each have laws that require a polluter to clean up and pay for damages associated with an oil spill. Unfortunately, the state legislatures rarely provided a mechanism for the state to secure the obligation. State claims will likely be treated as general unsecured claims unless they are associated with post-petition activity.

Can BP discharge all the costs associated with the spill in the underlying bankruptcy, including fines and penalties? According to the Code, the confirmation of a plan under Chapter 11 "discharges the debtor from any debt that arose before the date of such confirmation...." While there are limited exceptions to discharge for corporate debtors in § 1141(d), they do not except from discharge any claims related to environmental damages or fines and penalties associated with the corporation's conduct.

BP is precluded from discharging anything that is not a "claim" as defined by the Bankruptcy Code. While claim has been construed expansively by bankruptcy courts to facilitate the debtor's fresh start, courts have recognized that certain equitable remedies are not "claims." Courts have distinguished equitable remedies where there is a corresponding right to payment and equitable remedies that cannot be converted to a right to monetary damages. For example, under CERCLA, the federal government can order a polluter to clean up or it can clean up and then seek reimbursement. As a result, courts uniformly have construed an order to clean up under CERCLA as a "right to payment." In contrast, if a governmental entity issues an order to a polluter to "cease and desist" all future discharges, most courts have viewed the order as a non-dischargeable obligation. Courts distinguish orders that require the debtor to spend money (i.e. obtaining certain equipment to be in compliance with environmental laws) from orders that can be converted to a money judgment paid to the state. While four appellate courts have spoken on the issue, there is no unified national approach.

What if additional damages are discovered after the plan is confirmed, can a governmental or private entity or individual pursue BPEP outside of bankruptcy? As noted above, the confirmation of a plan under Chapter 11 "discharges the debtor from any debt that arose before the date of such confirmation." The key to answering the question above is determining when the debt "arose." When it comes to environmental damages, there is no consensus on the appropriate time frame. Bankruptcy courts tend to err on the side of the debtor's fresh start, however. Courts have developed a variety of flexible, fact specific tests to determine the appropriate time frame.

Heather Hughes, *Enabling Investment in Environmental Sustainability**

An extensive, public conversation about creating incentives for commercial actors to take more responsibility for environmental harm is underway. Very few participants, however, identify commercial finance law as a potential site for developing these types of incentives. This Article proposes an "environmental practices money security interest" (EPMSI) that could be added to Uniform Commercial Code (UCC) Article 9[3] to facilitate transactions that enable good environmental practices.

The concept of the "super-priority" security interest—a collateral-security device and priority rules designed to enable certain types of investments—is well established in commercial law. Article 9 contains rules governing two such interests: the purchase money security interest for acquisition of goods and the production money security interest in agricultural finance. The EPMSI would grant priority over earlier investors to financers whose extensions of credit enable debtors to invest in improving environmental impact.

Imagine a company that wants to renovate its manufacturing processes to reduce waste and utilize alternative fuels. Such renovation could require contracting with various experts, service providers, and engineers, as well as acquiring both tangible and intangible property. A company may want to undertake this type of improvement but be unable to do so because it lacks either internal funds or the capacity to issue low-risk debt to pay for the process. The company may lack the capacity to issue low risk debt because an existing secured creditor has a floating lien on the company's asset and this creditor is unable or unwilling to fund the renovation process. The proposed EPMSI rules would create a collateral-security device that private parties could elect to use in this type of situation....

---

* Originally published in 85 Indiana Law Journal 597 (2010). Reprinted with permission.

3. U.C.C. art. 9 (2005). This is the article of the UCC that governs secured transactions. "Secured transactions" are transactions in which a creditor makes a loan and takes as collateral a lien on personal property of the debtor. A lien is a type of property interest. Secured transactions create "security interests" in the debtor's property. Security interests are liens created by contract. UCC Article 9 and bankruptcy laws, in tandem, govern the order of priority of property interests in companies' assets.

Enabling Interests Under UCC Article 9

UCC Article 9 sets forth the order of priority in which various creditors take from an insolvent debtor's assets. Generally, these rules grant secured creditors priority over unsecured creditors. Secured creditors' priority ranks in the order in which each creditor came along—first in time, first in right. However, some security interests enjoy later-in-time priority, meaning they have priority over earlier secured creditors. These "super-priority" security interests enjoy an exception to the general rule to enable or facilitate the type of credit they involve.

It is important to recognize the difference between the concept of enabling interests in general and super-priority security interests that arise under UCC Article 9. There are numerous examples of enabling interests in every U.S. jurisdiction's laws. Most enabling interests arise pursuant to state statutes that create liens in favor of parties who extend credit for various types of goods and services, such as mechanics' liens, agricultural liens, and artisans' liens. Such liens are, of course, property interests. They are not security interests under Article 9 because they arise by statute and not by assignment. Security interests are consensual liens—property interests that arise by contract, not by statute or judgment.

In the context of Article 9, the purchase-money security interest is by far the most widely discussed super-priority interest. The purchase-money security interest enables a debtor to issue low-risk (high-priority) debt to acquire new equipment or inventory even though all of the debtor's assets are encumbered by a lien in favor of an earlier secured creditor.

Companies commonly finance operations and projects with loans secured by floating liens on the companies' assets. "Floating lien" is a short-hand (not a statutory) term for a security interest that attaches to after-acquired collateral and for which the code dates priority for future advances by the lender back to the date the lender first filed a UCC-1 financing statement or perfected its interest. A floating lien is a security interest that maintains its priority if enforced against property the debtor acquires after closing the transaction and, in many instances, after other creditors have come along. Floating lien creditors depend on the first-in-time, first-in-right rules to maintain priority over later creditors. Purchase-money and production-money creditors with later-in-time priority will defeat earlier floating lien creditors' claims, but only to the extent of the new value that the later creditor provided.

The reasoning or policies behind Article 9's special priority rules for certain security interests can be difficult to grasp. In essence, by permitting certain secured creditors to prevail over earlier secured creditors, the code, as Hideki Kanda and Saul Levmore explain, "compromises between the advantages and the disadvantages of 'new money.'"[36] The structure of and policies behind the PMSI, and the special priority rules that pertain to it, offer a framework for thinking about the proposed EPMSI.

---

36. Hideki Kanda & Saul Levmore, Explaining Creditor Priorities, 80 Virginia Law Review 2103, 2105 (1994) (arguing that the PMSI rules are justified because the first-in-time principle inhibits al-

Environmental-Practices-Money Security Interest

The concept of the EPMSI presents numerous, complex questions. Would creating such an interest conflict with basic facets of Article 9's approach to priority? Why should the UCC allocate environmental costs to secured parties and debtors? How does the EPMSI concept relate to Article 9's first-in-time, first-in-right priority system that grants later-in-time priority for purchase-money loans and, in some jurisdictions, for production-money loans?...

Conventional wisdom holds that the limitation of interests with later-in-time priority to new assets acquired with new value is key to the coexistence of floating liens and super-priority security interests. As Kanda and Levmore put it, Article 9 limits later-in time priority to creditors who are "virtually certain to be both value enhancing and non-risk-altering."[96] George Triantis, Jackson, and Kronman also emphasize the idea that super-priority-security-interest collateral is limited to specific assets acquired with the new value that the later creditor provides.[97] This limitation makes granting priority to purchase-money interests acceptable, these scholars find, because it makes risk of dilution of earlier creditors' claims negligible.

Much of the scholarly analysis of PMSI rules seems to assume an idealized form of purchase-money interest, rather than a reality in which purchase-money interests are risk altering. Kanda and Levmore, for example, overstate the extent to which limitations on PMSI collateral actually eliminate the potential for risk alteration. They may be perfectly correct that this is the objective of the rules—that we can explain the rules in reference to a desire to avoid risk alteration. But the rules do not always succeed at this.

As Professor Paul Shupack puts it, "Most real world transactions will be further away from an ideal PMSI" and will create some risk for existing creditors.[98] He continues:

> [A]lthough commercial debtors can be assumed to acquire goods in order to put them into enterprising activities, not all of these enterprises will be profitable. The PMSI, by giving the debtor leverage and thereby giving the debtor the opportunity to make purchases he or she would otherwise not have made, can increase risks to the general creditors.

Even in a case where a company acquires one valuable piece of equipment with purchase money credit on good terms, this investment could be risk altering. The equipment could be used to make a new product or to alter the company's processes

---

teration of risk, whereas later creditors have better information than earlier creditors to determine which shifts in risk are efficient).

96. Id. at 2132.

97. See [Thomas H. Jackson & Anthony T. Kronman, Secured Financing and Priorities Among Creditors, 88 Yale Law Journal 1143, 1179 (1979)]; George G. Triantis, Financial Slack Policy and the Laws of Secured Transactions, 29 Journal of Legal Studies 35, 47–50 (2000). Triantis emphasizes that the ideal balance between manager constraint and discretion—optimal financial slack—is struck by limiting the purchase-money creditor's interest to the value of the collateral acquired with the new funds....

98. Paul M. Shupack, Defining Purchase Money Collateral, 29 Idaho Law Review 767, 773 (1992).

in a way that causes losses. New equipment could require retraining of workers that slows production and sales, lowering the levels of receivables or inventory to which earlier creditors can look for security.

Secured creditors are aware of these kinds of risks, of course, and respond in a variety of ways. Many secured credit contracts contain provisions that give floating-lien creditors latitude to protect themselves in the event of risk alteration. Creditors may overcollateralize a loan to insulate themselves from the dilution risk presented by PMSIs. Loan-to-value covenants and further assurances provisions can ensure this kind of protection. Loan-to-value ratio covenants and further assurances clauses obligate the debtor to keep the secured party collateralized to a certain level and keep the security interest perfected. Or, secured creditors may require debtors to report any PMSIs and call their loans in response. Negative pledge clauses prohibit debtors from assigning security interests other than those contemplated by the security agreement at issue.

These basic insulation strategies could be effective in an EPMSI context as well. Though previously encumbered assets may be assigned to an EPMSI creditor, this later creditor's interest will be limited to the extent of new value given. If an earlier creditor were sufficiently oversecured, an EPMSI claim could amount to a portion of the value of the collateral securing the earlier interest such that the earlier creditor is sufficiently secured despite an EPMSI. This potential response to dilution risk raises questions, of course, about the costs of overcollateralization. Whether the benefits of a collateral security device like the EPMSI outweigh the costs it could create for debtors and secured creditors and whether these parties should bear such costs are separate questions presented below.

But novelty should not deter consideration of the EPMSI. Efforts to encourage commercial actors to bear costs of improving environmental effects are of recent vintage. States may want to consider enacting EPMSI provisions to the extent that they are seeking new ways to create incentives for commercial actors to fund and undertake new practices and processes to minimize environmental harm.

Secured Parties, Debtors, and Environmental Costs

The proposed EPMSI would put secured lenders in the position of either funding costs of improvements in environmental impact, or risking subordination to a financer who will. In some instances, engaging in environmental practices may yield very tangible returns for debtors; in others, the value of these practices may be harder to calculate or may be externalized. EPMSI rules would allocate to secured parties the costs of creating environmental benefits that could accrue to society at large.

The issue of creating costs that yield externalized benefits pervades thinking about responsibility for the environment. Why enact limits on carbon emissions that constrict businesses in one country or region when the benefits of reduced emissions are global? Why offer a tax credit that reduces revenue in one state to create environmental benefits that accrue across borders?

One could argue that the government subsidy approach to inducing "green" investment is better than an approach like the EPMSI because the tax base is the best available proxy for the beneficiaries of improvements in environmental impact. This work in no way argues against tax credits, subsidized financing (a couple examples of which are described below), or other government initiatives. This Article proposes collateral security rules that would complement these public initiatives.

The notion that costs of inducing "green" investment should accrue to the public because the public is the primary beneficiary of these measures raises a fundamental question in the context of environmental programs. Who should bear costs of improving the environment? If costs are always imposed on the public because the public benefits, then private actors have no incentive to reduce the harm they inflict—short of civil or criminal liability. On its own, a top-down regulatory approach has proven inadequate to remedy and deter environmental harm—hence the widespread focus in recent years on alternative mechanisms. At the same time, if certain private actors bear costs the benefits of which are externalized, and cannot stay solvent while doing so, then other costs to the public that we must consider are created. The EPMSI concept animates this tension in the context of commercial finance.

Institutional lenders recognize the connection between secured transactions and the environmental impact of debtors' activities. A long list of project financers has adopted the Equator Principles—standards for secured lending that include a commitment to fund only projects that meet certain environmental criteria.[121] Other major institutional lenders have adopted the Carbon Principles—commitments to encourage borrowers to invest in energy efficiency and reduce carbon emissions.[122] It is unknown, at the moment, what the Equator Principles' and the Carbon Principles' effects will be. For example, though the Equator Principles require subscribing banks to include covenants in project loan documentation under which the borrower agrees to maintain compliance with articulated environmental (and other) standards, lenders are not obligated to call an event of default if any such covenant is breached.

One could argue that secured parties are an ideal group to target for internalizing environmental costs because they are in a strong position to control companies' activities, and therefore, are in a strong position to control environmental impact. Legal scholars have advocated for secured lender liability under the Comprehensive Envi-

121. The Equator Principles: A Financial Industry Benchmark for Determining, Assessing and Managing Social & Environmental Risk in Project Financing (July 2006), http://www.equator-principles.com/documents/Equator_Principles.pdf ("The Equator Principles Financial Institutions (EPFI's) have consequently adopted these principles ... to ensure that the projects we finance are developed in a manner that is socially responsible ... and reflect sound environmental practices"). Numerous major U.S. and foreign lenders such as Bank of America, ABN AMRO, and Wells Fargo are Equator Principles financial institutions. Equator Principles: Institutions Which Have Adopted the Equator Principles, http://www.equator-principles.com/.

122. See, e.g., Press Release, Bank of America, Bank of America to Announce Adoption of Carbon Principles at Natural Res. Def. Council Tenth Annual Award Event (Apr. 1, 2008), http://bankofamerica.mediaroom.com/index.php?s=press_releases&items-8124.

ronmental Response Compensation and Liability Act (CERCLA) and for priority under Article 9 for environmental claims.[124]

The EPMSI differs in important ways from proposals for CERCLA liability for secured lenders and for priority in advance of secured lenders for environmental claimants. Generally, a secured lender is not liable under the CERCLA unless the lender controls activities on a site to such an extent that it is effectively an owner or operator of the business on the site. When a debtor pollutes, if the debtor's secured lender was participating in the management of the debtor's activities to a sufficient extent, then liability for cleanup extends to the secured lender.

Note that CERCLA liability relates to specific polluted sites. A lender can assess particular sites used by a debtor to gauge the risk of environmental liability. Also, a lender can use its monitoring power to prevent debtors from polluting a given site in a way that would create liability. In this sense, lenders have some power to determine whether they are at risk for CERCLA liability. The EPMSI presents a different type of risk. Under the proposed EPMSI rules, a secured lender's position could face dilution by a later, environmental-practices-money creditor to an extent that the lender could not assess in advance. The extent to which this is true in practice would depend in part on the formulation of EPMSI definitional provisions, the quality of debtors' disclosures, and the nature of the loan covenants that transactions contain.

Academic proposals to grant environmental claimants priority under Article 9 also seek to allocate environmental costs to secured lenders. Under this approach, environmental claims would be satisfied out of the debtor's assets before secured lenders' claims are satisfied. The basic proposal is that secured lenders' claims be subordinated to the claims of state actors that incur toxic waste cleanup costs, regardless of whether or not the secured lenders were owners or operators as defined in the CERCLA. Both this idea and CERCLA liability are, essentially, about ensuring that environmental claims get paid. They are about preventing scenarios in which environmental costs that are a company's responsibility are transferred to the public because the company cannot pay after its secured creditors satisfy their claims.

The point here is to recognize that others have sought to allocate environmental costs to secured lenders and to contrast the EPMSI to these liability-driven approaches to such allocation. Again, the concept of the EPMSI asks: why look exclusively to government subsidies to induce investment in environmental sustainability when commercial law devices also could do so? Proposals for CERCLA liability and environmental claimant priority, in theory, should incentivize better practices. If secured lenders could be liable for cleanup costs, then they should use their monitoring and directive power to ensure that debtors do not incur these types of liabilities.

---

124. See, e.g., Kathryn R. Heidt, Cleaning Up Your Act: Efficiency Considerations in the Battle for the Debtor's Assets in Toxic Waste Bankruptcies, 40 Rutgers Law Review 819 (1988); Kathryn R. Heidt, Corrective Justice from Aristotle to Second Order Liability: Who Should Pay When the Culpable Cannot?, 47 Washington & Lee Law Review 347 (1990); Lynn M. LoPucki, The Death of Liability, 106 Yale Law Journal 1 (1996) (arguing for priority for tort claimants generally).

The EPMSI is about incentivizing better practices in a more direct way. If a secured lender is unwilling to finance better environmental practices, then it will risk subordination to a financer who will. The EPMSI is not a measure to deal with costs of environmental liability after they arise. It is a measure to incentivize funding for new activities and investments to improve environmental impact going forward. It is a collateral-security device that companies and creditors could elect to use to fund activities that are environmentally progressive. Secured parties would have some choice under the EPMSI rules. They could figure out how to fund environmental practices themselves, attempt to contract around or minimize exposure to EPMSI creditor risk, or accept subordination to EPMSI creditors.

Many states currently incentivize investment in better environmental practices by offering tax credits. States offer tax deductions for investments in, for example, switching to solar power. Additionally, the federal government and state governments offer assistance with financing environmental practices. This assistance includes loan insurance, guaranty, grant, and low-interest loan programs to help businesses fund various investments in improved environmental sustainability. For example, California's Integrated Waste Management Board provides direct loans to businesses that use post-consumer or secondary waste materials to manufacture new products, or that undertake projects to reduce the waste resulting from the manufacture of a product. It also provides loans to California tire manufacturers and processors for the purchase of equipment that will be used to produce tire-derived material and products.

These types of programs assist with funding of investments in improved environmental impact, but they do not negate the potential value of a device like the EPMSI. These programs commit public resources in contexts where, with a measure like the EPMSI, private funding might become available. The proposed EPMSI could induce private financers to fund more environmental initiatives. Also, government financial assistance programs are especially important for activities that may not receive private funding regardless of whether or not debtors can issue high-priority debt to financers. The EPMSI may cause some of the activities currently undertaken with government financing assistance to become viable without government help. Government resources could then be devoted elsewhere, towards more funding of efforts for which private funds will be hard to procure in any event, or towards environmental cleanup and protection.

Government subsidies for "green" investment allocate the costs of inducing such investment to the public. One could argue that a device like the EPMSI that allocates costs to private parties is not as desirable as public subsidies because, if an EPMSI were enacted, secured lenders would charge more for credit and lend less, passing costs on to companies in ways that hinder growth. Allocating costs of environmental impact to secured creditors would cause secured creditors to restrict credit, which would hurt companies and could also hurt the environment.

The threat of credit constriction is a common refrain that secured creditors make in response to any proposal that involves reducing the scope of secured creditors' claims. The extent to which EPMSI rules would result in a level of credit constriction that would reduce available capital and value-adding investments presents a chain of unanswered questions.

We can assume that creditors, to some extent, will lend less if EPMSI rules were enacted. This fact does not justify rejecting consideration of the EPMSI concept. It just complicates fundamental questions surrounding the idea of an EPMSI. What is better: maximum access to credit or the capacity to issue high-priority debt to fund improvements in environmental impact? Responding to imminent environmental problems will be costly; failing to adequately respond would be much more costly. The perennial threat of credit constriction does not exempt UCC Article 9 from being a potential site for innovation as lawmakers search for ways to induce private investment in environmental sustainability. This Article does not set out to establish that a collateral security device like the EPMSI is better than or should supplant government subsidies to induce investment in environmentally sound practices. Rather, it seeks to show, in a concrete way, how we could enact commercial finance rules to induce "green" investment. Some may consider any proposal that would result in credit constriction to be bad or unjustified unless and until its benefits were proven to outweigh the costs associated with credit constriction. This type of proof is extremely difficult, if not impossible, to make. The difficulty of measuring in advance the benefits of a proposal like the EPMSI does not eliminate the proposal's value. Questions about how best to induce desirable modes and levels of investment are precisely what this work hopes to invoke.

Discussion Questions

1. The hardrock mining industry seems financially and otherwise unsustainable. What can states and countries do to solve the problems caused by such mining operations?

2. Could the pre-bankruptcy transfers Diamond describes at Pegasus Gold form the basis of a corporate veil-piercing claim or a fraudulent conveyance action? In other words, are the problems Diamond describes corporate law problems, bankruptcy law problems, or both (or neither)?

3. Do you think bankruptcies of large companies such as BP are a real possibility? Consider the coal industry, where a combination of increased environmental regulation and increasingly cheaper alternatives has pushed many coal companies (including the second and fourth largest) into bankruptcy. Bankruptcy renders these firms' "self bonds" essentially worthless, leaving the public to pick up the tab.

4. Do you think the current bankruptcy law deals effectively with environmental claims? Would you make any modifications to the current law to address some of these issues?

5. Do you agree with Gardina's recommendations to prevent debtor companies from discharging their environmental obligations?

6. Who would bear the costs and risks of EPMSIs? Are EPMSIs better or worse in this respect than taxes, grants, and low-interest loans?

Chapter 14

Sustainability and Intellectua Property Law

The law of trade secrets, patents, and trademarks can have a profound impact on innovative business practices that can help the environment. The first reading in this chapter introduces these categories and makes suggestions on how each should change to promote beneficial environmental technologies. The second reading deals with patent law and how it can be harnessed to mitigate the impact of global warming. The last reading focuses on environmental trademarks and the related problem of greenwashing, where a product purports to be socially and environmentally better than it really is. When reading this chapter, consider how intellectual property law intersects with sustainability and what changes need to be made to intellectual property law to further promote sustainable environmental practices.

Michael A. Gollin, *Using Intellectual Property to Improve Environmental Protection**

Intellectual property has had a neutral impact on the environment. Technical ingenuity thrives on the incentive system established by intellectual property law, which provides the prospect of remuneration for creative problem solving. An innovator can rely on the law of trade secrets, patents, copyrights, and trademarks to protect his or her new technology. Unfortunately, incentives for inventing and using environmentally beneficial technology have generally been no greater than those for environmentally harmful technology. Proprietary rights in destructive technology are indistinguishable from rights in beneficial technology.

Most environmental statutes include provisions intended to promote technical solutions to environmental problems.... Some laws, which are intended to eliminate harmful technologies or substances such as asbestos or polychlorinated biphenyls ("PCBs"), actually bring about radical innovation. Other laws encourage or require the use of beneficial technology. For example, a factory that discharges pollutants into the air or water may be subjected to a permit condition requiring the factory to employ pollution control or treatment technology, or the owner of a hazardous waste

---

* Originally published in 4 Harvard Journal of Law & Technology 193 (1991). Reprinted with permission.

site may be ordered to pump and treat contaminated groundwater using a sophisticated bioremediation system.

Just as intellectual property law does not generally distinguish between environmentally harmful and beneficial technology, environmental law does not generally take intellectual property incentives into account in seeking to protect the environment....

The Scope of Environmental Technology

Environmental technology includes: (1) industrial processes which minimize resource consumption and waste production, (2) consumer products which are environmentally benign throughout their life cycles, (3) recycling equipment and processes, (4) waste management technologies for solid and hazardous waste, (5) pollution control devices, and (6) products and methods for cleaning up pollution. Environmental technology is not limited to control equipment, but is also important in manufacturing, waste management, utilities, and the environmental service industry. This cross-cutting list of technologies has only recently come to be viewed as a discrete industrial sector with legal, technical, and commercial characteristics of its own.

The common thread linking these six categories of technology is the intention to solve environmental problems, and to fill the need for pollution control and prevention. Environmental technology innovation can help achieve ... (1) [a] net environmental benefit in comparison with exiting technologies, taking into account resources consumed, wastes produced, and risks to human health and the environment; (2) [r]educed costs of environmental compliance; and (3) [r]educed risk of environmental liability. In addition, as with all technology innovation, environmental technology can: (1) [r]educe costs of materials, (2) [r]educe costs of production, (3) [i]ncrease rates of production, and (4) [i]ncrease attractiveness of products in the marketplace. Ultimately, as with all innovation, an overarching goal is to gain a competitive advantage in the marketplace. Intellectual property protection can play a role in improving environmental protection by securing a marketplace advantage for environmental innovators.

The Technology Innovation Cycle

The technology cycle can be viewed as having three phases: invention, innovation, and diffusion. Invention is the implementation of a new idea or concept leading to a new product or process; innovation, the development and initial commercial transfer of an invention; and diffusion, the spread of a new process or product within or across markets. Environmental laws affect all three phases. The laws provide the impetus for invention by defining problems to be solved and needs to be filled. They may promote innovation and diffusion, for example, by requiring companies to use best available technology. Intellectual property laws also affect each of the three phases. They promote invention, and also facilitate development and diffusion by serving as assets that can be bought or sold.

Like any assets, intellectual property rights can be strong or weak and can be managed well or poorly. A skillful manager of environmental technology can find opportunities to create and utilize intellectual property rights even when faced with potential environmental liabilities, and turn compliance costs into competitive gains. For example, a company could invent a patentable method of cleaning up its own hazardous substances and then license the technology to others with similar problems. In this example, the impetus for the invention derives from both environmental liability and intellectual property laws. The resulting commercial exploitation of property rights in the invention leads to an abatement of pollution.

An Overview of Proprietary Rights in Environmental Technology Trade Secrets

Trade secrecy is a common law doctrine that has been codified in several statutes. A trade secret is defined in the Restatement (First) of Torts as:

> [a]ny formula, pattern, device or compilation of information which is used in one's business, and which gives him an opportunity to obtain an advantage over competitors who do not know or use it. It may be a formula for a chemical compound, a process of manufacturing, treating or preserving materials, a pattern for a machine or other device, or a list of customers.... Generally it relates to the production of goods, as, for example, a machine or formula for the production of an article. It may, however, relate to the sale of goods or to other operations in the business....[16]

This definition emphasizes that protection attaches only to information [that] provides a competitive advantage.

A slightly different formulation was adopted in the Uniform Trade Secrets Act:

> [I]nformation, including a formula, pattern, compilation, program, device, method, technique, or process, that: (i) derives independent economic value, actual or potential, from not being generally known to, and not being readily ascertainable by proper means by, other persons who can obtain economic value from its disclosure or use, and (ii) is the subject of efforts that are reasonable under the circumstances to maintain its secrecy.[17]

This definition adds the requirement that the trade secret owner take efforts to maintain secrecy....

The protection of trade secrets derives from the common law, but statutory protection of trade secrets has advanced in the states. More than half of the states have adopted the Uniform Trade Secrets Act. Criminal statutes protecting trade secrets have been adopted in a similar number of states, since civil damages are difficult to prove and collect, and are an insufficient deterrent. The economic incentive to misappropriate a trade secret is often greater than the prospect of damages from a civil

---

16. Restatement (First) of Torts § 757 comment b (1939).
17. Uniform Trade Secrets Act § 1, 14 U.L.A. 539 (1980).

lawsuit. However, as a practical matter, the high burden of proof in a criminal action will be hard to sustain in most trade secret cases.

Federal protection of trade secrets is found in the interstices of many statutes. The Trade Secrets Act, discussed below in the context of environmental legislation, provides criminal penalties for federal employees who disclose trade secrets unless authorized by law. The Freedom of Information Act provides some protection for trade secrets submitted to federal agencies. [Federal] agencies are not required to disclose such information in response to a FOIA request.... Moreover, many of the statutes establishing specific agencies contain provisions intended to protect trade secrets disclosed to the agencies. For example, the Patent Act provides that a patent application is secret and may not be disclosed without the applicant's permission until and unless a patent is granted. Environmental statutes also contain provisions protecting trade secrets, but the degree of protection varies substantially by statute.

One of the most important sources of trade secret protection, whether in a commercial or employment setting, is contract law, which allows individuals to obtain broader protection than otherwise afforded. Many disputes over trade secrets have their genesis in confidentiality or non-competition agreements. For example, a person may execute a confidentiality agreement, review the details of a secret process, and then use a very similar process for personal gain. More commonly, an employee may sign a non-competition agreement with a first employer, then leave for another job, where he or she uses techniques, formulas, or processes learned at the first job.

Summarizing the elements from above, a trade secret is information having commercial value that is not publicly known and is maintained in secret. The information potentially subject to trade secrecy is quite extensive. The following may constitute trade secrets: (1) [t]echnical information, e.g., chemical formulas, product specifications, equipment designs, process and engineering drawings, laboratory notebooks, invention disclosures, performance data, manuals, and risk assessments; (2) [b]usiness information, e.g., earnings reports, budgets, financial statements, tax returns, corporate minutes, stockholder identifies, business plans, and personnel records; (3) [m]arketing information, e.g., customer lists, sales estimates, and market analyses; and (4) [l]egal matters, e.g., contracts, negotiation materials, legal opinions, and material prepared for lawsuits.

... The task of protecting trade secrets in environmental technology is rendered extraordinarily difficult, however, by the broad disclosures required by environmental legislation and regulation. A pervasive feature of environmental regulation is the broad disclosure required. Environmental disclosure presents great risk to industry because much of the information required to be disclosed in, for instance, a permit application or an emissions report, relates to processes, equipment, and formulas at the heart of a company's competitive position. To alleviate the legitimate concern of industry that such disclosure may damage competitive advantage, and encourage full disclosure, most environmental statutes couple the duty to disclose with provisions protecting trade secrets....

Patent Law

Legal procedures for recognizing and rewarding invention were put in place in the eighteenth century. Patent law provides a well-established system for promoting innovation in environmental technology. The origins of patent protection in the United States are found in the Constitution. "The Congress shall have Power ... [t]o promote the Progress of Science and useful Arts, by securing for limited Times to ... Inventors the exclusive Right to their ... discoveries."[79] A patent is a grant from the government to an inventor, conveying "the right to exclude others from making, using, or selling the invention throughout the United States."[80] "Inventors disclose what they have discovered or invented, and society rewards them with a patent."[81]

The Patent Act of 1952 codifies the procedural and substantive requirements of the patent system. "Whoever invents or discovers any new and useful process, machine, manufacture, or composition of matter, or any new and useful improvement thereof, may obtain a patent therefor, subject to the conditions and requirements of [the Patent Act]."[83] Patentees are entitled to enforce their patents against infringers. A patentee may obtain an injunction against infringement, or a reasonable royalty and lost profits. Damages may be trebled, and in exceptional cases attorney fees can be awarded....

The substantive requirements for obtaining a patent include: (a) invention—a concept reduced to practice; (b) novelty—not known or used by others prior to invention and not published, in public use or on sale within one year prior to the date of the patent application, and (c) non-obviousness—the "subject matter as a whole would [not be] obvious at the time the invention was made to a person having ordinary skill in the art to which said subject matter pertains."[90] ... After issuance, a patent conveys a 17-year grant of exclusive rights, subject to payment of maintenance fees.*

Patents can protect inventors of advances in pollution control equipment and other environmental technology.... Some patents for environmental technology were issued well before the start of the environmental movement in 1970. The real boom in air pollution control technology, as with most environmental technology, began in the 1970s; patent disputes followed. For example, John Zink Co. v. National Airfoil Burner Co. involved a patented nozzle designed for smokeless emission of refinery waste gas. The court weighed environmental protection as a factor supporting validity in upholding the patent: the nozzle, invented "years before the popular concern with air pollution and the environment, is precisely the kind of invention the

79. U.S. Const. art. I, §8, cl. 8.

80. 35 U.S.C. §154.

81. [Robert P.] Merges, Commercial Success and Patent Standards: Economic Perspectives on Innovation, 76 California Law Review 803, 808 (1988) (calling the dual functions of the system the "disclosure" function and the "reward" function).

83. [35 U.S.C.] §101.

90. Id. §103.

* [The term is now twenty years from the date of filing the patent application.—Eds.]

framers of the Constitution wanted revealed and protected."[97] Thus, the environmental benefits of a patented invention can bolster the validity of a patent in an infringement lawsuit.

The patent regulations were amended in 1982 to provide for faster processing of environmental patents. These regulations permit a patent application for environmental technology to be made "special" and receive swifter processing. Environmental inventions are those [that] "will materially enhance the quality of the environment or materially contribute to the development or conservation of energy resources."[100] These regulations have not resulted in any great shift toward more rapid issuance of patents for environmental technology [however].

... In sum, the patent system offers many opportunities to enhance environmental technology innovation. Environmental patents should be made stronger and easier to obtain. Information from the patent literature should remain readily available to innovators and those seeking licenses for compliance purposes. Legislation and regulation affecting patent licenses must balance the interests of patentees and those required to use patented environmental technologies.

Trademarks

Trademark protection is relevant to environmental technology for several reasons. The trademark for an environmental product may be critical to its commercial success. The trade name and service marks of a services company are important assets.... Trademarks and the law of unfair competition govern the evolving efforts to introduce green labeling.

Trademarks are designed to identify the origin of goods or services; prevent mistake, deception and confusion with regard to origin; and protect goodwill. Trademark protection, like trade secret protection, has both federal and state components. Federal registration prevents use of a mark where it would "be likely to cause confusion, or to cause mistake or to deceive."[107] Common law provides certain additional protections. The Lanham Trademark Act creates a federal cause of action for unfair trade practices in addition to a cause of action for infringement of a registered trademark.[109]

Domestic and foreign trademark registrations and common law trademark protections are important to the success of any product or service. Since consumers are increasingly interested in environmentally safe products, trademark law can define the market for consumer environmental products. The recent advent of "green labeling" implicates trademark rights. Examples include statements regarding the environmental characteristics of a product, names connoting environmental benefits, and certification of environmentally benign characteristics by independent organi-

97. 613 F.2d 547, 559 (5th Cir. 1980).

100. 37 C.F.R. § 1.102(e).

107. 15 U.S.C. § 1114.

109. The elements of a Lanham Act unfair trade practice claim are: (1) False statements regarding products or services, (2) Likelihood of consumer deception, (3) Materiality of the deception to the purchasing decision, and (4) Likelihood of injury to defendant. See 15 U.S.C. § 1125(a).

zations such as Green Seal, Inc. and Green Cross Certification Co. These competing non-profit companies promote their "seal-for-sale" programs as alternatives to government certification....

Some states have taken action to implement green labeling as well.... The state labeling system is a creative approach that allows companies to achieve a competitive advantage for environmentally beneficial products. The opposite approach, one requiring companies to label products with warnings or labels disclosing the environmental harmfulness of their products, creates a competitive disadvantage. These approaches exemplify use of trademark concepts as an instrument of environmental policy....

Compulsory Patent Licensing

Generally, the right to exclude others from making, using, or selling a patented product or process is absolute. In theory, a patentee cannot be forced to make, use or sell the patented invention. In addition, she is not required to license the technology to others. As a result, the most appropriate technology for a given situation may be described and claimed in a patent, and yet cannot be used. From an economic viewpoint, a patentee would be unlikely to refuse a reasonable offer of payment or royalty. However, a company may refuse to allow competitors to take advantage of a patent in order to bring economic or public relations ruin upon the competitor.

... A statutory provision permits the United States and its contractors to use any patented technology upon payment of a reasonable royalty.[133] A federal contractor, subcontractor or any person who uses a technology or manufactures a product for the United States with governmental authorization and consent is protected from exposure to injunction, treble damages, and an award of attorneys' fees in a district court action. Rather, the worst consequences are an action in the Claims Court to determine whether a reasonable royalty is due.

The compulsory license statute can protect a party, for use of control or cleanup technology. When contracting with a federal agency [that] requires the use of a patented technology, the contractor may receive governmental authorization and consent specifying use of the patented technology. Such authorization and consent will establish the basis for a defense under Section 1498. Authorization and consent clauses are standard in government procurement contracts. EPA should make available its explicit authorization and consent to use particular environmental technology in permits and enforcement orders as well as contracts. Such authorization and consent will protect those required to use environmentally beneficial technology from exposure to injunctions and increased damages.

Even in the absence of express authorization and consent one could argue that EPA's requirement of particular proprietary technology for a permit to construct or operate a facility constitutes implied authorization and consent. For example, EPA may require a private party to use specific technology pursuant to the national con-

133. 28 U.S.C. § 1498.

tingency plan in a remedial action pursuant to CERCLA. The use of that cleanup technology would appear to be with the authorization and consent of the United States.

Negotiation of a favorable license will be preferable to litigation in the Claims Court over the reasonable royalty rate. Hence, the application of Section 1498 to environmental patents most likely will be limited to situations where a patentee has refused to grant a license.

The terms of Section 1498 do not specifically include states and municipal corporations within the definition of "person." Section 1498 embodies a policy belief that allowing federal agencies to use patented technologies serves the public good. For the same policy, provisions should be extended to states or towns that use a patented technology for environmental protection. However, the status of states and municipal corporations under Section 1498 remains unclear.

Alleged infringers may also avoid liability under the mandatory license provision of Section 308 of the [Clean Air Act]. Section 308 authorizes the Attorney General to seek a district court judgment requiring licensing on reasonable terms where certain conditions exist: (1) The patented invention is needed to achieve emission limitations, (2) No alternative methods are available, and (3) The patent reduces competition or monopolizes it.[138]

The legislative history limits the provision to patented technologies; mandatory licensing of trade secrets is not included. The legislation was intended to avoid the "super-monopoly" that could result from imposing environmental standards [that] necessitated use of patented technology. The statute guarantees all producers in a given field an adequate supply of technology with which to meet the statutory obligations of the CAA.

Commentators have criticized Section 308 as precedent for an onslaught of compulsory licensing provisions. However, Section 308 has never been invoked. The fear of compulsory licensing provisions appears unjustified, at least in the environmental arena. Since a patentee still receives a reasonable royalty for use of her invention, the patent system provides a sufficient incentive for innovation....

... Companies can use intellectual property assets in environmental technology to profit from environmental regulation. However, incentives require proper coordination. Intellectual property managers must be conversant with environmental affairs, because the market for environmental technology is largely defined by laws and regulations. By the same token, environmental managers should consider the existence of licenses, patents, trade secrets, and other intellectual property assets in selecting the best compliance strategies for their companies. Federal and state environmental agencies should develop an awareness of and sensitivity to the effect of governmental activity on the incentives to the public. There is, of course, no guaranteed way of en-

138. 2 U.S.C. §7608.

suring that beneficial technologies replace harmful ones. Nonetheless, increased reliance on intellectual property law can improve environmental protection.

Joshua Sarnoff, *The Patent System and Climate Change**

Over the next few decades, tens of trillions of dollars will be needed for the development and dissemination of a wide range of new technologies to upgrade infrastructure and to mitigate and to adapt to the effects of climate change (climate change technologies). As the Executive Secretary of the United Nations Framework Convention on Climate Change (the UNFCCC) put it, human "survival depends on our improvement of technology." Climate change is expected to cause dramatic changes to weather patterns, to adversely affect health (particularly for vulnerable populations), ecosystems, food production, and water availability, to displace populations and disrupt land and resource ownership, and to interfere with existing patterns of satisfying basic human needs. The amount of greenhouse gas emissions and the extent of climate change, as well as the problems that climate change will cause and how well society responds, will depend substantially upon the rapid development and widespread dissemination of a wide variety of new climate change technologies. The availability of substantial public funds and the huge potential private markets will attract new technological development and will encourage patenting (to differing degrees in various industries) in the hopes of appropriating returns. In turn, the costs of climate change mitigation and adaptation measures will depend on whether these climate change technologies are patented, on how they are licensed, and on what technological substitutes are affordably available....

The magnitude and social importance of these developments will place significant stress on the patent system and its use for scientific and technical innovation, technology development, and technology and product transfer and public dissemination. It will also focus attention on the patent system's theoretical justifications and alternatives to the patent system such as public domain treatment, public procurement, and creation of constructed commons. As with other serious global problems, such as access to medicines and the sharing the benefits of biodiversity and of the genomes of pathogenic organisms, climate change raises important human rights concerns. Thus, these issues are likely to bounce among international treaty regimes (through so-called regime shifting) as they arise at different times in different environmental, trade, and intellectual-property treaty fora. At the domestic level, governments and private institutions and actors will be forced to decide whether and what patent rights to grant or seek for climate change-related inventions, and how broadly to license them and what conditions to place on such licenses. Governments will also need to decide what kinds of creative discoveries should be treated as patent eligible inventions, what parameters to adopt for various patentability doctrines, what exceptions to

* Originally published in 16 Virginia Journal of Law & Technology 301 (2011). Reprinted with permission.

create to patent rights, and whether and how to regulate competition and prices in markets for patented climate change technologies.

... The range of technologies having climate effects, or accomplishing mitigation or adaption needs, is staggering. For example, one U.S. study identified hundreds of technologies in various categories, such as "end-use/infrastructure (e.g. transportation), energy supply (e.g. hydrogen), carbon capture-storage (e.g. geologic storage), non-CO_2 GHGs (e.g. methane from landfills), [and] measuring & monitoring capabilities (e.g. oceanic CO_2 sequestration)."[42] A European study identified fifty-one categories of technology, organized by industry sector, or by conservation or pollution reduction goals. Many studies have noted that the need for patents and how they operate may differ dramatically in regard to different kinds of technologies, industry sectors, and users and innovators.

To develop and disseminate the needed technologies, the Cancun Agreement contemplates substantial private funding (and wealth transfers to the developing [world, which will collectively be referred to as the "South"]) of technology development and deployment as well as the consequent creation of intellectual property rights in new technologies.[45] Although governments can play an important role in stimulating innovation and technology diffusion through mechanisms such as public provision of necessary infrastructure, subsidized research, and prioritized public procurement, there are limits to government resources (particularly at local levels), and the public sector "does not always have the resources required to push through new projects independent of the IP-related costs involved."[46] Given the political difficulties of committing to massive expenditures as public obligations, the choice to rely on private markets hardly comes as a surprise.

... [V]arious scholars offered a different international approach to addressing climate change. Specifically, the Hartwell Paper proposed a more indirect approach to mitigating climate change by harnessing coextensive social motivations to adopt carbon-free energy technologies, which will require "very substantially increased investment in innovation in non-carbon energy sources to diversify energy supply technologies."[51] Unlike the predominantly market-driven approach to technology of the Cancun Agreement, the Hartwell Paper recognized that "radical acceleration of decarbonization of economic activity ... will not be quickly or easily deployed [and thus] the primary RDD&D [research, development, demonstration and deployment]

---

42. [Thomas Brewer, Technology Transfer and Climate Change: International Flows, Barriers, and Frameworks, Brookings Global Economy and Development 4 (Draft 1, 2008)] (citing the U.S. Climate Change Technology Program).

45. [See UNFCCC, Draft Decision CP.16, Outcome of the work of the Ad Hoc Working Group on long-term Cooperative Action under the Convention, ¶¶95, 98, 99 (2010), http://unfccc.int/files/meetings/cop_16/application/pdf/cop16_lca.pdf.]

46. Chatham House, IPRs and the Innovation and Diffusion of Climate Technologies, at 3 (2007), http://www.chathamhouse.org.uk/publications/papers/view/-/id/722.

51. [Gwyn Prins et al., The Hartwell Paper: A New Direction for Climate Policy After the Crash of 2009 5 (2010), available at http://eprints.lse.ac.uk/27939.]

will have to be funded from the public purse."[52] The belief in the need for public funding was premised on a conclusion that "it is wrong to assume that a price on carbon can induce the generality of firms to undertake the requisite R&D," given incentives for "leakage" to lower cost or unrestricted carbon-emission markets and "offset games," and because "basic research, development, and demonstration cannot be easily patented ... [and thus] the market has no incentive to fund it."[54]

It remains to be seen whether the Hartwell Paper scholars are correct that insufficient private technology investment funds will flow relative to climate change technology development and dissemination needs. Existing government funding for climate change technology development and diffusion, although increasing, is certainly unlikely to be sufficient for the task....

Further, as recognized over fifty years ago by Fritz Machlup in his seminal report to the U.S. Congress, the patent system is only one of many, potentially overlapping alternative approaches to innovation, and the comparative advantage of patents to the alternatives is unproven and uncertain.[59] When insufficient market incentives exist for private development of technology in competitive markets,

> society has several choices: to make research grants or subsidies to selected industries or special private organizations; to promise prizes or bonuses for useful inventions made by private individuals or groups; to promise monopoly grants through patents; or to maintain governmental research agencies. It seems that the largest countries have adopted more than one of these possibilities.[60]

... Past proposals for international regulation of patent law in the context of climate change have included: (1) imposing new restrictions on patent eligible subject matter for climate change technologies ...; (2) revising requirements for disclosure (to increase information), application processing (to reduce processing times), and patentability requirements such as the obviousness threshold (either to promote or to restrict such patents); (3) reducing rights and/or patent terms, including altering infringement standards or creating exceptions and limitations; and (4) addressing licensing, misuse, and antitrust concerns, including imposing compulsory licensing regimes. Even those who foresee widespread international licensing of new climate change technologies at reasonable prices have argued for strict policing of antitrust laws to assure that vertical integration does not prevent competition, for mandatory cross-licensing to assure technology development, and for compulsory licensing to protect businesses in developing countries that are capable of manufacturing such technologies....

52. Id. at 24.

54. Id. at 33.

59. [See S. Subcomm. on Patents, Trademarks, and Copyrights, Comm. on the Judiciary, 85th Cong., An Economic Review of the Patent System 56, 62, 80 (Comm. Print 1958) (prepared by Fritz Machlup).]

60. Id. at 17.

III. Critical National and Public Policy Levers to Mitigate the Adverse Effects of Patents for Climate Change Technologies

National governments will face continuing and substantial domestic pressures to limit the scope and costs of patent rights in order to assure access to climate change technologies at affordable prices, to develop local capacity, and to attract competitive invention and investment from countries other than those where the patented technology is controlled. The obvious alternatives to refusals to license technologies (particularly if owned by foreign firms) for further research and development or to high prices for access to those technologies are to regulate the activities directly by adopting compulsory licenses or by imposing direct price regulations. The indirect alternatives are to regulate such conduct by treating restrictive licensing as a competition violation (i.e., as an abuse of dominant position) or by treating the patents themselves as essential facilities. These approaches will be highly controversial and may threaten substantial trade retaliation from the countries that have promised to transfer wealth and technology to the developing South, or may prompt technology and investment withholding by businesses in the developed North. Such direct or indirect regulation, moreover, may be largely ineffective in regard to assuring transfers of tacit knowledge. Compulsory licensing, price regulation, and antitrust treatment have been repeatedly resisted by the United States and (somewhat less so) other developed countries, particularly in foreign markets where they do not bear the costs but reap the benefits of exports. The developing South may be unwilling to resist such trade pressures, even if the threats and trade sanctions would be found illegal under WTO rules.

The six measures proposed below seek to avoid resort to these highly controversial approaches, although compulsory licensing, competition policy, and price controls will remain available and may operate in the background to induce broader and lower-cost voluntary licensing behaviors. Rather, the measures focus on achieving the greatest benefits for climate change innovation in both the developed and developing world in a manner that is generally recognized as consistent with existing international intellectual property treaty law. These measures thus promise a greater likelihood of being employed to develop the needed technologies while controlling the costs of supplying access to them and of transferring them to the developing South, particularly when the patent owners are unwilling to voluntarily adopt widespread and low-cost licensing approaches, generally or for Southern markets that are lacking in sufficient funds or innovation capacities.

Specifically, the first set of proposed measures focuses on protecting basic research and sequential innovation and use by assuring that significant additional creativity beyond basic scientific discovery is needed for patent eligibility, and by assuring robust experimental use, reverse engineering, and inter-operability exceptions to permit basic science to proceed unfettered by patent rights. They do so in order to allow scientific knowledge to flow to the developing South, and to permit downstream development and use of the creative patented technologies that do result. The next set of proposed measures seeks to assure that upstream owners of patented climate change technologies retain various rights when licensing their commercial development, so as to assure continued R&D and low-cost access. These measures include retaining power to authorize experimental and "humanitarian" uses for climate mitigation and adaptation needs, to change the default resort from exclusive to non-exclusively licensing unless the former has been demonstrated to be needed, and to clarify "march in" criteria to facilitate access when patent owners or their licensees fail to make the technology accessible at affordable costs. The final recommendation is to make greater use of exhaustion (parallel importation) of patented technologies, preferably on a regional rather than a full international level, when patent owners or their licensees voluntarily supply certain ... markets at low costs to achieve wider diffusion of the climate change technologies.

The basic premise of these measures is that they will best preserve the ability for both developed and developing countries to generate the needed, creative technologies and will be easier and less problematic for both the North and the South to adopt. By limiting the grant of rights to more creative applications, as well as by making clear that the grant of the patent does not include the right to prevent research and sequential innovation, inter-operation, or transfers across jurisdictions, the most serious concerns for technology development, access, and capacity building can be avoided. By retaining ownership powers and by clarifying the grounds for exercising them, both public funders and private patent owners can minimize the concerns over adversely effecting ex ante investment and innovation incentives that attend ex post government regulation to accomplish the same goals. Investors and inventors will know the limits of the patent rights, and can decide in advance whether the rewards warrant the limitations and risks. Such measures thus will be both simpler and fairer than imposing ex post regulatory constraints on broader ex ante grants of rights, as the limits will have been effectively consented to by the funding recipients and patent licensees.

Further, adopting such measures for climate change technologies should be less controversial and less threatening to the various patent system incentives than they would be for pharmaceuticals and other medical technologies. In the access to medicines context, massive investments are typically needed to recoup the costs of clinical trials (rather than of invention creation activity), copying costs are minimal, and first-mover advantages may therefore by insufficient to recoup investments. It also bears noting that investors and inventors do not need to recoup *all* of the positive spillovers of the inventions that they create and patent in order to be sufficiently motivated to invest time and effort in making them. As Mark Lemley has cogently noted, "[t]he effort to permit inventors to capture the full social value of their invention—and the rhetoric of free riding in intellectual property more generally—are fundamentally misguided. In no other area of the economy do we permit the full internalization of social benefits."[188]

188. Mark A. Lemley, Property, Intellectual Property, and Free Riding, 83 Texas Law Review 1031, 1032 (2005).

A. Broad Patent Eligibility Exclusions for Basic R&D to Direct Innovation to More Creative Applications

... For centuries and around the world, research discoveries of basic scientific principles, natural phenomena, and abstract ideas have been and remain excluded from the patent system. Originating in Europe, these exclusions for science, nature, and ideas were premised both on religious beliefs and deontological moral concerns, and corresponded to utilitarian beliefs that society was better off when scientific and natural discoveries were widely shared and free from patent property rights....

In the modern era, however, the scope of patentable subject matter has continuously expanded. Particularly regarding biotechnology, concerns have been raised that broad, "upstream" patent rights on scientific, natural, and abstract discoveries ... are being created that dominate and prevent too much sequential innovation. Further, such patent incentives may not be needed to fund and motivate these upstream discoveries, so granting patent rights only imposes corresponding social welfare losses.... Unless effectively checked, the expansion of patent eligible subject matter to science, nature, and ideas may prevent or unduly delay important climate change-related discoveries and their development into needed technologies. Accordingly, both the developed North and the developing South may wish to adopt expansive exclusions from patent eligible subject matter in regard to climate change science and mitigation and adaptation technologies....

... TRIPS specifically authorizes exclusions from patent eligible subject matter on environmental grounds under Article 27.2:

> Members may exclude from patentability inventions, the prevention within their territory of the commercial exploitation of which is necessary to protect *ordre public* or morality, including to protect human, animal or plant life or health or *to avoid serious prejudice to the environment*, provided that such exclusion is not made merely because the exploitation is prohibited by their law.[206]

Presumably, climate change is a now recognized as a sufficiently serious problem that excluding patentability for environmental sound technologies that make significant contributions to climate change would help to avoid serious prejudice to the environment within the meaning of Article 27.2....

However, an entirely different approach may be adopted that is clearly TRIPS-compatible and may provide greater protection against patent rights that would dominate sequential innovation and would tax dissemination of important climate change technologies. This approach is based on adopting a restrictive interpretation of the meaning of "invention" as used in Article 27.1 [to exclude uncreative applications of natural discoveries]....

---

206. Agreement on Trade-Related Aspects of Intellectual Property Rights, Apr. 15, 1994, 33 I.L.M. 81 (December 1993 text) [the TRIPS Agreement].

B. Robust Experiment Use and Inter-Operability Exceptions

Perhaps the greatest concern with patents for new technologies is their ability to impose costs on or preclude basic research and sequential innovation. For this reason, countries around the world typically adopt broad exclusions either for non-commercial and university-based research, or for research that will allow reverse engineering and development of clinical information for regulatory approval of pioneering and generic medical products. To the extent that countries do not already have such exceptions to patent rights in their laws, they may be well advised to adopt them....

The result [of adopting both heightened eligibility requirements and experimental use and regulatory approval exceptions] is likely to be greater technology transfer as well as greater development of local scientific and innovation capacity in the developing South.

C. Retained Research and Humanitarian Licensing Powers

In contrast to the previous measures, which focus on changing legal doctrines to protect basic research, sequential innovation, and inter-operability, public and private ownership powers and their exercise through contractual measures can largely accomplish the same goals. As Keith Maskus and Ruth Okediji have noted, contractual arrangements "govern the majority of inter-firm and intra-firm transfers of knowledge and technology in both domestic and international markets."[267] Thus, even without broad statutory experimental use and inter-operability exceptions from patent infringement rights, research tool and platform technology owners need not restrictively and expensively license or price their patented technologies. Private patent owners, or government agencies that permit private entities to take title to government funded inventions, could condition the grant or licensing of those ownership rights on contractual commitments not to enforce patents against experimental uses or uses for inter-operability purposes. Thus universities ... are increasingly choosing to reserve rights to enable continued experimentation and to "ensure broad access to research tools."[269] Without resorting to an explicit change to patent law doctrines regarding the scope of granted rights or limits on infringement, these measures could produce a contractual "research commons" through "common-use" licensing. This commons could extend not only to patented technologies but also to materials and databases of information, and for purposes of reverse engineering and inter-operability.

... These governmental and non-profit sector policies can also signal the private commercial sector to take similar actions....

---

267. Keith E. Maskus & Ruth Okediji, Intellectual Property Rights and International Technology Transfer to Address Climate Change: Risks, Opportunities and Policy Options 8 (2010).

269. See, e.g., National Research Council, Managing University Intellectual Property in the Public Interest 6 (2010) ... (discussing California Institute of Technology et al., In the Public Interest: Nine Points to Consider in Licensing University Technology 2 (Mar. 6, 2007) ...).

D. Presumptions of Non-Exclusive Licensing

Commentators have proposed various administrative and judicial powers to compel non-exclusive licensing. Non-exclusive licensing has proven much less problematic than exclusive licensing, in that it permits widespread use of the patented technology and the technology is more likely to be competitively priced, even if such licensing does raise the costs of (or "tax") uses for research that would otherwise be free under broad experimental use exceptions. But regulatory power to compel non-exclusive licensing is not needed if the default condition for acquiring title or licensing rights in government-funded and private inventions is to authorize non-exclusive licensing, except when it is first demonstrated that exclusive licensing is actually needed for commercialization. Accordingly, various commentators have recommended that developing countries ... should require that patents not be exclusively licensed unless it is clear in particular cases that doing so is necessary for commercialization....

E. Expansive and Clearer March-In Criteria

Under the Bayh-Dole Act, federal agencies granting title to federally funded inventions retain the statutory right:

> to require the contractor, an assignee, or exclusive licensee of a subject invention to grant a nonexclusive, partially exclusive, or exclusive license in any field of use to a responsible applicant or applicants, upon terms that are reasonable under the circumstances, and if the contractor, assignee, or exclusive licensee refuses such request, to grant such a license itself, if the Federal agency determines that such—
>
> ... (2) action is necessary to alleviate health or safety needs which are not reasonably satisfied by the contractor, assignee, or their licensees; or
>
> ... (3) action is necessary to meet requirements for public use specified by Federal regulations and such requirements are not reasonably satisfied by the contractor, assignee, or licensees....[300]

The power to march in, however, is subject to burdensome administrative and judicial appeals procedures....

This statutorily retained power to march in to compel third-party licensing or to directly authorize such licensing is highly controversial, as it can effectively act as an ex post regulatory compulsory license.... But unlike compulsory licensing, march-in rights are agreed to ex ante by federal funding recipients and in theory should be less objectionable when exercised. The problem arises because of the lack of clarity and foreseeability regarding the criteria on which and circumstances in which march-in power will actually be exercised.

Federal funding agencies thus [sh]ould develop such criteria up front....

---

300. 35 U.S.C. § 203(a).

F. Expansive Exhaustion (Parallel Importation) Criteria

Given the global nature of technologies and problems to be addressed, disputes over patent exhaustion are very likely to arise in the climate change context.* [Under] Article 6 of the TRIPS Agreement ... nations will remain free to provide either or both international and domestic exhaustion effect to patented goods sold in foreign and domestic markets, permitting low-cost resale and transfers from markets or market segments where patent holders have voluntarily placed goods on sale. To be fully effective, however, such domestic laws may also need to supersede contractual restrictions that would seek to avoid the exhaustion principles that would otherwise take effect, such as by limiting authority for certain kinds of sales or by treating contracts as licenses rather than sales....

Nevertheless, adopting such broad international exhaustion approaches may not be good policy, either for the developed North or for the developing South. First, as with ex post compulsory licensing, adopting such exhaustion selectively for particular technologies would likely invite trade retaliation. Further, aggressive international exhaustion doctrines may ultimately impose greater costs than benefits, not only based on their potential to diminish ex ante innovation incentives but also for the potential to acquire patented technologies at lower costs. The empirical literature on international exhaustion suggests that its economic effects are highly complex and heterogeneous across technologies....

Further, although parallel imports may help countries to obtain specific technologies at affordable prices, it may also exert a more general upward pressure on prices for the same and other needed technologies, precisely because suppliers can no longer rely on price arbitrage in different markets. For this reason, permissive regional exhaustion approaches should be found preferable to full international exhaustion. Such regional exhaustion permits arbitrage but only across relatively similar markets having comparable market structures and abilities to pay. It thereby permits price discrimination globally in ways that should better avoid diminishing both ex ante innovation incentives and willingness to supply markets in the first instance....

Eric L. Lane, *Consumer Protection in the Eco-Mark Era: A Preliminary Survey and Assessment of Anti-Greenwashing Activity and Eco-Mark Enforcement*†

We stand at the dawn of the Eco-mark Era—a period in which green branding, advertising environmentally friendly products and services, and touting sustainable business practices will be pervasive and profitable. The question is no longer whether

* [Under the exhaustion (or first-sale) doctrine, "[t]he unrestricted sale of a patented article, by or with the authority of the patentee, 'exhausts' the patentee's right to control further sale and use of that article by enforcing the patent under which it was first sold." In other words, the purchaser of a patented product acquires "the rights of any owner of personal property, including the right to use it, repair it, modify it, discard it, or resell it, subject only to overriding conditions of the sale." Jazz Photo Corp. v. International Trade Comm'n, 264 F.3d 1094 (Fed. Cir. 2001).—Eds.]

† Originally published in 9 John Marshall Review of Intellectual Property Law 742 (2010). Reprinted with permission.

businesses will highlight their sustainable practices and market environmentally friendly products and services, but how they will do so. Firms across industries are cultivating green brands and eco-marks—trademarks, service marks and certification marks that communicate environmentally friendly products, services or practices—to attract a growing segment of environmentally conscious consumers that are demanding green products and services.

However, the rise of green branding brings with it the temptation of "greenwashing," making false or misleading claims regarding environmentally friendly products, services or practices. Instances of greenwashing appear to be on the rise, and may already be a widespread problem. Fortunately, anti-greenwashing activity is becoming more common and effective as both public entities and private citizens take on the transgressors that engage in this behavior and hold them accountable.

In addition the prevalence of green brands and eco-marks has led to a spike in trademark litigation between clean tech companies and green organizations. In such cases, one party typically accuses another of trademark infringement by using a similar mark or some other false indication of source or sponsorship to create consumer confusion. While these lawsuits are nominally between two non-consumer entities, consumers nonetheless are affected by the outcomes of such disputes.

At the center of this storm of green branding, greenwashing and eco-mark activity stands the green consumer, whose purchasing decisions are motivated by a desire to preserve the environment. How is the green consumer faring in the Eco-mark Era? After all, although green branding is big business for the brand owners, it is the consumer whom trademark law is intended to protect. Whether a consumer is motivated by a particular level of quality, certain product features, safety concerns, or just a desire to use the same iPhone app as all of his friends, trademark law allows that consumer to be confident that the product or service he chooses is the one he wants, not a cheap imitation.

In the eco-mark context, the green consumer is motivated by a desire to consume responsibly, preserve the environment and factor the well being of our planet into her purchasing decisions. Whether one calls it morality, social activism or something else, the collective purchasing decisions of the growing number of green consumers could affect all of us as the behavior of society as a whole shifts in an attempt to curb global warming. Thus, the green consumer protection context is arguably more critical than consumer protection generally and attempts to deceive the green consumer may have a disproportionate effect on society....

Greenwashing, a term created by fusing "green" with "whitewash," means making false or misleading claims regarding environmentally friendly products, services or practices. As the dangers of climate change settle into the public consciousness and the number of consumers demanding environmentally friendly products and sustainable practices continues to grow, more brand owners become tempted to make lazy, unsubstantiated green claims, try to deceive green-leaning consumers or engage in other forms of eco-mark abuse to profit from this market. Instances of greenwashing appear to be on the rise, with some reports indicating it is already a widespread problem. TerraChoice Environmental Marketing Inc. ("TerraChoice"), a marketing agency, published a report initially called the "Six Sins of Greenwashing" and later revised to include a seventh sin.[33] The original TerraChoice report found that, of over 1,000 self-declared "green" products reviewed, all but one engaged in some form of greenwash by committing at least one of the sins. A British government agency, the Advertising Standards Authority ("ASA"), has seen complaints about U.K. advertisements making environmental claims nearly quadruple in a recent one-year period.[35]

But what exactly does greenwashing comprise? What is it that consumers and groups like TerraChoice are seeing in the marketplace that concerns them, and in connection with which products is it occurring? Instances of greenwashing typically involve products for which energy efficiency or fuel consumption are big selling points and product differentiators. These include products such as energy zapping home appliances, laptop batteries, gas guzzling automobiles and car tires. Another area subject to greenwash is products that many consumers fear contain dangerous chemicals or toxins, such as household cleaning products, paint or personal care items.

The TerraChoice report provides a definition of greenwashing sins and a useful breakdown of the common forms of greenwash. Broadly speaking, committing a sin consists of making an environmental claim that is either "demonstrably false" or misleading. The report breaks the sins into categories: (1) the sin of the hidden trade-off, (2) the sin of no proof of an environmental claim, (3) the sin of a vague environmental claim, (4) the sin of an irrelevant environmental claim, (5) the sin of the lesser of two evils and (6) the sin of fibbing.[41]

The sin of the hidden trade-off consists of promoting one particular green attribute of a product while ignoring other aspects of the product or its life cycle that may not benefit, or actually harm, the environment. The sin of no proof occurs when a claim of environmental benefit cannot be substantiated by the consumer through easily accessible information. A vague environmental claim is either ill-defined or overly broad such that consumers cannot understand what it means, e.g., "natural" or "chemical free" products. An irrelevant environmental claim may be true but is unimportant or unhelpful, such as the claim that a product does not contain chlorofluorocarbons ("CFCs"), which were banned almost 30 years ago. The sin of the lesser of two evils arises when a green claim may be true, but is made about a category of product that has an adverse environmental impact. Examples are organic cigarettes

33. [See Terrachoice Environmental Marketing, The Seven Sins of Greenwashing: Environmental Claims in Consumer Markets, at i (2009, available at http://sinsofgreenwashing.org/.]

35. See Advertising Standards Authority, Compliance Report: Environmental Claims Survey 2008, at 5 (2008), available at http://www.asa.org.uk/Resource-Centre/Reports-and-surveys.aspx....

41. [The seventh, later-added sin is the "sin of false labels," where a product "through either words or images, gives the impression of third-party endorsement where no such endorsement exists." See Sins of Greenwashing, supra note 33.]

or "green" herbicides. The sin of fibbing simply means that the claim is false and cannot be confirmed.

The U.S. Federal Trade Commission ("FTC") writes and publishes "Green Guides,"[49] which are instructive for both brand owners and consumers in assessing claims of environmental benefits. The Green Guides provide that such a claim "should be presented in a way that makes clear whether the environmental attribute or benefit being asserted refers to the product, the product's packaging, a service or to a portion or component of the product, package or service."[50] Claims should not overstate the environmental benefit, either expressly or by implication.[51] The relative specificity or generalization is a critical factor in determining the deceptiveness of an environmental claim, and the Green Guides warn against claims of general environmental benefits:

> It is deceptive to misrepresent, directly or by implication, that a product, package or service offers a general environmental benefit. Unqualified general claims of environmental benefit are difficult to interpret, and depending on their context, may convey a wide range of meanings to consumers. In many cases, such claims may convey that the product, package or service has specific and far-reaching environmental benefits [when that is not the case].[52]

Encouragingly, the recent rise in greenwashing has created a flood of green skepticism, and anti-greenwashing activity is increasingly visible and effective. In addition to the TerraChoice report and the FTC Green Guides, other detailed information about sustainable products, services and business practices is increasingly available to the public [on the internet]. Web sites such as ecolabelling.org provide independent verification and analysis of logos and labels that purport to communicate that products have met environmental standards.

Moreover, anti-greenwashing forces are well-informed, highly mobilized and very vocal. Notable transgressions and false claims instantly reach millions of concerned consumers through the green blogosphere. Green marketing expert Richard Seireeni has coined a term for this phenomenon, which is reflected in the title of his recent book, The Gort Cloud. In The Gort Cloud, Seireeni describes the "unorganized but interconnected network" that forms a community of like-minded eco-savvy individuals and organizations.[59] This community comprises, e.g., providers of green products and services, government agencies, non-governmental organizations, certifying organizations, green news organizations, green search engines, social networks, "trendspotter" web sites such as TreeHugger, advocacy groups, bloggers and green lifestyle movements. The Gort Cloud can make or break a company's green branding efforts; messages spread through the network can create a public relations nightmare

49. See Guides for the Use of Environmental Marketing Claims, 16 C.F.R. § 260.1 (2010).

50. Id. § 260.6(b).

51. Id. § 260.6(c).

52. Id. § 260.7(a).

59. [Richard Seireeni, The Gort Cloud: The Invisible Force Powering Today's Most Visible Green Brands 288–89 (2008).]

for a company that engages in greenwashing and attach a long-lasting stigma to a transgressor.[61]

In the legal arena, both public entities and private citizens are taking on greenwashing, and companies that engage in this behavior are increasingly being held accountable by consumers and governments acting on behalf of their green citizen consumers. The FTC uses its "Green Guides" to decide whether marketing claims regarding green products are valid or are deemed false advertising and may pursue transgressors. Government agencies around the world are using their investigative and enforcement powers to expose and punish greenwashers. These public enforcement actions tend to involve the "sins" of greenwashing including environmental claims that are misleading or cannot be substantiated. In addition, some governmental agencies run environmental or energy efficiency certification programs and police them to ensure their standards continue to be met by businesses that participate in the programs.

Courts are more aware of greenwashing and are allowing private lawsuits that target such transgressors to go forward.[67] In the courtroom, greenwashing is most appropriately classified, and typically litigated, as a species of false advertising. Greenwashing claims include federal causes of action under the Lanham Act, such as unfair competition claims under Section 43(a) and, in particular, Section 43(a)(1)(B) false advertising claims.[68] Greenwashing is also prosecuted under state consumer protection statutes and unfair competition and unfair business practices laws, as well as breach of warranty and unjust enrichment. Typically, these cases are consumer class actions where the class members bought a product allegedly because of false or misleading advertising of an environmental benefit. One consistent theme of private consumer greenwashing cases is the accusation that the performance levels or environmental benefits advertised cannot be achieved under normal operating conditions. Another common thread is the charge that a brand owner misrepresents its own green certification program as that of an independent, objective third party.

Combatting Greenwashers

Government agencies are paying more attention to green advertising claims. Examples include the FTC in the U.S., the ASA in the U.K. and the Australian Competition and Consumer Commission ("ACCC"). These consumer watchdogs provide a

---

61. See id. at 6–7 (detailing public relation issues encountered by companies such as Nestle, Proctor & Gamble, and BP).

67. See, e.g., Koh v. S.C. Johnson & Son, Inc., No. C-09-00927 RMW, 2010 WL 94265, at *3 (N.D. Cal. Jan. 6, 2010) (denying a corporate defendant's motion to dismiss in a greenwashing case brought by consumers).

68. See 15 U.S.C. § 1125(a):

(1) Any person who, on or in connection with any goods or services, or any container for goods, uses in commerce any word, term, name, symbol, or device, or any combination thereof, or any false designation of origin, false or misleading description of fact, or false or misleading representation of fact, which— … (B) in commercial advertising or promotion, misrepresents the nature, characteristics, qualities, or geographic origin of his or her or another person's goods, services, or commercial activities, shall be liable in a civil action by any person who believes that he or she is or is likely to be damaged by such act.

valuable notice function by setting guidelines—such as the FTC's Green Guides—that advertisers can review to stay informed of the parameters of permissible activity and adjust their marketing messages to stay in compliance. They also serve an investigative and enforcement function. Agencies such as these have pursued many advertisers and ruled against several purportedly green advertisements.[76]

The ASA, in particular, has made some notable rulings in recent years. In 2007 the British consumer watchdog required that the automaker Lexus pull an ad claiming that its hybrid SUV was "the world's first high performance hybrid SUV … [having] category-leading low CO_2 emissions."[77] The ad also included the phrase "High Performance. Low Emissions. Zero Guilt." The ASA found the ad misleading because it falsely implied that "the car caused little or no harm to the environment." The ASA also found that the ad's fine print was not prominent enough for consumers to read. This public enforcement action was a victory for [consumers interested in health and sustainability] and any other consumer considering buying the Lexus hybrid SUV for its purportedly environmentally friendly features.

Similarly, an ACCC probe forced Goodyear to admit that its Eagle LS2000 tire does not live up to claims made on the company's Australian web site that the tire is "environmentally-friendly," has "minimal environmental impact," improves fuel economy, and is produced by a process that results in reduced carbon dioxide emissions.[81] As a result of the ACCC investigation, Goodyear admitted that it could not substantiate these claims and deemed them false and misleading [and offered] a partial refund to anyone who purchased the tire during the time period these claims were on its web site.

In the U.S., a deal between the federal government and LG Electronics is another anti-greenwashing success story and a good example of how certification marks are supposed to work for the consumer. The case involved the U.S. government's Energy Star program, which seeks to aid investment in energy efficient products by providing information that consumers and investors can use to research and compare green product or project choices.[85] The program communicates product approval to consumers via the Energy Star certification mark. The U.S. Environmental Protection Agency ("EPA") owns a U.S. certification mark registration for its Energy Star design and works with the U.S. Department of Energy ("DOE") and manufacturers to award the Energy Star certification to products that meet particular energy savings standards.

---

76. E.g., Press Release, Federal Trade Commission, FTC Announces Actions Against Kmart, Tender and Dyna-E Alleging Deceptive 'Biodegradable' Claims (June 9, 2009), available at http://www.ftc.gov/opa/2009/06/kmart.shtm.

77. Advertising Standards Authority, ASA Adjudications on Lexus Ltd (May 23, 2007), http://www.asa.org.uk/asa/adjudications/Public/TF_ADJ_42574.htm.

81. Press Release, Australia Competition & Consumer Commission, Goodyear Tyres Apologises, Offers Compensation for Unsubstantiated Environmental Claims (June 26, 2008), available at http://www.accc.gov.au/content/index. phtml?itemId=833219.

85. See About Energy Star, http://www.energystar.gov/index.cfm?c=about.ab_index.

Many of LG's refrigerator models are Energy Star certified. However, ten of the models that had received the Energy Star certification evidently listed erroneous energy usage measurements on their labels. As it turned out, the refrigerators used more energy than advertised and did not actually meet the efficiency standards required to earn the certification. Clearly, consumer remedies were in order. The DOE and LG reached a settlement agreement to effect appropriate remedies.[91] As an initial measure, LG voluntarily withdrew the subject models from the Energy Star program [and offered] consumers free in-home modifications to improve the energy efficiency of the products [and] a one-time payment to consumers to cover the energy cost difference between the actual energy use of the product and the amount stated on the original label....

This is a good example of a certification program functioning to protect the consumer and combat greenwashing. The certifying organization, in this case the U.S. government, actively policed the companies using the mark and demanded remedial measures when those companies' products were not up to snuff. Public investigation of and enforcement against greenwashing, of which abuse of certification marks is a part, is making a difference because government agencies have the authority and the resources to shut down and alter the offending activity.

A second avenue for combating greenwashing is the private court action. These lawsuits ... often take the form of class actions whereby a class of consumers who purchased a particular product or class of products seeks recovery for alleged economic damages. In the greenwashing context, those damages are allegedly a result of the defendant's deceptive advertising of an environmental benefit of the product or class of products. Greenwashing legal claims, then, are a particular subset of false advertising that comprise claims under various state and federal U.S. consumer protection statutes, unfair competition and business practices laws and traditional theories of recovery such as breach of warranty and unjust enrichment.

Two lawsuits targeting the Honda Civic Hybrid, an individual action in state court and a federal class action, have achieved some success in combating allegedly deceptive advertising claims and forcing remedial action by the advertiser. Both cases highlight the disparities between the EPA's estimated automobile mileage data and the actual road figures and the question of whether car owners can adjust their driving habits to bridge the gap.

[The individual plaintiff] brought state and federal warranty claims and California state false advertising and deceptive practices claims relating to statements in Honda's Civic Hybrid brochures that diverge sharply from what [he] was told about driving habits and fuel efficiency. The brochure tells drivers that they do not have to do "anything special" to get "terrific gas mileage" and instructs them to "[j]ust drive the Hybrid like [one] would a conventional car and save on fuel bills." [On appeal], Cal-

---

91. Agreement Between the U.S. Dep't of Energy and LG Electronics, U.S. Dep't of Energy-LG Electronics U.S.A., Inc., Jan. 14, 2008, available at http://www.energystar.gov/ia/partners /manuf_res/DOE_LG_SettlementAgreement.pdf.

ifornia's 4th District Court of Appeal [ruled] that [the plaintiff] could go forward on the deceptive practices and misleading advertising claims [and] that a jury could find that the statements in the Honda brochure could mislead a reasonable consumer.[115] ... Accordingly, the case was remanded ... for further proceedings ... under the California Consumer Legal Remedies Act and California Unfair Competition Law, the two causes of action relating to deceptive advertising.

... Turning from cars to cleaning supplies, another green consumer class action has targeted the classic household cleaner, Windex, for alleged deceptive advertising. In March 2009, Wayne Koh filed a class action suit in federal court in U.S. District Court for the Northern District of California against SC Johnson & Son, Inc., accusing the maker of Windex of misleading consumers about the "environmental safety and soundness" of the cleaning product. The complaint states several California state law claims relating to unfair competition, false advertising, unlawful business practices and consumer protection violations.

At issue is the company's use of its Greenlist trademark [pictured right], and in particular, its placement of the mark on the Windex product labels. According to the complaint, the reverse side of the product label states, "Greenlist is a rating system that promotes the use of environmentally responsible ingredients." The complaint alleges that the Greenlist mark and accompanying statement falsely imply that the Greenlist designation is administered by a neutral third party when, in fact, it is owned by SC Johnson. Koh states that the use of the term "Greenlist" by environmental groups to designate environmentally friendly products and programs suggests that SC Johnson chose the term with the intent to convey third party approval. Moreover, SC Johnson is representing that Windex is made with natural and environmentally safe ingredients, the complaint states, while the company has not changed the ingredients of the cleaning product. According to the complaint, those ingredients include ethylene glycol n-hexyl ether, which is "not naturally derived and poses serious danger, including death, if ingested by wildlife and small children." The complaint further alleges that products bearing the Greenlist mark contain some of the same "non-natural toxic chemicals harmful to the environment and animals" as SC Johnson products without the label.

Whether SC Johnson truly is greening its cleaning products remains to be seen.... In January 2010 the court denied [SC Johnson's] motion [to dismiss] and held that Mr. Koh's allegations were sufficient to create a question of fact as to whether the Greenlist label was deceptive. As to the accusations about the Greenlist label, the brief explanation of the Greenlist program on the product label seems to be at least literally true.... It just happens that the system was developed and implemented by the maker of the product, not the government or a third party organization....*

115. See Paduano v. Am. Honda Motor Co., 169 Cal. App. 4th 1453, 1470 (Cal. Ct. App. 2009).

* [SC Johnson subsequently settled the lawsuit, agreeing to remove the Greenlist mark from its products.—Eds.]

The Rise of Eco-Mark Litigation

... Though trademarks' (and, necessarily, eco-marks') original and core purpose is to protect consumers, they are, of course, very important to the companies and organizations that own the marks and build valuable brands in and around them. Accordingly, it is no surprise that the rise of green branding in the Eco-mark Era has spawned a contemporaneous increase in trademark litigation between clean tech companies and organizations. While these lawsuits are nominally between two non-consumer entities, the green consumer nonetheless is affected by such disputes.

... The Biodegradable Products Institute (BPI) is a New York-based organization that promotes the use and recycling of biodegradable polymeric materials. BPI has a labeling program to certify plastic products that will safely and completely biodegrade and compost in accordance with the organization's standards. As with other certification marks, companies apply to BPI to have their products reviewed and, if the products pass muster, the companies can affix BPI's label to them. In 2003, BPI got a federal registration for its Compostable certification mark [pictured right] for polymeric products. According to the certificate of registration, BPI's mark certifies that "the plastic products will compost quickly, completely and safely."

In June of 2008, BPI sued several individuals operating EcoVision Alternatives (EcoVision), a Burlingame, California company that makes biodegradable bags and food containers, in federal court in Los Angeles for federal and state trademark infringement, counterfeiting and unfair competition.[247] The complaint alleged that EcoVision infringed BPI's certification mark by selling bags and containers that display the Compostable mark and by stating on its web site that its products are "BPI certified" when EcoVision never applied to BPI's labeling program and the products were not certified.

According to the complaint, this was not the first instance of infringement by the EcoVision crowd. The complaint stated that EcoVision wrongfully used BPI's certification mark previously when the company was operating under the name Biosphere Alternatives (Biosphere). At the time, BPI contacted Biosphere to ask them to stop using the mark and subsequently sent a cease and desist letter. BPI alleged that EcoVision was acting with full knowledge of its wrongdoing and malicious intent and therefore accused the company of willful infringement. The counterfeiting claim was a bit unusual for a certification mark infringement suit; counterfeiting is more typical where the infringing goods are high end consumer products like Rolex watches or Gucci handbags.... But BPI's motivation for bringing that claim is clear—in the case of willful use of a counterfeit mark, the federal trademark statute provides for a substantial damages award.[253]

247. Biodegradable Prod. Inst. v. Le, No. 08-cv-03661-FMC-VBK (June 4, 2008).

253. See 15 U.S.C. § 1117(c) ("Statutory damages for use of counterfeit marks.... (2) if the court finds that the use of the counterfeit mark was willful, not more than $2,000,000 per counterfeit mark per type of goods or services sold, offered for sale, or distributed, as the court considers just.").

Happily for green consumers, … this action … ended in an injunction. In December of 2008, the case was dismissed subject to the terms of a stipulated permanent injunction order. The order prohibited EcoVision, Biosphere and the individual defendants from using BPI's Compostable mark or any similar design, placing BPI's name or any similar name on any goods, or suggesting any affiliation with or sponsorship by BPI. This result helps to ensure that consumers can rely on the Compostable certification mark and BPI's approval in choosing products that truly are biodegradable and compostable.…

As green consumers continue to make purchasing decisions based on environmental considerations, it is important that they be able to do so based on complete and accurate product information. To that end, public and private organizations should continue to monitor and expose green brands owners that engage in greenwashing and other eco-mark abuse, and legal action should be taken against transgressors when necessary. Government agency investigations and certification mark enforcement litigation appear to be the most successful mechanisms for protecting the interests of green consumers, and these avenues ought to be used more. Through a combination of vigilance and selective enforcement, we can achieve effective consumer protection in the Eco-mark Era.

Discussion Questions

1. How has government regulation affected the use of intellectual property for sustainable practices? What changes should be made to these laws to better assure effective environmental practices?

2. Do you agree with the Cancun Agreement's primary focus on private, market-based innovation to generate climate-change technologies? What public efforts should be added to Sarnoff's proposals?

3. Are American consumers becoming more demanding in the type of "green" product they purchase? Do you think consumers in other countries have a similar viewpoint?

4. What marketing advice would you give to a firm looking to gain a competitive advantage in the market for "green" products and services?

5. Do you think that the FTC should expand the scope of the Green Guides? What are the advantages and disadvantages of a governmental as opposed to a private, independent third-party certification?

6. What do you think of the "Gort Cloud" as a way to police greenwashing claims? For another example of private greenwashing watchdogs, see Miriam A. Cherry & Judd F. Sneirson, "Chevron, Greenwashing, and the Myth of Green Oil Companies," 2 Washington & Lee Journal of Energy, Climate, and the Environment 133 (2012) (describing convincing spoofs of Chevron's green marketing campaign).

7. Can you think of a better way to police greenwashing?

Appendix

Sustainable Business in Practice

The businesses profiled below have successfully made sustainability a part of their operations. They represent a variety of industries and geographical areas, offering a diverse set of case studies for you to consider as you read the topic-specific materials in the previous chapters.

Matthew Tueth, *Fundamentals of Sustainable Business: A Guide for the Next 100 Years**

This [excerpt] features numerous real-world examples of diverse businesses that have incorporated remarkably effective processes yielding consistent financial, natural world, and social rewards. Although the following collection of profiled organizations is only a small sample of the broad ingenuity and commitment found in this movement, these illustrations will provide interesting and informative examples of the emerging face of sustainable business. Additionally, these real-world cases are snapshots in time compiled in late 2008; continued organizational evolution in each instance is assumed. Hopefully, these assorted descriptions of [triple-top-line] innovation put into practice will inform and inspire new participants who will put forth another wave of fearless transformations that will permeate and fill every business sector.

New Belgium Brewery, Fort Collins, Colorado—Beer Brewery

This mid-sized beer brewery was founded in 1991 by electrical engineer Jeff Lebesch and his wife, social worker Kim Jordan. A full-time sustainability officer position anchors the brewery's commitment to transitioning to sustainable business practices. The company generates 10%–15% of its electricity by burning the methane produced by bacteria at the on-site water purification plant, and the remaining 85%–90% of electrical demand is mitigated by the purchase of a corresponding amount of wind energy credits. These credits pay the difference between the cost of conventionally generated electricity and the higher cost of wind-generated electricity at a distant Wyoming facility. Brewery employees voted unanimously to use profit-sharing funds to finance the wind energy credits. During the winter months, induction fans draw in cold outside air to help cool the beer. In the warm months, evaporative coolers condition the air in the 55,000 square-feet packaging hall, so the need for energy-intensive refrigeration compressors is avoided. The company researched and imple-

---

mented the most efficient brewing procedures; consequently, it saves over $3,000 per month on off-site energy purchases and reduces carbon emissions by 8 million pounds per year.

Innovation teams have also reduced company water use (in short supply in this part of Colorado) by 50% through various recapture programs. Today, New Belgium uses only four gallons of water to brew a gallon of beer while the industry average is eight to 10 gallons. Spent grain from the brewing process is diverted from the company waste stream and sent to local farms where it is used as animal feed. Natural daylight from numerous windows, light tubes, and light shelves illuminates the indoor brewery facilities, and energy-saving motion sensor switches for electrical lighting are installed in most locations. Natural indirect daylight is diffuse, soft, and easy on the eye, while ... illuminating [a] surprising amount [of] surface detail for the employees. The interior walls of the packaging facility are made with locally procured beetle-killed pine lumber. New Belgium contributes 1% of total sales receipts to environmental non-profit organizations. Furthermore, this company gives each employee a new custom-built bike after one year of employment. In order to serve as an accessible business role model, the company offers on-site tours daily and off-site presentations as requested by local schools and organizations.

New Seasons Market, Portland, Oregon—Grocery Stores

This locally owned and operated company has nine store locations in the Portland area, nearly 1,800 employees, and an annual revenue of over $37 million. Founded in 1999 by Brian Rohter and Stan Amy, New Seasons Market (NSM) aspires to be the friendliest store in the Portland metro area and specializes in organic and health foods along with a variety of conventional grocery products. All NSM store bakeries are certified organic, and about one-third of the items offered in NSM stores are grown or manufactured in the Pacific Northwest. Plastic grocery bags have never been offered at any of the stores, and in 2008, more than a quarter of its customers received five cents for each grocery bag they brought in for transporting their groceries. Once a week from June through October, each store hosts five to seven local growers who bring in unique produce, homemade cheeses, and microbrew beers.

Each of the nine stores has an employee "green team" that works on continuous improvements that have included cycling and reprocessing systems, energy efficiency, waste reduction, and community and staff education. Ten percent of after-tax profits are donated to various community organizations. Each store provides three volunteers per day to serve shut-in senior citizens for the Meals-On-Wheels program, with three stores using only bicycles in the process. Two full-time nutritionists are hired by the company to teach wellness classes free of charge to all community members. New Season Market also supports their employees by providing loans of $200 to $2,500 for unexpected life situations regardless of the employee's credit history.

Google, Mountain View, California—Internet Information Access

Google was founded in 1998 by Larry Page and Sergey Brin near the southernmost extension of San Francisco Bay in California. This multi-billion dollar publicly-traded corporation provides all types of easily accessible world information via Internet search engines. With nearly 20,000 employees worldwide, Google earns revenue from advertising that is packaged inside various information search engines and services. Google adapts and grows using a loosely formed and flat corporate hierarchy with nearly all employees responsible for many different types of projects. For example, Google engineers spend one day per week working on special projects that particularly interest them, and this freedom of choice has resulted in some of the newer services offered, such as Gmail and Google News. Google work facilities are certainly non-conventional: offices are arranged in clusters of three to four workers and are furnished with couches; bicycles are commonly parked in hallways; workout facilities with exercise machines and shower rooms are standard; ping-pong and rollerblade hockey games are common; free healthy meals and snacks are available throughout the day in community cafeterias; on-site day care, massage, dentistry, and health care services are provided; and maternity and paternity leave is also available to employees.

Most facilities have abundant natural lighting, energy-management software, and evaporative cooling schemes. At the Google world headquarters in Mountain View, CA, leaders have installed a photovoltaic system of over 9,000 solar panels on the top of eight buildings and two carports that generates 30% of peak power demand; this system will pay for itself in 78 months and will continue to provide electricity for decades thereafter. All workers that walk, bike, or commute via mass transit to and from the headquarters complex can participate in a complimentary car-sharing program. Google's commitment to continuous innovation and to maintaining a small business atmosphere that values individuals and their abilities, product performance, and intelligent energy choices bodes well for the long-term future of this highly profitable information heavyweight.

Patagonia, Ventura, California—Outdoor Performance Clothing

In 1970, Chouinard Equipment, the predecessor organization of Patagonia, began championing sustainable business values when it decided to stop producing hard metal pitons for rock-climbing that were disfiguring rock walls and instead to manufacture aluminum climbing chocks that left the rock walls in near pristine condition. Patagonia founder Yvon Chouinard then made the decision to stop producing climbing hardware and to begin the design and production of high-performance outdoor clothing for rock and alpine climbing, backpacking, fly fishing, Nordic skiing, downhill skiing, and hiking. Recent year revenues for Patagonia are in the $250–$300 million range. A few highlights from Patagonia's long legacy of cutting-edge business innovation include the following: the opening of one of the first on-site employee day care centers in the U.S. in 1984, eliminating private offices in the same year to improve employee collaboration and communication, giving 1% of total sales revenue since 1985 to community-centered environmental groups to the tune of over $26 million, educating the public on a different sustainability theme each year by including articles in Patagonia merchandise catalogs and on the company Website, and allowing company employees a paid leave of two months to work for an environmental or sustainability organization of their choice. In 2006, the company began treating its wool products in a patented slow-wash process that eliminates the use of chlorine (toxin) and replaced the use of silver (heavy metal pollutant) for anti-microbial odor control with crushed crab and shrimp shells, with no loss of product performance quality.

Yvon Chouinard *also* understands the value of the people that work for him. He is an avid surfer and has started a custom of extending lunch break time when "surf's up" so employees may hit the waves at the company headquarters located on the Pacific Coast in Ventura, California. Patagonia also has a history of sponsoring numerous employee skiing and climbing trips throughout California and many other parts of the world. Some employees with unique situations enjoy flexible working schedules and job-sharing arrangements. This type of employee support has yielded a fiercely loyal workforce and a reputation for Patagonia as a wonderful place to work. Today, when a position becomes available at one of Patagonia's facilities, literally hundreds of job applications are submitted. But undoubtedly, employee performance expectations are exacting at Patagonia, and only the most productive, imaginative, and committed individuals are invited to carry on the extraordinary tradition.

In 2006, Patagonia built a new shipping and distribution center in Reno, Nevada with energy efficiency features that reduced conventional energy consumption by one-third. At the Ventura, California headquarters, [Chouinard purchases] wind energy credits for half of its electrical demand, and he has installed 360 photovoltaic solar panels on-site to produce another 12% of its electrical needs. In addition to the product-of-service take-back system for all worn-out Capilene® garments..., in 1996, Patagonia became one of the first major cotton garment producers to use only organically grown cotton for garments and they found that sales of these items rose 25%. With the financial success of Patagonia throughout the years, the company remains 100% privately owned by Chouinard. He has been approached many times by prospective buyers but has shunned all these lucrative offers. By preserving sole ownership, he has maintained control of Patagonia's legacy of solid profitability and contributing to a healthy natural world and human community.

Timberland, Inc., Stratham, New Hampshire— Footwear and Outdoor Clothing

Started in 1973, this New England-based company primarily manufactures boots and outdoor clothing, and it surpassed $1 billion in sales in 2007. Timberland has reduced energy consumption at its largest facilities by 40% and has *also* substantially reduced the use of toxic solvents and adhesives in its products. The company's distribution center in Ontario, California has a photovoltaic system that generates 60% of the on-site electricity demand. In 2004, Timberland began offering a $3,000 stipend for employees who choose to purchase a hybrid vehicle. The most distinguishing sustainable business project of the company came in 2007 when Timberland introduced its Green Index rating system for many products, which includes a sliding scale of 1–10 for climate impact, hazardous chemicals used, and natural resource consumption (more products were included in this system in 2008). By including the scores with each of Timberland's products, this company's leaders set new standards for environmental transparency to retail customers by providing an at-a-glance product comparison of natural world perturbations.

GoLite LLC, Boulder, Colorado—Outdoor Clothing and Equipment

Company founders Kim and Demetri Coupounas set out in 1998 to produce the best lightweight outdoor clothing and backpacking equipment possible. A task force with a dedicated budget now leads sustainable business initiatives at GoLite. One of their noteworthy accomplishments has been to help establish a regional, multi-company polyester reprocessing center that serves Boulder, Colorado and other Front Range, Colorado communities. Internally, GoLite has developed ... lines of clothing ... produced from 100% reprocessed polyester. Furthermore, ... performance fabric made with activated carbon from waste coconut shells is used for a number of other company' clothing items.

Employees for GoLite who ride bicycles to work can store them inside company buildings and use the showers and locker rooms provided for commuters. Full-time employees are offered one extra week of paid time off per year to volunteer for non-profit environmental organizations to field test company products. Golite also contributes 1% of all revenues to non-profit companies dedicated to natural-area preservation.

Aveda, Blaine, Minnesota—Hair Care, Skin Care, and Makeup Products

Privately founded in 1978 and now owned by Estee Lauder II Companies; Aveda expounds the three components of [the triple-top-line] through its mission statement, and the company has practices and policies that do indeed reflect that commitment. Sold in 26 countries, Aveda hair, skin, and make-up products are manufactured using 100% wind power from 19 wind farms in Minnesota. The corporate headquarters and distribution center are also powered by these wind power sources. Additionally, Aveda evaluates over 600 of its product ingredients for human and environmental safety and requires life-cycle analysis when designing merchandise packaging options. (Life-cycle analysis provides information, among other things that allows Aveda to select the least harmful packaging materials.) Prohibited materials for all products and packaging include polyvinyl chloride (PVC), heavy metals, and virgin forest products. Aveda has entered into some interesting partnerships to ensure product ingredients come from sustainable sources. For example, oil from the fruit of the rare Moroccan argan tree that is used in some skin care products is acquired from a cooperative of Berber women in Morocco. Only fruits fallen on the ground are gathered and processed by the women, with the spent fruit parts given to livestock and the hard shell cases burned as heating fuel. The Berber cooperative is involved in an argan reforestation project for the region and is currently supported by an Aveda two-year grant for new equipment and literacy training. Another indigenous-culture partnership involves the Mardu people of Australia and the responsible harvest of sandalwood, a medium-sized tree with wood that has a pleasurable scent and medicinal qualities. Aveda extracts the active ingredients of the sandalwood using a steam process rather than petrochemical solvents.

Each year in April, Aveda employees worldwide raise money for, and contribute to, various environmental grassroots organizations, such as Greenhouse Network,

Clean Air-Cool Planet, and Gulf Coast Restoration Network. Since 1999, company efforts have donated more than $11 million for these and dozens more non-profit organizations.

Frito-Lay, Plano, Texas—Snack Food Production

This $11 billion per year division of Pepsi-Co Inc. manufactures the familiar Lays, Ruffles, Doritos, Fritos, SunChips, and Cheetos brands of snack chips. Frito-Lay has concentrated efforts on energy and water-system improvements throughout its facilities. A rooftop solar water heater produces two-thirds of the hot water used by the corporate headquarters in Plano, Texas. The Frito-Lay service center in Phoenix, AZ has over 1,000 photovoltaic modules on the roof producing 200 kilowatts of electricity for the facility and is the seventh Frito-Lay distribution center that produces electricity on-site with photovoltaic systems. The Modesto, CA SunChips production center has installed solar-heating concentrators and collectors on the grounds, and this center uses the solar super-heated hot water to heat the facility's cooking oil. In the last ten years, Frito-Lay has saved over $40 million in energy savings from energy-efficiency improvements that cut electrical consumption by 22% and fuel consumption by 24%. Since 1999, this company has decreased its overall water consumption by 35% (1 billion gallons saved) by adapting various water-reclamation techniques in production processes nationwide.

Burgerville, Vancouver, Washington—Fast Food Restaurants

This Pacific Northwest fast-food company has 39 restaurants and 1,500 employees scattered throughout the states of Oregon and Washington. All of the energy consumed at the eateries and the corporate headquarters facility is offset by a corresponding amount of wind-power energy credits from a number of Washington locations. One of the most impressive accomplishments is an ongoing food-waste composting operation at each of the 39 restaurants with the rich compost returned to farms and gardens in the area.

This organization has developed an impressive list of regional food sources that supply the major part of its menu items. Beef is sourced from a co-op of family ranches near Antelope, Oregon, with no growth hormones or antibiotics given to the cattle. This regional year-round arrangement allows the company to serve meat that has never been frozen and to reduce food transportation costs. Buns and breads are baked by a large family-owned bakery, eliminating the need for preservatives and again minimizing food transportation costs. All cheese, sourced from a century-old co-op of small dairy farms, is free of hormones and antibiotics. These dairy ranchers all fence cattle from sensitive riparian corridors along streams and rivers and protect the integrity of salmon habitats. Premium Walla Walla sweet yellow onions are procured from the rolling hills in the Walla Walla area of southeastern Washington, while blackberries used in pies and other desserts come from the Willamette Valley of northwestern Oregon. The firm commitment of Burgerville to regionally locate all 39 company restaurants and to source nearly all food products inside Washington and Oregon not only provides high quality delicious food but also supports the region's farmers and ranchers, circulates wealth within the region, and contributes to a durable economic base.

All employees that work a minimum of 20 hours per week for six months are eligible for employer-subsidized health insurance at a cost of $15 per month. This rare opportunity for affordable health coverage in the fast-food industry costs Burgerville $3 million per year, but has lowered new employee training costs by decreasing worker turnover rate to one-third of pre-program levels and has built an unusually loyal and productive work force. Burgerville prominently publicizes company sustainable business innovations at each restaurant location, and this company has enjoyed double-digit restaurant sales increases during the recent period of change and improvement....

Wainwright Bank, Boston, Massachusetts—Commercial Bank

This publicly held commercial bank that employs 155 full-time employees tallied over $600 million in deposits and loans and claimed $6 million in net income in 2007. The Wainwright Bank Green Loan program was begun in 2001 and finances residential solar and wind energy, septic systems, replacement windows, and insulation projects. In order to reduce vehicle use, the company offers online banking and bill payment, no drive-up facilities (eliminates the pollution from idling vehicles in line), the ability for commercial customers to remotely scan and deposit checks, and public transportation subsidies for bank employees. In addition, loans for hybrid vehicles are offered at a 0.5% discount from the conventional vehicle loan rate.

The commitment to diversity in staff and client services is demonstrated by the 22 foreign languages spoken by Wainwright employees. Spousal insurance benefits are extended to all domestic partners of employees, and financial planning seminars for women are offered to encourage economic independence. The bank has committed over $75 million to finance well-built and affordable housing for low-income community members including the elderly, physically challenged, and mentally handicapped.

Wainwright Bank has made available millions of dollars in community development loans to non-profit organizations that are dedicated to environmental and sustainable causes, including The Trust for Public Land, Silent Spring Institute, Union of Concerned Scientists, and Earthwatch Institute. Over 30 other local and national non-profit organizations have chosen to bank with Wainwright. A three-year competitive-rate CD ... also functions as a line-of-credit collateral for the Equal Exchange, a fair trade coffee, tea, and cacao merchant that has helped establish over 30 farmer co-ops in 16 developing nations. The bank routinely distributes promotional materials to its local bank customers on such items as compact fluorescent light bulbs, wildflower seeds, and reusable shopping bags. Furthermore, two Wainwright Bank branch offices are LEED-certified.

Bazzani Associates, Grand Rapids, Michigan—
Commercial Real Estate Development

Founded in 1981 by sole proprietor Guy Bazzani, this real estate development and construction company began to embed [triple-top-line] values into its mission at the start of the new millennium. At that time, Bazzani recognized the opportunity to specialize in sustainable commercial facility development and has enjoyed increased economic, environmental, and social benefits from the change. Two examples typical of the company's successful and award-winning building projects include the following:

- The adaptive renovation of a historic commercial structure that serves as the company headquarters and includes a vegetative roof, combined efficiency improvements that lower utility rates by 40%, features conducive to particularly high indoor air quality, and a LEED silver rating.
- The reclamation of a brown field site (a former industrial location with a significant amount of pollution remaining on-site) into a four-unit commercial facility with a vegetative roof and a landscaped rain garden, which eliminates storm-water discharge; passive heating and lighting features; and high energy-efficiency design characteristics throughout.

The company routinely involves the neighboring community in project decisions and works to garner local support for the particular components of each project. Bazzani employees are also given paid time off to serve sustainable non-profit organizations....

Interface, Inc., Atlanta, Georgia—
Soft-Surface Floor Covering Manufacturer

Ray Anderson founded Interface in 1973 and today, 50-plus acquisitions later, the company has become the world's largest manufacturer of modular commercial carpeting and a leader in the production of broadloom carpeting, panel fabrics, and upholstery fabrics. The company owns manufacturing facilities on four continents, has offices in over 100 countries, and has seen profits increase from $191 million in 2003 to $378 million in 2007. Interface has saved over $370 million since 1995 by eliminating over two-thirds of its waste stream. The portion of reprocessed and bio-based materials used to manufacture products grew to 25% in 2007. Interface diverted 18 million pounds of refuse carpet from landfills in 2006, with 84% of this material reprocessed into new carpeting, 14% combusted for energy production, and 2% repurposed into new materials. Interface now uses renewable energy sources for over 27% of its current power demands and has reduced greenhouse gas emissions from its production processes by one-third since 1996.

The company offers low-VOC carpet brands for home or office ... ; when customers are ready to replace this carpet, Interface picks up the old carpet free of charge and reprocesses it into new carpeting. With its commercial ... brand, the company offers an option of using a VOC-free tile installation with ... small squares of PET (polyethylene terephthalate, a low toxicity polyester polymer) that reduce adverse toxic effects by 90% compared to conventional carpet adhesives.

Interface also values and keeps track of a number of employee metrics such as the average hours of training per employee per year, the percentage of females in management, and the number of employee family events held in all company locations. In 2007, Interface employees volunteered over 15,000 hours of work for various community organizations....

Herman Miller, Inc., Zeeland, Michigan—
Commercial Office Furniture Manufacturer

This publicly held global provider of office furniture began its tenure in 1923 in Zeeland, Michigan and has grown to over $2 billion in sales in 2008. HMI has a long history of environmental concern as evidenced by the policy of using only sustainably harvested hardwoods in its products since 1991 and becoming a founding member of the United States Green Building Council in 1993, the parent organization of the popular LEED building program. The company's beautiful and effective ... assembly plant building in Holland, Michigan was awarded the LEED Pioneer building status in 1995 for functioning as a pilot project for the development of the LEED rating system. Among other rewards, the facility has 30% lower utility costs and twice the production of the similarly sized building that it replaced....

Today the organization has new product designs evaluated and rated ... in three key areas: material chemistry toxicity, disassembly of the product, and the ability of materials to be reprocessed. Four models of Herman Miller chairs have received various levels of ... certification ... and all are PVC-free and quickly disassembled. Over 95% of the materials within them are able to be reprocessed and reused....

Herman Miller satisfies 28% of its electrical demand today by renewable energy sources; has reduced its hazardous waste, solid waste, and VOC emissions by more than 80% of base year 1994; and is well on its way to a complete elimination goal for all three by the year 2020. The organization also authored its first annual comprehensive sustainability report in 2007 that is open to the public in its entirety. On the social front, Herman Miller employees volunteered over 33,000 hours to community-based causes in 2006 alone. Other social efforts include a company-wide contest for employees who lower their personal carbon emissions; employees with the strongest reduction efforts receive locally grown organic produce or gift certificates for local bike shops....

Allianz SE, Munich, Germany—Insurance, Banking, Asset Management

With its beginnings in 1890, this global company now employs more than 180,000 workers and had $136 billion in total revenue in 2007. A core working group implements and manages sustainable business initiatives while reporting directly to the Board of Management and International Executive Committee. The company cultivates innovation with its "Ideas to Success" program, and over 60,000 ideas have been submitted by employees, with some of the company's greatest achievements coming from the front lines. For example, the idea to offer low-premium accident micro-insurance (low coverage with low premiums sold to low-income people) to nations like Colombia, using supermarkets as the intermediary, was an employee-submitted suggestion. To date, over 640,000 policies have been sold to many Colombians who had never been offered the opportunity for such an arrangement. In addition, death and disability, life, accident, and health micro-insurance are offered inside India, Indonesia, Egypt, and Senegal using various non-governmental organizations to broker the sales.

From 2006 to 2008, Allianz was the leading direct insurer on the Dow Jones Sustainability Index. The company now uses the G3 sustainability indicators (provided by the international non-profit organization Global Reporting Initiative) and has benchmarked its progress in economic, environmental, and social areas. Allianz has a standing requirement for all of its suppliers to pay a living wage, to abide by legal working hours and conditions, to eschew child labor or forced labor, and to have programs in place to minimize pollution, energy consumption, and materials exploitation. Included in a list of seven sustainable business products and services are a green-band-fund offering that invests in renewable energy and energy efficiency companies, an EU carbon fund that trades carbon-emission allowances, and wind-energy investment opportunities.

Allianz promotes from within while using an intranet system to advertise opportunities for advancement and a global talent management system that matches talents and career objectives with company needs. The company also retains active memberships in various sustainably focused external organizations including The Working Group on Principles for Sustainable Insurance, Transparency International, UN Global Compact, and Germany's Forum on Sustainability.

Co-operative Financial Services, Manchester, United Kingdom—
Consumer Cooperative

Founded in 2002, Co-operative Financial Services (CFS) includes a member-owned-and-operated commercial bank, a full-service Internet bank, insurance company, and investment firm that are part of the larger Co-operative Group, the largest consumer cooperative in the U.K., with over 6.5 million members. This organization features a wide variety of [triple-top-line] value-producing initiatives led by customers in its day-to-day operations. The 25-story tower company headquarters in Manchester has been equipped on three sides with over 7,200 vertically mounted photovoltaic panels as well as 24 roof-mounted wind turbines that generate 180,000 kilowatts and 56,000 kilowatts of electricity per year respectively. A peregrine falcon nesting box was also installed on the roof with a real-time camera mounted so that people can watch and learn about these beautiful birds that sometimes share urban skyscraper locales with humans. More than 87% of company written materials in 2007 were printed on totally chlorine-free paper with vegetable-based inks and waterless printing.

Perhaps even more impressive are some of the business practices instigated at CFS. Each year, members vote online to direct policies such as denying loans to companies that extensively pollute, exploit animals, or take advantage of struggling third-world nations. The organization offers special credit cards, through which CFS purchases and protects half an acre of Brazilian rainforest the first time the card is used and continue to donate 0.25% of all purchase amounts to protecting rainforest habitat. The holder of this credit card enjoys competitive basic terms and interest rates and also receives a 5% lower interest rate on all purchases made from selected businesses that demonstrate TTL practices. Similarly, the organization offers another credit card through which it makes donations to organizations like Amnesty International and Oxfam when the account is opened. All credit cards issued by [CFS] are not made from PVC but rather from polyethylene-terephthalate, which is a chlorinated hydrocarbon-free plastic material.

The [bank] branch has set aside a $50 million special fund to use for microloans to support small independent businesses in the world's poorest nations. A second special fund is available for locally based community development providers in the UK, and this loan is restricted to entrepreneurs disadvantaged in age, ability, or ethnicity.

CFS is especially supportive to the incarcerated population in the UK. The cooperative currently offers a pilot basic financial course in six prisons and intends to expand the program. CFS also sponsors an annual show of prisoner art works and uses sales revenue to re-invest in various rehabilitation projects for the prisoners.

The insurance branch offers discounted auto insurance policies for members who own high-mileage or electric vehicles. The organization provides access to a library of helpful information on pregnancy for all pregnant employees, and it provides the booklet "A Guide to a Working Pregnancy for Managers to all organization administrators. A special rest and relaxation facility for pregnant women employees was opened at CFS headquarters in 2007. The organization has also adapted a sustainable procurement strategy policy and releases an annual comprehensive sustainability report.

Switcher SA, Lausanne, Switzerland—Garment Manufacturer

Switcher is a small Swiss corporation founded in 1981 that manufactures and sells low-priced casual clothing items made from high-quality materials. The organization outsources much of its manufacturing processes but closely monitors and attempts to influence the production standards of its supply chain. All cotton suppliers are required to provide stock that contains only trace levels of heavy metals, pesticides, VOCs, and carcinogens. Every Switcher supplier must agree to an initial environmental and social performance audit and to work with Switcher to improve its production standards. All garment shipping boxes are bleached with a chlorine-free process, and the ink printed on the containers is free of heavy metals.

The company donated roof space atop its headquarters facility in Lausanne to Edisun Power Company for the installation of a 600-square-meter photovoltaic system that averages 10,000 kilowatt hours per month production for the customers of the utility. At a Switcher T-shirt supply-chain facility in Tirupur, India, textile mills are powered by seven wind turbines, and cafeteria meals for employees are cooked in a solar oven. The company co-financed a community water [re]cycling plant here and subsequently reduced water consumption by 95%.

Corporate managers at Switcher are held accountable for respectful treatment of all workers and for encouraging effective, free-flowing communication throughout the entire company. The organization offers four months of maternity leave for its female workers and the employee option of a part-time work schedule upon return. Employees at some of its developing world supply facilities are provided the opportunity to attend various educational classes, including environmental educational courses.

Precious Woods, Zurich, Switzerland—Sustainable Timber Harvesting

This publicly traded company with over $80 million in revenue in 2007 and 1,600 employees, specializes in sustainably harvested timber operations. Precious Woods has international operations in Costa Rica, Brazil, Nicaragua, the Democratic Republic of Congo, Gabon, and the Netherlands. The company adheres to the Forest Stewardship Council guidelines for harvest practices and processes nearly all hardwood materials in the locality of the extraction, employing mostly local workers. As part of its sustainable forestry strategy, the company leaves at least 20% of the harvestable timber uncut and never harvests along waterways or steep slopes, thus reducing adverse soil erosion effects. The company typically uses directional tree felling to minimize damage to uncut neighboring trees and takes care to prevent damage to the forest floor by using light equipment and cables to drag the logs to the skid trail where mobile loaders transport the timber to awaiting trucks.

Employees who harvest field timber in developing nations are provided with training and education programs that include communication skills, equipment safety procedures, disease prevention, first aid, and alcohol abuse. Precious Woods avoids timber harvest in areas inhabited by nomadic indigenous peoples and allows sedentary local peoples to continue to use company land in their customary ways.

Abengoa, Seville, Spain—
Sustainability Technology in Energy and Infrastructure

This publicly held parent company is organized into five separate units: solar, bioenergy, environmental services, information technology, and industrial engineering and construction. With nearly 14,000 employees and $4 billion in revenue in 2007, company operations include the design, construction, and operation of various types of solar technology and fuel cells. Solar power projects have been completed at multiple locations in Spain, the U.S., China, Algeria as well as Morocco that include concentrated solar power for large-scale commercial power plants and conventional and thin-film photovoltaic technology for smaller-scale applications. An example of other tangential technological developments is an on-board bus-fare collection system that uses magnetic strip swipe cards that allow quick and accurate fare crediting for passengers.

Abengoa offers on-site day care, fitness, and medical centers as well as maternity leave and flextime for most of its employees. In Seville, Spain where company headquarters are located, the Focus Abengoa Foundation operates inside the Los Venerables Hospital while also providing continual financial and administrative assistance to the community health-care provider. From this location, the company supports a variety of international community building programs including a four-decade-old collaborative program with a religious organization in Argentina, which operates three local community centers providing food, medicine, and job training for the poor, disabled, orphaned, or uneducated and school improvements in poverty-stricken areas of Argentina and Peru, making available clean water, electricity, and well-equipped kitchens....

The Black Sheep Inn, Cotopaxi, Ecuador—Sustainable Tourist Resort

This resort is located above 10,000 feet in the Andes Mountains, approximately 60 miles southwest of the capital city of Quito, Ecuador. Resort guests that arrive by bicycle receive a 10%–15% discount, depending on the length of stay. A 10-acre organic garden provides food for the guests and is supported by a passive solar-heated greenhouse and an attached chicken house that provides effective night heating with the dissipated body heat of roosting chickens. A variety of insect-repelling plants are used in the garden to safely keep crop pests at bay. Domestically raised animals include egg-laying ducks, geese, and chickens; llamas; and the famous black sheep. All resort food waste is either fed to the animals or composted and used for garden fertilizer. An electric water pump powered by two photovoltaic panels provides the power to move pond water for garden irrigation, a decorative fountain, and a waterslide. The Inn exclusively uses composting toilets set inside bathrooms with clear roofs and large windows that provide spectacular views of the Andes Mountains. Each bathroom is filled with small flower and vegetable gardens that are fertilized with the composted waste provided by resort guests. Laundry is done by hand with rainwater collected in roof cisterns and is line dried.

A small public library has been established by employee and guest donations for the nearby community with eight computers and over 1,000 books. The Black Sheep Inn has subsidized local school textbook purchases since 2002. The resort has supported local entrepreneurship by providing an interest-free loan that allowed a nearby family to open a horseback riding business for resort visitors. The Inn sells a variety of woven garments with all proceeds going directly to the local artisans. Furthermore, the Inn has co-sponsored a variety of community workshops with the U.S. Peace Corps in the areas of nutrition, public health, family planning, naturalist skills, and weaving.

Australian Gas Light Energy Limited, North Sydney, New South Wales—Electric Utility

This power company offers customers the opportunity to choose a percentage of "green power" (solar, wind, landfill methane, and biomass) they would like to buy throughout the year at a 5.5¢ per kWh premium. Customers may also opt for short-term 100% green power events, which provide unique educational opportunities about alternative energy choices. The utility uses a diverse energy source profile including coal, methane, hydroelectric, wind, solar, and cogeneration with macadamia nuts. Nut shells are burned to super-heat boiler water, 20% of which is used to process a local company's macadamia nut output, and the remaining 80% is used to generate electricity for the utility. At company's headquarters in Sydney, the company uses solar controlled window blinds and efficient heating, lighting, and ventilation systems to supplement its diverse power-source portfolio. Australian Gas Light Energy Limited is listed on the Dow Jones Sustainability World Index and publishes an annual sustainability report. The utility helps to build social capital by funding energy use in four homeless shelters, by matching all employee charitable contributions, and by partnering with Mission Australia, a non-profit organization that offers support services to the homeless Australians.

East Japan Railway Company, Tokyo, Japan—Rail Mass Transit

This major publicly held Japanese transit company, which had revenues of $27 billion in fiscal year 2008, serves over 16 million passengers daily with 53,000 employees. The company has pioneered the use of diesel/electric hybrid rail cars and is using fuel-cell powered electric trains on a limited trial basis. Photovoltaic panels are employed to provide a portion of the electricity for rail stations in Tokyo and Takaki, the general training center and the research and development facility of the company. Plastic fare cards with activated magnetic strips have replaced over 20 million paper tickets annually. These cards require a refundable deposit and, consequently, are nearly always returned for reuse. Hundreds of thousands of employee uniforms are made from the reprocessed plastic polymer *polyethylene terephthalate*, providing a second-generation use for this food and beverage container material. The company reclaims all of its food waste in its Tokyo train stations, composts the material, and sells the humus to local farmers and gardeners. More than 20 vegetative roofs have been installed on various company buildings, which cover more than 7,000 square meters throughout Japan.

The recent installation of sound-deadening walls and continuously welded rail tracks has reduced noise levels along selected routes by nearly two-thirds. The transit company has promoted local ecotourism in Japan[,] organiz[ing] over 400 nature hikes with nearly 200,000 participants in 2008. To increase the comfort level and safety of female passengers, East Japan Railway has introduced "women only" cars for late-night trips and morning rush-hour commuters. The company has also worked closely with local governments and childcare businesses to establish daycare centers for children near train stations for commuting workers. For employees that care for elderly family members (a common practice in Japan), adult daycare centers have been established at four different railroad company offices. The company has published and made available a yearly sustainability report since 2002....

Sharp Corporation, Tokyo, Japan—Electronics and Home Appliances

Founded in 1912 and incorporated in 1935, Sharp generated over $34 billion in revenues in 2007 and currently employs nearly 61,000 employees worldwide with a manufacturing operation that includes a wide variety of electronics devices and home appliances. Sharp has been the world's largest producer of photovoltaic systems from 2001 to 2008 and has also employed this energy technology inside some of its own facilities. The Kameyama complex in the western part of the Japanese large island of Honshu has over 47,000 square meters of photovoltaic equipment that generates over 5,200 kW of electricity (energy equivalent to service 1,300 homes). The liquid crystal display (LCD) plant and the distribution center have PV panels mounted on their roofs and outside walls; a third production facility has cutting-edge transparent thin PV film mounted on the south-facing windows. The complex also has four 250 kW fuel cells, which complement the PV system by contributing electricity to the complex at night and on cloudy days. On the industrial materials front, Sharp has made a number of technological advances that allow the reclamation, reprocessing, and re-use of a variety of product components. The company now separates and recovers the plastic polymer polypropylene from the waste stream, the soft metal indium from non-functioning LCD panels, and the silicon from old PV cells and reprocesses these materials into high-quality new components. Sharp is collaborating with five other electronics companies to operate 190 pick-up sites and 18 reprocessing facilities for nonfunctioning household appliances in Japan. The company also takes back, disassembles, and reprocesses outdated and non-functioning personal computers, office copy machines, and toner cartridges.

All Sharp employees receive one of three levels of environmental education based on their duties: the basic level includes current environmental issues; the expert level includes environmental policy and design-for-cycling topics; and the master level includes a comprehensive understanding of sustainable technology and products. Throughout the tenure of an employee, he/she is assisted in writing a professional development plan and in improving technological skills through in-house training. Sharp workers have the opportunity to participate in voluntary physical fitness, nutrition, and mental health programs. Sharp supports neighboring communities near its facilities by sponsoring local festivals and major tree reforesting projects and by opening company recreational facilities—tennis courts, gymnasiums, and ball fields—to the public.

Notes on the Contributing Authors

Sascha-Dominik Bachmann is an Associate Professor in Law at the Bournemouth University Law School in the United Kingdom.

Kelly R. Blackwood is a Senior Attorney at Bradley Arant Boult Cummings LLP in Jackson, Mississippi.

Dana Brakman Reiser is a Professor of Law at Brooklyn Law School.

Michael Braungart is a Professor of Process Engineering at the University of Applied Sciences in Suderburg, Germany, and a co-founder of McDonough Braungart Design Chemistry in Charlottesville, Virginia.

Marilyn Brown is a Professor at the Georgia Institute of Technology's School of Public Policy.

Sharon (Jess) Chandler is an engineer at Engineering and Technology Solutions in Kanagawa, Japan.

Jared Diamond is a Professor of Geography at the University of California, Los Angeles.

Jackie Gardina is a Professor of Law at Vermont Law School.

Susan N. Gary is the Orlando John & Marian H. Hollis Professor of Law at the University of Oregon School of Law.

Carola Glinski is a Postdoc at the University of Copenhagen Faculty of Law.

Michael A. Gollin is a Partner at Venable LLP in Washington, D.C.

Kent Greenfield is a Professor of Law and Law Fund Research Scholar at Boston College Law School.

Robert W. Hahn is the Executive Director of the American Enterprise Institute-Brookings Joint Center for Regulatory Studies and a Resident Scholar at the American Enterprise Institute.

Viva Hammer is currently Legislative Counsel for the United States Congress Joint Committee on Taxation.

Paul Hawken is an environmentalist, entrepreneur, and author. He is a founder of the Natural Capital Institute research organization as well as the retailer Smith & Hawken.

Keith H. Hirokawa is an Associate Professor of Law at Albany Law School.

Dennis D. Hirsch is a Professor of Law at Capital University Law School.

Heather Hughes is a Professor of Law at American University's Washington College of Law.

Mona Hymel is the Arthur W. Andrews Professor of Law at the University of Arizona James E. Rogers College of Law.

Robert C. Illig is an Associate Professor of Law and Dean's Distinguished Faculty Fellow at the University of Oregon School of Law.

Thomas W. Joo is the Martin Luther King Jr. Professor of Law at the University of California, Davis, School of Law.

Robert W. Kates is an independent scholar in Trenton, Maine and a University Professor Emeritus at Brown University.

Robert A. Katz is a Professor of Law at the Indiana University Robert H. McKinney School of Law.

David Kinley is a Professor of Law and holds the Chair in Human Rights Law at the University of Sydney Law School.

Eric L. Lane is an Adjunct Professor of Law at the Thomas Jefferson School of Law.

Alan S. Lederman is a Shareholder at Gunster, Yoakley & Stewart P.A. in Fort Lauderdale, Florida.

Anthony A. Leiserowitz is a Senior Research Scientist at the Yale University School of Forestry and Environmental Studies and Director of the Yale Program on Climate Change Communication.

Tory H. Lewis is an Associate at Friday, Eldredge & Clark LLP in Little Rock, Arkansas.

Amory B. Lovins is a physicist, environmental scientist, writer, and Chairman, Chief Scientist and a co-founder of the Rocky Mountain Institute.

L. Hunter Lovins is President and a co-founder of Natural Capitalism Solutions and a Professor of Business at the Bard College MBA Program in Sustainability.

John P. Manard Jr. is Of Counsel at Phelps Dunbar LLP in New Orleans, Louisiana.

Brett McDonnell is the Dorsey & Whitney Chair in Law at the University of Minnesota Law School.

William McDonough is a co-founder of McDonough Braungart Design Chemistry in Charlottesville, Virginia, and a former dean at the University of Virginia School of Architecture.

Nina A. Mendelson is the Joseph L. Sax Collegiate Professor of Law at the University of Michigan Law School.

Janet E. Milne is a Professor of Law and Director of the Environmental Tax Policy Institute at Vermont Law School.

Pini Pavel Miretski is on the Faculty of Social Sciences at the Hebrew University of Jerusalem.

Patrick O'Hara is a former attorney and current faculty member at the St. Joseph's Academy in Baton Rouge, Louisiana.

Antony Page is a Professor of Law at the Indiana University Robert H. McKinney School of Law.

Thomas M. Parris is President of ISciences LLC in Ann Arbor, Michigan.

Jeffrey Pfeffer is the Thomas D. Dee II Professor of Organizational Behavior at the Stanford University Graduate School of Business.

Benjamin Richardson is a Professor of Environmental Law at the University of Tasmania Faculty of Law in Australia.

David Malin Roodman is currently a Senior Advisor at the Open Philanthropy Project in San Francisco, California.

Joakim Sandberg is an Associate Professor of Practical Philosophy in the Department of Philosophy, Linguistics, and Theory of Science at the University of Gothenburg in Sweden.

Joshua Sarnoff is a Professor of Law at the DePaul University College of Law.

Christopher H. Schroeder is the Charles S. Murphy Professor of Law and Public Policy and Co-Director of the Program in Public Law at Duke Law School.

Nancy E. Shurtz is the B.A. Kliks Professor of Law at the University of Oregon School of Law.

Judd F. Sneirson is an Associate Professor of Law at Savannah Law School.

James Gustave Speth is a Professor of Law at Vermont Law School and is also a former dean at the Yale University School of Forestry and Environmental Studies.

Paulette L. Stenzel is a Professor of International Business Law at the Michigan State University Eli Broad College of Business.

Junko Tadaki is a Human Rights Officer at the United Nations Office of the High Commissioner for Human Rights.

Matthew Tueth is the Steelcase Professor of Sustainable Business at Aquinas College in Grand Rapids, Michigan.

David M. Uhlmann is the Jeffrey F. Liss Professor from Practice, Director of the Environmental Law and Policy Program, and the Distinguished Faculty Fellow in Sustainability at the University of Michigan Law School.

Cynthia Williams is the Osler Chair in Business Law at the Osgoode Hall Law School of York University in Toronto.

Adam Winkler is a Professor of Law at the University of California, Los Angeles, School of Law.

Michael P. Vandenbergh is the David Daniels Allen Distinguished Chair in Law, Director of the Climate Change Research Network, and Co-Director of the Energy, Environment and Land Use Program at Vanderbilt University Law School.

Joseph W. Yockey is a Professor of Law and the Michael and Brenda Sandler Faculty Fellow in Corporate Law at the University of Iowa College of Law.

Iris Marion Young was a Professor of Political Science at the University of Chicago. She passed away in 2006.

Table of Cases

Aronson v. Lewis, 46
Basic v. Levinson, 130
Beaty v. Lessee of Knowler, 77
Biodegradable Prod. Inst. v. Le, 425
Bd. of Trustees v. Mayor of Baltimore City, 164
BP Products N. Am., Inc., United States v., 302
Brehm v. Eisner, 46, 47
Bryan v. United States, 299
Carroll Towing Co., United States v., 283
Caterpillar, Inc., In re, 131
Cheff v. Mathes, 51
Citizens United v. Fed. Election Comm'n, 62
Cronin v. U.S. Dep't of Agric., 48
Davis v. Dyson, 85
Desimone v. Barrows, 85
Dodge v. Woolsey, 83
Dotterweich, United States v., 300
Elias, United States v., 302
Ethyl Corp. v. EPA, 288
In re—(see name of party)
Ira S. Bushey & Sons, Inc., United States v., 277
Kasky v. Nike, Inc., 192, 339
Kiobel v. Royal Dutch Petroleum Co., 332
Koh v. S.C. Johnson & Son, Inc., 421
Jazz Photo Corp. v. Int'l Trade Comm'n, 417
John Zink Co. v. Nat'l Airfoil Burner Co., 405
Laughlin, United States v., 299
Liggett Co. v. Lee, 77
Louisiana Mun. Police Employees' Ret. Sys. v. Pyott, 85
Massey, In re, 85
Metro Comm'n Corp. BVI v. Advanced Mobilcomm. Techs., 85
Midlantic Nat'l Bank v. N.J. Dep't of Envtl. Prot., 385
Miller v. Am. Tel. & Telegraph Co., 85
N.Y. City Employees' Ret. Sys. v. SEC, 38
Ohio v. Kovacs, 385
Paduano v. Am. Honda Motor Co., 424
Paramount Comm'ns v. Time, Inc., 51
Park, United States v., 300
Pollution Abatement Servs., In re, 279-80
Roth v. Robertson, 85
Salvagno, United States v., 302
Scrushy v. Tucker, 85
Sindell v. Abbott Labs., 284
Sinskey, United States v., 303
Smith v. Nat'l Transp. Safety Bd., 72
Smith v. Van Gorkom, 46
State Dep't of Envtl. Prot. v. Ventron Corp., 280
TSC Indus., Inc. v. Northway, Inc., 47
United States v.—(see name of party)
Ward v. Ritz Hotel, 271
White, United States v., 298
Williams, United States v., 305
W.R. Grace, United States v., 302

Index

Tables are indicated by T following page numbers.
Illustrations are indicated by *illu.* following page numbers.

A

Abengoa, profile of, 438
Acid Rain Program, carbon tax and, 240
acquisition/credit agreements, 200–201
act of God defense, 293–94
Adler, Timothy, 184–85
advertising, tax policy and, 256–61
  advertising, over-consumption and, 256–57
  advertising deductions, proposals limiting, 259–61
  consumption problems, 257–59
  labor, sustainability and, 257
Advertising Standards Authority (ASA), 419, 421–22
AES (power producer), reinvestment in natural capital by, 26
agriculture
  agriculture sector, carbon pricing initiatives of, 266T
  expenditures, in U.S. Budget (2015), 255T
  farm pollution, 226
  genetically modified organisms, 369–70
  good neighbor agreements, 207–15
  subsidies for, 373
Ahold, requirements on suppliers by, 196
air pollution. *See also* carbon tax, cap-and-trade *vs.;* clean air technologies, fiscal barriers to
  Acid Rain Program, carbon tax and, 240
  greenhouse gases (GHG), 240, 258–59
  ozone pollution, 226, 227, 233–34, 291
  regulation of, 288–89
Albertson, requirements on suppliers by, 196
Allianz SE, profile of, 435–36
Alternative Minimum Tax (AMT), 250
aluminum production sector (U.S.), 199, 203
Amalric, Franck, 176
American Law Institute, 280
anti-greenwashing. *See* eco-mark enforcement
apparel industry, global labor in, 315–20
  international justice, 318–20
  responsibility for, 316, 317, 320
  "sweatshops," conditions in, 315–16
  Workplace Code of Conduct, 338–39
apparel manufacturing, sustainable businesses in
  GoLite LLC, 431
  Patagonia, 429–30
  Switcher SA, in Switzerland, 437
  Timberland Inc., 430–31
Apple Inc. video of recycling process, 36
Applegate, John, 370
An Approach to Corporate Social Responsibility (Engle), 68–69
Arizona, groundwater depletion tax in, 230
Arthur D. Little (consulting firm), 27
Article 9 (UCC). *See* EPMSI, in commercial law
articles of incorporation, 78, 88–90
asbestos-related deaths, 302

Aspen Institute report, on social enterprise, 119–20
Australia, 173, 360
Australian Gas Light Energy Ltd., profile of, 439
automobile manufacturing sector (Europe), 197–98
automobile manufacturing sector (U.S.)
  ozone pollution by, 226, 227
  requirements on suppliers by, 197
  smog emissions by, 229
  tax subsidies/policies, 246–47
  taxes, on fuel economy, 234–35
  taxes, on gas, 229–30
Aveda, profile of, 431–32

B

B Lab, role of, 91, 95, 100, 116, 127
Baade, Hans, 336
Bachman, Sascha-Dominik, 348–61
Bainbridge, Stephen, 55
Bakan, Joel, 60
Baker, Edwin, 261
Baker, Larry C., 354, 358, 359–60
banking, as sustainable businesses, 433, 435–36
bankruptcy. *See* corporate polluters, bankruptcy by; EPMSI, in commercial law; hardrock mining, cleanup costs of
Bankruptcy Code, 384, 386–87, 389–90
Baxi, Upendra, 350, 352
Bayh-Dole Act, 416
Bazzani Associates, profile of, 433–34
beer brewery, as sustainable business, 427–28
Beitz, Charles, 319–20
Ben & Jerry's, as sustainable business, 116
benefit and B corporations, 87–90
  articles of incorporation, 88–90
  assessing benefit corporations, 97–102
  board composition, new governance and, 122
  community/environment provision, 88
  enforcement of, 99
  investors in, 120–21
  lawyers, roles of, 119–21
  in Oregon, 88–89
  states with, 91
  voluntary charter provisions, 89
  voluntary disclosure, by Starbucks, 153–54 *illu.*, 158
benefit corporation statutes, 90–102, 107–26
  B Lab, role of, 91, 95, 100, 116
  "benefit enforcement proceeding," 97
  branding, 101–2
  CICs, in U.K., 90, 99
  collaboration, within sectors, 116
  directors, role of, 93–94
  disclosure model, 100, 112–13, 114
  dual mission of, 96–98
  enforcement, 96–97
  funding, 100–101
  in Hawaii, 96, 100
  and L3Cs, 90, 99, 100
  in Maryland, 91, 92, 94, 96
  "new governance" principles, 108–9
  in New Jersey, 96, 100
  non-distribution constraint, asset locks and, 123–24
  public benefit requirement, 92–93
  public officials, regulatory role of, 99
  self-regulation, 111–18, 123
  shareholder enforcement role, 98–99, 120–21
  social audits, 124–25
  state laws, 110, 115
  statutory authorization, 91–92
  statutory revision, 123
  sustainability, 102, 109–10
  third-party standard-setters, 94–95, 98, 113
  in Vermont, 96, 100
  in Virginia, 96
Benson, Melinda, 13
Benyus, Janine *(Biomimicry)*, 22
Berle, Adolf A. *(The Modern Corporation and Private Property)*, 135–39
BHP Billiton (Papua New Guinea), pollution by, 332, 379
Bierman-Lytle, Paul, 23
Biodegradable Products Institute (BPI), certification mark, 425–26
biological models, redesign production of, 17, 22–23

Biomimicry (Benyus), 22
biotechnology, patents of, 414
The Black Sheep Inn, profile of, 438–39
Blackwood, Kelly R., 292–94
Blair, Margaret, 51
boards of directors
 of B corporations, 93–94, 122
 board pluralism, 53–56
 codetermination, concerns about, 56
 diversity of, 55, 122–23
 social enterprise, in Minnesota, 105
 stakeholder boards, changing to, 53–56
Bomann-Larsen, Lene, 174
BP Deepwater Horizon oil spill, 236, 390–93
Brandeis, Louis D. (Justice), 77, 134–35
branding, of benefit corporations, 101–2
Braungart, Michael, 28–35
Brennan, Troyen A., 287
British Petroleum, values of, 321
Brown, Marilyn A., 245–52, 267
building industry, sustainability in, 19, 35, 230, 247
Burgerville, profile of, 432–33
"business judgment rule," 40, 46

C

CAFOs (Concentrated Animal Feeding Operations), GNAs and, 213, 214
California
 CalPERS, 161, 164, 177
 carbon dioxide legislation (2006), 240
 Google, as sustainable business, 428–29
 Honda, deceptive advertising by, 423–24
 Patagonia, as sustainable business, 429–30
Campagna, Julie, 359
Canada, 360, 373, 380–81
Cancun Agreement, on climate change, 410
Cane, Peter, 286
Capitalism and Freedom (Friedman), 63–64, 364
carbon emissions, reduction of. *See* carbon tax, cap-and-trade *vs.*
carbon pricing initiatives, 265–67T
Carbon Principles, 397
carbon reduction markets, 26
carbon tax, cap-and-trade *vs.*, 237–43, 239T
 administrability of, 238–39
 carbon allowances, 238, 244
 carbon impact, material failure to disclose, 129–32
 cross-border regional plans, 245
 efficacy of, 242–43
 efficiency *vs.* economic growth, 241
 equity *vs.* incidence, 241–42
 political feasibility of, 239–40
 revenue from, 228
carpet industry, sustainable practices by, 29–35, 32–33, 36
CERCLA of 1980, 294, 385, 388–89, 398
Chambers, Rachel, 350, 356, 357
Chandler, Sharon (Jess), 245–52, 267
China, natural resources use by, 202
CH2M Hill (engineering firm), 23
Chouinard, Yvon, 430
Christmann, Petra, 206
civic investor thesis. *See* UO (universal owner) thesis
Clay, Don R., 298
Clean Air Act (CAA), 211, 288–89, 302, 408
Clean Air Act (CAA) Amendments of 1990, 240
clean air technologies, fiscal barriers to, 245–52
 fiscal incentives, 251
 fiscal penalties, 251–52
 fiscal policies, 249–51
 generally, 245–46
 tax subsidies, 246–47
 taxes, on capital *vs.* operating expenses, 247–49
 unfavorable tariffs, 249
Clean-up Assurance and Polluter Accountability Act (S. 452), 390
Clean Water Act (CWA), 294, 299, 303
climate change, patent system and, 409–17
 Cancun Agreement, 410
 climate change, scope of, 409–10
 expansive exhaustion, 417

Hartwell Paper, 410–11
humanitarian licensing powers, 415
inter-operability exceptions, 415
international regulation, 411
limiting patent regulation, 411–17
march-in criteria, 416
non-exclusive licensing, 416
public policy, patenting technologies and, 412–13
R&D exclusions, 414
technologies, effects of, 410
climate change ("green"), 3–7
American business, greening of, 4–5
applying sustainability to, 15
changing attitudes, of consumers, 6–7
deforestation, cost of, 25–26
economy-wide investors and, 177–78
Al Gore on, 3–4
interpretive release on, by SEC, 157
meta-study of (2012), 186–87
Silicon Valley and, 5–6
weather, damage from, 25–26
Oprah Winfrey on, 3–4
Clinton, Bill, NAFTA and, 367
closed-loop manufacturing theory, 23
Co-operative Financial Services, profile of, 436–37
Coca-Cola (Colombia), human rights violations by, 331
codes of conduct, 191–94, 337–40
Coffee, John, 80
Collins, Ronald, 261
Collins Pine, reinvestment in natural capital by, 26
Colorado, 380–81, 427–28, 431
commercial office furniture manufacturer, as sustainable business, 435
commercial real estate, as sustainable business, 433–34
Community Interest Companies (CICs), 90, 99, 104–5
compliance, costs of, 66–75
advising clients, 69–72
altruism, 68
contract law *vs.* public law, 74–75
"efficient investment in compliance" paradigm, 68–69
law-as-price, 69, 73
malum in se vs. *malum prohibitum*, 70–72, 85, 297–98
penalties, 69
public law theory, efficient breach of, 66–67, 72–75
rational-choice theory, 67–68
complicity-based doctrine, in SRI, 170–73
complicity, legal concept of, 172–73
deontological ethics, 171
negative orientation of, 172
regulations, for Norwegian fund, 170–71
reputational risks, for SRI, 173
consumerism, advertising tax and. *See* advertising, tax policy and
consumers, green branding and, 203, 418–23
contract law. *See* codes of conduct; global governance, supply-chain contracting in; good neighbor agreements (GNAs)
Convention against Torture (CAT), 345
Cooter, Robert, 67–68
copper mining, pollution from, 378–79
corporate change, environment and, 57–61
business press, on green trend, 57
corporations of the future, 61
CSR and, 58–59
"new capitalists," 58
required, by law, 59–60
shareholder primacy, as obstacle to, 60–61
voluntary, to green initiatives, 57–58
corporate charters, 59
corporate compliance, with law. *See* compliance, costs of; corporate governance; shareholders; "ultra vires" doctrine
corporate culture, 118, 311, 315
corporate decisionmaking, 42–50, 307–15
corporate culture and, 311, 315
due care, duty of, 44–47
"enlightened stakeholder theory," 44
generally, 41–42
laws, protecting interests of employees, 309, 311, 312–13

NEPA assessments, 48–49
officer/board power, employees and, 310, 313
organizational forms and, 311, 314–15
political feasibility, 312
shareholder power, employees and, 310, 313
stakeholder assessments, 49–50
stakeholder theory, CSR and, 42–44, 308
stakeholders, employees as, 307–15
unions and, 310, 312, 314

corporate governance, 9–12. *See also* corporate change, environment and; corporate decisionmaking; global governance, supply-chain contracting in
"gearing up" framework, 11–12, 35
management-centered corporations, 37–41
principles of, 10
responsible corporate officer doctrine, 300–301
study on, 188
"triple bottom line" approach, 10–11, 35, 58
X-efficiency theory, 308

corporate law. *See also* corporate decisionmaking; "ultra vires" doctrine
corporate lobbying, 60
corporate personhood, 59
corporate structure change, CSR and, 50–56
directors and managers, personal liability for, 59
good faith consideration of all information, due care in, 47–50
managerial discretion, due care in, 44–47
needed government actions, 59–60
stakeholder assessment, as NEPA model, 48–50

corporate polluters, bankruptcy by, 383–93
accountability of, 384
Bankruptcy Code, 384, 386–87, 389–90
bankruptcy law, 386–87
BP bankruptcy (hypothetical), 390–93
case law, 385
under CERCLA, 388–89
environmental disasters, costs of, 383–84
environmental obligations, 387–89
jurisdiction, in cleanup laws *vs.* federal bankruptcy, 385–86
"polluter pays" principle, 385
solutions, 389–90

corporate structure change, CSR and, 50–56
non-equity investors, inclusion of, 51–53
to stakeholder boards, 53–56
stakeholder-oriented corporate law, 51–53
wealth, changing definition of, 50–51

corrective justice, deterrence *vs.*, 283–85, 286–87

Costco Wholesale, requirements on suppliers by, 196

Counseling at the Limits of the Law (Pepper), 69–72

Coupounas, Demetri, 431

Coupounas, Kim, 431

Craig, Robin, 13

creditors, as stakeholders, 81–82

Cridland, John, 359

CSR (corporate social responsibility)
corporate decisionmaking, due care in, 41–50
corporate structure change and, 50–56
management-centered corporations and, 37–41
principles of, WTO and, 364–66
self-regulation, torts and, 269–74
by TNCs, profit maximization *vs.*, 337
in U.N. *Norms,* 356

CVS, annual sales by, 196

D

DaimlerChrysler, requirements on suppliers of, 197

Databases for State Incentives for Renewables and Efficiency (DSIRE), 251

de Graaf, Frank, 180
Delaware, fiduciary law in, 45, 84–85
deontological ethics, 171
deterrence, corrective justice *vs.*, 283–85, 286–87
Deutsche Bank Group, meta-study of responsible investing by, 186–87
Deva, Surya, 349, 358
Diamond, Jared, 377–83
disclosure, 129–40. *See also* SEC, transparency by; social corporate transparency
  material disclosure, by management, 129–32
  model, in benefit corporation statutes, 100, 112–13, 114
  as regulatory mechanism, history of, 133–40
discount/variety retail sector (U.S.), 195–96
divine command doctrine, 171
double dividend theory of environmental taxation, 220–25, 225T
Dow Chemical, business model change by, 24–25, 32
due care, fiduciary duty of, 44–50
  constituency statutes, 45–46
  in Delaware, 45
  generally, 44–45
  good faith consideration of all information, by management, 47–50
  managerial discretion, 45–46, 160
due diligence, standard of, 270–74
DuPont, rent-a-solvent concept use by, 32
Durning, Alan, 257

E

East Japan Railway Co., profile of, 439–40
Easterbrook, Frank, 66–67, 72
Eccles, Robert, 173, 188
eco-mark enforcement, 417–26
  anti-greenwashing activists, 420–21
  eco-mark litigation, 425–26
  FTC "Green Guides," 421
  green branding, 417–18
  greenwashers, combatting, 421–25
  greenwashing, 418–20
Ecological Tax Reform (von Weizscker), 228
economic instruments, in environmental taxation, 231–36
  price-based *vs.* property-based instruments, 232 *fig.*
  revenue-raising function, 235–36
  tax base, tax rate and, 233–35
  tax reform *vs.* fiscal reform, 232 *fig.*
economic theories, in environmental taxation, 217–25
  differences, summary of, 225T
  effects, on environmental goal, 221–22
  effects, on revenue use, 223–24
  effects, on tax rate, 222–23
  theories, generally, 217–21
The Economics of Welfare (Pigou), 226–27, 243–44
EcoVision, eco-mark infringement by, 425–26
Ecuador, sustainable business in, 438–39
EITI (Extractive Industry Transparency Initiative), 115
electricity supply market
  fiscal policies for, 247–48
  production tax credit (PTC), 251
  sustainable business in, 439
  utility pricing policies, 249
  wind energy, 263–65
electronics/home appliances, sustainable business in, 440–41
Elkington, John, 9, 35
employees, as stakeholders, 307–15. *See also* human sustainability
  increasing employee involvement, 309–15
  sustainability and, 307–9
  ultra vires doctrine and, 82–83
EMS (Environmental Management System) standards, 198, 199, 200, 205, 206–7
Energy Policy Act (EPAct) of 2005, 248, 249, 250
energy sector (U.S.), 253–54T, 258, 265T
Energy Star certification mark, 422–23
Engle, David *(An Approach to Corporate Social Responsibility)*, 68–69

environmental law
  corporate change, environment and, 57–61
  due diligence standard, in tort, 270–74
  environmental assessments, by NEPA, 48–49
  environmental procurement requirements, 204–6
  environmental procurement standards, 201–4, 206–7
  statutory requirements, SEC and, 150
environmental movement, 3–7, 152, 153–54 *illu.*, 158, 287–89
environmental regulation, 281–92, 294–305. *See also* good neighbor agreements
  citizen suit provisions, 282
  deceptive/misleading conduct, 303–4
  deterrence *vs.* corrective justice, 283–85, 286–87
  environmental crimes program, 295–96
  environmental movement, 287–89
  environmental risks, in tort, 289–92, 290T
  environmental standards, 281–83
  equity courts, 285
  generally, 281
  harm prevention, 285–86
  improper waste management practices, 294–95
  mental state requirements, 298–99
  public health/environmental harms, 301–2
  responsible corporate officer doctrine, 300–301
  Rivers and Harbors Act of 1899, 294
  violations, 296–98, 304–5
environmental taxation, 217–45
  carbon tax *vs.* cap-and-trade, 237–43
  "polluter pays" principle, 226–30
  theories, tax rate and, 217–25
  in U.S., 231–36
environmental technologies, 401–9
  compulsory patent licensing, 407–9
  generally, 401–2
  patent law, 405–6
  scope of, 402
  sustainable business using, 438
  technology innovation cycle, 402–3
  trade marks, 406–7
  trade secrets, proprietary rights in, 403–4
Environmental Trade Measures (ETMs), 371–72
environmentalist philosophies, 35–36
EOC, EEO-1 annual report, 149
EPA (Environmental Protection Agency)
  bankruptcy, by corporate polluters, 384
  CERES, 150, 181, 365
  cost of meeting standards, 23, 381
  lead in gasoline, regulation by, 288
  Toxic Release Inventory, 86, 155, 209
EPMSI, in commercial law, 393–400
  CERCLA liability *vs.*, 398
  EPMSI concept, 395–96
  Equator Principles, 397
  green investment, costs of, 397
  incentivizing environmental practices, 399–400
  secured parties/debtors, 396, 397–98
  "super-priority" security interest, 393
  UCC Article 9, enabling interests under, 394
Equator Principles, 200, 397
ESG (environmental, social, governance) factors. *See also* fiduciary duty
  definition, 159
  ESG arguments, 163–65
  ESG performance, research on, 186–90
  financial relevance of, 165–67, 185–86
Esty, Daniel *(Green to Gold)*, 58
ethanol, 249, 251–52
European Union, 362, 369–70, 371
Exchange Act of 1934, 148
Executive Order No. 13514, 14
Exxon Valdez oil spill, 301

F

fair trade movement, WTO and, 372
faith-based investing. *See* complicity-based doctrine, in SRI
Falke, Josef, 273–74
fast food restaurants, as sustainable businesses, 432–33

Federalist Papers (Madison), 56
Fiat, requirements on suppliers by, 198
fiduciary duty, of due care, 44–50
  constituency statutes, 45–46
  in Delaware, 45
  generally, 44–45
  good faith, by management, 47–50
  managerial discretion, 45–46, 160
  social investors, studies of, 168–69
  of trustees, 161, 164
fiduciary duty, SRI and, 159–69
  beneficiaries, considerations of, 167–69
  beneficiaries, prudent investing and, 181, 190
  definitions, 159, 160–61
  ESG arguments, 163–65
  ESG factors, financial relevance of, 165–67, 185–86
  Freshfields report, 160, 162–63, 165–66, 167, 169, 190
  of institutional investors, 160–62
  of managers, to shareholders, 136
  reputational risks, to businesses, 173
  SRI, statistics, 159, 160
  state law litigation, 40–41
Fischel, Daniel, 66–67, 72
fisheries
  bankruptcy by corporate polluters and, 384
  certified by MSC, 195–96, 204, 205, 206
  fishing subsidies, 373
floor covering manufacturer. *See* Interface Inc., as sustainable business
Ford, Henry, 28, 31
Ford Motor Company, requirements on suppliers by, 197, 206
Forest Stewardship Council, 26
forestry sector/standards, 202, 250–51, 266T, 437–38
fossil-fuel divestment, costs of, 184–85
France
  CSR in stock selection, study of, 187–88
  long-term sustainability in, 179–80
  Pension Reserve Funds, UO thesis rationale, 176–77
  "Tobin" tax, 369
Frankfurter, Felix, 134, 139–40
fraud, 79–80, 129–32
Freedom of Information Act (FOIA), 404
Freshfields report, 160, 162–63, 165–66, 167, 169, 190
Friedman, Milton *(Capitalism and Freedom),* 63–64, 86, 364
Frito-Lay, profile of, 432
FTC "Green Guides," 420, 421

G

Gakidou, Emmanuela E., 323
The Gap, human rights violations by, 331
Gardina, Jackie, 383–93
Gary, Susan, 183–90
GATT (General Agreement on Tariffs and Trade), 362, 363, 370, 372, 373–74
GE (General Electric), 58, 194
General Mining Act of 1872, 383
General Motors, requirements on suppliers by, 197
Germany, 228, 310, 435
Ginsburg, Douglas, 72
Glinski, Carola, 191–94, 216, 269–74, 306
global governance, supply-chain contracting in, 194–207
  acquisition and credit agreements, 200–201
  environmental procurement requirements, 204–6
  environmental procurement standards, 201–4, 206–7
  insurance agreements, 201
  supply agreements, study of, 194–200
Global Reporting Initiative Sustainability Reporting Guidelines, 157
global warming, 37–41, 129–32
  "business judgment rule," 40
  classification of, in tort law, 290–91
  definitions, 37
  energy consumption and, 258–59
  material disclosure, management duty, 129–32
  shareholders, policymaking by proposals, 38–40
  state law fiduciary duty litigation, 40–41

globalization
  apparel industry, 318–20
  Equator Principles, 200
  social investors and, 144–45, 168–69, 179
  Starbucks report (2014), 152, 153–54 *illu.*, 158
GNAs. *See* good neighbor agreements
gold mining, pollution from
  in Colorado, 380–81
  in Montana, 380, 382, 383, 400
  in New Guinea, 379
GoLite LLC, profile of, 431
Gollin, Michael A., 401–9
good neighbor agreements (GNAs), 207–15
  concerns about, 215
  environmental audits, 208
  EPA regulations and, 209–10
  examples of, 211–12
  nuisance actions *vs.* statutes, 207–8
  principles of, 211–15
  public participation methods, 209–10
  TRIs, of large/small farms, 209
Goodyear, misleading advertising by, 422
Google, as sustainable business, 428–29
Gore, Al, 3, 6–7
The Gort Cloud (Seireeni), 420–21
Grasberg-Ertsberg mine, pollution from, 379
Green to Gold (Esty & Winston), 58
green trend, in business. *See also* eco-mark enforcement
  "green consumerism," 250
  green labeling, 406–7
  reliably green companies, 59–60
  statistics, 57, 58
Greenfield, Kent, 50–56, 75–84, 86
greenhouse gases (GHG), 240, 258–59. *See also* clean air technologies, fiscal barriers to
grocery stores, as sustainable businesses, 428
Gulf oil spill
  clean-up costs for, 236
  tort litigation for, 292–94, 384
  Trust Fund, 236, 391–93

H

hair/skin care, makeup products, as sustainable business, 431–32
Hammer, Viva, 263–65
Hand, Learned, 283
handicapped, needs of, 30
hardrock mining, cleanup costs of, 377–83
  "assurance" costs, 381
  bankruptcy, as strategy, 380–81
  environmental problems from, 378–79
  future of, 382–83
  laws governing, 383
  statistics, 377
  taxpayer liability and backlash, 381–82
  "walkaway restoration" policy, 379–80
Hartwell Paper, on climate change, 410–11
Hawken, Paul, 16–28
Hawley, James, 176
Henkin, Louis, 334
Herman Miller, Inc., profile of, 435
Hewlett-Packard, requirements on suppliers by, 198
Hirokawa, Keith H., 13–15
Hirsch, Dennis D., 154–56
Hoepner, Andreas, 183
Hoerner, J. Andrew, 229
Hoffman, Andrew J., 109, 116–17
Hohfeld, Wesley N., 341
Holliday, Chad, 251–52
Holocaust, Deutsche Bank's complicity in, 345
Home Depot, requirements on suppliers by, 196
home improvement/hardware retail sector (U.S.), 196
Honda, practices of, 197, 423–24
Hoovers report, of supply-chain contracting, 195–200
housing/building sector, carbon pricing initiatives by, 267T
Hughes, Heather, 393–400
human rights. *See Norms on Responsibilities of TNCs with Regard to Human Rights* (UN); TNCs (transnational corporations)

human sustainability, 321–29
  employee mortality, organizational effects on, 322–25
  environmental/social sustainability *vs.*, 326–28
  in fast food restaurants, 433
  health insurance, in U.S., 323, 329
  inequality, effects of, 324–25
  layoffs, effects of, 323–24
  at Patagonia, 430
  profitability *vs.* employees, 321–22, 327
  research agenda for, 328–29
  work hours/stress, effects of, 324
Hurricane Katrina, tort liability from, 292–94
Hymel, Mona, 256–61, 268
Hypercars, 20–22

I

IATTC, dolphin protection program by, 372
IBM, supplier conduct principles of, 198
Illig, Robert C., 3–7
Illinois Tool Works, requirements on suppliers by, 199
Impact Investing Benchmark, 189
"An Inconvenient Truth" (DVD), 3–4, 6
industry sector, carbon pricing initiatives of, 266T
insurance agreements, environmental provisions in, 201
intellectual property. *See* eco-mark enforcement; environmental technologies; patents
Interface Inc., as sustainable business, 18, 23, 24, 364, 434
International Covenant on Civil and Political Rights (ICCPR), 345
International Labor Organization (ILO), 335–37, 347
international law. *See also* environmental technologies; TNCs (transnational corporations); WTO (World Trade Organization)
  international labor standards, 145, 151
  international treaties, 143, 169
investing. *See* SRI
Ioannou, Ioannis, 188
IRS Tax Reform Act of 1986, 247
ISO 14001 Environmental Management System standard
  benefit corporations, 95
  certification process, 365–66
  compliance, by suppliers, 205, 206–7
  in manufacturing sectors, 197, 199
ISOs (Independent System Operators), tariffs by, 249

J

Japan
  energy use by, 22
  pollution from mining in, 378
  sustainable business in, 439–40, 440–41
Jenkins, Alec, 247
Jensen, Michael, 44
John Deere, requirements on suppliers by, 199
Johnson, Jack, waste by music industry and, 216 n.
Johnson, Jennifer L., 340
Johnston, Keith, 180
Jones, William C., 125
Joo, Thomas, 37–41, 129–32

K

Kaelin, Albin, 29
Kant, Immanuel, deontological approach of, 171, 172
Kanzer, Adam, 186
Kaplan, Robert, 43
Kates, Robert W., 12–13
Katz, Robert A., 102–7
Keynes, John M., 312
Kinley, David, 331–48, 350, 356, 357
Kleiner Perkins Caufield & Byers firm, 5–6
Koh, Wayne, 424
Komatsu, requirements on suppliers by, 199
Kristof, Nicholas, 347
Kritzman, Mark, 184–85
Kroger, annual sales of, 196
Kurtz, Lloyd, 189–90

L

Land, Edwin, 18
land ownership, forest resources *vs.*, 250–51

Lane, Eric L., 417–26
Langbein, John H., 162
Lanham Trademark Act, 406, 421
L3Cs (low-profit limited liability companies), 90, 99, 100, 103–4
least cost abatement theory
effect, on environmental goal, 222
effect, on revenue use, 224
effect, on tax rate, 223
generally, 220
summary, 225T
Lederman, Alan S., 261–63
Leiserowitz, Anthony A., 12–13
Lemley, Mark, 413
Lewis, Tory H., 207–15
Lexus, misleading advertising by, 422
LG Electronics, misleading advertising by, 422–23
liability, for injustice in global apparel industry, 316–17
liability, of shareholders, 274–81
controlling interest, risk and, 279–81
limited liability, 274–78
Light, Andrew, 14–15
Living Downstream (Steingraber), 36
Loblaw, annual sales of, 196
Lovins, Amory B., 16–28
Lovins, L. Hunter, 16–28
Lowe's, requirements on suppliers by, 196
lumber/timber operations sector (U.S.), 198–99
Lyondell Chemical Co., clean up costs from pollution by, 384

M

MacDonnell, Lawrence, 13
Machlup, Fritz, 411
MacMillan Bloedel, costs for failure to invest in natural resources, 26
Madison, James *(Federalist Papers)*, 56
malum in se vs. malum prohibitum, 70–72, 85, 297–98
management
integrity of, disclosure and, 143–44
managers, CSR proposals and, 42–43
managers, ultra vires doctrine and, 82–83
responsible corporate officer doctrine, 300–301
at Starbucks, 152–53, 158
management-centered corporations, 37–41. *See also* corporate decision-making
"business judgment rule," 40
"monism," definition, 40 n.48
shareholders, policymaking by proposals, 38–40
state law fiduciary duty litigation, 40–41
Manard, John P., Jr., 292–94
Mann, Michael, 245
Marcal Paper Mills Inc., clean up costs from pollution by, 384
Margolis, Joshua D., 165–66
Marmot, Michael, 322
Maskus, Keith, 415
Massachusetts, sustainable business in, 433
McDonnell, Brett H., 307–15, 330
McDonough, William, 28–35
McMillon, Doug, 321
McWane, Inc., prosecution of, 303
Means, Gardiner C. (*The Modern Corporation and Private Property*), 135–39
Meidinger, Error, 202
Menard, annual sales of, 196
Mendelson, Nina A., 274–81, 306
Michigan, sustainable business in, 433–34, 435
Milne, Janet E., 217–25, 231–36, 243
mining industry, pollution from. *See* hardrock mining, cleanup costs of
Minnesota, sustainable business in, 431–32
Minnow, Nell, 175
Minor, Dylan, 184
Miretski, Pini Pavel, 348–61
Mitchell, Ronald, 201
Mitsubishi Heavy Industries, requirements on suppliers by, 199
Model Business Corporation Act (1979), 77
The Modern Corporation and Private Property (Berle & Means), 135–39
Monks, Robert, 175
Montana, gold mining pollution in, 380, 382, 383

Montreal Protocol, 233–34
morality. *See also* SRI (socially responsible investing)
  apparel industry and, 318–20
  limited liability, moral hazards of, 275, 276–77
Motorola, sustainable business practice by, 23
MSC certification program, 206
music concerts, waste management and, 216 n.

N

NAFTA, international trade agreements and, 367
National Environmental Policy Act (NEPA) of 1969, 48–49
natural capitalism, 16–28
  biological models, redesign production of, 17, 22–23
  business models, change, 17, 24–25
  California Rice Industry Association, 27
  definition, 16–17
  electricity profits, 18–19
  expenses, accounting for, 17
  failure to protect/reinvest, costs of, 26
  "management-intensive rotational grazing" method, 26–27
  natural resources, increase productivity of, 16, 18–22
  reinvest in, 17, 25–28
  sewage to clean water, 27
negligence, in tort law, 271, 283
Netherlands, environmental tax use by, 227
New Belgium Brewery, profile of, 427–28
New Guinea, pollution from mining operations in, 378–79
New Hampshire, sustainable business in, 430–31
New Jersey, environmental protection in, 230, 389
New Mexico, reclamation costs of copper mining in, 383
New Seasons Market, profile of, 428
New South Wales, sustainable business in, 439
New York
  BPI certification, 425–26
  fiduciary responsibilities in, 85
  incorporation statute, 77–78
  Teachers Retirement System, SRI and, 161
New Zealand, layoffs in, 324
NGOs (non-governmental organizations), role of, 203, 332, 367–68
Nike, Inc.
  articles of incorporation, 78
  corporate responsibility of, 11–12
  human rights violations by, 331
  Kasky v. Nike (2003), 339
  reputation of, contractors and, 82
Nissan, requirements on suppliers by, 197, 206
Norms on Responsibilities of TNCs with Regard to Human Rights (UN), 348–61
  appraisal of, 357–61
  Article 1, 352
  development of, 351–54
  history and failure of, 348–50
  legislative context and relevance of, 350–51
  Part I, 354
  Preamble, 352, 358–59
  press release on, 348
  shortfalls of, 354–57
Norton, Bryan, 15
Norton, David, 43
Norway, complicity-based doctrine in, 170–73, 175, 228
nuclear reactor income tax credit, 261–63

O

Office Depot, requirements on suppliers by, 197
Office Max, annual sales, 197
office products retail/distribution sector (U.S.), 197–98
O'Hara, Patrick, 292–94
oil mining/drilling process, 378
oil pollution, 201, 236, 390–93. *See also* Gulf oil spill
Oil Pollution Act of 1990, 236, 292, 385
Oil Spill Liability Trust Fund, 236, 391–93

Okediji, Ruth, 415
O'Neill, Onora, 318–19
Oregon, sustainable business in, 428
Organization of Economic Cooperation and Development (OECD), 335–37, 367
OSHA requirements/standards, 23, 149–50
The Overspent American (Schor), 260
ozone pollution, 226, 227, 233–34, 291

P

Page, Antony, 102–7
Parris, Thomas M., 12–13
Patagonia, as sustainable business, 116, 118, 364, 429–30
Patent Act of 1952, 405
patents, 405–6, 407–9. *See also* environmental technologies
Pepper, Stephen *(Counseling at the Limits of the Law),* 69–72
personal computers sector (U.S.), 198
PET (polyethylene terephthalate), 29
Peugeot, requirements on suppliers by, 197–98
Pfeffer, Jeffrey, 321–29
pharmaceuticals/medicines, access to, 413
Phillips-Van Heusen (Guatemala), human rights violations by, 331
Pigou, Arthur C. *(The Economics of Welfare),* 218, 226–27, 243–44
Pigouvian theory
  effect, on environmental goal, 221
  effect, on revenue use, 223–24
  effect, on tax rate, 222
  generally, 218
  policy choice, 220
  summary, 225T
Plerhoples, Alicia, 125
Plum Organics, culture of, 118
Pogge, Thomas, 319–20
politics, corporations and
  apparel industry, political responsibility for, 320
  "clean elections" cause, 59
  political feasibility, of carbon tax, 239–40, 245
  political feasibility, of employee involvement, 312, 314
  unions and, 310, 312, 314
"polluter pays" principle, 218–20, 226–30
  cost allocation, 218–20
  criticisms of, 229–30
  effect, on environmental goal, 221, 227
  effect, on revenue use, 224, 228
  effect, on tax rate, 223, 224
  environmental harm, history of taxing, 226–27
  regulations, limits of, 227
  summary, 225T
  tax shifting, 228
  taxation policy, generally, 226, 230
pollution regulation, by GNAs, 207–15
population sector, carbon pricing initiatives, 267T
portfolio management, ESG investing, 183–90
  ESG factors, 185–86
  ESG performance, studies on, 186–90
  governance and, study on, 188
  Impact Investing Benchmark, 189
  negative screening *vs.* best-in-class screening, 183
  portfolio diversification, 183
  securities, high ratings and costs, 187
  SRI, costs of, 183, 184–85
  UO thesis and, 178
Posner, Richard A., 162
Post, James, 364
Potlatch, requirements on suppliers by, 199
Potoski, Matthew, 206
Prakash, Aseem, 206
"precautionary principle," GMOs and, 369–72
Precious Woods, profile of, 437–38
Preston, Lee, 364
prudent man/investor rule, 161, 180–82, 190
public law, contract law *vs.,* 74–75
public policy
  duty to obey law, 76
  expulsion of unwanted corporations, 59
  social policy reforms, 63–65

R

Ratner, Stephen R., 344
RCRA of 1976, 294, 298, 299
Red Sky at Morning (Speth), 59
reflexive law, green business and, 154–56
  environmental norms, internalization of, 155–56
  reflexive law, definition, 154
  stakeholder assessment proposal, 49–50
  systems theory, 156
  TRI rankings, 155
Reiser, Dana Brakman, 90–102
Renault, requirements on suppliers by, 198
Renneboog, Luc, 183, 188
Repetto, Robert, 60
Restatement (First) of Torts, 403
Revelli, Christophe, 187–88
Revised Model Business Corporation Act (1999), 77
Richardson, Benjamin J., 166–67, 170–82, 190
Rio Tinto, code of conduct of, 338
Roodman, David M., 226–30, 243, 244
Roosevelt, Franklin D., 134, 135
Royal Dutch/Shell (Nigeria), human rights violations by, 332
Rule, Troy, 361
running shoes, 11–12, 33–34. *See also* Nike, Inc.
Rwanda, TNC's complicity in genocide in, 345

S

SafetyKleen, business model change by, 24–25
sales tax, disparity in, 248
Sam's Club, goals of, 321
Sandberg, Joakim, 159–69, 190
Sandmo, Agnar, 228
Sarbanes-Oxley Act, 215
Sarnoff, Joshua, 409–17
SC Johnson & Son, Inc., deceptive advertising by, 424
Schepel, Harm, 273–74
Schindler, business model change by, 24
Schor, Juliet (*The Overspent American*), 260
Schroeder, Christopher H., 281–92
Schultz, Howard, 152, 153–54 *illu.*, 158
Schwartz, Gary T., 284, 286
Scott, Lee, 321
SEC, transparency by, 132–51
  on climate change, 157
  controlling interest, of shareholders, 280
  disclosure, 60, 133–34
  disclosure requirement of, 141–44, 157
  history of, 133–40
  MD&A disclosure obligations, 130–32, 156–57
  "ordinary business" rule, 38
  Regulation S-K, disclosure obligations, 130, 132–33
  requirement, filing supply agreements, 200
  Rule 10b-5, material disclosure, 129–30
  S.A. 8000 standard (labor relations), 145, 151, 332
  social disclosure models, 148–51
Section 45 PTC (wind energy), 263–65
Section 45J credit (nuclear reactor), 261–63
securities law. *See* management-centered corporations; reflexive law, green business and; SEC, transparency by; Starbucks, global responsibility report (2014)
Seireeni, Richard (*The Gort Cloud*), 420–21
self-regulation
  codes of conduct, 191–94
  deregulation *vs.*, 123
  external engagement and, 111–13
  incentivizing, 113–18
  reflexive law, green business and, 154–56
  tort law consequences of, 269–74
Serafeim, George, 188
Seventh Generation, 117
shareholders. *See also* liability, of shareholders
  control-based liability, for corporate torts, 274–81
  CSR and, 42–44
  derivative actions by, 89–90

enforcement role of, 98–99
managerial fiduciary responsibility, to, 136
managerial integrity, disclosure and, 143–44
role, in B corporation statutes, 98–99, 120–21
shareholder primacy, 84–85, 309
shareholder proposals, exclusions of, 38–39
ultra vires doctrine and, 79–81
Sharp Corp., profile of, 440–41
Shavell, Steve, 207–8
Shurtz, Nancy E., 237–43, 244, 265–67
Silicon Valley, 5–6, 125
snack food production, as sustainable business, 432
Sneirson, Judd F., 9–12, 41–50, 84–85, 87–90
social corporate transparency, 132–51. *See also* SEC, transparency by
accountability, to public, 136, 138–39, 148, 151
accountability, to shareholders, 146–47, 150
Justice Brandeis, influence of, 134–35
of domestic statutes, compliance with, 142–43
for economic investors, 141–43, 144–45
expanded social disclosure, 147–49
Felix Frankfurter, influence of, 139–40
of international treaties, compliance with, 143, 169
managerial integrity, 143–44, 147
mandatory disclosure, 132–33
The Modern Corporation and Private Property, influence of, 135–39
power, social *vs.* economic, 135
"property" *vs.* "ownership," 136–37
securities valuation, 137
separation of ownership from control, 135–36
social auditing format, 150
social disclosure, definitions/categories of, 140–41, 149
social disclosure, of compliance with statutes, 141–43
social disclosure, of corporate social policies, 144–46
for social investors, 141, 145–46, 147–48, 168–69
social responsibility, of corporate management, 137–38, 146–47
social enterprise law. *See* benefit corporation statutes
social enterprises, 102–8. *See also* benefit corporation statutes; sustainable businesses
CICs, 104–5
culture of, 118
definitions, 102–3
increasing number of, 105–7, 107–8
L3Cs, 103–4
in Minnesota, 105
mission drift, 117–18 n.214
self-regulation, external engagement and, 111–13
self-regulation, incentivizing, 113–18
self-reporting, 157
socially responsible corporations, 105, 152, 153–54 *illu.*
study of, 125
transaction costs, 106
social welfare legislation, to benefit stakeholders, 63–64
Sony (U.S.), EMS requirement by, 198
South Africa, SRI in, 173, 339
Spain, sustainable business in, 438
Speth, James Gustave, 57–61
SRI (socially responsible investing), 159–90
complicity-based doctrine, 170–73
cost, 184–85
definitions, 159
ESG arguments, 163–65
ESG factors, financial relevance of, 165–67, 185–86
ESG performance, research on, 186–90
fiduciary duty and, 159–69
leveraged-based responsibility, as rationale for, 173–75
long-term investing approach, 178–82
portfolio theory, diversification and, 183

pressure from, in supply-chain contracting, 204
prudent investing, 180–82, 190
"sphere-of-influence" approach, 174–75
sustainability paradigm, investors and, 180
universal owner (UO) thesis, 175–79, 182
UNPRI report (2006), 179
valuing, 183–90
stakeholders, corporate governance and, 63–66, 112, 307–15
Starbucks, global responsibility report (2014), 152, 153–54 *illu.*, 158
states, as stakeholders
benefit corporation statutes, 110, 115
innovations by, using environmental taxes, 230
production tax credit (PTC), 251
sales tax moratoria by, 248
ultra vires doctrine, 78–79
Steelcase, sustainable upholstery fabric design by, 29–35
Steingraber, Sandra (*Living Downstream*), 36
Stenzel, Paulette L., 362–74
Stout, Lynn, 51
Sunstein, Cas, 54–55
Superfund taxes, 235–36
Surrey, Stanley S., 252
sustainability concept, 13–15, 102, 109–10
sustainable businesses, 9–36, 427–41
Abengoa, Spain, 438
Allianz SE, Germany, 435–36
Australian Gas Light Energy Limited, New South Wales, 439
Aveda, Minnesota, 431–32
Bazzani Associates, Michigan, 433–34
The Black Sheep Inn, Ecuador, 438–39
Burgerville, Washington, 432–33
Co-operative Financial Services, U.K., 436–37
corporate governance, new paradigm for, 9–12
definitions, 9
East Japan Railway Co., Japan, 439–40
Frito-Lay, Texas, 432
GoLite LLC, Colorado, 431
Google, California, 428–29
Herman Miller, Inc., Michigan, 435
Interface, Georgia, 434
natural capitalism, 16–28
New Belgium Brewery, Colorado, 427–28
New Seasons Market, Oregon, 428
Patagonia, California, 429–30
Precious Woods, Switzerland, 437–38
Sharp Corp., Japan, 440–41
sustainability concept, definition, 13–15
Switcher SA, Switzerland, 437
Timberland, Inc., New Hampshire, 430–31
Wainwright Bank, Massachusetts, 433
waste, redesigning to eliminate, 28–35
Sweden, sustainability by, 228, 229, 324
Switcher SA, profile of, 437
Switzerland, sustainable business in, 437

T

Tadaki, Junko, 331–48
tailings dams, failures of, 378–79
tax subsidies, 245–68
advertising, tax policy and, 256–61
carbon pricing initiatives, 265–67T
clean air technologies, fiscal barriers to, 245–52
nuclear reactor income tax credit, 261–63
U.S. Budget (2015), 252, 253–55T
wind energy, 263–65
taxation. *See* environmental taxation; tax subsidies
Taylor, Glenn, 206
ter Horst, Jenke, 183, 188
TerraChoice Environmental Marketing Inc., 419–20
Texas, sustainable business in, 432
Thel, Steve, 134
Thompson, Paul, 15
Thornton, Rosy, 164, 165
3M Corporation, CSR behavior by, 364–65
TIAA-CREF, SRI by, 177
Timberland, Inc., profile of, 430–31

TNCs (transnational corporations), 331–61
codes of conduct, 337–40
complicity in crimes by, 345
human rights abuses by, 331–32
human rights norms and, 343–44
International Labor Organization (ILO), 335–37, 347
international law governing, 332
international legal rights of, 333–34
labor rights and, 346–48
liabilities/duties of, 340–41
OECD, 335–37, 367
private legal rights of, 344–45
profit maximization *vs.* CSR, 337
public functions of, 343
regulation of, 332–33
right to life and, 345–46
third-party duty of, 341–43
UDHR, 334–35
UN Global Compact, 336–37
UN *Norms* on, 348–61
"Tobin" tax, 369
Todd, John, 27
torts/crimes, sustainability and. *See* environmental regulation; Hurricane Katrina, tort liability from; liability, of shareholders; self-regulation
tourism industry, sustainable businesses in, 438–39
trade secrets, proprietary rights in, 403–4
trademark rights, 406–7, 425–26. *See also* eco-mark enforcement
transportation sector (U.S.), 246–47, 266T, 439–40
"triple bottom line" approach, 10–11, 35, 58
TRIPS Agreement, 414, 417
trustees, fiduciary duty of, 161, 167–69, 181, 182
Tueth, Matthew, 35, 427–41
Tyler, Tom R. *(Why People Obey the Law)*, 86

U

UCC Article 9. *See* EPMSI, in commercial law
Uhlmann, David M., 294–305
"ultra vires" doctrine, 75–84
creditors, as stakeholder, 81–82
duty to obey law, 76
history of, 76–77
implications for corporate practice, 83–84
legal *vs.* illegal activities, 77–78
managers and employees, as stakeholders, 82–83
profits and, 75–76
shareholders, as stakeholder, 79–81
state, as stakeholder, 78–79
Uniform Prudent Investor Act (UPIA), 183
Uniform Trade Secrets Act, 403
United Kingdom
EITI, 115
employment reporting in, 149
greenwashing in, 419
long-term sustainability in, 179–80
SRI, statistics, 160
sustainable business in, 436–37
on U.N. *Norms,* 360
USS, investing in SRI by, 161, 162, 164, 176, 177
United Nations
Brundtland Commission, 102
Fiduciary II, 162, 190
Freshfields report by, 160, 162–63, 165–66, 167, 169, 190
Global Compact, 193, 336–37
"Guiding Principles for Business and Human Rights," 348
limitations on force/firearms use, 346
Norms on TNCs, 348–61
"sphere-of-influence" approach, 174
studies by (2008), 177
UNEP-FI, study by, 181, 187
United States
Budget (2015), 252, 253–55T
compliance with WTO by, 362
consumption rates in, 257–58
cost, decrease CO2 in, 241
dolphin protection by, 372
Energy Star certification mark, 422–23
environmental harm *vs.* tax revenue in, 228
environmental taxation in, 231–36
ethanol, import tariff on, 249

Europe *vs.*, on use of environmental taxation, 244
farm subsidies, 373
fishing subsidies, 373
gas taxes in, 229–30
GMOs and, 370–71
health insurance in, 323
liability, for cleanup from hardrock mines, 381–82
NAFTA and, 367
statistics, hardrock mining in, 377
on U.N. *Norms*, 353, 358, 361
wind energy in, 263–65
United States Code (U.S.C.)
Title 18, 303–4
Title 28, Section 1498, 407–8
Universal Declaration of Human Rights (UDHR), 334–35, 345
"unmarketables," 34
Unocal, articles of incorporation, 78
UNPRI report (2006), 179
UO (universal owner) thesis, 175–79
conceptual weaknesses of, 177
definition, 175–76
economy-wide investors, 177–78
institutional funds using, 177, 182
as investment rationale, 176–77
portfolio management, 178
U.S. Constitution, on patent law, 405
USS (Universities Supperannuation Scheme)
fiduciary duty, SRI investing by, 161, 162, 164
UO thesis used by, 176, 177

V

Vandenbergh, Michael P., 194–207
venture capitalists, in benefit corporations, 120–21
Viviani, Jean-Laurent, 187–88
Volkswagen, environmental requirements on suppliers by, 197–98
von Weizscker, Ernst Ulrich *(Ecological Tax Reform)*, 228

W

Wachovia Bank, exclusion of shareholder proposal by, 38–39
Wainwright Bank, profile of, 433
Wal-Mart, 144–45, 195–96, 321
Walgreens, annual sales of, 196
Walsh, James P., 326
Ward, Halina, 339
Washington, sustainable business in, 432–33
waste, redesigning to eliminate, 28–35
biological metabolism, 28–31
definitions, 28–29, 31, 32
factory effluent/influent incongruity, 30
"monstrous hybrids," 33–35
product of service, 31–32, 33
project, compostable upholstery fabric design, 29–35
technical metabolism, 31–33
"unmarketables," 34, 36
water pollution
from hardrock mining, 378
from oil spills, 236, 277, 292–94
regulations for, 227
taxes on, 23, 227
TDMLs in GNAs, 213, 214
water, as "good," 373–74
wealth redistribution, by stakeholder boards, 53–54
Weissbrodt, David, 350, 351
West Virginia, Buffalo Creek disaster, 378
wetlands cases, criminal prosecutions of, 305
White, Allen, 60–61
Why People Obey the Law (Tyler), 86
Wiggen, Oddny, 174
Williams, Andrew, 176
Williams, Cynthia A., 66–75, 132–51
Wilper, Andrew, 329
wind energy, 263–65
Windex, deceptive advertising by, 424
Winfrey, Oprah, 3–4
Winkler, Adam, 63–66, 85
Winston, Andrew *(Green to Gold)*, 58
Wolseley, annual sales by, 196
Wood, Stepan, 173, 174
work law. *See also* apparel industry, global labor in; corporate governance; human sustainability
international labor standards, 145, 151
labor, sustainability and, 257

S.A. 8000 standard (labor relations), 145, 151, 332
workers, protections for, 65, 332
WTO (World Trade Organization), 362–74
budget, 362
Committee on Trade and Environment (CTE), 363
CSR principles and, 364–66
environmental education, 368–69
environmental NGOs, 368
ETMs and, 371–72
fair trade movement, 372
GATT, 362, 363, 370, 372, 373–74
powers of, 362–64
precautionary principle, on GMOs, 369–71
reform difficulties of, 367–68
reform suggestions, 368–69
subsidies for agriculture, 373
water, as "good," 373–74
WuDunn, Sheryl, 347

Y

Yockey, Joseph W., 107–26
Young, Iris M., 315–20, 330

Z

Zhang, Chendi, 183, 188
Zortman-Landusky gold mine, pollution from, 380